LIVES AND DEATHS

The Series in Death, Dying, and Bereavement
Consulting Editor
Robert A. Neimeyer

Nord—*Mutiple AIDS-Related Loss: A Handbook for Understanding and Surviving a Perpetual Fall*
Harvey—*Perspectives on Loss: A Sourcebook*
Davies—*Shadows in the Sun: The Experiences of Sibling Bereavement in Childhood*
Werth—*Contemporary Perspectives on Rational Suicide*
Leenaars—*Lives and Deaths: Selections from the Works of Edwin S. Shneidman*
Klass—*The Spiritual Lives of Bereaved Parents*

FORMERLY THE **SERIES IN DEATH EDUCATION, AGING, AND HEALTH CARE**
HANNELORE WASS, CONSULTING EDITOR

Bard—*Medical Ethics in Practice*
Benoliel—*Death Education for the Health Professional*
Bertman—*Facing Death: Images, Insights, and Interventions*
Brammer—*How to Cope with Life Transitions: The Challenge of Personal Change*
Cleiren—*Bereavement and Adaptation: A Comparative Study of the Aftermath of Death*
Corless, Pittman-Lindeman—*AIDS: Principles, Practices, and Politics, Abridged Edition*
Corless, Pittman-Lindeman—*AIDS: Principles, Practices, and Politics, Reference Edition*
Curran—*Adolescent Suicidal Behavior*
Davidson—*The Hospice: Development and Administration, Second Edition*
Davidson, Linnolla—*Risk Factors in Youth Suicide*
Degner, Beaton—*Life-Death Decisions in Health Care*
Doka—*AIDS, Fear, and Society: Challenging the Dreaded Disease*
Doty—*Communication and Assertion Skills for Older Persons*
Epting, Neimeyer—*Personal Meanings of Death: Applications of Personal Construct Theory to Clinical Practice*
Haber—*Health Care for an Aging Society: Cost-Conscious Community Care and Self-Care Approaches*
Hughes—*Bereavement and Support: Healing in a Group Environment*
Irish, Lundquist, Nelsen—*Ethnic Variations in Dying, Death, and Grief: Diversity in Universality*
Klass, Silverman, Nickman—*Continuing Bonds: New Understanding of Grief*
Lair—*Counseling the Terminally Ill: Sharing the Journey*
Leenaars, Maltsberger, Neimeyer—*Treatment of Suicidal People*
Leenaars, Wenckstern—*Suicide Prevention in Schools*
Leng—*Psychological Care in Old Age*
Leviton—*Horrendous Death, Health, and Well-Being*
Leviton—*Horrendous Death and Health: Toward Action*
Lindeman, Corby, Downing, Sanborn—*Alzheimer's Day Care: A Basic Guide*
Lund—*Older Bereaved Spouses: Research with Practical Applications*
Neimeyer—*Death Anxiety Handbook: Research, Instrumentation, and Application*
Nord—*Multiple AIDS-Related Loss: A Handbook for Understanding and Surviving a Perpetual Fall*
Papadatou, Papadatos—*Children and Death*
Prunkl, Berry—*Death Week: Exploring the Dying Process*
Ricker, Myers—*Retirement Counseling: A Practical Guide for Action*
Samarel—*Caring for Life and Death*
Sherron, Lumsden—*Introduction to Educational Gerontology. Third Edition*
Stillion—*Death and Sexes: An Examination of Differential Longevity, Attitudes, Behaviors, and Coping Skills*
Stillion, McDowell, May—*Suicide Across the Life Span—Premature Exits*
Vachon—*Occupational Stress in the Care of the Critically Ill, the Dying, and the Bereaved*
Wass, Corr—*Childhood and Death*
Wass, Corr—*Helping Children Cope with Death: Guidelines and Resource. Second Edition*
Wass, Corr, Pacholski, Forfar—*Death Education II: An Annotated Resource Guide*
Wass, Neimeyer—*Dying: Facing the Facts. Third Edition*
Weenolsen—*Transcendence of Loss over the Life Span*
Werth—*Rational Suicide? Implications for Mental Health Professionals*

LIVES AND DEATHS

Selections from the Works of Edwin S. Shneidman

Edited by

Antoon A. Leenaars

BRUNNER/MAZEL
Taylor & Francis Group

USA	Publishing Office:	BRUNNER/MAZEL *A member of the Taylor & Francis Group* 325 Chestnut Street Philadelphia, PA 19106 Tel: (215) 625-8900 Fax: (215) 625-2940
	Distribution Center:	BRUNNER/MAZEL *A member of the Taylor & Francis Group* 47 Runway Road, Suite G Levittown, PA 19057 Tel: (215) 269-0400 Fax: (215) 269-0363
UK		BRUNNER/MAZEL *A member of the Taylor & Francis Group* 1 Gunpowder Square London EC4A 3DE Tel: +44 171 583 0490 Fax: +44 171 583 0581

LIVES AND DEATHS: Selections from the Works of Edwin S. Shneidman

1 2 3 4 5 6 7 8 9 0

Printed by Braun-Brumfield, Ann Arbor, MI, 1999.
Cover design by Nancy Abbott.

A CIP catalog record for this book is available from the British Library.
The paper in this publication meets the requirements of the ANSI Standard Z39.48–1984 (Permanence of Paper).

Library of Congress Cataloging-in-Publication Data

Shneidman, Edwin S.
Lives and deaths : selections from the works of Edwin S. Shneidman / edited by Antoon A. Leenaars.
p. cm. — (Series in death, dying, and bereavement)
ISBN 1-58391-010-7 (case : alk. paper). — ISBN 1-58391-011-5 (paper : alk. paper)
1. Suicide—Pyschological aspects. 2. Bereavement—Psychological aspects. 3. Suicide—Sociological aspects. I. Leenaars, Antoon A. II. Title. III. Series.
RC569.S469 1999
616.85'8445—dc21 99-18296
CIP

ISBN 1–58391–010–7 (case)
1–58391–011-5 (paper)
ISSN 1091–5427

CONTENTS

Section B: Suicide Notes

Section C: Administrative and Programmatic

Section D: Clinical and Community

Section E: Psychological Autopsy and Postvention

PREFACE

To borrow here and there from a previous preface by Edwin Shneidman to a collection of pieces by Henry A. Murray: There are few endeavors in life that meet Sigmund Freud's dictum for happiness, "love and work." This book is one such happy occurrence. This enterprise, long urged on Dr. Shneidman, finally "set sail" on January 2, 1996, but when that agreement came, it seemed such a heavy responsibility for me to assume singly that I immediately conscripted friends of his (and mine) to assist me by constituting themselves an informal "committee," the crew, to help make the final selections and to edit the interstitial materials. They are Nancy H. Allen, Pamela Cantor, Robert E. Litman, John T. Maltsberger, and Nina Murray. We corresponded several times on major and detailed issues. The form of this book reflects their efforts, and I am grateful to each of them.

The seventh member of the crew—truly the first mate—was Jeanne Shneidman. Anyone who knows the Shneidmans will immediately grasp that her efforts were essential. And finally, my wife, Susanne Wenckstern, acted as the committee's personal secretary. For many realistic and personal reasons, and because of my deep attachment to both Jeanne and Susanne, I dedicate my efforts in this book to them.

Dr. Shneidman was, of course, *ex officio* captain of the group. The list of papers was compiled on June 29, 1996 in the Shneidman galley, with an update on May 13, 1998—keeping in mind that the final table of contents represents a compromise between the press for greater inclusion and the need to restrict the list to the most representative pieces. In consultation with the committee and with Dr. Shneidman, we decided to divide the selections into five categories: Psychological Assessment, Logic, Melville and Murray, Suicide, and Death. And further, the section on Suicide might itself be divided into five parts: Definitional and Theoretical, Suicide Notes, Administrative and Programmatic, Clinical and Community, and Psychological Autopsy and Postvention. The title of this volume was my selection, associating to both Murray's and Shneidman's endeavors in studying human lives.

Since my early studies of suicide notes, Dr. Shneidman has been pivotal to my thinking. I am proud to state that he has been the most important intellectual influence in my life. He taught me that the seas of life and death are vaster than had ever been charted. I am honored now again to have this opportunity to bring a selection of his work before a new and wider audience.

Antoon A. Leenaars

PERMISSIONS

In order of appearance in the text, grateful acknowledgment is made for permission to reprint.

Chapter 1 A Note on the Experimental Study of the Appraisal Interview. *Journal of Applied Psychology,* 1943, *27,* 196–205. With permission of American Psychological Association.

Chapter 2 MAPS of the Harvard Yard. *Journal of Personality Assessment,* 1986, *50,* 436–447. With permission of Lawrence Erlbaum Associates, Inc.

Chapter 3 Personality and "Success" Among a Selected Group of Lawyers. *Journal of Personality Assessment,* 1984, *48,* 609–616. With permission of Lawrence Erlbaum Associates, Inc.

Chapter 4 The Psychological Pain Assessment Scale. *Suicide and Life-Threatening Behavior,* 1999, *29.* With permission of E. Shneidman.

Chapter 5 The Logic of Politics. In M.A. May and L. Arons (Eds.), *Television and Human Behavior.* New York: Appleton-Century-Crofts, 1963, pp. 178–199. With permission of E. Shneidman.

Chapter 6 On "Therefore I Must Kill Myself." *Suicide and Life-Threatening Behavior,* 1982, *12,* 52–55. With permission of Guilford Publications, Inc.

Chapter 7 Melville's Cognitive Style: The Logic of *Moby-Dick.* In J. Bryant (Ed.), *A Companion to Melville Studies.* Westport, CT: Greenwood Press, 1986, pp. 543–564. With permission of Greenwood Publishing Group, Inc.

Chapter 8 The Deaths of Herman Melville. In H. P. Vincent (Ed.), *Melville and Hawthorne in the Berkshires.* Kent, OH: Kent State University Press, 1968, pp. 118–144. With permission of The Kent State University Press.

Chapter 9 Some Psychological Reflections on the Death of Malcolm Melville. *Suicide and Life-Threatening Behavior,* 1976, *6,* 231–242. With permission of Guilford Publications, Inc.

Chapter 10 A Possible Classification of Suicidal Acts Based on Murray's Need System. *Suicide and Life-Threatening Behavior,* 1980, *10,* 175–181. With permission of Guilford Publications, Inc.

Chapter 11 Remarks at a Memorial Service for Henry A. Murray, Memorial Church, Harvard University, October 3, 1988. With permission of E. Shneidman.

Chapter 12 "Suicide" and "Suicidology": A Brief Etymological Note. *Life-Threatening Behavior,* 1971, *1,* 260–263. With permission of Guilford Publications, Inc.

Chapter 13 A Formal Definition, with Explication. *Definition of Suicide.* New York: Wiley, 1985, pp. 202–213. With permission of E. Shneidman.

Chapter 14 Suicide on My Mind, *Britannica* on My Table. *The American Scholar,* 1998, *67(4),* 93–104. With permission of the Phi Beta Kappa Society.

Chapter 15 Suicide. *Encyclopaedia Britannica.* Chicago: William Benton, 1973, Vol. 21, 383–385. With permission of Encyclopaedia Britannica, Inc.

Chapter 16 Perturbation and Lethality as Precursors of Suicide in a Gifted Group. *Life-Threatening Behavior,* 1971, *1,* 23–45. With permission of Guilford Publications, Inc.

Chapter 17 A Conspectus of the Suicidal Scenario. In R. W. Maris, A. L. Berman, J. T. Maltsburger and R. I. Yufit, (Eds.), *Assessment and Prediction of Suicide.* New York: Guilford Press, 1992, pp. 31–49. With permission of Guilford Publications, Inc.

Chapter 18 Suicide as Psychache. *Journal of Nervous and Mental Disease,* 1993, *181,* 147–149. With permission of Waverly Press.

Chapter 19 Some Characteristics of Genuine Versus Simulated Suicide Notes. In P. J. Stone, D. C. Dunphy, M. S. Smith, and D. M. Ogilvie (Eds.), *The General Inquirer: A Computer Approach to Content Analysis.* Cambridge: MIT Press, 1969, pp. 527–535. (With D. M. Ogilvie and P. J. Stone). With permission of MIT Press.

Chapter 20 Suicide Notes Reconsidered. *Psychiatry,* 1973, *36,* 379–394. With permission of The George Washington University Medical Center.

Chapter 21 Self-Destruction: Suicide Notes and Tragic Lives. *Voices of Death.* New York: Harper and Row, 1980, pp. 41–76. With permission of Kodansha America, Inc.

Chapter 22 Letters of Enforced Death Versus Suicide Notes. *Journal of Psychology and Judaism,* 1995, *19,* 153–160. With permission of K. Kaplan, Editor-in-Chief.

Chapter 23 The Los Angeles Suicide Prevention Center: A Demonstration of Public Health Feasibilities. *American Journal of Public Health,* 1965, *55,* 21–26. (With N. Farberow). With permission of The American Public Health Association.

Chapter 24 The NIMH Center for Studies of Suicide Prevention. *Bulletin of Suicidology,* 1967, *1,* 2–7. With permission of E. Shneidman.

Chapter 25 Some Reflections of a Founder. *Suicide and Life-Threatening Behavior,* 1988, *18,* 1–12. With permission of Guilford Publication, Inc.

Chapter 26 *How To Prevent Suicide.* Public Affairs Pamphlet. New York: Public Affairs Pamphlets, 1967, No. 406. (With P. Mandelkorn). With permission of E. Shneidman.

Chapter 27 Psychotherapy with Suicidal Patients. In T.B. Karasu and L. Bellak (Eds.), *Specialized Techniques in Individual Psychotherapy.* New York: Brunner/Mazel, 1980, pp. 305–313. With permission of Brunner/Mazel.

Chapter 28 Aphorisms of Suicide and Some Implications for Psychotherapy. *American Journal of Psychotherapy,* 1984, *38,* 319–328. With permission of E. Shneidman.

Chapter 29 Letter to Editor: Rational Suicide and Psychiatric Disorders. *New England Journal of Medicine,* March 26, 1992, Vol. 326, No. 13, p. 889. With permission of Massachusetts Medical Society.

Chapter 30 The Psychological Autopsy. In L. I. Gottschalk et al. (Eds.), *Guide to the Investigation and Reporting of Drug-Abuse Deaths.* Washington, D.C.: USDHEW, U.S. Government Printing Office, 1977, pp. 179–210. With permission of E. Shneidman.

Chapter 31 Comment: The Psychological Autopsy. *American Psychologist,* 1994, *39,* pp. 75–76. With permission of American Psychological Association.

Chapter 32 An Example of an Equivocal Death Clarified in a Court of Law. *Suicide as Psychache.* Northvale: Jason Aronson, Inc., 1993, pp. 211–246. With permission of Jason Aronson, Inc.

Chapter 33 Postvention: The Care of the Bereaved. In R.O. Pasnau (Ed.), *Consultation in Liaison Psychiatry.* New York: Grune and Stratton, 1975, pp. 245–256. With permission of W. B. Saunders Co.

Chapter 34 Orientations toward Death: A Vital Aspect of the Study of Lives. In R. W. White (Ed.), *The Study of Lives.* New York: Atherton Press, 1963, pp. 200–227. With permission of Simon & Schuster.

Chapter 35 Clinical Thanatology and Psychotherapy: Some Reflections on Caring for the Dying Person. *Omega,* 1979, *10,* 1–8. (With L. Feigenberg). With permission of Baywood Publishing Company, Inc.

Chapter 36 Final Thoughts and Reflections. *The Suicidal Mind.* New York: Oxford University Press, 1996, pp. 157–166. With permission of E. Shneidman.

Chapter 37 Dedication (to Parents). *Voices of Death.* New York: Harper & Row, 1980. With permission of E. Shneidman.

PART

I

PSYCHOLOGICAL ASSESSMENT

There are discernible stages of development in Shneidman's intellectual approach to suicide, a topic which has been his life-long professional focus. Foremost, he believes that, in the study of large issues like mental disorders, there is a "natural progression" from conceptualization, to understanding, and then to application and practice. Shneidman thought, "We ought to know what we are treating," and he believes that we will treat such problems as suicide more effectively only when we develop a clear vocabulary in terms of which we can assess and treat the problem. When the answers come, they may come in terms we currently cannot imagine. In mental health especially, he prefers the concept of assessment to the notion of diagnosis. (This has led him to a rather critical view of the *DSM* approach to mental pain.) Shneidman disapproves of the practice of pretending to understand a person by means of a diagnostic label, and on this point he quotes his mentor, Henry Murray: "Never denigrate a fellow human being in fewer than 2,000 words." He has also followed Murray's lead in his interest in thematic projective techniques—like Murray's Thematic Apperception Test (TAT)—with his own Make-A-Picture-Story (MAPS) Test. He has a continuing interest in the narrative aspects of a human life, in their "unity thema" and their prominent psychological threads.

The four chapters in this section reflect some of Shneidman's interests in the assessment process. The first, dated 1943, was his first publication, when a Captain in the Army during World War II, five years before his Ph.D. degree. It is a unique study done in a live setting, specifically, an examination of the interview process in a municipal civil service setting. Somehow, he persuaded the Los Angeles Civil Service Commission to recall a number of applicants who had been interviewed (with the usual substantive questions), in relation to a city clerk's position. In the second, experimental interview, they were asked simply to respond to some Rorschach ink blot cards. (None of the judges and none of the applicants knew anything about that procedure.)

The results of the study seemed to suggest that raters' judgments did not depend on the content of the answers as much as on such items as appearance, demeanor, bearing, fluency of speech, and self-assurance, independent of the content of the interview. It was an early look at personality assessment in the employment process based on Shneidman's challenging the then time-honored question-and-answer format. In a way, it set the stamp for all his future research studies: somewhat daring, somewhat iconoclastic, and involving the application of the method of difference.

The great psychological enthusiasm of the 1940s and 50s was projective techniques like the Rorschach and the TAT. During those years, Shneidman was president of the Society for Projective Techniques, edited *Thematic Test Analysis,* and was keenly interested in the power of projective narrative methods like the TAT and the MAPS Test. Chapter 2 presents an example of his studies of projective methods. It is a case study wherein the MAPS Test was given to a young undergraduate, a participant in Dr. Murray's longitudinal studies of Harvard men. It was written as a chapter for a book intended as a sequel to Murray's *Explorations in Personality* that never made it into print. The chapter attempts to place the subject's MAPS Test responses within a larger array of psychological assessment procedures. What makes a person the whole person that he is? Shneidman has expressed a longing to know how that young man has fared in life, and what, if any, predictive power there was in that earlier MAPS Test performance, an endeavor of all assessment.

Chapter 3 relates to another long-range study—one of the most formidable longitudinal psychological studies ever undertaken, the Terman Study of Gifted Children. Lewis Terman began that study at Stanford in

1921, and it continues to this day. In 1969, Shneidman was at the Center for the Advanced Study of the Behavioral Sciences (on the Stanford campus), and obtained permission to have access to the Gifted Study files. Later he interviewed, over a period of several years, about 30 of the Terman Study men. This paper reports on 11 lawyers among them, looking to see what adjectival traits seemed to be associated with the most successful among them and the least successful among them. As Daniel Goleman has pointed out in his recent book on emotional intelligence, it takes more than just high IQ to make a grand success in life. This chapter touches on what some of those other life-enhancing attributes might be.

"The Psychological Pain Assessment Scale"—the last item in this section—is Shneidman's latest publication on assessment. The paper is a first report of a new psychological instrument, the Psychological Pain Assessment Scale (PPAS) whose purpose is to measure psychological pain, i.e., introspectively felt hurt, inner anguish, mental aching—what he called "psychache." The subject is asked to measure the psychological pain in 10 TAT-like pictures, depicting various pleasant, innocuous or woeful human situations and to report the psychological pain at the worst moment of his/her life. The goal of the approach is to make an operational statement of inner pain, especially as it relates to suicide. It is thus easy to see that assessment has been a core aspect of Shneidman's career. The papers in this section, in fact, cover a half century of work in psychological assessment.

1

CHAPTER

A Note on the Experimental Study of the Appraisal Interview

In the selection or promotion of candidates for positions in the public service, the personnel technician must make a sharp distinction between the written and oral parts of the examination. The latter has the unique function of appraising the candidate's general fitness or ability in terms of his personal qualifications for a specific class of employment rather than his knowledges or skills related to that work. The fact that such appraisals can be made only in the oral interview gives it a particular importance and makes the present lack of knowledge of the underlying factors which determine its course especially conspicuous.

The purpose of the present paper is to suggest a method for the experimental study of the problems of the appraisal interview. The experiment to be reported grows out of the difficulty which confronts the interviewers (usually a board of two or more persons) of creating a situation in which the appraisal of general fitness can be made without asking questions which relate to the candidate's specific knowledge, information, or skill with respect to the job.

Specifically, the purpose was to set up two interview situations: in one the candidates were questioned in the usual manner by an interview board, while in the other they were asked to react not to formal ques-

Reprinted from *Journal of Applied Psychology,* 1943, *27,* 196–205. With permission. The author conducted the study while holding the position of Personnel Technician with the City of Los Angeles, California.

tions but to a set of stimuli that were neutral insofar as the job in question was concerned. In both cases the members of the interview boards appraised the candidates in terms of a specific set of traits. The neutral stimuli selected for the experimental interviews were the Rorschach series of ink blot cards. It should be emphasized that the intent was to use the Rorschach material because it presented a neutral stimulus situation for the candidates. This study was in no way concerned with the theory or methods of interpretation usually associated with the Rorschach technique. Indeed, the oral raters for the experimental interview board[1] had never seen nor heard of the Rorschach procedure before.

The use of ink blots in the interview situation creates certain definite changes in the role of the interviewer. Strictly speaking, he no longer interrogates in a give-and-take conversation, but he limits his behavior largely to the observation of each candidate. The verbal responses of each candidate—except those on being introduced to and taking leave of the oral board—are confined to his spoken interpretations of the series of ink blot cards. The situation changes in character from an interview which is social and reciprocal to an appraisal which is relatively static and uni-directional, lacking the shifting inter-play of conversation.

There were two hypotheses on which this study was premised: (1) the more uniform stimulus situations engendered by the use of the ink blots would result in greater uniformity of ratings among the judges in the experimental interviews; and (2) the standardization of the interview procedure would eliminate the criticism that a series of interviews does not present nearly identical situations to all candidates.

☐ Procedure

The ten standardized 7¼ by 9½ inch cards which constitute the essential part of the Rorschach test, contain ink blots of different shapes. The figures on the cards are partly black and gray, partly colored. In adapting the procedure of administration of the Rorschach technique to the interview situation, the subject was seated to face the group of three oral raters, one of whom handed him the cards. Each candidate in the experimental interview, after being introduced to the members of the oral board, was instructed by one member of that body:

> This interview is probably a little different from some you may have taken. Rather than ask you questions, we are merely going to ask you to interpret ten ink blots. You will be handed the blots one at a time and asked: "What might this be?" When you have finished with each blot you are to return it to us and we shall hand you the next one. There are no other instructions or rules. Here is the first card. What might this be?

When questions were asked by the candidate, he was answered with: "That is entirely up to you." No information regarding the use, purposes, or possible significance of the interview was given any candidate at that time.

The subjects were candidates in an examination for the class, Deputy Clerk—Deputy Marshal, given approximately one month before the experimental interviews by the Los Angeles City Civil Service Commission. Only those employed at that time by the Commission were used as subjects in the second interviews.

Two days before the experimental interviews and a few days after the eligible register for Deputy Clerk—Deputy Marshal became legal, the subjects, who had all been bona fide and serious candidates in the examination, were notified by the Director of Examinations that protests on the oral interview grades had necessitated the re-scheduling of the interviews with another oral board. While this kind of situation is highly improbable according to the rules under which the Commission operates, it may be assumed that the subjects took the Director's words in good faith and did not display significantly less concern, incentive, or legitimate effort in the experimental interview than they did in the first.

The traits rated were Personal Appearance, Mental Alertness, Ability of Self-Expression, Manner and Bearing, Ability to Get Along Well with Others, Adaptability to New Work, and Summary Rating. The degrees of endorsement, made on a graphic rating scale, were Inadequate, Borderline, Suitable, Good, and Outstanding.

At the completion of each of the fifteen experimental interviews, the candidate was directed into an adjoining room where he was informed that the interview was not a re-test and was asked not to reveal the nature of the interview. He was then given a page on which he was requested to check one of three possible answers to three questions relating to a comparison of the conventionally conducted interview and the interview with ink blots; to state the number of civil service interviews he had taken previously; to indicate whether or not he had ever seen the blots before; and to write any comments he felt inclined to make.

At the end of the day, after all the subjects had been interviewed, the oral examiners were asked to fill out a special questionnaire on which they indicated the degree of their general endorsement of this type of interview and wrote their comments relative to the use of ink blots as a means of obtaining an estimation of candidates' personal qualifications.

☐ Results

A summary of the checks made on the Report Sheet for Candidates by the fifteen subjects is presented next:

1. ". . . I like this interview
   (*a*) better than the conventional interview 4
   (*b*) neither more nor less 4
   (*c*) not so well as 7
2. "As compared to the conventionally conducted interview, this type of interview put me
   (*a*) more at ease 3
   (*b*) equally at ease 6
   (*c*) less at ease 6
3. "In regard to accuracy and fairness, I would rate this type of interview as
   (*a*) superior to the customary interview 4
   (*b*) not significantly different from 2
   (*c*) inferior to the customary interview" 9
4. The candidates indicated that they previously had taken from two to ten civil service interviews.
5. Four of the fifteen candidates stated that they had seen the blots before.

The total of the 1(*a*), 2(*a*), and 3(*a*) responses—"better," "more," and "superior"—is 11; the total of the 1(*b*), 2(*b*), and 3(*b*) responses—"neither more nor less," "equally," and "not significantly different from"—is 12; and the total of the 1(*c*), 2(*c*), and 3(*c*) responses—"not so well as," "less," and "inferior"—is 22. Therefore, 11 responses indicated that the interview with ink blots was preferred to the conventional interview; 12 indicated that it was neither better nor worse; while 22 indicated that it was thought inferior.

On the qualitative side, certain important points were made by the candidates. The following quotations are extracts from the comments written by the subjects after they had been interviewed.

1. Two of the candidates misinterpreted the experiment as a psychoanalytical study.

> Frankly, I do not feel quite competent to judge this type of interview as I really do not know just what they are driving at. It seemed more like a Freudian experiment to me than anything else.
>
> Because I am aware of the limitations of the psychoanalytic techniques and of the Rorschach test in particular, I would hesitate to endorse the use of such techniques in civil service examinations. . . .

2. Two of the candidates mentioned some advantages of using this type of subject matter in the oral interview.

> It is an improvement, from my point of view, to give the candidate some objective problem to solve. This method brings out the characteristics of

> the candidate more clearly, I believe, than the artificial situation of making conversation from topics usually drawn from the application blank.
>
> From the standpoint of the raters, this type of interview seems to offer many desirable features. It allows them an opportunity to examine visible characteristics of a candidate (clothes, manner, etc.) at greater length and more carefully than in an ordinary interview. It also calls into play the candidate's adjustment to this type of situation. . . . Another advantage of this type of rating is that it eliminates the necessity of a rater's knowing anything about the candidate's experience or education, the knowledge of which often colors a rater's judgment of other qualities possessed by a candidate. . . .

3. Another person wrote of disadvantages and limitations inherent in the use of the ink blots.

> The interchange of ideas that verbal intercourse makes possible seems to me to be of the greatest value in judging or rating personality. It seems that both the oral examiners and the candidates are at a disadvantage in this type of interview. I cannot see that it gives a person an adequate means of presenting his personality, although it may give the examiners the opportunity to determine a trait or two which more conventional interviews would not do. . . .

4. Two subjects thought that more comprehensive directions should have been given.

> This type of interview would be more valuable if the candidate was aware of why he was being asked to interpret meaningless ink blots. The procedure makes the candidate feel ill at ease in that often it is really quite difficult to put any meaning into what he is asked to interpret.
>
> I think that the ratings in an oral interview using this technique have the advantage of being relatively free from bias that they would be subject to in an interview in which experience is discussed. However, to get a good display of personal traits, I think that more comprehensive instructions should be given the subject. . . .

5. Two individuals commented on the public relations problems that would have been involved had this type of interview been used as part of a regular examination procedure.

> . . . As far as substituting this type of interview for the conventional type which is associated with civil service examinations, I believe that this would be a very unwise move. The average candidate would not accept it as being practical and I think that public opinion would thus be alienated from the efficiency of the merit system principle.
>
> . . . What the general public who heard of this would think of the Commission and would publish in newspaper columns or satirize in movies is still another problem. Certainly though, this is an interesting attempt to improve what up to now has been a weak point in the examination procedure.

6. The other comments were concerned with general dissatisfaction with, or concern about, the candidate's own behavior in the experimental interview situation.

The comments made by the three oral examiners after the fifteen experimental interviews were concluded constitute perhaps the most valuable data secured from this study. These comments are presented in verbatim form, labelled A, B, and C.

Comment A

An interesting way of conducting an oral interview. It has considerable possibilities. If the candidate can forget the interview board and concentrate on examining the blots (and several did) the examiners get a fine idea of the "workings of the candidate's mind." It does give the examiners a fine opportunity to judge personal appearance without obviously staring at the candidate. Self-expression is well brought out because the candidate is given full opportunities and does not have to be thinking of an answer to a definite question. Surely alertness is well tested in this type of examination because the examiner can observe the candidate's reactions to the various blots. I do feel that there is the possibility that the candidate is perhaps not put fully at ease with only one of the examiners giving the preliminary instructions and the other two remaining mute. However, I believe that for the purpose of this examination, and almost all others, a fair and accurate picture can be drawn of the several qualities on which the candidates are to be graded.

Comment B

Thinking of an interview a person will think of possible questions and answers. Being given something new, an examiner has a chance to see what that person will do when faced with a problem he has had no time to think through. In dealing with people, one has to change quickly from one type to another. This test gives the examiner a good idea what a candidate will do and shows the candidate's reaction to change, which is sometimes the only difference between a good and bad employee.

Comment C

There appear to be restrictions upon the candidates' opportunity to express themselves. This may be a good thing and eliminate unnecessary and confusing talk as well as more nearly standardize the scope of expression heard by the oral board. I could not see that candidates were either more or less at ease than those I have seen in the conventional type. The rapport seemed to improve as each candidate became more accustomed to the situation, i.e., after he had seen about four cards.

The attempt at so-called objectivity in the oral situation should, it seems to me, be in terms of the situation established for both the board members and the candidates. The simple instructions, the freedom of the board members from a responsibility of "keeping questions and answers flowing," the nearly identical situations for all candidates tend to increase the objectivity. For an opinion upon the validity, I would rather see some objective correlation made, if possible. The control of the situation and the more standard stimuli among candidates seem to offer a more adequate and fair basis for judging suitability.

I like the method for these off-hand reasons: (1) Freedom of board from burden of questions and attempts to secure questions of so-called revealing nature. (2) Standard questions and attempts to secure subject matter for discussion at least on a par with "Why are you interested in this job?" (3) Ease of administering. (4) Possibility of more valid data for test research. (5) Time consumed aspect is up to candidates, not a burden on the board nor a clock watching requirement on members' part. (6) Information revealed seems to lend itself fairly well to check list form, more especially the traits Mental Alertness, Ability of Self-Expression, Manner and Bearing, and Adaptability. Appearance and Summary Evaluation would be obtainable on any method used.

The criticisms associated with standardized paper and pencil and miniature tests will be directed at this form of oral interview. Clear explanation to candidates stated in the bulletin and continued at the time of the interview can in part off-set this. To this end, I believe a few additional instructions might be used; maybe only a sentence enlarging upon the fact that this is used instead of questions and is to evaluate certain factors required for the job and listed in the bulletin.

What are the reactions and suggestions of those taking the oral today? They should be interesting and valuable.

☐ Statistical Data

In the case of both the original and experimental interviews, the fifteen series of ratings of the three judges on each board were averaged for each trait, although the three ratings on each trait were considered as a sum. The rank-difference correlations between the ratings on each particular trait in the two interviews and the probable errors of these correlations are presented in Table 1-1.

The correlations between the same traits in the different interviews, computed by the rank-difference method, range from .03 ± .18 to .41 ±

TABLE 1-1. Rank-difference correlations between average trait ratings of original and experimental interview boards

Trait	rho	PE(rho)
Appearance	.07	.18
Alertness	.08	.18
Expression	.20	.18
Bearing	.04	.18
Congeniality	.41	.15
Adaptability	.17	.17
Summary	.03	.18

.15. The correlation of the trait of "Appearance," .07 ± .18, is significant in that it is statistically insignificant. Of all the traits measured, it might be assumed, a priori, that the appearance of any candidate would be evaluated similarly by two comparable groups of raters regardless of the difference in the nature of the interview which existed in this case. At least in regard to this trait, one must conclude that the two boards rated with measurably different biases.

On the other hand, the rank-difference correlation between the two interviews on the trait called "Ability to Get Along Well with Others," or "Congeniality," was .41 ± .15, the highest measure of agreement obtained. In spite of the relatively large probable error, this correlation is strikingly high in light of the fact that this trait is one of the most nebulous and vague of all the aspects of personality rated.

The rank-difference correlations between the initial interview scores and the experimental interview scores, when but seven traits are considered (with the data for "Education," "Experience," and "Interest in the Work" omitted), between the written part of the examination and the initial interview scores, and between the written part of the examination and the second or experimental interview scores were found to be non-significant.

While there was no general significant agreement between the two boards, the indices showing the relative agreement among the raters themselves demonstrate which of the two groups displayed relatively more unanimity and agreement in its appraisals. These data are presented in Table 1-2 in the form of rank-difference correlations, and their probable errors, among the three examiners of each oral interview board.

In terms of the relative reliabilities of the two groups of raters, the correlations, and their measures of significance, shown in Table 2, reveal

TABLE 1-2. Rank-difference correlations of ratings among examiners of original and experimental interview boards

	Original Interview Board						Experimental Interview Board					
	A & B		B & C		A & C		X & Y		Y & Z		X & Z	
Trait	rho	PEρ	rho	PEρ	rho	PEρ	rho	PEρ	rho	PEρ	rho	PEρ
Appearance	.74	.09	.47	.14	.73	.09	.50	.14	.37	.16	.49	.14
Alertness	.46	.15	.39	.16	.51	.13	.55	.13	.78	.07	.72	.09
Expression	.39	.16	.24	.17	.45	.15	.51	.14	.82	.06	.56	.13
Bearing	.81	.06	.35	.16	−.02	.18	.52	.13	.55	.13	.50	.18
Congeniality	.65	.11	.48	.14	.73	.09	.59	.12	.85	.05	.58	.12
Adaptability	.65	.11	.62	.11	.84	.06	.42	.15	.66	.10	.74	.08
Summary	.74	.08	.52	.13	.67	.10	.47	.14	.83	.06	.66	.10

that (1) the order of magnitude of the correlations is about the same in the two groups; and (2) the correlations for both groups show both considerable variability among raters and an amount of agreement and disagreement with respect to traits that is usually expected from oral interview boards. That is, both boards behaved much the same in spite of the introduction of a drastically different method of interviewing. This fact would appear to minimize the error involved in the use of the two board technique.

☐ Discussion

There are certain sources of error in the experiment as a whole that may be considered in the interpretation of the statistical data.

1. The most serious error arises from the fact that the original board had an enormously greater range of experience in interviewing candidates for positions in the class of Deputy Clerk—Deputy Marshal. This board worked together for a longer period of time and thereby set up important psychological relationships that could not be present in the experimental oral board.

2. The fifteen subjects used in the experiment were a rather select group of the total number of 186 called to the initial interviews. All fifteen were employed at the time of the experiment by the Commission in a clerical-technical class, indicating that they had already successfully passed through a competitive selection process.

3. The low order of the inter-board correlations on the several traits may be a commentary on the interview process itself, indicating that the same rating form and similar instructions to raters may not yield appreciably better results than might be expected from informal, unstandardized estimates. The facts are, however, that neither the total group nor the raters in the two interviews were the same.

4. It might be expected that the correlations between ratings on the same traits in the two interviews would tend to be low because of the deletion in the experimental interview of three traits discussed and rated in the initial interview, which might have influenced other ratings made at that time. These traits were "Evaluation of Education," "Evaluation of Experience," and "Interest in the Work"—the three which obviously could not be rated from responses to ink blots. In the first interview, the ratings on "Education" and "Experience" for the fifteen candidates subsequently re-interviewed, were generally high, while the ratings on "Interest" were strikingly low.

5. Although the data presented in Table 1-2 might be taken to indicate otherwise, the difference in the kind of interviews would seem to be an

operative variable. The first interview was of the type that might be described as conversational or social, in that the verbal responses were in the nature of continual stimulation and response among the candidate and the raters. The experimental interview, on the other hand, employed not this "circular" type of response that engenders a psychological barrier between the interviewer and the interviewee, and which characterizes the true interview, but was more "linear" and mechanical, in that the verbal responses made during the interview were almost entirely from the candidates to the raters. In the second or "observational" interview situation, the same traits had to be appraised on the basis of manifestations of different qualities of response than those employed in the original interview, as there were few of the nuances of behavior that come from a social conversation.

☐ Suggestions

With the possibility of some future experimentation along this line in mind, these major changes of procedure may be suggested: (1) The need of a large enough number of candidates to give significance to the statistical results is evident. (2) The use of the same oral raters for both the initial and experimental interviews is recommended. While it might then be possible that the raters' judgments in the second interview would be influenced by their ratings in the first, the uncontrollable variable introduced by having "comparable" interview boards would be eliminated.

☐ Endnote

[1]The original oral interview board consisted of a professor of psychology and two employment interviewers from two California State Employment Agencies. The experimental interview board included a professor of public personnel administration, a principal of a large business school, and a branch head librarian.

2

CHAPTER

MAPS of the Harvard Yard

The Make-A-Picture-Story (MAPS) Test was given to 14 undergraduates who were studied intensively at the Harvard Psychological Clinic by Henry Murray and his colleagues from 1959 to 1962. A case study of one of these subjects is presented to illustrate the use of the MAPS Test in drawing inferences about personality characteristics.

Imagine that we are standing in Harvard Yard on some spectacular New England autumn morning, and our attention is directed to a typical Harvard undergraduate as he moves briskly from one class to another. Imagine further our stopping him and asking for some directions: "Can you direct us to Wigglesworth Hall? The Leverett Towers? The Widener Library?" We note that he points out each of them (with appropriate courtesy) before he hurries on. We concluded that his cognitive maps of the Harvard Yard are well delineated and that they are, in his mind, clearly seen. But as he leaves us we wonder what else is in his head and in his heart. What constellations of personal need and press, of negative and positive affect, might be mapped out to describe the being and essence of him?

At this point, the reader may note that the title of this article involves a fair play on words in that I present some Make-A-Picture-Story (MAPS) Test findings about a group of Harvard undergraduates. All members of this group are young men who volunteered, during the 1960s, to be stud-

---

Reprinted from *Journal of Personality Assessment*, 1986, *50*, 436–447.

ied and trained at the Baleen,[1] Professor Henry A. Murray's center for personality research. The MAPS Test is a modification of Murray's Thematic Apperception Test (TAT)—it has been called a "little first cousin" of the TAT—the essential difference being that the background pictures and the human figures are physically separate from each other, and hence subjects are required to populate each background picture before telling the story to a situation that they have in part themselves created. It might be said that the purpose of this article is to provide a slim Baedeker of the MAPS of the Harvard Yard; or in other words, for me, as a cicerone who loves his beat, to describe some local statistics and a few of the points of special interest found among 14 Harvard Yard natives who were studied with MAPS test material.

In order to move on to the next point, we have to leave the Yard and transport ourselves to the nearby Loeb Theater on Brattle Street, so that some analogies from the drama can come easily to mind. What play is being presented? What is it all about? Who is (i.e., what is the personality of) the author? Anyone who has ever looked at the photographs or stills in the foyer of a theater and tried, by imagination, to anticipate the nuances of character in the full play—or for that matter, anyone who has looked at the pictures in an illustrated book and has in this manner attempted to anticipate the plot or character development of the story—has already participated in the essential process involved in interpreting a MAPS Test Figure Location Sheet (FLS). From our glances at the photograph of that solemn young man addressing his thoughts to a skull or of a handsome British Naval Captain seemingly in benign conversation with a roly-poly female aboard a 19th-century man-of-war, we often "get the picture" as to what the total piece is about and what the characters "are up to." Thus, MAPS Test interpreters can be said to be, among other things, part drama critic because their task is to scan the stills of the dramatis personae exhibited in the foyer of the subjects' psychodramatic playhouse and then to write critiques (hopefully including praise for demonstrated strengths as well as criticism for visible flaws) of the playwrights themselves.

We can continue to employ our dramaturgical analogy to describe the materials of the MAPS Test. The "scenery" is chosen from among 22 background pictures, 8½ × 11 in., printed achromatically on thin cardboard. With two exceptions, there are no figures in any of the pictures. (There is an ambiguous human head in the bottom left corner of the dream background and a humanlike lump in the bed of the bedroom background.) There are unstructured or ambiguous backgrounds such as the blank card, the abstract doorway, and the dream background; semistructured background such as the stage, the forest, the cave, and the landscape; and definitely structured backgrounds in the remaining 15 backgrounds, including the living room, street, bathroom, and bridge.

The "company of players" is made up of 67 figures. A distinguishing feature of the MAPS method is that it offers the subject the opportunity to select the figures, as well as to enliven and interpret them. In the MAPS Test, a 6-ft human figure is 5½ in. tall; all others are scaled proportionally. Any figure can be placed on any background without violating one's sense of proportion. The figures are depicted with various facial expressions and are in various poses; some are partially clothed or nude. The types of figures include male adult, female adult, children, minority group figures such as blacks, two animal figures (a dog and a snake), figures of indeterminate sex, legendary and fictitious characters, silhouettes, and figures with blank faces.

The Figure Location Sheet is a printed form representing "pictorial synopses" of each scene, on which there are lightly printed, reduced reproductions of all the background pictures. This form enables the examiner to record the subject's total choice and exact placement of the test figures. The Figure Location Sheet indicates the dramatis personae of the subject's imaginal productions.

The Figure Identification Card, representing the "cast of characters," contains a miniature picture as well as a verbal description of each figure. This enables the examiner to identify each figure he or she records on the Figure Location Sheet by means of a simple numerical code.

It only needs to be added that if the subject's verbatim remarks are the "plays," then the psychologist's interpretations constitute the psychologically oriented assessment of the playwright.

How are these materials used in actual practice? The MAPS Test is administered by presenting the subjects with approximately 10 (of the 22) backgrounds, 1 at a time, with the instruction to populate each background picture with 1 or more of the 67 human figures that they have placed out on the table before them. After subjects have selected and placed figures on the background picture, they are then requested, as in the TAT, to tell a story to this figure-on-the-background situation, indicating who the characters are, what they are doing and thinking and feeling, and how the story turns out. The exact details of administration are published elsewhere (Shneidman, 1951).

On occasion, in clinical practice, it happens that the subject will not give any verbal responses but will be willing to select and place the test figures on the backgrounds. Examples of this phenomenon have been obtained with mute subjects (Shneidman, 1960), deaf subjects (Bindon, 1957), and very young subjects (Spiegelman, 1956). In these cases, where one must depend entirely on the Figure Location Sheet, it has been demonstrated that the interpretations still retain clinical meaningfulness.

In analyzing the FLS, the interpreter does well to attend to the "formal" aspects of the completed form. These aspects would include such items as the following: the number for figures (paucity of figures, over-inclusion, etc.); the placement of figures (upside down, off the background, in the air, at sharp angles, etc.); the appropriateness of the figures (e.g., a nude figure on the street); the general "tenor" of the figures (hostile, sexual, frightened, etc.); conspicuous absence in the choice of figures (e.g., no female figures of any kind); the relationships among figures (the kinds of figures that are generally coupled with other figures); and any differences in the "figure-handling" in the relatively unstructured backgrounds (e.g., the dream or the blank) as opposed to the ways in which the subject populates the more structured backgrounds like the bridge or the cemetery (Proud, 1956). A résumé of these formal signs, especially as they apply to schizophrenic subjects, is given in a separate monograph (Shneidman, 1948).

In general, one interprets a MAPS Test protocol in rather the same way in which he or she would interpret a TAT protocol. We know that there are many—around 36—published ways of interpreting the TAT. Murray readers will know that 17 of these approaches were brought together in a single volume, *Thematic Test Analysis* (Shneidman, 1951), where they are described by their authors and illustrated, all using the same case. In that study, it was possible to group the different methods of interpretation in terms of five primary approaches: normative, hero-oriented, psychodynamic, interpersonal, and formal. In addition, it was possible to distill some 20 "report areas" that any comprehensive psychological test report might reflect, including, for example: intrapsychic conflicts, self-concept, personality defensive mechanisms, quality of perception, idiosyncratic logical styles, and so forth. As a result, it appears that the most sensible recommendation as to a method of thematic test analysis would be the one that combined the best elements of all these approaches and included as many of the test report areas as applicable.

The dissertations and publications relating to the MAPS Test can be divided among these categories: (a) basic manuals and texts (Shneidman, 1948, 1951, 1952); (b) references having to do primarily with children and adolescents, ranging in age from 3½ to 15 (Bindon, 1957; Fraimow, 1950; Joel, 1948; Shneidman, 1960; Spiegelman, 1956); (c) references relating to use with adults, all male subjects (Conant, 1950; Fantel & Shneidman, 1947; Farberow, 1950; Fine, 1952; Hooker, 1957; McDonald, 1952; Shneidman, 1948, 1952, 1955, 1961; Smith & Coleman, 1956); (d) articles and monographs dealing with methodological and research issues (Charen, 1954; Edgar & Shneidman, 1958; Fine, 1955; Proud, 1956; Spiegelman, 1956; Van Krevelen, 1954); and (e) general review articles (Goldenberg, 1951).

Let us turn to the Baleen MAPS Test data. The MAPS Test was administered to 14 (of the 21) Harvard undergraduates studied intensively at the Baleen by Dr. Murray and his associates from 1959 to 1962. The MAPS Tests were given early in 1962, at a time when all the subjects were seniors, around 21 years of age. Of the 14 tests, 12 were administered by Dr. Daniel Slobin (Dr. Slobin is currently, 1985, Professor of Psychology at the University of California at Berkeley), who was then a graduate student in the Department of Social Relations; the other 2 were administered by me. The 7 subjects who were not tested could not meet their appointments or were not available by virtue of illness or absence from the city. No systematic selective factor seemed evident in the self-choice of the 14 MAPS Test subjects from among the total group.

The remainder of this article discusses, as an illustration, the MAPS Test protocol of one Baleen subject: the young man whose code name was Tandy.

□ Tandy

Figure 2-1 is a photographic "mock-up" of what the backgrounds and the figures actually look like, as Tandy selected and placed them. First, let us examine Tandy's choice and placement of the figures on the backgrounds.

These comments on the figure location are speculations, surmises, and guesses on the basis of only the subject's choice and placement of figures as to (a) what story the subject probably would have told to the scene that he has created and (b) what psychodynamic import that scene and the story might have for him in his total psychological makeup.

A tachistoscopic peek at the figure location shows two, three, or four figures on each background. No figures are in any bizarre positions, seemingly, at first glance, and they appear to be interacting in healthy, outgoing ways. One additional impression is that in the less structured backgrounds—dream, blank, doorway—Tandy seems to be able to expand his mind more freely. From this I tentatively hypothesize that he uses the structure of a situation to impose an abiding structure on himself.

What do we see when we look briefly at each background?

Living room. The focus seems to be on the competent, giving male. No competition from the female, yet surrounded by noncompetitive females (black maid, little girls). He is a hero but only by carefully arranged comparison. (The reader can compare this surmise with Tandy's actual story, which is presented later.)

Street. Virile policeman and frightened, incapacitated woman and child. The puppy is the psychological center of the scene. The policeman

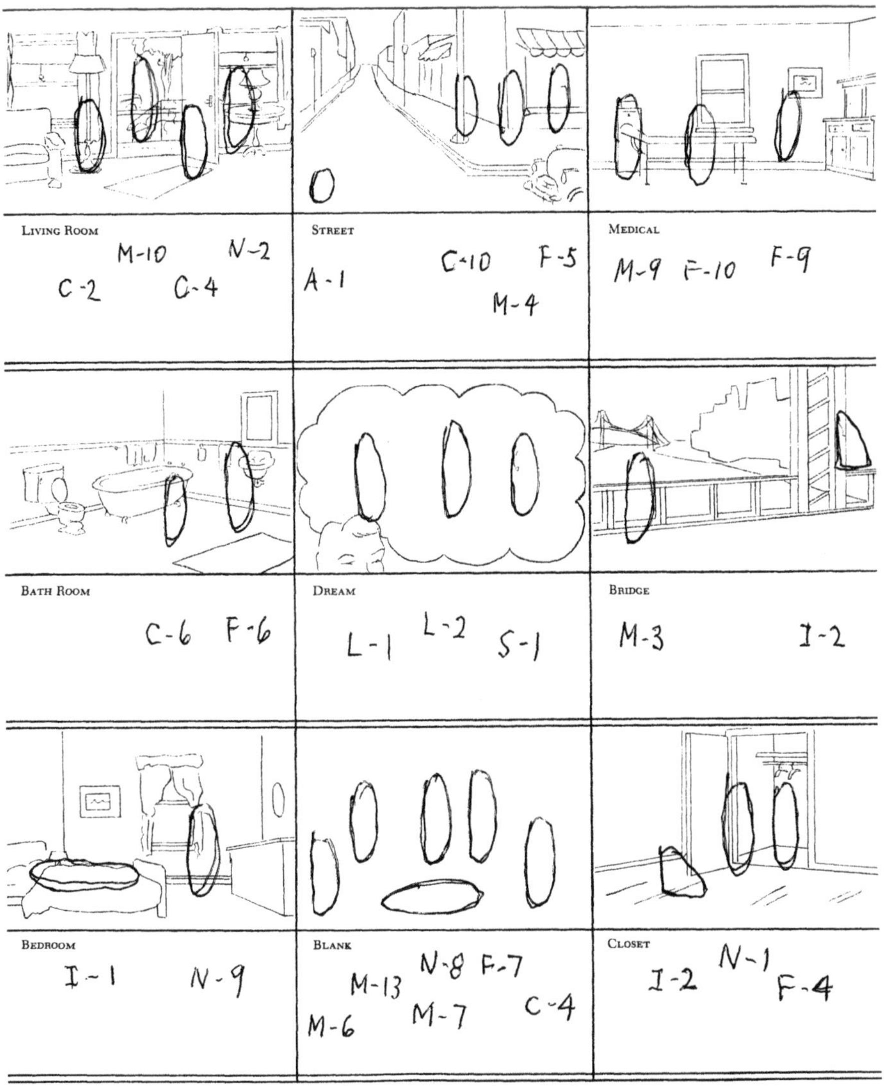

FIGURE 2-1. Tandy's MAPS Test Figure Location Sheet.

is doing something, even if it turns out to be only a trivial action. Thus, a legitimate goal of behavior can be an inconsequential difference so long as it is a difference.

Medical. Doctor (competent male) and no comparable females. Females are either too young or too old. One is his ancilla, and he will save the other, but not compete with either.

Bathroom. Young mother and young boy. The rather sexless roles are reversed. The bathroom is heterodesexualized.

Dream. He or she—the figure in the lower left-hand corner—has a dream of male omnipotence (king and pirate) and an enigmatic figure—the first silhouette of hope.

Bridge. A despondent and ambiguous figure. Despondent because ambiguous? A male military figure still is a doll. Can "it" save anyone from anything?

Bedroom. A supine and ambiguous figure and a second upright female. We know who is at home, but who is on first?

Blank. Male with gun kills and frightens all other men, women, and children. Hostility on the part of one creates helplessness on the part of another. Hostility is thus terribly powerful and awfully taboo.

Doorway. His own selection. The figures are an old black, a slattern female, and an ambiguous crouching figure. This is a curious group to use on a symbolic background, often representing hope or escape. Is the theme one of encapsulated sexuality related to the depressed figure that was used on the bridge? (See Tandy's story.)

☐ Summary from the FLS

There is an overall impression of constrained sexuality and constrained expression generally in this record of an individual in good contact with reality but in poor communication with any richness within himself. There is a kind of inertness, a malaise, a sense of psychic ennui, and a concern with tempests in teapots. He appears to ruminate as to how he can be original, but has only pedestrian notions of creativity. His FLS seems rather superficial and ordinary. It has obsessive elements, and it raises questions of his having genuine lacunae of permissible fantasy content.

Tandy's perception style is that of the furtive glance; he is a shunner. To his perceptions he says: You are there, but I do not need to look. And to evil he says: Evil is bad; there is too much evil; it will never go away. His position with his two primate friends sitting on their haunches is one of holding his hands in front of his eyes. He is the "see no evil" member of the trio.

Now we can turn to his stories beginning with his living room story:

LIVING ROOM (Selected Figures: M-10, C-2, C-7, N-2)

Of course some of the characters are pointing the wrong way, too. Let's see, we have a door with a car parked out in front. The maid has opened

> the door. Of course it doesn't look like a house that might have a maid. Let's say there's a gentleman coming in with a gift under his arm. A baseball bat, I suppose, for his son's birthday, let's say. Not a very imaginative story. Can't very well put a girl in. That's fine. A little fellow walking toward him. Too bad it shows some determination. Should be sort of joyful. "For me, Daddy?!" A little girl off to the left, with her back turned, and a rather wry look on her face and her hands crossed before her, looking as though she were making every effort not to see her father come home, even though it's quite an occasion. Let's see, the little boy and the little girl have a fight. How complicated do they have to be? Well, the father's come home from work. There's been a squabble between the two children, which might, or might not, be usual. If there's a maid, it might be the type of family with squabbles between the children. Where's the wife? That's a good question. The man is looking as though he's expecting his wife, looking around. Maybe his wife isn't home. The children have been left at home all afternoon with the maid. Let's assume there isn't any mother. Let's assume it's just a housekeeper and babysitter as well. It's not a birthday, because obviously the two presents are different, one with a bow and the other a baseball bat. One feminine and the other masculine. Let's say, for the time being, or permanently, that the father likes each of his children equally. He's come home to a motherless house with the two children. Let's assume that the girl has her back turned by accident, you know, she was standing in that position for quite a while, well, would call it just being stubborn, contrary. The father comes in and notices that there's something not quite right. He calls to her and says he has a present for her. A present for both of the children. She runs to her father and takes her present and opens it up. The boy takes his baseball bat and goes out of the house, which immediately leaves the field free for the little girl, gives her a chance to talk out or live out her little squabble with her brother. So we've disposed of the boy who has gone out to try his new bat. I'm wondering what's in the package for the little girl. What's for a little girl like a baseball bat for a little boy? Candy would be too foolish. Clothing? A doll! Let's say this doll now gives her an opportunity to wander off somewhere and begin playing with it. Leaves the father to his dinner and to his maid who opened the door for him, to his evening of paper work. However, he doesn't have a briefcase. Let's say he's a widower. If he's a widower, he might spend the evening going out. And that's as far as I can carry this little scene at the front door. Except that somewhere in the course of it, the children come back in for dinner. [How would you title this?] Friday Afternoon at 5:30 or 6 o'clock or something like that.

Consider Tandy's titles to his nine MAPS Test stories: Living Room: "Friday Afternoon at 5:30 or 6 o'clock"; Street: "The City Is No Place to Bring up a Puppy Dog"; Medical: "The Trouble of Bringing Children into the World"; Bathroom: "The Pleasure of Doing as You're Told"; Dream: "The

Defining of Himself"; Bridge: "Fact and Fancy; Freedom and Authority; the Dream of Becoming Involved"; Bedroom: "Insistence Versus Indolence"; Blank: "The 4:10, Right on Time"; and Doorway (which he chose): "The Perversity of Being Considerate." A number of thoughts suggest themselves after reading these titles: (a) his notion of daring to be bad is a variation of being good; (b) his great manifestations of independence and courage consist of taking minor liberties with conventional dependency patterns; (c) his disdain of evil has an effect on his approach to ordinary experiences. I am reminded of something I heard a long time ago about Titchener: He was a person of rigid German temperament whose peculiar notion of being an American was to behave like a constricted Englishman. I am emphasizing Tandy's limited degrees of perceptual freedom. He is focused, and what he is focused on he sees clearly and unambiguously. But he seems to focus on discrete items, sometimes fragmenting what to most of us would be a series. He is a man who knows what he knows, but the price of this concrete precision is that he plays close to home and is fearful of extended trips of either abstract imagination or enriching inner experience. Thus, there is a dissociative quality, a discreteness, of what should be "all of a piece."

In his story to the medical background, as he begins to show a small amount of imagination, he feels constrained to say: "I'm afraid I'm fudging a little because I'm drawing on books I just finished reading. I could tell a beautiful science fiction story about this, but it would hardly be fair." And in the doorway story he states: "I'm afraid this is going to lead to nothing, as far as stories go. I can't put it in concrete form at all. Makes me recall a book I finished last night called *Portrait of a Lady.* No, that's too much, I can't impose this on that concrete situation . . ." And in the dream he concludes his story:

> I don't see how thought can have consequence in action. I think this, the way I set it up, is something of a memory. Something to be smiled at or enjoyed. [What might you call this story?] It's all tied up with the fact that he sees himself rather nebulously, nevertheless most definite of all the characters. Another result of my reading *Huckleberry Finn* too carefully. Too much identity. It's very interesting because you can think of his identity being brought out, delineated, by being placed against the backdrop of others' actions. I'd like to work on the word identity, but I cannot. Title: "The Defining of Himself."

Tandy's solution to his perceptual impasse in relation to evil is interesting: He reduces the basic thematic problem of evil to activity. To embrace evil leads to the frustration of passivity and dependency, frustrated dependency brings about despair and rejection, and eventually ends up in death: "I don't want the girl involved with the corpse because she's too carefree for that ______." The major ally of frustration is creativity, which, by unstructuring the field and potentially permitting anything, may produce despair. Because each person carries within himself the instrument of his own perturbation, individuals must be on careful guard within themselves. The way out of this trap, and the way to eschew evil, is to be cautious, passive, careful, psychologically prudent; to concentrate on the moment and on the raindrop; to attend carefully to nuances and to details: "the young boy was 17 or 18, 19, really admires his friend who plays the pirate, because obviously he must have a hairy barrel chest. And he also admires the king, because the king is exquisitely made up with a tremendous double chin, chalky white face, and otherwise rather chubby, gross features, and he has a quaint gait about him [dream]." And his first lines to the bedroom background: "Oh, oh, a bedroom. Nice, frilly curtains, a picture on the dresser, and two pillows on the bed. It's hardly a boy's room. If it's not a boy's room, let's put a boy in it and say he doesn't belong. Now we have a reason for him being there . . ."

Time and temporal sequence are very important to Tandy, but mostly the present. He uses the present to think about how he will carefully recover fragments (of memory) from the past and how he will carefully pace himself (in fantasy) into the future. The key word is fragments. "I'd like to see some connection," he says. Each subject was, after several test backgrounds, permitted to choose a background himself. Tandy chose the doorway (selected Figures F-4, N-1, and I-2) and told the following story:

> Originally, when I saw this rectangle, I thought it was a door. Obviously, the future. I'm trying to think of a series of different characters all at the door to the future. The young man . . . I would have labeled "The Thinker, but not do-er." Then I would have had the little girl obviously racing into the future, playfully, tumbling along. Or I would have had the elder girl, more quietly, seriously, and considerately stepping into the future. I would like to have had a gradation of ages all in the process of entering the future. I can't find the figures. Here we go. Here's an elderly man . . . where's our old woman? . . . I want something in the future as a warning . . . therefore I want the elderly black man with his arms outspread barring her advance, or holding her back from stepping on alone. And she, by stepping on, unaware, refuses to acknowledge the existence of this warning, and steps past him, past this elderly black, and walks on alone. Now there's a young fellow, this do-nothing, sitting back here at the portal, just staring away moodily. I'd like to see some connection between the girl and him. She's going on alone and he is sitting on his seat, not going with her. Now, what would it be like if we had a fellow with his back turned, so he could be going too? A triangle, trying to make a triangle. Now what is the black warning them of? Even though he's leaving lots of space for everyone to walk around, he's nevertheless a quite potent, massive figure firing away. I

> don't mean to imply that his character is connected with these two. I wish to use him as a symbol, of a premonition or of an actual fact, which, I don't know. The main thing is that the girl is going on alone, and the fellow is, for some reason, remaining, sitting in the present. The girl has more strength of character, more determination coupled with an equivalent to a quiet willingness to go on, but somehow the fellow hasn't got his legs moving, he's sitting, the brave and courageous one going after her, walking beside her, but his half of the way is barred by this elderly man. Why is it barring only his way, and not the girl's? What is there in the future that says that he can't come? What is the elderly woman doing? The elderly woman doesn't fit. How do we know that the girl is the most decisive of the three? But the young man is, perhaps after all, what shall I say, well, the most correct, doing the most proper thing, considering the circumstances. Does he want to go with her? If we took the black away, it would be said almost without the shadow of a doubt that he wishes, but can't quite bring himself, to do so. But if we leave the black there blocking his half of the way, then we feel that, well, I feel that the one who is sitting there, resting his head on his arms, is somehow justified in holding back, somehow justified in his lassitude. Now if we assume this, then the girl is being driven into the future, rather than running into the future, which must be because of something unhappy in the past, which is this side of the arch. Perhaps nothing happened on this side of the arch. They have nothing in common, they have no past, therefore they have no future. But still something holds him from going into the future. It's not the fact of growing older, because then it would have been the older woman . . . something forcing obedience, or forcing abstinence, but it's so general I can't attempt to tell you what kind of reality. If I take the block away, and have the fellow stand and walk beside the girl . . . that would apply unity. It's a curious thing. The block isn't really the idea of growing old as I said. Somehow I can't give up the feeling that his staying back is justified, perhaps I should reverse the roles and have him walking off into the future and her seated and starting and not being able to follow. I'm afraid this is going to lead to nothing.

All these are Tandy's fear about himself and are, as a matter of fact, the focus of our interest in him too.

Professor Murray has lamented about the trained incapacity of professional psychologists, specifically their penchant to reduce human personality to elements and then to describe these elements in words having mostly derogatory connotations—using "the sharper instruments of depreciation"—in other words, to accentuate the negative in attempting to encompass the person. I fear that I have not been blameless in respect to this charge and would like to put my comments about Tandy in a more proper, or at least a more positive, perspective. These MAPS Test records, as a group, should be seen as reflecting the good strengths and vivid intellects of exceptional young men, behaving successfully in a rather special environment.

About a quarter century ago, Tandy was a senior at Harvard. Now he is about 44 years old, in the middle of his middle life. Where is he today? What did he do with his life? What are the characteristics of his outer life and his inner styles of living it?

Dr. Murray—now 92 years old—knows the precise details of these questions, but understandably he cannot reveal these confidences. But I am permitted to ask a few questions of him: Was the MAPS Test of 25 years ago anywhere near the mark for Tandy as he was then or as he is today? Or would a Rorschach Test interpreted by the incomparable Bruno Klopfer have told us much more of what we ought to know?

Endnotes

[1]The Harvard Psychological Clinic was called the Baleen. Baleen is the mouth plate sieves (called whalebone) in the throat of the *Mystacoceti*, including the giant 100-ft blue whale. Baleen is old French for whale. (Moby Dick was an *Odontoceti*, or toothed whale.)

References

Bindon, D.M. (1957). Make-A-Picture-Story (MAPS) Test findings for rubella deaf children. *Journal of Abnormal and Social Psychology, 55,* 38–42.

Charen, S. (1954). The interaction of background and characters in picture test story telling. *Journal of Clinical Psychology, 10,* 290–292.

Conant, J.C. (1950). *A comparison of thematic fantasy among normals, neurotics and schizophrenics.* Unpublished doctoral dissertation, University of Southern California.

Edgar, C.L., & Shneidman, E.S. (1958). Some relationships among thematic projective tests of various degrees of structuredness and behavior in a group situation. *Journal of Projective Techniques, 22,* 3–12.

Fantel, E., & Shneidman, E.S. (1947). Psychodrama and the MAPS Test. *Rorschach Research Exchange and Journal of Projective Techniques, 11,* 42–47.

Farberow, N.L. (1950). Personality patterns of suicidal mental health patients. *Genetic Psychology Monographs, 42,* 3–79.

Fine, R. (1952). Interpretation of Jay's Make-A-Picture-Story method: The Case of Jay: Interpretions and discussion. *Journal of Projective Techniques, 16,* 449–453, 462–473.

Fine, R. (1955). Manual for a scoring scheme for verbal projective techniques (TAT, MAPS Test, etc.). *Journal of Projective Techniques, 19,* 310–316.

Fraimow, L.S. (1950). *The use of the Make-A-Picture-Story (MAPS) Test with mentally retarded children and children of normal intellectual development.* Unpublished master's thesis, Pennsylvania State University, State College, PA.

Goldenberg, H.C. (1951). A resume of some MAPS Test results. *Journal of Projective Techniques, 15,* 79–86.

Hooker, E. (1957). The adjustment of the male overt homosexual. *Journal of Projective Techniques, 21,* 18–31.

Joel, W. (1948). The use of the MAPS Test with disturbed adolescents. *Rorschach Research Exchange and Journal of Projective Techniques, 12,* 1–10.

McDonald, F.R. (1952). *The effect of different cultural pressures on projective test performances of Negroes.* Unpublished doctoral dissertation, University of Southern California.

Proud, A.P. (1956). *Responses to picture-thematic stimulus material as a function of stimulus structure.* Unpublished doctoral dissertation, University of California, Los Angeles.

Shneidman, E.S. (1947). The Make-A-Picture-Story (MAPS) Test: A preliminary report. *Journal of Consulting Psychology, 11,* 315–325.

Shneidman, E.S. (1948). Schizophrenia and the MAPS Test. *Genetic Psychology Monograph, 38,* 145–224.

Shneidman, E.S. (Ed.). (1951). *Thematic test analysis.* New York: Grune & Stratton.

Shneidman, E.S. (1952). Manual for the MAPS Test. *Projective Techniques Monograph, 1* (Whole No. 2), 1–92.

Shneidman, E.S. (1960). The MAPS Test with children. In A.L. Rabin & M.R. Haworth (Eds.), *Projective techniques with children* (pp. 130–148). New YorK: Grune & Stratton.

Smith, J.R., & Coleman, J.C. (1956). The relationship between manifestations of hostility in projective techniques and overt behavior. *Journal of Projective Techniques, 20,* 326–334.

Spiegelman, J.M. (1956). A note on the use of Fine's scoring system with the MAPS Tests of California. *Journal of Projective Techniques, 20,* 442–444.

Van Krevelen, A. (1954). A study of examiner influence on responses to MAPS Test materials. *Journal of Clinical Psychology, 10,* 292–293.

3

CHAPTER

Personality and "Success" Among a Selected Group of Lawyers

As part of a larger study, eleven subjects—male, Caucasian, native-born, early 70s, lawyers, life-long (since 1922) participants in the Terman Study of the Gifted—were interviewed. From the edited tapes, seven qualified raters evaluated various measures of life success and completed a 100-item Q-sort for all subjects. In general, the very highest successes were related to contentment, self-confidence, openness and spontaneity, a wide range of cultural interests, and relative freedom from pervasive feelings of hostility, irritability and dissatisfaction. The general results are corroborated by Terman Study data available for these same subjects for years 1922, 1927, and 1940. Some implications of these findings for child-rearing, marriage and the possible governance of one's life are explored.

This study seeks to identify certain characteristics of personality which distinguish different degrees of success-in-life among members of a relatively successful group. The group is made up of 11 practicing lawyers, average age early 70s, each of whom has been a subject (for almost all his life) in the Terman Study of the Gifted.

The Terman Study was formally begun in 1921.[1] Lewis M. Terman, then professor of psychology at Stanford University, together with his coworkers, searched the public schools of the cities of California for exceptionally bright youngsters (Seagoe, 1975). His stated purposes were "to discover what gifted children are like as children, what sort of adults

Reprinted from *Journal of Personality Assessment,* 1984, *48,* 609–616. With permission.

they become, and what some of the factors are that influence their development" (Oden, 1968, p. 5). That study, begun a half-century ago, continues to this day.

Of the original 1,528 subjects, 857 were males and 671 were females. The sample was composed of children (mean age 9.7 years) with Stanford-Binet IQs of 135 or higher—the mean IQ was over 150. An enormous amount of data has been collected. At the time of the original investigation in 1921–22, the information included a developmental record, health history, character trait examination, home and family background, school history, character trait ratings and personality evaluations by parents and teachers, interest tests, school achievement tests and the like. Subsequently, there has been a long series of follow-ups, by mail—in 1924, 1925, 1936, 1940, 1945, 1950, 1955, 1960, 1972, 1977, and 1982—and with personal visits in field studies (1921, 1927, 1940, and 1950) in which the subjects and their families were interviewed and data from intelligence tests, personality tests and questionnaires were obtained. In 1982 a considerable amount of the Study data was put on computer tape.

The Terman studies have catalyzed two generations of thought, research, attitudinal changes and educational developments. Detailed descriptions of the subjects at various ages, as well as summaries of the important findings are available in a series of publications by Terman, his chief coworker, Melita Oden and Robert and Pauline Sears (Cox, 1926; Oden, 1968; Sears, 1977, 1978; Sears & Barbee, 1977; Terman, 1925, 1940).

Almost everyone in the psychological and pedagogical worlds now knows the basic findings of the Terman Study: That intellectually gifted children—far from being, as once was thought, spindly, weak and maladjusted or one-sided—are, on the whole, more physically and mentally healthy and successful than their less-than-gifted counterparts.

☐ Subjects

In 1981, with permission from Professor Robert Sears, the author interviewed 45 Terman Study subjects. The interview sessions typically lasted about an hour and a half and were open-ended in response to the request to tell about oneself and one's life. In general, the group can be described as all Caucasian, U.S.-born males in their early 70s. (There are, of course, women in the Terman Study, but none of them was seen in this present group.) Among the 45 subjects who were seen, there were 11 men with L.L.B. degrees—all of whom were practicing attorneys at the time of the interviews, all born between 1910 and 1914. These 11 lawyers constitute the subjects for this present study.

Raters

There were seven raters (or evaluators) in this study. Four—called Behavioral Science Raters—included a marriage and family counselor, a psychiatrist in private practice, a professor of psychiatry, and the author. Three of the raters—called Lawyer Raters—are practicing attorneys. Except for the author, none of the raters knew any of the subjects personally.[2]

Rating Forms, Rating Results and Trichotomization of the Group

Except for the author (who interviewed the subjects) all the raters were supplied with a copy of the cassette recordings of each of the 11 interview sessions. The recordings were the sole source of data from which they made their assessments.

The Rating Page presented the raters with the task of making ratings from 1 to 9 ("Most Successful" to "Least Successful") for the following four items: Occupational Life, Marital Life (relationship with spouse), Family Life (relationship with children), and Overall Self-Fulfillment (life fulfillment as a total person).

Oden (1968), a long-time staff member of the Terman Study, compared Terman Study subjects who had been relatively successful with those who were less so. In the present study I decided to follow Oden's pattern and trichotomize the group in order to focus on the two extremes by selecting the three subjects (from the 11) who received the highest ratings and the three subjects who received the lowest ratings on occupational success and overall life success—and to compare these two groups, leaving out the middle five subjects. (Among the raters, the ratings were almost identical on degree of occupational success for each of the 11 subjects.)

It should be pointed out that *all* 11 men in this study are comparatively capable and effective. There is some temptation simply to call the two groups High and Low, or Most Successful and Least Successful, but, in each case, the second label is both mildly perjorative and not totally accurate. For these reasons, the two sets of subjects will be referred to simply by number: 1-2-3 and 9-10-11. The meaning of 1-2-3 is fairly clear: they are the highest ranked people in a small group of practicing lawyers, probably at or near the head of their profession as compared with any group of lawyers. The meaning of 9-10-11 is not so clear. That they received the relatively lowest rankings in this admittedly select group does not tell us where they would rank in a larger group of, say, all the living 70-year-old lawyers in California, and it would therefore be inaccurate to label them simply as Low and Least Successful.

The three Behavioral Science raters evaluated all 11 subjects. After the Trichotomization was made, only six subjects (1-2-3 and 9-10-11) were rated and Q-sorted by the three Lawyers raters—with no word, of course, as to their groupings.

In the ratings for Occupational Life, the mean score (on the nine-point scale) for the 1-2-3 group was 2.11 and for the 9-10-11 Subjects 4.72; for Overall Self-Fulfillment, the two means were 2.11 and 5.50. Subjects 4-5-6-7-8 received mean ratings (by the Behavioral Science raters only) of 3.20 and 3.66 on these two dimensions.

There were no significant differences between Subjects 1-2-3 and 9-10-11 on the Family Life ratings, but there were striking differences on the Marital Life ratings: 2.33 compared with 6.55. Relative lack of success in one's professional life is matched with difficulty in the marriage.

☐ The Q-Sort Method

The Q-Sort Method, developed by Stephenson (1953), "is a language instrument . . . which aims to permit the comprehensive description of an individual's personality in a form suitable for quantitative comparison and analysis" (Block, 1961). It focuses on the salient features within an individual's personality. It permits direct comparisons—by means of statistical correlations—between evaluations by different raters of the same individual, between evaluations (by the same or different raters) of different individuals, or between evaluations of the same individual at different times—all in terms of the same set of descriptive items about personality.

In the present study, 100 items were used. Seventy of these items are taken directly from the Q-set developed by Block (1968, 1977); the remaining 30 were devised by the author for this study to analyze the full set more appropriate for this group of subjects. The 100 items are listed in Table 3-1.

☐ Caveat

In its essence, this study involves very few cases—two groups of three subjects—who were rated by seven judges. It follows that the findings have to be viewed as tentative and suggestive at best. Nonetheless, the findings seemed too interesting in their own light to suppress even

TABLE 3-1. 100 Q-sort items

1. absent-minded	27. *depressed	52. jealous	78. sentimental
2. affected	28. disorderly; disorganized	53. lazy	79. shrewd
3. *afraid of failure	29. dissatisfied	54. likable	80. *shy
4. ambitious	30. dramatic	55. *lonely	81. sincere
5. *angry	31. dull	56. *outgoing	82. sophisticated
6. *anxious	32. easily embarrassed	57. *over-sensitive	83. *spontaneous
7. assertive	33. easily hurt	58. *perfectionistic	84. stubborn
8. bossy	34. energetic	59. persevering	85. *submissive
9. calm	35. *even-tempered	60. poised	86. suspicious
10. *capable	36. fair-minded	61. *procrastinating	87. sympathetic
11. cautious	37. feminine style and manner	62. *productive	88. tactless
12. charming		63. reasonable; thoughtful	89. timid
13. competitive	38. *forebearing; patient	64. rebellious	90. touchy; irritable
14. *compulsive	39. frank; open; candid	65. *religious	91. unconventional
15. confident	40. friendly	66. resentful	92. undecided; confused
16. *conforming	41. *frustrated	67. reserved; dignified	93. unhappy
17. *conscientious	42. guileful; deceitful	68. *responsible	94. uninterested; indifferent
18. considerate	43. helpless	69. restless	95. versatile
19. *contented	44. hostile	70. *rigid	96. *vulnerable
20. cooperative	45. idealistic	71. sarcastic	97. warm
21. *creative	46. imaginative	72. *secure	98. withdrawn
22. *critical of others	47. impulsive	73. self-controlled	99. worried
23. *critical of self	48. inadequate	74. self-indulgent	100. wise
24. cruel; mean	49. intelligent	75. selfish	
25. defensive	50. introspective	76. self-pitying	
26. dependent	51. *introverted	77. sense of humor; witty	

100 items: 70 items from the 70-item Block Q-Set, and 30 added items which are identified with an asterisk.

though the sample was meager. The compromise was to publish these data and reflections with appropriate notice to the reader.

☐ Q-Sort Results

Inspection of the interrater correlations (see Table 3-2) permits at least the following observations: That, in general, Behavioral Science raters agree more with each other than do Lawyer raters; and that both sets of raters agree more with each other on Subjects 1-2-3 than they do on Subjects 9-10-11.[3]

Raters tend to agree more with one another as to what is fine, good, successful than they do with each other when the Subjects are seen as slightly less so. To use an analogy: A number of men looking at one woman might agree that she is an absolute beauty but, looking at other only slightly less attractive persons they might have many minor differences about rating them as "neat," "handsome," "striking," "interesting-looking," etc. There seems to be more diversity of opinion about less-than-first-rate persons than there is about the clear "winners."

In general, for Subjects 1-2-3, the degree of agreement (as measured by the correlations between Q-sortings) among any two of the six raters

TABLE 3-2. Interrater Q-sort correlations

Raters			Subjects					
Beh. Sc. and Beh. Sc.	Beh. Sc. and Lawyer	Lawyer and Lawyer	1	2	3	9	10	11
A-B			.71	.67	.60	.47	.63	.52
A-C			.68	.72	.75	.35	.12	.53
B-C			.76	.71	.64	.49	.27	.63
	A-D		.53	.47	.72	.42	.03	.50
	A-E		.74	.71	.68	.31	.14	.56
	A-F		.55	.65	.38	.28	.15	.33
	B-D		.54	.45	.51	.31	.09	.40
	B-E		.70	.59	.55	.12	.17	.55
	B-F		.36	.53	.52	.36	.29	.48
	C-D		.42	.45	.52	.37	.37	.67
	C-E		.77	.77	.55	.00	.19	.57
	C-F		.56	.63	.49	.41	.06	.31
		D-E	.39	.52	.58	.23	.50	.51
		D-F	.44	.34	.39	.22	.06	.34
		E-F	.64	.56	.55	.47	.10	.37

TABLE 3-3. Most characteristic and least characteristic Q-sort items for subjects 1-2-3 & 9-10-11

Subjects 1-2-3		Subjects 9-10-11	
Beh. Sc. Raters	**Lawyer Raters**	**Beh. Sc. Raters**	**Lawyer Raters**
	Most Characteristic		
	4. Ambitious		
10. Capable	10. Capable		
	13. Competitive	11. Cautious	
17. Conscientious	17. Conscientious	17. Conscientious	
19. Contented			25. Defensive
36. Fair-minded		29. Dissatisfied	27. Depressed
	49. Intelligent	41. Frustrated	
	56. Outgoing	55. Lonely	41. Frustrated
63. Reasonable	63. Reasonable		55. Lonely
68. Responsible		68. Responsible	67. Reserved
72. Secure	72. Secure	96. Vulnerable	
73. Self-controlled	73. Self-controlled		
81. Sincere			
	82. Sophisticated		
	Least Characteristic		
	1. Absent-minded		2. Affected
	5. Angry	19. Contented	
24. Cruel		21. Creative	21. Creative
	27. Depressed	24. Cruel	24. Cruel
23. Disorganized			30. Dramatic
43. Helpless		37. Feminine oriented	37. Feminine oriented
44. Hostile			39. Frank; candid
48. Inadequate	48. Inadequate	46. Imaginative	46. Imaginative
53. Lazy	53. Lazy	47. Impulsive	47. Impulsive
90. Irritable		78. Sentimental	
92. Undecided			91. Unconventional
93. Unhappy			
94. Uninterested		97. Warm	

was almost the same—with an average correlation of about .60 and not too much variation from the correlation. However, for Subjects 9-10-11, the correlations for the three Subjects were not only lower—with an average correlation of about .30—but also more varied among the three Subjects, with most discrepant correlations (from .63 to .03) being within the one Subject with the lowest interrater correlations. When a rated Subject is "ambiguous" or "controversial" or raises issues of life style about which there are different commonsense points of view, then not only will the raters tend to disagree about that Subject among themselves but they may also rate him differently vis-a-vis the other Subjects whom they assess.

For each Q-sort word, there were nine judgments—three Subjects (1-2-3 or 9-10-11) times three raters. In this study, a Q-sort item was selected for comment if it appeared six or more times (of a possible nine) among the 13 "Most" or 13 "Least" items. The results are indicated in Table 3-3.

For Subjects *1-2-3*, the *most* characteristic Q-sort items of the Behavioral Science raters are: Contented, fair-minded, responsible and sincere; of the Lawyer raters: Ambitious, competitive, confident, intelligent, outgoing and sophisticated; and for both sets of raters: Capable, conscientious, reasonable and self-controlled.

The *least* characteristic items for Subjects 1-2-3 by the Behavioral Science raters are: Cruel, disorganized, helpless, hostile, irritable, undecided, unhappy and uninterested; for the Lawyer raters: Absent-minded, angry and depressed; for both sets of raters: Inadequate and lazy.

For Subjects *9-10-11*, the *most* characteristics items of the Behavioral Science raters are: Cautious, conscientious, dissatisfied, responsible and vulnerable; for the Lawyer raters: Defensive and depressed; and for both groups of raters: Frustrated and lonely.

The *least* characteristic items for Subjects 9-10-11 by the Behavioral Science raters are: Contented, sentimental and warm; for the Lawyer raters: Affected, dramatic, frank and unconventional; and for both groups of raters: Creative, cruel, feminine orientation, imaginative and impulsive.

Two items appear as *most* characteristic of *both* groups (1-2-3 and 9-10-11): Conscientious and responsible; and one item that is *least* characteristic of *both* groups: Cruel. Only one item is *most* characteristic of the 1-2-3 group and *least* characteristic of the 9-10-11 group: Contented.

□ Some Longitudinal Data

Much information is on file for Subjects 1-2-3 and 9-10-11 for year 1922, when they were seven to twelve years old. Included in the data are sets of "Ratings on Physical, Mental, Social and Moral Traits." The ratings were made by the subject's parent—the mother in five of the six ratings. Each item was rated on a 13-point rating scale, with the middle rating designed as "Average for his Age." Ratings for several of these same items for these subjects also exist for years 1927–1928 and 1939–1940.

Findings are separated in this study if there were differences of over 2 points on a 13-point scale between the mean scores of the two groups of three subjects. The tentative nature of these findings is re-emphasized.

In 1922, at ages seven to twelve, the mothers of Subjects 1-2-3 rated them slightly higher than the mothers of Subjects 9-10-11 rated their sons on these traits: Leadership, popularity, sociability, mood stability, and musical appreciation.

In 1927, when the subjects were 12 to 17, a truncated form of 12 (of the 25) traits was used. Although there are not data for all the subjects in this present study, nonetheless Subjects 1-2-3 were again slightly higher on leadership and popularity and, additionally, on sociability.

In 1939–1940 (at ages 24 to 30)—in self-ratings—Subjects 1-2-3 rated themselves, compared with the self-ratings of Subjects 9-10-11, as slightly less moody, with more close friends, having more interest in art and music, with lower feelings of inferiority and less interest in religion.

Over those almost 20 years (from 1922 to 1940), Subjects 1-2-3, compared with Subjects 9-10-11, seemed to be more stable, more socially skilled with their peers, and more diversified in their interests. These differences, evidenced as early as age seven—and may very well have existed before—continued at ages 12 to 17 and were visible at age 30.

A previous study with Terman Study subjects (Shneidman, 1970)—which did not include any of the 11 lawyer subjects of this present study—found that the character and personality characteristics relating to at least one vital life decision—specifically, whether or not an individual committed suicide at the age of 55—were definitely discernible from the case history and rating scale materials by the time the individual was age *thirty.*

☐ Discussion

What do the findings of this small study with few subjects—the Q-sort results and the trait ratings over several years—permit us to say? First, that the two groups, Subjects 1-2-3 and 9-10-11, are somewhat different. They have different qualities of personality; they function differently; and they make different impressions on others.

Most of the six raters—Behavioral Scientists and Lawyers—believed that it was *most* characteristic of Subjects 1-2-3 to be capable, conscientious, responsible and fair-minded, and *least* characteristic of them to be inadequate or lazy; further, the raters believed that for Subjects 9-10-11 it was *most* characteristic of them to be frustrated and lonely, and *least* characteristic to be creative, imaginative and impulsive.

In words other than those on the Q-sort items, the personality correlates of "success/happiness" (for those three subjects in the profession of the Law, at least) seem to be these: Energy, talent, derring-do, conscience and sanguinity. Conversely, one might infer that it is best—if one can—to eschew incapacitating hostility. The items angry, cruel, hostile and irritable—a syndrome of negativity—were *least* characteristic of the 1-2-3 Subjects.

On the other hand, caution, depression, dissatisfaction, frustration, and loneliness were *most* characteristic of the 9-10-11 group, and *may*—one must be careful not to infer causality from correlational data—have inhibited their creativity, imagination, and freedom to act on appropriate impulse. In addition, the members of the 9-10-11 group are not as sentimental, and it is uncharacteristic of them to have the "softer" orientations or interests. They would be more apt to be engaged in or found at a physical sports event than at a library or concert.

In general, the Q-sort items identified with Subjects 1-2-3 describe their social and intellectual and interpersonal capacities and skills, whereas the items identified with Subjects 9-10-11 describe their personality attributes and—to stretch a word—their "neuroses." It seems as though in speaking about a highly credentialled and obviously successful person, one tends to speak of his professional attributes and to say things like he is competent and reasonable and fair, whereas in speaking about a person who is somewhat less successful, one might speak in rather different terms, touching more upon his psychological state and say such personal things as he is unhappy and discontented.

The other source of information, the trait-rating data, tend, if anything, to corroborate the Q-sort findings. From as early as ages seven to twelve—and how much earlier we do not know—and again at ages 17 and 29, Subjects 1-2-3, compared with Subjects 9-10-11, are rated by their parents and by themselves as being slightly more stable (less moody), more social (less isolated) and more diversified in their interests (less estranged from art and music). It would appear that the best life-long success is found in the all-around person with social skills, emotional stability, and diversified cultural interests. This general notion first propounded by the Terman Study findings in 1925—as opposed to the then-popular misconception of the bright child as being spindly and neurotic—of a healthy personality in a healthy body is borne out by this present study, even among subjects all of whom are at the higher end of a continuum of success.

Keeping in mind the social milieu in which these subjects lived—born around 1910 in peaceful (and segregated) California and living through most of this century—the following *reflections*—not necessarily causally connected to these data—come to mind: While one can assert the importance of good parents and a happy childhood for a successful life, and—

from a previous study (Shneidman, 1971)—one can also note that often an important ingredient of a long life's happiness is a congenial and supporting spouse in a good marriage.

In that earlier study of those relatively few Terman Study subjects who committed suicide—a clearly *unhappy* outcome of a life—the role of the spouse was often critical: A competitive or indifferent spouse (as opposed to a supporting mate) seemed to make a vital difference in the outcome of some lives. But, of course, this formulation begs the question of how it is that viable and happy marriages (or stressed and competitive marriages) are made in the first place.

If we look again at the trait ratings and the Q-sortings (and the interview comments as well), we sense the related texture of work and family and the ways in which the two enhance (or depreciate) the other. What is perhaps a fresh insight into Freud's dictum of *Liebe und Arbeit* is the importance of the conjunction: that love *and* work are not separate aspects of a life but are intertwined as obviously different expressions of somewhat different roles of *one* life. And we sense in a finely developed and rich life there is the importance of other features: Normalcy, perspicacity, tenacity and—tagging Pasteur's dictum onto Freud's—luck. Chance favors the prepared mind (as Pasteur said), but it also helps the situation if that mind is tranquil and tenacious. Regrettably, the data of this study do not tell us how all these beneficent attributes of psyche are to be achieved. There are, happily, rich opportunities for further research.

☐ Endnotes

[1]The present study was conducted under arrangements made to interview the subjects (at UCLA) and to have confidential access to the research records (at Stanford University) by Professor Robert Sears who, with Professor Lee J. Cronbach, is one of the scientific executors of the Terman Study. The author is especially grateful to Mrs. Eleanor Walker, staff member of the Gifted Study, for her help in preparing relevant data and for advice and guidance along the way. I deeply appreciate the generosity of Norman Sprague, M.D., for his tangible support of this study.

[2]In the interests of honoring the subjects' sense of privacy, it was deemed best to omit the names of the raters and to tender my gratitude to each one in private.

[3]I wish to thank two UCLA students, Misses Deborah Allen and Lisa Weinstein, who graciously helped with these computations.

☐ References

Block, J. (1961). *The Q-sort method in personality assessment and psychiatric research.* Springfield, IL: Thomas.

Burks, B., Jensen, D.W., & Terman, L.L. (1930). *Genetic studies of genius, Volume III: The promise of youth: Follow-up studies of a thousand gifted children.* Stanford: Stanford University Press.

Cox, C.M. (1926). *Genetic studies of genius. Volume II: The early mental traits of three hundred geniuses.* Stanford: Stanford University Press.

Oden, M.H. (1968). The fulfillment of promise: 40-year follow-up of the Terman gifted group. *Genetic Psychology: Monographs, 77,* 3–93.

Seagoe, M.V. (1975). *Terman and the gifted.* Los Altos, CA: William Kaufmann.

Sears, P., & Barbee, A.H. (1977). Career and life satisfaction among Terman's gifted women. In J. Stanley, W. George, and C. Solano (Eds.), *The gifted and the creative: Fifty-year perspective.* Baltimore: Johns Hopkins University press.

Sears, P.S. (1979). The Terman genetic studies of genius, 1922–1972. In *The gifted and the talented: Their education and development.* Chicago: University of Chicago Press.

Sears, R.R. (1977). Sources of life satisfaction of the Terman gifted men. *American Psychologist, 32,* 119–128.

Shneidman, E. (1970). Perturbation and lethality as precursors of suicide in a gifted group. *Life-threatening behavior, 1,* 23–45.

Stephenson, W. (1953). *The study of behavior: Q-technique and its methodology.* Chicago: University of Chicago Press.

Terman, L.M. et al. (1925). *Genetic studies of genius, Volume I: Mental and physical traits of a thousand gifted children.* Stanford: Stanford University Press.

Terman, L.M., & Oden, M.H. (1947). *Genetic studies of genius. Volume IV: Twenty-five years' follow-up of a superior group.* Stanford: Stanford University Press.

Terman, L.M., & Oden, M.H. (1959). *Genetic studies of genius, Volume V: Thirty-five years' follow-up of the superior child.* Stanford: Stanford University Press.

4

CHAPTER

The Psychological Pain Assessment Scale

The purpose of the Psychological Pain Assessment Scale (PPAS) is to investigate *psychological* pain by providing *pictures* to illustrate it. Psychological pain is the introspective experience of negative emotions such as anger, despair, fear, grief, shame, guilt, hopelessness, loneliness, loss—called "psychache" (Shneidman, 1993, 1998). The goal of the PPAS is to offer an instrument that might permit explorations of relationships between heightened psychache and suicidal acts. The challenge is to depict various degrees of psychache so that intra- and interpersonal comparisons might reliably be made.

There is a vast literature on *physical* pain. From that source, Thomas Syndenham's timeless (1683) written description of *gout* is especially to the point.

> The victim goes to bed and sleeps in good health. . . . He is awakened by a severe pain in the great toe. . . . The pain, which was at first moderate, becomes more intense. With its intensity, the chills and fevers increase. After a time this comes to its height, accomodating itself to the bones and ligaments of the tarsus and metatarsus. Now it is a violent stretching and tearing of the ligaments—now it is a gnawing pain and now a pressure and a tightening. So exquisite and lively meanwhile is the feeling of the parts affected that it cannot bear the weight of the bedclothes. . . .

Reprinted from *Suicide and Life-Threatening Behavior,* 1999, *29.* With permission.

Somewhat over one hundred years later, in 1799, the English printmaker, James Gillray drew a picture of gout. It is of a man's swollen foot; on it there is a muscular fire-breathing gargoyle-like creature, waving a serrated tail, with dragon-like fangs and predatory claws, demonically biting and scratching the ball of an inflamed foot. One does not need to see much more to sense the excruciating pain of incapacitating gout.

Another notable illustration of this genre—called "The Headache"—is George Cruikshank's 1819 medical caricature which shows a barely conscious man seated in a chair being tortured by six devil-like creatures who are variously banging, drilling, probing, lancing, draining and hectoring his vulnerable head.

There can, of course, be psychological pain that accompanies physical pain, but, importantly, there can be psychological pain in the absence of physical pain. How to depict it is the problem.

Murray's (1935) Thematic Apperception Test (TAT), is a device that uses pictures as stimuli. Could the TAT technique be modified by focusing on the psychological pain within each of several pictures? My own interest in pictorial thematics test spans a half-century, first with Murray's TAT and then with my own Make-A-Picture-Story (MAPS) Test (Shneidman, 1951, 1999). It was from these thoughts and others that the PPAS was developed.

The materials for the PPAS consist of a single sheet of paper folded so as to make four 8 by 11 inch pages. The items on page 1 request some identifying information, briefly explain the concept of psychological pain, and ask the subject to rate his or her psychache—from 1 to 9—as of the present moment.

Page 2 and the top half of page 3 consist of five TAT-like pictures about which the subject is asked to rate the psychological pain of the principle characters. A few words about the provenance of these pictures may be in order; it is a somewhat personal one: All these pictures are from a set of postcards that my father—who was an amateur Sunday painter—brought with him to the United States from Czarist Russia around 1910. That collection of over one hundred cards was mostly of solemn and serious, even lugubrious, pictures with a few *fin de siecle* beauties thrown in for spice and variety. As a child I perused them dozens of times; they are certainly among the shaping influences in my life. Here is a brief description of the five pictures, as well as whatever text appears on either the front or verso side of the card:

A. *First Steps:* This appears to be a mother helping her infant child to learn to walk. They are both well groomed. The scene is somewhat suffused with tenderness, affection, and every hope for a future filled with locomotion and love. On the back, the word "Postcard" is printed in Russian, Polish and Italian.

B. *The Strike.* The back of this card has the word "Postcard" in Russian, French and Polish. The words "The Strike" in English, are at the bottom of the picture. The picture depicts a man, with downcast visage, standing in the doorway of a brick house, his wife and infant child right behind him. In the background there is an adult figure with hand to cheek. They all look poor and miserable.

C. *Departure for the War.* On the back of the postcard it says "Depart pour la Guerre" and "Auszug in den Krieg." The painter is F. C. Baude. The scene is in a turn-of-the-century French farmhouse. A French soldier, who is leaving for war, is kissing his baby good-bye. (It is probably the Franco-Prussian war from the date of it and the look of his uniform.) The chief character is the young mother-wife who is seated at the table, her head bowed in her arms, overcome with grief and apprehension. She may never see her husband again. Baude's picture is a remarkable depiction of severe psychological pain.

D. *Adam and Eve and the Corpse of Abel.* This card has the title in Russian, Hebrew and German. The German reads "Adam und Eva an der Leiche Abels." The picture depicts the world's charter parents holding the dead body of their son who has been murdered by his brother.

E. *Thoughtful Woman.* Here is a portrait of a rather handsome young woman looking somewhat pensive and thoughtful, gazing, as it were, off into the future. What is she thinking? How is she feeling? On the back, it says "Postcard" in English, French, German, Italian, and Russian.

Are any of these people suicidal? There is much psychache in the world that is *not* accompanied by thoughts of suicide, but in my view there is no suicide that is not touched by intolerably felt psychological pain (together with psychological constriction and the thanatophilic thought that being dead is preferable to being alive). And further: the source or polluted wellspring of suicidal feelings is frustrated or thwarted psychological *needs.*

For me, these psychological needs are best described by Henry A. Murray in *Explorations in Personality* (1938) (see Figure 4-1). It is the thwarting or blocking of one or more of these needs—different needs in different people—that produces the psychache that pushes the suicidal scenario. It is in terms of these needs that mollifications of the suicidal urges can be achieved. The PPAS ought to help in this task, inasmuch as it is specifically designed to focus on the relevant psychological action in the mind.

The bottom half of page 3 asks the subject to rate the *worst* psychological pain ever personally experienced, and then to indicate which feelings were operative in that pain. There are also two brief questions about previous suicide attempts, if any.

NEED FORM

Subject ________________________ Sex___ Age___ Rater______Date______

____ ABASEMENT. The need to submit passively; to belittle self.
____ ACHIEVEMENT. To accomplish something difficult; to overcome.
____ AFFILIATION. To adhere to a friend or group; to affiliate.
____ AGGRESSION. To overcome opposition forcefully; fight, attack.
____ AUTONOMY. To be independent and free; to shake off restraint.
____ COUNTERACTION. To make up for loss by restriving; get even.
____ DEFENDANCE. To vindicate the self against criticism or blame.
____ DEFERENCE. To admire and support, praise, emulate a superior.
____ DOMINANCE. To control, influence and direct others; dominate.
____ EXHIBITION. To excite, fascinate, amuse, entertain others.
____ HARMAVOIDANCE. To avoid pain, injury, illness and death.
____ INVIOLACY. To protect the self and one's psychological space.
____ NURTURANCE. To feed, help, console, protect, nurture another.
____ ORDER. To achieve organization, order among things and ideas.
____ PLAY. To act for fun; to seek pleasure for its own sake.
____ REJECTION. To exclude, banish, jilt or expel another person.
____ SENTIENCE. To seek sensuous, creature-comfort experiences.
____ SHAME-AVOIDANCE. To avoid humiliation and embarrassment.
____ SUCCORANCE. To be taken care of; to be loved and succored.
____ UNDERSTANDING. To know answers; to know the hows and whys.
100

FIGURE 4-1. Need form. Adapted from Henry A. Murray, *Explorations in Personality* (1938).

Page 4: Probably the most important aspect of the PPAS is what the subject writes in the essay describing psychological pain. The instruction on page 4 reads: "Please describe below how your worst psychological pain felt, what the circumstances were, and how it worked out." This essay form, like responses to TAT cards, permits the subject to spin a tapestry, to tell a unique story, to reveal personal thresholds, and to relate a psycho-dynamically-laden narrative. If one is looking for a manual for interpreting thematic materials, the one that comes first to mind is *Thematic Test Analysis* (1951). That volume contains the detailed interpretive accounts of 17 skilled psychologists all analyzing the same case.

It is relatively easy for any tyro or journeyman to describe, often in pejorative technical terms, the pathology and the limitations of personality and character in any record, but it takes a skilled clinician to find the coping mechanisms and the ego strengths. When we use the PPAS, we can look for assets and strengths; characteristics and features of the inner life that have kept that person *alive* and that are life-promoting and life-sustaining, especially items in the past that permitted that person to endure the unendurable and to tolerate the intolerable, for that is what *not* committing suicide involves. One searches in the PPAS (in both the questionnaire part and in the contents of the essay) for these clues and, conversely, for clues that might be precursors of committing suicide in the future.

From the standpoint of the *clinician,* the goal of the PPAS is to assess the patient's mental anguish, present and past, especially as it might relate to suicide; from the standpoint of the *researcher,* the goal of developing the PPAS is to explicate the concept of psychache, to explore its theoretical dimensions, to begin the process of developing operational meaning (and eventually to metricize the concept), and to explore some of the relationships between psychache and suicidal behaviors.

The obvious central implication of this approach for therapy (help, redress, prevention) is to reduce the person's heightened perturbation, thwart the heightened lethality but centrally address (and seek to mollify) the particular psychological needs that are distressing *that* particular individual, and do all these in therapeutic exchanges that are tailor-made for that person's disposition of psychological needs. (Shneidman, 1971, 1980, 1986, 1993, 1996). The basic formula is: Elevated psychache plus constricted perceptions of life's options plus thanatophilic thoughts (preference for being dead over being alive) equals suicide. Psychache is the elevated psychological pain caused by frustrated psychological needs created by destructive (catadynic) life events. Listen to the three basic elements of a prototypical suicide note: ". . . I cannot take (stand, endure) this *pain* any longer. . . . this is the *only* thing to do (way to go). . . . I am tired; I'd be better off *dead.* . . ."

The PPAS has been administered without any ill effects to individuals in the United States, in Israel, and in the Ukraine with seeming usefulness. These individuals include males and females; undergraduate students, medical residents, physicians, rabbis, professors, firemen, psychiatric patients, and sundry others. The psychological, introspective, phenomenological sector of suicide—where I believe the real destructive work is done—merits all the attention it can get.

☐ References

Murray, H.A. (1935). *Manual for the Thematic Apperception Test.* Cambridge, MA: Fellows of Harvard University.

Murray, H.A. (1938). *Explorations in Personality.* New York: Oxford University Press.

Shneidman, E.S. (Ed.) (1951). *Thematic Test Analysis.* New York: Grune and Stratton.
Shneidman, E.S. (1971). Perturbation and Lethality as Precursors of Suicide in a Gifted Group. *Life-Threatening Behavior, 1(1),* 23–45.
Shneidman, E.S. (1980). A Possible Classification of Suicidal Acts Based on Murray's Need System. *Suicide and Life-Threatening Behavior, 10,* 175–181.
Shneidman, E.S. (1986). *Definition of Suicide.* New York: John Wiley and Sons.
Shneidman, E.S. (1993). Suicide as Psychache. *Journal of Nervous and Mental Disease, 181,* 147–149.
Shneidman, E.S. (1996; pb 1998). *The Suicidal Mind.* New York: Oxford University Press.
Shneidman, E.S. (1998). Further Reflections on Suicide and Psychache. *Suicide and Life-Threatening Behavior, 28(3),* 245–250.
Shneidman, E.S. (1999). The TAT: A Paradise of Psychodynamics. In M.T. Gieser and M.I. Stein (Eds), *Evocative Images: The Thematic Apperception Test and the Art of Projection.* Washington, DC: American Psychological Association.

PART

II

LOGIC

Ever since he took courses in logic as a college freshman in UCLA in 1934, Shneidman has been keenly interested in making explicit the latent logical components of everyday thought. He says he "devoured" the courses. He especially liked the deductive explication of the Aristotelian syllogism into its 64 implications (some valid, some not), and the power of Mill's canons of induction, especially the practical applications of Mill's method of difference, which, as we saw in the first paper and shall see later (under "Suicide Notes"), dramatically changed his life. He mentions two other books on logic which have had a distinct influence on his views of logic, especially as they gave insights into how logic might be applied in the overall study of suicide. They are Nakamura's monumental *Ways of Thinking of Eastern Peoples* and Rescher's slim book, *Temporal Modalities in Arabic Logic.* These two volumes show that there are legitimate, widespread other-than-Aristotelian ways of thinking, and raise the possibilities that there may be many idiosyncratic logics even in the Western world, and that it might be important and useful to examine the logical styles exhibited in *each* suicidal person.

This part contains three chapters: Chapter 5, a prize-winning paper on the logic of politics, specifically a detailed analysis of the syllogistic styles and cognitive maneuvers of John F. Kennedy and Richard Nixon in their presidential debates of 1960; Chapter 6, a brief paper on the importance of that seemingly innocuous conjunction "therefore" that occurs in every syllogism (as in the suicidal thought . . . "therefore I must kill myself."); and Chapter 7, a somewhat detailed look at Herman Melville's elaborate cognitive styles and special logics as he used them in his masterpiece, *Moby-Dick.*

It is Shneidman's belief that it can be vitally important for a psychotherapist to understand the patient's idiosyncratic logical style—and then not to agree with that patient's major premise when that premise is the keystone to the patient's lethal (suicidal) syllogistic conclusion. ("People who have committed a certain sin ought to be dead; I am a person who has committed that sin; *therefore,* I ought to be dead"). Shneidman's view is that psychotherapy contains these cognitive components and it is often prudent, if not necessary, for the therapist to make them explicit and to deal with them.

5

CHAPTER

The Logic of Politics

When significant political figures speak nowadays, people listen. Our common sense tells us that we are living in a time of political activities of such extreme importance that national and international decisions can affect not only the subtle tenor of our lives but indeed whether or not we shall survive at all. If this time is, as it has been called, "the age of anxiety," it is probably fair to say that the burden of that anxiety revolves around political actions and political crises—and their implications for global destruction.

Of the many attributes of political speeches (or any kind of verbalization, for that matter) which might be the focus for analysis, one avenue of investigation which has been relatively neglected (but which nonetheless might prove to be extremely important) relates to the *cognitive* aspects and the psychological concomitants of these cognitive aspects. We apply the label "psychologic" to the joint analysis of the logical and psychological elements of a text. We propose to outline a specific method for psychological analysis of the stimulus materials and to illustrate the application of that new method of analyzing political thinking by using materials from some particularly interesting examples.

We are a nation of millions of television sets; we are a nation of almost constant political elections and of intense political interests. We are also living in a world where the other nations include both tangible friends and potential foes. Television influences our elections and our interna-

---

Reprinted from M. A. May and L. Arons (Eds.). *Television and Human Behavior.* (New York: Appleton-Century-Crofts, 1963, pp. 178–199. With permission.

tional relationships, and it is extremely important for us to know more about the television stimuli that our own political leaders transmit and the "impact" which they produce at home and abroad. We must also learn more about the "meaning" (and implications to us) of the televised materials from our international brethren—especially those with keen sibling rivalry.

The purpose of this essay is to present the outlines for a logical model, a model which might be employed in any one of several settings and which would provide a conceptual scheme for translating the logical elements contained in verbal stimuli into their related psychological attributes. Assuming that each individual has—along with his universal and culturally common ways of thinking—some idiosyncratic ways of thinking, the purpose of this paper is to set up a system whereby one can convert these into their psychological attributes. The implication here is that the important impact of the logical aspect of the verbal stimulus is not in the logic which it portrays, but rather in the personality attributes which it implies. A second purpose of this essay is to give content to this notion by way of example and, further, to suggest (in the last section of this paper) some experiments which would be required to test the appropriateness and fruitfulness of the model itself.

The framework of suppositions contained in this essay can be stated in terms of the following:

1. That, given the typescript of a televised speech (address, debate, program, etc.) of a specific political personage, it is possible to analyze meaningfully the unique logical elements or styles of thinking which are latently contained within it.
2. That, given this cognitive analysis, it is then possible systematically to infer specific personality or psychological characteristics that accrue to that individual. The assumption here is that the style of a man's thinking is directly related to other aspects of his personality and that meaningful inferences as to personality or psychological traits can be made from an analysis of an individual's thinking patterns.
3. That, further, in an election situation, given the two candidates' logical styles (and their inferred psychological characteristics), it may be possible to make specific predictions over and above chance expectations as to the impact of the two candidates upon television audiences.
4. That those voters who are television viewers are influenced not entirely by what a candidate says (in that it may be confusing or essentially similar to what the other candidate says), or by what a candidate looks like, but in some significant part by the candidate's "personality" (the kind of person he "is"), which they (consciously or unconsciously) infer in part from his styles of thinking.

5. That most voters have in mind the "kind of person" they would like to see occupy a particular office at a particular time, and they will tend to vote for that candidate whose "projected" personality (as inferred in part from the candidate's styles of thinking, etc.) comes closest to the average "model" that the voters have in mind.
6. That a basis for making predictions of the outcome of elections is available through "matching" candidates' personalities with voters' personality models.

☐ Relevant General Background and Philosophic Assumptions

There are several diverse sources of materials which are relevant to this essay.

1. Behavioral Analysis. There are respectable numbers of previous psychological researches which relate styles of thinking to psychological (or behavioral) variables. Examples would include the investigations of the effects of various experimental variables on the logical styles of *normal* subjects. Along these lines are studies of the effects on syllogistic reasoning of drugs (Andrews, 1940), of anxiety (Beier, 1951), of negative premises (Woodworth & Sells, 1935), etc. Also there are investigations of the developmental aspects of styles of thinking. In this connection, the work of Piaget (1932) and Werner (1957) on the development of different types of reasoning in people of various ages immediately comes to mind. There is extensive literature on the investigation of the styles of thinking of *aberrant* persons, limited largely to schizophrenic and brain-damaged patients. In this connection, one would want to make reference to the work of Goldstein (1944), Kasanin (1944), Vigotsky (1934), von Domarus (1944), Arieti (1955), Cameron (1938), Sullivan (1944), and Rapaport (1951). The work on the "logic of suicide" by Shneidman (1961a) in which are analyzed various attributes of logical thinking in genuine and simulated suicide notes also furnishes relevant background.

2. Content Analysis. Also directly related to this essay are important works in the area of content analysis, which have been concerned with the description of the stimulus pattern in communication. In this connection, reference should be made to the work of Berelson (1952) in communications research, of Lasswell et al. (1949) in "the language of politics," of George (1959) in propaganda analysis, of Osgood et al. (1957) and his semantic differential, and of the volume on content analysis edited by Pool (1959).

3. Thematic Apperception Analysis. Most directly related are the stimulating concepts from Murray (1938) and his host of followers (Shneidman, 1951b) in the tradition that is called thematic apperception test analysis—a tradition which encompasses a large variety of approaches applicable to the analysis of verbal responses to pictorial stimulus materials.

4. Concern with the Importance of the Stimuli. Our problem reflects our general need to "understand" (and to predict) behavior better than we do. In behavioral science, a basic formulation is that of "stimulus-organism-response" (S-O-R). There has generally been too little systematic study of the properties of the stimulus. This is true not only in television research but throughout psychological science as well. Cornell Professor James J. Gibson has stated the following about the stimulus in psychology: "It seems to be that there is a weak link in the chain of reasoning by which we explain experience and behavior, namely, our concept of the stimulus. . . . Enough has been said to show that in the twentieth century we have inherited a mixed batch of ideas about the stimulus. We constantly use the term but seldom define it. We take it for granted. We have behavior theory in full bloom, and perception theory in ripened complexity, but who ever heard of stimulus theory?" (Gibson, 1960)

There is great need to understand the potentiating properties of the television stimulus. The current study ties in with the growing interest in the psychology of the stimulus and the growing general awareness that understanding the nature of the stimulus is particularly important for understanding the operation of mass communication, especially for television.

5. Philosophic Background. The notion that there are different logical styles (or different styles of thinking) is given intellectual permissiveness particularly by the writings of the American philosophers Charles Sanders Peirce (1955), William James (1907), and John Dewey (1938), especially in those parts of their works which relate to logical systems. For this writer, the philosophic father of this notion is Peirce. In order for the reader better to follow the subsequent analyses, it will be useful, at the outset, to indicate some general suppositions which underlie the argument in this paper. It is assumed that:

(a) Thought is common to all. All individuals—possibly excluding neonates and unconscious persons—mentate, reason, cerebrate, deduce, induce, come to conclusions, etc. Thought is not too good for common people.

(b) Individuals think in various ways. There is not one way of thinking, but many ways. In this paper we are not talking about "correct" thinking, but just thinking. People think as they do, often believing they are thinking aright. People do not just make mistakes; there are good reasons for their seeming to be unreasonable. In this paper, we are interested in the *processes* of "concludifying"[1] which the individual thinker traverses. We wish to recapitulate the "concludifying" so that we can infer (from the individual's patterns of concludifying) the psychological "reasons" (or personality variables) which, for him, are consistent with his being "unreasonable" (that is, reasoning as *he* does).

(c) The concept of "error" in relation to modes of thinking has, in the past, been applied somewhat narrowly, if not superciliously. "Error" has ordinarily implied a departure from a particular (theoretical) standard of thinking, usually that attributed to Aristotle when he was thinking about thinking. Our position is that a madman's thinking or a feebleminded person's thinking is as bona fide as the thinking of a genius, and further, is as "reasonable"—given the thinker's premises and accepting his modes of thinking as possible modes of thinking. (It is not implied for a moment that thoughts are of equal value.) The marriage between an individual's patterns of thinking and other aspects of that individual's personality is binding whether "in sickness or in health." We are interested in how people do think, not in how they ought to think. "Reasoning," to quote William James, "is always for a subjective interest."

(d) This "nonevaluative" point of view toward thinking provides a lever to understand (rather than to score or evaluate) the reasoning of the other individual. The main point of this approach is that the thinking of an individual is best understood by assuming that the other person's thinking is logical for that person doing the thinking. Then one is in the position to cast about to see what logical assumptions—no matter how "illogical" from our point of view—would have been made for that individual to have thought as he did.

(e) After one has identified the "idiosyncratic logical position" of the individual thinker, he may then proceed to inquire as to what kind of psychological state in that individual would be consistent with (or even, so to speak, compel) that individual's adopting the logical position which he apparently assumed.

(f) By supplying these intervening variables of idiosyncratic logical position and concomitant psychological status, one can better understand aberrant or unusual thinking in terms of psychological states, and aberrant or unusual psychological states in terms of ways of thinking. A bridge between these offers a most-interesting road to explore.

(g) A word of caution is in order. The way that a man thinks on occasion is not necessarily the way that he must think at all times. Specific idiosyncratic ways of thought need not be globally characteristic of an individual, but may occur only with specific content or in specific situations, so that there may well be intraindividual variations in ways of thoughts which might account, within that individual, for the "logic of prejudice," the "logic of neurosis," the "logic of suicide," etc. Intensive idiographic (intrapersonal) studies would be important in pursuing this approach.

(h) It is believed that this approach to the analysis of the stimulus, if consistently carried out, could clarify a number of problems in the psychology of thinking, which purely logical or purely experimental approaches cannot handle. We would hope that data could be analyzed to obtain meaningful findings about human psychology.[2]

Brief Overview of Proposed Method and Illustrative Materials

If different individuals may have different ways of reasoning, what becomes of paramount importance is the development of a system or procedure for delineating the specific characteristics of a man's logical styles, and then, in some manner explicating the specific psychological characteristics that would be consonant with a particular logical style. In line with this approach (and with our general concern with the nature of the stimulus), three concepts, which are basic to the development of this essay, must be defined. They are as follows:

1. The *idiologic* or "styles of thinking" represent the latent stimulus in this approach, that is, therein is contained the individual patterning and arrangement of logical nuances (in, for example, the political speech coming out of the television set) which serve as the basis (after appropriate conversion to other forms described below) of the listener's response. In this essay, the word "idiologic" is used as roughly synonymous with individual "styles of thinking." Every human (except perhaps newborns and some severe neurological cases) thinks. Individuals think differently. They have different styles of thinking. There are many individual idiosyncratic ways of cognizing, mentating, intellectualizing, inferring, deducing, inducing, reasoning, cerebrating—*thinking*. Idiologic refers to all those things which can be said—given the text of a speech, etc.—about the syllogistic structure, the idiosyncrasies of either induction or deduc-

tion, the form or the content of the (explicit or implied) premises, the gaps or unwarranted conclusions, etc.—indeed, anything that a logically oriented investigator who understood the approach propounded in this paper might wring from a manuscript if he put his mind to it. The idiologic properties of the stimulus are made up of idiosyncracies of reasoning and cognitive maneuvers, both described later.

2. The *contralogic* or "method of rationalizing logical idiosyncrasies" is our technique for clarifying the latent stimulus. Briefly described, the speaker's contralogic would be that theoretical logical system (which might be operating unconsciously in the mind of the speaker) which would serve to undo or rectify or make reasonable the apparent idiosyncrasies of the speaker's logical positions. Its purpose is to permit us to see what is required—what the speaker must implicitly believe—to logically "explain" the speaker's own special logic. This concept of contralogic will be elaborated and illustrated later.

3. The *psychologic* or "psychological traits relevant to styles of thinking" correspond to the psychological impact of the stimulus, that is, the psychological traits or portion of his "personality" which the speaker conveys or imparts by means of his particular logical styles or his ways of thinking. It is to this (implied) aspect of the logical stimulus that potential voters would primarily respond. Some of the specific psychological traits which can be inferred from styles of thinking will be listed and some examples given.

An impetus for the development of this presentation was the 1960 Kennedy-Nixon "Great Debates" and the possibility of analyzing these unique television exchanges. It seemed evident from viewing the debates that Kennedy and Nixon "thought" differently from each other, that they had different styles of thinking and were thus prone to different ranges and kinds of logical errors; also that these differences in logical styles could be systematically analyzed and that they carried with them substantially different personality impacts. As social science data, however, the debate materials raise questions. Are there meaningful methods for such analysis? What was the impact of the Great Debates? What did they tell us about the candidates? Could one have predicted the outcome of the election from an analysis of the Great Debates? Can one, having analyzed aspects of the thought processes of Kennedy and Nixon, now make predictions (better than chance) as to the manner in which each of these individuals would cognize (or think through) some present or future issue? In addition to the questions listed above for the Kennedy-Nixon debates, one might pose some additional general questions. Can one believe that the best prediction of a man's future behavior is an extrapolation from his past behavior in similar situations? Specifically, by knowing something about the manner in which, for example, Khrushchev or Castro thinks today, can we predict how either of these individuals will cognize or "solve" some conflict situation (that might inexorably involve us) tomorrow? And, are there specific techniques for predicting behavior which can be applied to leaders—helpful and hostile—on the international scene?

Results from the analysis of these debates are presented as illustrative material in the delineation of our method. The analysis itself made use of verbatim texts of two of the four debates (*The New York Times*, Sept. 27, 1960 and Oct. 8, 1960). The first two debates involved approximately 22,000 words of which approximately 20,000 were divided almost equally between Kennedy and Nixon. The numbers of separate, discrete statements (usually one or two paragraphs in length and in almost every case in response to a question by a member of the panel of newscasters) by the two main participants in the first two debates were 25 for Kennedy and 24 for Nixon. An analysis of the logical components of the first and then of the second debate indicated that the results for these first two debates were so similar that it was feasible to combine each participant's logical tabulations and to present the two debates as one unit.[3]

☐ The Idiologic or "Styles of Thinking"; The Latent Stimulus

Idiologic has been described as the explication of the ways in which a specific individual cerebrates in his processes of coming to conclusions. With our approach, his idiologic is assessed by way of his (1) idiosyncrasies of reasoning and (2) his cognitive maneuvers.

Idiosyncrasies of reasoning are, essentially, an individual's deductive gambits or tactics. They are the styles of his reasoning, his ways of "syllogizing" and "concludifying" and include what would ordinarily be subsumed under "logical fallacies." Our list is an extension and a rearrangement of the currently "traditional" logical fallacies as might be found in any standard textbook on logic, such as Copi (1953). A brief description of each idiosyncrasy, and the percentages for Kennedy and Nixon in the first two debates are presented in Table 5-1.

Cognitive maneuvers relate to the manner of development of thought, and describe the linear flow of the argumentation. The cognitive maneuvers, so to speak, deal with the interstices between the specific idiosyncrasies of reasoning. Table 5-2 lists these cognitive maneuvers with percentages for Kennedy and Nixon in the first two debates.

TABLE 5-1. Idiosyncrasies of reasoning

	Per Cent Kennedy	Per Cent Nixon
I. Idiosyncrasies of Relevance. Those features of the argumentative style involving the intrusion of conceptual elements extraneous to the argument		
A. *Irrelevant premise.* Premise is irrelevant to the conclusion it is purportedly instrumental in establishing.	9	5
B. *Irrelevant conclusion.* Conclusion is irrelevant to the major body of premises which purportedly establish it.	7	3
C. *Argumentum ad baculum.* Appeal to force or fear in one or more premises where the conclusion in question does not involve these concepts.	2	0
D. *Argumentum ad hominem.* Appeal to real or alleged attributes of the person or agency from which a given assertion issued in attempting to establish the truth or falsity of that assertion.	1	4
E. *Argumentum ad misericordium.* Appeal to pity for oneself or for an individual involved in the conclusion where such a sentiment is extraneous to the concepts incorporated in the conclusion.	1	0
F. *Argumentum ad populum.* Appeal to already present attitudes of one's audience where such attitudes are extraneous to the concepts incorporated in the conclusion.	3	12
G. *Argumentum ad vericundium.* Appeal to authority whose assertions corroborate or establish the conclusion where no premises are asserted to the effect that the authority is dependable or sound.	2	0
H. *False cause.* Falsely judging or implying a causal relationship to hold between two events.	1	4
J. *Complex question.* A premise or conclusion of an argument contains a qualifying clause or phrase the appropriateness or adequacy of which has not been established.	0	2
K. *Derogation.* A premise or conclusion contains an implicit derogation of an individual or group, where the concepts expressing derogation are neither relevant nor substantiated.	1	5
II. Idiosyncrasies of Meaning.		
A. *Equivocation.* The use of a word or phrase which can be taken in either of two different senses.	7	2

TABLE 5-1. (*Continued*)

	Per Cent Kennedy	Per Cent Nixon
B. *Amphiboly.* An unusual or clumsy grammatical structure obscuring the content of the assertion incorporating it.	5	3
C. *Opposition.* The phrasing indicates an opposition or disjointedness of elements which are in fact not opposed or disjointed.	3	1
III. Enthymematic Idiosyncrasies. Argument contains suppressed premises or conclusion.		
A. *Contestable suppressed premise.* A suppressed premise, necessary for rectifying initial invalidity of argument, is contestable.	5	4
B. *False suppressed premise.* A suppressed premise necessary for rectifying initial invalidity of argument is false, either logically or empirically.	3	3
C. *Plausible but not obvious suppressed premise.* A suppressed premise necessary for rectifying initial invalidity of argument is plausible but not obvious.	4	2
D. *Suppressed conclusion.* The conclusion, while determined by the context of discussion, is never explicitly asserted, so that the point allegedly established by the argument is not brought clearly into focus.	0	1
IV. Idiosyncrasies of Logical Structure.		
A. *Stranded predicate.* A predicate occurs in a premise which occurs neither in the remaining premises nor in the conclusion, the function of such recurrence being to bind or relate the isolated predicate to other predicates.	6	7
B. *Novel final predicate.* A predicate occurs in the conclusion which does not occur in any premise.	7	6
C. *Stranded term.* A term occurs in a premise which occurs neither in the remaining premises nor in the conclusion.	5	5
D. *Novel final term.* A term occurs in the conclusion which does not occur in any premise.	4	4
E. *Top-heavy predicate structure.* Stranded predicates outnumber novel final predicates.	6	3
F. *Bottom-heavy predicate structure.* Novel final predicates outnumber stranded predicates.	1	2
G. *Balanced predicate structure.* Number of stranded predicates equal to number of novel final predicates.	2	3

TABLE 5-1. (*Continued*)

	Per Cent	
	Kennedy	Nixon
H. *Top-heavy term structure.* Stranded terms outnumber novel final terms.	5	3
J. *Bottom-heavy term structure.* Novel final terms outnumber stranded terms.	1	1
K. *Balanced term structure.* Number of stranded terms equal to number of novel final terms.	3	5
V. Idiosyncrasies of Logical Interrelations.		
A. *Truth-type confusion.* A confusion between unquestionable assertions on the one hand (logically true assertions, definitions, and "bald" empirical truths), with empirically questionable assertions on the other hand.	2	6
B. *Inconsistency.* Making conflicting or contradictory assertions.	1	1
C. *Identification of conditional with its antecedent.* Treating an assertion of the form $A \rightarrow B$ (if A, then B) as equivalent to A.	0	2
D. *Illicit distribution of negation.* Treating an assertion of the form $\sim(A \rightarrow B)$ (it is false that if A, then B) as equivalent to $\sim A \rightarrow B$ (if it is false that A, then B).	1	0
E. *Illicit derivation or normative from descriptive.* Attempt to derive an assertion of the form I(P) (it is imperative that P—usually occurring as "Therefore we should . . ." "Therefore we must . . . ," and the like) from assertions not of that form—in effect, from assertions not incorporating imperatives.	2	1
Total	100	100
N	(229)	(267)

Resume of the Idiologic of Kennedy

Kennedy's logical style is meandering and loose-knit and tends to be top-heavy (IV-E–IV-K)[4] and impulsive (I-A, I-B, V-E). He is somewhat prone to irrelevancies, both with respect to the premises and conclusion (I-A, I-B), but the distinctive feature of his irrelevancies is that whole sentences tend to be irrelevant rather than isolated concepts in otherwise relevant sentences (I-A, I-B, IV-A–IV-E). In effect, on occasion, the whole conceptual framework can be "off-base" rather than isolated details. His style is

TABLE 5-2. Cognitive maneuvers

		Kennedy	Nixon
1.	Switch from a normative to a descriptive mode.	0	1
2a.	Switch from a descriptive to a normative mode.	0	1
b.	Switch from descriptive to emotive or personal mode.	7	5
3a.	Switch from an emotive or personal mode to a descriptive one.	5	3
b.	Switch from an emotive or personal mode to a normative one.	0	1
5*	Enlarge or elaborate the preceding, relevantly or irrelevantly.	8	6
7.	Use an example, relevantly or irrelevantly.	3	3
8.	Deduce or purport to deduce from the preceding.	3	3
9.	Change emphasis, with continuity or warrant or without continuity or warrant.	2	2
10.	Make a distinction between two preceding notions, a preceding notion and a new notion, or between two new notions, with or without warrant, justification, relevance.	4	6
11.	Branch out.	4	3
12.	Synthesize or summarize.	4	3
14.	Obscure or equivocate by phrasing or context.	7	5
16.	Smuggle a debatable point into a context which is semantically alien to it.	6	8
17.	Paraphrase or otherwise render as equivalent statements which, in general, are not to be taken as syntactically identical, with or without warrant.	2	2
21.	Give a premise or assumption for a statement explicit or implicit in the preceding.	5	6
25.	Be irrelevant.	7	10
26.	Repeat or rephrase.	2	1
28.	Allege but not substantiate.	4	6
31.	Deny or reject with or without warrant.	3	3
35.	Agree with the whole but take issue with a part, implicitly or explicitly.	1	1
39.	Accept conditionally.	3	2
41.	Render another's assertion stronger or weaker by paraphrase.	1	2
42.	Digress.	1	2
42a.	Initiate discontinuities.	4	2
44.	Perpetuate or aggravate discontinuities.	2	1
46.	Go toward greater specificity.	5	6
47.	Go toward greater generality.	1	1
48.	Transfer or attempt to transfer authority or responsibility.	2	1
50.	Attack.	4	4
	Total	100%	100%
	N	(725)	(678)

*Not all numbers are represented because items in which neither Kennedy nor Nixon had any tabulations are omitted in this present list.

abundant, prolix, and comprehensive. It is spontaneous, natural, and relatively unvaried. (When restricted to cohesive arguments, the drop in idiosyncratic features is considerably less marked than with Nixon.) Again, it is straightforward, undevious, and impersonal (I-D–I-K). There is a marked idiosyncratic proneness toward ambiguity, a proneness toward double meanings and overlapping meanings of concepts (II). He thinks in a many-faceted continuous, "both-and," inclusive style (II), that is, in terms of qualitative continua rather than in terms of discrete concepts (II, V-D–V-F). He thinks in broad terms and tends to overlook small structural details (I-A, II, V-D–V-F).

Resume of the Idiologic of Nixon

In general, Nixon's logical style is cohesive, balanced, and univocal (I-A, I-B, II). His style is cerebral, controlled, and deliberate—capitalizes on emotive potentialities (I-D–I-F, I-K) offered by discursive argumentative contexts, but his style changes abruptly in cohesive argumentative contexts—hence he also displays great variety in style (depending on whether the context is cohesive or discursive). His style is detailed and balanced, with some emphasis on economy of concepts (I-A, I-B, IV, V). He is prone to invoking considerations about special circumstances in attempting to establish a conclusion (I-D, I-E), and also, appeals "to the gallery," that is, makes statements with "mass appeal" incorporating popular or "folksy" phraseology (I-F). He is prone to derogating his opponent without establishing the alleged charge—usually by innuendo or suggestion (I-K). He shows propensities toward irrelevancies of an emotive nature which influence the listener's acceptance of an argument. While his thinking style is detailed (II, V-F) and balanced (I-A, I-B, IV-G, IV-K), there is considerable idiosyncratic confusion about logical and causal interrelationships (V-A, V-C, I-H) and a hesitancy in drawing consequences from a position or situation (V-C). Tends to be "either-or" rather than "both-and" (II).

☐ The Contralogic or the Method of Rationalizing Logical Idiosyncrasies

The process of converting the ideological properties into *psychological* attributes is accomplished by means of the contralogic. To follow the presentation of this idea, the reader is asked to refer to the illustrations in Table 5-3. In the first column, idiologic, appear individual idiosyncrasies of reasoning as defined above and listed in Table 5-1. The second (and pivotal) column, contralogic, involves one's taking the position that all

TABLE 5-3. Illustration of method of logical analysis

Column I—Idiologic.	Column II—Contralogic.	Column III—Psychologic.
Sample of specific way of thinking, in terms of idiosyncrasies of logic	*Logical conditions under which the logical idiosyncrasy is rationalized*	*Psychological state concordant with contralogic*
Example taken from von Domarus, and Arieti: "Switzerland loves freedom; I love freedom; therefore I am Switzerland." Fallacy: identification in terms of attributes of the predicate (or undistributed middle). III-B, IV-G, IV-K.	If one supplies the implicit premise that Switzerland is the *only* member of the class of freedom-lovers (and if I loved freedom), then it would follow, without logical error, that I would *have* to be Switzerland.	The reasoning reflects a psychological state in which the range of attention is constricted and narrowed (to one member of a class). Psychological symptons: intense concentration, oblivion to ordinary stimuli, hypesthesia, acute withdrawal, and, at its extreme, catatonia.

logical formulations can be thought to demonstrate some sort of straightforward reasoning (for that individual who is doing the reasoning) if one will only supply the logical conditions under which the apparent error would be "true" (i.e., in effect the "new" logic would neutralize or rationalize the error). In the third column, psychologic, are those psychological and psychiatric conditions which are concordant with the contralogic advanced in Column II (i.e., psychological states which would be involved, if this "new" logic is to make psychological sense).

The following presents for Kennedy and Nixon a hypothetical tailor-made set of constructs developed from our analysis of the first two Great Debates. These constructs may be said to represent the private, covert logical-system assumptions—the contralogic—which were operating (most likely unbeknownst to the persons themselves) in the minds and thinking processes of these two principals.

It should be stated that these resumés of the contralogic of the two men are not meant either to represent the ways these individuals think, nor in any way to imply a "clinical description" of these individuals, but rather, the purpose is to describe what could be the latent or unspoken or "unconscious" epistemological and metaphysical positions—"philosophies of life"—of these two individuals which would be consistent with the idiologics which they manifested.

The mental or psychological characteristics that one could infer from these particular constellations of contralogic are indicated in the next section.

Resume: Contralogic of Kennedy

Everything is related to everything else (I-A)[5] and, furthermore, related in a dynamic sense. There being many things that can bear a given relation to a given thing (II-A), the world allows extensive change and permutation by man. There are no boundaries or limitations to action—the universe can be manipulated by the will of man, and desire and actuality can be made to accord with that will (II-A, V-E). The means appear incidental and have value primarily as they efficiently implement the desired ends (I-A, IV-E). Reality is given, i.e., is independent of what men think or desire it to be, but that reality can be manipulated and changed to accord with man's desires (I-D, I-F). It is important to know the causal laws operating in that world (I-H).

Resume: Contralogic of Nixon

Subjective desires and attitudes are identified with the objective world (I-D, I-F, I-K). Value statements have cognitive import (I-D, I-K, V-A). The world is what each man legislates that it is (V-A). The implementation of goals is not important (I-H, V-C)—one projects his subjective feelings and desires onto the world. The emphasis is not on causal relationships operating in the outside world, but on perfecting the inner subjective self (I-H, V-C). Truth is man-made—there are no objective conditions (I-D, I-F). Acceptability to man is the criterion for truth; argumentation is developed to influence others' acceptance to one's subjective desires and attitudes (I-D, I-F).

☐ The Psychologic or Psychological Traits Relevant to Styles of Thinking. The Psychological Impact of the Stimulus

We have developed a set of thirteen relevant psychological traits or dimensions with our method; these appear in Table 5-4. Two observations concerning the nature of these traits will be clarifying. First, it should be noted that these do not encompass the entire spectrum of psychological

TABLE 5-4. Psychological traits relevant to patterns of thinking

	1 2 3	4	5 6 7
A.	Wide-ranged, diverse, broad-scoped	vs.	Narrowed, constricted, focused
B.	Flexible, pliable, adaptable, mobile	vs.	Rigid, fixed, inflexible, dogmatic
C.	Rational, reasoning, reality-oriented	vs.	Autistic, poor reality orientation, projection of standards
D.	Spontaneous, uninhibited, creative, original	vs.	Inhibited, conforming, tradition-oriented
E.	Objective, open-minded, nonhostile, unprejudiced	vs.	Prejudiced, biased, infusion of hostile affect
F.	Consistent, reliable, steady, unvarying	vs.	Changeable, variable, unreliable, inconsistent, fluctuating
G.	Positive, builds on past achievements, extends accepted positions	vs.	Contrary, iconoclastic, "perverse," negative
H.	Systematic, organized, cohesive, methodical	vs.	Unsystematic, unorganized, loose, scattered, disjointed
I.	Combinatory, extrapolating, seeing implications, holistic	vs.	Atomistic, piecemeal, detailed
J.	Dichotomous, binary, "either-or"	vs.	Continuous, neutralistic, "both-and"
K.	Goal-directed, planful, purposeful, persevering	vs.	Easily diverted, lacking in direction and planning, labile
L.	Aggressive, assertive, declarative, decisive	vs.	Apologetic, defensive, equivocating, indecisive
M.	Action or "fact" oriented: mentation used primarily as a means to external rewards	vs.	"Mentation" oriented: theoretical, philosophic, puzzle-solving—for the pleasure of the mentation

traits which are part and parcel of human personality, but rather are limited to those aspects of personality having to do with ways of thinking. For example, some persons tend to be more-or-less dichotomous, discrete, binary, "either-or" in their thinking, as opposed to others who appear more or less neutralistic, looking for middle ground and compromise, believing in the possibility of "both-and." These are psychological dimensions, *and* they influence styles of thinking—as anyone who has ever contrasted the "logic" of Khrushchev and Nehru would readily see. The traits listed, thus, are extrapolations from the individual's thinking patterns, and refer to the cognitive or intellective or mental aspects of the individual's personality and do not necessarily imply anything about other aspects of his personality.

Second, since we are presenting essentially a theoretical logical model, the personality attributes of the individuals described will be "theoretical" descriptions in the sense that the descriptions indicate how these individuals might think (and act) if they were left entirely to their own thinking devices. With a prominent public figure we can assume that there will be little opportunity, at least in his public life, to manifest uncensored impulse or officially to speak or act without a great deal of forethought, discussion, and consultation with advisers. However, the point can be made that such individuals may tend to choose advisers who are largely psychologically compatible and that even after consultation, the individual himself may well proceed in his own logically idiosyncratic way.

And finally, one may ask why we infer psychological characteristics from the contralogic (Table 5-3: Column II) rather than directly from the manifest idiologic (Table 5-3: Column I). The apparent psychological characteristics of an individual may be different than when inferred from the contralogic. The contralogic, moreover, seems a more powerful method. It enables the psychologician to make meaningful statements about the individual's psychological states, frequently when the manifest logic is cryptic. Once converted into the contralogic, however, one can see what must have been going on in that person's mind, what that person's logical systems must have been in order that the way he was thinking would make sense to him. The contralogic and the psychological characteristics derived thus are basic to our method.[6]

In the following we present the psychological characteristics which can be derived for Kennedy and Nixon, from the particular constellations of contralogic inferred from the logical analysis of the two debates. The traits are primarily in terms of the attributes listed in Table 5-4. The references included with the descriptions are to particular logical idiosyncrasies (Tables 5-1 and 5-2), from which the contralogic itself was derived.

Resume: Psychologic of Kennedy

Our analyses suggest that in the cognitive sphere, Kennedy tends to be impatient (I-A, I-B, II), spontaneous (note the great difference in idiosyncrasies when restricted to cohesive arguments). He appears goal-oriented but disdainful of details (I-A, I-B, II, IV-E, IV-H, V-E), apparently regarding achievement of goals to be important and unmindful of incidental consequences resulting from their achievement (I-A, I-B, II, V-D, V-E). In effect, he is goal-oriented but not analytic. He seems willing to take risks (I-A, IV-E, IV-H). He is relatively nonintrospective. (Again note the great difference in idiosyncrasies when restricted to cohesive contexts). In many of his relationships he is impersonal (I-D, I-E, I-F, I-K). His orientation is toward realistic facts (I-H, V-A); he is objective, open-minded (I-D, I-K). For him considerations of psychic economy appear unimportant, in that he wants to bring everything to bear in achieving a goal. There seems no undue anxiety regarding failure or waste of effort (I-A, I-B, IV-E, IV-H). Certain courses of action are mandatory when given states of affairs prevail—he feels each man has a unique destiny to fulfill (V-E). He feels he must drive himself to his own. He tends to see things on a qualitative continuum: he is continuous, "both-and" (II), but not especially compromising (I-F). He seems to prefer to use all means available for instrumenting a goal rather than take time to seek out the most effective solution (I-A, IV-E, IV-H). He appears constructive (I-K) but somewhat iconoclastic (V-D, V-E)—forceful, impulsive, driving (II, V-E). He is not troubled by conflict, and he functions well under pressure; he is persevering, energetic, driven (II, I-D).

Resume: Psychologic of Nixon

Nixon can be described as systematic, organized, methodical, planful (as indicated in marked drop in idiosyncrasies in cohesive arguments (I-A, I-B, II, IV-E–IV-K, V). However, he seems to have limited scope (II, V-C, V-E), and gives more attention to details of manner of execution of an act and to its peripheral consequences than to the over-all efficacy of that act (I-A, I-B, I-H, IV-E–IV-K, V-A, V). He has some anxiety about making decisions—apparently feeling that decisions involve a commitment to one extreme or another (IV-G, IV-K, V-C). He tends to be concerned about consequences and prefers to have his position judged for its intrinsic merits rather than for what may follow from that position (V-C). He seems to value compromise, balance, equilibrium (IV-E–IV-K), and is painstaking, cautious, piecemeal, inhibited, (I-A, I-B, IV, V-C, V-E, V). He tends to fear imbalance (IV-E–IV-K) and direct attack, but he himself attacks indirectly by innuendo and suggestion (I-D–I-F, I-K, especially I-F). He appears labile, opportunistic (I-D, I-F, I-J, I-K, also note marked drop in idiosyncrasies in cohesive arguments). He dichotomizes the universe into "good" and "bad," "we" and "they" (I-D, I-F, I-K). He dislikes conflict and prefers to resolve it quickly (II, IV-G, IV-K, V-S, V). He is apt to react personally to criticism (I-D, I-F, I-K). He is analytic, intelligent, but sensitive emotionally—easily diverted (I-D, I-F, I-K). He emphasizes economy of concepts and orderliness rather than action and effectiveness (II, IV, V-E, V).

Whereas Kennedy's image came through as a "doer," albeit he might impulsively do some "wrong" things, Nixon's image came through as a man who might "deliberately" do the wrong things, but they would be done with careful attention to detail.

☐ Some Research Proposals

The chief value of all theoretical models is that they serve as stimuli and guides for research. In our case we have a model directed largely toward the properties of the *stimulus* in the basic S-O-R formulation of behavioral science. We are concerned with cognitive aspects—styles of thinking—and have developed a rationale for translating the manifest logical structure of verbal stimulus material (idiologic) into latent psychological characteristics (psychologic) conveyed by the speaker, through a mediating contralogic.

As we have pointed out, the model was developed in connection with political debates, and we shall propose empirical tests with voting behavior. First, however, we wish to present certain methodological considerations.

Methodological Considerations

It is important that there be a high order of consistency or concordance among psychologicians in the outcomes obtained when applying the method. While there should be little difficulty in training persons who have appropriate backgrounds, concordance should be checked, particularly in connection with the contralogic and psychologic.

The stability of patterns of logical style over time, should be investigated. While our analysis of patterns shown by Kennedy and Nixon revealed that results were very similar for the first two debates, we have little knowledge of how much stability we can normally expect over a period of time, and the conditions which make for greater or less stability. This is important in connection with the problem of selecting "representative" material for experimentation, as well as for other problems.

If the impression a person conveys to others is not alone a matter of what he says, but also of how he goes about saying it (his logical style), it should be possible to validate this experimentally. One approach which comes to mind would be to adapt the thirteen psychological traits (Table 5-4) for use with experimental Subjects (Ss). Experimental materials might be obtained, for example, from intercollegiate debate scripts. From these, one which showed definitely contrasting patterns of logical style on the part of the debaters would be selected. An experimental script would be derived, restricted to a manageable number of debaters.

The resulting script would be videotaped (or filmed), using performers who were not known to the Ss. In preparing the tapes the performers' roles would be rotated to control for other personal factors (i.e., appearance and other visual and auditory nonverbal cues). Ss would be assigned at random to the experimental groups, one group for each version of tape. To provide a control, each experimental tape would be preceded by a brief "neutral" (taped) interview of each of the performers. Ss would check scales for each performer at the conclusion of the interview, and then told they would have an opportunity of seeing these persons in action. Ss would check scales again at the conclusion of the experimental tape. Pretests should be done on the adaptation of the scales, and to determine procedures more precisely. For example, it might be desirable to separate the control and experimental sessions, or to include an additional criterion—one which more nearly approaches the behavioral in character. If the experiment were conducted at a university, the experiment might be placed in a mock voting context, and the Ss required to vote (for an official in the local community government, president of student government, etc.). Since the psychological impressions conveyed by logical style may not be readily verbalizable by members of an audience, a behavioral criterion could have great value.

Empirical Field Tests—Voting Behavior

The studies indicated below are illustrative of a larger number which can be related to our model. They involve the following hypothesis: The winner will be the candidate whose psychological profile (derived from logical analysis of spontaneous verbal campaign material) comes closest to the "personality style" appropriate for the time and place. In times of comparative tranquility we would expect the winners to have profiles of psychological traits (Table 5-4) close to the average or midpoints of the scales. However, in times of great crisis (war, economic upheaval) the winners would be those candidates whose profiles reflect qualities toward the extremes deemed necessary by the electorate to meet the particular crisis situation.

1. As one test of our major hypothesis, we propose a three-wave field test, making use of a panel of representative adults. The first wave of interviewing would take place very early in the campaign. Respondents would be questioned on the candidate for whom they expected to vote, knowledge of the candidates, and extent of exposure to speeches (very few at this time) or other material on the candidates. In addition, an appropriate adaptation of the psychological character-

istics scale would be used to secure the respondent's evaluation of each candidate and of the requirements for the office itself "in times like these." The second wave of interviewing (three to four weeks before election day) and the final wave (during the week after the election) would cover essentially the same ground, except that in the postelection interview, respondents would be asked whether they had voted and the candidate for whom they voted. The standard household and personal characteristics information would be secured, together with party affiliation and other information usual in political polls. Appropriate pretesting of the questionnaires and procedures would be necessary.

Concurrently, speeches of the candidates would be analyzed for the psychological characteristics revealed by styles of thinking. These results would be related to those of the survey. Their relation to the extent of exposure to candidate speeches should be particularly interesting. In addition to serving as a test of our hypothesis, the study data should provide methodological insights, for example, the stability of candidate profiles, of voter evaluation (and reliability of our scales), and the interrelations of the two.

2. A second study could be restricted to cases in which the same candidate ran (successfully or unsuccessfully) for the same office two or more times. Here again, one would relate the nuances and differences in psychological patterns manifested by the same candidate in different campaigns with the differences in voting patterns at the times of those respective elections. The approach employed would generally parallel the first study except that only one wave of interviewing would be required. New representative samples would be drawn for each election in such a longitudinal study. This study could throw considerable light on why it is that mayors, governors, and other officials manage to get elected time after time.

The foregoing studies by no means exhaust the possible uses of the theoretical model for generating empirical research not only in the field of political behavior but in other areas as well—mass communication, advertising, education, in fact in any area in which it is important to learn more about how behavior in general can be influenced through projection of more effective verbal stimuli.

☐ Endnotes

[1]"Concludifying" is the author's term and refers to the logical maneuvers, the logical gambits, the sequences of logical activities, etc., by which an individual reasons, thinks, men-

tates, cognizes, or arrives at a conclusion. An example of this process, with the illustrious Samuel Johnson as the thinker—in which he first asserts a belief, then points out a distinction, then accepts another's objection as an unavoidable consequence of his own position, etc.—is given on page 6 of Susan Stebbing's *A Modern Introduction to Logic,* 2nd ed., New York, Harper and Bros., 1933.

[2]A more extensive discussion of the rationale of this method is presented in the author's chapter in Kagan and Lessor's recent book (Schneidman, 1961a). The application of this approach to a psychological case study is given in "The Case of El" (Schneidman, 1961b).

[3]It is, of course, essential in analyzing a man's styles of thinking (as recorded in his spoken thoughts) to be sure that it is *his* speech, and not his ghost writer's, that one is analyzing. In the case of the Kennedy-Nixon materials it was fairly obvious that although both participants had been briefed—with the exception of the opening statement in the first debate which *could* have been ghost-written or group written and memorized by the speaker—the material was extemporaneous and unrehearsed.

[4]References are to Table 5-1.

[5]References are to Table 5-1.

[6]It would, of course, be theoretically possible to construct different contralogics from any one given idiologic. These different contralogics could be made from the point of view of different major language-logic orientations, such as standard average European (Whorf, 1956), Chinese, Hopi, Eskimo, and even Russian, as opposed to American. In this present approach we limit our contralogic to the standard average European (SAE) point of view.

References

Andrews, T. C. (1940). The Effect of Benzedrine Sulfate on Syllogistic Reasoning. *Journal of Experimental Psychology, 26,* 423–431.

Arieti, S. (1955). *Interpretation of schizophrenia.* New York: Robert Bruner.

Beier, E. G. (1951). The Effect of Induced Anxiety on Flexibility of Intellectual Functioning. *Psychological Monographs, 65.*

Berelson, B. (1952). *Content analysis in communication research.* Glencoe, Ill: Free Press.

Cameron, N. (1938). Reasoning Regression and Communication Schizophrenia. *Psychological Monographs, 50,* 1–33.

Copi, L. M. (1953). *Introduction to Logic.* New York: The Macmillan Company.

Dewey, J. (1938). *Logic: The Theory of Inquiry.* New York: Henry Holt and Company.

George, A.L. (1959). *Propaganda Analysis: A Study of Inferences Made from Nazi Propaganda in World War II.* Evanston: Row, Peterson.

Gibson, J. J. (1960). The Concept of the Stimulus in Psychology. *American Psychologist, 15,* 694–703.

Goldstein, K. (1944). Methodological Approach to the Study of Schizophrenic Thought Disorder. In J. S. Kasanin (Ed.), *Language and Thought in Schizophrenia.* Berkeley: University of California Press.

James, W. (1907). *Pragmatism.* New York: Longmans, Green and Company.

Kasanin, J. S. (1944). Disturbance of conceptual thinking in schizophrenia. In Kasanin, J. S. (Ed.) *Language and thought in schizophrenia.* Berkeley: University of California Press.

Lasswell, H. D., Leites, N., et al. (1949). *The language of politics.* New York: G. W. Stewart.

Murray, H. A. (1938). *Explorations in personality.* New York: Oxford University Press.

Osgood, C. E., Suci, G. J., & Tannenbaum, P. H. (1957). *The measurement of meaning.* Urbana: The University of Illinois Press.

Peirce, C. S. (1955). *Philosophic Writings of Peirce.* New York: Dover Publications.
Piaget, J. (1932). *The language and thought of the child* (2nd ed). London: Routledge and Kegan Paul Limited.
Pool, I. de S. (Ed). (1959). *Trends in content analysis.* Urbana: University of Illinois Press.
Rapaport, D. (Ed). (1951). *Organization and pathology of thought.* New York: Columbia University Press.
Shneidman, E. S. (Ed). (1951). *Thematic test analysis.* New York: Grune and Stratton.
Shneidman, E. S. (1961a). Psycho-logic: A personality approach to patterns of thinking. In J. Kagan & G. Lessor (Eds.), *Contemporary issues in thematic apperceptive methods.* Springfield: Charles C. Thomas.
Shneidman, E. S. (1961b). The logic of El: A psycho-logical approach to the analysis of test data. *Journal of Projective Techniques, 25,* 390–403.
Sullivan, H. S. (1944). Language of Schizophrenia. In J. S. Kasanin (Ed.), *Language and thought in schizophrenia.* Berkeley: University of California Press.
Vigotsky, L. S. (1934). Thought in Schizophrenia. *Archives of Neurology and Psychiatry, 31,* 1063–1077
Von Domarus, E. (1944). The Specific Laws of Logic in Schizophrenia. In J. S. Kasanin (Ed.), *Language and thought in schizophrenia.* Berkeley: University of California Press.
Werner, H. (1957). *Comparative psychology of mental development* (Rev. ed.). New York: International Universities Press.
Whorf, B. L. (1956). *Language, thought and reality* (Ed. John B. Carroll). New York: John Wiley and Sons.
Woodworth, R. S., & Sells, S. B. (1935). An Atmosphere Effect in Formal Syllogistic Reasoning. *Journal of Experimental Psychology, 18,* 451–460.

6 CHAPTER

On "Therefore I Must Kill Myself"

This article focuses on the word "therefore" (and its near synonyms) and the role that it plays in syllogistic and nonsyllogistic reasoning, particularly in the phrase " . . . therefore I must kill myself." It is shown that the traditional Aristotelian role of the syllogistic conjunction ("therefore") is greater than an automatic connection or transformation between the premises and the conclusion, and is, in fact, a bridge with a rather wide range of psychological and temporal dimensions. Some practical implications for the treatment of suicidal persons are cited.

Perhaps the most important word in life is the common word "therefore"—especially when it is followed by the word "I." Although the word is not used often in ordinary speech, it is implied in almost every decision that a person makes (based on some unspoken reasoning in the mind): it is the logical bridge between almost every thought and every action (or deliberated inaction). Among all the ". . . therefore, I . . ." sequences that are possible in the mind, one of the most important ones is contained in the words: ". . . therefore I must kill myself."

This short paper focuses on the apparently simple conjunction "therefore."

When someone says "therefore," we take it for granted that that person has come to some sort of decision or resolution. "Therefore" implies that the speaker has been thinking and, more than that, coming to conclusions.

Reprinted from *Suicide and Life-Threatening Behavior,* 1982, *12,* 52–55. With permission.

"Therefore" is the pivot-word in the syllogism. Almost everybody knows the following bits of information about the Aristotelian syllogism:

1. A *syllogism* is usually made up of three statements; the first two are called premises and the third one, following the word "therefore" (or "then," "hence," "consequently," "accordingly," or "so") is called the conclusion. A well-known example: All men are mortal, / Socrates is a man, / Therefore, Socrates is mortal.

2. There are four (and only four) kinds of statements (each containing a subject and a predicate) that can be made. They are called:

A. Universal affirmative. All Subject is Predicate (e.g., All men are mortal).
E. Universal negative. No S is P (e.g., No cow is a bird).
I. Particular affirmative. Some S is P (e.g., Some cattle give milk).
O. Particular negative. Some S is not P (e.g., Some women are not beautiful).

3. There are 64 "moods" of the syllogism—consisting of the 64 possible combinations of the A, E, I and O statements—of which exactly 16 are considered valid, i.e., reasonable or logical. The others are invalid because they commit one or more logical errors.

4. It is generally believed that not much need be said about the word "therefore." There is very little discussion of it in all of logic. It is thought to be simply the *automatic* process—the colorless conjunction—between the premises and the conclusion. It is viewed as a sort of clearing of the throat after the "whereases" before one gives the punch line (the conclusion) of the cognitive resolution.

But, as we shall see, "therefore" is not always a totally simple or automatic or innocuous logical operation.

Nicholas Rescher in his monograph *Temporal Modalities in Arabic Logic* (1967), quoting from "The Sun Epistle" by the 13th century Persian logician al-Qazmini al-Katibi and from the 10th century Persian philosopher Avicenna states: "A [temporal] theory of modal propositions was superadded to or superimposed [by the Persians] upon the basic [Aristotelian] theory of absolute, unmodalized categorical propositions of the standard A, E, I and O types. When a proposition of this sort is modalized, it bears a modal qualifier such as 'necessarily,' 'perpetually,' 'non-necessarily' or 'non-perpetually' . . . ." So that in Persian logic of centuries ago, there were four basic modal relationships:

1. A is necessarily true whenever B is true—called a chronologically constant necessary correlation.
2. A is true whenever B is true—called a chronologically constant correlation.

3. A is true at some time when B is true—called a chronologically occasional correlation.
4. A is possibly true at some time when B is true—called a chronologically occasional possibility correlation.

Thus there are two dimensions in Arabic logic that are not prominent in Western (Aristotelian) logic: (a) a *temporal* dimension of ubiquity and occasionality; and (b) a *possibility* dimension of necessity (certainty) and probability.

At the very least, these additions to and refinements of the classical Aristotelian syllogism have direct implications for the inexorability of the bridge from premises to the conclusion, the bridge contained in the word "therefore." It is not at all my thought to give total credit for this insight to Avicenna or al-Qazmini; the bulk of the credit goes to universal common sense, to the recognition of the ordinary person that there is a *range of inexorability* in any deductive logical process from the premises to the conclusion. It is not fixed and automatic.

We all know that there are bridge-words between thought and action. Words like "might," "ought," "should," "must"—which convey *various* amounts of psychologic *push.* The point is that *not all "therefores" are psychologically identical,* or to put it another way: not all equal signs are equally equal. Thus the word "therefore" cannot be taken for granted as a word which means "always" or "under all circumstances" as in the syllogism about Socrates. In *that* example, Socrates is *always* mortal, but that example simply illustrates the confinements of traditional Aristotelian syllogisms.

The even broader implication is that deductive reasoning in the mind is clearly not limited to the syllogistic format *in the first place.* The mind does much more than simply "syllogize." It does something which I have called "concludify"—coming to conclusions. The mind is constantly concludifying, not always syllogizing, and certainly not always thinking without making some of the classical logical "errors." Indeed, most thinking by most people most of the time is replete with the so-called logical errors. That is how most thinking is actually done. My analysis of the logical (or mentational) styles of the two protagonists in the 1960 Kennedy-Nixon debates irrefutably illustrates this point (Shneidman, 1963, 1969).

It would seem that our classical Western logic (which is assumed by Westerners to be "the way things really are" or the way the mind works) is really only "professional" logic, that is, the logic that is supposed to be employed when the Greek logicians were professionally thinking about thinking (or logicizing about logic). It is not (and never has been) the man-at-home's logic, when, say, even the great Socrates was involved in ordinary talk (and according to legend, often engaged in extraordinary argument) with his wife Xantippe. In *real* life, we reason (and act) in a variety of ways including the so-called invalid moods of the syllogism and involving a great deal of *non*-syllogistic deductive conclusions. We do very little "concludifying" in a computer-like automatic way, especially in the processing that occurs just preceding the act of "thereforing." We have not one logic as a computer does, but many ways of saying therefore. When we make a conclusion, we have not one binary switch but a whole rheostat of many degrees—of inexorability, necessity, "push," have-to-do-itness.

In relation to suicide, we can logically (in our own lights) conclude at different times "therefore I must commit suicide" where, on different occasions the "force" of the "therefore" may reflect different degrees of inexorability—such as I may commit suicide, ought to commit suicide, should, might, shall, must commit suicide, now, in the future, under certain circumstances, etc. "Therefore" is not a simple automatic binary act of the mind; it is an enormously complicated dimension in human thinking involving a range—unlike an electronic off-and-on switch—of inexorability. All this is excitingly clear to me as I conduct intensive analyses of the logics of self-destruction contained within several lengthy suicide diaries and many suicide notes with which I am currently obsessed. All future logical (cognitive) analyses of suicide materials will have to attend to the nuances of the conjunction in the fatal inner arguments of the mind.

There are implied syllogisms in almost every suicidal utterance—in almost every suicide note and certainly in every diary of a suicide. In suicide prevention work, the word "therefore," hitherto thought by many to be entirely perfunctory and totally inflexible, is really a rather complex idea with a variety of meanings. There is an old rule in psychotherapy that it is the patient's inflexibles—the "musts" and "can'ts"—that need to be reexamined. What we have done here is to extend this rule from the content of the patient's premises and conclusions to the process of cognition itself contained in the word "therefore." The very manner of the patient's stepping from premises to conclusions may itself be as constricted as his premises and also contribute to the total effect of a lethal syllogism.

The practical implications are obvious. In psychotherapy with a suicidal person, one can be free to touch not only upon his constriction as it relates to his substantive positions—" . . . the only thing I can do is either X or suicide," but one can also choose to deal with that same constriction as it inhibits the mental shifts within the reasoning process itself, thus mollifying his pattern of thinking from " . . . therefore I *must* kill myself" to " . . . therefore I may kill myself," or " . . . therefore I might kill myself under certain circumstances or at another time," or " . . . therefore I can think about killing myself as a substitute for actually doing it."

References

Rescher, N. (1967). *Temporal modalities in Arabic logic.* New York: The Humanities Press. Also (1967) Dordrecht, Holland: D. Reidel Publishing Company.

Shneidman, E. S. (1963). The Logic of Politics. In M. A. May and L. Arons (Eds.), *Television and human behavior.* New York: Appleton-Century-Crofts.

Shneidman, E. S. (1969). Logical content analysis: An explication of styles of concludifying. In G. Gerbner, et al. (Eds.), *The analysis of communication content.* New York: John Wiley & Sons. (The latter reference also contains a detailed logical analysis of a suicide note.)

7

CHAPTER

Melville's Cognitive Style: The Logic of *Moby-Dick*

From the first exciting moment that one looks at *Moby-Dick* from a logician's point of view, it is startlingly clear that the book (as a living entity) and Melville-Ishmael (as driving intellects) have rich and textured *ways* of *thinking* that are consistent with and advance the main psychological thrust and message of the book. After dramatically telling us who his logician is ("Call me Ishmael"), Melville begins the journey with an extended syllogism, or sorites.[1] First he summarizes the argument in a rather straightforward and beguiling fashion:

> Some years ago—never mind how long precisely—having little or no money in my purse, and nothing particular to interest me on shore, I thought I would sail about a little and see the watery part of the world. It is a way I have of driving off the spleen, and regulating the circulation.

But then, Melville-Ishmael becomes explicit and reveals the bitter underlying meaning of this sorites:

> Whenever I find myself growing grim about the mouth; whenever it is a damp, drizzly November in my soul; whenever I find myself involuntarily pausing before coffin warehouses, and bringing up the rear of every funeral I meet; and especially, whenever my hypos get such an upper hand of me, that it requires a strong moral principle to prevent me from deliber-

---

Reprinted from J. Bryant (Ed.), *A Companion to Melville Studies*. Westport, CT: Greenwood Press, 1986, pp. 543–564. With permission.

ately stepping into the street, and methodically knocking people's hats off—then, I account it high time to get to sea as soon as I can.

In case any reader has lost sight of the argument (that getting away, egressing, is Ishmael's substitute for knocking people's heads in, for committing mayhem or *murder*), Melville-Ishmael tells us straightforwardly: "This is my substitute for pistol and ball. With a philosophical flourish Cato throws himself upon his sword: I quietly take to the ship" (*MD*, p. 12).

The argument can be restated this way: When my bodily humors (hypos) are such that they make me feel like committing murder, I (Melville-Ishmael), instead, commit a partial or symbolic suicide by burying myself for an extended time in a ship at sea. Furthermore, by a subtle process that intermixes fate (or chance) and my conscious (and unconscious) selections, I make this egression on a ship that is ruled by a crazy captain-monarch whose madness takes the form of a monomaniacal murderously revengeful impulse that is coupled with a self-destructive capacity to destroy not only himself but all his crew around him, myself included.

No one now can miss the point: *Moby-Dick* is about *suicide*, specifically suicide *as an alternative to murder.* The first chapter is about it; the last chapter is about it. Self-destruction is the psychological topic that frames the entire work. All of the glorious text in between is interstitial to the "book ends" of self-sought death.

And still further *Moby-Dick* is about the covert, subintentioned, beneath-the-surface ways [" . . . as if the infatuated man sought to run more than half way to meet his doom . . . " (*MD*, p. 220)], in which a person can demean, truncate, limit, narrow or diminish himself. It is about the moieties of life, "living on with half a heart and half a lung" (*MD*, p. 160), short of death itself. It is about the unconscious elements, "the gliding great demon of the seas of life" (*MD*, p. 162), in self-induced destruction. The exploration of this world of the sub-surface stream of the mind makes this book an endlessly unfathomable excitement.

☐ A Brief Overview of Logic

The history of logic is a long and interesting one.[2] Here, in an admittedly oversimplified view of Western logic, I have identified five major names or sets of names.

Aristotle dominates logic as Mt. Everest might dominate the plains of Kansas. He is the source of the concept of the syllogism. Refinements and improvement of his system have constituted most of the art and science of logic in the Western world for the past 2,500 years. Other than prayer, the principal occupation of the monasteries of the Middle Ages seems to have been a cerebral beadcounting of the Aristolelian syllogistic forms. What is considered to be correct, reasonable, sensible, or logical today is usually defined in terms of the traditional Aristotelian rules for reasoning. The bulk of Aristotle's logic is *deductive* consisting of identifying all the statements (as either true or false) that are implied or imbedded in premises or syllogisms.

Inductive logic, however, is another rather different kind of reasoning. It flows from any number of actually observed facts to one empirical generalization or conclusion. Two giants are identified with this approach. *Francis Bacon,* who spoke of the kinds of rational lapses people are liable to make when they attempt these inductions, linked such errors to false Gods and called them Idols—Idols of the Cave, of the Tribe, of the Marketplace, and of the Theater. Second, *John Stuart Mill,* in *The System of Logic* (1843), propounded a set of basic rules (or Canons) for establishing causality inductively. These are the Methods of Difference, of Agreement, of Agreement and Difference, of Residues, and of Concomitant Variation.

Since the nineteenth century there has been a major refurbishing of Aristotelian logic, sparked in large part by the insight that mathematics is itself a form of logic. Associated with this development are Frege, Boole, De Morgan, Peirce, Peano, Russell, and Whitehead, and the "Vienna Circle" (Carnap, Wittgenstein, Reichenbach)—all of whom believed that the single proper function of philosophy was to clarify language. Their doctrine of Logical Positivism, which totally eschews the traditional topics of philosophy (such as cosmology, epistemology, ethics, aesthetics), has had an enormous impact on Western thought, perhaps, in part, because of the sanctified position in which we moderns hold mathematics and precision.

Not many people think of *Freud* as a giant among logicians. Some, myself included, believe that one of Freud's major contributions is to the world of thought and logic. His emphasis on unconscious processes and on the concept of ambivalence showed us that the dichotomy deemed to be absolutely basic to Aristotelian thinking (A *vs.* non-A) was not necessarily psychologically sound. One could both love and hate at the same time; a person could simultaneously wish to die and entertain fantasies of rescue and intervention. Freud changed Aristotle's monologic to a more psychologically sophisticated dualogic. For our purposes what is especially interesting is that Melville anticipated Freud in this important respect.

Most of us take it for granted that Greek-European-American logic is the only logic of the world. Of course, this is not so. There are ancient

Eastern logics that are predicated on styles of thinking that are fundamentally different from Western ways of reasoning. Hajime Nakamura's monumental book, *The Ways of Thinking of Eastern Peoples* (1967), for instance, explicates the dimensions of Japanese, Chinese, and Indian logics. Indeed, the Whorf-Sapir hypothesis (that our thinking is inescapably filtered through our language) should alert us that there are at least as many basic logics as there are language types, so we might expect a Standard Average European logic, an Arabic logic, a Chinese logic, a Hopi logic, an Eskimo logic, and so on.

There is much more then to deductive logic than classical Aristotelian syllogistic reasoning. Human beings employ many ways of coming to conclusions that are simply not accounted for in traditional logic. Furthermore, many gambits of reasoning that receive poor marks in the Aristotelian system are better understood not as "errors" but as "idiosyncrasies of reasoning," that is, as part of cognitive style in which these idiosyncrasies seem to work quite well and to "make sense" to the person who employs them. In this chapter I will distinguish at least four kinds of deductive logic. I call these (1) Denotative Deductive Logic, (2) Connotative or Conditional Deductive Logic, (3) Non-summative Deductive Logic, and (4) Paralogic.

☐ Denotative Deduction

Denotative Deductive Logic is the traditional Aristotelian logic. It depends solely on its formal structure. In this system, language sentences are represented by their denotated place, for example, Subject *(S)* or Predicate *(P)*, etc. All *S*s are equal; all *P*s are equal. Any *P* is equal to any other *P*. There is no flexibility about it. The well-known syllogism about Socrates's mortality is equally and inflexibly true of Plato, Descartes, Smith, Jones, or anybody. It simply asserts that when all *S* is *P* (all men are mortal) then every *S* is *P* (any man is mortal).

Using Subjects and Predicates, we may generate four kinds of propositions: Universal affirmative (all *S* is *P*), universal negative (no *S* is *P*), particular affirmative (some *S* is *P*), and particular negative (some *S* is not *P*). Traditionally, these are labeled *A, E, I,* and *O* propositions, respectively.

A syllogism consists of two propositions and a conclusion, each one of them being an *A, E, I,* or *O* statement. There are then sixty-four possible combinations (called *moods* of the syllogism)—*AAA, AAE, AAI,* and so on—of which only sixteen are logically valid. (Sound reasoning is supposed to be confined to these sixteen moods of the syllogism.) The other combinations contain logical errors and are considered invalid.

Not unexpectedly, *Moby-Dick* has some interesting examples of straightforward valid Aristotelian syllogisms. They occur throughout the work. When, for instance in Chapter 17, Ishmael wishes to enter his room at the inn, he discovers Queequeg performing Ramadan. Here is a paraphrase of his *AAA* syllogism:

1. The room was locked even though sufficient time has elapsed for Queequeg to have completed his ritual. ("Towards evening, when I felt assured that all his performances and rituals must be over, I went up to his room and knocked at the door; but no answer. I tried to open it, but it was fastened inside. 'Queequeg,' said I softly through the key-hole:—all silent. 'I say, Queequeg! why don't you speak? It's I—Ishmael.' But all remained still as before. I began to grow alarmed. I had allowed him such abundant time; I thought he might have had an apoplectic fit.")
2. Through the key-hole, Ishmael espies the shaft of Queequeg's harpoon. ("I looked through the key-hole; . . . I was surprised to behold resting against the wall the wooden shaft of Queequeg's harpoon. . . . ")
3. Ishmael knows that Queequeg never leaves his room without his harpoon. ("That's strange, thought I; but at any rate, since the harpoon stands yonder, and he seldom or never goes abroad without it.")

The syllogistic conclusion: "therefore he must be inside here, and no possible mistake" (*MD*, p. 78).

But this straightforward syllogism is not totally straightforward. Curiously, it has a conditional quality about it. Queequeg "seldom or never goes abroad without it" (*MD*, p. 78). The word "seldom" introduces a continuum in the "always-never" dichotomy, but Melville treats the situation as though it were a dichotomy when he adds: " . . . and no possible mistake" (*MD*, p. 78). Figure 7-1 shows a schematization of the syllogism, employing the traditional Venn circles.

Another, much more dramatic example is from Chapter 44, "The Chart."

> Often, when forced from his hammock by exhausting and intolerably vivid dreams of the night, which, resuming his own intense thoughts through the day, carried them on amid a clashing of phrensies, and whirled them round and round in his blazing brain, till the very throbbing of his life-spot became insufferable anguish; and when, as was sometimes the case, these spiritual throes in him heaved his being up from its base, and a chasm seemed opening in him, from which forked flames and lightnings shot up, and accured fiends beckoned him to leap down among them; when this hell in himself yawned beneath him, a wild cry would be heard through the ship; and with glaring eyes Ahab would burst from his

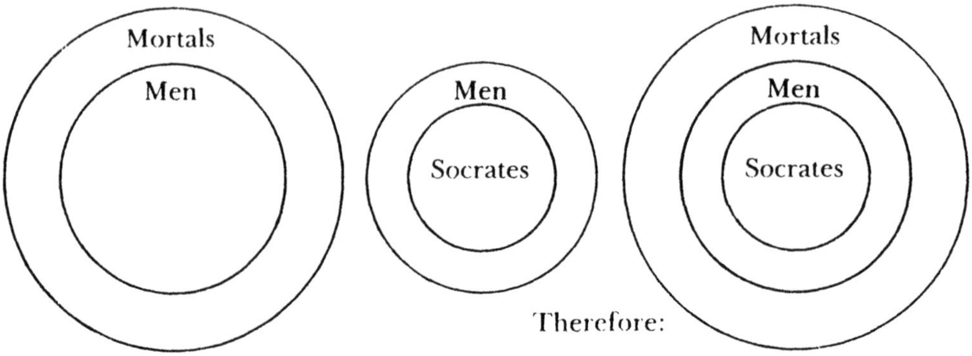

All men are mortal	Socrates is a man	Socrates is mortal

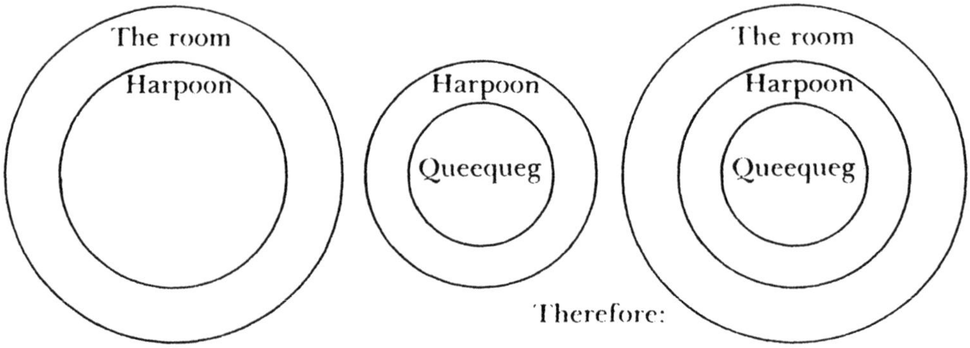

The harpoon is in the room	Where the harpoon is, there is Queequeg	Queequeg is in the room
Queequeg (seldom or) never leaves his room without his harpoon	Ishmael sees, through the keyhole, Queequeg's harpoon in the room	Queequeg must be inside the room

FIGURE 7-1. Examples of Aristotelian syllogistic reasoning.

> state room, as though escaping from a bed that was on fire. Yet these, perhaps, instead of being the unsuppressable symptoms of some latent weakness, or fright at his own resolve, were but the plainest tokens of its intensity. For, at such times, crazy Ahab, the scheming, unappeasedly steadfast hunter of the white whale; this Ahab that had gone to his hammock, was not the agent that so caused him to burst from it in horror again. The latter was the eternal, living principle or soul in him; and in sleep, being for the time dissociated from the characterizing mind, which at other times employed it for its outer vehicle or agent, it spontaneously sought escape from the scorching contiguity of the frantic thing, of which, for the time, it was no longer an integral. But as the mind does not exist unless leagued with the soul, therefore it must have been that, in Ahab's case, yielding up all his thoughts and fancies to his one supreme purpose; that purpose, by its own sheer inveteracy of will, forced itself against gods and devils into a kind of self-assumed, independent being of its own. Nay, could grimly live and burn, while the common vitality to which it was conjoined, fled horror-stricken from the unbidden and unfathered birth. Therefore, the tormented spirit that glared out of bodily eyes, when what seemed Ahab rushed from his room, was for the time but a vacated thing, a formless somnambulistic being, a ray of living light, to be sure, but without an object to color, and therefore a blankness in itself. God help thee, old man, thy thoughts have created a creature in thee; and he whose intense thinking thus makes him a Prometheus; a vulture feeds upon that heart for ever; that vulture the very creature he creates. (*MD*, pp. 174–75)

The syllogism in this chilling paragraph may be paraphrased as follows:

1. In each human being, there are two aspects of the self: "The characterizing mind" and "the eternal living principle or soul."
2. In times of great emotional intensity, these two (which should, in their normal functioning, be united) can become separated by a psychological chasm and thus become dissociated from each other.
3. In extreme cases of such dissociation (such as Captain Ahab's), by sheer power of will, one of the two elements, specifically the unsouled mind, can assume a grim (but empty) existence of its own.
4. *Therefore*, the manifestations of the tormented spirit that others see is but a hollow vessel; a man without a soul; an empty being. Such a man is a blankness, a nullity doomed by his self-created, self-destroying psychological vulture.

Melville's extraordinary passage is filled with prefigurings. In one paragraph, Melville anticipates Eugen Bleuler (1857–1939), who coined the term "schizophrenia," implying a schism between thought and feeling, a cleavage or fissure between the basic mental functions of intellect and emotion. Furthermore, it presages Jung's (1875–1961) notions of the persona, the shadow as well as existential ideas of the hollow man, the empty person, the meaningless life, the estranged individual, the affectless human ("All visible objects, man, are but as pasteboard masks. But in each event—in the living act, the undoubted deed—there, some unknown but still reasoning thing puts forth the mouldings of its features from behind the unreasoning mask" [*MD*, p. 144].) It also anticipates the basic psychoanalytic concept of the Unconscious proposed by Freud (1856–1939) and, then necessarily, of various layers of personality functioning ("Hark ye yet again—the little lower layer" [*MD*, p. 144] and "how all this came to be . . . how to their unconscious understandings . . . all this to explain, would be to dive deeper than Ishmael can go" [*MD*, p. 162].) In all, this passage, like a frigate filled with a thousand ideas, is indeed a fully packed syllogism.

Even these few syllogisms give us some idea of Melville's deductive logical style. *Moby-Dick* is filled with logical arguments. The book itself can be seen as one immense sorites.

The major premise of *Moby-Dick* might go something like this: There is a natural order in the universe, an order between one individual and another and between the individual and nature. (By implication, there are strict limitations to any individual's autonomy and power.) The first minor premise would be: To depart from or to challenge this natural order always results in some corrective redress or balance by nature, usually felt as retaliative punishment by the offending individual. The second minor premise: Ahab's monomaniacal, revengeful drive could have remained his own crazy business, but his overwhelming hubris openly taunted the Fates and thus became a matter between him and the natural order. Conclusion: Ahab had to be punished; he had to be destroyed, even if it meant the death of almost everyone around him. The admonition "Look not too long in the face of the fire, O man!" (*MD*, p. 354) can also be read as "Beware! Do not over-tempt the Fates. You may go only so far, even (or especially) in your megalomania."

But there are other *kinds* of logic in *Moby-Dick*. Let us try to harpoon two or three of them.

☐ Conditional Deduction

There is, of course, more to deductive logic than the classical textbooks say. There is a kind of logic, conditional logic, that purists would never admit. Connotative or *Conditional Deductive Logic* is reasoning which embodies the notion that the correctness of reasoning may depend on the time or place or circumstance. These "circumstances" may even include the emotional, psychological, or ethical state-of-mind of the logician. In other words, the logic depends, in part, on the connotative overtones of the words. Symbols alone will not do—not all *S*s or *P*s are alike.[3]

Logic itself is contextual or conditional. This idea is as unacceptable to Aristotelian logic as the idea that the sum of a group of numbers depends on anything other than invariable addition. But thinking (reasoning, coming to conclusions) is more complicated than mathematics precisely because it is touched by psychological and other contextual factors. All these notions lead us to a second, closer look at the seemingly least important word in the syllogism, the bridge-word "therefore."

First, however, a brief but necessary aside. Among the 216,014 words in *Moby-Dick* there are 17,560 different word forms. From among these, I have selected a set of twenty-five "logical words" including key conjunctions or conjunctive adverbs ("therefore" and "hence") and such words as "both" and "half" that reflect Melville's concern with simultaneous opposites, oxymorons, moieties, and ambivalences. The twelve "logical words" used most frequently are then (629 times), half (137), both (124), because (92), therefore (67), since (65), hence (32), thinking (28), concluded (19), thereby (28), whereas (18), and whenever (15).[4]

At first, the most innocuous word in the syllogism seems to be a simple conjunction. When someone says "therefore," we assume that that person has come to some sort of decision or resolution. "Therefore" implies that the speaker has not only been thinking but, more than that, coming to conclusions. It is the pivot-word in the syllogism.

It is generally believed that not much need to be said about "therefore." There is relatively little discusion of it in Western logic. It is simply that automatic process—the colorless conjunction—between the premises and the conclusion. It is viewed as a sort of clearing of the throat after the "whereas," the signal before one gives the punch line (the conclusion) of the cognitive resolution. It turns out that "therefore" does not always indicate a totally simple or automatic or innocuous operation.

By examining Melville's use of "therefore" and "hence" we can better understand his style of thinking—the ways in which he is traditionally Aristotelian and the ways in which he is idiosyncratically, uniquely Melvillean in his thinking. Not unexpectedly, most of Melville's usage of "therefore" is straightforwardly syllogistic, as in the following example:

> Now, the Pequod had sailed from Nantucket at the very beginning of the Season-on-the-Line. No possible endeavor then could enable her commander to make the great passage southwards, double Cape Horn, and then running down sixty degrees of latitude arrive in the equatorial Pacific in time to cruise there. Therefore, he must wait for the next ensuing season. (*MD*, p. 173)

There are many instances in *Moby-Dick* of this kind of not-very-exciting syllogism and sorites, all of them grist for any schoolman's mill.

But Melville was capable of a much more subtle kind of "thereforing." And it is in these non-Aristotelian variations of syllogistic reasoning, specifically in his conditional, almost Persian ways of thinking that Melville creates a new language and a new logic and adds to the tone of *Moby-Dick* that sense of special inevitability and doom.

Melville's strength as a subtle logician does not lie in his traditional syllogisms. It begins to show itself in the nuances he gives to the reasoning process, his conditional uses of "therefore" (and "hence"). In the following example, Queequeg's illiteracy, an idiosyncratic circumstance in the world rather than a universal logical rule, shapes the logical structure.

> Shaking off the sleet from my ice-glazed hat and jacket, I seated myself near the door, and turning sideways was surprised to see Queequeg near me. Affected by the solemnity of the scene, there was a wondering gaze of incredulous curiosity in his countenance. This savage was the only person present who seemed to notice my entrance; because he was the only one who could not read, and, therefore, was not reading those frigid inscriptions on the wall. (*MD*, p. 40)

Father Mapple provides another telling example of conditional thinking:

> "Shipmates, God has laid but one hand upon you; both his hands press upon me. I have read ye by what murky light may be mine the lesson that Jonah teaches to all sinners; and therefore to ye, and still more to me, for I am a greater sinner than ye." (*MD*, p. 50)

In this case, the "therefore" has more intensity (as if one had turned up the volume on a rheostat) for Father Mapple than it does for others—"still more to me" (*MD*, p. 50). All men are sinners, but some men are greater sinners than others. And what Jonah teaches to all sinners, he teaches much more to those who are greatest sinners: "God had laid but one hand upon you; both his hands press upon me" (*MD*, p. 50).

And reasoning can even depend on even more subjective states. Indeed, the very logic by which Ahab is able to track and find the object of his hate contains a way of reasoning that is interfused with personal, experiential, intuitive, conditional elements.

In addition, philosophical elements condition the logical flow. In Chapter 72, "The Monkey-Rope," the narrator muses as follows:

> So strongly and metaphysically did I conceive of my situation then, that while earnestly watching his motions, I seemed distinctly to perceive that my own individuality was now merged in a joint stock company of two:

> that my free will had received a mortal wound; and that another's mistake or misfortune might plunge innocent me into unmerited disaster and death. Therefore, I saw that here was a sort of interregnum in Providence; for its even-handed equity never could have sanctioned so gross an injustice. And yet still further pondering—while I jerked him now and then from between the whale and the ship, which would threaten to jam him—still further pondering, I say, I saw that this situation of mine was the precise situation of every mortal that breathes; only, in most cases, he, one way or other, has this Siamese connexion with a plurality of other mortals. If your banker breaks, you snap; if your apothecary by mistake sends you poison in your pills, you die. (*MD*, p. 271)

All this is prologue to the main act. The psychological nuances in Melville's paragraphs on death and suicide and Melville's daring notion of partial suicide (like burying oneself in a whaling ship at sea) are a kind of subintentioned or unconscious way of cutting oneself off from life, short of overt death. Consider:

> Death seems the only desirable sequel for a career like this; but Death is only a launching into the region of the strange Untried; it is but the first salutation to the possibilities of the immense Remote, the Wild, the Watery, the Unshored; therefore, to the death-longing eyes of such men, who still have left in them some interior compunctions against suicide, does the all-contributed and all-receptive ocean alluringly spread forth his whole plain of unimaginable, taking terrors, and wonderful, new-life adventures; and from the hearts of infinite Pacifics, the thousand mermaids sing to them—"Come hither, broken-hearted; here is another life without the guilt of intermediate death; here are wonders supernatural, without dying for them. Come hither! bury thyself in a life which, to your now equally abhorred and abhorring, landed world, is more oblivious than death. Come hither! put up *thy* gravestone, too, within the churchyard, and come hither, till we marry thee!"
>
> Hearkening to these voices, East and West, by early sun-rise, and by fall of eve, the blacksmith's soul responded, Aye, I come! And so Perth went a-whaling. (*MD*, p. 402)

Continuing to focus on this issue of subintentioned death wherein the individual plays a latent or covert role in hastening his own demise, let us examine the final chapters of *Moby-Dick*, especially as they touch on Ahab's death.

There is a certain persuasive logic to the manner of Ahab's death, which might be called a victim-precipitated homicide; he dared, and made, the murderous death-white whale kill him. He could not rest until he was so taken. He invited death by the risks that he ran. He permitted suicide. To what empty purpose would any further voyages have been, if he *had* killed the symbol of his search, the object of his hate? His death on that voyage by Moby Dick came at the right time, for in his unconscious wish it was perfect, the only, the "appropriate" death.

After forty solitary years at sea, Ahab had little in the way of self-possessions or personal belongings. His wife, he said, was already a widow; his interest in the possible profits from the voyage was nil; his withdrawal from meaningful material possessions (and his loss of joy with them) is perhaps best indicated by his flinging his "still lighted pipe into the sea" (ch. 30) and dashing his quadrant to the deck (ch. 118), both rash acts for a captain.

In Ahab's conscious mind, he wanted to kill, but we know that self-destruction can be "murder in the 180th degree." Figuratively speaking, the barb of his harpoon was pointed toward him; his brain thought a thrust, but his arm executed a retroflex. Was his death an "accident?" If he had survived his psychodynamically freighted voyage and had returned unharmed to Nantucket's pier, that would have been a true accident. Men can die for nothing—most men do—but a few big-jointed men can give their lives for an internalized something. Ahab would not have missed this opportunity for the world.

What further evidence can be cited bearing on the issue of subintentioned cessation? With his three harpooneers before him, with their harpoons turned up like goblets, Ahab commands, in this maritime immolation scene: "Drink, ye harpooneers! drink and swear, ye men that man the deathful whaleboat's bow—Death to Moby Dick! God hunt us all, if we do not hunt Moby Dick to his death!" (*MD*, p. 146). Kill or be killed; punish or be punished; murder or suicide. The two are intertwined in one inexorable logic.

☐ Non-Summative Deduction

There is more; the little lower layers. Let us go down to a deeper tier, to a more submerged stratum, to a sub-sub-sub-basement, where psychologists (not librarians) dwell. In this spirit, I propose that there is still a third kind of deductive logic, one that is an integral piece of the inner logical life of Melville-Ishmael. What I call *Non-summative Deductive Logic* asserts that one thought can actually be a half, or two, and that the two can even be contradictory while embraced in the same thought. In other words, moieties, ambivalences, and oxymorons can all be integral parts of the flow of thought.

One of two key words can signal a major shift in emphasis. Words like "both" and "half" tell us that we are dealing with modes of logic that are clearly outside the ordinary Aristotelian mold. At the Try Pots Inn, when

Ishmael answers Mrs. Hussey's query, "Clam or Cod?" with " 'Both,' says I; and let's have a couple of smoked herring by way of variety" (*MD*, pp. 64,66), he is asserting the possibility of the simultaneous presence of *A* and non-*A*, and something even more thrown in for variety. It is decidedly non-Aristotelian. On a much more profound level, the line "On life and death this old man walked" (*MD*, p. 200) clearly asserts the possibility of psychological simultaneity of logical opposites.

The use of "both" is critical in Melville's expanded logical style and his understanding of ambivalence.

Melville knows that it is humanly possible, even if it is logically strained, that "even Christians could be both miserable and wicked"; that one can "boldly dip into the Potluck of both worlds" (*MD*, p. 57); and that there is no rule of nature that one has to choose, as a rule of life, between clam or cod. " 'Both,' says I." This seemingly innocuous statement reflects more than gustatory greediness. It is a paradigm of life itself. In a single act, we can do something that has two different uses. Queequeg's tomahawk pipe can both brain his foes and soothe his soul (*MD*, p. 93); the whaleboat hull is "both balanced and directed" by one central keel (*MD*, p. 455); and Ahab plunges his harpoon into Moby Dick with both steel and curse (*MD*, p. 468). The point is that Ahab and every one of us have within us different warring forces: good and evil, light and dark, land and sea, order and disorder, love and hate, flesh and ivory limbs. Without these contradictory psychological richnesses, we would be as two-dimensional as "pasteboard masks."

In a sense, the converse of simultaneity-of-opposite ("both") is a moiety ("half"). "Half" suggests fractions, partials, moieties. It implies ambivalences, ambiguities, dualities, and, by extension, duplicities. (This expanded logic shows the way of *Moby-Dick* and of works beyond *Moby-Dick; Pierre*, "Bartleby," "Benito Cereno," *The Confidence-Man*, and *Billy Budd* would have no life without it.)

Melville's writings have their fair share of moieties, partials and parts, especially in relation to death, specifically partial death.

> . . . some deep men . . . are left living on with half a heart and half a lung. . . . (*MD*, p. 160)

> His voice was like that of one with lungs half gone—hoarsely suppressed, a husky whisper. No wonder that, as in this state he tottered about, his private servant apprehensively followed him. (*Tales*, "Benito Cereno," p. 245)

> Now, which was Samoa? The dead arm swinging high as Haman? Or the living trunk below? . . . For myself, I ever regarded Samoa as but a large fragment of a man, not a man complete. . . . And the action at Teneriffe over, a great Nelson himself—physiologically speaking—was but three-quarters of a man. (*Mardi*, p. 78)

Melville understood the importance of the non-Aristotelian coexistence of *A* and non-*A*. Was Socrates mortal or immortal? In a sense (by virtue, in part, of this very question): both. Was Ahab's goal survival or self-destruction? "On life and death this old man walked" (*MD*, p. 200). Even these few illustrations illuminate the close relationship between the style of logic and the basic theme in *Moby-Dick*. A suicidal person such as Ahab is basically ambivalent, thinking with simultaneity-of-opposites. He wants to flee unbearable circumstances, and, at the same time, he has active fantasies of magical intervention to be like a Catskill eagle:

> And there is a Catskill eagle in some souls that can alike dive down into the blackest gorges, and soar out of them again and become invisible in the sunny spaces. And even if he for ever flies within the gorge, that gorge is in the mountains; so that even in his lowest swoop the mountain eagle is still higher than other birds upon the plain, even though they soar. (*MD*, p. 355)

In the Aristotelian sense, *Moby-Dick* is not a logical book and Ahab is not a logical character. We can reasonably conclude that Melville was not, himself, a logical person when he wrote it—for which we can be eternally grateful.

Part of Melville's marvelous illogicality stems from the fact that he was a self-taught depth psychologist. It may be as accurate to say that Melville was a pre-Freudian as it is to state that Freud was a post-Melvillean. Melville wrote about the unconscious in 1851, five years before Freud was born. When in *Moby-Dick* the author-narrator says, "what the White Whale was to them or . . . to their unconscious understandings . . . " (*MD*, p. 162) or "through infancy's unconscious spell . . . " (*MD*, p. 406) or the phrase "the little lower layer . . . " (*MD*, p. 144) he is telling us that he understands the dualities, the admixtures, the contradictions, the ambivalences, the ambiguities, and the layers of the human mind.

Ambivalence is the non-Aristotelian idea that contradictories can coexist psychologically, like the simultaneous feelings of love and hate toward the same person. (Nowadays, ambivalence is considered to be an essential psychoanalytic idea.) The first-cousin of ambivalence is the oxymoron. It involves a union of opposites for epigrammatic effect. Among the best known examples in English are from *Romeo and Juliet*: "Feather of lead, bright smoke, cold fire, sick health" and, of course, "parting is such sweet sorrow." Melville's oxymoronic gem is his short poem "Art" wherein

> unlike things must meet and mate . . .
> And fuse with Jacob's mystic heart,
> To wrestle with the angel—Art.
> (*Poems*, p. 231)

There are two points about the logic in this poem. The first is that the juxtaposition of opposites—after conflict, sacrifice, and struggle—creates something tangible and worthwhile, Art. The second point reinforces the first. Jacob's wrestling with the angel (*Genesis* XXXII:25–33) results in both a blessing (his new name, Yisrael) as well as an injury (in "the hollow of his thigh"). Reflecting on the latter, we think of symbolic castration. So again, castrative injury, sacrifice, sweat, blood, tears, effort, pain, loss are all part of the price of their opposites: victory, creativity, and almost everything in life that has value—Art and Love. These values not only have their opposites, but, as part of a larger opposite, have their "price." Ahab, for instance, certainly wounded, perhaps, even killed the object of his hate, but at a price that a more rational man—one who is not crazy, not wildly vindictive, not obsessively hateful, not rigidly monomaniacal—would have prudently long before decided not to pay.

To exist with the knowledge of ambivalences, dualities, and oxymorons is a more complicated challenge than to live in the more simple world of the sixteen valid moods of the Aristotelian syllogism. And even more frightening, for unlike the ordered Aristotelian world, there are no magic talismanic formulas to guide us. Melville tells us as much in his profound summation in Chapter 114 of the human course of life itself, that there is no single set of fixed stages of life—totally at odds with what Shakespeare and countless others (Erik Erikson, in our time) would have us believe.

> . . . the mingled, mingling threads of life are woven by warp and woof; calms crossed by storms, a storm for every calm. There is no steady unretracing progress in this life; we do not advance through fixed gradations, and at the last one pause:—through infancy's unconscious spell, boyhood's thoughtless faith, adolescence' doubt (the common doom), then skepticism, then disbelief, resting at last in manhood's pondering repose of If. But once gone through, we trace the round again; and are infants, boys, and men, and Ifs eternally. (*MD*, p. 406)

I believe that the greatest oxymoronic passage in *Moby-Dick* is the stunning opening paragraph of "The Funeral":

> 'Haul in the chains! Let the carcase go astern!'
>
> The vast tackles have now done their duty. The peeled white body of the beheaded whale flashes like a marble sepulchre; though changed in hue, it has not perceptibly lost anything in bulk. It is still colossal. Slowly it floats more and more away, the water round it torn and splashed by the insatiate sharks, and the air above vexed with rapacious flights of screaming fowls, whose beaks are like so many insulting poniards in the whale. The vast white headless phantom floats further and further from the ship, and

> every rod that it so floats, what seem square roods of shark and cubic roods of fowls, augment the murderous din. For hours and hours from the almost stationary ship that hideous sight is seen. Beneath the unclouded and mild azure sky, upon the fair face of the pleasant sea, wafted by the joyous breezes, that great mass of death floats on and on, till lost in infinite perspectives. (*MD*, p. 261–62)

What is to be noted especially in this superlative passage is the breathtaking shift in mood between the first eight lugubrious sentences and the last lilting sentence—from horror and rapaciousness to the most pacific calm. Indeed, the last sentence itself contains this same dramatic contrast in the shift in tone between the first three phrases and the last two. It is the connotative tension in this passage that rivets and chills us. This description is a paradigm, if not of the actualities, then of the omnipresent tensions (whatever their character) in our own lives. In *Moby-Dick* it is the logic of tension and the aberrant ways in which these tensions are reduced that, together, provide the central implicit drama beneath the surface of the written text.

☐ Paralogic

As though all this were not enough, there is still one more kind of logic we must consider. It is an openly flawed way of reasoning, a cryptologic, an illogic, a crazy logic, a *paralogic.* The topic of paralogical thinking in *Moby-Dick* has to be of some special interest to us, even though it may be somewhat painful to look too closely at it. Let us look briefly but openmindedly at the issue.

"N.B.," wrote Melville in March of 1877 at the bottom of a letter to his brother-in-law John C. Hoadley, *"I ain't crazy"* (*Letters,* p. 260). He underlined the words for emphasis. But his disclaimer has not prevented a swirl of controversy about his mental health. Independent of this, the family tried to get him to see an alienist, the esteemed Dr. Oliver Wendell Holmes. Recently, some newly found correspondence from Elizabeth Melville and Melville's brother-in-law, Samuel Shaw has revealed rather explicitly that in 1868 Melville was viewed as having more than ordinary perturbation (Walter D. Kring and Jonathan S. Carey, Donald Yannella and Hershel Parker). While there is no evidence, in my opinion, that Melville suffered from what we today would call schizophrenia, it nonetheless provides an intellectually engaging exercise to turn to the topic of "language and thought in schizophrenia." In doing this I am not for a moment attempting to imply the oversimplistic notion that insanity and genius are identical, or that they are similar or just a hair's breadth apart. It is more sensible to say that there are "differences." Both the insane person and the genius are, almost by definition, "different" from the sane and the ordinary; but they are different in radically diverse ways. Principally, the genius is effective and makes sense, whereas the insane person is not and does not.

In "The Specific Laws of Logic in Schizophrenia" (1964), Elhard von Domarus puts forth the view that schizophrenic thinking involves erroneous reasoning in terms of attributes of the Predicate (instead of thinking, as most of us do, in terms of attributes of the Subject) and it commits the error of the "undistributed middle term."

A few examples should clarify the principle. A female patient claims that she is the Virgin Mary. Elucidation of her thinking reveals that her basic syllogism is the following: The Virgin Mary was a virgin; I am a virgin; therefore I am the Virgin Mary. Another example: A patient on a closed ward continually shouted that he was Switzerland. Various personnel asked him if he had Swiss ancestry, if he had been to Switzerland or if he wished to visit there—all of which served only to irritate him and disturb him further. "You don't understand," was his agitated reply. Then one day, in response to his shouted assertion, "I am Switzerland!" a new doctor on the ward told him that he would do everything he could to get him out of the locked ward. The patient's demeanor changed immediately and dramatically. "At last," he said, "someone understands me." The syllogistic reasoning, in terms of attributes of the predicate was this: Switzerland loves freedom; I love freedom (I want to get off this locked ward); therefore, I am Switzerland (see Figure 7-2).

Not all examples of reasoning in terms of the attributes of the Predicate have such fervent content. In Chapter 82, "The Honor and Glory of Whaling," Melville provides a rather benign and innocuous example, in which the latent syllogism can be schematized as follows:

A most noble episode in English history is that St. George was in actuality battling against a great whale.

> St. George's whale might have crawled up out of the sea on the beach; and considering that the animal ridden by St. George might have been only a large seal, or a sea-horse; bearing all this in mind, it will not appear altogether incompatible with the sacred legend and the ancientest draughts of the scene, to hold this so-called dragon no other than the great Leviathan himself. (*MD*, p. 305)

Therefore (reasoning in terms of attributes of the Predicate), all Nantucket whalemen are comparable to St. George and by good rights ought to be considered to be knights of the most noble order of St. George and should not be looked down on by anyone.

I. It is as though the person thought this way:

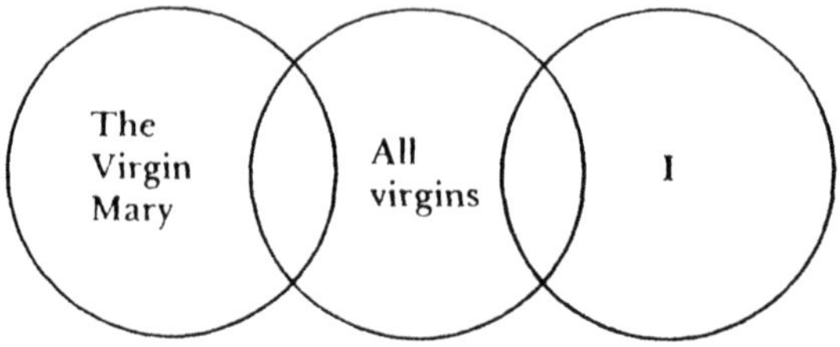

II. What the person actually does is this:

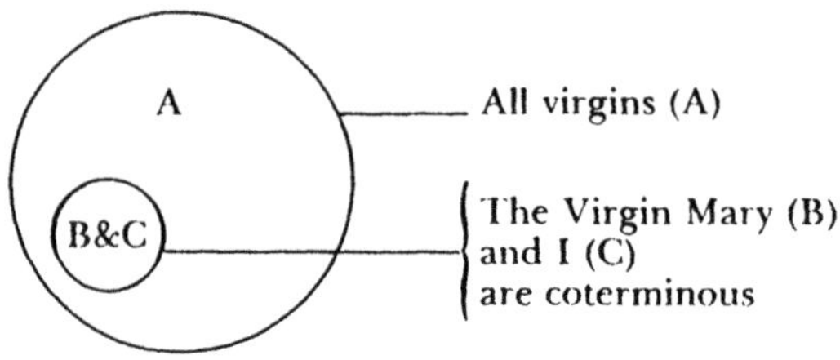

A	B	C	Therefore:
Those who are virgins	The Virgin Mary	I am a Virgin	I am The Virgin Mary
Those who are swift	Some Indians are swift	Some stags are swift	Some Indians are stags
Those who love freedom	Switzerland loves freedom	I love freedom	I am Switzerland
Those who have grand designs & immutable needs	The Fates have grand designs & immutable needs	I have grand designs & immutable needs	I am of the Fates—the Fates' Lieutenant

III. What the person should logically do is this:

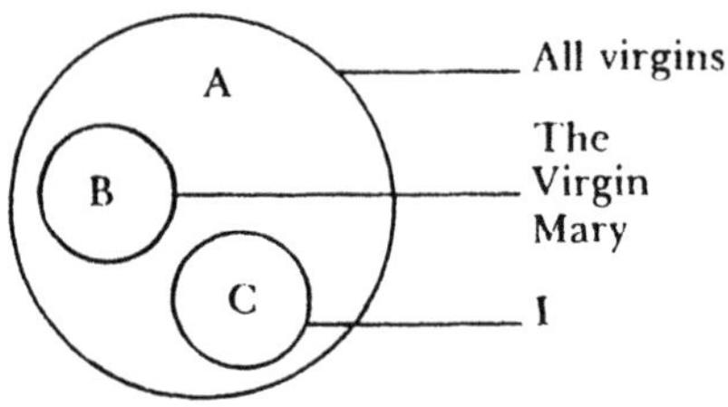

FIGURE 7-2. Examples of reasoning in terms of attributes of the predicate; or, fallacies of the inadequately distributed middle terms

> Thus, then, one of our own noble stamp, even a whaleman, is the tutelary guardian of England; and by good rights, we harpooneers of Nantucket should be enrolled in the most noble order of St. George. And therefore, let not the knights of that honorable company . . . [ever] eye a Nantucketer with disdain, since even in our woollen frocks and tarred trowsers we are much better entitled to St. George's decoration than they. (*MD*, p. 305)

Melville is clearly spoofing. He knows that the syllogism "St. George killed a whale; Nantucket whalers kill whales; therefore Nantucket whalers are equal with St. George" doesn't quite "hold water." But other times, Melville-Ahab uses an identical flawed logic in a totally serious way, filled with urgency and passion. What are we to make of the logic of this tirade by Ahab: "Swerve me? The path to my fixed purpose is laid with iron rails, whereon my soul is grooved to run" (*MD*, p. 147). A locomotive runs on rails; my soul runs on rails; therefore—it has a wild Whitmanian ring—I am a locomotive.

And, again, in a great credo passage from "The Chase—Second Day":

> Starbuck, of late I've felt strangely moved to thee; ever since that hour we both saw—thou know'st what, in one another's eyes. But in this matter of the whale, be the front of thy face to me as the palm of this hand—a lipless, unfeatured blank. Ahab is for ever Ahab, man. This whole act's immutably decreed. 'Twas rehearsed by thee and me a billion years before this ocean rolled. Fool! I am the Fates' lieutenant; I act under orders. Look thou, underling! that thou obeyest mine. (*MD*, p. 459)

The underlying syllogism of this passage takes its very strength from the attributes of the Predicate: The Fates have grand designs and immutable needs; I have grand designs and immutable needs; therefore, I am part of the Fates, "the Fates' lieutenant."

All this, and several syllogisms cited above, are diagrammatically represented in Figure 7-2. The diagram makes it evident that while some of *A* is *B*, and some of *C* is *B*, *A* is not *C*. Paralogical thinking makes the mistake of believing that because *A* and *C* can be mentioned in the same breath (in relation to *B*) they are co-equal. It is the *wish* to do so even in the absence of the necessary logical supports that creates this fantasized bridge. It is the logic of yearning and of passion, not the logic of common sense.

Again, in "The Chase—First Day," just prior to the one that contains the passage about the Fates' lieutenant, Ahab, in response to a statement by Starbuck about an omen, declaims:

> Omen? omen?—the dictionary! If the gods think to speak outright to man, they will honorably speak outright; not shake their heads, and give an old wives' darkling hint.—Begone! Ye two are the opposite poles of one thing;

> Starbuck is Stubb reversed, and Stubb is Starbuck; and ye two are all mankind; and Ahab stands alone among the millions of the peopled earth, nor gods nor men his neighbors! (*MD*, p. 452)

Confused in his logic, Ahab desires to be straightforward in his speech in order to communicate his deeper emotional needs. He does not seem to care that what he says contains a truly megalomaniacal bit of tortured reasoning. Here is what he implies: The extended universe—*all* that one can imagine—is made up of two and only two units: (a) *All* humankind (represented by their monotonous duplicated opposites, Starbuck and Stubb), and (b) one Ahab—"nor gods nor men his neighbors!" (*MD*, p. 452) Does Ahab really mean that he is somehow outside humankind?—"that man makes one in a whole nation's census—a mighty pageant creature formed for noble tragedies" (*MD*, p. 71).

Ahab is so wrought up that he does not care how far he goes; he seems to have the need to show just how desperately he feels by making overextended assertions to the world: "Talk not to me of blasphemy, man; I'd strike the sun if it insulted me. . . . Who's over me? Truth hath no confines" (*MD*, p. 144). And it does not matter if such a man has some defects:

> Nor will it at all detract from him, dramatically regarded, if either by birth or other circumstances he have what seems a half wilful over-ruling morbidness at the bottom of his nature. For all men tragically great are made so through a certain morbidness. Be sure of this, O young ambition, all mortal greatness is but disease. (*MD*, p. 71)

But what kind of morbidness or disease or madness did Ahab have? In the Preface to *Language and Thought in Schizophrenia* (1964), the noted American psychiatrist Nolan D. C. Lewis, speaking of schizophrenia, says that:

> Among those presenting features repeatedly emphasized in this connection are (1) fundamental or fancy-born inconsistencies more or less foreign to normal or average life; (2) shut-in tendencies, with a sense of something wrong or unusual going on in the environment; (3) indulgence in vague artistic fantasies, with daydreaming and partial withdrawal from reality . . . ; (4) automatic and dissociated thought processes, often with projection . . . ; (5) odd mental influences, with transformation experiences; (6) grotesque incongruities of judgment, with accounts of fantastic episodes; (7) scatterings of thought and speech . . . combined with oddities of statement and fantastic action; (8) impulsive episodes and vagueness, with shifts of emotional reactions . . . or with other evidence of marked disorganization in language such as neologisms . . . (pp. viii-ix)

With a few slight shifts of emphasis, this explication of schizophrenic language and thought sounds like a harsh description of the goings-on in *Moby-Dick*. Some examples of all eight of the symptoms are present. On these grounds, a schizophrenic "syndrome" might be said to be present in *Moby-Dick*. But we would be illogical to say so.

The language and thought in *Moby-Dick* are not schizophrenic. There are a thousand differences, but the vital difference is that what Melville says, albeit in his idiosyncratically bold and lofty way, *makes sense*. From a strictly traditional point of view, the text of *Moby-Dick* is filled with logical mistakes, but it does not make *aesthetic* or *psychological* errors; rather it uses all these devices to heighten tension, to create grand efforts, and to *further communication*. It is the opposite of schizophrenic gibberish; it is Art which, by taking risks and stretching the "limits of governable imagination," communicates projectively with each active mind that confronts it.

Melville tells us that Ahab is special; Melville knew that *he* was special. A special person creates a special "bold and nervous lofty language" (*MD*, p. 71), a language that obviously is different from everyday talk and yet enables him to communicate while retaining some important measures of independence to speak-and-think his own way. It is a language-and-logic which is effective precisely because of the special modes of thought and persuasive logic that it so cunningly employs.

That is what a great writer is: a person who creates a new language, a fresh way of thinking and talking, a different style of language and thought; one who possesses an idiosyncratic way of seeing the world and reports his vision in a unique way. Possessing more than a fresh-sounding cadence or an individualized different accent or dialect, a great writer needs the unhesitating talent to be an Aristotle and forge a style of *logic* copyrighted in a private patent office of which he or she is the sole proprietor and the most enthusiastic defender. Every great author is his or her own logician, eligible to be included in the select company of Aristotle, Avicenna, Bacon, Mill, and Whitehead. There are *many* styles of logic in the world, most of them yet to be formulated. Any standard textbook of logic would, if it were read, cripple the mind of a potential Proust or Joyce. Melville knew that standard philosophy and logic have to be diluted to meet *individual* tastes: "Adler & Taylor came into my room. . . . We talked metaphysics continually . . . under the influence of the whiskey" (1849 *Journal*, p. 12). More importantly, Melville also knew the larger corollary truth: "There are some enterprises in which a careful disorderliness is the true method" (*MD*, p. 304). A great writer must think his or her own logic, forge a new genre; be a true "original." The names are few. In nineteenth-century America we have Whitman,

Poe, Clemens, Dickinson, and, rising above all, "like a snow hill in the air," Herman Melville.

Endnotes

[1]The typical form of the syllogism consists of three statements (each with a subject and predicate); the first two are premises, and the third, which follows logically from them, is the conclusion. A commonly quoted syllogism is: All men are mortal; Socrates is a man; therefore Socrates is mortal. An extended syllogism with three or more premises (the number is almost unlimited) is called a sorites.

[2]See Alonzo Church's excellent discussion of the history of logic in the *Encyclopaedia Britannica* (1973).

[3]Quoting from "The Sun Epistle" by the thirteenth-century Persian logician al-Qazwini-al-Katibi and from the tenth-century Persian philosopher Avicenna, Nicholas Rescher points out that the Persians introduced temporal and quantitative qualifiers of the basic Aristotelian absolute categories of "all" and "none," such as "necessarily," "perpetually," "non-necessarily," or "non-perpetually." In the Persian logic of centuries ago there were four basic modal relationships:

A. A chronically constant necessary correlation (i.e., *A* is necessarily true when *B* is true).
B. A chronologically constant correlation (i.e., *A* is true whenever *B* is true).
C. A chronolgically occasional correlation (i.e., *A* is true at some time when *B* is true).
D. A chronologically occasional possibility correlation (*A* is possibly true at some time when *B* is true).

Thus, it can be seen that there are two dimensions in Arabic logic that are not at all prominent in Western (Aristotelian) logic: (1) a temporal dimension of ubiquity and occasion; and (2) a possible dimension of necessity (certainty) and probability.

[4]Other "logical words" used with less frequency are argument, conclude, concluding, conclusion, deduction, denote, denoted, denotes, follows, inasmuch, premised, and whereupon. See *A Concordance to Melville's Moby-Dick* (1978). H. Cohen & J. Cahalan (Eds.), Ann Arbor, MI: University Microfilms. A more recent concordance is by Eugene F. Irey (1982). New York: Garland. There are also, in dissertation form, concordances for *Clarel* (Larry Wegener; *Mel. Diss.*, #487) and *Billy Budd* (Charles Murray; *Mel. Diss.*, #505).

References

Church, A. (1973). Logic, history of: Modern logic. *Encyclopaedia Britannica.*

Cohen, H., & Cahalan, J. (Eds.). 1978. *A concordance to Melville's Moby-Dick.* 2 vols. Ann Arbor, Mich.: University Microfilms International.

Kring, W. D., & Carey, J. S. (1975). Two discoveries concerning Herman Melville. *Proceedings of the Massachusetts Historical Society, 87,* 137–41.

Lawrence, T. E. (1935). *Seven pillars of wisdom.* New York: Garden City Publishing Co.

Lewis, N. D. C. (1964). Preface. In J. S. Kasanin (Ed.), *Language and thought in schizophrenia.* New York: W. W. Norton.

Murray, C. J. *A concordance to Melville's* Billy Budd. Doctoral dissertation, Miami (Ohio) University, 1979. [*Mel. Diss.*, #505]

Nakamura, H. (1967). *The ways of thinking of Eastern peoples.* New York: UNESCO.
Rescher, N. (1967). *Temporal modalities in Arabic logic.* New York: Humanities Press.
von Domarus, E. (1964). The specific laws of logic in schizophrenia. In J. S. Kasanin (Ed.), *Language and Thought in Schizophrenia* (pp. 104–114). New York: W. W. Norton.
Wegener, L. E. (1978). *A concordance to Herman Melville's Clarel: A poem and pilgrimage to the Holy Land.* Doctoral dissertation, University of Nebraska. [*Mel. Diss.*, #487]
Yannella, D., & Parker, H. (1981). *The endless, winding way in Melville: New charts by Kring and Carey.* Glassboro, NJ: Melville Society.

PART

III

MELVILLE AND MURRAY

Shneidman is eager and happy to assert that Henry Murray has been the center of his intellectual life. He readily admits that he has tried all his adult life to emulate Murray in whatever ways he thought he might succeed, but that his interest in Herman Melville actually predated his association with Murray, although it was enormously reinforced by that relationship. Shneidman has stated that Melville was his main hobby. (Dr. Shneidman even has a Melville room in his home). For much of the last half of the 20th century, Murray was the foremost amateur Melville scholar in America. His psychoanalytical writings on Melville forever changed the tenor of English-department scholarship.

In 1920, before the great Melville revival in the United States, a distinguished English literary figure, Viola Meynell, wrote in a foreword to *Moby-Dick*: "Herman Melville has here endowed human nature with writing that I believe to be absolutely unsurpassed. To read it and absorb it is the crown of one's reading life." Shneidman believes that. He has read and collected Melville since his college days. The heart and jewel of his Melville collection—which Shneidman gave to UCLA—are the three volumes of the 1851 English edition of *The Whale*, which Murray sent to Shneidman, by ordinary post, unannounced. Shneidman admits that he sometimes obsesses about Melville, seeing in him all the precursors of depth psychology from Freud and Jung to the present, and the deepest insights into the 19th and 20th centuries' unresolvable tensions between Christianity and capitalism—between avowed benignity and rapacity.

This part consists of four chapters: two on Melville and two on Murray. Chapter 8 is a careful counting—done before the advent of computer-generated concordances—of all the death and death-related words in Melville's eleven novels, from *Typee* (1846) to *Billy Budd* (1891). (*Billy Budd* lay unknown until 1921.) These varying emphases on death themes in Melville's writings are then related to what, in general, was happening in Melville's life. Shneidman wrote this paper with Murray in mind, to be delivered at a special meeting (at Williams College) of the Melville Society, of which Murray was then president. It was his way of trying to show his loving feelings for his benefactor.

The paper presented in Chapter 9 also involved Murray in a way. It was a psychological autopsy—a procedure invented by Shneidman and his colleagues Norman Farberow and Robert Litman at the Los Angeles Suicide Prevention Center in the 1950's to help the coroner certify the mode of equivocal deaths more accurately. This chapter presents a psychological autopsy of Malcolm Melville, Herman's eldest son, who died at age 18, from a pistol wound to his right temple. Shneidman devised a case of a contemporary (fictional) 18 year-old Los Angeleno, as though it were a real coroner's case. Dr. Murray came out from Cambridge and participated in that event. The recommendation to the coroner would have been for suicide (as opposed to accident or homocide), as the mode of death.

In Chapter 10, Shneidman argues that suicides can be understood, along with other approaches, in terms of Murray's writings on psychological needs (e.g., the need for achievement, the need for shame-avoidance, the need for succorance, etc.). These twenty-some psychological needs are given their exhaustive definitions in the hundred pages of Chapter 3, "Aspects of Personality," in Murray's *Explorations in Personality*, which is Shneidman's basic text. It is no surprise that Shneidman would apply Murray's need-oriented personology to his own field, suicidology.

Chapter 11 reprints Shneidman's remarks at Murray's memorial service on October 3, 1988. On that solemn occasion, Shneidman turned to Melville to express his deepest feelings.

8

CHAPTER

The Deaths of Herman Melville

I feel that I have about as much right to be here in this select company as has a copy of *The Refugee* or *Redburn: or the Schoolmaster of a Morning* to be in a definitive edition of the *Complete Writings*. For my intrusion, you must blame entirely my all-bestowing benefactor, Professor Henry A. Murray, who, in a myriad of wonderful and mysterious ways of which he alone in this world is capable, led me to Melville and, of equal importance in the charting of my own course, to an abiding and appropriate concern with the dark as well as the light compass-headings of the human voyage. And now my travels have brought me to this gam.

A gam is it? I, who should be listening silently in the dark corner of the cabin, have been, with Captain Murray's urgings, emboldened to speak. In this trade-around of tales, the ship that I report from is a curious composite of ill-fated craft: it has torn timbers from the *Pequod,* rotted spars from the *San Dominick,* broken planks from the *Parki.* I speak, of course, about the vessels of death—and would include even fragments from one of Melville's earliest published writings: "The Death Craft." In short, I am the scrivener-mate from the ever-pressing *Thanatopsis.*

Surely, "death" is one of those patently self-evident terms, the definition of which, it is felt, need not detain a thoughtful mind for even a moment. Every adult person knows instinctively what he means by it. The

In H. P. Vincent (Ed.), *Melville and Hawthorne in the Berkshires.* Kent, OH: Kent State University Press, 1968, pp. 118–144. With permission.

dictionary defines death as the act, or event, or cause, or occasion of dying, or of the end of life, or of cessation. In these terms, by "the death of Herman Melville" one could refer only to a description or a discussion of what occurred to Melville on September 21, 1891—or by legitimate extension, one might choose to include those events and factors which immediately preceded Melville's physical death, or which were causally related to it. But what can one possibly mean by the *deaths* of Herman Melville?

Melville, in *Pierre*, quoting the highest power, provided us with an operational definition of death as "the last scene of the last act of man's play." But perhaps there is more—"the little lower layer." The main issue for this paper is whether or not the *concept* of death need only be dichotomous—granting that the *event* of death involves a distinct irreversible physiological termination and psychological cessation of one's viable existence. Specifically, the question is whether or not it is possible for us to talk about such matters as death equivalents, substitutes for death, and especially partial deaths, such as deaths of aspects of the self.

On the Death Certificate which has been used in the United States and in many European countries for over the last half century, among other entries, there is stated the *cause* of death and *mode* of death. Currently, in the handbook for all those countries that report to the United Nations there are listed some 130 causes of death. These include asphyxiation due to drowning, myocardial infarction, cerebral hemorrhage, etc. More importantly for our present consideration is that in addition to the cause of death, the mode of death is stated. In the current—and in my opinion, grossly inadequate—classification of modes of death, four modes are indicated. They are: natural, accident, suicide, and homicide, the initial letters of which, for your mnemonic convenience, spell N-A-S-H. Each one of us must end up in one of the barren conceptual crypts. It is immediately apparent that the cause of death does not always automatically indicate its mode. For example, one might die of asphyxiation due to drowning in a suicidal, accidental or homicidal mode. But by far the greater inadequacy of this traditional classification of modes of death and in the concept of modes of death itself, lies in the fact that it emphasizes relatively adventitious and often trivial elements in the death of a human being. This is so because it omits entirely the psychological role of the individual in his own demise. The N-A-S-H classification is Cartesian and apsychological in its spirit. For example, it is a relatively unimportant difference to me whether the light fixture above me falls and I am invaded by a lethal chandelier (accidental mode), or someone about me coughs and I am invaded by a lethal virus (natural mode), or someone shoots a gun at me and I am invaded by a lethal bullet (homicidal mode), in light of the fact that I do not wish (intention) any of these to occur. To be blunt about it, my own overriding interest in my own Death Certificate, if by some illogical magic I could ever be permitted to see it, would be almost entirely in the date.

In order to avoid the inadequacies of this conceptual morass, I have proposed, at the Suicide Prevention Center in Los Angeles—an organization which I helped direct for a number of years before I was recently persuaded to move to the Nation's Capitol by the promise of "an opportunity to paint on a broader canvas"—that all human deaths be classified among three types: intentioned, sub-intentioned, and unintentioned. An *intentioned* death is any death in which the decedent plays a direct, conscious role in effecting his own demise. An *unintentioned* death is any death—whatever its determined cause and apparent conventional mode—in which the decedent plays no effective role in effecting his own demise—where death is due entirely to independent physical trauma from without, or to non-psychologically-laden biological failure from within. But most importantly—and what I believe to be characteristic of the vast majority of all deaths—*sub-intentioned* deaths where the decedent plays some, partial, covert, or unconscious role in hastening his own demise. The objective evidences of the presence of these roles lie in such behavioral manifestations as, for example, poor judgment, imprudence, excessive risk-taking, abuse of alcohol, misuse of drugs, neglect of self, self-destructive style of life, disregard of prescribed life-saving medical regimen, and so on, where the individual himself fosters, facilitates, exacerbates, or hastens the process of his dying.

At the Suicide Prevention Center we have participated with the Chief Medical Examiner-Coroner of Los Angeles County in assessing the psychological role of the deceased individual in his own death, especially in puzzling or cryptic deaths or deaths which are equivocal as to mode of death. We do this by careful and selective interview of a number of his surviving relatives and acquaintances.[1] What might be of especial interest to members of the Melville Society is my own attempt to illustrate this procedure, which I have labelled the "Psychological Autopsy," by a detailed analysis of the enigmatic and equivocal death—was it accident or suicide or what?—of Captain Ahab. This analysis appeared in an essay entitled "Orientations toward Death" published in 1963 in the book *The Study of Lives*[2]—a volume written in honor of Dr. Murray by several of his colleagues and former students.

It is important to note that the role of sub-intention is not at all limited to dying behaviors. Indeed, the main point of this presentation is to assert the importance of the role of the individual—his conscious and unconscious needs, conflicts, thrusts—not only in his dying (his death style), but also in his living (his life style), the latter consisting in part of the ways in which individuals (all too rarely nowadays) elevate, ennoble, expand or actualize their lives, or, conversely, the ways in which they (all too often) diminish, narrow, attrit, or truncate aspects of their inner and outer lives, or what we can now explicitly refer to as the partial deaths of their psychic and social selves.

We can be sanguine that Melville would not have, in principle, resisted this concept of sub-intention, certainly not on the grounds of its involving unconscious motivation. Melville was a veritable cerebral-fluid brother of Freud. His *Moby-Dick* and *Pierre*, to name two instances, rest, in no insignificant part, on the concept of sub-intentioned motivations. Consider, from *Moby-Dick*, Melville's explanation of the aboundingly empathic response of Ahab's crew in terms of "their unconscious understandings," which Melville reified as "the subterranean miner that works in us all."

I now further buttress my position with a quotation from our President. Professor Murray, in his paper "Dead to the World: Or the Passions of Herman Melville,"[3] an address which he gave under the auspices of the Suicide Prevention Center in Los Angeles in October, 1963, aware of our studies attempting to relate the permanent cessation of suicide to the temporary interruption of sleep,[4] asked the following questions:

> Why not some other related condition such as a temporary or permanent cessation of a part of psychic life, the cessation of affect, feeling almost dead, for example; or the cessation of an orientation of conscious life, the cessation of social life, dead to the outer world; or the cessation of spiritual life, dead to the inner world, for example. . . . It might be well to take account of different degrees or changes of degrees of life, near cessation, as good as dead; or trend toward cessation, dying.

The concept of partial death—death of an aspect of the self—is now the pivotal and critical concept for our consideration. Its manifestations—and again I quote from my authority—are

> . . . as if the person's primal spring of vitality had dried up, or as if he were empty or hollow at the very core of his being. There is a striking absence of anything but the most perfunctory and superficial social interaction.

This is accompanied by withdrawal from his society, grave social refusal, or even where the fires of feeling are still burning, they burn without glow or warmth, or pleasure-giving purpose. It has to do with repudiation of one's society, of ostracizing people, cutting them dead; it also relates to society's repudiation and ostracism of the person. Thus there are deaths of aspects of the inner self, and deaths of aspects of the outer or social self. Buchanan's failure to find Melville in America—

> I sought everywhere for this Titan who was still living somewhere in New York, but no one seemed to know anything of the one great writer fit to stand shoulder-to-shoulder with Whitman on that continent. . . .

is a poignant example of Melville's not being totally socially alive, a partial social death which lasted for some "forty torpid years."

This may be the point to supply a brief but clear example of an individual who participated, sub-intentionally, in his own fate—in this case a broken jaw, lucky for him, not lethal. I refer, of course, to Radney, the chief mate of the *Town-Ho*, "the infatuated man [who] sought to run more than half way to meet his doom,"—an excellent example of the moiety of self-participation in the sub-intentioned act.

Parenthetically, we can note that Melville is filled with moieties, partials, and parts, especially of the human body. I quote a few from many:

Moby-Dick:

> . . . some deep men . . . are left living on with half a heart and half a lung . . .

Benito Cereno:

> . . . His voice was like that of one with lungs half-gone—hoarsely suppressed, a husky whisper. No wonder that, as in this state he tottered about, his private servant apprehensively followed him.

Mardi:

> Now, which was Samoa? The dead arm swinging high as Haman? Or the living trunk below? . . . For myself, I ever regarded Samoa as but a large fragment of a man, not a man complete. And the action at Tenerife over, great Nelson himself—physiologically speaking—was but three quarters of a man.

Melville had an intimate association with the idea of partial death: About it, he might have said: "I am quick to perceive a horror and could still be social with it." It is debatable whether *Moby-Dick* is as much about terminal death as it is about partial death, and especially about suicidal equivalents:

> . . . whenever it is a damp, drizzly November in my soul . . . then I account it high time to get to sea as soon as I can. This is my substitute for pistol and ball. With a philosophical flourish, Cato throws himself upon the sword; I quietly take to the ship.

And again:

> . . . to the death-longing eyes of such men, who still have left in them some interior compunctions against suicide, does the all-contributed and all-receptive ocean alluringly spread forth his whole plain of unimaginable, taking terrors, and wonderful, new-life adventures; and from the hearts of infinite Pacifics, the thousand mermaids sing to them—"Come hither, broken-hearted; here is another life without the guilt of intermediate death; here are wonders supernatural, without dying for them. Come

hither! bury thyself in a life which, to your new equally abhorred and abhorring, landed world, is more oblivious than death. Come hither! put up *thy* gravestone, too, within the church-yard, and come hither, till we marry thee"!

Before we turn to Melville's further explications of these qualitative nuances of death in the human spirit (including his own), I shall, as background material, attempt to present some few quantitative evidences of the extent of Melville's interest in the topics of death. I must confess that I present these quantitative data with both serious misgivings and deep trepidations. To reduce the grand scope of Melville's poetic outpourings to chart and figures can only remind one of Whitman's poem, "When I heard the Learn'd Astronomer":

When I heard the learn'd astronomer,
When the proofs, the figures, were ranged in columns
  before me,
When I was shown the charts and diagrams, to add, divide,
  and measure them,
When I sitting heard the astronomer where he lectured with
  much applause in the lecture-room,
How soon unaccountable I became tired and sick,
Till rising and gliding out I wander'd off by myself,
In the mystical moist night-air, and from time to time,
Look'd up in perfect silence at the stars.

Eleven of Melville's books—*Typee, Omoo, Mardi, Redburn, White Jacket, Moby-Dick, Pierre, Israel Potter, The Piazza Tales, Confidence Man,* and *Billy Budd*—were examined, and a notation was made for each of five types of death material.[5] A brief definition and some examples of these five death categories will now be given.

A. Any reference to the death of the chief protagonist, including his wishes about death, his ideation concerning death, threats of death to him (either by himself or by others), or actions which might result in his death.

B. The actual death of specific characters other than the chief protagonists, either in an individual or a group, such as the entire crew of a ship.

C. Any reference to death relating to other than the chief protagonists: Threats of death, actions which might involve the character in destruction, death thoughts, and so on.

D. Death in nature, and references to death in the environment. Examples would be storms, violence, natural destruction. Other examples would include references to the dark, hostile, destructive, death-dealing aspects of nature and of life in general.

E. Discourse on death, including historic references to naval battles where death occurred; philosophic dissertations on death; metaphysical discussions of death.

The result of this study was the tabulation of 1802 references to death. Table 8-1 and Figure 8-1 reflect these data from among the eleven books. In the Figure, the solid line represents the manner in which Melville distributed the totality of his eighteen hundred thoughts of death *among* these eleven works; the dotted line indicates the relative concentration per page of death talk *within* each of these eleven works. Of what Melville said about death, he seems to have said most of it—about thirty per cent—in *Moby-Dick,* and next most in *The Piazza Tales, Mardi,* and *Pierre*—14, 13 and 12 per cent, respectively. The vast majority—seventy per cent—of Melville's death thoughts is contained in these four books.

The dotted line in Figure 8-1, reflecting the concentration of death talk per page, was computed by comparing the number of death items per book with the number of pages in the Constable Edition of that book, and then reducing those ratios so that their sum was 100 per cent. These data indicate that there was relatively more death talk per page in *The*

TABLE 8-1. Death in Melville

		Among all Books		Within Each Book		
		No. of Items[a]	Per-cent	No. of Pages[b]	% Thoughts per Page	Per-cent[c]
Typee	1846	92	5	340	27	6
Omoo	1847	52	3	375	14	3
Mardi	1849	243	13	769	32	7
Redburn	1849	89	5	403	22	5
White-Jacket	1850	109	6	504	22	5
Moby-Dick	1851	538	30	725	74	16
Pierre	1852	218	12	505	41	9
Israel Potter	1855	63	3	225	28	6
Piazza Tales	1856	246	14	271	91	20
Confidence Man	1857	49	3	336	15	3
Billy Budd	1891	103	6	114	90	20
		1802	100%	4567	456	100%

[a]For five death categories: Cessation of chief protagonist, death of anyone, death in nature, discussion of death, and general cessation.
[b]Constable Edition.
[c]Percentage of thoughts per page divided by 4.5 in order to reduce 456 to 100%.

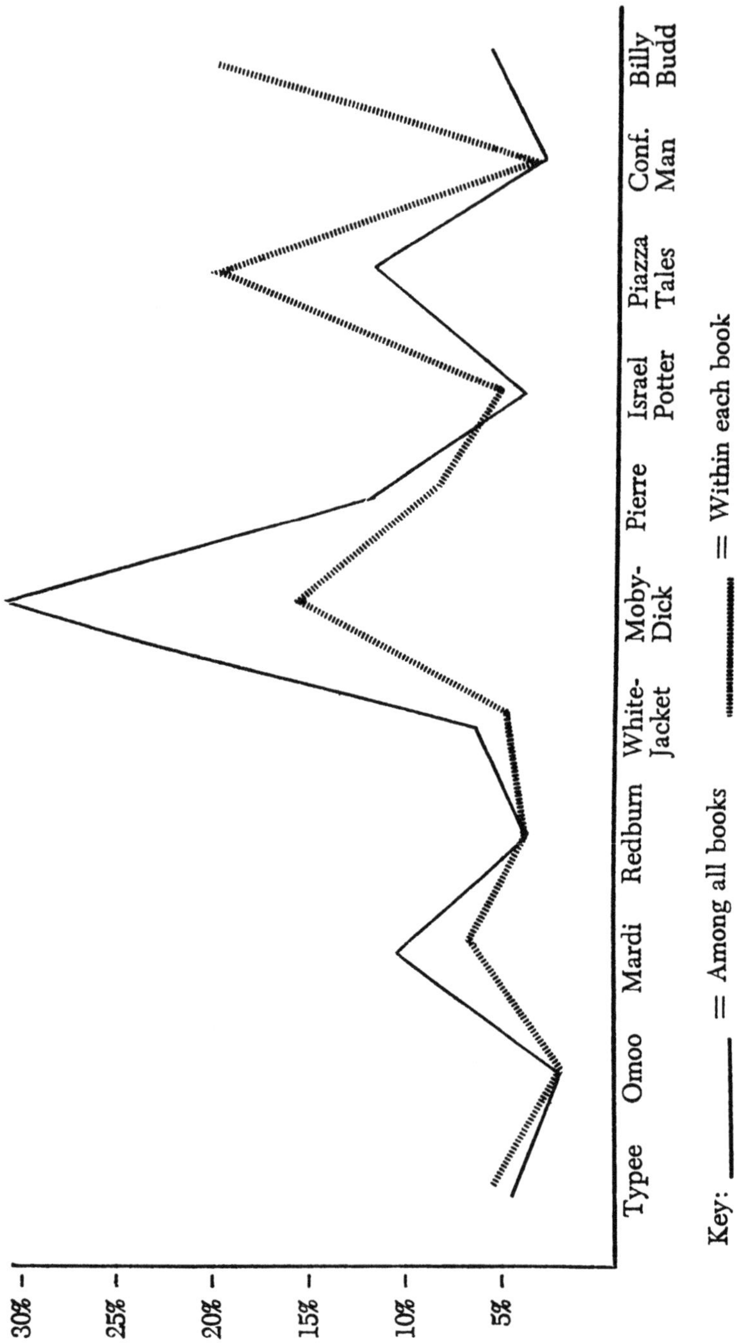

FIGURE 8-1. Death in Melville.

Piazza Tales and *Billy Budd* than in any other books, and next highest concentration in *Moby-Dick*.

The distribution of the five death categories among the eleven books is indicated in Table 8-2. These data show us that most of the items (36 per cent) were in the "Discourses on Death" category; least (7 per cent) in the "Death in Nature" category. Among the interesting items contained within Table 8-2 is the fact that 45 per cent of the death talk in *Pierre* relates to the death of the chief protagonist.

The quality of the references to death varies among the books: *Mardi* is more philosophic, reflecting a fantasied wish for idealization of society; *Moby-Dick* is concerned more with actual death and symbolic substitutes for death as portrayed through the struggle of man with his internal and external environments; *Pierre* obsesses about death in the individual psyche, an introspective accounting of the psychodynamics of death; *The Piazza Tales* also deals with death in the environment, but the environment pitted against man; and in *Billy Budd* the emphasis is on the interplay of death-movements among the chief characters—Billy, Captain Vere, and Claggart.

In brief summary, we found some 1800 death thoughts distributed among some 4500 printed pages of Melville's writing, or about one death thought for every 2 1/2 pages. The most death-laden book is *Moby-Dick*, next *Mardi*, *Pierre*, and *The Piazza Tales;* the most death-concentrated books are *The Piazza Tales* (which followed *Moby-Dick* by three years) and *Billy Budd* (which followed *Moby-Dick* by almost forty years). Death remained in Melville's mind and flowed from his pen from *Mardi* on, that is, from the time that Melville was only thirty years old.

My saying "only thirty years old" would seem to indicate that some other standards or separate criteria are implied. And so they are. The main notion here is that of an appropriate time of life—an idea based in turn on the concept of stages or phases of life in the total human life cycle. The most famous explication of this notion is in Shakespeare's seven ages of man. In our own time, the psychoanalyst Erik Erikson has written about eight psycho-social stages in the human life cycle; Jung has discussed the two main ages of man; Gerald Heard has described his five ages of man, and Charlotte Buhler has delineated the several main stages in the human course of life, to name a few.

One main point that all these writers imply is that each major period of life is a special time—a time with its own modal special problems, conflicts, crises, ordeals and mysteries. To give one example, adolescence—the teen years—is a time when the main problem is that of separation from the family and the movement into young adulthood, the latter movement carrying with it the problems of how to find and hold love,

TABLE 8-2. Analysis of Melville death items

	Typee	*Omoo*	*Mardi*	*Redburn*	*White Jacket*	*Moby-Dick*	*Pierre*	*Israel Potter*	*Piazza Tales*	*Conf. Man*	*Billy Budd*
Number of Items, 1802	92	52	243	89	109	538	218	63	246	49	103
Death Categories:											
A. Any reference to death of chief protagonist, including wishes, ideation, threats, etc.	18%	5%	10%	15%	12%	11%	45%	20%	26%	8%	33%
B. Actual death of specific characters other than chief protagonists	3%	10%	10%	13%	8%	10%	11%	22%	18%	16%	27%
C. Death in nature; death in the environment.	11%	11%	8%	4%	5%	13%	4%	5%	8%	6%	1%
D. Discourses on death; discussion of death; historic references to death.	28%	31%	51%	37%	43%	26%	34%	32%	29%	57%	33%
E. Any reference to death relating to characters other than chief protagonists: wishes, thoughts, threats.	39%	43%	21%	30%	32%	39%	7%	21%	19%	12%	7%
	100%	100%	100%	100%	100%	100%	100%	100%	100%	100%	100%

the role of romantic love and its relationship to sexuality, how to begin a career, and how to establish and support a family.

Building on these concepts, I have elsewhere[6] indicated that psychological crises can occur to a person *within* a period of his life (what I call *intra*-temporal crises); in the interstices *between* periods of his life (*inter*-temporal crises); or, occasionally, there are those crises which occur in individuals who are *out-of-phase* with what ought to be their own period of life (what I call *extra*- temporal crises). This group includes individuals who have "too early" savored experiences "beyond their years," and in this sense, are too old for their age (inappropriately precocious in life-development); and, conversely, it includes individuals who are not "grown up emotionally," who are sheltered not only from experience, but from reflection (regarded in life's ways). These individuals are, in terms of their chronological age, out of tune with the modal psychological issues and conflicts that ought to be occupying their psyches. Experiences that come "too early" (such as at too early an age having to be one's own parents, or having to integrate the impact of sexuality, or having to face annihilation) put one out of phase with one's own years. These individuals may be said to suffer from "information overload" or what might be called "stimulus inundation."

Listen to Melville in early out-of-phase *Redburn:*

> Talk not of the bitterness of middle-age and after life; a boy can feel all that, and much more, when upon his young soul the mildew has fallen; and the fruit, which with others is only blasted after ripeness, with him is nipped in the first blossom and bud. And never again can such blights be made good; they strike in too deep, and leave such a scar that the air of Paradise might not erase it.

Again, from *Redburn:*

> I had learned to think much and bitterly before my time; all my young mounting dreams of glory had left me; and at that early age, I was unambitious as a man of sixty. . . . Cold, bitter, cold as December, and bleak as its blasts, seemed the world then to me; there is no misanthrope like a boy disappointed; and such was I, with the warm soul of me flogged out by adversity.

Mostly, when Melville was producing these refractory images of his own inner life, his deeper concerns were about his own obsessing intoxication with the enigmatic and unanswerable issues that are more grim even than those of misery and death, namely, eternal and total cessation, naughtment, and annihilation.

And even more and still worse: Had Melville been able to postpone his invested concern with these depressing topics until a more proper time in his own life, he might have been a more measured and sanguine soul, but precocious psyche that he was, he encountered these core issues out of phase with his own life, too early, in his twenties and thirties, and then they could only be for him unconquerable phantoms and monsters, leviathans and krackens.

To answer a soul's need to deal with the issue of one's own annihilation before he is thirty-five is to tackle God's world in off-season, at hurricane time, and then one is faced only with the tortured choice of what nature of wreck will ensue—utter, partial, immobilizing, fatal—but not, alas, with the happier alternatives between wreck or safety, between escape or deep spiritual success, between destructive or positive affective transactions.

On the occasion of Dr. Murray's address in Los Angeles, he stated:

> It occurred to me that a roughly analogous study might be made of the . . . cycle of affective transactions in the works of certain Romantic authors—authors whose credo encourages them to give vent in apt and telling words, to emotions of all sorts. I need not tell you the name of my first choice among eligible authors.

I have taken what I consider to be a reasonable calculated risk and assumed that it could have been no other than Melville that he had in mind. If this were so, what can we now say about Melville's credo?

Melville's credo was to say Yes; Yes to his own sense of right; Yes to his fealties to the depths of his own thought and inner experience; but like any other brave man who feels overcome by vastly superior forces, never to say Yes to the commands of others or of fate or of nature to surrender. Melville had several mottoes, for example: *Ego non baptizo te in nomine patris*—you know the rest—but his credo seems to have been this: *better to be drowned as a daring fool than be hanged as an uncommitted or timid coward.* And this, as we shall see, was just a partial reflection of his great, self-ennobling, courage-building, autonomous sense of pride. He voices this credo over and over. But first, concerning his sense of autonomy:

Moby-Dick:

> I'd strike the sun if it insulted me.
>
> I, myself, am a savage, owing no allegiance but to the King of Cannibals; and ready any moment to rebel against them.
>
> . . . the queenly personality lives in me and feels her royal rights . . .
>
> Here I am proud as Greek God . . .

And in a letter to Hawthorne, April 16, 1851:

> The man who, like Russia or the British Empire, declares himself a sovereign nature (in himself) amid the powers of heaven, hell, and earth. He

> may perish, but so long as he exists, he insists upon treating with all Powers upon an equal basis.

And now, to the core and substance of Melville's credo:

Moby-Dick, about Bulkington:

> Better it is to perish in that howling infinite than to be ingloriously dashed upon the lee, even if that were safety.
>
> Oh man! Admire and model thyself after the whale. Do thou too remain warm among ice. Do thou, too, live in this world without being of it. . . . Retain, O man! in all seasons a temperature of thine own.

Pierre:

> For now am I hate-shod! On these I will skate to my acquittal! No longer do I hold terms with aught. World's bread of life, and world's breath of honour, both are snatched from me; but I defy all world's bread and breath. Here I step out before the drawn-up worlds in widest space and challenge one and all of them to battle.

Jimmy Rose:

> I still must meditate upon his strange example, whereof the marvel is, how after that gay, dashing, nobleman's career, he could be content to crawl through life, and peep about among the marbles and mahoganies for contumelious tea and toast, where once like a very Warwick he had feasted the huzzaing world with Burgundy and venison.

And from his letters:

June 1, 1851: To Hawthorne:

> All Fame is patronage. Let me be infamous: there is no patronage in *that.* . . .
>
> To the dogs with the head! I had rather be a fool with a heart, than Jupiter Olympus with his head. . . .

March 3, 1849: To Duyckinck:

> . . . then had I rather be a fool than a wise man.—I love all men who *dive.* Any fish can swim near the surface, but it takes a great whale to go down stairs five miles or more; & if he don't attain the bottom, why, all the lead in Galena can't fashion the plumet that will. . . .

Along with his many other ambiguities, Melville, with his great zest for life, was a death-intoxicated man. His concerns with thoughts related to death and diminution appear through his works as a *leitmotif,* subliminally haunting the reader with their baleful expressions of grandeur and woe. Nor are we surprised to find these thoughts in the man who asked so urgently about life's purposes and life's moralities.

What made this issue laden with even more than ordinary anguish was that, for Melville, death meant more than physical demise or even more—if one can imagine it—than psychological cessation; it meant complete, that is, eternal, annihilation. More than do or die; it was exult or never-have-been. The essence of his credo, from Melville's third book, *Mardi*—and one of my own favorite Melville passages—written when he was 29, reads as follows:

> Oh, reader, list! I've chartless voyaged. With compass and the lead, we had not found those Mardian Isles. Those who boldly launch, cast off all cables; and turning from the common breeze, that's fair for all, with their own breath, fill their own sails. Hug the shore, naught new is seen; and "Land ho!" at last was sung, when a new world was sought.
>
> That voyager steered his bark through seas, untracked before; ploughed his own path mid jeers; though with a heart that oft was heavy with the thought that he might only be too bold, and grope where land was none.
>
> So I.
>
> And though essaying but a sportive sail, I was driven from my course, by a blast resistless; and ill-provided, young, and bowed to the brunt of things before my prime, still fly before the gale;—hard have I striven to keep stout heart.
>
> And if it harder be, than e'er before, to find new climes, when now our seas have oft been circled by ten thousand prows—much more the glory!
>
> But this new world here sought, is stranger far than his, who stretched his vans from Palos. It is the world of mind; wherein the wanderer may gaze round, with more of wonder than Balboa's band roving through the golden Aztec glades.
>
> But fiery yearnings their own phantom-future make, and deem it present. So, if after all those fearful, fainting trances, the verdict be, the golden haven was not gained;—yet, in bold quest thereof, better to sink in boundless deeps, than float on vulgar shoals; and give me, ye gods, an utter wreck, if wreck I do.

In any complete recitation of Melville's unusual combination of gifts, pressures, heritage, and inner thrusts, the role of his private sense of warranted and unwarranted overweening pride must be given the great emphasis it obviously merits. At the outset, we can, following Nietzsche, distinguish pride from vanity—where the former comes mostly from inner feelings and the latter from outside re-enforcement and feedback, as in the case, for example, of poets. With Melville, it is pride, not vanity, which we mean.

It would appear that Melville's inner sense of pride stemmed largely from two main sources: Pride in his family and lineage; but mostly the pride that came from his recognition of his own active, first-rate, self-contained inner life, dealing creatively—and with a sure sense of its own extraordinary capacity—with core cultural and cosmic psychic issues. Melville not only had a self-sustained sense of being of somewhat noble birth, but he also had the feeling of being a more than somewhat gifted man.

His pride in his family is clearly indicated in his books—in *Moby-Dick,* he writes: "It touches one's sense of honor, particularly if you come of an old established family in the land, the Van Rensselaers, or Randolphs, or Hardicanutes."—and explicitly stated in his letters, as, for example, his letter to his mother (May 5, 1870), and to his cousin (August 27, 1876).

As for his pride in himself, as early as 1839, when he was 19, Melville wrote in his *Fragments from a Writing Desk* about his own "mind endowed with rare powers"; all through his letters he writes either with the exaggerated modesty of a proud man or the proper self-respect of a proud man. For example, he writes to his father-in-law: "I hope the perusal of this little narrative of mine will offer you some entertainment." He describes himself in his letters as "conceited," "garrulous," filled with "selfishness" and "egotism." He was hungry to read the reviews and notices of his own works. He wrote to his brother to send him "every notice of any kind" and to John Murray to send him all the reviews of his books. He had an enormous appetite for recognition and fame. Melville was obviously deeply wounded by the critics of *Mardi* and of *Moby-Dick.* After the *New York Literary World*'s review of *Moby-Dick,* he cancelled his subscription to that journal.

Now, if one believes in the power of the self-fulfilling prophecy, the role of pride can be a salutary one. It enhances one's self-confidence and increases effectiveness, but the negative side of this coin is that it also makes one vulnerable. It is like an Achilles heel in an Olympic athlete.

The enemy of pride is criticism, rejection, verbal abuse. I need not take the time in this presentation to recite the criticisms which were levelled at the heart of Melville. The public, represented by the critics, liked his tobacco and wood-chopping works but railed and hooted when he wanted to say the things most meaningful to him. We all know his letter to Hawthorne in 1851: "What I feel most moved to write, that is banned,—it will not pay. Yet, altogether, write the other way I cannot." And, from *The Confidence Man,* the tale of Charlemont, a story of aristocratic pride—and its concomitant fear of dependency and vulnerability, the key lines of which are:

> When both glasses were filled, Charlemont took his, and lifting it, added lowly: "If ever, in days to come, you shall see ruin at hand, and, thinking you understand mankind, shall tremble for your pride; and, partly through love for the one and fear for the other, shall resolve to be beforehand with the world, and save it from a sin by prospectively taking that sin to yourself, then will you do as one I now dream of once did, and like him will you suffer. . . ."

In a situation where one has been verbally abused and behaviorally constrained, one can generally react in one of two global ways. He can protest and advance his best efforts and products, but if he takes this course he demonstrates how deeply he cares and how grievously he has been hurt. This tack will make him more vulnerable, more pitiable, and often subject to more abuse. It is a course which runs directly counter to the instincts of a proud man. The other course is to be disdainful, ignoring one's critics as though they did not exist, as though they were dead, reducing them to the unimportant position of impotence by robbing them of their power to influence and especially of their power to hurt. But this maneuver, by its very nature, tragically can be executed only at the price of one's own total or partial self-ostracism and thus at the expense of the death of part of one's social and hence psychological self.

In Stedman's Introduction to the 1892 edition of *Typee,* we read a contemporary illustration of Melville's social death:

> Mr. Melville would have been more than mortal if he had been indifferent to his loss of popularity. Yet he seemed contented to preserve an entirely independent attitude, and to trust to the verdict of the future. The smallest amount of activity would have kept him before the public; but his reserve would not permit this. That he had faith in the eventual reinstatement of his reputation cannot be doubted . . . Our author's tendency to philosophical discussion is strikingly set forth in a letter from Dr. Titus Munson Coan to the latter's mother, written while a student at Williams College . . . The letter reads in part:
>
> " . . . when I left him he was in full tide of discourse on all things sacred and profane. But he seems to put away the objective side of his life, and to shut himself up in this cold north as a cloistered thinker."

One human experience not inconsistent with pride is hate or hostile affect. Hostility can take many forms, including verbal criticism, verbal retaliation, physical abuse, and in its most extreme form, complete disregard of the other person—especially conscious disregard. There is great reciprocity in interpersonal or intergroup hostility and, as we know, great danger of escalation of this type of reciprocity. Some hostility is retaliatory, but much of hostility is anticipatory—to get one's blows in first. Melville had more than his fair share of hate—conscious and unconscious: against his parents—his mother and father for separate reasons—against society, and against Christendom—all the forces that he saw as wanting him to surrender and to acquiesce. Granted that his global hate was long repressed by his fear of retaliation; but who can gainsay his attacks on Christianity in *Omoo,* and on Western society in *Typee*?

We see this combination of pride, fear and hate in Ahab's address to the Candles:

> Oh! thou clear spirit of clear fire, whom on these seas I as a Persian once did worship, till in the sacramental act so burned by thee, that to this hour I bear the scar; I now know thee, thou clear spirit, and I know now that thy right worship is defiance. To neither love nor reverence wilt thou be kind; and e'en for hate thou canst but kill; and all are killed. No fearless fool now fronts thee. I own thy speechless, placeless power; but to the last gasp of my earthquake life will dispute its unconditional, unintegral mastery in me. In the midst of the personified impersonal, a personality stands here. Though but a point at best; whencesoe'er I came; wheresoe'er I go; yet while I earthly live, the queenly personality lives in me, and feels her royal rights, But war is pain, and hate is woe. Come in thy lowest form of love, and I will kneel and kiss thee; but at thy highest, come as mere supernal power; and though thou launchest navies of full-freighted worlds, there's that in here that still remains indifferent. Oh, thou clear spirit, of thy fire thou madest me, and like a true child of fire, I breathe it back to thee.

Nor need we look too far, nor inappropriately exercise our imagination to divine Melville's attitudes about duplicity and criticism, and especially about critics.

White-Jacket:

> How ere these officers to *gain glory?* How but by a distinguished slaughtering of their fellowmen? How were they to be promoted? How but over the buried heads of killed comrades and messmates?
>
> Do you straighten yourself to think that you have committed a murder, when a chance falling stone has often done the same? Is it a proud thing to topple down six feet perpendicular of immortal manhood, though that loft living tower needed perhaps thirty good growing summers to bring it to maturity? Poor savage! And you account it so glorious, do you, to mutilate and destroy what God himself was more than a quarter of a century in building?

Moby-Dick:

> There's a most doleful and most mocking funeral! The sea-vultures all in pious mourning, the air-sharks all punctiliously in black or speckled. In life but few of them would have helped the whale, I ween, if peradventure had had needed it; but upon the banquet of his funeral they most piously do pounce. Oh, horrible vulturism of earth! from which not the mightiest whale is free.

Encantadas:

> If some books are deemed most baneful and their sale forbid, how, then, with *deadlier* facts, not dreams of doting men? Those whom books will hurt will not be proof against events. Events, not books, should be forbid.

And from his letters:

April 23, 1848: To Lemuel Shaw:

> I see that *Mardi* has been cut into by the London Atheneum and also burnt by the common hangman in the Boston Post.
>
> There is nothing in it, cried the dunce, when he threw down the 47th problem of the 1st book of Euclid—there's nothing in it.—This with the posed critic.

Dec. 13, 1850: To Evert Duyckinck:

> . . . I don't know but a book in a man's brain is better off than a book bound in calf—at any rate it is safer from criticism.

Jan. 18, 1886: To John W. Henry Canoll:

> For what can one do with the Press? Retaliate? Should it ever publish the rejoinder, they can.

Perhaps his penultimate comment, from *Moby-Dick,* about the revengers in life: "Sharks . . . like hungry dogs 'round a table where red meat is being carved."

And for pure, undiluted heartbreaking hate, no other passage in our literature is so concentrated as this one from *Moby Dick:*

> All that most maddens and torments; all that stirs up the lees of things; all truth with malice in it; all that cracks the sinews and cakes the brain; all the subtle demonisms of life and thought; all evil, to crazy Ahab, were visibly personified, and made practically assailable in Moby Dick. He piled upon the whale's white hump the sum of all the general rage and hate felt by his whole race from Adam down; and then, as if his chest had been a mortar, he burst his hot heart's shell upon it.

For some, the often highly exciting and sometimes superb narrative novels—*Typee, Omoo, Redburn, White Jacket, Israel Potter*—remain primarily as valued interstices between Melville's more profound identity-seeking and death-focused labors, those works that sprang out of his deeper shaping and crushing concerns, cemented as they were to both his self and his *post-self.*

The self or ego relates to the core of one's active functioning, his cognitive and emotional masterings and maneuvers in the present life; the post-self, on the other hand, refers to the ways in which one might live on, survive, or have some measure of impact or influence after the event of his own physical death—for example, through one's children (in whom Melville did not before their deaths seem to have that deep an investment, and in whom, after the premature deaths of his sons, he could not have any hope), or through one's published works, in a selected few of which Melville most was deeply invested.

Here are some samples of Melville's thoughts concerning the concept that I have labelled the post-self:

Redburn:

> Peace to Lord Nelson where he sleeps in his mouldering mast! but rather would I be urned in the trunk of some green tree, and even in death have the vital sap circulating round me, giving of my dead body to the living foliage that shaded my peaceful tomb.
>
> . . . how much better would such stirring monuments be full of life and commotion, than hermit obelisks of Luxor, and idle towers of stone; which, useless to the world in themselves, vainly hope to eternalize a name, by having it carved, solitary and alone, in their granite. Such monuments are cenotaphs indeed; founded far away from the true body of the fame of the hero; who, if he be truly a hero, must still be linked with the living interests of his race; for the true fame is something free, easy, social, and companionable. They are but tombstones that commemorate his death, but celebrate not his life . . .

Moby-Dick:

> It may seem strange that of all men sailors should be tinkering at their last wills and testaments . . . After the ceremony was concluded upon the present occasion, I felt all the easier; a stone was rolled away from my heart. Besides, all the days I should now live would be as good as the days that Lazarus lived after his resurrection; a supplementary clean gain of so many months or weeks as the case might be. I survived myself . . .
>
> . . . I now leave my cetological System standing thus unfinished, even as the great Cathedral of Cologne was left, with the cranes still standing upon the top of the uncompleted tower. For small erections may be finished by their first architects; grand ones, true ones, ever leave the copestone to posterity . . .
>
> . . . immortality is but ubiquity in time . . .

And from his letters:

April 5, 1849: To Evert Duyckinck:

> All ambitious authors should have ghosts capable of revisiting the world, to snuff up the steam of adulation, which begins to rise straightway as the Sexton throws his last shovelfull on him.—Down goes his body and up flies his name.

April 23, 1849: To Lemuel Shaw:

> These attacks are matters of course, and are essential to the building up of any permanent reputation—if such should ever prove to be mine . . .

June 1, 1851: To Hawthorne:

> What "reputation" H.M. has is horrible. Think of it! To go down to posterity is bad enough, any way; but to go down as a "man who lived among

> the cannibals"! When I speak of posterity, in reference to myself, I only mean the babies who will probably be born in the moment immediately ensuing upon my giving up the ghost. I shall go down to some of them, in all likelihood.

Dec. 10, 1862: To Samuel Savage:

> I once, like other spoonies, cherished a loose sort of notion that I did not care to live very long. But I will frankly own that I have now no serious, no insuperable objections to a respectable longevity. I don't like the idea of being left out night after night in a cold church-yard.

The concept of the post-self is, of course, directly related to the notion of annihilation. To cease as though one had never been, to be "oblivionated," to accept defeat, to abandon any hope of love or fame, any hope of impact or memory-in-the-mind-of-another beyond one's death, to be obliterated, to be ostracized, to be muted, to be naughted, to be expunged from history's record—that is a fate literally far worse than death.

Not unexpectedly, Melville had a few things to say on these issues: *Lightning-Rod Man:*

> Think of being a heap of charred offal, like a haltered horse burned in his stall; and all in one flash!

Israel Potter:

> Few things remain. . . . He was repulsed in efforts after a pension by certain caprices of law. His scars proved his only medals. He dictated a little book, the records of his fortunes. But long ago it faded out of print—himself out of being—his name out of memory.

Redburn:

> But all is now lost; I know not who he was; and this estimable author must need share the oblivious fate of all literary incognitos.

White-Jacket:

> it is a good joke, for instance, and one often perpetrated on board ship, to stand talking to a man in a dark night-watch, and all the while be cutting the buttons from his coat. But once off, those buttons never grow on again. There is no spontaneous vegetation in buttons.

Pierre:

> Unendurable grief of a man, when Death itself gives the stab, and then snatches all availments to solacement away. For in the grave is no help, no prayer thither may go, no forgiveness thence come; so that the penitent whose sad victim lies in the ground, for that useless penitent his doom is

> eternal, and though it be Christmas-day with all Christendom, with him it is Hell-day and an eaten liver forever.

From his letter to Hawthorne, June 1, 1851:

> Though I wrote the Gospels in this Century, I should die in the gutter.

Implicit in the preceding is a board hypothesis, the contents of which run roughly as follows: that aspects of Melville's personality are to be found distributed (in either a direct or a refractory way) among his fictional characters; and further, there is implied a refinement of this general notion in the specific sub-hypothesis which proposes that within particular books there can be found a range of characters some of whom reflect a particular segment or portion of Melville's personality, and who, in their totality may yield the entire secret combination that unlocks the tantalizing safe. Related to this latter hypothesis is an article by the Italian critic Eugenio Montale (1960, *Sewanee Review, 68,* 419–422) which mentioned, but certainly does not endorse—nor do I—the interpretation that the three principal characters of *Billy Budd* stand as different "narcissistic projections of the three ages of the author." More to the point and better documented: Professor Bezanson, in his "Introduction" and discussion of "The Characters" in the Hendricks House edition of *Clarel,* plausibly and convincingly advances the proposition that several of the main characters were intended to represent different aspects or potentialities of Melville's nature, and—what is especially relevant to our own present concerns—specifically that Mortmain embodied Melville's wish for self-annihilation. I quote, liberally, from Professor Bezanson:

> . . . in the two decades after *Moby Dick,* Melville's descent into self had made him acquainted with an underworld of recalcitrant shades: the sense of defeat, willful isolation, unmanageable moods, fear of death, anxiety over his own physical and mental health. . . . These darker elements of Melville's sensibility are channeled into the striking series of monomaniacs who followed one another so ominously through the poem: . . . From his first appearance Mortmain is committed by name ("Death Hand") and symbol (his black skull cap) to *self-annihilation.* The roots of his personal malaise, running subtle and deep, have flowered into political, philosophic, and religious despair. . . . Consumed by psychic fury, driven to *intolerable introversion,* Mortmain has no strength left to hold back his own will to self-destruction.

I assume that every student of Melville is well acquainted with Professor Murray's explication of Melville's psychological positions over time in relation to his own annihilation. Quoting from Dr. Murray, they go something like this[7]:

In *Mardi* (1847), Melville's position was: "If I fail to reach my golden haven, may my annihilation be complete; all or nothing."

In *Moby Dick* (1851); "I forsee my annihilation, but against this verdict I shall hurl my everlasting protest."

In *Pierre* (1852): "I am confronted by annihilation, but I cannot make up my mind to it."

In 1856, in London, as recorded by Hawthorne: "I have pretty much made up my mind to be annihilated."

And in *Billy Budd* (1891): "I accept my annihilation."

After Melville's early successes with *Typee* and *Omoo,* and the excitement of his being challenged for veracity and for his criticism of missionaries, but not for his style nor genre nor philosophic exploration, when he dared then to write his first real romance and turned, after the first one hundred pages of *Mardi,* to the infinite perspectives of his own ruminations and discovered, as consequence, that he was met with a grape-shot barrage of annihilating criticism, the issue for him was forever joined.

Thereafter, his most vital dialogue of the mind concerned itself with whether or not he could fully live, express himself openly, be printed publicly, be read widely, be adjudged fairly; or whether he would need to print himself privately, eschew critical support, retreat from public view, write to his own soul's need—all partial deaths of his talents, his energies, his natural desires, and his interplay with his own time.

Out of Melville's combination of his great sense of inner pride, his bravura inner life style, his imperious reaction to hostility and to criticism, his conscious and unconscious attrition of the social side of his literary life—out of all of these diverse elements grew his concern with death and annihilation and his enormous investment in his post-self. In this sense, Melville wrote not so much for his own time as he did for any appropriate (that is, any appreciating) time to follow—for what Leyda has called a "posthumous celestial glory." Melville was partially dead during much of his own life, but he more than compensated for that lugubrious limitation by writing in such a way that he could realistically plan to live mostly after he had died. "On life and death this old man walked."

Endnotes

[1]Litman, R. E., Curphey, T. J., Shneidman, E. S., Farberow, N. L., & Tabachnick N. D. (1963). Investigations of equivocal suicides. *Journal of the American Medical Association, 184,* 924–929.

[2]Shneidman, E. S. (1966). Orientations toward death: A vital aspect of the study of lives. In R. W. White (Ed.), *The study of lives.* New York: Atherton Press; reprinted with discussion in the *International Journal of Psychiatry* (1966) *2,* 167–200.

[3]Murray, H. A. (1967). Dead to the World: Or the passions of Herman Melville. In E. S. Shneidman (Ed.), *Essays in self-destruction.*

[4]Shneidman, E. S. (1964). Suicide, sleep and death: Some possible interrelations among cessation, interruption and continuation phenomena. *Journal of Consulting Psychology, 28,* 95–106.

[5]My great apprecaition to Miss Jan Kramer of the Los Angeles Suicide Prevention Center for her enormous effort and help in this connection, is here expressed.

[6]Sleep and self-destruction: A phenomenological approach. (1967). In *Essays in Self-Destruction.*

[7]Murray, H. A. Introduction. *Pierre, or the ambiguities.* (pp. xiii–ciii). New York: Henricks House (Farrar Straus).

☐ Epilogue

Sometime during the writing of "The Deaths of Herman Melville" Murray sent Shneidman this note about Herman Melville and death.

☐ Rambling Thoughts and Queries

Henry A. Murray:
Harvard University, Cambridge, Massachusetts, U.S.A.

1. The question is: What is the nature and chronological incidence of HM's preoccupation with death *before its season* (say 70), not death in old age. 2. Death may be (a) organic life cessation or (b) psychic life cessation. 3. What impresses us is (a) trend of action toward danger of death (with a full description of perils involved), (b) premonitions of disaster and death (fated and predetermined), and (c) a final image of a tragic hero (a brave man overcome by vastly superior forces, and who yet refuses to surrender, to say *Yes*). Not until Billy Budd does a hero say Yes (bless the hand that chastised him). 4. What is the nature and the incidences of (a) a trend toward the danger of death, descriptions of perils to be encountered—(including the danger of ostracism: social death).

1. HM's going whaling, the perils of the whale.

2. His invasion of a cannibal community—cannibal rites *(Typee).*

3. Melville heroes who court danger, who attack others (Taji killing the priest Aleema, in *Mardi*), who commit acts which will result in ostracism.

4. HM's attacks on Christianity in *Omoo* and on Society (Western) in *Typee* and from then on. Attacks on his parents, attacks on critics.

[NB: One explanation of this might be: (a) an early fear of danger, (b) counteracted later by a courageous movement towards extreme danger (pride overcoming fear) with (c) premonition of defeat (coming out of repressed fear).]

[NB: Another explanation might be (a) a long-repressed (by fear) global *hate* against the world—first the parents and then Society and Christendom *in toto*—i.e., all forces that want him to surrender, say *Yes*. These two explanations go together and are all summed up in Ahab's address to the Candles. This would be derived from parricide (as described by Freud) and ego pride (not described by Freud).]

5. What is the nature and incidences of premonitions of disaster and death throughout Melville's work and in Melville's life (letter to Hawthorne, 1851, confession to Hawthorne, 1856).

6. What is the nature and the incidences of (a) actual tragic deaths (including references to Christ) and of (b) annihilations (character assassinations) of great men, geniuses, self, heroes misunderstood by the world (Lombardo, etc., etc.), Hawthorne (in essay on H)—*Pierre, Confidence Man*, etc. The frequency of suicide of some sort as the cause of death.

7. Another angle relative to social death (ostracism) would date back to the trauma of birth (expulsion from the claustrum) and later rejection by the mother, etc., which would lead the proud young HM to react by bringing about his own egression (running off to sea, etc.). In several places (Bulkington) the Land is compared to a safe but slavish life in Society, and the Sea to freedom which may lead to death (social), followed by an apotheosis.

All references to piteous forlorness (Ishmaels, orphans), uncharitable treatments are indications of dependency (poor me) and the miseries of being an outcast, all this has reference to HM's reaction to character assassination by the critics of *Pierre* and to a less extent, by the critics of *Moby-Dick*, and I am inclined to think now that he had an enormous appetite for recognition, fame. (He was hungry for all the English and American reviews of *Typee* and *Omoo*, and he was deeply wounded by the critics of *Mardi*. After the *N.Y. Literary World's* review of *Pierre*, he stopped his subscription. He was too proud to acknowledge that he cared what the critics said and to this extent was dependent on them.)

8. Maybe your paper might show the steps that led up to "I have pretty much made up my mind to be annihilated," and serve to explain it to some extent. I quoted it to Conrad Aiken, who has not been fully appreciated—his name is rarely mentioned nowadays—and he said that was *exactly* what he felt. (He has made one abortive sub-intentioned attempt at suicide). What does "to be annihilated" mean? To accept defeat? Not to fight back anymore? To abandon my hope of fame? Of Love? To stop writing? To let the critics obliterate my name, oblivionate me, mute me? To accept ostracism? To let go of my hold on life? To commit suicide?

Forgive me please if all of this is irrelevant to your purpose. It is all old hat to you, I know.

9

CHAPTER

Some Psychological Reflections on the Death of Malcolm Melville

Malcolm Melville died on September 12, 1867, at age 18 from—to quote his death certificate—a "pistol shot wound in [his] right temporal region." Contemporary designations of the mode of his death changed within hours from suicide, to accident, to death while of unsound mind. Historically, the mode of his death has remained equivocal. In order to approach this enigma a "psychological autopsy" of an equivocal death case as identical to Malcolm Melville's as was possible was conducted as though it were a genuine current "open" case at the Los Angeles Suicide Prevention Center in 1973. That procedure resulted in a near-unanimous judgment by the center staff that the most accurate certification of the death as described was "probable suicide," which would then be certified as "suicide." In this paper the assertion is made that Herman Melville himself had been a psychologically "battered child" and, in a way typical for battered children, psychologically battered his own children when it came his turn to be a parent. The further assertion is made that, for Malcolm, his father was suicidogenic; and established this penchant in Malcolm (through his neglect, active rejection, fearsomeness, and his fixed attention to his own writing—*Redburn, White Jacket,* and *Moby Dick*) within the first 2 years of Malcolm's life. For Malcolm, the psychological basis of his suicidal state was isolated desperation—a ubiquitous characteristic of most suicides. Malcolm had a deep unconscious feeling of not being wanted by his father; that it would

Reprinted from *Suicide and Life-Threatening Behavior,* 1976, *6,* 231–242. With permission.

Presented at the meeting of the Melville Society, December 28, 1975, in San Francisco, California.

> be better if he were out of the way, dead. On the morning of his death, the choice for Malcolm was between the memory of his mother's kiss a few hours before and the terror of (and the need to protect himself against) his father's rage to come.

I wish to begin on solid ground, by making at least one statement with which everyone will agree: Herman Melville is the hero of the Melville Society. There is general agreement among us that his work represents a veritable Everest of art. He is the man whom we seek to understand and whose gifts we are eager to share with those not fortunate enough to know them as we do, but he ought not to be a pasteboard figure for us. My own small efforts do not preclude my looking at his all too-human characteristics as well as his towering strengths. He is my hero, not my villain; but for Malcolm, he was suicidogenic. Trained by his unconscious reactions to his own childhood, he in turn created the psychological climate for Malcolm's suicide.

The sum and substance of my speculations is that, psychologically, the groundwork for Malcolm's self-destructive behavior was laid in the first 2 years of his life. The basic unconscious charge to the boy from his father was that Malcolm should not get in the way, should not grow up, should not live out his own life. From the beginning, it would be better for his father if he, Malcolm, were simply not around the house. The first 2 years of life were "Shadows present, foreshadowing deeper shadows to come."

In order to view Malcolm's death in the perspective of his life, one reasonable approach would be to create a detailed life chart. A document of this sort would be in the tradition of Adolph Meyer, the famous American psychiatrist of the early part of this century. Meyer developed what is now called, by the rather few who remember him, the Meyerian life chart. On it one lists in several columns the events of a life, year by year, then looks for concomitances in the life patterns. In preparing a life chart one obviously begins at the beginning. Thus I have begun my reflections with thoughts of what Malcolm's first few years of life (vis-a-vis his father) must have been for him. It makes psychological sense to me to say that Melville was the following kind of father as seen through the baby Malcolm's eyes: Significantly he was absent and rejecting and, second, when he was present, he was actively fearsome and rejecting. In short he was a frightening figure. It seems fairly clear that what Melville did, without malice, but out of his own driven, creative neurotic force, was to inculcate perturbation in his first-born son.

In *Redburn*, composed in the year in which Malcolm was born (1849), Melville, in what is certainly a rather poignant passage and surely one of the least insightful passages of all his writings, wrote:

> I was then but a boy. Some time previous my mother had removed from New York to a pleasant village on the Hudson River, where we lived in a small house, in a quiet way. Sad disappointments in several plans which I had sketched for my future life; the necessity of doing something for myself, united to a naturally roving disposition, has now conspired within me, to send me to sea as a sailor. . . . Added to these reminiscenses, my father, now dead. . . . (Chap. 1, p. 3)
>
> It was with a heavy heart and full eyes, that my poor mother parted with me; perhaps she thought me an erring and a willful boy, and perhaps I was; but if I was, it had been a hardhearted world, and hard times that had made me so. I had learned to think much and bitterly before my time; all my young mounting dreams of glory had left me; and at that early age; I was as unambitious as a man of sixty. . . . Cold, bitter cold as December, and bleak as its blasts, seemed the world then to me; there is no misanthrope like a boy disappointed; and such was I, with the warm soul of me flogged out by adversity. (Chap. 2, p. 10)

Even if one makes allowances for the differences between character and author, one has compassion for Melville, for in a very direct sense this had certainly happened to him. But I am reminded of the cold, harsh, empirical, clinical truth that the parents of battered children—Malcolm and Stanwix in this case—have, as their most conspicuous item of their own case histories, the fact that they themselves were battered children. Melville—who had compassion for himself as a rejected child—rather than being a compassionate father, became what is alas too frequently seen nowadays in the clinic, a rejecting father, and in turn battered his own children psychologically.

Another important item to note is that *Moby Dick* was probably begun around February, 1850, and finished in September, 1851. According to Elizabeth, Melville was, in this period, "working under unfavorable circumstances, sitting at his desk all day, and not eating until four or five o'clock and then riding to the village after dark" (Leyda, p. 412). At this same time infant Malcolm was in the house, crying, teething, needing his mother's attention to stay alive. Melville, in a chapter on good and bad temper, in *White Jacket* (written when Malcolm was an infant), penned these lines:

> But of all chamber furniture in the world, best calculated to soothe a bad temper, and breed a pleasant one, is the sight of a lovely wife. If you have children, however, that are teething, the nursery should be a good way upstairs; at sea, it ought to be in the mizen-top. Indeed, teething children play the very deuce with a husband's temper. I have known three promising young husbands completely spoil on their wives' hands by reason of a teething child, whose worrisomeness happened to be aggravated at the time by the summer complaint. With a breaking heart, and my hand-

> kerchief to my eyes, I followed those three hapless young husbands, one after the other to the premature graves. (Chap. 12, p. 46)

Baby Malcolm in the deep recesses of his forming unconsciousness was an intruder. The newly forming unconscious speaks to itself in curious ways. The message could have been: It would be better if he were gone. One of the prices for Melville's writing *Moby Dick* was to offer Malcolm as a sacrifice.

At the 1973 convention of the American Psychological Association I presented (in a symposium honoring Dr. Murray) a paper entitled "A Psychological Autopsy of Malcolm Melville's Death." This is not the occasion to repeat the full contents of that paper, but I wish to report one interesting, empirical finding. First, however, I need briefly to give some background.

Some years before, when I was codirector of the Los Angeles Suicide Prevention Center, I labeled a procedure that had been worked out jointly between the prevention center and the coroner's office as the "psychological autopsy" (Shneidman, 1974, pp. 131–149). In most countries of the world today and in all of the 50 states of this country there is a fairly uniform death certificate. On each, there is an entry that asks the certifying physician to indicate what he considers to be the causes of the death, and, in addition, there is an item that asks him to check whether that death is accidental, suicidal, or homicidal. It is fairly reasonable to suppose that if none of these is checked, then what is implied is that the death was natural. Currently, according to the latest revision of the International Classification of Diseases and Causes of Death, there are 137 causes of death. Everyone who died must be certified as having died of one or more of these 137 causes. On the other hand, the words "natural," "accident," "suicide," and "homicide"—the acronym of which is NASH—refer not to the 137 causes of death, but to four *modes* of death. It is also immediately clear, if one reflects on it at all, that cause of death does not automatically tell one the mode of death. For example one can die of asphyxiation due to drowning or of crushing injuries to the head, accidentally, suicidally, or homicidally. A sizable number of the cases that come to any coroner's attention—perhaps 10% to 15%—for certification are *equivocal* as to the mode of death, that uncertainty usually lying between the mode of accident and suicide. The cause of death is usually easy to determine with today's technology. The purpose then of the psychological autopsy, which interviews relatives and friends and acquaintances of the decedent seeking to ascertain the decedent's intentions vis-à-vis his own death, is to clarify the mode of death of equivocal deaths.

A few years ago I determined to conduct a psychological autopsy on Malcolm Melville's death and arranged to do this at the Los Angeles Suicide Prevention Center. Only one staff member was in on the secret. The case was presented to the full staff as a contemporary case. The facts were presented as close to the historical record as information from solid biographical sources could provide. At that meeting Professor Leon Howard represented himself as the uncle of the dead boy and Professor Alan Sandy as his high school teacher of English and baseball coach. The case was presented as though it were an equivocal case coming from the Coroner's Office for consultation. The staff asked a number of questions and treated the occasion with the seriousness that such an occasion would require. After some 3 hours of questions and discussion, 18 members of the staff then voted as follows: suicide, 3; probable suicide, 13; suicide/accident undetermined, 2; accident, 0. Homicide and natural death were not considered. In the certification of any death, a "probable suicide" is certified under the rubric "suicide." Thus the overwhelming consensus at the suicide prevention center—16 of 18—was that Malcolm's death would today be certified as a suicide.

Suicide is almost always an enigmatic act. The article on suicide in the 1973 *Encyclopaedia Britannica* (Shneidman, Vol. 21, pp. 383–385) begins by stating that a dozen individuals can kill themselves and have done 12 psychologically different deeds. There is no simple formula for self-destruction. The earlier (circa 1910) traditional psychoanalytic formulation of the inner dynamics of suicide as being hostility directed toward the introjected, ambivalently seen, love object—what I have called murder in the 180th degree—is today no longer accepted as a universal formula, even among psychoanalysts. The roles of other psychodynamic states, such as anguish, pain, impotent rage, shame, guilt, and frustrated dependency—the latter especially—are all currently recognized as capable of being the primary motivating psychological forces in a suicidal act.

Nevertheless—speaking as one who in his own work and writings has pressed for a multifaceted approach to the understanding of suicidal acts—I believe, without contradicting the above, that some generalizations about suicide can usefully be made. My own work with suicidal persons and more recently a return to an intensive study of suicide notes emboldens me to generalize that the suicidal individual (with very few exceptions) is in a state of *isolated desperation*. That person has positioned himself or has been positioned—they can be the same in the mind—into a dark corner where there is no hope (by way of human contact or communication) of relief; the person is desperate and there is no one (capable of helping) to turn to.

Listen to this brief excerpt of a contemporary young person, about Malcolm's age, who committed suicide and fortuitously survived. She jumped from a sixth story balcony. This verbatim record dramatically illustrates the narrowing field of consciousness, the constriction of the focus of attention, the tunnel vision, the closed world of the suicide, as well as the anguishing, close to bursting depression felt by the person in an acute suicidal state. We see confusion and panic, sparked by the sense of isolated desperation.

> Well, after that I was out of danger more or less, at that point, and they pretty much let me wander around the hospital as I pleased. And there was some question about my husband letting me return home, to the apartment, because he thought I was going to make another attempt and he couldn't bear to live with that. And it was just all up in the air, it was sort of like, well you go and find a place to stay and there was no place for me to stay. And I don't know anyone here and so it turned out that I was going to be staying in some sort of welfare kind of arrangement which was going to be fixed or arranged by the social worker. All of a sudden there I was out in the middle of nowhere without any money, and my husband wasn't going to let me come back to the house and I was desperate. And then I went into a terrible state. So at this point I was supposed to be making these arrangements myself. I could barely even spaek, you know, the social worker was calling various agencies and then turning the telephone over to me so I could tell my story and I could even barely remember my name let alone my date of birth or anything like that and I thought my God in Heaven, I can hardly even—and I was not functioning at all and these people are going to throw me into the street. And I didn't want to go to a psychiatric ward because I was really frightened that I would wind up—I would possibly have a psychotic episode or something like that. I was so desperate I felt my God, I can't face this thing, going out, and being thrown out on the street. And everything was like a terrible sort of whirlpool of confusion. And I thought there's only one thing I can do. I just have to lose consciousness. That's the one way to get away from it. The only way to lose consciousness I thought was to jump off something good and high. I just figured I had to get outside, but the windows were all locked. So I managed to get outside. I just slipped outside. No one saw me. And I got down to the ground by walking across that catwalk thing, sure that someone would see me, you know, out of all those windows. The whole building is made of glass. And I just walked around until I found this open staircase. As soon as I saw it I just made a beeline right up to it. And then I got to the sixth floor and everything just got very dark all of a sudden, and all I could see was this balcony. Everything around it just sort of blacked out. It was just like a circle. That was all I could see, just the balcony. And I went over it. I climbed over it and then I just let go. I was so desperate. Just desperation. And the horribleness and the quietness of it. The quiet. Everything became so quiet. There was no sound. And everything sort of went into slow motion as I

> climbed over the balcony. I let go and it was like I was floating. I blacked out. I don't remember any part of the fall.

If we accept the diagnosis of Malcolm's death as a suicide as accurate and if, further, we take the role of isolated desperation as a valid model for the suicidal state, then we have to ask about the sources of Malcolm's isolated desperation. At the outset it would not seem unreasonable to speculate that it had at least two components: (a) a deep sense of guilt and shame in relation to his mother, together with a sense of powerless yearning to protect her from any overbearing behavior of her husband; and (b) a rather overpowering terror of his father, coupled, not illogically, with a sense of impotent hostility toward him.

That same week of the meeting at the Los Angeles Suicide Prevention Center (a few years ago), there was a premeeting at UCLA to rehearse the presentation to be made a few days later at the suicide prevention center. The purpose of the meeting was to see that the presentations were clear and to remove any quaintness and anachronisms from the 1867 record. That premeeting at UCLA and the meeting at the suicide prevention center were illumined and bewitched for all of us who attended by the presence of two giant Melvilleians, Henry Murray and Leon Howard, coming to honor Melville from opposite poles of our terraqueous globe.

The different approaches were far more interesting to me than even a comparison of the (essentially similar) Ionian and Aegian waves from a nonexistent Corinthian shore. At that meeting, Dr. Murray talked about Melville's children's terror of their father and the apparent absence of love in the home. Dr. Murray said that he had had a chance to talk to one of the Melville daughters and it was a terrible experience for her even to recall her father. He further reported that there were times when they separated Malcolm from his father as though they did not get on together. And there were stories about Melville's liking to carve the roast beef at the dining table in a menacing way. Dr. Murray used the words "ritualized, emphasized, exaggerated aggression, something you could say could be translated in a dream into a human being; one source of the terror of his father." Dr. Murray further said that:

> There is a question whether down in his marrow Malcolm thought of his father as coming into his room and punishing him. I would be inclined to put the pistol on the side of a fantasied self-defensive act on the part of Malcolm. He would have slept with his pistol whether loaded or unloaded and the thematic meaning of the pistol would be to defend himself against the punishing father[1]. . . . Home is usually a place where you get support and protection, but it was the most dangerous place in New York City for Malcolm.

These remarks uttered with some sense of pain by Dr. Murray and repeated by me here with that same sense of pain are not, however, inconsistent with a whole new wave of current feeling about Melville as father. Some current examples include Robert Penn Warren (1967, pp. 79–80) who states that Melville "was an 'unnatural' father, made life at home very difficult for his children, and was the chief cause of the failure of Stanwix and the suicide of Malcolm who was in terror of him." He further refers to Melville's "defective parental sense."

Very recently, Edwin Miller, in his biography, *Melville* (1975), wrote:

> Melville must also have recognized that Malcolm's act gave a horrible reality to a motif running through his fiction that revealed a personal preoccupation with suicide. Malcolm had, as it were, acted out his father's fantasy. . . . The first-born son, Malcolm grew up in a household in which the father was monomaniacally dedicated to his writing. Sometimes it must have seemed to him that nothing else mattered to his father. Always moody and irascible, the father did not improve in disposition after the departure of Hawthorne from Lenox in 1851. . . . Herman's favorite cousin termed him "a very strict parent," and her judgment was an outsider's. Only Malcolm and the other children knew the whole story. Even they did not realize how their father unwittingly imitated the stern sea captains who manhandled greenhorns into manhood aboard ships. If as a youth Herman fled authority, he later exercised it with a heavy hand. In *White Jacket* he wrote fiercely against the tyrannical flogging aboard warships, but in a jocular letter to his brother Tom on May 25, 1862, he commended his treatment of "those young ones": "Strap them, I beseech you. You remember what the Bible says . . . about spareing the strap & spoiling the child."[2] (Chap. 20, p. 318)

And Melville's great grandson, Paul Metcalf, implied in Genoa (1965) that Melville was an unconsciously destroying father.

> And there were the children:
> Mackey,
> Stanny,
> Bessie,
> & Fanny,
> hovering at the edge of the storm, the vortex, and
> killed, crippled or withered, according to the order of birth, to how
> near in time (the father's *space*) they came
> to the eye of it.
> Melville—as good a parent as, say, Columbus was an administrator—was more of a prophet:
>
> There was the letter to Mackey, 1860: "Whilst the sailors were aloft one of the yards, the ship rolled and plunged terribly; and it blew with sleet and hail, and was very cold & biting. Well, all at once, Uncle Tom saw something falling through the air, and then heard a thump, and then—

> looking before him, saw a poor sailor lying dead on the deck. He had fallen from the yard, and was killed instantly." (*Mackey, you shall die violently*. . . . Chap. 3, p. 73)

Let me touch briefly on the possible effects of one possibly important item in the physical environment of Malcolm's home. For some years of Malcolm's life, how many I am unable to ascertain, in the parlor of a pedestal rested a larger-than-life-size marble bust of Antinous. It was an obvious favorite of his father's. Was it not so that this beautiful young man was revered in classical times for his spontaneously having committed suicide for his emperor? What might have been the intertwined psychological impact on Malcolm (relating to the relationship between filial loyalty and suicide) of the latent message contained in his father's choice of their household god?

From his earliest days Malcolm might have felt in the recesses of his unconscious mind that his father wanted him out of the way, out of the house, forever, gone, dead. As an infant and young boy, and later as a young man when he could be directly compared with his father (in terms of holding a job, and becoming aware of the secrets of sexuality, growing up and having his own adventures, and who knows, perhaps writing books), the two were then competitors, albeit indirect ones, but never on an equal footing. At the deepest level the alternatives for Malcolm were too painful for words: patricide or suicide.

There are other reasonable views of this matter, however. Professor Howard, playing his role perfectly at the Los Angeles Suicide Prevention Center as a dead boy's uncle, in response to a question by a staff member, "Was he close to anyone in his family?" said the following:

> He was the oldest of four. He had a brother who was 2 years younger and two sisters. There was approximately 2 years spacing. I don't think he was close with any of them. His younger brother admired him very much and was greatly disturbed over what had happened. But I don't know very much about their relationship. His parents, I think, feel [sic]very much the way I feel about it, in the first place, he knew enough about guns not to have been particularly careless. The carelessness explanation is not a reasonable one from what we know of him. He had no reason for deliberate suicide so that is equally unacceptable. The family would prefer to have it accident because there is a certain stigma attached to suicide. There is nothing that the family can arrive at to make them believe that it was not an accident—although an accident is entirely implausible.

Later in that 3-hour session, the following brief colloquy occurred between Professor Howard and the one staff member who knew the true identity of the decedent. (That person is Mr. Samuel Heilig, who is Chief Psychiatric Social Worker at the Los Angeles Suicide Prevention Center.)

Mr. H: *I'm puzzling whether or not he was just terribly frightened about what was going to happen that evening when his father came home.*

Prof. H: *That would not fit into any pattern that I was aware of.*

Mr. H: *Well, your sister said something in another direction when I talked with her. She thought all of the children were afraid of the father. That he could have these sudden outbursts that would terrify the whole family and her.*

Prof. H: *Well then, you have more direct information than I have.*

Mr. H: *She said all the children were very fearful and would tread very carefully when he was around.*

Prof. H: *She would not have told me this. This would be a commentary on the marriage that would be private and that would be kept secret from me.*

At this point someone else made a statement about some aspect of the young man's personality and the discussion moved to other topics.

In that sonorous first paragraph of "The Funeral" in *Moby Dick* (Chap. 69, pp. 343–344), which begins with two roared commands, Melville has written one of the most extraordinary oxymoronic passages in all literature, specifically by juxtaposing in a dramatic shift in mood the description of what happens to the beheaded and stripped whale as being "rapacious . . . insulting . . . murderous . . . hideous," in the first eight sentences, to these serene and pacific words of the last sentence—floating "beneath the unclouded and mild azure sky, upon the fair face of the pleasant sea, wafted by the joyous breezes, the great mass of death floats on and on till lost in infinite perspectives."

There is an oxymoronic quality too to Malcolm's suicide. The oxymoronic quality of Malcolm's suicidal act (as well as his sense of impotent isolated desperation) is conveyed in the barest description of that fatal act: Malcolm Melville, recent recipient of a military uniform, at age 18, fatally wounded in the temple by his own pistol—whilst in his bed in his night clothes.

This oxymoronic quality which infused some of Melville's most moving passages also, as Miller states, dominated his behaviors in which he confused his children by his double messages, what we today call "double binds."

It would be interesting to know if Malcolm ever poured over the opening lines of *Moby Dick*. When Malcolm was about a year old, his father wrote a prescription for an antidote to suicide. It is egression, or escape; but apparently for the remainder of Malcolm's life, Melville systematically withheld that cure from his son. Consider the confusion for Malcolm latent in the opening paragraph of *Moby Dick:*

	Comment
Call me [a wanderer]. . . . I thought I would sail about a little and see the watery part of the world.	Mackie, you are 18—the age at which I was teaching school. I have taken your latch-key from you. You are to be home each evening by eleven o'clock. And don't keep your mother up.
Whenever I find myself growing grim about the mouth; whenever it is a damp, drizzly November in my soul;	"Mackie . . . was always obliging and affectionate. . . ." (Davis & Gilman, letter number 172, p. 228)
. . . and especially whenever my hypos get such an upper hand of me, that it requires a strong moral principle to prevent me from deliberately stepping into the street and methodically knocking people's hats off. . . .	"Mackie never gave me a disrespectful word in his life, nor in any way ever failed in filialness." (Ibid)
—then, I account it high time to get to sea as soon as I can.	"Any boy, who disobeys his mother, or worries her. . . .—such a boy is a poor shabby fellow; and if you know such boys, you ought to cut their acquaintance." (Ibid)
This is my substitute for pistol and ball. . . . I quietly take to the ship.	Malcolm, what is your substitute or way of escape? Or is it pistol and ball?

On the fatal morning of September 11, 1867, in the inner duel in Malcolm's mind between the memory of a mother's kiss earlier that morning and the fears of a father's disapproval and wrath to come, the greater potency lay with the power of blackness—in his infant, childhood, and lifelong sense of isolated desperation.

☐ Endnotes

[1]It is interesting that at the meeting at the Los Angeles Suicide Prevention Center (which Dr. Murray could not attend), the chief psychiatrist of the center, Dr. Robert Litman, made this statement: "I think he was carrying the gun around with the fantasy that he would shoot his father. To protect himself."

[2]See Davis and Gilman, letter number 162, p. 214.

☐ References

Davis, M. R., & Gilman, W. H. (Eds.) (1960). *The letters of Herman Melville.* New Haven: Yale University Press.

Leyda, J. (1951) *The Melville log.* (Vol. 1.) New York: Harcourt, Brace.

Melville, H. (1969). *Redburn: His first voyage.* Evanston and Chicago: Northwestern University Press and the Newberry Library. (Original work published 1849).
Melville, H. (1970). *White Jacket or the world in a man-of-war.* Evanston and Chicago: Northwestern University Press and the Newberry Library. (Original work published 1850).
Melville. H. (1851). *Moby-Dick: Or, the whale,* New York: Harper & Brothers.
Metcalf, P. (1965). *Genoa.* Highlands, North Carolina: Jonathan Williams.
Miller, E. H. (1975). *Melville.* New York: George Braziller.
Shneidman, E. S. (1973). Suicide. In *Encyclopaedia Britannica.* Chicago: William Benton.
Shneidman, E. S. (1974). *Deaths of man.* New York: Penguin Books.
Warren, R. P. (Ed.) (1967). *Selected poems of Herman Melville.* New York: Random House.

10

CHAPTER

A Possible Classification of Suicidal Acts Based on Murray's Need System

Recently, Baechler (in his book *Suicides*) stated that the central question for suicidological investigation was: "What kind of people seek what solutions to what problems by means of suicide?" It can be argued that the principal problems of human beings relate to the frustration of their satisfaction of a variety of psychological needs. Thus, a full accounting of human needs might furnish a psychologically meaningful basis for a better understanding of suicidal events. Happily, such an explication already exists (in Henry Murray's *Explorations in Personality*). A classification of suicidal acts based on Murray's need system is proposed. A brief example is given.

Recently (1980), I reviewed Jean Baechler's remarkable book, *Suicides*. I concluded by stating that it was "a landmark book, clearly one of the two or three most important books written on this subject in the last 100 years." To cannibalize further from my review:

> After mentioning—and practically dismissing—the three traditional approaches to the study of suicide: moral and philosophical analysis, the analysis of individual cases, and the use of statistics—Baechler states that "the problem of suicide must be taken up again on an entirely new basis. . . . I will base my argument on the following definition: *Suicide denotes all behavior that seeks and finds the solution to an existential problem by making an attempt on*

Reprinted from *Suicide and Life Threatening Behavior*, 1980, *10*, 175–181. With permission.

> *the life of the subject.*" (Italics in original). Essentially, suicide is a response to a problem; the center of suicidological investigation should therefore be the following question: "*What people seek what solutions to what problems by means of suicide?*" Baechler's formulation is breathtakingly simple and straightforward. It does not even implicitly assume a psychodynamic or a social force or an epidemiologic point of view. It says, about suicidal phenomena: Come, let us observe together, unbiased, from the *victim's* point of view.

The remainder of this brief article contains some thoughts born subsequent to my writing that review, indirectly stimulated by Baechler's book. I begin by stating that suicide is an act which serves a purpose (or purposes); further, to understand a suicidal act we must seek to find the purposes it was intended to accomplish. The philosopher who then, understandably, comes immediately to mind is the great inventor of pragmatism, Charles Sanders Peirce. One of Peirce's key ideas is contained in this credo: "Consider what effects, that conceivably might have practical bearings, we conceive the object of our conception [behavior] to have. Then our conception of these effects is the whole of our conception of the object [act]." (Hartshorne & Weiss, 1935). About suicide, Peirce might have posed these questions: "What will it do (accomplish)? What's in it for that person?"

We now approach the programmatic definition of a "self-inflicted death" *as a lethal response*—intentioned or subintentioned; univalent or ambivalent—*to some situation seen as a problem*—that situation always residing in the victim's mind, but certainly capable of being formed and influenced by external circumstances, interactions, events, trauma, etc.

In order to understand suicide in this kind of context, we need to ask a much more broad question, which, I believe, is the key: What purposes do most *human acts* in general intend to accomplish? The best non-detailed answer to that question is that, in general, human acts are intended to satisfy a variety of human *needs*. There is no compelling *a priori* reason why a typology (or classification or taxonomy) of suicidal acts might not *parallel* a classification of general human needs. Indeed, such a classification of needs exists. It can be found in Murray's *Explorations in Personality* (1938). These needs—21 in number—include the need for abasement, achievement, affiliation, aggression, autonomy, counteraction, defendance, deference, dominance, exhibition, harm avoidance (including pain avoidance), infavoidance (relating to humiliation), inviolacy, nurturance, order, play, rejection, sentience, sex, succorance and understanding. *There,* in Murray's list of human needs, is a ready-made, viable, useful taxonomy of *suicidal* behaviors.

Let us now look at each of these needs in more detail, keeping in mind that each need can be related to a specific (psychological) kind of suicidal act. The definitions are paraphrases from Murray (Hall & Lindzey, 1957). In Murray's discussion of needs, he further refines their place in human psychology by distinctions between covert and overt needs, between focal and diffuse needs, proactive and reactive needs, random and focused activities.

In each case, the lethal suicidal act represents an effort by an individual to resolve a (real or fancied or exaggerated) problem either through the medium of satisfying that particular need (which, by the nature of the act, leads to death), or, pushed by a strong overriding general need to satisfy that particular need specifically by means of a suicidal solution. The following is a list of Murray's manifest needs, each one of which can be related to suicidal acts—which can then be labeled by the name of the need. For example, a suicidal death that might appropriately be identified primarily with the need for achievement (abbreviated as n-Ach) would accordingly be called—however peculiar it sounds on first hearing—an Achievement suicide, and similarly, for the other 20 needs. Had I the space, I could illustrate each of these 21 suicide-need types with a case history.

☐ Abasement

To have a need to submit passively to external force. To accept blame, criticism, punishment. To surrender. To be resigned to fate. To admit inferiority, error, wrongdoing, or defeat. To atone. To blame or belittle the self. To seek punishment, illness, and misfortune.

☐ Achievement

To accomplish something difficult—the act of suicide itself. To master or organize ideas or human beings, including oneself. To do this as rapidly and as independently as possible. To overcome obstacles. To excel oneself. To rival and surpass others. To increase self-regard by the successful accomplishment of some task.

☐ Affiliation

To draw near or join an allied other (an other who resembles the subject or who likes the subject). To please and will affection of a loved person. To adhere and remain loyal to a friend.

☐ Aggression

To overcome opposition forcefully. To revenge an injury. To injure or hurt another. To oppose forcefully or punish another. (See Baechler's discussion of Aggressive suicides).

☐ Autonomy

To get free, shake off restraint, break out of confinement. To resist coercion and restriction. To avoid or quit activities prescribed by domineering authorities. To be independent and free to act according to impulse. To defy convention.

☐ Counteraction

To make up a failure by restriving. To obliterate a humiliation by resumed action. To overcome weakness, to repress fear. To efface a dishonor by action. To maintain self-respect and pride on a high level.

☐ Defendance

To defend the self against criticism or blame. To conceal or justify a misdeed, failure, or humiliation. To vindicate the self.

☐ Deference

To support a superior. To honor another. To yield eagerly to the influence of an allied other. To emulate an exemplar. To conform to custom. (See Baechler's discussion of Oblative suicides.)

☐ Dominance

To control one's human environment. To influence or direct the behavior of others by action. To dissuade, restrain, or prohibit.

☐ Exhibition

To make an impression. To be seen and heard. To excite, amaze, fascinate, shock, intrigue, or entice others.

☐ Harmavoidance

To avoid pain. To escape from a dangerous situation. To take "protective" measures. (See Baechler's discussion of Escapist suicides.)

☐ Infavoidance

To avoid humiliation. To quit embarrassing situations or to avoid conditions which may lead to belittlement, scorn, derision, or indifference of others.

☐ Inviolacy

To preserve self-respect. To maintain psychological distance, pride.

☐ Nurturance

To gratify the needs of another person, especially one who is weak, disabled, tired, inexperienced, infirm, defeated, humiliated, lonely, dejected, sick, mentally confused. To help or protect another.

☐ Order

To put things or ideas in order. To achieve arrangement, organization, balance, tidiness and precision.

☐ Play

To act for "fun" without further purpose. To participate in games, gambling, carnivals, orgies. To take excess risks. (See Baechler's discussion of Ludic suicides.)

☐ Rejection

To separate oneself from a disliked person. To exclude, abandon, or remain indifferent to another person. To snub or jilt another.

☐ Sentience

To seek and enjoy sensuous experiences.

☐ Sex

To further erotic feelings. To have heightened sexual feelings (by, for example, momentarily hanging oneself).

☐ Succorance

To wish to be nursed, supported, sustained, surrounded, protected, advised, guided, indulged, forgiven, consoled, loved. To attempt to remain close to a devoted protector.

☐ Understanding

To seek the answer to general questions (about God, the hereafter, etc.). To be interested in theory. To speculate, formulate, analyze, and seek to experience the answer.

Most suicides represent *combinations* of various needs, so that a particular case of suicide might properly be subsumed under two or more different need categories. Example: a person who commits suicide by means of Russian Roulette largely because of a scandal in which that person's honor and reputation were impugned. Such an act (incident, occurrence or event) would seem to have at least two components; The need to avoid criticism, humiliation, blame, together with the need somehow to vindicate oneself, or, *Defendance;* and, secondly—because in this case the technique of committing suicide is too dramatic to be disregarded—the need, in these dire straits, to play with one's life, to gamble with fate, to take excessive risks, to leave life itself up to chance, or *Play.* (I shall use the word Ludic here instead of Play simply because the topic is too lugubrious to use the word with the more frivolous connotations.) Thus in this case, we might label that death as a "Defendance-Ludic suicide."

To me, such an approach makes more sense than any single talismanic psychodynamic formulation; it ought—to mix images—bury the ghost of Durkheim; it makes most demographic information only tangentially relevant; and, even as an admirer of Baechler's book on suicide, it is obviously more catholic and more flexible that Baechler's four categories of Aggressive, Escapist, Oblative and Ludic suicides. Certainly, it is more helpful than the moral, philosophic, religious arguments about suicide. Peirce himself, in his 1905 paper on "Issues of Pragmaticism," touched on this last item (see Weiner, 1958). Discussing, rather critically, the Christian tradition about suicide, Peirce wrote:

> For though it is a wrench to part with life, which has its charms at the very worst, just as it is to part with a tooth, yet there is no *moral* element in it whatever.

There is never a suicide without some keen needs. There are many pointless deaths, but never a needless suicide.

References

Baechler, J. (1979). *Suicides.* New York: Basic Books.

Hall C. C., & Lindzey, G. (Eds.) (1957). *Theories of personality.* New York: John Wiley. Chapter 5 (Murray's Personology).

Hartshorne, C., & Weiss, P. (Eds.) (1935). *The collected papers of Charles Sanders Peirce.* (Vol. 5, p. 2). Cambridge, MA: Harvard University Press.

Murray, H. A. (1938). *Explorations in personality.* New York: Oxford University Press.

Shneidman, E. S. (1980). A genuine classic in suicidology: A review of Jean Baechler's *Suicides. Contemporary Psychology, 25,* 108–109.

Weiner, P. P. (Ed.) (1958). *Values in a universe of chance: Selected writings of Charles S. Peirce* (p. 209). Garden City, NY: Doubleday Anchor.

11

CHAPTER

Remarks at a Memorial Service for Henry A. Murray, Memorial Church, Harvard University, October 3, 1988

Henry A. Murray had a full life, yet nothing for Harry was ever finally done. His major written contributions—the most regal in American psychology—were entitled explorations, preparations, scaffoldings, prolegomena. Harry's rule was that one can have only the latest clarifications, never the final one. Life, the world, the universe is an open system. He conceptualized death as an endless voyage among the infinite galaxies. At this very micro-second, Harry is moving along, refining, revising, taking in and digesting new sciences and articulating hitherto undreamed ideas on that inter-galactic cruise that, for the last years of his long, productive and inspiriting life, he was ready to start. He took much from all of us but gave back more than could a regiment of ordinary mortals. We miss him. We wish we could hear his voice. Here is the voice of Herman Melville.

> And like a frigate, I am full with a thousand souls; and as on, on, on I scud before the wind. . . . Aye, many, many souls are in me. In my tropical calms, when my ship lies tranced on eternity's main, speaking one at a time, then all with one voice—an orchestra of many bugles and horns, rising and falling, and swaying, in golden calls and responses. . . . Yet not I, but another; God is my Lord, and though many satellites revolved around

> me, I and all mine revolve round the great central Truth, sunlike, fixed and luminous forever in the foundationless firmament. (*Mardi,* Ch. 119, Dreams).
>
> . . . Those who boldly launch, cast off all cables, and turning from the common breeze, that's fair for all, with their own breath fill their own sails. Hug the shore, naught new is seen; and "Land ho!" at last was sung when a new world was sought. . . . But fiery yearnings their own phantom future make, and deem it present. So if after all these fearful, fainting trances the verdict be the golden haven was not gained, yet, in bold quest thereof, better to sink in boundless deeps than float on vulgar shoals; and give me, ye gods, an utter wreck, if wreck I do. (*Mardi,* Ch. 169, Sailing On).
>
> . . . With other men, perhaps, such things would not have been inducements; but as for me, I am tormented with an everlasting itch for things remote. I love to sail forbidden seas, and land on barbarous coasts. Not ignoring what is good, I am quick to perceive a horror, and could still be social with it. . . . By reason of these things, then, the whaling voyage was welcome; the great flood-gates of the wonder-world swung open, and in the wild conceits that seayed me to my purpose, two and two there floated into my inmost soul, endless processions of the whale, and, midmost of them all, one grand hooded phantom, like a snow hill in the air. (*Moby-Dick,* Ch. 1, Loomings).
>
> So that there are instances among them of men, who, named with scripture names—a singularly common fashion on the island—and in childhood naturally imbibing the stately dramatic thee and thou of the Quaker idiom; still, from the audacious, daring, and boundless adventure of their subsequent lives, strangely blend with these unoutgrown peculiarities, a thousand bold dashes of character, not unworthy a Scandinavian sea-king, or a poetical Pagan Roman. And when these things unite in man of greatly superior natural force, with a globular brain and a ponderous heart; who has also by the stillness and seclusion of many long night-watches in the remotest waters, and beneath constellations never seen here at the north, been led to think untraditionally and independently; receiving all nature's sweet or savage impressions fresh from her own virgin, voluntary and confiding breast, and thereby chiefly, but with some help, some accidental advantages, to learn a bold and nervous lofty language—that man makes one in a whole nation's census—a mighty pagaent creature formed for noble tragedies. (*Moby-Dick,* Ch. 16, The Ship).

One key idea for Harry was that life was—in the special way he defined the word—a "spiritual" pilgrimage, focused on the search for essential truths. These truths could be represented not only in carefully chosen words, but in artistically rendered objects in wood or stone, or in music or paint or in relationships themselves, just as the search for truth itself should be touched by beauty; converting the very process of the search into Art. Melville said:

In placid hours well-pleased we dream
Of many a brave unbodied scheme.
But form to bend, pulsed life create—
What unlike things must meet and mate:
A flame to melt—a wind to freeze;
Sad patience—joyous energies;
Humility—yet pride and scorn;
Instinct and study; love and hate;
Audacity—reverence. These must mate,
And fuse with Jacob's mystic heart,
To wrestle with the angel—Art.

Thus it can be truly said that in his way of living, Harry was a supreme artist, and if we view his life as a vast, almost century-long panorama, we see that he created a living montage of intense and complex beauty. It was the brilliance and the beauty of the process of his being that, for many of us, made knowing him the apogee of our lives.

To have known him, to have loved him
  After loneless long;
And then to be estranged from life,
  And neither in the wrong;
And now for death to set his seal—
  Ease me, a little ease, my song!

PART

IV

SUICIDE
Section A: Definitional and Theoretical

Shneidman's main contributions have been theoretical. He is an inveterate inventor of words. Shneidman has made up words and concepts—suicidology, psychological autopsy, postvention, subintentioned death, psychache—when he felt them to be required to reflect some nuance of his thought, and he has given renewed emphasis to well-established words and concepts—perturbation, constriction, lethality—when he felt that they were more accurate than some of the current technical jargon.

There are seven selections in this section, given to definitions and theory. Chapter 12 discusses the page on "Suicide" from the *Oxford English Dictionary (OED)*. We learn that the word is a fairly recent one, and did not exist until the 18th century. An interesting addendum to that short article, which was first printed in 1971, is that in 1987 the word "Suicidology" has entered the definitive pages of the *OED*.

In Chapter 13 we find Shneidman at serious business: the defining of his territory. It is a chapter from his *Definition of*

Suicide. There he presents a psychologically oriented definition of suicide and then explains (except for prepositions and conjunctions) every single word of it.

In Chapter 14, the entries on "Suicide" in twenty successive printings (involving fifteen editions) of the *Encyclopaedia Britannica (EB)* from 1777 to 1997 were reviewed. The paper was published in *The American Scholar,* the official journal of the International Academy for Suicide Research. The changing emphases, attitudes and social mores are reflected in the tone and contents of the articles written in this 220-year span. An overview supports Dr. Shneidman's idea that definitions are important—and that the *EB* has played an important cultural role.

No one, including Shneidman, turns down an invitation to write for the *Encyclopaedia Britannica.* He, in fact, developed his intellectual roots on those books as an adolescent. Apparently, after reviewing the previous articles on suicide in the *EB,* Shneidman decided he would not reproduce the usual tables of statistics of suicide among various countries at various times but, instead, introduce a potpourri of then-current (1973) and avant-garde ideas about suicide. That article met with mixed reviews. Murray wrote Shneidman: "Your encyclopaedia article is . . . a wonderfully, condensed, coherent and sophisticated survey of the whole conglomerate of today's knowledge of suicide that exists—handsomely written to a marked extent in your own terminology. I couldn't help thinking that this was possibly the timely moment [for you] to consider a shift of focus for a renaissance of spirit and mind after lying fallow for a season." For the record, Shneidman was not at all keen at having that article reproduced in this volume, although, obviously, he was willing to share Murray's letter on that topic.

Chapter 16 involves individuals who were subjects in Lewis Terman's famous study of gifted children in California and is Shneidman's most important empirical study. In a separate sub-project, Shneidman demonstrated that early clues to suicide committed when individuals were in their fifties existed in the life history materials and could be discerned as early as age thirty. This assumes that full life histories are available (as was the case in the Terman Study). The implications of this paper for prevention are quite extensive.

A conspectus is a survey or outline of a subject. This is what Chapter 17 attempts: to give a survey of the psychological aspects of suicide in terms of its common and ubiquitous characteristics.

Chapter 18 is vintage Shneidman. It is brief, personal, and focused around a single idea, and that idea is expressed in a neologism that has been tailor-made for that particular occasion. Shneidman believes that insofar as suicide is psychological, it stems from that person's psychache, from personal anguish, perturbation and pain. Given this central idea, all the rest is explication of the details.

12

CHAPTER

"Suicide" and "Suicidology": A Brief Etymological Note

In 1621, when Robert Burton, under the pseudonym of Democritus Junior, published *The Anatomy of Melancholy,* the word "suicide" was, according to the *Oxford English Dictionary,* not to be invented for yet another thirty years (1651). It is interesting, now, to note the somewhat elaborate verbal constructions and euphemisms (from John Lyly's *Eupheus,* written in 1580) that Burton used in order to convey the concept of suicide. For example, in his section called "Evil Prognostics of Melancholy" Burton (1652, pt. 1, sec. 4, mem. 1) states:

> Seldom this malady melancholy procures death, except (which is the greatest, most grievous calamity, and the misery of all miseries) *they make away themselves,* which is a frequent thing, and familiar amongst them. 'Tis Hippocrates observation and Galen's sentence. . . . In such sort doth the torture and extremity of his misery torment him, that he can take no pleasure in life, but is in a manner *enforced to offer violence unto himself,* to be freed from his present insufferable pains. So some (saith Fracastorius) in fury, but most in despair, sorrow, fear, and out of the anguish and vexation of their souls, *offer violence to themselves,* for their life is unhappy and miserable. They can take no rest in the night, or sleep, or if they do slumber fearful dreams astonish them [italics added].

And here is Burton's (1652, pt. 3, sec. 4, mem. 2, subsec. 5) accounting of the *methods* of what he has called "offering violence unto oneself":

Reprinted from *Life-Threatening Behavior,* 1971, *1,* 260–263. With permission.

> Most part these kind of persons make away themselves, some are mad, blaspheme, curse, deny God, but most offer violence to their own persons, and sometimes to others. . . . Felix Plater hath collected many examples. A merchant's wife that was long troubled with such temptations, in the night rose from her bed, and out of the window broke her neck into the street; another drowned himself desperate as he was in the Rhine; some cut their throats, many hang themselves.

Then, as now: jumping, drowning, cutting, hanging. (Poisoning is neither mentioned nor indexed by Burton.) Today's most frequently used methods—gunshot and barbiturates—were not available then.

Even in the contemporary technical literature on suicide one sometimes sees the phrase "felo de se," meaning, as the *Oxford English Dictionary* states: a felon of himself, specifically from Blackstone, 1769; one who "deliberately puts an end to his own existence, or commits any unlawful malicious act the consequence of which is his own death." This phrase did not come into general use until the seventeenth century—although there is a record of its use in Latin (cited in the OED) as early as 1250.

The *OED* indicates that the earliest use of "suicide" was essentially a Latinizing of the concept of self-killer or self-destroyer.[1] The term was apparently not used until 1651. A. Alvarez claims that he found the word a little earlier in Sir Thomas Browne's *Religio Medici,* written in 1635, published in 1642. By the mid-eighteenth century, the word seems to have been generally known to literary men in England. In the nineteenth century, French writers—Boismont, Durkheim, Quetelet—did much with the word. Today, "suicide" is everyone's word, the almost international labeling for—as a recent definition has it—"the human act of self-inflicted, self-intentioned cessation" (*International Encyclopedia of the Social Sciences,* 1968, vol. 15, pp. 385–89).

On the other hand, "suicidology" is a far more recent term. I first used it in a 1964 review of Louis I. Dublin's book *Suicide: A Sociological and Statistical Study*—a review that I entitled "Grand Old Man of Suicidology" (Shneidman, 1964). At the National Institute of Mental Health—1966 to 1969—I employed the word in a number of ways: to describe aspects of a new training program (Fellowships in Suicidology—1967); as part of the title of a new journal (*Bulletin of Suicidology*—1967); to label a new profession (the American Association of Suicidology—1968); as a descriptive term in an encyclopedia article (cited above—1968); and whenever I thought that the word—defined as "the scientific and human study of human self-destruction"—was useful and relevant, which turned out to be pretty much all of the time.

I have since learned that the word "suicidologie" was used earlier by Dutch Professor W. A. Bonger. In *Het Zelfmoordvraagstuk,* N. Speijer (1969, p. 15) writes:

Inmiddels is het woord suicidologie in de laatste tijd naar voren gekomen. In juli 1967 verscheen zelfs het eerste nummer van het *Bulletin of Suicidology*, uitgegeven door het US Department of Health, Education and Welfare; Public Health Service. In het voorwoord van dit Bulletin lezen we: "Initiation of the Bulletin signals the inauguration of a new profession, suicidology, the study of suicidal phenomena and their prevention."

Het is wel interessant te weten dat onze landgenoot *Bonger* deze term reeds in 1929 gebruikte. In zijn voordracht voor het Psychiatrisch-Juridisch Gezelschap op 9 februari 1929 zei hij: "De wetenschap van de selfmoord, the *suicidologie* (cursivering van mij) zou men haar kunnen noemen, is ruim een eeuw oud." (p. 3).

In this brief linguistic note it needs to be added that the word "suicidology," whether in Dutch or English, is an etymological impurity, combining as it does a Latin stem with a Greek suffix. This cogent point has been made to me more than once, especially by my colleagues in *socio-logy*.

Endnote

[1]Interesting enough, the word *suicide* "was never used by the ancient Romans. Instead they employed circumlocution: *sibi morten consciscere* (to procure one's own death); *vim sibi inferre* (to cause violence to oneself); *sua manu cadere* (to fall by one's own hand)" (Choron, 1972, p. 91).

References

Burton, R. [Democritus Junior](1652). *The Anatomy of Melancholy.* London: Hen. Crips & Lodo: Lloyd.

Choron, J. (1972). *Suicide.* New York: Charles Scribner's Sons.

International Encyclopedia of the Social Sciences. (1968). Vol. 15. New York: Macmillan Co. & Free Press.

Shneidman, E. S. (1964). Grand Old Man of Suicidology. *Contemporary Psychology, 9,* 370–71.

Speijer, N. (1969). *Het Zelfmoordvraagstuk.* Arnheim: Van Loghum Slaterus.

13

CHAPTER

A Formal Definition, with Explication

My principal assertion about suicide has two branches. The first is that suicide is a multifaceted event and that biological, cultural, sociological, interpersonal, intrapsychic, logical, conscious and unconscious, and philosophical elements are present, in various degrees, in each suicidal event.

The second branch of my assertion is that, in the distillation of each suicidal event its essential element is a *psychological* one; that is to say, each suicidal drama occurs in the *mind* of a unique individual. Suicide is purposive. Its purpose is to respond to or redress certain psychological needs. I have said before that there are many pointless deaths but there are no needless suicides. Suicide is a concatenated, complicated, multidimensional, conscious and unconscious "choice" of the best possible practical solution to a perceived problem, dilemma, impasse, crisis, desperation.

To use an arborial image: The psychological component in suicide is the "trunk" of it. An individual's biochemical states, for instance, are the roots. An individual's method of suicide, the contents of the suicidal note, the calculated effects on the survivors, and so on, are the branching limbs, the flawed fruit and the camouflaging leaves. But the psycho-

---

Reprinted from E. Shneidman. *Definition of Suicide.* New York: Wiley, 1985, pp. 202–213. With permission.

logical component, the problem-solving choice—the best solution to the perceived problem—is the main trunk.

We may now proceed to my proposed definition of suicide.

Currently in the Western world, suicide is a conscious act of self-induced annihilation, best understood as a multidimensional malaise in a needful individual who defines an issue for which the suicide is perceived as the best solution.

Now I shall attempt an exegesis of this definition by clarifying the meaning of each word.

Currently. What is meant to be implied in this study of suicide is a contextual endeavor, embedded in the historical epic or era in which it occurs and in which it is either historically or concurrently studied. For example, if it were possible it would not be enough simply to contrast suicide rates in pre-Christian Rome with suicide rates in Rome today. The whole meaning of this act for the person who did it and the contemporary witnesses is vastly different from that time to now. I would believe that the definition of suicide offered in this book will have to become out of date in time and would not be applicable to apply without appropriate modification even to suicidal occurrences as recent as the nineteenth century.

Western World. There are publications of studies of suicides in Africa (Bohannan, 1960), in Hong Kong (Yap, 1958), and other places around the world. I believe that this proposed definition is applicable only to the Western world (which may very well, in certain circumstances, include Japan and other countries.) But this cautionary needs to be cited so that cross-cultural comparisons do not make the error of assuming that a suicide is a suicide.

Suicide. Two comments about this word. First is that after much thought I have concluded we are well advised to use this word rather than to venture on a substitute for it or to create a neologism. The use of the word admittedly has some disadvantages, but it has such wide usage that it is tactically best to employ it.

The second point is that an examination of a number of previous definitions of suicide reveals that the word is often (perhaps typically) used with not one, but two meanings. These two meanings are: The definition of the *act* of self-destruction, and some delineation of the *person* who commits the act. I have followed this practice in my proposed definition.

Conscious. What is implied here is that first of all suicide—at least the kind of suicide we are talking about—is limited to *human* acts. We shall not be concerned at all with migrating lemmings or mourning dogs in as much as (as we shall see) suicide devolves in part on reportable intention.

A second important issue reflected in this word is the entire domain of the unconscious mind. The use of the word conscious in this definition is not meant to gainsay or to deny the notion that there may be important (even vital or anti-vital) unconscious elements in a total suicidal scenario. Rather it is meant to indicate that, by definition, suicide can occur only when an individual has some conscious mediation or, better, some conscious intention to stop his or her own life. There is always an element of some awareness and conscious intentionality in suicide.

This is not to say there are not many deaths—I would venture to assert even a majority of all deaths—that do not have a *subintentioned* quality to them. A subintentioned death is any death other than a suicidal death (accidental, natural, or homicidal) in which the decedent has played some significant covert, latent, unconscious role in hastening his or her demise. No suicide is a subintentioned death. Rather, every suicide is an intentioned death with a conscious advertent element in it.

Act. This word is meant to carry some special meanings. One direct implication is, I believe, that we should totally eschew the words "attempt" or "threat" when they are preceded by the adjective "suicidal." (I am now obviously discussing other than lethal suicidal acts.) I make this suggestion because the words attempt and threat are often used in either a judgmental pejorative way, impuning even the worthlessness of the person or the seriousness of the personal crisis which in part impelled the act, as in the phrase "We sewed her up and sent her home. It was *only* a suicide attempt." My suggestion is that we reject the words "attempt" and "threat" and try to describe every suicidal act. Instead, we should use words like suicidal act, event, occurrence, deed, maneuver, phenomenon, and indicate our *lethality rating.* The lethality rating that might run, say, from 1 to 9, is the common-sense ascription of the probability of that act or deed or event having a lethal outcome. (In this sense *any* act, deed, or event in the world can be rated on a lethality dimension.) The main merit of the use of the word "act" is that it clarifies and appropriately simplifies what suicide is; namely, a behavior which leads to death.

Two ratings should be made for each suicidal act or event or deed: Lethality, as indicated above, and *perturbation;* as discussed below. The rating of perturbation—also from 1 to 9—is an indication of how upset, agitated, depressed, psychotic, or perturbed the individual was deemed to be at the time of doing the act. It is very important in assessing a suicidal act (or treating a suicidal person) to distinguish between how perturbed the individual is and how lethal that individual is.

No one has ever died from elevated perturbation alone. It is elevated lethality which is dangerous to life. The two concepts need to be separated in order to have a clear understanding of the total event and the chief protagonist in it.

Self-Inflicted. The fulcrum word in the definition of suicide is the word self-inflicted. If suicide is anything, it is a *mort ius dese,* a death by oneself. This would seem to be clear enough although there are problems with the biblical incident in which Saul asked another soldier to kill him and in cases of what are now called assisted suicides. But in these instances the suicidal person changes only the voice of the grammar of the event and instead of killing himself directly has himself killed at one remove only by the asked for action of another agent.

In the same sense the suicide is also self-inflicted even in the instance when Seneca was ordered by the mad Roman emperor Nero to kill himself. We can reasonably assume that until the moment of that imperial order, Seneca had no intention of killing himself but after the order he then consciously intended to kill himself when he did because the alternative—disgrace, enforced death, or punishment to his family—was worse.

Annihilation. This word is meant to imply that the life of an individual is the life as that individual experiences it. It is the life of the mind. (The activities of the mind are the products of a living brain. No brain, no mind; no mind, no life.) One's life is the history—the introspective history—of one's mind. Suicide is the stopping or cessation of consciousness. It is redundant to say "forever." Cessation is thus distinguished from interrupted states (i.e., sleep, coma, anesthetic unconsciousness) and altered continuation states (i.e., intoxication, fugue states, psychotic states). Termination is what others see to have happened to your body. You can never experience cessation—being dead. A committed suicide results in cessation but we know that often the person who does it wants only a stopping of the flow of unbearable anguish or intolerable emotion or a change of "locale" from this world to a hoped for other existence. But operationally speaking, suicide is a conscious act of self-inflicted cessation. Synonyms are cessation, nothingness, oblivionation, and naughtment.

These seven terms above, especially terms three to seven, define the *act* of suicide. The remaining eight terms define the *actor,* the person who does the act.

We have already defined what suicide is. It is the consciously intended act of self-inflicted cessation. Every definition is a tautology and it turns upon itself in a more or less obvious way. A definition is like an equation in which the word and its meaning have equal weight on the two sides of the copula (usually the word "is"). Now having defined the act, we shall go on and explicate some of the omnipresent characteristics of the actor (limited, of course, to "currently in the Western world").

Multidimensional. No single learned discipline is sufficient to explain any individual suicidal event. I believe it is most accurate to define (in addition to the definition above) suicide as a biological/biochemical/sociocultural/sociological/interpersonal/intrapsychic/philosophic/existential event. It is certainly possible to write about suicidal phenomena from, say, a sociological point of view (as Durkheim has done with great success) or from a psychodynamic point of view (as Menninger has done, also with great success). But those are simply elaborations of one point of view and cannot be thought to tell the whole story. The main point is that suicide is a multidimensional event and requires, for its understanding, a multidisciplinary approach.

Malaise. The history of suicide is a record that involves words like sin, crime, and disease. Battin, in her recent book (1982), reminds us that even today "the narrower definition used in the Catholic tradition" (which emphasizes the moral signification under which the act is done synonymous with "morally repugnant self-killing") "seems closest to much ordinary usage." The notion of suicide as sin is very much present in current talk of it. A contemporary scientist, on the other hand, eschewing religion, has attempted to express suicide in medical terms, insisting that suicide is best understood not as a sin, not as a crime, and certainly not as a disease. From everything we know about a human event as complicated as suicide, we can be certain that such human disorders as malaria, syphilis, and tuberculosis are not accurate paradigms of suicide. In this sense suicide is more akin to delinquency or prostitution or craziness. I believe it is best conceptualized as a malaise, not a disease (for which we might hope to find a virus, coccus). It is a state of being, a human malaise.

Perturbed. In the assessment of any (living) potentially suicidal person, evaluations along two continuum should be made: How oriented toward death the individual is (lethality), and how upset or disturbed the individual is (perturbation). By its very definition no one commits suicide who is not highly lethal. We know, of course, it is possible to be highly perturbed and not to be highly lethal at the same time—the living presence of many disturbed individuals attests to this. But our clinical observations affirm to us that no one commits suicide who is unperturbed. Consider: If a totally unperturbed individual were to commit suicide (so to speak "for no reason at all,") that, in itself would be an aberrant act. There are several implications and corollaries of the above statements. It is not implied that all, or even most, individuals who commit suicide are insane or psychotic. It is implied that some elevated state of perturbation is necessarily present. This could be as relatively "innocuous" as the truncated scope of choices induced by severe psychical pain, sudden threat of torture, loss of health, or loss of status. The point is that an individual in his or her normal or modal state of being-in-the-world (by which is meant being in his or her accustomed world) does not ever commit suicide. Some elevated perturbation is the trigger, the *sine qua non,* the omnipresent component of the suicidal act.

One obvious and important implication (supported by the totality of my clinical experience) is that the most effective way to treat a potentially suicidal (highly lethal) person is for the helping person to address not the lethality directly, but the perturbation. The most effective way to treat a suicidal person is to do whatever is humanly possible to decrease the lethality to a point below its critically explosive level. This means that one is not limited to addressing the suicidal individual's psyche. Instead, one attempts to make whatever changes are required in that individual's inter-personal relationships (especially with his or her significant others) and with other aspects of that person's environment, job, jail, cancer, and so on.

Needful. It is difficult to conceptualize an individual's committing suicide apart from that individual's seeking to satisfy certain inner-felt needs (of course, these needs always operate within the context of a surrounding psychological situation—and there is something to be said for the subsidiary role of the environmental determinants of action). The reader will recall the discussion of suicide in relation to Murray's classification of human needs. That approach is not the be all and end all but it certainly is a good beginning and perhaps the very best set of useable terms now available. I dare to repeat my own dictim in this matter: There are many pointless deaths but there can never be a needless suicide.

It might be argued that the word "needful" is unnecessary (almost redundant) in this definition in that every living individual is needful. The point of including this word in the definition of suicide is to focus on the fact that aside from whatever else suicide represents, it focally involves the attempt to fulfill some urgently felt psychological needs. Operationally, these heightened unmet needs make up, in large part, what the suicidal person feels (and reports) as his or her perturbation.

Individual. Fedden (1938) distinguishes between two kinds of suicide: personal and institutional (or sacrificial) suicide. In this he is simply wrestling, as Deshaies and others have, with the tag end of sacrificial suicide, not knowing where to put it and needing to create a separate category for it. Just as we do not believe in the "mob mind" or in the "collective unconscious," so we do not believe in institutional suicide. All suicides are individual acts. Granted that they reflect degrees of social or societal or group pressure. At the furthest remove, all suicide might be considered institutional or social to some degree in the sense that the individual has learned about it. There is no history of a feral person (that is, a person raised by animals) ever committing (i.e., inventing) suicide.

The task of the suicidologist who wishes to understand or to assess a suicidal act, whether that of a samurai warrior, a traditional Hindu widow that has practiced suttee, or a child at Jonestown, is no different from assessing a suicide of a middle class Westchester teenager who kills herself by taking an excessive amount of barbiturates and permits herself to drown in her swimming pool.

In each case what is to be rated is the intention of the decedent vis-a-vis death. We can now answer the question that was discussed by European intellectuals during World War II. That question was: If you kill yourself when the Gestapo knocks on your door, have you,—without any moral judgment in it (except, perhaps, about the Gestapo)—committed suicide? What else would you call it? (Accident? Natural death? Homicide?) In a terrible sense all suicides—*every* suicide—is committed because the real or figurative or imagined or hallucinated "Gestapo" is knocking at the psychic door.

If one could arrange it—and one cannot—it would be "appropriate" to die at one of the apogees of one's life; but it would be pointless if it were done. To commit suicide at the high point (when one is healthy, successful, happy, etc.) would be pointless and aberrant. The examples in Durkheim of individuals who kill themselves on the occasion of attaining sudden wealth are always referred to as being "overwhelmed" by their "good fortune." One man's apogee is another man's perigee.

It seems sensible to say that no person left entirely to his or her own devices would commit suicide. A feral adult would not have the conceptualization of suicide and, more importantly, that concept without which suicide has absolutely no meaning, death. In that sense and in the further sense that many, perhaps most, suicidal events are intensely dyadic (involving some significant other), suicide may be said to be an interpersonal and certainly an intracultural event. But in its essence suicide is always an individual occurrence. It is separate people who kill themselves (albeit on occasion in a group setting) and always, as I have indicated, within a cultural nexis. All this may sound fairly obvious but those readers whose orientations are tenaciously sociological may well take umbrage at the seemingly rather innocuous, words. To do so would be to misunderstand what I wish to say: Suicide is always an individual event, *but* (or *and*) it always occurs in an individual who, willy-nilly, holds one or more citizenships in one or more cultures and who can never emigrate to *no where* (there is *no where* in suicide). In addition, there can be no suicide without some independent conceptualization of death, nullity, naughtment, cessation, and surcease and their opposites survival, continuance, and immortality. The emphasis on the individual does not at all preclude interest and concern with social (including economic) and especially cultural forces as they reside or swirl within the individual psyche.

Defines. Psychic life is perception (and imagining and thinking and feeling). Perception involves, by its very nature, distortion by the living brain which performs the act of perceiving. We are "defining" our world all the time, misperceiving it in our own idiosyncratic way—albeit with such commonplace agreements that no one but a sophist would quibble over a vast percentage of our perceptions. All this to say that the word "defines" and the subsequent key word "issue" need to be discussed together since an issue is always defined by someone; that is, the very act which makes some matter in the world an image in the first place.

Inasmuch as the various words in this definition are organically related to one another, an additional point can be made about the word "defines." We have already indicated that the individual who commits suicide is perturbed. More specifically that perturbation is manifested by a constriction and narrowing of the perceptional "diaphragm" in the camera of the mind. There is a narrowing and a tunneling and a closing down—much more light is needed for an ordinary common-sense "picture" of what is going on. This means that the very act of defining is done with some constriction and is not done in the relatively more open way of which that individual is capable. Operationally it means that fewer options than would ordinarily occur to that individual are present for the perturbed mind's consideration. A suicidal individual who is defining any issue is not at his etymological best. He is rather like Dr. Samuel Johnson might have been if he had worked on his famous *Dictionary* with a mind truncated by drugs, fatigue, or extraordinary emotional stress.

Issue. There is a notion in the watered-down popular misconception of psychoanalytic theory that if the individual (usually in the course of psychotherapy) need only discover that one traumatic incident or moment in the earlier life at which point the complexes were fixed. We can call this "the magic moment" theory of the neuroses. It is a point of view that looks for *the* cause of relatively complex nexi of human behaviors. In the same sense there is some danger of focusing on the issue in a suicidal drama. At the outset we are aware that the causes of suicide are multiple and layered. We can speak of primary causes, sustaining causes, resonating causes, exacerbating causes, and precipitating causes. (Most discussions of the causes of suicide—for instance, ill health, financial failure, emotional rejection—deal only with precipitating situations.) Nonetheless it makes sense in the linguistic analysis of the typical suicidal scenario to speak of *the* issue which is paramount in the consciousness of the suicidal person. The implication of this view is that the unconscious factors (the psychodynamics) which admittedly do play an important role in the entire suicidal drama play their role indirectly by making what could be an issue in an individual's life *the issue* around which that individual then conducts a life-or-death debate.

Perceived. No brain, no life. Everything we experience is processed through our living brain. In that sense all perception has some idiosyncratic components. The words "perceive" and "misperceive" are synonymous. There is some distortion, by definition, in all perception. In the cases of suicidal individuals, the issue is the extent of this distortion. Our definition of suicide could have as easily read ". . . for which the suicide is misperceived as the best solution." The pathology in suicidal perception is linked most directly with the *constriction* of the individual's then-present perceptual processes. This tunneling or focusing of the mind's set seems stimulated by the increase in perturbation. It is a commonplace observation that when one is upset, one does not (or is unable to) think clearly. Operationally, "clearly" implies capacity internally to scan and to choose among several viable options. Confusion is not so much a jumbling of possible options as it is a falling away of viable options and an arbitrarily operational focusing on only one seemingly possible solution (i.e., suicide) where more than one solution is realistically possible.

Best. Suicide is an act done by a perturbed individual who (with a somewhat truncated perception of the options possible in the world) decides that cessation is the *best* possible solution that he can choose. Pascal, in his *Pensèes,* talked about the Bet Situation (in which he asserted each individual must bet his soul on whether or not God exists). In a comparable way we can say that the suicidal person places himself in a Bet Situation where, under duress, he jumps to what he considers to be the best choice among the possible options—all of which may be noxious or offensive in some degree; an *aristos,* the best one can do under the circumstances. One implication of this view is that the treatment of the suicidal person almost always involves an effort to broaden the scope or range of his perceptions—"to widen his blinders" and to increase the number of more or less onerous options available in his consciousness.

Solution. We have described suicide as an act or a deed. We have said that it is an event done in the service of certain unfilled psychological needs. It is all purposeful; its purpose is to solve a problem. In the mind of the chief protagonist suicide is a solution—*the* solution—to a perceived problem, dilemma, challenge, difficulty, seemingly inescapable, intolerable situation. "It was the only thing I could do. What else could I do? It was the best way out of that terrible situation." In this sense every suicide is not only a solution; it is an *aristos*—the best that one can do.

In this definition, "suicide" has an adaptive and a self-serving function. Suicide is always done in the individual's "best interests;" that is, in the service of the individual's most pressing yearnings (to be free of intolerable emotion). In this sense, suicide can be said to be a selfish act. The individual's first fealty is not to his own preservation, but to himself. In this paradoxical sense, we are reminded of Richard Dawkin's brilliantly reasoned (but not totally convincing) presentation, *The Selfish Gene* (1976), whose major thesis is "that a predominant quality to be expected in a successful gene is ruthless selfishness" (p. 2). Neither for Dawkins (in his book), nor for me (in this context), is it a moral judgment to say that both successful evolution and "successful" suicide are ruthlessly committed self processes—the "best" that can be done under the circumstances.

☐ References

Battin, M. (1982). *Ethical issues in suicide.* Englewood Cliffs, NJ: Prentice Hall.

Bohannan, P. (1960). *African homicide and suicide.* New York: MacMillan.

Dawkins, R. (1976). *The selfish gene.* New York: Oxford University Press.

Fedden, H. (1938). *Suicide: A social and historical study.* London: Peter Davies.

Yap, P. (1958). *Suicide in Hong Kong.* London: Oxford University Press.

14

CHAPTER

Suicide on My Mind, *Britannica* on My Table

I think it is safe to say that ours is the only dining room in West Los Angeles on whose table—an eight-foot-long, two-hundred-pound behemoth on which I have taken my meals for many years—rest piles of photocopies of articles on suicide, all of which were printed in the *Encyclopaedia Britannica* over the past 220 years. They represent the convergence of two crucially important strands in my own life. Indeed, as I look at the articles, arrayed before me in fanlike tiers, I get the odd feeling that the old oak table on which I have eaten so many thousands of dinners has been set not with its customary china and silver but with my intellectual autobiography.

My special relationship with the *Britannica* is long-standing. It is relevant to report that I was a sickly child and stayed home from school a great deal. The reader can readily imagine the sort of boy I was: frail, bookish, and undersized (I was small to begin with, and continued to shrink, comparatively speaking, as I was double-promoted four times in elementary school—entirely my mother's doing). Our house, fifteen miles and seventy years from the one in which my wife and I live today, resembled those of many Eastern European Jewish immigrant families with intellectual aspirations. There were copies of Shakespeare, Tolstoy, Melville, Dostoyevsky, Conrad, and Mann, diligently assembled from the local Lincoln Heights Library's list of "The 100 Best." There was a

Reprinted from *The American Scholar*, 1998, *67(4)*, 93–104. With permission.

windup Victrola and records of operatic arias sung by Caruso and Farrar. And in the center of all this—the jewel in the Shneidman family's cultural crown—there was the Ninth Edition of the *Britannica,* enshrined in a Stickley bookcase with glass doors and its own little key. The suite of Craftsman furniture to which the bookcase belonged also included a sofa, a chair, and a table. All of them are in my home today.

Among the happiest hours of my childhood were those spent alone at home, circa 1925. My parents would be working in their clothing store, my brother and sister would be in school, and I would be in my parents' pleasant bedroom, tucked in their 1910 Grand Rapids mahogany bed between two billowy white sheets, listening to Farrar sing Gilda and reading the encyclopedia. I have little doubt that more than half of what I know today I learned from the pages of the Ninth Edition of the *Encyclopaedia Britannica.* I suspect that this accounts for my essentially nineteenth-century ideas about science. And I muse that my frenetic and nervous way of studying (or reading or writing)—a lifelong habit—could well be a happy remnant of the fact that my first earnest perusals of "The Geometry" or "Kant" were interrupted every few minutes by the need to leap out of my parents' bed either to change the 78-rpm record or to wind the Victrola. It seems unlikely that I would so deeply love the intellectual life today had I not initially found my young mind's independence within such a cozy and easeful setting.

Fast-forward to 1949, the year that, quite by accident, I met my life's second great strand. I was thirty-one, working as a clinical psychologist at the Brentwood Veterans Administration hospital. On that particular morning I was in the sub-basement of the old Los Angeles Hall of Records, in the coroner's vault, looking at file folders containing the records of certified deaths. The director of my hospital had asked me to prepare letters to two young widows whose husbands had recently committed suicide while they were hospital patients. My intention was to look at the two men's folders, make some notes, and get back to work.

The first folder contained something I had not seen before: a genuine suicide note. The second folder did not. Who could stop at this point? I looked at several dozen folders. It seemed that every so often I would open a folder—about one out of every fifteen suicide folders—and find a suicide note. I did a quick count of the folders on one shelf and estimated that I was standing in a room that contained approximately two thousand suicide notes. I felt like a cowpoke who, wandering home drunk on a dark night, stumbles into a pool of oil and is just sober enough to realize he has found his fortune.

Had I indulged my initial urge to read the letters right there in the coroner's vault, I might have learned a good deal about individual human tragedy, but I would have done nothing to advance the study of suicide, which was then an almost nonexistent field. Instead, in a decision that changed my life, I made photocopies of more than seven hundred genuine suicide notes and put them aside *without* reading them, so that my colleague Norman Farberow and I could later compare them, in blind controlled studies, with simulated suicide notes that would be elicited from nonsuicidal people. The result was the first work on suicide notes—and indirectly on suicide itself—that followed scientific protocols. My subsequent career—helping to found the Los Angeles Suicide Prevention Center, developing a program in suicide prevention for the National Institute of Mental Health, thinking about suicide, writing about suicide—all dates from that morning in the sub-basement of the Hall of Records. Since that day, I have been continuously intrigued by the topic of suicide and drawn to people who are on the brink of self-destruction. I am not a suicidal person myself; my fascination is, I suppose, partly voyeuristic and partly scientific. I have always been attracted to excitement, and few things could be more exciting than the pursuit of understanding in a virgin field that involved such strong and intimate human emotions.

The reader can surmise what it meant to me, a quarter century after I happened upon those suicide notes, to be invited to contribute my own seven pages of printed text, headed "Suicide," to volume 21 of the 1973 edition of the *Encyclopaedia Britannica,* the same set of books that once was my Testament, Koran, and Upanishads.

I have come close to implying that the Ninth Edition of the *Encyclopaedia Britannica* was a kind of father figure to me. It is true that I treated those books and the information in them with a respect bordering on awe, that they were authoritative, that they spoke to me ex cathedra. At that time, all these sentiments were also true of my unquestioned attitudes toward my father. Writing my own article for the *EB* was a psychological landmark; it gave me a voice of my own. I suddenly felt like Ernest Pontifex, in *The Way of All Flesh,* who was finally able to contravene his father without feeling that he was either destroying or betraying him.

Before I wrote my 1973 article, I looked at two or three earlier pieces. It did not occur to me then to view them as documents of intellectual history; I merely wished to identify my predecessors' pitfalls—such as an overreliance on dreary tables of statistics—so I could avoid stepping into them myself. I wrote the article and proudly added the Fourteenth Edition of the *Britannica* to the Ninth Edition that still reposed in the glass-fronted Stickley bookcase that I had inherited. Two and a half decades passed. Then, as I approached the age of eighty, I had another thought. It was, perhaps, the sort of retrospective notion one is unlikely to have in one's twenties or even fifties, when the habit of looking back is not so fully developed. Why not examine the articles on suicide in *all* the editions since the first one, in 1768?

The idea allowed me simultaneously to become, all over again, the unformed child in a soft bed who had learned about the world from his parents' encyclopedia, and also to read these articles on suicide—including my own—and see, from the emancipated vantage point of old age, their flaws, their anachronisms, their generational gaps of knowledge. If the *Britannica* was the most authoritative popular repository of knowledge during the various eras of its existence, would not its successive treatments of suicide reflect, in a long chronological march, our culture's changing attitudes toward the subject that had consumed my life? With the help of the Chicago staff of the *EB*, the New York Public Library, and Harvard's Houghton Library, I assembled copies of the encyclopedia's fourteen different articles on suicide. Together, they told a story—the attempt, over time, to answer such crucial questions as: Is suicide a sin? Is it a crime? Is it the responsibility of the individual or of society? What causes it? Can human suffering be reduced to statistics? How can suicide be prevented? *Should* it be prevented? And that story is what is now spread out, with my wife's indulgence, all over our dining table.

The *Encyclopaedia Britannica*, while not the first encyclopedia—its forerunners include the remarkable *Encyclopédie ou Dictionnaire raisonné des Sciences, des Arts et des Métiers* of Diderot and d'Alembert, published in France starting in 1751—has remained the most constant and influential. Its first edition was published in Edinburgh in 1768. There have been fourteen editions since then, of which the Eleventh Edition, of 1910, is generally considered the greatest. Roughly speaking, a new edition was published every ten or twenty years (in the interim there were sometimes several printings with minor variations) until the Fourteenth Edition, in 1929. Thereafter, for over a half century, there were only relatively modest alterations: some articles were dropped, some added, some contributors replaced. With the Fifteenth Edition, in 1974, there was a radical restructuring of the overall format of the *EB:* the time-honored, strictly alphabetical arrangement was dropped in favor of a thesaurus-like approach, including a one-volume Propaedia (an overview), a Micropaedia (a comprehensive survey), and a Macropaedia (topics discussed in detail). The latest version of the *Britannica*, "published" in 1994, is on CD-ROM—a hundred pounds of books reduced to about an ounce.

There was no article on suicide in the first edition of the *Encyclopaedia Britannica*. That is understandable; the word itself was fairly new. (The words *suicide* and *encyclopedia* seem to have a common vintage and perhaps even a common creator. The vintage is the fifth decade of the seventeenth century, 1642 for *suicide* and 1646 for *encyclopedia;* the creator is

Sir Thomas Browne, the author of *Religio Medici*.) However, in 1777, when the Second Edition of the *EB* was published, it contained a memorable article called "Self-Murder."

"Self-Murder" is one page long. Whatever else can be said about it, it is not dull. It jerks you awake with the first sentence, hectors and shakes you until the finish, and, at the very end, makes an unconvincing attempt to soften its Draconian stance. It has the smell of fire and brimstone, the sound of a wrathful sermon by Cotton Mather. The article begins with a beautifully expressed but horrendously cruel definition: "SELF-MURDER, the pretended heroism, but real cowardice, of the Stoic philosophers, who destroyed themselves to avoid those ills which they had not the fortitude to endure, though the attempting it seems to be countenanced by the civil law, yet was punished by the Athenian law with cutting off the hand which committed the desperate deed." It continues in a vein that joins the religious and the legal:

> And also the law of England wisely and religiously considers, that no man hath a power to destroy life but by commission from God and the author of it; and as the suicide is guilty of a double offence; one spiritual, in invading the prerogative of the Almighty, and rushing into his immediate presence uncalled for; the other temporal, against the king, who hath an interest in the preservation of all his subjects; the law has therefore ranked this among the highest crimes, making it a peculiar species of felony; a felony committed on one's self.

And it concludes with an answer to the obvious question: If the felon is dead, how can human laws punish him?

> They can only act upon what he has left behind him, his reputation and fortune; on the former, by an ignominious burial in the highway, with a stake driven through his body; or the latter, by a forfeiture of all his goods and chattels to the king, hoping that his care for either his own reputation or the welfare of his family would be some motive to refrain him from so desperate and wicked an act. . . . And tho' it must be owned that the letter of the law herein borders a little on severity; yet it is some alleviation, that the power of mitigation is left in the breast of the sovereign, who upon this (as on all other occasions) is reminded by the oath of his office, to execute judgment in mercy.

The last sentence strikes me as conveying the same dubious comfort as a hangman's blessing. The anonymous author of this mean-spirited little article—whose only mention of prevention is its approving note on the custom, prevalent at the time, of besmirching the self-murderer's reputation and confiscating his worldly goods—is clearly far more interested in flagellating the suicide than in keeping him alive.

By 1788, when the Third Edition was published, the word *suicide* had gained sufficient currency to constitute the article's title. And this time the *EB* had much more to say: five pages' worth, starting with a far briefer and more neutral definition: "SUICIDE, the crime of self-murder, or the person who commits it." The first section of the article is a historical survey of suicide among the Jews, the ancient Greeks, the Brahmins, the Hindus, the Japanese, the Scythians, the tribes of Scandinavia, and others. The tone of this report can be gathered from the paragraph on suicide among the Jews:

> Suicide is one of those crimes which we are led to believe not common among savage nations. The first instances of it recorded in the Jewish history are those of Saul and Ahitophel; for we do not think the death of Samson a proper example. We have no reason to suppose it became common among the Jews till their wars with the Romans, when multitudes slaughtered themselves that they might not fall alive into the hands of their enemies. But at this period the Jews were a most desperate and abandoned race of men, had corrupted the religion of their fathers, and rejected that pure system which their promised Messiah came to Jerusalem to announce.

This anti-Semitic burst was reprinted through four editions, until 1852.

As for the causes of suicide in England, they are ascribed to "the variableness of the climate, the great use of animal food, strong spiritous liquors and to tea, and to the sulphurous exhalations of the pit-coal used as fuel. . . . We are rather surprised that coal is mentioned even as a distant cause of suicide, for it is one of the blessings of our island; and a good coal fire we have always found rather conducive to good spirits rather than injurious to them." It is rare to find such a cozy passage in the staid pages of the *EB*.

Having disposed of history and causation, the article moves on to the aspects that had constituted the entirety of the 1777 article: the morality and legality of suicide. It reasserts that suicide is a felo-de-se (a felony against oneself), a crime against God and the king. But it ends with a sentence that indicates that the times are changing: "Suicide, we find, is a common and increasing evil; but it is a difficult matter to find an effectual remedy. . . . Punishment will not be a preventive, even if it could be always inflicted; and that it is seldom inflicted, though the laws have decreed it, is well known." This concluding emphasis on prevention, complete with a humble acknowledgment of its difficulty, sounds surprisingly modern.

The historical portions of this entry appeared essentially unchanged for sixty-four years in the Fourth (1801), Fifth (1815), Sixth (1820), and Seventh (1830) Editions.

But changes were coming. The entry for "Suicide" in the Eighth Edition (1852–1860) in many ways repeats the contents of the Seventh. However, it is notable for including landmark quotations from two major nineteenth-century intellectual figures.

The first quotation is from Henry Thomas Buckle, chess prodigy and scientifically minded historian. Buckle believes that "the progress of every people is regulated by principles . . . as certain as those which govern the physical world." Buckle tries to show the constancy of suicide rates over years and points to the folly of enacting laws against it. He states that

> suicide is merely the product of the general condition of society, and that the individual only carries into effect what is a necessary consequence of preceding circumstance . . . [thus] we are able to predict within a small limit of error the number of voluntary deaths for each ensuing period, assuming, of course, that the social circumstances do not undergo marked change.

Buckle's morally neutral stance, which transfers blame from the individual to his society, neatly moves suicide from the purview of religion to that of social science and presages the key role that demography was soon to play in its study.

The second quotation is from the great philosopher and economist John Stuart Mill. In his essay "On Liberty"—in which he opposed any legislation that would interfere with the sale of poisons on the ground that it would exert unnecessary state control over individual freedom—he wrote (and is quoted in the 1860 *EB*) as follows:

> When there is not a necessity, but only a danger of mischief, no one but the person himself can judge of the sufficience of the motive which may prompt him to incur the risk of buying [poison]. In this case therefore (unless he is a child, or delirious or in some state of excitement or absorption incompatible with the full use of the reflecting faculty), he ought, I conceive, be only warned of the danger, not forcibly prevented from exposing himself to it.

This prescient paragraph contains the core arguments of current controversies and debates: Do people own their own lives (and deaths), or are we as a society responsible for saving our fellows from their own errors?

Mill's libertarian voice was destined to be outshouted by the subsequent inundation of articles that concentrated on numbers rather than ethics. The Ninth Edition (1875–1889) contains a six-page article by Wynnard Hooper, a financial journalist who, tellingly, also wrote the pieces on statistics and population. (This was the edition that dominated my childhood; I do not, however, remember reading this article then.)

Hooper includes five tables of European suicide statistics and one table for certain American states, and discusses these figures in terms of race, sex, climate, population density, occupations, seasons, and methods of suicide. He concludes that "it cannot be said that any satisfactory result has been obtained from these investigations, owing no doubt to the fact that the phenomenon is too minute to furnish numbers large enough for the proper application of the statistical method." His article marks a radical swing to the demographic and statistical approach, reflecting and foreshadowing the work of Morselli, Durkheim, Halbwachs, and Dublin. It cut the pattern for the next hundred years.

The Tenth Edition (1902) contains an unmemorable two-page article, essentially a shortened version of the article in the previous edition, by H. H. Littlejohn, a professor of forensic medicine at the University of Edinburgh. Littlejohn also wrote the article on suicide in the great Eleventh Edition of 1910; it was not one of the edition's high points. Like Buckle and Hooper, Littlejohn regards suicide as "a sign of the presence of maladies in the body politic [which] deserve careful consideration." He asserts that "suicide as a whole conforms to certain general laws, and is influenced by conditions other than mere individual circumstances or surroundings." His article, mainly concerned with British suicide statistics for the 1880s and 1890s, was repeated in the Twelfth (1921) and Thirteenth (1926) Editions.

The article on suicide in the Fourteenth Edition (1929–1940) went through numerous versions in different printings. The first, in 1929, was a two-page article by S. de Jastrzebski, the assistant registrar general of Great Britain, that included updated figures for sex and age and for methods of suicide in England and Wales as well as an interesting and highly topical section on the "Influence of the World War":

> The following figures [for 1911–1914, 1915–1918,1921–1925], relating as they do to nine of the belligerent countries and two non-belligerents closely affected by war conditions show beyond any possibility of doubt the profound effect produced upon the suicide-rate by the World War. . . . In every case the war period is marked by a notable decline in the suicide-rate. To the theory that nervous strain is one of the prime causes which lead to self-destruction, they give a complete and emphatic contradiction.

The 1955—1961 printings of the Fourteenth Edition contained a short piece by Ruth S. Cavan, an American sociologist, which was perhaps the most succinct and most comprehensive to date. Within the compass of a single page, it includes pithy paragraphs on a variety of subtopics: international comparisons; age, sex, and marital conditions; urban-rural rates; methods of suicide; suicide and other means of violent death; and interpretations. Cavan concludes:

> Although suicide rates differ with various social conditions, the explanation does not lie in external forces but in the attitudes and emotions of people. . . . Some people are subjected to greater social pressures than others. Finally, some countries provide more adequate guidance and counselling facilities than others, to which the harassed person may turn for help.

This brief bit of wisdom touches both the inner and the outer worlds of suicide with more empathy than any of Cavan's predecessors had shown.

My turn came in 1973, in an article that deliberately owed little to its forerunners. Its seven pages contained not a single statistical table. (As I reread them in the company of the other articles on my dining table, I felt that in my urge to rescue the study of suicide from the numbing forces of statistics, I had gone too far and given short shrift to the field's legitimate demographic aspects.) The sections included: definition, complexities of definitions, major threads of study, psychological characteristics of suicide, attempted suicide, partial death and substitutes for suicide, suicide and religion, suicide and the law, myths about suicide, romantic suicide and the artist, statistics on suicide, suicide notes, and prevention-intervention-postvention.

One example will suffice to convey the article's general tenor. Under "Main Threads of Suicidal Study," there are several paragraphs about the locus of blame for suicide. Saint Augustine and Saint Thomas Aquinas called suicide a grievous sin and located its source within the deficient person; Rousseau emphasized the natural and innocent state of man and transferred the locus of blame from man to society; Hume tried to sanitize suicide entirely by arguing that it was neither a crime nor a sin; Durkheim focused on society's inimical effects on the individual; and Freud, eschewing the notions of sin and crime, gave suicide back to the individual but put the main locus of action in the unconscious mind. In other words, I attempted to present a variety of views on suicide instead of the single opinions that had dominated most of the earlier articles. My own expressed opinion is that each instance of suicide is a multidimensional event (with biological, physiological, sociocultural, and existential components), but that the main trunk of the suicidal tree is the psychological drama that occurs in the individual's mind: the need to escape from unbearable psychological pain—what I call psychache—tied to some notion of death or cessation as the effective exit. Here is the heart of what—now that I have read all the earlier articles—I feel the *EB* had previously omitted: a recognition of suicide as a response to individual human suffering, a tragedy that befalls real people.

This article had a noteworthy personal consequence. For many years—from 1950, when I met him, until his death in 1988 at the age of ninety-five—the psychological epicenter of my intellectual life was Henry A. Murray: physician, psychoanalyst, biologist, Melville scholar, director of the Harvard Psychological Clinic, and author of *Explorations in Personality.* (There is a marvelous portrait of Henry Murray in the winter 1969 issue of THE AMERICAN SCHOLAR, by then-editor Hiram Haydn.) Murray's peerless writings influenced me more than any others, and I tried to spend as much time as possible in his presence. I was at Harvard for two extended stays—as research associate in the early sixties and as visiting professor in the late sixties, and I flew to Boston as often as I could arrange it. It was one of life's high privileges for me to know him and to be made, by him, much more than I otherwise could have been.

In 1963, in a paper about Melville titled "Dead to the World," Murray had defined suicide as "no more than an urgently felt necessity to stop unbearable anguish, that is, to obtain relief by interrupting the stream of suffering." He asked: "For what is suicide in most instances but an action to put an end to intolerable affect?" You can see right away that my main ideas about the central role in suicide of psychological pain and negative emotions all flow from his fountain. In any event, in February 1973, Harry wrote me:

> Your encyclopaedia article is masterful . . . handsomely written to a marked extent in your own terminology. I couldn't help thinking that this was possibly the timely moment to consider a shift in focus of spirit and mind after lying fallow for a season.

That paragraph changed my life. I knew Harry well enough to put aside his hyperbolic praise and to know that the real meat of that paragraph—his covertly intended message—lay in the serious criticism implied in the second sentence. He was telling me what I already knew inside: that I was temporarily burned out on the topic of suicide and ought to consider a shift of focus for a while. Harry's note resonated with my own suspicion, which I had not fully admitted to myself until I read his words, that my *EB* article had been a mite too discursive and idiosyncratic. Accordingly, I shifted my clinical focus from patients who were suicidal to cancer patients who were coming to death unwillingly. I transformed myself from clinical suicidologist to clinical thanatologist, someone who deals with illness and mourning. When I returned to suicide a few years later, I believe I did so with a refreshed vision of self-destruction as well as a better understanding of the dynamics involved in the wrestling match with death. I would write a more seasoned encyclopedia article today.

My piece was superseded in the Fifteenth Edition (1974–1984) by a wise and comprehensive five-page article by the late Erwin Stengel, professor of psychiatry at the University of Sheffield. Its most innovative section is headed "Suicide in the Future," and Stengel's predictions are not particularly rosy. He writes:

> It is difficult to imagine man in the future without this potential, which has sometimes been proclaimed as one of the basic human freedoms. There are no prospects of an antisuicidal substance in the foreseeable future. There are certain aspects of present-day society that make a decline in the incidence of suicidal acts unlikely [including] the increased number of the aged . . . the young [who] are more openly aggressive . . . the continued increase in population. The outlook for suicide would be very black indeed if it were not for the strong urge to self-preservation inherent in the individual and in society. The emergence of nonprofessional movements toward self-help in the struggle against suicide can be seen as a manifestation of this tendency.

Here is a man who, though he thoroughly understood the value of statistics, also understood that suicide is a *philosophical* act. This is manifestly an encyclopedia article and not a novel. But Stengel's empathetic sadness, deepened by his own background as a refugee from the Nazis, clearly shows through his prose and, in my view, makes it finer. Inexplicably, there are printings of the Fifteenth Edition in which Stengel's indispensable essay on suicide does not appear. In these cases, I strongly advise the reader to seek another printing.

In the 1985–1997 printings of the Fifteenth Edition there is a half-page article in the Micropaedia (Stengel's piece is in the Macropaedia). Its concluding paragraph is especially topical:

> No single approach can be expected to succeed in substantially reducing the incidence of suicide, but early detection and treatment of mental disorders are important deterrents. Since the 1950s special centres and organizations for the prevention of suicide have been created in many countries. . . . The telephone is commonly used as a means of communication between lonely and desperate individuals in need of support and advisers who are available by day and night. There is evidence that this kind of service may help to avert suicidal acts.

The *Encyclopaedia Britannica*—along with our society—has obviously traveled several light-years since 1777, when it excoriated suicide as cowardly, sinful, illegal, and shameful. The emphasis has shifted to the question, "How can we help?"

My march through the centuries is complete, but a few ideas still swirl in the wake of my dual obsessions, suicide and the *EB*. The first idea is that there might be something to learn from similar *Britannica* surveys of other socially sensitive tag words. One might look, from 1768 (or whenever the word first appears) to the present date, at *Addiction, Adultery, Childhood, Homosexuality, Insanity,* and so forth. Scholars in different fields could suggest candidates for the word list. Put together, these would yield a lexicographic history of the past two centuries that might give some fresh insights into the evolution of our cultural trends.

My second idea returns to the study of suicide. Why not take a look at the word in *dictionaries* of the past couple of hundred years? Authoritative definitions are important. Indeed, dictionaries might provide us with a microcosm of what was happening in the encyclopedias of their times.

I believe I have good reason, beyond the fact that it is my own field, to think that our society's views of suicide are important to all of us. I learned from a study I once did with the coroner of Marin County, California, that more than a quarter of all deaths—*all* deaths, not just overt suicides—are probably interlaced with threads of imprudence, disregard, excess, indifference, or ennui that bring an end to life sooner than is necessary. In other words, some people who have died what I call "subintentioned deaths" from heart attacks or automobile accidents may have a good deal in common with people who are termed "suicides." In that sense alone, suicide is everybody's business, and we disregard it at the risk of moving up the dates on our own tombstones.

The definition of any important term such as *suicide* gives it power—and also gives it honorific, neutral, or pejorative overtones. Denotation influences connotation. The connotative meanings of a word govern society's responses to it. These community responses can cover a wide range: in the case of suicide, one extreme includes scorn, indifference, and punishment, and the other extreme includes empathy and therapy. And even *within* the realm of therapy, the very modalities are influenced by definition. Whether the therapeutic response is primarily pharmacological (pills), surgical (lobotomy), electrical (shock), institutional (hospitalization), or psychodynamic (talk)—differences that are not trivial—may depend on the inner, unspoken definition of suicide and its connotative associations that one's physician happens to hold.

Anthropologically speaking, dictionaries and encyclopedias are the two key books in any literate society. Each of us lives within (or rebels against) the reigning mores, and those mores are reflected in and created by words. Much of our English-American Zeitgeist is reflected in the long history of the *Encyclopaedia Britannica.* As I look at the piles of articles fanned out on my dining table, I feel that the pages, though they all deal with death, are in some sense alive, and that they are spreading their exhalations into many vast and tiny places.

15

CHAPTER

Suicide

No one really knows why human beings commit suicide. Indeed, the very person who takes his own life may be least aware at the moment of decision of the essence (much less the totality) of his reasons and emotions for doing so. At the outset, it can be said that a dozen individuals can kill themselves and "do" (or commit) 12 psychologically different deeds. Understanding suicide—like understanding any other complicated human act such as drug or alcohol misuse or antisocial behaviour—involves insights drawn from many fields that touch on man's entire psychological and social life.

□ Definition of Suicide

In this article the definition of suicide will be treated in two ways: first, a definition is put forward, and then some of the difficulties and complexities involved in defining the term are discussed. Briefly defined, suicide is the human act of self-inflicted, self-intentioned cessation.

Suicide is not a disease (although there are those who think so); it is not, in the view of the most detached observers, an immorality (although, as noted below, it has often been so treated in Western and other

Reprinted from *Encyclopaedia Britannica,* 1973, vol. 21, 383–385. Chicago: William Benton. With permission.

cultures); and, finally, it is unlikely that any one theory will ever explain phenomena as varied and as complicated as human self-destructive behaviors. In general, it is probably accurate to say that suicide always involves an individual's tortured and tunneled logic in a state of inner-felt, intolerable emotion. In addition, this mixture of constricted thinking and unbearable anguish is infused with that individual's conscious and unconscious psychodynamics (of hate, dependency, hope, etc.), playing themselves out within a social and cultural context, which itself imposes various degrees of restraint on, or facilitation of, the suicidal act.

This definition implies that committing suicide involves a conceptualization of death; that it combines an individual's conscious wish to be dead and his action to carry out that wish; that it focuses on his intention (which may have to be inferred by others); that the goal of action relates to death (rather than self-injury or self-mutilation); and that it focuses on the concept of the cessation of the individual's conscious, introspective life. The word "suicide" would seem to be clear enough, although such phrases as "self-inflicted" (in the incident in which Saul asked another soldier to kill him) and "self-intentioned" (when Seneca was ordered by Nero to kill himself) add to the complications of finding a clear-cut definition of suicide.

Complexities and Difficulties with Definitions

If the definition of suicide is complicated, there are even more confusions of meaning when the adjective "suicidal" is used. Some of the current confusions relating to the term "suicidal" are as follows:

(1) The word "suicidal" is used to cover a number of categories of behaviour. For example, it may convey the idea that an individual has committed suicide, attempted suicide, threatened suicide, exhibited depressive behaviour—with or without suicidal ideation—or manifested generally self-destructive or inimical patterns.
(2) There also is confusion with respect to the temporal aspects of suicidal acts. One sees "suicidal" used to convey the information that an individual was self-destructive, is currently self-destructive, or will be so. Most diagnoses in this field are post hoc definitions, labeling an individual as "suicidal" only after he has attempted or committed suicide.
(3) Serious confusion relating to suicidal phenomena may occur if the individual's intentions in relation to his own cessation are not con-

> sidered. "Suicide" may be defined for medical, legal, and administrative purposes. In the United States and Great Britain (and most of the countries reporting to the World Health Organization), suicide is defined (by a medical examiner or coroner) as one of four possible modes of death. There are 140 possible causes of death but only four modes. An acronym for the four modes of death is NASH: natural, accident, suicide, and homicide. This traditional, fourfold classification of all deaths leaves much to be desired. Its major deficiency is that it emphasizes relatively adventitious details in the death. Whether the individual is invaded by a lethal virus (natural), or a lethal bullet (homicide), or a lethal steering wheel (accident) may be a trivial difference to the deceased, who may be more interested in the date of his death. More importantly, the NASH classification of death erroneously treats the human being in Cartesian fashion, as a biological machine, rather than appropriately treating him as a motivated psychosocial organism. It also obscures the individual's intentions in relation to his own cessation and, further, completely neglects the contemporary concepts of psychodynamic psychology regarding intention, purpose, and the multiple determination of behaviour including unconscious motivation.

It may make more sense eventually to eschew the category of suicide entirely—along with the other NASH categories—and instead to classify all deaths in terms of the role of the individual in his own demise: (1) intentional, (2) subintentional—cases in which an individual has played partial, latent, covert, or unconscious roles in hastening his own demise—or (3) unintentioned. The problems of certification would then be no more difficult than they are at present, but such a classification would serve to put man back into his own dying and death and, in addition, would reflect the 20th-century view of man that emphasizes both the conscious and unconscious aspects of his intentionality.

The Word

Suicide is a relatively recent word. According to *The Oxford English Dictionary,* the word was first used in 1651 by Walter Charleton when he said, interestingly enough, "To vindicate ones self from . . . inevitable Calamity, by Sui-cide is not . . . a Crime." The exact date of its first use is open to some question. Edward Phillips in the 1662 edition of his dictionary, *A New World in Words,* claimed invention of the word: "One barbarous word I shall produce, which is suicide." Curiously enough he does not derive it from the death of oneself but says it "should be derived from 'a sow' . . . since it is a swinish part for a man to kill himself."

The British poetry critic Alfred Alvarez in 1971 claimed that he found the word was used even earlier, in Sir Thomas Browne's *Religio Medici,* written in 1635 and published in 1642, in the following passage: "Herein are they not extreme that can allow a man to be his own assassin and so highly extoll the end by suicide of Cato."

The word "suicide" does not appear in Robert Burton's *Anatomy of Melancholy* (1652 edition) nor in Samuel Johnson's *Dictionary* (1755). Before the introduction of the word, other terms, mostly circumlocutions and euphemisms relating to self-murder, were used—among them self-destruction, self-killing, self-slaughter, *sibi mortem consciecere* (to procure one's own death), *vim sibi inferre* (to cause violence to oneself), and *sui manu cadere* (to fall by one's own hand). Burton's phrases for suicide include "to make way with themselves" and "they offer violence to themselves." The traditional (and current) German term is *Selbstmord*—self-murder.

It may well be that in light of current concepts and facts about human self-destruction a new (and more accurate) term may eventually come into general usage. In the 1960s a relatively new word, suicidology, was introduced. *Suicidologie* was used in a text by a Dutch professor, W. A. Bonger, in 1929, but did not become widely known. Independently, the word was used by Edwin S. Shneidman in a book review (1964) and then in the *Bulletin of Suicidology* (1967) and at the first convention of the American Association of Suicidology, which met in 1968. Since then the word has come into general use. Suicidology is defined as the scientific study of suicidal phenomena.

☐ Main Threads of Suicidal Study

The modern era of the study of suicide began around the turn of the 20th century, with two main threads of investigation, the sociological and the psychological, associated with the names of Émile Durkheim (1858–1917) and Sigmund Freud (1856–1939), respectively. Much earlier, during classical Greek times, suicide was viewed in various ways, but, in classical Rome, in the centuries just before the Christian era, life was held rather cheaply and suicide was viewed either neutrally or even positively. The Roman Stoic Seneca said: "Living is not good, but living well. The wise man, therefore, lives as well as he should, not as long as he can. . . . He will always think of life in terms of quality not quantity. . . . Dying early or late is of no relevance, dying well or ill is . . . even if it is true that while there is life there is hope, life is not to be bought at any cost."

Historically it seems that the excessive martyrdom and penchant toward suicide of the early Christians frightened the church elders sufficiently for them to introduce a serious deterrent. That constraint was to relate suicide to crime and the sin associated with crime. A major change occurred in the 4th century with a categorical rejection of suicide by St. Augustine (354–430). Suicide was considered a crime, because it precluded the possibility of repentance and because it violated the Sixth Commandment relating to killing. Suicide was a greater sin than any sin one might wish to avoid. This view was elaborated by St. Thomas Aquinas (1225–74), who emphasized that suicide was a mortal sin in that it usurped God's power over man's life and death. Although neither the Old nor the New Testament directly forbids suicide, by 693 the Council of Toledo proclaimed that an individual who attempted suicide was to be excommunicated. The notion of suicide as sin took firm hold and for hundreds of years played an important part in Western man's view of self-destruction.

The Christian injunctions against suicide seemed paradoxically to rest on a respect for life (especially the life of the soul in the hereafter) and were a reaction to the light way in which life was held by the Romans. If those were the church's original motivations, however, they went awry and the results were excessive and counterproductive, and resulted in degrading, defaming, impoverishing, torturing, and persecuting individuals (who had attempted suicide, committed suicide, or were the survivors) whom they had originally tried to protect and succor.

The French philosopher Jean Jacques Rousseau (1712–78), by emphasizing the natural state of man, transferred sin from man to society, making man generally good (and innocent) and asserting that it is society that makes him bad. The disputation as to the locus of blame—whether in man or in society—is a major theme that dominates the history of suicidal thought. David Hume (1711–76) was one of the first major Western philosophers to discuss suicide in the absence of the concept of sin. His famous essay "On Suicide," published in 1777, a year after his death, was promptly suppressed. That well-reasoned essay is a statement of the Enlightenment position on suicide. The burden of the essay is to refute the view that suicide is a crime; it does so by arguing that suicide is not a transgression of our duties to God, to our fellow citizens, or to ourselves. He states that ". . . prudence and courage should engage us to rid ourselves at once of existence when it becomes a burden. . . . If it be no crime in me to divert the Nile or Danube from its course, were I able to effect such purposes, where then is the crime in turning a few ounces of blood from their natural channel?"

Whereas Hume tried to decriminalize suicide, Rousseau turned the blame from man to society. In the 20th century, the two giants of suicidal theorizing played rather different roles: Durkheim focused on society's inimical effects on the individual, while Freud—eschewing the notions of either sin or crime—gave suicide back to man but put the locus of action in man's unconscious.

Durkheim's best-known work, *Le Suicide* (1897), established a model for sociological investigations of suicide. There have been many subsequent studies of this genre. The monographs and books by R. S. Cavan on suicide in Chicago (1926), of Calvin F. Schmid on suicide in Seattle (1928) and Minneapolis (1933), of Peter Sainsbury on suicide in London (1955), of Louis I. Dublin and Bessie Bunzel (1933), and of Andrew F. Henry and James F. Short, Jr., on suicide in the U.S. (1954) all fall within the sociological tradition of taking a plot of ground—a city or a country—and figuratively or literally reproducing its map several times to show its socially shady (and topographically shaded) areas and their differential relationships to suicide rates.

According to Durkheim suicide is the result of society's strength or weakness of control over the individual. He posited three basic types of suicide, each a result of man's relationship to his society. In one instance, the "altruistic" suicide is literally required by society. Here, the customs or rules of the group demand suicide under certain circumstances. Harakiri and suttee are examples of altruistic suicides. In such instances, however, the persons had little choice. Self-inflicted death was honourable; continuing to live was ignominious. Society dictated their action and, as individuals, they were not strong enough to defy custom.

Most suicides in the United States are "egoistic"—Durkheim's second category. Contrary to the circumstances of an altruistic suicide, egoistic suicide occurs when the individual has too few ties with his community. Demands, in this case to live, do not reach him. Thus, proportionately, more individuals, especially men, who are on their own kill themselves than do church or family members.

Finally, Durkheim called "anomic" those suicides that occur when the accustomed relationship between an individual and his society is suddenly shattered. The shocking, immediate loss of a job, a close friend, or a fortune is thought sufficient to precipitate anomic suicides; or, conversely, poor men surprised by sudden wealth also have been shocked into anomic suicide.

The students and followers of Durkheim include Maurice Halbwachs in France and Ronald W. Maris and Jack D. Douglas in the United States.

Douglas, especially, has argued that Durkheim's constructs came not so much from the facts of life and death as from official statistics, which themselves may distort the very facts they are supposed to report.

As Durkheim detailed the sociology of suicide, so Freud fathered psychological explanations. To him, suicide was essentially within the mind. Since men ambivalently identify with the objects of their own love, when they are frustrated the aggressive side of the ambivalence will be directed against the internalized person. The main psychoanalytical position on suicide was that it represented unconscious hostility directed toward the introjected (ambivalently viewed) love object. For example, one killed oneself in order to murder the image of one's loved-hated father within one's breast. Psychodynamically, suicide was seen as murder in the 180th degree.

In an important exegesis of Freud's thoughts on suicide by Robert E. Litman (1967, 1970), he traces the development of Freud's thoughts on the subject, taking into account Freud's clinical experiences and his changing theoretical positions from 1881 to 1939. It is evident from Litman's analysis that there is more to the psychodynamics of suicide than hostility. These factors include the general features of human condition in Western civilization, specifically, suicide-prone mechanisms involving rage, guilt, anxiety, dependency, and a great number of specifically predisposing conditions. The feelings of helplessness, hopelessness, and abandonment are very important.

Psychodynamic explanations of suicide theory did not move too much from the time of Freud to that of Karl Menninger. In his important book *Man Against Himself* (1938), Menninger (in captivating ordinary language) delineates the psychodynamics of hostility and asserts that the hostile drive in suicide is made up of three skeins: (1) the wish to kill, (2) the wish to be killed, and (3) the wish to die. Gregory Zilboorg refined this psychoanalytic hypothesis and stated that every suicidal case contained strong, unconscious hostility combined with an unusual lack of capacity to love others. He extended the concern from solely intrapsychic dynamics to the external world and maintained that the role of a broken home in suicidal proneness demonstrated that suicide has both intrapsychic and external etiological elements.

In addition to the sociological and psychological approaches to the study of suicide, there is a third main contemporary thrust that might be called the philosophical or existential. Albert Camus, in his essay *The Myth of Sisyphus,* begins by saying: "There is but one serious philosophic problem and that is suicide." The principal task of man is to respond to life's apparent meaninglessness, despair, and its absurd quality. Ludwig Wittgenstein also states that the main ethical issue for man is suicide. To

Camus, Wittgenstein, and other philosophers, however, their ruminations were never meant as prescriptions for action. Arthur Schopenhauer (1788–1860), the philosopher of pessimism, lived to a fairly ripe age and died of natural causes.

Psychological Characteristics of Suicide

Suicide has been related to many emotions: hostility, despair, shame, guilt, dependency, hopelessness, ennui. The traditional psychoanalytic position, first stated by Wilhelm Stekel at a meeting in Vienna in 1910, is that "no one kills himself who has not wanted to kill another or at least wished the death of another." This thought became translated into the psychoanalytic formulation that suicide represented hostility toward the introjected (ambivalently identified) love object. Currently, even psychodynamically oriented suicidologists believe that although hostility can be an important psychological component in some suicides, other emotional states—especially frustrated dependency and hopelessness and helplessness—often play the dominant role in the psychological drama of suicide. If there is one general psychological state commonly assumed to be associated with suicide it is a state of intolerable emotion (or unbearable or "unrepeatable despair")—what Herman Melville, in his masterpiece on self-destruction, *Moby Dick,* called "insufferable anguish."

Over and above the emotional states related to suicide, there are three important general psychological characteristics of suicide:

1. The first is that the acute suicidal crisis (or period of high and dangerous lethality) is an interval of relatively short duration—to be counted, typically, in hours or days, not usually in months or years. An individual is at a peak of self-destructiveness for a brief time and is either helped, cools off, or is dead. Although one can live for years at a chronically elevated self-destructive level, one cannot have a loaded gun to one's head for too long before either bullet or emotion is discharged.
2. The second concept is ambivalence. Few persons now dispute that Freud's major insights relating to the role of unconscious motivation (and the workings of what is called the unconscious mind) have been one of the giant concepts of this century in revolutionizing our view of man. The notion of ambivalence is a critical concept in 20th-century, psychodynamically-oriented psychiatry and psychology. The dualities, complications, concomitant contradictory feelings, attitudes,

and thrusts toward essentially the same person or introjected image are recognized hallmarks of psychological life. The dualities of the mind's flow constitute a cardinal feature of man's inner life. One can no longer ask in a simple Aristotelian way, "Make up your mind." To such a question a sophisticated respondent ought to say: "But that is precisely the point. I am at least of two, perhaps several, minds on this subject." A law has equal force whether it is passed in the Senate by a 100–0 or a 51–49 vote; so has a bullet. The paradigm of suicide is not the simplistic one of wanting to or not wanting to. The prototypical psychological picture of a person on the brink of suicide is one who wants to and does not want to. He makes plans for self-destruction and at the same time entertains fantasies of rescue and intervention. It is possible—indeed probably prototypical—for a suicidal individual to cut his throat and to cry for help at the same time.

3. Most suicidal events are dyadic events, that is, two-person events. Actually this dyadic aspect of suicide has two phases: the first during the prevention of suicide when one must deal with the "significant other," and the second in the aftermath in the case of a committed suicide in which one must deal with the survivor-victim. Although it is obvious that the suicidal drama takes place within an individual's head, it is also true that most suicidal tensions are between two people keenly known to each other: spouse and spouse, parent and child, lover and lover. In addition, death itself is an extremely dyadic event.

The cold sociological truth is that some modes of death are more stigmatizing to the survivors than are other modes of death and that, generally speaking, suicide imposes the greatest stigma of all upon its survivors. The British physician John Hinton deals with this in his book *Dying* (1967). Hinton also comments that the notes left by the suicidal subject often cause further anguish.

Suicide notes provide an unusual window into the thoughts and feelings of a suicidal person. Various surveys in different places indicate that about 15% of individuals who commit suicide leave suicide notes—although the actual range is from 2 to 20%. By the 1970s fewer than 20 systematic studies of suicide notes had been completed. One of the first scientific studies of suicide notes was by W. Morgenthaler (1945) in a monograph that reported 47 suicide notes (in German) from Bern, Switz. The best-known reports in the United States are by Edwin S. Shneidman and Norman L. Farberow (1947, 1970) in their studies of genuine suicide notes and elicited matched notes written by nonsuicidal persons. Suicide notes have been subjected to a number of types of analyses: by emotional states, logical styles, "reasons" stated or implied, death wishes, language characteristics, relations to persons, and by computer count of key "tag words." In general these analyses indicate that (1) it is possible to distinguish between genuine and simulated suicide notes, and, more importantly, (2) genuine suicide notes are characterized by dichotomous logic, greater amount of hostility and self-blame, use of very specific names and instructions to the survivor, more decisiveness, less evidence of thinking about thinking, and more use of the various meanings of the word "love."

The Two Fundamental Aspects of Death and Suicide

Twentieth-century philosophers, especially Percy Bridgman (1938), pointed out that there is an epistemological characteristic unique to death, specifically that there are two fundamental aspects of death: the private aspect, as an individual lives it himself (my death); and the public aspect, as one can experience, in reality, the death of another (your death). In death (and suicide) there is a key difference between the principal actor and the observer. One major implication of this key difference is that I can observe and experience your death (just as you can observe and experience my death), but I can never experience my own death for if I could, I should still be alive.

Some of this kind of thinking operates in suicide, especially when it is seen as a psychologically magical act. Just as Melville wrote that "All evil, to crazy Ahab, were visibly personified and made practically assailable in Moby Dick," so to the suicidal mind, using this same tortured logic, the whole world is "made practically assailable" and can be thought to be expunged by destroying oneself.

The fantasies of one's own suicide can represent the greatest possible combination of omnipotence and potential realization of effectiveness—greater even than one's fantasies of the assassination of another, group revenge, mass murder, or even genocide. Any "average" individual can say: "From my point of view, suicide destroys all"—and it can be done.

These inferred psychodynamics of suicide (relating to delusions of annihilation) are thought by psychoanalysts to have their origins in the earliest notions of an individual's infantile omnipotence. The literature of suicide in Western man, however, continually emphasizes that suicide can be an individual's final act, his final escape hatch, his final revenge—often misconstrued as a final "right." This unique epistemological dual characteristic of death (the difference between my death and your death) is fundamental to an understanding of suicide.

☐ Attempted Suicide

Although it is obvious that one has to "attempt" suicide in order to commit it, it is equally clear that often the event of "attempting suicide" does not have death (cessation) as its objective. It is an acknowledged fact that often the goal of "attempted suicide" (such as cutting oneself or ingesting harmful substances) is to change one's life (or to change the "significant others" around one) rather than to end it. On the other hand, sometimes death is intended and only fortuitously avoided. After that, one's life—what has been called "a bonus life"—is forever somewhat different. Alfred Alvarez, who himself made a serious suicide attempt, said that survivors have a changed life, with entirely different standards.

Erwin Stengel, a student of attempted suicide, in his arguments and statistical presentations, seems to suggest, in the main, that persons who attempt suicide and those who commit suicide represent essentially two different "populations"—with admittedly some overflow from the first to the second. It is useful to think of two sets of overlapping populations: (1) a group of those who attempt suicide, few of whom go on to commit it, and (2) a group of those who commit suicide, many of whom have previously attempted it. A great deal has to do with the lethality of the event. Lethality is roughly synonymous with the "deathfulness" of the act and is an important dimension in understanding any potentially suicidal person. Avery D. Weisman in 1972 distinguished three aspects of lethality: that of intention (ideation and involvement); that of implementation (risk and rescue); and that of intercession (resources, relief, and reorientation). The ratio between suicide attempts and commits is about 8 to 1—1 committed suicide for every 8 attempts.

Suicide attempts have many meanings and, whatever their level of lethality, ought to be taken seriously. A person who attempts suicide because he believes that there is no use living may not necessarily mean that he wants to die but that he has exhausted the potential for being someone who matters.

☐ Partial Death and Substitutes for Suicide

Sometimes the very life-style of an individual seems to truncate and demean his life so that he is as good as dead. Often alcoholism, drug addiction, mismanagement of physical disease (such as diabetes or Buerger's disease), and masochistic behaviour can be seen in this light. A study of gifted individuals (with IQ's over 140) indicated that conspicuous failure in adult life—a kind of "partial death"—was sometimes the "price" for life as a substitute for overt suicide.

The chief theorist of the concept of partial death is Karl Menninger. Much of his conception is explicated in *Man Against Himself.* Menninger writes of (1) chronic suicide, including asceticism, martyrdom, neurotic invalidism, alcohol addiction, antisocial behaviour, and psychosis; (2) focal suicide—focused on a limited part of the body—including self-mutilations, malingering, multiple surgery, purposive accidents, impotence, and frigidity; and (3) organic suicide, focusing on the psychological factors in organic disease, especially the self-punishing, aggressive, and erotic components. In the 1970s, the focus was on concepts such as indirect self-destructive behaviour. There have been many studies of alcoholism and drug addiction and diabetes and on aspects of homicide (on both the murderer and the victim) as suicidal equivalents. In relation to the role of the homicidal victim in his own death, the work of Marvin Wolfgang (1958) has been particularly interesting.

A related concept is that of "subintentioned death." That concept asserts that there are many deaths that are neither clearly suicidal nor clearly accidental or natural but are deaths in which the decedent has played some covert or unconscious role in "permitting" his death to occur, sort of "accidentally," or by "inviting" homicide, or, by unconsciously disregarding what could be life-extending medical regimen, and thus dying sooner than "necessary." Losing the "will to live" and so-called voodoo deaths—as well as many deaths in ordinary society—can be viewed as subintentional deaths. Obviously, this view of death changes the nature and statistics of suicide dramatically.

This concept of a reduced level of life as a substitute (or psychological "trade") for suicide itself presents fascinating philosophic, social, psychological, and moral questions that relate to whether or not there actually is an irreducible suicide rate among human beings. Is there a price for civilization? Indeed, a price for life? Litman, reflecting on Freud's work, agrees with Freud's general schematic view and that there is a suicidal trend in everyone. This self-destructiveness is controlled through constructive habits of living and loving, but when they break down, the individual may easily be forced into a suicidal crisis. To keep alive one must keep his thoughts, feelings, and aspirations in a vital balance.

☐ Suicide and Religion

In the Western world it has been traditionally said that the suicide rate is higher among Protestants than among Catholics or Jews and that the latter group shows significantly low suicidal figures. By the 1970s it was known, however, that the role of religion in relation to suicide is more complicated and that religious affiliation serves both to inhibit and, at other times, to facilitate suicide. At the outset it is important to distinguish between religious beliefs and religious (social) affiliation. Durkheim not unexpectedly emphasized the sociological aspects of religion. He stated: "If religion protects one from the desire for self-destruction, it is not because it preaches to him, with elements of religious origin, respect for one's person; it is because it forms a social group." A nationwide study in the United States indicated that the pro rata suicide rate among veterans—a fairly representative group of U.S. citizenry—for Catholics and Protestants was about equal to the numbers (and percentages) of Protestants and Catholics in the country generally. Much more important than nominal religious affiliation would be a number of subtleties of religious belief: the feeling of group belongingness, belief in an omnipotent God, belief in the efficacy of prayer, belief in a hereafter or existence after death, and other issues relating to death in general. Results of a national U.S. survey of 30,000 persons reported by Shneidman in 1970 indicated that a sizable percentage (57%) of individuals of all religious backgrounds (and with a variety of intensities of religious belief) did not believe in any life after death and that over one-third indicated that religion had played either a relatively minor role or no role at all in the development of their attitudes toward death (and toward suicide). Just as in the 20th century there has been an enormous "secularization" of death—the physician and hospital in many ways replacing the clergyman and the church in relation to the anxieties surrounding death—so too has there been a secularization of suicide. Few of the current debates about suicide are on primary religious grounds; when the ethics of suicide are debated, those usually are in terms of such concepts as "freedom" and "life," *i.e.*, how free an individual should be to take his own life and how far "benign intervention" should go in an attempt to save an individual's life before the intervention is intrusive and robs him of more than his life is worth.

When Durkheim spoke of religion as a source of social organization (holding individuals together with common beliefs and practices), he was not only speaking of social integration but he was also, from a psychological point of view, referring to personal identification. Walter T. Martin and Jack P. Gibbs (1964) proposed a theory relating status integration with suicide and Henry and Short (1954) discussed the positive relationship between suicide and status and the negative relation between suicide and the strength of a relational source. In general it appears that a person who is uneasy in his religion (or in his irreligion) or changes his religion several times (like a person who is uneasy in his marriage or has several marriages) is more likely to commit suicide, not so much on purely religious (or marital) grounds but because of his general perturbation and lack of good self-concept, which underlie his uneasy search for certainty and stability in his life.

☐ Suicide and the Law

Not surprisingly, the history of suicide and the law closely parallel and reflect—often with significant lags—the major cultural and philosophic attitudes toward suicide. Probably the most important single legal change was the passage of the Suicide Act in England in 1961 that (1) finally abolished criminal penalties for committing suicide—considering that in the 19th century (as late as 1823), a London citizen who committed suicide was buried at a crossroads in Chelsea with a stake pounded through his heart; (2) no longer made survivors of suicide attempts liable to criminal prosecution; and (3) as a kind of quid pro quo for the liberalization of the first two measures, increased the penalties (up to 14 years' imprisonment) for aiding and abetting a suicidal act. Earlier, the Homicide Act of 1957 changed the charge against a survivor of a suicide pact from murder to manslaughter.

In the United States, most aspects of suicide are not against the law. As of the early 1970s a comparatively small number of states (9) listed suicide as a crime, although no penalties (such as mutilation of bodies or forfeiture of estates) were exacted. In such states suicide attempts are either felonies or misdemeanours and could result in jail sentences, although such laws are selectively or indifferently enforced. Two states (Nevada and New York) repealed such laws, stating in effect that although suicide is "a grave social wrong" there is no way to punish it. Eighteen states—Alaska, Arkansas, California, Florida, Kansas, Louisiana, Michigan, Massachusetts, Minnesota, Mississippi, Missouri, Montana, Nevada, New Mexico, New York, Oregon, Wisconsin, and Wyoming—have no laws against either suicide or suicide attempts but specify that to aid, advise, or encourage another person to commit suicide is a felony. In the more than 20 other states, there are no penal statutes referring to suicide.

In the early 1970s, especially in Great Britain, there was some movement (among some eminent lawyers, theologians, philosophers, and physicians) toward the legalization of voluntary euthanasia; proposals were to repeal the aiding and abetting aspect of suicide laws so that a physician might, on a patient's request, assist him to his own voluntary death.

Some Oddities of Suicide

The lore about suicide contains a large number of interesting and esoteric items about various cultures. Suicide was thought, for example, to be absent among so-called primitive cultures, but it is evident that this is not so. Studies were made of suicide in Africa (Paul Bohannan, 1960), India (Verrier Elwin, 1943; Upendra Thakur, 1963), Hong Kong (Yap Powmeng, 1958), and Japan (Ohara, 1961). Practically every popular article on suicide routinely contains a statement about the kamikaze pilots who flew and died for Japan in World War II. Also, in relation to Japan, one often reads of the practice of hara-kiri or seppuku, which is the ritual act of disemboweling oneself and was limited to the samurai warrior and noble classes. General Tōjō, who attempted hara-kiri at the end of World War II, was saved by U.S. doctors, only to be hanged later by a military tribunal. In 1970 the well-known Japanese author Mishima Yukio (*q.v.*) committed seppuku (with ritual self-disemboweling and decapitation) at the age of 45. In general, however, suicide in contemporary Japan is more "Western" than otherwise—often done with barbiturates. In a discussion of suicide in 19th-century India one finds references to suttee, the custom in which Hindu widows threw themselves onto the funeral pyres of their husbands.

Six suicides are recorded in the Old Testament: Abimelech, Samson, Saul, Saul's armour bearer, Ahithophel, and Zimri. The most famous and among the most frequently cited suicides perhaps, are Socrates' drinking hemlock and Cato's throwing himself upon his sword. The apocryphal stories of Bismarck's contemplating suicide, Napoleon's attempting suicide, Washington's despondency, and Lincoln's depression keep reappearing in articles on suicide—including this one.

Myths of Suicide

Following is a summary of some of the more outstanding misconceptions of suicide:

Fable: Persons who talk about suicide do not commit suicide. *Fact:* Of any ten persons who will themselves commit it, eight have given definite warnings of their suicidal intentions.

Fable: Suicide happens without warning. *Fact:* Studies reveal that the suicidal person gives many clues and warnings regarding his suicidal intentions.

Fable: Suicidal persons are fully intent on dying. *Fact:* Most suicidal persons are undecided about living or dying, and they "gamble with death," leaving it to others to save them. Almost no one commits suicide without letting others know how he is feeling.

Fable: Once a person is suicidal, he is suicidal forever. *Fact:* Individuals who wish to kill themselves are suicidal only for a limited period of time.

Fable: Improvement following a suicidal crisis means that the suicidal risk is over. *Fact:* Most suicides occur within about three months following the beginning of "improvement," when the individual has the energy to put his morbid thoughts and feelings into effect.

Fable: Suicide strikes much more often among the rich, or, conversely, it occurs almost exclusively among the poor. *Fact:* Suicide is neither the rich man's disease nor the poor man's curse. Suicide is represented proportionately among all levels of society.

Fable: Suicide is inherited or "runs in the family." *Fact:* It follows individual patterns.

Fable: All suicidal individuals are mentally ill, and suicide always is the act of a psychotic person. *Fact:* Studies of hundreds of genuine suicide notes indicate that although the suicidal person is extremely unhappy, he is not necessarily mentally ill.

Romantic Suicide and the Artist

Since at least the 16th century, specifically in the Italian commedia dell'arte, there has been a character named Harlequin who typically wears a multicoloured suit and a black mask—and has a connection with death. Indeed to be loved by Harlequin was to be married to death. This is the idea of death as a lover; it relates to the romanticization of death itself. As a refinement of this idea, suicide has historically been thought to be a romantic kind of death. One specific myth is that suicide is caused by unrequited love. Suicide pacts (portrayed romantically in *Mayerling* and in *Elvira Madigan*) are depicted as the essence of intense love. One result of this mystique is a belief that especially sensitive people, artists—poets, painters, and writers—are unusually prone to commit suicide and, indeed, add to their reputations as artists by committing suicide. Perhaps the best-known novel of this genre is Goethe's *The Sorrows of Young Werther*, published in 1774 when the author was 24 years old and credited, in the mythology of suicide, with having created a veritable epidemic of romantic suicides throughout Europe. By the 1970s the list of suicides of artists was sufficiently long and vivid to persuade an uncritical student of suicide that the sensitivity of the artist is somehow related to the special nature of a romantic suicidal death. The list includes Van Gogh, Virginia Woolf, Hart Crane, the Italian writer Cesare Pavese, Randall Jarrell, Modigliani, Jackson Pollock, Mark Rothko, Ernest Hemingway, John Berryman, Sylvia Plath, Mishima, and Kawabata Yasunari. Perhaps the best description and analysis of suicide and the creative literary artist is by the English poetry editor and critic Alfred Alvarez in his book *The Savage God: a Study of Suicide* (1971). Maksim Gorki attempted suicide when he was 19. One of the most romanticized suicides in Western literature is that of the English poet Thomas Chatterton (1752–70), who took poison at the age of 17. This particular death illustrates the notion (or myth) "that those with more life and passion go soon"—that the best die young. It reminds one of those who have died "too young"—Byron, Shelley, Keats, Mozart—and the particular poignancy of an untimely death of an especially beautiful or gifted person. We tend to be essentially undemocratic about death and suicide—because we tend to believe that some deaths level (or elevate) certain people more than others.

Statistics on Suicide

The demographic use of statistics on suicide perhaps were given their greatest impetus by John Graunt and Johann Peter Süssmilch. Graunt was a London tradesman who, in 1662, published a small book of observations on the London bills of mortality. He separated various bits of information contained in these rolls of names of the dead into separate categories and organized the information systematically, finally constructing mortality tables—the first attempt to organize data in that manner. Of great significance was his success in demonstrating the regularities that can be found between medical and social phenomena when one deals with large numbers. He demonstrated how an analysis of the mortality statistics could be used to the advantage of physicians, businessmen, and government.

Much of what is known today as statistical information came into existence with the work of Süssmilch, a Prussian clergyman who in 1741 in his analyses of vital data from church registers created political arithmetic, or what is now called vital statistics. It is important to keep in mind that statistics, particularly statistics on suicide, are in part socially manufactured data—mostly by coroners and physicians. Suicidal deaths are notoriously underrepresented and obviously vary from country to country dependent not only on the number of suicides that in fact occur in each country but also on deeply ingrained cultural folkways relating to the social, cultural, and religious attitudes of that country.

There are several sources of suicide statistics. Louis Dublin's text, *Suicide* (1963), is a standard source; the World Health Organization (WHO) booklet, *The Prevention of Suicide* (1968), is another. *Suicide in the United*

States, 1950–1964 (1967) and *The Facts of Life and Death* (1970), both published by the U.S. Department of Health, Education, and Welfare, are standard sources in the United States. In general, the reported suicide rate for the United States is between 10 and 12 per 100,000, which places the United States about in the middle of the countries that report to the United Nations. Austria, West Germany, Hungary, Japan, Czechoslovakia, Denmark, Finland, Sweden, and Switzerland report rates of over 25 per 100,000 population, and Italy, the Netherlands, and Spain report rates under 10 per 100,000. The number of suicides in the United States per year is given at about 22,000 but many experts believe the actual number to be at least twice as high.

In any discussion of the statistics of suicide—keeping in mind their tenuous character—it is important to distinguish among rank, rate, and number. Currently, in the United States, suicide is ranked among the first five causes of death for white males from 10 to 55. For example, suicide is the second-ranked cause of death for white males age 15–19, but one must appreciate that the first leading cause of death, accidents, yields 627 chances in 100,000 of the individual's dying from that cause, while suicide yields (only) 88 chances in 100,000. Generally, in the early ages when suicide is high, it occupies that rank because the other killers like heart disease, malignant neoplasms (cancer), vascular lesions of the central nervous system (stroke), and cirrhosis of the liver are not then common.

In general, statistics on suicide in the 19th and 20th centuries indicate that more men than women commit suicide (about 3 to 1) and that more women than men attempt suicide (again about 3 to 1). In the early 1970s there was evidence that the ratio for committed suicide seemed to be changing, moving toward (but not yet achieving) an equal proportion between the sexes. Statistics relating to race and ethnic origin seem to be undergoing changes, probably reflecting general changes in attitude toward the concept of race and ethnicity. In the United States it was reported for years that suicides among Whites far outnumbered suicides among Blacks, but the rate for Blacks seems to be changing, moving closer to that for Whites. Whether this reflects the effects of urban ghetto living, the effects of identifying with "the white man's problems," or simply better and more accurate record keeping are all issues for further study. Some studies (conducted in England and Australia) that followed individuals who emigrated either to the United States or to Australia seem to indicate that the suicide rates of specific groups such as Hungarians, Italians, Poles, and Irish appear, for a generation or so, to be closer to the rates of the homeland than to the rates of the adopted country. In these data, there are many methodological issues that are also yet to be resolved.

In relation to suicide statistics, a standard textbook on sociology published in 1972 reported that sociologists still made continuous reference to the work of Durkheim. Rates derived from Durkheim's studies show that suicide rates for Protestants have been consistently higher than those for Jews or Catholics. In the early part of the 20th century the Jewish rate in the Netherlands was higher than the Protestant, and during the depression, in Toronto, Canada, Catholic rates also were higher than Protestant. The inference is that the time, the place, and the social circumstances are all important factors.

In the matter of comparative national statistics, Alvarez points out that U.S. Pres. Dwight D. Eisenhower blamed the high Swedish suicide rate on what too much social welfare can do. But the present rate in Sweden, Alvarez notes, is about the same as it was in 1910, before comprehensive social welfare programs were begun and is actually ranked ninth on a table published by WHO. The countries of Central Europe who show the highest rates: Hungary has the highest national rate; Austria and Czechoslovakia are third and fourth. The highest suicide rate in the world is that of West Berlin; its rate is more than twice that of West Germany as a whole. The city, it has been suggested, is a model of what Durkheim called anomie—alienated not only geographically but also in cultural, social, and political aspects. Countries like Ireland and Egypt, where suicide is considered by many a mortal sin, have rates among the lowest in the world, bearing out Stengel's conclusion that highly industrialized and prosperous countries tend to have comparatively high suicide rates. Alvarez concludes that official statistics reflect only a fraction of the true figures, which a number of authorities reckon to be anywhere from a quarter to a half again as large. Because of religious and bureaucratic prejudices, family sensitivity, differences in the proceedings of coroners' hearings and postmortem examinations, and the shadowy distinctions between suicides and accidents—in short, the unwillingness to recognize the act for what it is—knowledge of the extent to which suicide pervades modern society is diminished and distorted.

A certain sizable percentage of deaths that are certified by coroners or medical examiners—estimated to be between 10 and 15%—are equivocal as to what the actual mode of death ought to be; this uncertainty usually lies between suicide or accident. A procedure, called the psychological autopsy, has been developed to deal with these equivocal deaths. Essentially, the psychological autopsy involves the use of social and behavioural scientists (psychologists, psychiatrists, social workers, and other trained personnel) who interview relatives and friends of the decedent with the goal of developing information about the decedent's intention vis-à-vis his own death in the days just before the death.

Clues—verbal ("You won't be seeing me around"); behavioural (e.g., giving away prized possessions or marked changes in patterns of eating, sexuality, interests); or situational (e.g., the loss of a loved one)—are deemed to point more to suicide than to accident. In the absence of such clues, a recommendation for a non-suicidal or "undetermined" mode of death should be made to the certifying official.

☐ Suicide Vention (Prevention, Intervention, Postvention)

The Latin word *venire* means "to come" or "to do." In relation to any event (e.g., suicide) one can act before, during, or after—corresponding to prevention, intervention, and postvention. These terms also correspond roughly to the public health concepts of primary, secondary, and tertiary prevention.

Prevention If, as this article has suggested, suicidal phenomena are existential-social-psychological-dyadic events, then obviously primary prevention is enormously complicated—almost tantamount to preventing human unhappiness. Some students of human nature believe that the urge toward self-destruction is ubiquitous and that a certain amount of it is an evitable and constant price of civilization, if not of life itself. Primarily, prevention would relate to the principles of good mental hygiene in general.

Intervention Intervention relates to the treatment and care of suicidal crisis or suicidal problems. On this score, suicide prevention centres could be more accurately labeled suicide intervention centers. A great deal has been learned about practical techniques for effective suicide intervention. There is a vast literature on therapy and treatment of suicidal persons in various settings—in the community, in suicide prevention and crisis intervention centers, in poison-control centers, in outpatient offices, and in both medical and mental hospitals. In general, most of the suggestions for care have in common the stressing of good rapport, working with the "significant others" in the suicidal person's life, using the available community resources for referral (for emotional support, legal aid, financial help, employment, individual and group psychotherapy, hospitalization), and focusing on the reduction of the person's "lethality" during the period of suicidal crisis. Much of the suicide prevention work borrows from the theory of crisis intervention developed by Erich Lindemann (1944) and Gerald Caplan (1964). In the United

States, the theoretical and empirical work of the Los Angeles Suicide Prevention Center, established in 1955, and in Great Britain, the work of the Samaritans, established in 1953, has been widely emulated.

In 1960 there were fewer than a half-dozen suicide prevention centers in the United States; a decade later there were over 200. Typically they are telephone-answering centres; maintaining 24-hour service, they serve as short-term resources, are theoretically modeled in terms of the concept of crisis intervention, and use both professional and lay volunteer staff.

Suicide is best understood as a socio-psychological, existential human event that calls for compassionate response to an individual in an emotional and philosophic crisis. Obviously suicide is not solely a medical problem and many kinds of persons including volunteers—provided they are carefully selected, well-trained, and continuously supervised—can serve as lifesaving agents in the prevention of suicide. The lay volunteer has been described as probably the most important single discovery in the history of suicide prevention. Nonetheless, professionally trained persons—psychologists, psychiatrists, social workers—continue to play the primary roles in suicide prevention and especially in research.

Postvention This term, introduced by Shneidman in 1971, refers to those things done after the dire event has occurred that serve to mollify the aftereffects of the event in a person who has attempted suicide, or to deal with the adverse effects on the survivor-victims of a person who has committed suicide. It is offering psychological services to the bereaved survivors. It includes work with the surviving children, parents, and spouses. Much of postventive work has been focused on widows. Studies show that survivors are apt to have a higher morbidity and mortality rate in the year following the death of their loved one than comparable persons who are not survivors of such a death. It may well be that the major public mental-health challenge in suicide lies in offering postventive help to the survivor-victims. The development of postvention is part of the current new view of the special psychological needs relating to death.

☐ Bibliography

Emile Durkheim, *Suicide* (1897; Eng. trans. by J. A. Spaulding and G. Simpson, 1951); Sigmund Freud, "Mourning and Melancholia" (1917), in *The Standard Edition of the Complete Psychological Works*, vol. 14 (1965); Karl A. Menninger, *Man Against Himself* (1938); Edwin S. Shneidman and Norman L. Farberow (eds.), *Clues to Suicide* (1957), *The Cry for Help*

(1961); Glanville Williams, *The Sanctity of Life and the Criminal Law* (1957); Louis I. Dublin, *Suicide: a Sociological and Statistical Study* (1963); Erwin Stengel, *Suicide and Attempted Suicide* (1964); Paul Friedman (ed.), *On Suicide* (1967); Jack D. Douglas, *The Social Meanings of Suicide* (1967); Robert E. Litman, "Sigmund Freud and Suicide," Henry A. Murray, "Dead to the World," in E. S. Shneidman (ed.), *Essays in Self-Destruction* (1967); U.S. Public Health Service, *Suicide in the United States, 1950–1964* (1967); Arnold Toynbee *et al., Man's Concern with Death* (1969); World Health Organization, *Prevention of Suicide* (1968); Edwin S. Shneidman, "Suicide, Lethality and the Psychological Autopsy," in E. S. Shneidman and M. Ortega (eds.), *Aspects of Depression* (1969); N. L. Farberow, *Bibliography on Suicide and Suicide Prevention* (1969); E. S. Shneidman (ed.), *On the Nature of Suicide* (1969); E. S. Shneidman, N. L. Farberow, and R. E. Litman, *The Psychology of Suicide* (1970); A. Alvarez, *The Savage God: a Study of Suicide* (1971); Jacques Choron, *Suicide* (1972).

(E. S. SH.)

16

CHAPTER

Perturbation and Lethality as Precursors of Suicide in a Gifted Group

Thirty cases, for whom longitudinal personality data were available from 1921 to 1960, were analyzed. All the cases were Caucasian males with high I.Q.'s. Five individuals had committed suicide (all by gunshot), 10 (matched) individuals had died natural deaths from cancer or heart disease, and 15 were still living. A blind clinical analysis was conducted primarily in terms of two guiding concepts, perturbation and lethality, by means of a Meyerian "life chart" and a "psychological autopsy," respectively. The results indicated that four of the five cases deemed to be most suicidal had, in fact, committed suicide—a chance probability of 1 out of 1,131. The prodromal clues—instability, trauma, and personality controls—are discussed. The role of the "significant other" and the "burning-out" of affect seem to be paramount. Suicide is seen as a discernible part of a life style and as a predictable outcome, in a person of 50, by the time that individual is 30 years old.

☐ Introduction and Background

The two principal assertions in this paper are (*a*) that discernible early prodromal clues to adult suicide may be found in longitudinal case his-

Reprinted from *Life-Threatening Behavior*, 1971, *1*, 23–45. With permission.

tory data and (*b*) that it is useful to conceptualize these premonitory clues in terms of *perturbation* and *lethality*.

The data from which evidence for these assertions was obtained are those of the longitudinal study of 1,528 gifted people initiated by Lewis M. Terman in 1921.[1] Terman and his co-workers searched the public schools of the cities of California for exceptionally bright youngsters. His purposes were "to discover what gifted children are like as children, what sort of adult they become, and what some of the factors are that influence their development" (Oden, 1968). That study, begun a half-century ago, continues to this day.

Of the original 1,528 subjects, 857 were males and 671 were females. The sample was composed of children (mean age 9.7 years) with Stanford-Binet I.Q.'s of 140 or higher—the mean I.Q. was over 150—and an older group of high school students (mean age 15.2 years) who scored within the top 1 percent on the Terman Group Test of Mental Ability. The present analysis will be limited to male subjects, of whom approximately 80 percent were born between 1905 and 1914.

An enormous amount of data has been collected. At the time of the original investigation in 1921–22, the information included a developmental record, health history, medical examination, home and family background, school history, character trait ratings and personality evaluations by parents and teachers, interest tests, school achievement tests, and the like. Subsequently, there has been a long series of systematic follow-ups by mail or by personal field visits: in 1924, 1925, 1936, 1940, 1945, 1950, 1955, and 1960. Another follow-up study is planned for the near future. In the field studies (1921, 1927, 1940, and 1950), subjects and their families were interviewed, and data from intelligence tests, personality tests, and questionnaires were obtained.

The Terman studies have catalyzed two generations of thought, research, attitudinal changes, and educational developments. Detailed descriptions of the subjects at various ages, as well as summaries of the important findings, are available in a series of publications authored by Professor Terman and his chief co-worker, Melita Oden (Oden, 1968; Terman, 1925, 1940; Terman & Oden, 1947, 1959). Among longitudinal studies (Stone & Onque, 1959) the Terman Study is unique in many ways, including the extent to which its staff has continued to maintain contact with the subjects for nearly half a century. As of 1960, only 1.7 percent of the 1,528 subjects had been lost entirely.

Almost everyone in the psychological and pedagogical worlds now knows the basic findings of the Terman Study: that intellectually gifted children—far from being, as was once thought, spindly, weak, and maladjusted or one-sided—are, on the whole, more physically and mentally healthy and successful than their less-than-gifted counterparts. An unusual mind, a vigorous body, and a well-adjusted personality are not incompatible.[2]

A mortality summary for the Terman gifted group is as follows: In 1960—when the median age was 49.6—there had been 130 known deaths, 83 male and 47 female. The mortality rate was 9.8 percent for males and 7.2 percent for females—8.6 percent for the total group. According to Dublin's life tables (Dublin, Lotka, & Spiegelman, 1949), 13.9 percent of white males, 10.1 percent of white females, and 12 percent of a total cohort who survive to age 11 will have died before age 50. In 1960, the figures indicated a favorable mortality rate in the Terman group lower than the general white population of the same age.

By 1960, 110 of the 130 Terman group deaths—61 percent—had been due to natural causes. (Cardiovascular diseases ranked first with males, and cancer was first among females.) Accidents accounted for 19 male deaths, while only 5 females died in accidents. Five men had lost their lives in World War II. There were no homicide victims. One death was equivocal as to mode and could not be classified. As of 1960, suicide was responsible for 14 male and 8 female deaths; by 1970 there were 28 known deaths by suicide—20 men and 8 women.

An inspection of the listing of suicidal deaths (Table 16-1) suggested that there were several subgroups: student suicides, 30- and 40-year suicides, and middle-age suicides. Among the 28 suicides—of both sexes, ranging in age from 18 to 63 (a 45-year span), year of death from 1928 to 1968 (40 years), using a variety of lethal methods (pills, poison, drowning, guns)—there was a subgroup of 5 persons—numbers 14 to 18—all of whom were male, Caucasian, with I.Q.'s over 140, born about the same time (between 1907 and 1916), 4 of whom committed suicide within a year of each other (1965 or 1966), were in the "middle period" of their lives (ages at death 43, 50, 51, 53, and 58), and used the same method (all gunshot). This special subgroup seemed to offer a unique opportunity for an especially intensive investigation.[3]

A listing of all those subjects who had died indicated that there were 10 other males, born about the same time (1910 to 1914) as the 5 suicides, who had died of natural causes (either cancer or heart disease) during the same years that 4 of the 5 suicides had killed themselves (1965–66). The opportunity for a natural experiment, using blind analyses, was evident.

Thirty cases were selected to include the 5 suicides, the 10 natural deaths, and 15 individuals who were still alive. The latter two subgroups were matched with the 5 suicides in terms of age, occupational level, and father's occupational level. That these three subgroups are fairly well matched is indicated by the information in Table 16-2. (The reader should keep in mind that all 30 subjects were male, Caucasian, Califor-

TABLE 16-1. The 28 suicides in the Terman study as of 1970

	Age at Suicide	Year of Birth	Year of Suicide	Marital Status	Education	Occupational Level*	Method of Suicide
Men							
1.	18	1910	1928	S	High School	S	Poison
2.	19	1916	1935	S	2 yrs. college	V	Gunshot
3.	24	1908	1932	S	AB+	Grad S	Drowning
4.	28	1910	1938	S	MA	II	Poison
5.	33	1913	1946	M,D,M	High school	III	Barbiturate
6.	34	1913	1947	S	2 yrs. college	III	Carbon monoxide
7.	35	1904	1939	S	Ph.D.	I	Gunshot
8.	37	1909	1946	M	1 1/2 yrs. coll.	II	Poison
9.	42	1905	1947	M	2 yrs. college	II	Not known
10.	42	1916	1958	M,D,M,D,	AB * 3 yrs	I	Barbiturate
11.	45	1911	1956	M	3 yrs. college	II	Barbiturate
12.	45	1911	1956	M	AB, MA, LLB	IV	Carbon monoxide
13.	45	1913	1958	M	MD+	I	Poison
14.	43	1910	1953	M^4,D^4	2 yrs. college	II	Gunshot
15.	50	1916	1965	M,D,	BS	Inc.	Gunshot
16.	51	1915	1966	M,D,M	High school	III	Gunshot
17.	53	1913	1966	M	LLB	I	Gunshot
18.	58	1907	1966	M^3,D^3	2 yrs. college	I	Gunshot
19.	61	1905	1966	S	MA	Ret (1)	Barbiturate
20.	63	1905	1968	M,D,M	Ph.D.	I	Barbiturate

TABLE 16-1. (*Continued*)

	Age at Suicide	Year of Birth	Year of Suicide	Marital Status	Education	Occupational Level*	Method of Suicide
Women							
1.	22	1914	1936	S	2 yrs. college	S	Gunshot
2.	30	1905	1935	S	AB	A (librarian)	Carbon monoxide
3.	30	1913	1943	M	2 yrs. college	H	Gunshot
4.	32	1917	1949	W	3 yrs. college	A (physical therapist)	Barbiturate
5.	37	1916	1953	M^5D^4	2 yrs. college	A (writer)	Barbiturate
6.	40	1915	1955	M,D	3 yrs. college	H	Barbiturate
7.	44	1910	1954	M	MA	H	Barbiturate
8.	44	1910	1954	M,D	BS	A (social worker)	Barbiturate

*Occupational levels—Men: I. Professional; II. Official, managerial, and semiprofessional; III. Retail business, clerical, sales, skilled trades, and kindred; IV. Agricultural and related; V. Minor business, minor clerical, and semiskilled occupations.
Occupational groupings—Women: A. Professional and semiprofessional; B. Business (includes secretarial and office work as well as work in other business fields); H. Housewife.

TABLE 16-2. Occupations and ages for the suicide, natural death, and living subjects

	Suicide (N=5)	Natural (N=10)	Living (N=15)
Occupational Level			
I—Professional	2	5	7
II—Official, managerial, semiprofessional	2	4	6
III—Retail business, clerical and sales, skilled trades	1	1	2
Fathers' Occupational Level			
I—Professional	—	2	5
II—Official, managerial, semiprofessional	4	6	6
III—Retail business, clerical and sales, skilled trades	—	1	4
IV—Agricultural and related occupations	—	—	—
V—Minor business or clerical and semiskilled	1	1	—
Year of Birth			
1907	1	—	—
1908	—	—	—
1909	—	—	—
1910	1	1	3
1911	—	3	3
1912	1	1	4
1913	—	2	1
1914	—	3	3
1915	1	—	1
1916	1	—	—

nian, middle- and upper-middle-class, had I.Q.'s over 140, and were members of the Terman Gifted Study.) Each folder was edited by Mrs. Oden so that I could not tell whether the individual was dead or still alive. (Death certificates, newspaper clippings, and other "death clues" were removed.) The cases came to me, one at a time, in a random order. Although I was "blind" as to the suicide-natural death-living identity of each case, I did know the total numbers of cases in each subgroup.

☐ Rating of Perturbation (The Life Chart)

The cases were analyzed in terms of two basic continua (by which every life can be rated): perturbation and lethality. Perturbation refers to how upset (disturbed, agitated, sane-insane, discomposed) the individual is—rated, let's say, on a 1 to 9 scale[4]—and the latter to how likely it is that he will take his own life. (Lethality is discussed in the next section below.) For each of the 30 cases a rough chart of the individual's perturbation in early childhood, adolescence, high school, college, early marriage, and middle life was made. Clues were sought relating to tranquillity-disturbance, especially evidences of any *changes* and variations in the levels of perturbation. An attempt was made to classify the materials under such headings as "Early prodromata," "Failures," and "Signatures"—each explained below.

A "life chart" was constructed for each case, roughly following the procedures developed by Adolf Meyer (1951, 1952). In each case the folders were examined more or less chronologically in an attempt to order the materials in a temporal sequence while keeping in mind a number of related skeins.

One example of perturbation (from an individual who turned out to be among the five homogeneous suicides): A high school counselor wrote about one young man that he was "emotionally unstable, a physical roamer and morally erratic, excellent to teachers who treat him as an adult but very disagreeable to others." At the same time, the home visitor wrote: "I like him tremendously; he is better company than many teachers." Ten years later the subject himself wrote: "My gifts, if there were any, seem to have been a flash in the pan."

Early Prodromata

Under this category were included early important interpersonal relationships, especially with the subject's father and mother. The folder materials contained ratings by the subject of his attitudes and interactions with each of his parents. Some information relating to relationships with parents may be of special interest. In the 1940 questionnaire materials—when the modal age of the male subjects was 29.8 years—there was a series of questions concerning earlier conflict and attachment to mother and father. The responses of the five individuals who, as it turned out, made up the homogeneous suicide group seemed to have three interesting features: (*a*) in answer to the question "Everything considered, which was your favorite parent—father, mother, had no favorite?" only one of the five answered "father"; (*b*) in answer to the question about the amount of conflict between the individual and his father and the individual and his mother, two of the five indicated moderate to severe conflict with the father, whereas none of the five indicated moderate or severe conflict with the mother; (*c*) the one suicide who was most obviously rejected by his father (and who indicated that he had had conflict with him) was the only one (of the five) to indicate that "there has been a person . . . who had had a profound influence on his life." He wrote: "My father, I think, has been responsible for a code of ethics stressing honesty and fair dealing in all relations." It was this man's father who insisted that he come into the family business and then called him stupid when he, for reasons of his own temperament, did not show the same amount of aptitude for business that his older brother demonstrated.

In general, for the five suicidal subjects, for reasons that are not completely clear, it seemed that the relationships with the father were more critical than the relationships with the mother. It may be that any exceptionally bright, handsome young child tends to be mother's darling and, for those same reasons, tends to be father's rival—hence the built-in psychological tendency for there to be more friction between father and son than between mother and son. (It all sounds vaguely familiar; I believe that there is a Greek play about this theme.)

In the perusal of the records, evidence of trauma or stress in early life was sought: the death of a parent, divorce of the parents, stress (either overt or subtle) between the parents, or rejection of the subject by either parent. In retrospect, I had in mind a continuum ranging from tranquil and benign at one end to stressful and traumatic at the other.

The folder materials indicated that at the time the study began practically all of the subjects were described in essentially positive terms. For example, among the five subjects who, as it turned out, were the five homogeneous suicides, the following early descriptions by the home visitor appeared: "Attractive boy, well built, attractive features, charming." "Round chubby boy; very sweet face." "Winning little fellow, very fine all-around intelligence. The mother has excellent common sense and much is due to her." "Friendly, cheerful, freckled boy." "Tall for his age."

At the beginning, the psychological picture for most Terman youngsters was benign. However, in two of five homogeneous suicide cases there were, at an early age, already subtle prodromal clues of things to come: "He is the constant companion of his father but he is not his father's favorite." (A few years later, at age 14, a teacher wrote about this child: "This boy's parents are of two minds; his mother is for college, his father thinks that college is of no value to a person who expects to take up the business. The boy does not show very much hardmindedness. His type is more the theoretical, he prefers ideas to matter.") During the same year, his mother wrote that the child's worst faults were "his lack of application and irresponsibility"—perhaps not too unusual at age 14.

Another example: A child is ranked by his mother as "average" in the following traits: prudence, self-confidence, optimism, permanence of mood, egotism, and truthfulness. We do not know, of course, how much of this is accurate perception or how much is self-fulfilling prophecy.

Still another example: At age 14 there is a series of letters from the head of his boarding school. (The parents were away on an extended trip.) The headmaster wrote letters having to do with the boy's veracity, perhaps revealing his own special emphases: "We have every hope of making him a straightforward young man. We are people he cannot bluff, and with consistent vigilance the boy will be able to overcome his difficulties." A few years later his mother wrote: "His success will depend a good deal on his associates."

Least Successful

In Melita Oden's (1968) monograph she presented a number of measures and comparisons between the 100 Terman subjects ranked as most successful and an equal number adjudged to be least successful. For each of the 30 cases that I have analyzed, I tried to make some judgment along a success-failure continuum. In the end, 8 cases were labeled as conspicuous successes and 5 cases as failures. As it turned out, none of those cases rated by me as "most successful" subsequently committed suicide, whereas 3 of the cases rated as "least successful" killed themselves.[5]

An example: a very bright young boy (I.Q. 180) who did very well in high school, both academically and in extracurricular activities. When he was 15 years old Professor Terman wrote of him: "I think there is no doubt that he would make a desirable student at Stanford." Within a year, at age 16, he had entered Stanford and flunked out. Eventually, after working as a clerk, he returned to college after one year and graduated. He earned a law degree going to an evening law school. He then became an attorney in a large law firm. He was described as unsocial and shy. In his forties he says he was inclined to drink rather heavily, but not sufficiently to interfere with his work. His wife is described as vivacious and he as withdrawn. After a heart attack, his income suddenly became half of what he had been earning. He described himself as much less interested than his peers in vocational advancement or financial gain.

Signatures

In each case I looked for some special (albeit negative) indicators that might in themselves, or in combination, be prodromatic to suicide. For example, alcoholism, homosexuality, suicide threats, conspicuous achievement instability, depression, neurasthenia, and dyspnea could be listed. All 5 of the homogeneous suicides had one or more of these signature items. An additional 8 (of the 30 cases) also had signature items.

These items in themselves did not necessarily point to suicide, but when taken in combination with other features in the case they constituted an important aspect of the total prodromal picture.

Another example, this one emphasizing the lifelong instability of the individual: At age 7 his mother wrote that "he is inclined to take the line of least resistance." At the same time, the teacher rated him high in desire to excel, general intelligence, and originality; average in prudence, generosity, and desire to know; and low in willpower, optimism, and truthfulness. She indicated that, though he came from a good home, he was inclined to be moody and sulky. At age 8 his mother said he was strong-willed and liked to have his own way, that school was easy, and that he was making excellent grades. At age 10 his parents divorced. At age 12 the teacher reported that he was not a very good student and was doing only fair work, that he had rather lazy mental habits. At age 16 he graduated from high school with a C average. He did not attend college. In his twenties he became an artist. He was married. During World War II he was in the army. After the service he was unemployed and was described by his wife as "immature, unstable, irresponsible and extravagant." Because of his many affairs his wife, although stating she was fond of him, left him. She called him impulsive, romantic, and unstable. In his thirties he worked for a while as a commercial artist. He wrote to Professor Terman: "I am a lemon in your group." He indicated, as a joke, that his "hobby" was observing women from a bar stool. He remarried. He wrote to Professor Terman in relation to his art work that he "received much acclaim from those in the immediate audience," but that his works had not yet been displayed in any shows. His life was a series of ups and downs, some impulsive behaviors, and lifelong instability, although his status improved markedly in the late 1950s.

Apropos "up and downs" in general, any sudden *changes* in life status or life style can be looked upon as suspicious (i.e., prodromal to suicide), especially a change which marks a decline of status, position, or income. Generally, in suicide prevention work, one views any recent changes in life style as possible serious indicators of suicidal potential.

☐ Rating of Lethality (The Psychological Autopsy)

In addition to the life chart, the second procedure employed was one that I had some years before labeled "the psychological autopsy." This procedure is a retrospective reconstruction of an individual's life that focuses on lethality, that is, those features of his life that illuminate his intentions in relation to his own death, clues as to the type of death it was, the degree (if any) of his participation in his own death, and why the death occurred at that time. In general, the main function of the psychological autopsy is to help clarify deaths that are equivocal as to the *mode* of death—usually to help coroners and medical examiners decide if the death (which may be clear enough as to cause of death, e.g., asphyxiation due to drowning or barbiturate overdose) was of an accidental or suicide mode. Clearly, the *psychological* autopsy focuses on the role of the decedent in his own demise.

In the last few years, a number of individuals have written on this topic: Litman and his colleagues (Litman, Curphey, Shneidman, Farberow, & Tabachnick, 1963) have presented a general overview of its clinical use; Curphey (1961) has written of the use of this procedure from the medicolegal viewpoint of a forensic pathologist; and Weisman and Kastenbaum (1968) have applied this procedure to study the terminal phase of life. Elsewhere (Shneidman, 1969b), I have indicated that three separate types (and uses) of the psychological autopsy can be discerned. Each is tied to answering a different primary question as follows: (*a*) why did the individual commit suicide? (*b*) why did the individual die at this time? and (*c*) what is the most accurate mode of death in this case? Given a death which is clear as to *cause* of death but which is equivocal as to *mode* of death, the purpose of this type of psychological autopsy is to clarify the situation so as to arrive at the most accurate or appropriate mode of death—what it "truly" was. This original use of the psychological autopsy grew out of the joint efforts of the Los Angeles County chief medical examiner-coroner (then Dr. Theodore J. Curphey) and the staff of the Los Angeles Suicide Prevention Center as an attempt to bring the skills of the behavioral sciences to bear relevantly on the problems of equivocal deaths. In those 10 percent of coroner's cases where the mode of death is questionable or equivocal, this equivocation usually lies between the modes of accident and suicide. Here are three simplified examples:

1. *Cause of death:* asphyxiation due to drowning. Woman found in her swimming pool. Question: did she "drown" (accident), or was it intentional (suicide)?

2. *Cause of death:* multiple crushing injuries. Man found at the foot of a tall building. Question: did he fall (accident), or did he jump (suicide)? Or, even, was he pushed or thrown (homicide)?

3. *Cause of death:* barbiturate intoxication due to overdose. Woman found in her bed. Question: would she be surprised to know that she was dead (accident), or is this what she had planned (suicide)?

An outline for a psychological autopsy is presented in Table 16-3.

In the usual application of the psychological autopsy, the procedure is to interview close survivors (relatives and friends) of the decedent in

TABLE 16-3. Outline for psychological autopsy

1. Identifying information for victim (name, age, address, marital status, religious practices, occupation, and other details)
2. Details of the death (including the cause or method and other pertinent details)
3. Brief outline of victim's history (siblings, marriage, medical illnesses, medical treatment, psychotherapy, previous suicide attempts)
4. "Death history" of victim's family (suicides, cancer, other fatal illnesses, ages at death, and other details)
5. Description of the personality and life style of the victim
6. Victim's typical patterns of reaction to stress, emotional upsets, and periods of disequilibrium
7. Any recent—from last few days to last 12 months—upsets, pressures, tensions, or anticipations of trouble
8. Role of alcohol and drugs in (*a*) overall life style of victim and (*b*) in his death
9. Nature of victim's interpersonal relationships (including physicians)
10. Fantasies, dreams, thoughts, premonitions, or fears of victim relating to death, accident, or suicide
11. Changes in the victim before death (of habits, hobbies, eating, sexual patterns, and other life routines)
12. Information relating to the "life side" of victim (upswings, successes, plans)
13. Assessment of intention, i.e., role of the victim in his own demise
14. Rating of lethality
15. Reactions of informants to victim's death
16. Comments, special features, etc.

order to reconstruct his role in his own death. In the present study, I was, of course, limited to an examination of folder materials.

All the criteria that have been discussed above—perturbation, including early prodromata, failure, and signatures—were combined into one judgment of that individual's lethality, that is, the probability of his committing suicide in the present or the immediate future. In this process of judgment I was guided by two additional governing concepts: (*a*) the key role of the significant other and (*b*) the concept of a partial death (or chronic suicide or "burned-out" life).

The Crucial Role of the Significant Other

In an adult who is suicide prone, the behavior of the significant other, specifically the wife, seems either lifesaving or suicidogenic. My reading of the cases led me to feel that the wife could be the difference between life and death. In general, a wife who was hostile, independent, competitive, or nonsupporting of her husband who had some of the suicidal prodromata seemed to doom him to a suicidal outcome, whereas a wife who was helpful, emotionally supportive, and actively ancillary seemed to save a man who, in my clinical judgment at least, might otherwise have killed himself.

To the extent that these global clinical impressions of the important role of the spouse, in some cases, are correct, then, in those cases, there is an equal implication for suicide prevention, specifically that one must deal actively with the significant other. A regimen of therapy or a program of education must not fail to include the spouse; indeed it might be focused primarily on the wife and only secondarily on the potential suicide himself. Of course, the conscious and unconscious attitudes of the wife toward her husband must be carefully assessed. In a situation where the wife is deeply competitive (and might unconsciously wish him dead), using her as an auxiliary therapist would at best be an uphill climb. It is possible that in some cases a separation might be a lifesaving suggestion. All the above is not to impugn the wife; rather it is to involve her appropriately. It could very well be that, had the study focused on female suicides, the above prescription would be in relation to the complementary role of the husband.

The Concept of a Partial Death

This concept is well known in suicidology. In the technical literature it was given its most well known presentation by Karl Menninger (1938) in *Man Against Himself.* On valid psychological grounds it denies the dichotomous nature of psychological death and asserts that there are some lives that are moieties and only partial existences. Henry Murray (1967) expands this theme in his paper "Dead to the World":

> When I chose the phrase "dead to the world," I was thinking of a variety of somewhat similar psychic states characterized by a marked diminution or near-cessation of affect involving both hemispheres of concern, the inner and the outer world. Here it is as if the person's primal springs of vitality had dried up, as if he were empty or hollow at the very core of his being. There is a striking absence of anything but the most perfunctory and superficial social interactions; output as well as intake is at a minimum. . . . I have been talking about a diminution or cessation of feeling, one component of consciousness, on the assumption that this condition is somewhat analogous to a cessation of the whole of consciousness. If the cessation of feeling is temporary it resembles sleep; if it is permanent (a virtual atrophy

> of emotional life) it resembles death, the condition of the brain and body after the home fires of metabolism in the cortex have gone out. In a feelingless state the home fires are still burning but without glow or warmth.

That last statement about the home fires burning led me to think of a "burned-out" person—a person whose whole life was a kind of chronic suicide, a living death, a life without ambition and seemingly without purpose.

In the lethality ratings of the 30 cases, those that gave me the greatest difficulty were the chronic, nonachieving, "partial death" lives. I decided that I would rate this type of person among the first 12 in lethality, but not among the first 5. I did this with the conviction that this very style of living was in itself a kind of substitute for overt suicide; that in these cases, the *raison d'être* for committing overt suicide was absent, in that the truncated life itself was the significant inimical act (Shneidman, 1963).

☐ Results of Blind Clinical Analyses

On the day that I completed the blind analysis of the 30th case, I wrote a memorandum to Professor Sears that included the following:

> My analysis of the data and possibly the data themselves do not permit me to state with anything like full confidence which 5 cases were suicidal. The best that I can do—from my subjective ratings of each individual's perturbation and lethality—is to rank order 11 of the cases as the most likely candidates for suicidal status. I should be somewhat surprised if any of the other 19 individuals committed suicide. The rank order for suicide potential is as follows . . .

Then we—Mrs. Oden, Mrs. Buckholtz, and I—met to "break the key."

The facts revealed that the individual whom I had ranked as number 1 had, in fact, committed suicide, my number 2 had committed suicide, number 3 was living, number 4 had committed suicide, number 5 had committed suicide, and number 6 had committed suicide. Numbers 7 and 9 were living; numbers 8, 10, and 11 had died natural deaths. For the statistical record, the probability of choosing four or five of the five suicide cases correctly by chance alone is 1 out of 1,131—significant at the .000884 level. Obviously, the null hypothesis that there are no discernible prodromal clues to suicide can be discarded with a fair degree of confidence.

Table 16-4 presents a summary of the blind analysis data in terms of a brief vignette, signature items, success-failure ratings, perturbation ratings, lethality ratings, and suicide probability ranking for all 30 subjects.

TABLE 16-4. Blind ratings and outcomes for 30 matched male Terman study subjects

No.	Notable Characteristics	Signatures	Life Success	Pertur-bation	Lethal-ity	Suicide Rank	Postscript
1	NP hospitalization; divorced; great perturbation; talks of suicide at 15 and 20	Suicide threats	C−	7–8	High	1	Committed suicide
2	Deaf; professional; low drive for worldly success	Nonachiever	C	3–4	Low	12+	Living
3	Flunked out of college; obtained LLB; shy; ups and downs; drop in income; alcohol	Alcohol; ups and downs	C	6–7	High	2	Committed suicide
4	Insurance man in heart attack rut	—	B	3–4	Low	12+	Died—heart
5	Ambitious bank officer	—	B	3–4	Low	12+	Died—cancer
6	Brilliant professor of medicine; textbook author; good life	—	A	1–2	Low	12+	Died—cancer
7	Set back at adolescence by home stresses; obese; no college aspirations; withdrawn; low-level job; underachiever; stabilized	Underachiever; stabilized	C−	6–7	?	11	Died—heart
8	Physician; too high standards for people; tones down	—	B+	5–6	Low	12+	Died—heart
9	Hand-driving rancher; dominated by mother	—	B	5–6	Low	12+	Died—cancer
10	Stable geologist; steady life	—	A	1–2	Low	12+	Living
11	Lithographer; brilliant; no family back-up;	Underachiever	C	5–6	Low	12+	Living
12	Multimarried; emphysemic; inventor; ups and downs	Dyspnea; failure	C	6–7	High	4	Committed suicide
13	Scion of business fortune; straight success line; father helpful and supportive	—	A	4–5	Low	12+	Living
14	Quietly successful in own small business; tranquil life	—	B	3–4	Low	12+	Living
15	Had all advantages; did rather well but not superlatively	—	B	3–4	Low	12+	Living
16	Neurasthenic; esoteric mother; underachiever; chronic suicide	Depression; neurasthenia	C−	6–7	?	7	Living

17	Artist; unstable; flighty; impetuous; willful	Instability	B−	7–8	?	5	Committed suicide
18	Insurance man; stable life; interesting siblings	—	B	3–4	Low	12+	Living
19	Brilliant child and siblings; needed a father; stabilized by second wife	—	B	4–5	Low	12+	Living
20	Pleasant man; pleasant life; pleasant family; likes work	—	B	2–3	Low	12+	Living
21	Early genius; hiatus; never fully recovers; wife commits suicide	—	B	5–6	Mdn	12+	Died—heart
22	Shy, depressed artist; multiple illnesses; making it	Depression; ill	B	6–7	?	9	Living
23	Unhappy; forced into father's business; rejected by father; always second to sibling; 4 divorces; unstable; downhill; alone	Depression; instability	B+	7–8	?	6	Committed suicide
24	Average school administrator; ordinary stresses	—	B	4–5	Low	12+	Living
25	Well-adjusted, stable attorney; great relationship with father; good life success	—	A	2–3	Low	12+	Living
26	Depressed engineer; hypomanic wife; his job holds him	Depression	B	6–7	Mdn+	8	Died—cancer
27	Scientist; brilliant beginning; wife drains him; good but not great	—	B+	3–4	Low	12+	Living
28	Engineer; overcame adolescent crisis and parents' divorce; good marriage; has grown steadily	—	B	4–5	Low	12+	Died—heart
29	Author; asthmatic; depressed; strong support from wife	Dyspnea; depression	A−	5–6	?	10	Died—cancer
30	Professional; stormy life; alcoholic; competing wife	Alcohol; instability	B−	6–7	?	3	Living

(The "Postscript" information was not available to me when I made these ratings and was added to the chart after all the other ratings and rankings had been made.)

Much of my analysis of these 30 cases was inferential, sometimes even intuitive—which is to say that not every clue or cognitive maneuver can be recovered, much less communicated. But for what it is worth, I deeply believe that a number of experienced professional persons could have done as well. Indeed, I feel that the volumes of information generated in the past 20 years by suicidologists furnish the working concepts and the background facts for making precisely this kind of (potentially lifesaving) judgment every day of the year in the practical clinical situation. Knowledge of this sort is now an established part of the new discipline of suicidology.

One striking result was that among those who committed suicide in their fifties, the pattern of life consistent with this outcome seemed clearly discernible *by the time they were in their late twenties.* The data subsequent to age 30 served, in most cases, primarily to strengthen the impression of suicidal outcome that I had formulated at that point. Those relatively few cases in which this earlier impression was reversed in the thirties and forties had one or two specific noteworthy elements within them: (*a*) a psychologically supporting spouse or (*b*) a "burning-out" of the individual's drive and affect. In the latter cases, this condition of psychological aridity and successlessness seemed to be the price for continued life.

What were some of the main clinical impressions relating to adult suicide in this gifted male group? In the briefest possible vignette, my main overall clinical impression might be formulated in this way: the *father,* even in his absence, *starts* the life course to suicide; *school and work* (and the feelings of inferiority and chronic low-grade hopelessness) *exacerbate* it; and the *wife* can, in some cases, effect the *rescue* from it (or otherwise play a sustaining or even a precipitating role in it).

Among the five homogeneous suicides, three types of suicidal prodomata—relating to instability, trauma, and control—could be differentiated.

Instability

In general, suicide is more likely to occur in a life where there has been instability (rather than stability). As used here, instability is practically synonymous with perturbation.

Chronic Instability

Evidences of chronic, long-term instability would include neuropsychiatric hospitalization, talk or threat of suicide, alcoholism, multiple divorces, and any unusually stressful psychodynamic background—even though these bits of evidence occurred in as few as one of the five cases. Examples: Mr. A: NP hospitalization, divorce, talk of suicide at 15 and at 20; Mr. B: unstable personality, divorced, flighty behavior, few stabilizing forces; Mr. C: unhappy man, rejected by father, always second-best, four marriages, highly perturbed.

Recent Downhill Course

A recent downhill change that occurs in a career marked by ups and downs, that is, a generally unstable life course, was characteristic of suicidal persons. Specifically, these changes include a marked sudden decrease in income, sudden acute alcoholism, a change in work, and divorce or separation, especially where the wife leaves the husband for another man. In general, a sudden, inexplicable change for the worse is a bad augury. This means that in an individual with an up and down history, the most recent bit of information can be singularly irrelevant, if not outright misleading. Examples: Mr. D: highly recommended for university, flunked out of college, went back to school, earned an LL.B. degree, shy, alcoholic, sudden drop in income, up and down course, does not "burn out"; Mr. E: inventor, multiple marriages, up and down course, severe emphysema. (N.B., dyspnea can be an especially incapacitating symptom and has been related to suicide in special ways [Farberow, McKelligott, Cohen, & Darbonne, 1966].)

Trauma

Early Childhood or Adolescent Trauma

Examples would include acute rejection by one or both parents, lack of family psychological support, and separation or divorce of the parents. A crisis in adolescence can turn a life toward lower achievement.

Adult Trauma

This includes poor health, such as asthma, emphysema, severe neurosis, obesity, and multiple illnesses. Another major type of adult trauma relates to the spouse, either rejection by the wife for another man or being married to a hyperactive (and competing) wife, who has changed from the woman he married. Examples: Mr. F, a depressed engineer whose top security job in aerospace holds him together; and Mr. G, who has a complicated, hypomanic, and successful wife toward whom he is deeply ambivalent.

Controls

Outer Controls

These are the compensations or stabilizing influences in individuals who, without these assets from other than within themselves, would be more perturbed than they are and might commit suicide. Examples: the stabilizing work of Mr. F, mentioned above; the stabilizing wife of asthmatic Mr. H, a woman who nurses him and keeps the world from inappropriately intruding upon him or exhausting him. She husbands his limited energies.

Inner Controls

These inner controls are not the usual strengths or positive features or assets of personality or character. They are the negative inner controls of default. One such is what occurs in some individuals who are perturbed early in their lives, who, if they survive, stabilize or simmer down or "burn out" in their fifties or sixties.

Examples: Mr. J: He was psychologically traumatized during adolescence by home stresses. He has no hobbies, no college aspirations, is withdrawn, and works as a mechanic and caretaker.

Mr. K: Extremely high I.Q. He is neurasthenic, has a mother with esoteric tastes, experiences back and shoulder pains just like his father, and is unable to hold a job as a professional. He calls himself "an unsuccessful animal." He ends up working as a clerk in a large company. His stance is that—to use an example from Melville—of a contemporary Bartleby ("I prefer not to"), what Menninger (1938) has called a "chronic suicide," where the truncated life itself can be conceptualized as a partial death.

☐ Discussion

Whereas the clinical challenge is to be intuitive, to display diagnostic acumen, and to manifest therapeutic skill, the scientific challenge is to state theory and to explicate facts in a replicable way. I feel obligated to address myself to the theoretical side of this issue.

I shall begin with low-level theory, that is, an explication of the specific items that guided my thinking in choosing the individuals whom I believed had committed suicide. Some 10 items were in my mind: (*a*) early (grammar school, adolescence, or college age) evidences of instability, including dishonesty; (*b*) rejection by the father; (*c*) multiple marriages; (*d*) alcoholism; (*e*) an unstable occupational history; (*f*) ups and downs in income; (*g*) a crippling physical disability, especially one involving dyspnea; (*h*) disappointment in the use of one's potential, that is, a disparity between aspiration and accomplishment; (*i*) any talk or hint of self-destruction; and (*j*) a competitive or self-absorbed spouse. In summary, this low-level theoretical explication states that a bright male Caucasian who committed suicide in his fifties was apt to be: rejected by his father, adolescently disturbed, multimarried, alcoholic, occasionally unsettled or unsuccessful, disappointed in himself and disappointing to others, unstable, lonely, and perturbed with a penchant for precipitous action.

At a somewhat deeper level, and thus more theoretical, are the elements of rejection, disparity between aspiration and accomplishment, instability, and perturbation. At a still deeper level (and even more theoretical) is the notion that the suicidal person is one who believes that he has not had his father's love and seeks it symbolically without success throughout his life, eventually hoping, magically, to gain it by a singular act of sacrifice or expiation. The most theoretical formulation might be stated as follows: those gifted men who committed suicide in their fifties did not have that internalized viable approving parental homunculus that—like a strong heart—seems necessary for a long life.

It is interesting to reflect that the five gifted suicidal persons of this study constituted an essentially nonpsychotic group. This assertion is not to gainsay that each of them was severely perturbed at the time of the suicide, but they were not "crazy"; that is, they did not manifest the classical hallmarks of psychosis such as hallucinations, delusions, dereistic thinking, and the like. Their perturbation took the form—prior to the overt suicidal act—of alcoholism, other than one marriage (single, divorced, or multiple marriages), and chronic loneliness, occupational ups and downs, impetuosity and impulsivity, and inner (as well as overt) agitation. Although, as it is in most suicidal persons, one can suppose that their thought processes were circumscribed ("tunnel vision") and tended to be dichotomous ("either a happy life or death"), there was no direct evidence to indicate that they were psychotically bizarre or paleological (Schneidman, 1969a).

As has been noted by Oden (1968), the "magic combination" for life success among the gifted is not a simple one. For suicide also the equation is a combination of obvious and subtle elements. Many factors, none of which alone seems to be sufficient, appear to coexist in a suicidal case. And, as in any equation, there are factors on both the positive (life-loving, biophilic, suicide-inhibiting) and the negative (death-loving, necrophilic, suicide-promoting) sides.

In the algebra of life and death, the wife may play an absolutely vital role, holding her spouse to life or, at the worst, stimulating or even provoking him to suicide. Every suicidologist knows that suicide is most often a two-person event, a dyadic occurrence, and for this reason, if no other, the management and prevention of suicide almost always has to involve the significant other. With high suicide risk gifted males, my impression is that the most important lifesaving task is not directly to the potentially suicidal person, but through the wife—especially in concert with the family physician.

Currently, there is a small number of retrospective studies seeking to establish some of the early precursors of suicide among special populations presumed to be intellectually superior, specifically physicians and university graduates. A few words about each.

Blachly and his colleagues (Blachly, Disher, & Roduner, 1968) have made an analysis of 249 suicides by physicians reported in the obituary columns of the *Journal of the American Medical Association* between May 1965 and November 1967. Deaths from suicide exceeded the combined deaths from automobile accidents, airplane crashes, drowning, and homicide. The mean age of the suicidal group was 49. Blachly and his associates mailed questionnaires to the next of kin (usually the widow); about 30 percent of the inquiries were returned, many with extensive comments. The suicide rate varied greatly among the medical specialties, ranging from a low of 10 per 100,000 among pediatricians to a high of 61 per 100,000 among psychiatrists. A résumé of Blachly's main findings is presented in Table 16-5.

Paffenbarger and his associates (Paffenbarger & Asnes, 1966; Paffenbarger, King, & Wing, 1969) have completed analyses of over 50,000 medical and social histories (including physical and psychological evaluations) of former male students at the University of Pennsylvania and at Harvard covering a 34-year period from 1916 to 1950. Their original focus was on individuals who subsequently died of coronary heart disease. The data drew their attention to those who had committed suicide—whom they then compared with their nonsuicidal cohorts. The 4,000 known deaths included 225 suicide deaths. Their findings relative to suicide point to paternal deprivation through early loss or death of the father, loneliness and underjoining in college, dropping out of college, and feelings of rejection, self-consciousness, and failure during the college years.

TABLE 16-5. Summary of findings of three studies of precursors to suicide among intellectually superior subjects

Present Clinical Impressions*	Blachly's Tabular Results	Paffenbarger's Statistical Findings
a. early (before 20) evidences of instability, including dishonesty	a. mentally depressed or disturbed	a. college education of father
b. actual or felt rejection by the father	b. prior suicidal attempt or statement of suicidal intent	b. college education of mother
c. multiple marriages	c. heavy drinker or alcoholic	c. father professional
d. alcoholism	d. drug addiction or heavy drug user	d. father dead
e. an unstable occupational history	e. "inadequate" financial status	e. parents separated
f. ups and downs in income (not to mention ups and downs in mood)	f. death of close relative in decedent's childhood	f. cigarette smoker in college
g. a crippling physical disability, especially one involving dyspnea	g. suicide of relative	g. attended boarding school
h. disappointment in the use of potential, i.e., a disparity between aspiration and accomplishment	h. seriously impaired physical health	h. college dropout
i. any talk or hint of self-destruction		i. nonjoiner in college
j. a competitive or self-absorbed spouse		j. allergies
		k. underweight
		l. self-assessed ill health
		m. self-consciousness
		n. subject to worries
		o. feelings of being watched or talked about
		p. insomnia
		q. secretive-seclusiveness
		r. "anxiety-depression" index (including nervousness, moodiness, exhaustion, etc.)

*Of course, not all of these features occurred in any one suicidal case; conversely, some of these features occurred in as few as one suicidal case. It was the "total impression" that counted most.

Dr. Caroline Thomas (1969)—like Paffenbarger, a cardiologist—is studying the causes of death among 1,337 former medical students of the Johns Hopkins University School of Medicine from 1948 to 1964. Her present project—as did Paffenbarger's—began as a study of the precursors of coronary heart disease but, in light of the data (14 suicides among the 31 premature deaths) shifted to include precursors of suicide. That project is currently in the hypothesis stage. Interesting results should be forthcoming.

What may be of especial interest in Table 16-5 are the common elements or threads in the findings of these three projects and the clinical findings of this present study. To what extent these findings relate only to the intellectually superior and to what extent they are ubiquitous is a matter for further study; nonetheless it is not premature to say that, on the basis of currently known data, it would appear that the common findings would seem to have general application.

Endnotes

[1]This study was conducted while the author was a Fellow at the Center for Advanced Study in the Behavioral Sciences, 1969–70. Arrangements were made for confidential access to the research records by Professor Robert R. Sears who, with Professor Lee J. Cronbach, is one of the two scientific executors of the Terman Study. The data themselves are the property of Stanford University. The author is especially grateful to Mrs. Melita Oden and Mrs. Sheila Buckholtz, long-time staff members of the Gifted Study, for their extensive help in preparing relevant data for his use and for advice and guidance along the way.

[2]As part of the Terman Study of the Gifted, Catharine M. Cox (1926) completed a comprehensive retrospective study of the childhood intelligence of 301 historically eminent men born after 1450. Of the individuals discussed in her study, 119 were thought to have I.Q.'s of 140 or higher. (As examples, here are some names—1 person in each of the five-step I.Q. intervals from 140 to 190: Carlyle, Jefferson, Descartes, Hume, Pope, J. Q. Adams, Voltaire, Schelling, Pascal, Leibnitz, and J. S. Mill.) As to suicide among this extraordinary group, so far as can be ascertained, only 1 of the 301 eminent men died by killing himself—Thomas Chatterton, at age 17.

[3]In the technical literature on suicide, one does not find many anamnestic or case history reports for individuals who have *committed* suicide. (Materials for attempted suicides are another story; the data for them are far more plentiful.) Only four sources—spread over a half-century—come to mind: Ruth Caven's (1928, pp. 198–248) extensive diaries of two young adults, Binswanger's (1958) detailed report of 33-year-old Ellen West, Kobler and Stotland's (1964, pp. 98–251) extensive reports of four hospitalized patients—ages 23, 34, 37, and 56—in a "dying hospital," all of whom committed suicide within the same month, and Alvarez' (1961) annotated bibliography.

[4]The following point must be strongly emphasized: a basic assumption in this entire scheme is that an individual's orientations toward his cessation are biphasic; that is, any adult, at any given moment, has (*a*) more or less long-range, relatively chronic, pervasive, habitual, characterological orientations toward cessation as an integral part of his total psy-

chological makeup (affecting his philosophy of life, need systems, aspirations, identification, conscious beliefs, etc.); and (*b*) is also capable of having acute, relatively short-lived, exacerbated, clinically sudden shifts of cessation orientation. Indeed, this is what is usually meant when one says that an individual has become "suicidal." It is therefore crucial in any complete assessment of an individual's orientation toward cessation to know both his habitual *and* his at-that-moment orientations toward cessation. (Failure to do this is one reason why previous efforts to relate "suicidal state" with psychological test results have been barren.)

[5]Among the 20 men who committed suicide, at least 3 were considered outstandingly successful by gifted group standards: 2 in the 1960 study and 1 who died in 1938 who had a brilliant record until his death at the age of 28. Conversely, 3 were considered least successful: 2 in 1940 (they had died before 1960) and 1 in the 1960 evaluation (Oden, 1968).

References

Alvarez, W. C. (1961). *Minds that came back.* Philadelphia: Lippincott.

Binswanger, L. (1958). The case of Ellen West. In R. May, E. Angel, & H. F. Ellenberger (Eds.), *Existence* (pp. 237–364). New York: Basic Books.

Blachly, P. H., Disher, W., & Roduner, G. (1968). Suicide by physicians. *Bulletin of Suicidology,* 1–18.

Cavan, R. S. (1928). *Suicide.* Chicago: University of Chicago Press.

Cox, C. M. (1926). The early mental traits of three hundred geniuses. *Genetic Studies of Genius* (Vol. 2). Stanford: Stanford University Press.

Curphey, T. J. (1961). The role of the social scientist in the medicolegal certification of death from suicide. In N. L. Farberow & E. S. Shneidman (Eds.), *The cry for help.* New York: McGraw-Hill.

Dublin, L. I., Lotka, A. J., & Spiegelman, M. (1949). *Length of Life.* New York: Ronald Press.

Farberow, N. L., McKelligott, W., Cohen, S., & Darbonne, A. (1966). Suicide among patients with cardiorespiratory illnesses. *Journal of the American Medical Association, 195,* 422–428.

Kobler, A. L., & Stotland, E. (1964). *The end of hope.* New York: Free Press of Glencoe.

Litman, R. E., Curphey, T. J., Shneidman, E. S., Farberow, N. L., & Tabachnick, N. D. (1963). Investigations of equivocal suicides. *Journal of the American Medical Association, 184,* 924–29.

Menninger, K. A. (1938). *Man against himself.* New York: Harcourt, Brace.

Meyer, A. (1951). The life chart and the obligation of specifying positive data in psychopathological diagnosis. In E. E. Winters (Ed.), *The collected works of Adolf Meyer: Vol. 3* (pp. 52–56). Baltimore: The Johns Hopkins Press.

Meyer, A. (1952). Mental and moral health in a constructive school program. In E. E. Winters (Ed.), *The collected works of Adolf Meyer: Vol. 4* (pp. 350–370). Baltimore: Johns Hopkins Press.

Murray, H. A. (1967). Dead to the world: The passions of Herman Melville. In E. S. Shneidman (Ed.), *Essays in self-destruction.* New York: Science House.

Oden, M. H. (1968). The fulfillment of promise: 40-year follow-up of the Terman gifted group. *Genetic Psychology Monographs, 77,* 3–93.

Paffenbarger, R. S., Jr., & Asnes, D. P. (1966). Chronic disease in former college students. III. Precursors of suicide in early and middle life. *American Journal of Public Health, 56,* 1026–36.

Paffenbarger, R. S., Jr., King, S. H., & Wing, A. L. (1969). Chronic disease in former college students. IX. Characteristics in youth that predispose to suicide and accidental death in later life. *American Journal of Public Health, 59,* 900–908.

Shneidman, E. S. (1963). Orientations toward death: A vital aspect of the study of lives. In R. W. White (Ed.), *The study of lives.* New York: Atherton Press. Reprinted, with discussion, in *International Journal of Psychiatry,* 1966, *2,* 167–200; and in Shneidman, E. S., Farberow, N. L., & Litman, R. E., (1970), *The psychology of suicide.* New York: Science House.

Shneidman, E. S. (1969a). Logical content analysis: An explication of styles of "concludifying." In G. Gerbner et al. (Eds.), *The analysis of communication content.* New York: John Wiley & Sons.

Shneidman, E. S. (1969b). Suicide, Lethality and the psychological autopsy. In E. S. Shneidman & M. J. Ortega (Eds.), *Aspects of depression.* Boston: Little, Brown & Co.

Stone, A. A., & Onque, G. C. (1959). *Longitudinal studies of child personality.* Cambridge: Harvard University Press.

Terman, L. M. (1925). *Genetic studies of genius: I. Mental and physical traits of a thousand gifted children.* Stanford: Stanford University Press.

Terman, L. M. (1940, October 4). Psychological approaches to the biography of genius. *Science, 92,* 293–301.

Terman, L. M., & Oden, M. H. (1947). *Genetic studies of genius: IV. The gifted child grows up.* Stanford: Stanford University Press.

Terman, L. M., & Oden, M. H. (1959). *Genetic studies of genius: V. The gifted child at mid-life.* Stanford: Stanford University Press.

Thomas C. B. (1969). Suicide among us: Can we learn to prevent it? *Johns Hopkins Medical Journal, 125,* 276–85.

Weisman, A. D., & Kastenbaum, R. (1968). The psychological autopsy: A study of the terminal phase of life. *Community Mental Health Journal Monograph, 4,* 1–59.

17

CHAPTER

A Conspectus of the Suicidal Scenario

The Experience of Suicide: Accounts of Three Cases

Let us consider some verbatim excerpts from the case transcripts of three failed suicides—each of whom performed an act that is ordinarily fatal, and fortuitously, against all realistic odds, survived to tell us something about the inside view of the suicidal scenario. What are the common threads of psychological gold and silver in the ore and slag of these heated reports? Both as a preview to all of the following text and as a guide to the proactive reading of the three excerpts, let us keep in mind these half-dozen key words (to be defined and discussed in this chapter): *pain, needs, frustration* (of needs), *constriction, ambivalence,* and *cessation* (of pain).

> *Immolator:* I remember sitting in the car, and it was sort of like a blank in my mind. I felt very calm. I felt a kind of hush over my body. That everything was going to be OK. And I remember then pouring the gasoline first over the front seat, and of course over myself to a great extent. Even then, no thoughts went through my head at all of the pain that it was going to entail, the misery, hurt, any of that. I guess I didn't think that burns would really hurt, but none of that went through my head. It just felt good. It was

Reprinted from R. W. Maris, A. L. Berman, J. T. Maltsberger & R. I. Yufit (Eds.), *Assessment and Prediction of Suicide.* New York: Guilford Press, 1992, pp. 31–49. With permission.

the first time, in fact, that I had felt at peace, that I wasn't hurting inside. And for once it seemed like I had taken care of my problems and that my pain would just go away. It was not going to exist any more, especially my mental pain. And I remember very slowly striking the match and at that moment the fumes ignited, just a tremendous explosion.

Jumper: I was so desperate, I felt, "My God, I can't face this thing." Everything was like a terrible whirlpool of confusion. And I thought to myself, "There's only one thing to do: I just have to lose consciousness." That's the only way to get away from it. The only way to lose consciousness, I thought, was to jump off something good and high. I just figured I had to get outside. I just slipped out. No one saw me. And I got to the other building by walking across that catwalk thing, sure that someone would see me, you know, out of all those windows. The whole building is made of glass. And I just walked around until I found this open staircase. And as soon as I saw it, I just made a beeline right up to it. And then I got to the fifth floor and everything got very dark all of a sudden, and all I could see was this balcony. Everything around it just blacked out. It was just like a circle. That was all I could see, just the balcony. I climbed over it and I just let go. I was so desperate.

Shooter: There was no peace to be found. I had done all I could and was still sinking. I sat many hours seeking answers and all, but there was a silent wind and no answers. The answer was in my head. It was all clear now: Die. The next day a friend of mine offered to sell me a shotgun. I bought it. My first thought was, What a mess this is going to make. The next day I began to say goodbye to people. Not actually saying it, but expressing it silently. I didn't sleep. The dreams were reality and reality dreams. One by one I turned off my outside channels to the world. My mind became locked on my target. My thoughts were, Soon it will all be over. I can obtain the peace I have sought so long for. The will to survive and succeed had been crushed and defeated. I was like a general alone on a battlefield being encroached upon by my enemy and its hordes: fear, hate, self-depreciation, desolation. I felt I had to have the upper hand, to control my environment, so I sought to die rather than surrender. Destiny and reality began to merge. Those around me were as shadows, apparitions, but I was not actually conscious of them, only aware of myself and my plight. Death swallowed me long before I pulled the trigger. I was locked within myself. The world through my eyes seemed to die with me. It was like I was to push the final button to end this world. I committed myself to the arms of Death. There comes a time when all things cease to shine, when the rays of hope are lost. As I look back on that day it is as if this was another person's life. I was ending. I placed the gun under my chin. Then I remember a tremendous explosion of lights like fireworks consumed within a brilliant radiance. Thus did the pain become glorious, becoming an army rallied to the side of death to help destroy my life which I could feel leaving my body with each rushing surge of blood. I was engulfed in total darkness.

It is possible to conceptualize the commonalities of these (and all other) suicides in terms of the basic and omnipresent elements of the suicidal scenario—a "conspectus" of suicide, as it were. These fundamentals are as follows:

1. A sense of unbearable psychological *pain,* which is directly related to thwarted psychological *needs.*
2. Traumatizing *self-denigration*—a self-image that will not include tolerating psychological pain.
3. A marked *constriction* of the mind and an unrealistic narrowing of life's actions.
4. A sense of *isolation*—a feeling of desertion and the loss of support of significant others.
5. An overwhelmingly desperate feeling of *hopelessness*—a sense that nothing effective can be done.
6. A conscious decision that *egression*—leaving, exiting, or stopping life—is the *only* (or at least the best possible) solution to the problem of unbearable pain.

All these elements combine to result in suicide.

☐ The Ten Commonalities of Suicide

In previous publications (Shneidman 1985, 1986, 1987, 1989, 1990), I have referred to "the ten commonalities of suicide"—specifically, the common psychological features in human self-destruction. They are reproduced in Table 17-1 and are discussed briefly below. But first, a few preliminary remarks.

TABLE 17-1. The ten commonalities of suicide

I. The common purpose of suicide is to seek a solution.
II. The common goal of suicide is cessation of consciousness.
III. The common stimulus in suicide is intolerable psychological pain.
IV. The common stressor in suicide is frustrated psychological needs.
V. The common emotion in suicide is hopelessness-helplessness.
VI. The common cognitive state in suicide is ambivalence.
VII. The common perceptual state in suicide is constriction.
VIII. The common action in suicide is egression.
IX. The common interpersonal act in suicide is communication of intention.
X. The common consistency in suicide is with lifelong coping patterns.

Note From Shneidman, E. S. (1985). *Definition of Suicide.* New York: Wiley. Copyright © 1985 by Edwin S. Shneidman.

Suicidal phenomena can be understood in various ways. (I discuss these different approaches at the end of the chapter.) Clearly, one of the principal ways is the psychological approach, and the key to the psychological understanding of suicide is *pain*—psychological pain, the pain that the suicidal individual feels in *that* situation in his or her life. In this sense, suicide is a practical act intended to stop the unbearable flow (in consciousness) of intolerable pain. As Murray (1938) says in his great book, *Explorations in Personality,* suicide is clearly not adaptive, but it is just as clearly uniquely adjustive. Similarly, Baechler (1975), in his intensive book-length essay on suicide, tells us that in order to understand a specific case of suicide we must know what problem it was intended to solve. And Kelly (1961), in a way that is both philosophical and psychological, views suicide by proposing that each individual has his or her own private (unique, idiosyncratic) epistemology—his or her personal construct of the world—and that a suicide is to be understood as that individual's efforts to validate this personal construct.

Let us now consider the ten psychological commonalities of suicide (see Table 17-1), together with some illustrative quotations from the three suicidal vignettes presented above:

1. The Common Purpose of Suicide Is To Seek a Solution

First of all, suicide is not a random, pointless, or purposeless act. To the sufferer, it seems to be the only available answer to a real puzzler: "How am I to get out of this? What am I to do?" Its purpose is to seek a solution to a perceived crisis—the problem of overwhelming pain—that is generating intense suffering. To understand what a suicide is about, one must know the psychological problems it was intended to resolve. The general question one must put to the suicidal person is this: "What is going on?"

> "And for once it seemed like I had taken care of my problems."
> "And I thought to myself, 'There's only one thing to do . . .' "
> "The answer was in my head."

2. The Common Goal of Suicide Is Cessation of Consciousness

Suicide is both a moving toward and a moving away. The common practical goal of suicide is the stopping of the painful flow of consciousness. Suicide is best understood not so much as a movement toward a reified Death as it is in terms of "cessation"—the complete (and irreversible) stopping of one's consciousness of unendurable pain. Suicide, as R. E. Litman (personal communication, 1990) points out, involves not only pain, but the individual's unwillingness to tolerate that pain, the decision not to endure it, and the active will to stop it. This means that in psychotherapy one needs to focus on the amelioration of the pain, as well as the "character" that has chosen not to tolerate it.

> "It [the mental pain]] was not going to exist any more."
> "I felt, 'My God, I can't face this thing . . . I just have to lose consciousness.' "
> "Die. . . . Soon it will all be over."

3. The Common Stimulus in Suicide Is Unendurable Psychological Pain

In any close analysis, suicide is best understood as a combined movement toward cessation *and* a movement away from intolerable, unendurable, unacceptable anguish. It is psychological pain of which I am speaking: "metapain," the pain of feeling pain. From a traditional psychodynamic view, hostility, shame, guilt, fear, protest, longing to join a deceased loved one, and the like have singly and in combination been identified as the root factor(s) in suicide. It is none of these; rather, it is the pain involved in any or all of them, together with the unwillingness to endure that idiosyncratically defined pain. Psychological pain is the center of suicide and constitutes the chief hurdle that must be lowered before any kind of therapy can be effectively lifesaving. The basic clinical rule is this: If the level of suffering is reduced (often just a little bit), the individual can choose to live.

> "It was the first time . . . that I wasn't hurting inside. And for once it seemed . . . the [mental] pain would just go away."
> "I was so desperate."
> "I can obtain the peace I have sought so long for."

4. The Common Stressor in Suicide Is Frustrated Psychological Needs

The psychological pain that is central to suicide is driven, created by, and sustained by frustrated, blocked, or thwarted psychological needs. Suicide is best understood not so much as an unreasonable act—every suicide seems logical to the person who commits it (given that person's major premises, styles of syllogizing, and constricted focus)—as it is a reaction to unfulfilled psychological needs.

In order to understand suicide in this kind of context, we need to ask a much broader question, which I believe is the key: What purposes do most human acts (including suicide) intend to accomplish? The best nondetailed answer to that question is that, in general, human acts are intended to satisfy a variety of human needs. There is no compelling *a priori* reason why a typology (or classification or taxonomy) of suicidal acts might not parallel a general classification of human needs. Such as classification of psychological needs can be found in Murray's *Explorations in Personality* (1938). Murray's discussion of human needs is a ready-made, viable taxonomy of the essential underpinnings of suicidal behaviors. Table 17-2 presents a partial listing of Murray's explication of psychological needs.

TABLE 17-2. A partial listing of the Murray psychological needs

Abasement. To submit passively to external force. To accept injury, blame, criticism, punishment. To surrender. To become resigned to fate. To admit inferiority, error, wrongdoing, or defeat. To confess and atone. To blame, belittle, or mutilate the self. To seek and enjoy pain, punishment, illness, and misfortune.

Achievement. To accomplish something difficult. To master, manipulate, or organize physical objects, human beings, or ideas. To do this as rapidly and independently as possible. To overcome obstacles and attain a high standard. To excel oneself. To rival and surpass others. To increase self-regard by the successful exercise of talent.

Affiliation. To draw near and enjoyably cooperate or reciprocate with an allied other (who resembles the subject or who likes the subject). To please and win affection of a respected person. To adhere and remain loyal to a friend.

Aggression. To overcome opposition forcefully. To fight. To attack or injure another. To oppose forcefully or punish another.

Autonomy. To get free, shake off restraint, break out of social confinement. To resist coercion and restriction. To avoid or quit activities prescribed by domineering authorities. To be independent and free to act according to desires. To defy convention.

Counteraction. To master or make up for a failure by restriving. To obliterate a humiliation by resumed action. To overcome weakness; to repress fear. To efface a dishonor by action. To seek for obstacles and difficulties to overcome. To maintain self-respect and pride on a high level.

Defendance. To defend the self against assault, criticism, or blame. To conceal or justify a misdeed, failure, or humiliation. To vindicate the ego.

Deference. To admire and support a superior. To praise, honor, or eulogize. To yield eagerly to the influence of an allied other. To emulate an exemplar. To conform to custom.

Dominance. To control one's human environment. To influence or direct the behavior of others by suggestion, seduction, persuasion, or command. To dissuade, restrain, or prohibit.

Exhibition. To make an impression. To be seen and heard. To excite, amaze, fascinate, entertain, shock, intrigue, amuse, or entice others.

TABLE 17-2. (*Continued*)

Harmavoidance. To avoid pain, physical injury, illness, and death. To escape from a dangerous situation. To take precautionary measures.
Infavoidance. To avoid humiliation. To quit embarrassing situations. To avoid conditions that lead to scorn, derision, or indifference of others. To refrain from action because of fear of failure.
Inviolacy. To protect the self. To remain separate. To resist attempts of others to intrude upon or invade one's own psychological space. To maintain a psychological distance. To be isolated, reticent, concealed, immune from criticism.
Nurturance. To give sympathy and gratify the needs of another person, especially an infant or someone who is weak, disabled, tired, inexperienced, infirm, defeated, humiliated, lonely, rejected, sick, or mentally confused. To feed, help, support, console, protect, comfort, nurse, heal; to nurture.
Order. To put things or ideas in order. To achieve arrangement, organization, balance, tidiness, and precision among things in the outer world or ideas in the inner world.
Play. To act for "fun" without further purpose. To like to laugh and make jokes. To enjoy relaxation of stress. To participate in pleasurable activities for their own sake.
Rejection. To separate oneself from a negatively viewed person. To exclude, abandon, expel, or remain indifferent to an inferior person. To snub or jilt another.
Sentience. To seek and enjoy sensuous experience. To give an important place to creature comforts of taste, touch, and the other senses.
Succorance. To have one's needs gratified by the sympathetic aid of another person. To be nursed, supported, sustained, protected, loved, advised, guided, indulged; forgiven, consoled, taken care of. To remain close to a devoted protector. To have a supporter.
Understanding. To ask and answer questions. To be interested in theory. To speculate, formulate, analyze, and generalize. To want to know the answers to general questions.

Note. Adapted from Murray, H. A. (1938). *Explorations in Personality* (pp. 142–242). New York: Oxford University Press. Copyright © 1938 by Oxford University Press. Adapted by permission.

Most suicides represent combinations of various needs, so that a particular case of suicide may properly be understood in terms of two or more different need categories. There are many pointless deaths, but never a needless suicide. If the frustrated needs are addressed, the pain they cause will be lessened, and the suicide will not occur. The therapist's function is to decrease the patient's acute discomfort and to increase the patient's comfort. One way to operationalize this task is to focus on the thwarted needs. Questions such as "Where do you hurt?" can be useful in clarifying the suicidal picture.

The assessment of needs related to suicide may be a more complicated epistemological task than the identification of the other commonalities of suicide. Psychological needs are more conceptual and abstract, and there is more inference necessary to name them. One requires access to a detailed anamnestic record or case history for the raw data from which inferences can reasonably be made. In the case of the shooter whose words are quoted above, I have concluded that the half-dozen most important needs (see Table 17-2) related to his suicidal state were the needs for dominance, autonomy, counteraction, succorance, affiliation, and order. These constitute a quite different constellation of vital psychological needs from the frustrated needs that ignited the immolator or those that pushed the jumper. I should note also that the use of the language of psychological needs immediately and radically changes the way in which one then conceptualizes that individual's suicidal behavior, and in which one can think of ways to help the suicidal person.

> "I was like a general . . . being encroached upon by my enemy and its hordes: fear, hate, self-depreciation, desolation."

5. The Common Emotion in Suicide Is Helplessness-Hopelessness

In the suicidal state, there is a pervasive feeling of helplessness-hopelessness: "There is nothing I can do [except to commit suicide] and there is no one who can help me [with the pain that I am suffering]." Underlying all of the emotions—hostility, guilt, shame—is the emotion of impotent ennui, the feeling of helplessness-hopelessness. The most effective way to reduce the elevated lethality is to reduce the elevated perturbation of which the feelings of helplessness-hopelessness are an integral part.

> "There comes a time when all things cease to shine, when the rays of hope are lost."

6. The Common Cognitive State in Suicide Is Ambivalence

The (non-Aristotelian) accommodation to the psychological realities of mental life—simultaneous contradictory feelings (such as love and hate toward the same person)—is called "ambivalence." It is the common internal attitude toward suicide: to feel that one has to do it, and at the same time to yearn (even to plan) for rescue and intervention. The therapist uses this ambivalence, and plays for time so that the affect rather than the bullet can be discharged.

> "[I was] sure that someone would see me [and rescue me] . . . The whole building is made of glass."

7. The Common Perceptual State in Suicide Is Constriction

Suicide is not best understood as a psychosis, a neurosis, or a character disorder (100 percent of suicides are highly perturbed). It is more accurately seen as a more or less transient psychological constriction of affect and intellect. A synonym for "constriction" would be a "tunneling" or "focusing" or "narrowing" of the range of options usually available to that individual's consciousness when the mind is not panicked into dichotomous thinking: either some specific (almost magical) good solution or cessation; *Caesar aut nihil;* all or nothing. The range of life choices has narrowed to two—not very much of a range. The usual life-sustaining images of loved ones are not even within the mind. The fact that suicide is committed by individuals who are in a special constricted condition suggests that no one should ever commit suicide while disturbed. It takes a mind capable of scanning a range of options greater than two to make a decision as important as taking one's life. At the outset, it is vital to counter the suicidal person's constriction of thought by widening the mental blinders and increasing the number of options beyond only two dichotomous options of either achieving a magical resolution or being dead. The dangerous word that the therapist must be alert for is the word "only."

> "[It] was sort of like a blank in my mind. . . . I didn't think that burns would really hurt . . ."
>
> " 'There's only one thing to do . . . That's the only way . . . ' The only way to lose consciousness, I thought, was to jump off something good and high. . . . [E]verything got dark all of a sudden . . . Everything around it just blacked out. It was just like a circle. That was all I could see . . ."
>
> "My mind became locked on my target. . . . I sought to die rather than surrender."

8. The Common Action in Suicide Is Egression

"Egression" or escape is a person's intended departure from a region of distress. Suicide is the ultimate egression, besides which all others (running away from home, quitting a job, deserting an army, leaving a spouse) pale. The therapist needs to give the person other exits, other ways of doing something. (The therapist and those close to the patient also need to close a possible lethal exit by, for example, removing a gun.) This notion is very much related to expanding the patient's constriction.

> "It [I] was not going to exist any more . . ."
> "I just have to lose consciousness."
> "I committed myself to the arms of Death."

9. The Common Interpersonal Act in Suicide is Communication of Intention

Perhaps the most interesting finding from large numbers of psychological autopsies of suicidal deaths is that in most cases (80 percent) there were clear verbal or behavioral clues to the impending lethal event. Individuals who are intent on committing suicide (albeit ambivalent about it) consciously or unconsciously emit signals of distress, whimpers of helplessness, or pleas for response; or they provide opportunities for rescue in the usually dyadic interplay that is an integral part of the suicidal drama. The common interpersonal act of suicide is paradoxical communication of intention with the usual verbal and behavioral clues.

> "The next day I began to say goodbye to people."

10. The Common Consistency in Suicide Is with Lifelong Coping Patterns

In suicide, one may be initially thrown off the scent because suicide is an act that, by definition, that individual has never committed before; thus, there seems to be no precedent. And yet there are some deep consistencies with lifelong coping patterns. The therapist must look at previous episodes of deep perturbation, distress, duress, and threat, and at the person's capacity to endure psychological pain, for patterns of egression in that person's life.

> "I felt I had to have the upper hand, to control my environment, so I sought to die rather than surrender."

A Theoretical Model of Suicide

It is now possible to combine these ten items into a more succinct theoretical model. Let us imagine a cube (see Figure 17-1) made up of 125

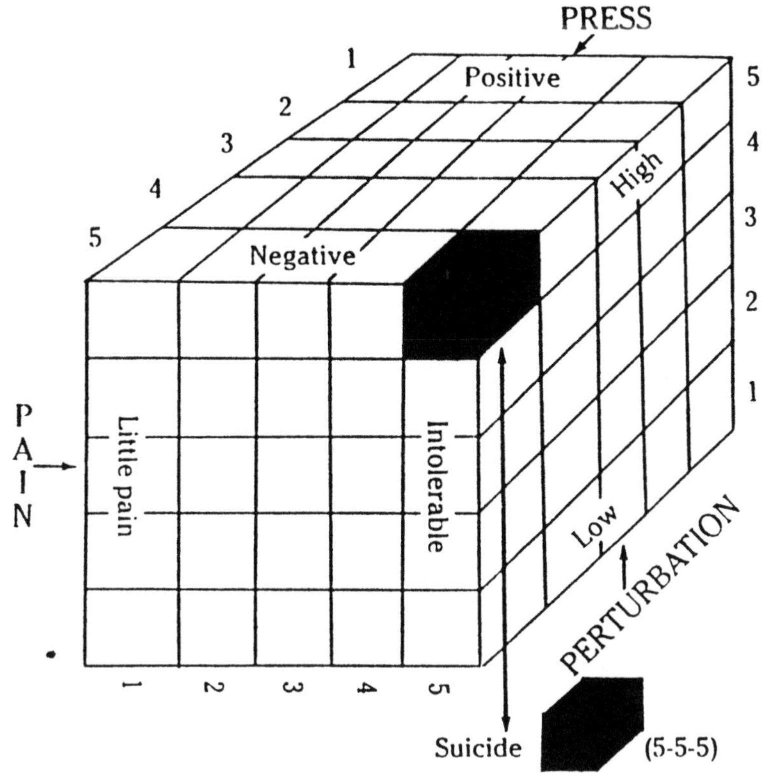

FIGURE 17-1. A theoretical cubic model of suicide. From Schneidman, E. S. (1987). "A Psychological Approach to Suicide." In G. R. VandenBos & B. K. Bryant (Eds.), *Cataclysms, crises and catastrophes: Psychology in action.* Washington, DC: American Psychological Association. Copyright © 1987 by the American Psychological Association. Reprinted by permission.

cubelets, with twenty-five squares on a plane, and five cubelets in each row and each column. I call these three faces of the cube (and the three corresponding components of this theoretical model) "pain," "perturbation," and "press," which are defined as follows:

1. *Pain.* "Pain," represented on the front of the cube, refers to the psychological pain resulting from thwarted psychological needs. The leftmost column of cubelets represents little or no pain, the next column some bearable pain, and so on until the rightmost column, which represents intolerable psychological pain.
2. *Perturbation.* "Perturbation," assigned to the side plane of the large cube, is a general term meaning the state of being upset or perturbed.

Ranked here on a five-point rating scale, perturbation includes everything in the *Diagnostic and Statistical Manual of Mental Disorders,* third edition, revised (*DSM-III-R* 1987). In relation to suicide, perturbation includes (a) perceptual constriction, and (b) a penchant for precipitous self-harm or inimical action. "Constriction" refers to the reduction of the individual's perceptual and cognitive range. At its worst, the individual reduces the viable options to two, and then to one. On this plane in the cube, the bottom row reflects open-mindedness, wide mentational scope, and relatively clear thinking. The top row reflects constriction of thought, tunnel vision, and a narrowing of focus to few options, with cessation, death, and egression as one (and ultimately the only) solution to the problem of pain and frustrated needs. "Penchant for action" refers to something akin to impulsiveness—a tendency to get things over with; to bring them inappropriately to a quick resolution; to have little patience and low tolerance for open and stressful situations; to jump to conclusions; and to jump at opportunities for more immediate resolution. The row of cubelets at the bottom reflects a high tolerance for ambiguity, a capacity for patience and waiting. As we move upward on this plane, we come closer to this tendency for precipitous and consummatory action, this lethal impulsivity. That is what the topmost row on the side plane represents.

3. *Press.* Murray (1938) may have had the word "pressure" in mind when he decided to use the word "press" ("press" is both the singular and the plural form) to represent those aspects of the inner and outer world or environment that impinge on, move, touch, or affect the individual and make a difference. The term refers to the things dones *to* the individual (and the way they are incorporated and interpreted), to which he or she reacts. There is positive press (good genes and happy fortune), and there is negative press (conditions or events that perturb, threaten, stress, or harm the individual). It is the latter that are relevant to suicide. Press includes both actual and imagined events, in the sense that everything is mediated by the mind. In this cubic model, press ranges from positive (in the back row of the top plane) to negative (in the front row of the top plane).

In this theoretical cube of 125 cubelets, there is only one cubelet that is numbered 5-5-5. Not every individual who is in a 5-5-5 cubelet commits suicide—he or she may commit homicide, or go crazy, or become amnesic, or destroy a career—but in this conceptual model no one commits suicide *except* those in the 5-5-5 cubelet (maximum pain, maximum perturbation, maximum negative press). The implications for therapy and lifesaving redress would seem to be obvious: Reduce any of these three dimensions from a 5 to a 4 (or less); preferably, reduce all three. Individuals can lead long, unhappy lives as 4s and 3s, but the specific goal in suicide prevention is to remove the individual from the 5-5-5 cubelet—to save his or her life. All else (demographic variables, family history, previous suicidal history) is peripheral, except as those and other factors bear on the presently felt pain, perturbation, and negative press.

☐ Conclusion: Fields Contributing to Suicidology

Now, finally, to put this presentation of the psychological approach to suicide in a wider perspective, I can speak of a variety of fields of knowledge that have a legitimate interest in suicidology (see Table 17-3). Each of these approaches can contribute to our knowledge of suicidal phenomena. In this same sense, any one of them errs when it claims that *its* sector represents the whole circle of etiology—that it is clearly the only way to achieve a real understanding of suicide. Furthermore, propo-

TABLE 17-3. Various contemporary approaches to the study of suicidal phenomena

Sector	Key References	Principal Assertion: That Suicide is Best Understood Primarily—
Life history	Allport (1937) Murray (1967) Runyon (1982)	As an episode in a long life history; precursors of the suicidal death can be seen in previous patterns of response to comparable life situations.
Personal documents	Allport (1942) Schneidman & Farberow (1957) Leenaars (1988)	Through the analysis of such personal documents as letters, diaries, autobiographies, and especially suicide notes.
Demographic; epidemiological	Graunt (1662) Süssmilch (1741) Dublin (1963) Hollinger & Offer (1986)	In terms of census data (the statistics for sex, age, race, religious affiliation, marital status, socioeconomic status, etc.).
Systems theoretical	Blaker (1972) Miller (1978) Tyler (1984)	As an act within a living system; both the individual and the individual-within-the-society are considered as living systems.

TABLE 17-3. (*Continued*)

Sector	Key References	Principal Assertion: That Suicide is Best Understood Primarily—
Philosophical; theological	Pepper (1942) Fowles (1964) Choron (1972) Battin (1982)	In terms of answers to questions such as these: What is the purpose of life? Are there forces beyond ourselves? What is our relation to the universe? Is there life after death?
Sociocultural	Hendin (1964) Lifton, Kato, & Reich (1979) Iga (1986)	In terms of sociocultural data (e.g., knowledge of various countries and cultures such as Sweden, Japan, etc.).
Sociological	Durkheim (1897/1951) Douglas (1967) Maris (1981)	In terms of an individual's relationship to his or her society (estrangement from it, ties to it).
Dyadic and family	Pfeffer (1986) Richman (1986)	In terms of the stressful interaction between two people or within a family nexus.
Psychiatric	Kraepelin (1883/1915) American Psychiatric Association (1987)	In terms of mental illnesses (e.g., depression, schizophrenia, alcoholism).
Psychodynamic	Freud (1910/1967) Zilboorg (1937) Menninger (1938) Litman (1967)	In terms of unconscious conflicts, especially unconscious hostility toward the father; suicide is seen as unconscious murder.
Psychological	Murray (1938) Shneidman (1985)	In terms of psychological pain, produced by the frustration of psychological needs.
Constitutional	Roy (1986) Kety (1986)	As an expression of inborn (constitutional or genetic) factors.
Biological; biochemical	Bunny & Fawcett (1965) Asberg, Nordstrom, & Traskman-Bendz (1986)	As a result of biochemical imbalances in the body fluid (blood) or organs (brain).

nents of all the approaches need to be vigilant that they do not confuse concomitance (events [in the brain, in the blood, in society, in interpersonal relations, within the psyche] that happen at the same time as heightened suicidality) with causality (events that necessarily must precede the onset of a suicidal state). It is the causally related events that present us with reasonable avenues to effective prevention.

☐ References

Allport, G. (1937). *Personality: A psychological interpretation.* New York: Holt, Rinehardt & Winston.

Allport, G. (1942). *The use of personal documents as psychological science.* New York: Social Science Research Council.

American Psychiatric Association (1987). *Diagnostic and statistical manual of mental disorders* (3rd ed., rev.). Washington, DC: Author.

Asberg, M., Nordstrom, P., & Traskman-Bendz, L. (1986). Biological factors in suicide. In A. Roy *Suicide* (pp. 47–71). Baltimore: Williams & Wilkins.

Baechler, J. (1979). *Suicides,* (B. Cooper, Trans.) New York: Basic Books.

Battin, M. P. (1982). *Ethical issues in suicide.* Englewood Cliffs, NJ: Prentice-Hall.

Blaker, K. P. (1972). Systems theory and self-destructive behavior. *Perspectives in Psychiatric Care, 10,* 168–172.

Bunney, W. E., & Fawcett, J. A. (1965). Possibility of a biochemical test for suicide potential. *Archives of General Psychiatry 13,* 232–239.

Choron, J. (1972). *Suicide.* New York: Scribner's.

Douglas, J. D. (1967). *The social meaning of suicide.* Princeton, NJ: Princeton University Press.

Dublin, L. I. (1963). *Suicide a sociological and statistical study.* New York: Ronald.

Durkheim, E. (1951). *Suicide: A study in sociology* (J. A. Spaulding & and G. Simpson, Trans.). Glencoe, IL: Free Press. (Original work published 1897)

Fowles, J. (1964). *The Aristos.* Boston: Little, Brown.

Freud, S. (1967). Comments on suicide. In P. Friedman (Ed.), *On suicide* (E. Fitzgerald, trans.), (pp. 140–141). New York: International University Press. (Original work published 1910)

Graunt, J. (1662). *Natural and political annotations . . . upon the bills of mortality.* London.

Hendin, H. (1964). *Suicide in Scandinavia.* New York: Grune & Stratton.

Hollinger, P. C., & Offer, D. (1986). *Sociodemographic, epidemiologic and individual attributes of youth suicides.* Bethesda, MD: Department of Health and Human Services.

Iga, M. (1986). *The thorn in the chrysanthemum: Suicide and economic success in modern Japan.* Berkeley: University of California Press.

Kelly, G. A. (1961). Suicide: The personal construct point of view. In N. Farberow & E. S. Shneidman (Eds.), *The cry for help* (pp. 255–280). New York: McGraw-Hill.

Kety, S. (1986). Genetic factors in suicide. In A. Roy (Ed.), *Suicide* (pp. 41–45). Baltimore: Williams & Wilkins.

Kraepelin, E. (1915). *Textbook of psychiatry.* (Original work published 1883)

Leenaars, A. A. (1988). *Suicide notes.* New York: Human Sciences.

Lifton, R. J., Kato, S., & Reich, M. R. (1979). *Six lives/six deaths.* New Haven, CT: Yale University Press.

Litman, R. E. (1967). Sigmund Freud on suicide. In E. S. Schneidman (Ed.), *Essays in self-destruction,* (pp. 324–344). New York: Science House.
Maris, R. (1981). *Pathways to suicide: A survey of self-destructive behaviors.* Baltimore: Johns Hopkins University Press.
Menninger, K. A. (1938). *Man against himself.* New York: Harcourt, Brace and World.
Miller, J. G. (1978). *Living systems.* New York: McGraw-Hill.
Murray, H. A. (1938). *Explorations in personality.* New York: Oxford University Press.
Murray, H. A. (1967). Dead to the world: The passions of Herman Melville. In E. S. Shneidman (Ed.), *Essays in self-destruction* (pp. 7–29). New York: Science House.
Pepper, S. (1942). *World hypotheses.* Berkeley: University of California Press.
Pfeffer, C. (1986). *The suicidal child.* New York: Guildford.
Richman, J. (1986). *Family therapy for suicidal individuals.* New York: Springer.
Roy, A., (Ed.). (1986). *Suicide.* Baltimore: Williams & Wilkins.
Runyan, W. M. (1982). *Life histories and psychobiography: Explorations in theory and method.* New York: Oxford University Press.
Shneidman, E. S. (1973). Suicide. In *Encyclopaedic Britannica: Vol. 21* (14th ed.). Chicago: William Benton.
Shneidman, E. S. (1980). *Voices of death.* New York: Harper & Row.
Shneidman, E. S. (1984). Aphorisms of suicide and some implications for psychotherapy. *American Journal of Psychotherapy, 38,* 319–328.
Shneidman, E. S. (1985). *Definition of suicide.* New York: Wiley.
Shneidman, E. S. (1986). Some essentials of suicide and some implications for response. In A. Roy (Ed.), *Suicide* (pp. 1–16). Baltimore: Williams & Wilkins.
Shneidman, E. S. (1987). A psychological approach to suicide. In G. R. VandenBos & B. K. Bryant (Eds.), *Cataclysms, crises and catastrophes: Psychology in action* (pp. 147–183). Washington, DC: American Psychological Association.
Shneidman, E. S. (1989). A multidisciplinary approach to suicide. In D. Jacobs & H. Brown (Eds.), *Suicide: understanding and responding: Harvard Medical School Perspectives* (pp. 1–30). Madison, CT: International Universities Press.
Shneidman, E. S. (1990). A life in death: notes of a committed suicidologist. In C. E. Walker (Ed.), *A history of clinical psychology in autobiography* (pp. 225–292). Pacific Grove, CA: Brooks/Cole.
Shneidman, E. S., & Farberow, N. (Eds.). (1957). *Clues to suicide.* New York: McGraw-Hill.
Süssmilch, J. (1941). *Die göttliche ordnung in den veränderungen des menschlichen geschlechts, aus der geburt, dem tode, und der fortflanzug desselben erwiesen.* Berlin: J. C. Spenser.
Tyler, L. (1984). *Thinking creatively.* San Francisco: Jossey-Bass.
Zilboorg, G. (1937). Considerations in suicide with particular reference to that of the young. *American Journal of Orthopsychiatry, 7,* 15–31.

18

CHAPTER

Suicide as Psychache

As I near the end of my career in suicidology, I think I can now say what has been on my mind in as few as five words: *Suicide is caused by psychache* (sik-ak; two syllables). Psychache refers to the hurt, anguish, soreness, aching, psychological *pain* in the psyche, the mind. It is intrinsically psychological—the pain of excessively felt shame, or guilt, or humiliation, or loneliness, or fear, or angst, or dread of growing old or of dying badly, or whatever. When it occurs, its reality is introspectively undeniable. Suicide occurs when the psychache is deemed by that person to be unbearable. This means that suicide also has to do with different individual *thresholds* for enduring psychological pain(Shneidman, 1985, 1992).

All our past efforts to relate or to correlate suicide with simplistic nonpsychological variables, such as sex, age, race, socioeconomic level, case history items (no matter how dire), psychiatric categories (including depression), etc., were (and are) doomed to miss the mark precisely because they ignore the one variable that centrally relates to suicide, namely, intolerable psychological pain; in a word, psychache.

By its very nature, psychological pain is tied to psychological needs. In general, the broadest purpose of most human activity is to satisfy psychological needs. Suicide relates to psychological needs in that suicide is a specific way to stop the unbearable psychachical flow of the mind. Furthermore, what causes this pain is the blockage, thwarting, or frustration

Reprinted from *Journal of Nervous and Mental Disease*, 1993, *181*, 147–149. With permission.

of certain psychological needs believed by that person (at that time and in those circumstances) to be vital to continued life.

Suicide is not adaptive, but adjustive in the sense that it serves to reduce the tension of the pain related to the blocked needs. Murray's (1938) monumental volume *Explorations in Personality* provides a comprehensive list of psychological needs, and their definitions: abasement, achievement, affiliation, aggression, autonomy, counteraction, defendance, deference, dominance, exhibition, harmavoidance, infavoidance, inviolacy, nurturance, order, play, rejection, sentience, succorance, and understanding.

There is an integral relationship between suicide and happiness—or rather the absence of it. Genuine happiness—contrary to the 19th and 20th century materialistic notions that narrowly identified happiness with the mere absence of pain and the presence of creature comforts—has a special magical quality (Spender, 1988). There is a mundane happiness of comfort, pain avoidance, and psychological anesthesia. But genuine, magical happiness has relatively little to do with creature comfort; rather, it is the kind of ecstasy and consuming exuberance that one can experience only in a benign childhood. To the extent that suicide relates to happiness, it relates in people of any age—not to lack of mundane happiness but to the loss of childhood's magical joys.

A principal task for contemporary suicidology is to operationalize (and metricize) the key dimension of psychache. One way to begin is to ask the simple question, "How much do you hurt?" (Kropf, 1990).

One trenchant way to understand any individual is to rank order (or Q-sort) the prepotency among the 20 needs, that is, to define or characterize that individual's personality in terms of his or her weightings among all the needs. This can be done by assigning, for that individual, a number to each need, so that the total sum for the individual adds up to 100. This permits us to rate various individuals (or a single individual over time) by use of the constant sum method. The task is simple and takes only a few minutes. (Try it by rating yourself; then rate a well-known public figure, have colleagues rate that same figure, rate your patients after each session, rate suicidal patients, and rate nonsuicidal patients.)

In relation to suicide, there are, within any individual, two sets of dispositions or sets of relative weightings among the 20 psychological needs. They are: a) those psychological needs that the individual lives with, that define his or her personality in its day-to-day intrapsychic and interpersonal functioning—the *modal* needs; and b) those few psychological needs, the frustration of which that individual simply cannot tolerate; the needs that person would die for—the *vital* needs. Within an individual, these two kinds of needs are psychologically consistent with each other. The vital needs come into play when the individual is under threat or duress. This special disposition of needs can be elicited by asking an individual about his precise reactions to the failures or losses or rejections or humiliations—the dark moments—previously in his life.

By means of an intensive psychological autopsy (Shneidman, 1977), it should be possible to identify (or label) every committed suicide in terms of the two or three prepotent needs the frustration of which played a major role in that death. (With 20 needs, we have a possible taxonomy of a few hundred different "types" of suicide.)

The prevention of suicide (with a highly lethal person) is then primarily a matter of addressing and partially alleviating those frustrated psychological needs that are driving that person to suicide. The rule is simple: Mollify the psychache.

In the progression to a suicidal outcome, I believe that we can distinguish seven components. They are:

a. the vicissitudes of life; those stresses, failures, rejections, and catabolic and social and psychological insults that are omnipresent by virtue of living.
b. various approaches to understanding human behavior. Suicidal behavior (as is all behavior) is obviously multidimensional, which means, in practice, that its proper explication has to be multidisciplinary. The relevant fields for suicidology include biochemistry (and genetics), sociology, demography-epidemiology, psychology, psychiatry, linguistics, and so on. The reader should appreciate that *this* paper is limited to the psychological approach to suicide, without derogating the importance of other legitimate approaches.
c. the vicissitudes of life as they are perceptually funneled through the human mind and apperceived (or appreciated) as ecstatic, pleasurable, neutral, inconsequential, or painful. If there is extreme psychache, a necessary condition for suicide is present. "I hurt too much."
d. the perception of the pain as unbearable, intolerable, and unacceptable, another necessary condition for suicide, in addition to psychache. "I won't put up with this pain."
e. the thought (or insight) that cessation of consciousness is the solution for the unbearable psychache, still another necessary condition. In a phrase, death is preferable to living, with death as a means of egression or escape. "I can kill myself."
f. a lowered threshold for enduring or sustaining the crippling psychache, a final necessary condition for suicide. A priori, people with more or less equal amounts of psychache might have radically different overt outcomes depending upon their different thresholds for

tolerating or enduring psychological pain. (In life, pain is ubiquitous and inescapable; suffering is optional.)

g. the suicidal outcome. "I hurt too much to live."

About now, the alert and restive reader might be asking, What about depression? As everyone knows, depression is a serious psychiatric syndrome, well recognized and relatively treatable. But depression is not the same as suicide. They are quite different. For one thing, they have enormously different fatality rates. One can live a long, unhappy life with depression—not true of an acutely suicidal state. Theoretically, no one has ever died of depression—it is not a legitimate cause of death on the death certificate—but many people, too many, have died of suicide. Vast numbers of people suffer from minor or major depressions. Depression seems to have psychological, biochemical, and probably genetical components. The use of medications in treatment is on target. It is, so to speak, a biological storm in the brain. Suicide, on the other hand, is a phenomenological event, a transient tempest in the mind. It is responsive to talk therapy and to changes in the environment. Suicide is not a psychiatric disorder. Suicide is a nervous dysfunction, not a mental disease. *All* persons who commit suicide—100% of them—are perturbed, but they are not necessarily clinically depressed (or schizophrenic or alcoholic or addicted or psychiatrically ill). A suicidal crisis is best treated on its own terms. It is a deadly serious (temporary and treatable) psychache (Table 18-1).

Depression never causes suicide; rather, suicide results from severe psychache, coupled with dysphoria, constriction of perceptual range, and the idea of death as preferable to life. By themselves, the clinical symptoms of depression are debilitating, but, by their nature, not deadly. On the other hand, severe psychache by itself may be life threatening. Correlating suicide with DSM categories is irrelevant to the real action in the mind's main tent. Depression merits treatment for itself, but then to assert that suicide is essentially depression is either a logical mistake, a conceptual confusion, or a professional gambit. In any case, it is past time to make this correction.

Here, finally, after over 40 years of experience as a suicidologist, is a tight summary of my current beliefs about suicide.

1. The explanation of suicide in humankind is the same as the explanation of the suicide of any particular human. Suicidology, the study of human suicide, and a psychological autopsy (of a particular case) are identical in their goals: to nibble at the puzzle of human self-destruction.
2. The most evident fact about suicidology and suicidal events is that they are multidimensional, multifaceted, and multidisciplinary, con-

TABLE 18-1. Symptoms of depression—characteristics of suicide

Depression*	Suicide
1. Sadness	1. In great psychological pain (psychache)
2. Apathy	2. Cannot stand the pain (lowered threshold for suffering)
3. Loss of appetite or increased appetite	3. Sees ending life as an escape (death as solution)
4. Insomnia or sleeping far more than usual	4. Sees no possibilities other than death (constriction)
5. Feeling physically agitated or slowed down	5. May or may not have symptoms of depression (suicide as a mental state)
6. Fatigue and lack of energy	
7. Feelings of worthlessness or great guilt	
8. Inability to concentrate or indecisiveness	
9. Thoughts of death or suicide	

*The source (for Depression) was *The New York Times,* August 5, 1992 (by permission).

taining, as they do, concomitant biological, sociological, psychological (interpersonal and intrapsychic), epidemiological, and philosophical elements.

3. From the view of the psychological factors in suicide, the key element in every case is psychological pain: psychache. All affective states (such as rage, hostility, depression, shame, guilt, affectlessnes, hopelessness, etc.) are relevant to suicide only as they relate to unbearable psychological pain. If, for example, feeling guilty or depressed or having a bad conscience or an overwhelming unconscious rage makes one suicidal, it does so only because it is painful. No psychache, no suicide.
4. Individuals have different thresholds for enduring or tolerating pain; thus, the individual's decision not to bear the pain—the threshold for enduring it—is also directly relevant.
5. In every case, the psychological pain is created and fueled by frustrated psychological needs. These needs have been explicated by Murray (1938, pp. 142–242).
6. There are modal psychological needs with which the person lives (and which define the personality) and there are vital psychological needs whose frustration cannot be tolerated (which define the suicide). Within an individual, these two kinds of needs are psychologi-

cally consistent with each other, although not necessarily the same as each other.

7. The remediation (or therapy) of the suicidal state lies in addressing and mollifying the vital frustrated needs. The therapist does well to have this template (of psychological needs) in mind so that the therapy can be tailor-made for that patient. Often, just a little bit of mollification of the patient's frustrated needs can change the vital balance sufficiently to save a life.

References

Kropf, J. (1990). *An empirical assessment of Murray's personological formulation of suicide.* Unpublished doctoral dissertion, California School of Professional Psychology, Fresno, CA.

Murray, H. (1938). *Explorations in personality.* New York: Oxford University Press.

Shneidman, E. S. (1977). The psychological autopsy. In L. Gottschalk et al. (Eds.), *Guide to the investigation and reporting of drug abuse deaths.* Rockville, MD: ADAMHA.

Shneidman, E. S. (1985). *Definition of suicide.* New York: Wiley.

Shneidman, E. S. (1992). A conspectus of the suicidal scenario. In R. W. Maris et al. (Eds.), *Assessment and prediction of suicide.* New York: Guilford.

Spender, S. (1988). Introduction to the second edition. In P. O'Connor, *Memoirs of a public baby.* New York: W. W. Norton.

IV

SUICIDE
Section B: Suicide Notes

Since the day in 1949 when Shneidman discovered the trove of suicide notes in the vaults of the Los Angeles County Coroner's office, he has never left the topic of suicide as his principal professional concern. When he realized that he was in a coroner's vault with thousands of *genuine* suicide notes, he immediately thought of the possibility of comparing them, in a blind study, with *simulated* notes which could be elicited from non-suicidal people. His old friend John Stuart Mill and his method of Difference handed Shneidman a career, and, indirectly, created suicidology.

This section consists of four selections. The first, Chapter 19 (with Daniel Ogilvie and Philip Stone, in which Shneidman is the junior author), is a report of a study using Harvard's General Inquirer, a 1960s pioneer computer. Thirty-three pairs of genuine-and-simulated suicide notes, assembled by Shneidman and Farberow, were subjected to a computer analysis. Using special combinations of "tag words," the machine, through brute power, could successfully identify the genuine notes and, in this way, threw light on the inner workings of suicide itself. The thesis—that notes provide insights into the act—seemed to be supported, if not proved.

Chapter 20, "Suicide Notes Reconsidered," is antithetical in mood. It takes a long second look at the exuberant notion that "suicide notes are the golden road to the understanding of suicide," and argues instead that individuals who commit suicide are, by and large, in a constricted frame of mind; further: that if a person were capable of penning a full and explanatory psychological note, that person would probably have the wits to resist the inner suicidal impulses. In a word, we must not expect too much from suicide notes.

It would seem that in Chapter 21 Shneidman has attempted to force a synthesis between the two views that suicide notes are enormously rich sources of psychological data and the contrary view that suicide notes are pedestrian and banal. This paper, taken from his *Voices of Death*, asserts and seeks to illustrate the point that suicide notes—which, after all, are the penultimate act of that person's life—can be very informative when they are placed within the context of the thousand details of that person's life. Using that approach, then, almost every word in the suicide notes is illuminated by the life, and many details of the life are tragically illustrated by the contents of the notes.

Chapter 22, "Letters of Enforced Death versus Suicide Notes," is Shneidman's most recent statement on the value of personal documents in science, once more following the tradition of Allport (1942).

Taken all together it appears that Shneidman never forgot his suicidological "roots"—the notes in the coroner's files, and the usefulness of Mill's method of difference in wresting secrets from nature's vaults.

19

CHAPTER

Some Characteristics of Genuine Versus Simulated Suicide Notes

The Notes and the Problem[1]

Thirty-three genuine suicide and 33 simulated suicide notes were made available to members of the research team by Edwin S. Shneidman. The genuine notes were selected from 721 suicide notes collected from folders of suicide cases in Los Angeles county for the ten-year period of 1945 to 1954. This sample included only those notes written by suicide victims who were male, Caucasian, Protestant, native born, and between the ages of 25 and 59. For comparative purposes, simulated suicide notes were obtained from nonsuicidal individuals who were all also male, Caucasian, Protestant, and native born, and who were matched with genuine note writers with respect to age and occupational level. The simulated note writers were instructed to make their notes sound as real as possible, to write as if they were actually planning to take their own life. Through the use of the General Inquirer, we were able to distinguish between genuine and simulated suicide notes.

Reprinted from P. J. Stone, D. C. Dunphy, M. S. Smith, and D. M. Ogilvie (Eds.), *The General Inquirer: A Computer Approach to Content Analysis,* Cambridge, MA: MIT Press, 1969, pp. 527–535. (With D. M. Ogilvie and P. J. Stone). With permission.

The Dictionary[2]

The dictionary used in this study was the Harvard II Psychosociological Dictionary (forerunner of our current dictionary.) That category system, like the Harvard III Dictionary, was divided into first-order tags (discrete, independent categories) and second-order tags (nonindependent categories). The first-order tags were subdivided into *ROLES, OBJECTS, EMOTIONAL STATES,* and *ACTIONS.* All **Things** were either *ROLES* or *OBJECTS,* and all **Processes** were either *EMOTIONAL STATES* or *ACTIONS*. The second-order tags were classified as referring to either *INSTITUTIONS, STATUSES, QUALITIES,* or *SYMBOLIC REFERENTS.*

First Inspection of Tag Score Differences

The genuine and simulated notes were processed separately. The tags that appeared to differentiate between the sets (total difference of .03 percent or greater) are presented in Table 19-1.

Roughly summarizing the differences revealed in Table 19-1, we found that the genuine suicide notes are slightly more diversified in their use of the eight general categories in our theoretical scheme. With the exception of *EMOTIONAL STATES* and *INSTITUTIONS,* the genuine notes have relatively higher counts on some tags under all categories. On the other hand, the simulated notes do not have any higher scores in the following categories: *OBJECTS, STATUSES,* and *QUALITIES.* Moreover, the simulated notes make relatively little use of the *ROLES* category.

More specifically, the greatest difference seems to be that the genuine note writers concentrate more heavily on tags referring to **Things** *(ROLES* and *OBJECTS)* and *qualities,* whereas the simulated note writers have their heaviest concentration on tags referring to **Processes**. The use of tags under **Things** and *qualities* by genuine note writers appears to represent a greater emphasis on specifics. On the other hand, the high counts on tags under **Processes** might well reflect a more general use of words indicating the operation of cognitive processes for the simulated note writers (words such as think, sense, if, goals). Another difference between the two types of notes is the tendency for the genuine notes to use sentences with words referring to themselves in the first person and to others (male and females), whereas the simulated note writers tend to refer more to themselves and others simultaneously by using the word "we." Equally interesting is the complete absence of tags under *EMOTIONAL STATES* for the genuine notes. This reflects a relative lack of direct references to emotion. Also we find that the genuine notes are high

TABLE 19-1. Tags that discriminate between genuine and simulated notes

FIRST-ORDER TAGS			
Things			
ROLES		***OBJECTS***	
(Genuine)	**(Simulated)**	**(Genuine)**	**(Simulated)**
SELF*	SELVES	ARTIFACT	
OTHER		PLACE	
MALE-ROLE			
FEMALE-ROLE			
Processes			
EMOTIONAL STATES		***ACTIONS***	
(Genuine)	**(Simulated)**	**(Genuine)**	**(Simulated)**
	ANXIETY-FAIL	COMMUNICATE	THINK
	ANXIETY-UNABLE	POSSESS	SENSE
	DISTRESS	GET	IF
		ATTACK	NOT
			MOVE
			AVOID
			DIRECT
			GOALS
SECOND-ORDER TAGS			
INSTITUTIONS		**STATUSES**	
(Genuine)	**(Simulated)**	**(Genuine)**	**(Simulated)**
	ACADEMIC	HIGHER-STATUS	
QUALITIES		***SYMBOLIC REFERENTS***	
(Genuine)	**(Simulated)**	**(Genuine)**	**(Simulated)**
QUANTITY-REFERENCE		SEX-THEME	DEATH-THEME
BAD		MALE-THEME	UNDERSTATE

*Tags that appear in this table are those which had comparatively "high" counts for the set (genuine or simulated) under which they are listed.

on the symbolic tags SEX-THEME and MALE-THEME, possibly indicating an underlying concern with sex which is not recognized on the conscious level.

Leftover Revelations

The words that were not found in the dictionary and thereby were printed out as leftovers were reviewed. First it was found that the dictionary defined a higher percentage of words in the simulated notes (92 percent) than were defined for the genuine notes (86 percent). In other words, 8 percent of the words in the simulated notes were not defined, whereas 14 percent of the words from the genuine notes went without definition. In addition to this finding, the words in the two lists differed in content. Specifically, 64 percent of the leftover words from the genuine notes could be classified in one of the following five categories: proper names, places, objects, numbers, and time. By contrast, only 32 percent of the leftover words from the simulated notes could be classified under these categories. This finding supports one of our initial interpretations of the differences between the sets of notes were further divided into differences on tag counts between the two sets of notes. That is, the genuine note writers used very specific, concrete references in their messages.

Retrieving and Judging Sentences

Previous to processing the genuine and simulated notes, they had been coded and syntax marked. For our purposes, this was important in two respects. First, pronouns could be identified. If the writer referred to his sister by using the pronoun "you," the information that "you" meant sister and sister meant female was not lost. Second, since sentence "parts" (subject, verb, object, and so on) had been specified, initial tag-score differences with respect to parts of speech. For example, the summary score for the tag FEMALE-ROLE revealed that genuine note writers referred to females more frequently than did simulated note writers. Further inspection of the printout revealed that the greatest difference lay in the genuine notes' references to females in the *subject* position of the sentence (154 occurrences of female as subject for the genuine notes compared to 64 occurrences for the simulated notes). Making use of this rather substantial difference, we retrieved all sentences from both sets of notes that matched our Female-as-Subject specification.

Working from the printout of the retrieval of these sentences, we found that all sentences from both genuine and simulated notes could be classified under one of the following three categories:

1. Writer is making a request or is giving an instruction or command to a woman.

   Examples: You (female) get in touch with Mary Jones (female) at once.
   You (female) please get a lawyer.
   You (female) be happy.
   You (female) teach him (son) to grow into a fine man.

2. Writer is giving information or expressing opinions (given as information) about a woman.
   Examples: She lives close by.
   Soon she (daughter) will dominate you.
   She packed her bag.
   Mother meant good.
3. A woman has acted upon the writer, over and above straight information.
   Examples: She kept after me.
   Helen (female) gave it (pen) to me.
   And (wife) left me.
   But she (mother) drove me to my grave.

Table 19-2 gives the percentage distribution of sentences retrieved and classified from both genuine and simulated notes with respect to these categories.

We see that genuine note writers gave a smaller percentage of instructions to females, but they had a higher percentage of sentences giving information about women and sentences implying that a woman had directed action toward the writer. The latter two findings seemed reasonable, but the first finding created difficulties insofar as it was incongruent with our evolving notion of a suicide victim's terse concreteness. An investigation of those sentences in which the writer was giving commands or instructions indicated that they could be further classified into two relatively clear categories. These categories were

1. Instructions are of a specific nature.
   Examples: You (female) tell my folks.
   You (female) please take care of my bills.

TABLE 19-2. Classifications of "female-as subject" retrievals

	Genuine	Simulated
Instruction	29%	45%
Information	55%	50%
Female acting upon writer	15%	06%
	$n = 152$	$n = 64$

Independently rated by three judges not familiar with the materials with 95 percent agreement.

2. Instructions are of an unreasonable or vague nature.
   Examples: You (female) do not be mean with me, please.
   You (female) find a new life for yourself.

Three judges who were not familiar with the materials independently judged these "instruction" sentences as belonging either in the *specific* or *vague* categories. There was complete agreement among raters. The results showed that when genuine writers gave instructions, 55 percent of these instructions were specific and direct. Only 25 percent of the instructions given by the simulated note writers had this quality; the other 75 percent were of a vague, noninstrumental nature.

Moving away from the women in the lives of genuine and simulated suicide note writers, we recall that another difference between the two sets of notes appeared when we considered tags under the **Processes** division of first-order tags. The simulated notes were overrepresented by tags falling under this division. Quite generally, we remarked that this might reflect a greater use of decision-making words on the part of the pretenders. To investigate this possibility further, we chose to concentrate on sentences that were retrieved on the basis of containing words that had been defined by the tag THINK. Fifty-nine sentences were recovered from the genuine set compared to 54 sentences from the simulated set.[3] It was noted from these retrievals that two types of words were responsible for raising the tag count for THINK. The first type included words such as think, recall, reason, remember, explain, consider, decide, and so forth. The second type included the words know, knew, known. Normally when words in the first list are used in a sentence they serve to indicate that the writer is attempting to solve a problem or is using his reasoning processes in some way, for instance, "I am thinking of all the problems we have shared." On the other hand, when "know" is used in a sentence, it indicates that a problem has been solved, knowledge has been gained, a decision has been made; for example, "I knew that if I went to the doctor, I would. . . ."

This distinction within the category THINK differentiated between the genuine and simulated notes in the following manner. Fifty-eight percent of the genuine notes originally retrieved as matching the specification THINK contained a form of the word "know." When the distribution is viewed in a slightly different manner, 19 of the 33 genuine notes contained sentences using a form of the word "know." By contrast, only 8 of the 33 simulated suicide notes contained "know" sentences.

We may conclude that the simulated note writers tended to use words indicating the operation of problem-solving modes, whereas the genuine note writers' use of the word "know" reflects the fact that a final decision has been made. Partial substantiation of this view is gained when we recall that, along with the tag THINK, other tags referring to intellectual processes (SENSE, IF, ACADEMIC) were more frequently used by the simulated note writers than by the genuine note writers.

Discussion and Summary

Before summarizing the results of our analysis, it is instructive to review briefly the results of these same paired notes in an analysis conducted by Gottschalk and Gleser (1960). By using a hand method of classifying words into objects, processes, spatial relations, and so forth (a method similar to our computer method), they summarized that the categories of words that typify genuine suicide notes include a relatively high percentage of references to people and things, places or spatial relations, and a relatively low percentage of references to cognitive processes. We too found that genuine notes had a relatively high percentage of references to people, places, and things when we (1) compared the frequencies of tags under *ROLES* and *OBJECTS* and (2) compared the two lists of leftover words. The results of our analysis of *specific* versus *vague* requests made by the note writers using "Female-as-Subject" warrant us to note the possibility that the genuine note writers not only made more specific mention of names, places, and objects but they were much more specific in their entire final communicative attempt than were the simulated note writers. Again, in line with Gottschalk and Gleser's findings, we pointed out that the simulated note writers used a large number of words that were defined by the tags indicating the use of cognitive processes. The results of the analysis of the tag THINK and the high counts on tags SENSE, IF, and ACADEMIC for the simulated note writers added support to this finding. Contrasting these results for simulated note writers we found that genuine suicide note writers tended to use the word "know" more often. This finding can also be viewed as another example of the genuine note writers' specificity as opposed to the generality of the simulated notes.

As a demonstration of the usefulness of these findings in discriminating between the genuine and simulated notes, Stone carried out the following procedure. First he developed a discriminant function for distinguishing between the first 15 pairs of notes. The three factors that, when combined, best discriminated between these pairs were

1. References to concrete things, persons, and places (higher for genuine notes).
2. Use of the word "love" in the text (higher for genuine notes).
3. Total number of references to processes of thought and decision (higher for simulated notes).

The first and third criteria were taken from the findings just discussed. The addition of the second factor (use of the word "love") was the result of further exploration of the text word differences between these 15 documents.

The discriminant function developed from these factors was simple and straightforward: the score on the third measure was subtracted from the sum of the scores of the first two measures. This index correctly discriminated 13 of the 15 pairs of notes.

Stone, who was not familiar with the remaining 18 pairs of notes, then applied the discriminant function to them. After making his predictions on the basis of the index scores, we found that he had correctly separated 17 of the 18 paired notes.

More elaborate functions for discriminating between real and simulated suicide notes could be obtained by combining stepwise multiple regression techniques with the tree-building procedures. Our further explorations have shown that the task becomes much more difficult, however, if the notes are not available in matched pairs, as they were for Stone. Assuming that age and socioeconomic information is available, a more realistic procedure would be to collect more notes and develop separate discrimination formulas and norms as needed for each major age and socioeconomic group.

In summary, the question asked at the outset of this study was "Can we find differences between genuine suicide notes and simulated suicide notes by using the General Inquirer procedures?" We found that we could find differences and that those differences were substantial. More often than was true of the simulated notes, genuine notes contained specific information, used names of people, places, and things, made frequent mention of women, and gave instructions to others that were concrete enough to be actually carried out. By contrast, the simulated suicide notes contained a greater percentage of "thinking" words, suggesting that the issue of suicide was being pondered, reasoned with, and probably rationalized.

☐ Endnotes

[1]For more complete information about these notes and the research related to them, the reader is referred to *Clues to Suicide,* edited by E. S. Shneidman and Norman L. Farberow (New York: McGraw-Hill, 1957).

[2]Since an understanding of the results of this study is not contingent upon a full understanding of the dictionary that was used, a complete presentation of the tag categories will not be undertaken here.

[3]For the most part, genuine notes were longer than simulated notes. Thus, even though more THINK sentences were retrieved from the genuine set, the percentage difference of such sentences remains in the simulated note writers' favor.

References

Gottschalk, L. A., & Gleser, G. (1960). An analysis of the verbal content of suicide notes. *British Journal of Medical Psychology, 33,* 195–204.

Shneidman, E. S., & Farberow, N. L. (Eds.) (1957). *Clues to suicide.* New York: McGraw-Hill.

20

CHAPTER

Suicide Notes Reconsidered

I have read scores of letters from suicides, but none of them ever told the truth.

—Isaac Bashevis Singer[1]

I'm sorry, but somewhere I lost the road, and in my struggle to find it again, I just got further and further away.

There should be little sadness, and no searching for who is at fault; for the act and the result are not sad, and no one is at fault.

My only sorrow is for my parents who will not easily be able to accept that this is so much better for me. Please folks, it's all right, really it is.

1:30 p.m.—The ultimate adventure begins!

Car to Helen or Ray (needs a tune up). Money to Max and Sylvia. Furniture to George (plus $137.00 I owe him).

I wanted to be too many things, and greatness besides—it was a hopeless task. I never managed to learn to really love another person—only to make the sounds of it. I never could believe what my society taught me to believe, yet I could never manage to quite find the truth.

2:15 p.m.—I am about to will myself to stop my heart beat and respiration. This is a very mystical experience. I have no fear. That surprises me. I thought I would be terrified. Soon I will know what death is like—how many people out there can say that?

Reprinted from *Psychiatry*, 1973, *36*, 379–394. With permission.

†In a slightly modified form, this paper was presented as the presidential address of the Division of Clinical Psychology at the 81st annual meeting of the American Psychological Association, Montreal, August 27, 1973.

The above suicide note (reproduced with a few minor emendations) was found a few years ago in the pocket of a 30-year-old psychiatrist who committed suicide, with sleeping pills, deep in a forest of a midwestern state. Later in this article, we shall have occasion to contrast that note with another type of death message, also written by a 30-year-old psychiatrist in the period preceding his death—but a death of a radically different kind.

Almost without a flagging of interest, for nearly a quarter of a century, I have been keenly concerned with trying to unlock the mysteries of suicidal phenomena by using suicide notes as the possible keys. It is almost a basic tenet of suicidology that suicide notes are written in the context of the suicidal act, usually within a few minutes of the death-producing deed. On the face of it, suicide notes would seem to offer a special window, unparalleled among socio-psychological phenomena, into the thinking and feeling of the deed itself. And yet, a dozen and a half research studies by a score of qualified investigators over the past fifteen years have not produced those new insights and information which that amount of focus and effort would have led us legitimately to expect. How to account for these essentially disappointing results? That question is the topic of this paper.

Suicide notes are not like letters or diaries, which are written at leisure, often away from the scene of action. Suicide notes would seem to be comparable to battle communiqués, filled with the emotion of the current scene and describing some special aspects of the contemporary dramatic event.

And yet, as one reads dozens and hundreds of suicide notes, one finds that many of them tell pretty much the same story. What is most disappointing is that most suicide notes, written at perhaps the most dramatic moment of a person's life, are surprisingly commonplace, banal, even sometimes poignantly pedestrian and dull. It is obviously difficult to write an original suicide note; it is almost impossible to write a note which is really informative or explanatory.

Without a doubt, suicide notes are valuable and fascinating documents. They furnish extremely important data for the study of suicide. But they are not the royal road to an easy understanding of suicidal phenomena. The perusal of a suicide note is usually a disappointing process, nor has the study of notes in large number, comparing groups of them, first one way and then another, yielded findings that have thrown completely new light on suicidal behavior in general.

Suicide notes are rather special documents. They obviously fall under the category of what has been called "personal documents" as discussed in the pioneer monograph of Gordon Allport (1942). It is interesting to reflect that in Allport's comprehensive listing of personal documents—

autobiographies, confessions, diaries, memoirs, logs, letters,[2] etc.—it apparently did not occur to him to include suicide notes. Allport's monograph is to be recommended to any serious student of personal documents, suicide notes included. In it, he lists over a dozen reasons why personal documents are written, including the following: Special pleading, exhibitionism, desire for order, literary delight, securing personal perspective, relief of tension, assisting in therapy, redemption and social re-incorporation, scientific interest, public service and example, and desire for immortality. One can see that the writing of suicide notes encompasses these reasons as well as such others as confession, attribution of blame, removal of guilt, pleading for understanding, coercive demand for action, etc.

The importance of the use of personal documents in psychological science is not to be under-estimated. Indeed it may well be that we will learn more about suicidal phenomena from a close study of personal documents written over an extended period of time—diaries, journals, letters, and autobiographies—than from any other sources. Nor should we neglect biographies of persons who have committed suicide, for example the several biographies of Thomas Chatterton, the English genius who committed suicide at age 17 (Shneidman, 1971a).

The study of suicide notes is a relatively recent occurrence although there is a nineteenth-century study of Brierre de Boismont (1856) in which he published his analysis of 1328 suicide notes expounding essentially moralistic viewpoints. In 1944 Curt Michael published a collection of 166 suicide notes written by known personalities from antiquity up to modern times emphasizing the ubiquitous human elements and focusing on the changes and attitudes toward life and death reflecting the prevailing culture. In 1945 W. Morgenthaler published a monograph on suicide notes in which he reproduced verbatim (in German) 47 notes from Berne, Switzerland, dating from 1928 through 1935.

Shneidman and Farberow can be said to have begun the scientific study of suicide notes in 1957 by employing John Stuart Mill's methods of difference and residues, specifically by eliciting suicide notes from non-suicidal persons and then analyzing substantial numbers of both genuine and simulated notes in "blind" studies (where the identity of the note, genuine or simulated, was not known to the raters doing the analyses). A set of 33 paired and matched genuine and simulated suicide notes—all 66 notes written by Protestant, caucasian male adults in Los Angeles County in the period 1945 to 1955—has been used in over half a dozen different studies: the logic of suicide (Shneidman & Farberow, 1957b); changes in suicidal dynamics over age (Farberow, 1957); the socioeconomic and psychological variables of suicide (Shneidman & Farberow, 1960); suicidal life-space (Bjerg, 1967); a phenomenological study of suicide notes

(Jacobs, 1967); a re-study of suicide and age (Darbonne, 1969); and the effects of knowledge of manner of death in judging suicide notes (Hood, 1970).

There are recent studies, focusing on the emotional content of suicide notes, from Denmark (Wagner, 1960), Wales (Capstick, 1960), and Pennsylvania (Tuckman, Kleiner, & Lavell, 1959), and a study from Illinois analyzing the effects of motivational level on language (Osgood & Walker, 1959). In addition to the studies which have compared genuine notes with simulated notes, one of the studies sagaciously compared suicide notes with "ordinary letters" to friends and relatives (Osgood & Walker, 1959).

Suicide notes have been analyzed with a number of emphases: in terms of emotional states (Morgenthaler, 1945; Shneidman & Farberow, 1957a; Wagner, 1960; Bjerg, 1967; Jacobs, 1967); in terms of logical styles (Shneidman and Farberow, 1957b; Tripodes, 1968; Neuringer, 1961, 1964, 1967; Shneidman, 1969; Neuringer & Lettieri, 1971); stated or implied reasons for suicide (Capstick, 1960); levels of death wishes (Farberow, 1957); language characteristics (Osgood and Walker, 1959; Tuckman, Kleiner, & Lavell, 1959; Gottschalk & Gleser, 1960; Darbonne, 1969); relations to persons (Shneidman & Farberow, 1960); and computer count of key "tag" words (Ogilvie, Stone, & Shneidman, 1966).

One study, by Tripodes (1968), compared materials "before suicide" and materials "at the time of suicide." The former were Thematic Apperception Test protocols of persons who subsequently committed suicide; the latter were genuine suicide notes, albeit not of the same persons. The most important finding of this study is that the styles of reasoning and the patterns of logic are different at the time of suicide than they are some weeks or months before; specifically, at the time of suicide a person is more constricted, irrelevant, scattered, and disorganized in his logical style. He simply is not at his cerebral best at the moment of truth.

As a whole, these studies indicate that (1) it is possible to distinguish between genuine and simulated suicide notes, and, more importantly, (2) genuine suicide notes are generally characterized by dichotomous logic, a greater amount of hostility and self-blame, more use of very specific names and instructions to the survivors, less evidence of thinking about how one is thinking, and more use of the various meanings of the word "love."

Overall summary reports of suicide note studies have been listed by Bjerg (1967), reported in a concise summary by Frederick (1969), and presented and discussed by Lester (1972).

But in general the results of all these studies have been fragmentary and not as illuminating as one would have wished. In almost every case, the results have reflected more the method of analysis than the suicidal state of man, and although some of the findings are extremely interesting from several theoretical points of view, they have not provided an open sesame into the understanding of human self-destruction. In a word, the results of these carefully done studies, taken as a whole, have been deeply disappointing.

If this assessment of the relative barrenness of most suicide notes is correct, what might account for this characteristic? In order to generate a hypothesis I must digress slightly to speak of a closely related topic, *death.* These particular thoughts are sparked by two recent books on death by Kübler-Ross (1969) and by Weisman (1972). I have reviewed Kübler-Ross's book elsewhere (1971) and need not repeat my appraisal of that humane and warm volume except to say in this context that the main burden of her book is her assertion that there are five stages of dying (denial, anger, bargaining, depression, and acceptance). While I was drawn to the human and compassionate aspects of her book, I could not agree with her five stages of dying. In my own experience with dying persons (admittedly less intensive than hers)—individuals dying of leukemia, cancer, histiocytosis, etc.—I have never seen these five stages in any one person, must less seriatim. What I have seen is a *variety* of emotional postures, mood states, and existential positions, in a variety of different orders, always interspersed, though not necessarily between each stage, by *denial* (i.e., denial of the fact that the individual is dying). The key concept is denial. Intermittent denial is the ubiquitous psychological feature of the dying process (Shneidman, 1973). During the dying process, there are periods of constricted focus, tunneled vision, blinded view, and simple denial of the life-threatening illness and of the threat of death.

As its very title, *On Dying and Denying,* indicates, Avery Weisman's recent book (1972) focuses on the pivotal and ubiquitous role of *denial* in the dying process. Weisman discusses the purposes of denial in the following words:

> . . . denial is expressed in words, actions, and fantasies, but these are what people *do* in order to counter, categorize, and orient themselves in the presence of danger. . . . Although a potential danger is about to evoke denial, a common threatened danger is a *jeopardized relationship with a significant key person.* Hence, the purpose of denial is not simply to avoid a danger, but to prevent loss of a significant relationship . . . even when there seems to be no one in particular who threatens or could be threatened by a patient's illness, termination, or death, the patient himself may deny because he wants to maintain the *status quo* of already existing relationships. . . .

Nor is denial seen as a unitary, unchanging process, at one or another point in the dying process. Weisman (1972), says: "The balance between denial and accepting changes like a kaleidoscope during fatal illness; all fragments constantly re-arrange themselves into new patterns."

When a person comes to commit suicide his faculties of attention are constricted. There is a narrowing of focus of his perceptual field and he suffers from what might be called tunnel vision. Ringel has written about the "narrowing of the field of consciousness." Alvarez (1972) has called this "the closed world of suicide," which he describes in this way: "Once a man decides to take his own life he enters a shut-off, impregnable but wholly convincing world . . . where every detail fits and each incident reinforces his decision." Further, he says: "Each of these deaths has its own inner logic and unrepeatable despair. . . . [Suicide is] a terrible but utterly natural reaction to the strained, narrow, unnatural necessities we sometimes create for ourselves" (pp. 283–284).

This narrowing of the field of consciousness, the "closed world of suicide," the constriction of focus of attention, or the "tunnel vision" that one finds during the actual moments of a suicidal deed are dramatically illustrated in the following excerpt of a (beautiful and brilliant) 25-year-old woman who, in a transient period of acute confusion and panic, jumped several stories from a hospital balcony and—sustaining (only) several fractures of one leg and hip, a pneumothorax and some organ ruptures—miraculously survived. Two days previously she had ingested fifty 100-mg. sodium secobarbital tablets, had been discovered by her landlady, had been brought to the hospital and treated in the emergency room, and then had been placed in a hospital room. She said about that attempt: "I was pretty isolated at that time. Precisely at the moment of my 25th birthday I sort of went into a kind of panic state and things got worse and worse." She stated that she was angry that she had complicated everything by winding up in a hospital. I asked her what happened then. Here is a verbatim segment:

> Well, after that I was out of danger more or less and at that point they pretty much let me wander around the hospital as I pleased. And there was some question about my husband letting me return home, to the apartment, because he thought I was going to make another attempt and he couldn't bear to live with that. And it was just all up in the air, it was sort of like, well you go and find a place to stay and there was no place for me to stay. My sister wouldn't let me come stay with her and I don't know anyone here and so it turned out that I was going to be staying in some sort of welfare kind of arrangement which was going to be fixed or arranged by the social worker. All of a sudden there I was out in the middle of nowhere without any money, and my husband wasn't going to let me come back to the house and I was desperate. And then I went into a terrible state. So at this point I was supposed to be making these arrangements myself. I could barely even speak, you know, the social worker was calling various agen-

> cies and then turning the telephone over to me so I could tell my story and I could even barely remember my name let alone my date of birth or anything like that and I thought my God in Heaven, I can hardly even—and I was not functioning at all and these people are going to throw me into the street. And I didn't want to go to a psychiatric ward because I was really frightened that I would wind up—I would possibly have a psychotic episode or something like that. I was so desperate I felt my God, I can't face this thing. Going out, and being thrown out on the street. And everything was like a terrible sort of whirlpool of confusion. And I thought to myself there's only one thing I can do, I just have to lose consciousness. That's the only way to get away from it. The only way to lose consciousness, I thought, was to jump off something good and high. I just figured I had to get outside, but the windows were all locked. So I managed to get outside. I just slipped outside. No one saw me. And I got down to the ground by walking across that catwalk thing, sure that someone would see me, you know, out of all those windows. The whole building is made of glass. And I just walked around until I found this open staircase, and, as soon as I saw it I just made a beeline right up to it. And then, I got to the 5th floor and everything just got very dark all of a sudden, and all I could see was this balcony. Everything around it just sort of blacked out. It was just like a circle. That was all I could see, was just the balcony. And I went over it. I climbed over it and then I just let go. I was so desperate. Just desperation. And the horribleness and the quietness of it. The quiet. Everything became so quiet. There was no sound. And everything sort of went into slow motion as I climbed over the balcony. I let go and it was like I was floating. I blacked out. I don't remember any part of the fall. Just, just going. I don't remember anything after going over that balcony. I don't remember crying or screaming. I think I was panting from the exertion and the strain of running up all those stairs. And then, when I woke up I was having a dream, which seemed very weird. At that point I was in intensive care and I was looking at the patterns on the ceiling, you know the sort of metal inserts that are like this, and there's a light in the middle of each one. . . .

Writing of the suicide of several young poets, Boris Pasternak (1959), the famous author, has stated:

> A man who decides to commit suicide puts a full stop to his being, he turns his back on the past, he declares himself bankrupt and his memories to be unreal. They can no longer help or save him, he has put himself beyond their reach. The continuity of his inner life is broken, and his personality is at an end. And perhaps what finally makes him kill himself is not the firmness of his resolve but the unbearable quality of this anguish which belongs to no one, of this suffering in the absence of the sufferer, of this waiting which is empty because life has stopped and can no longer feel it. (pp. 88–89)

If this sense of personal emptiness is at all true of the suicidal person, is it any wonder that suicide notes, written at the very moment when an individual has lost touch with his own past, are concerned with the moment's minutiae and are relatively arid and psychologically barren?

One of the main functions of the personality is to protect itself from other aspects of itself. An individual cannot continually stare into the horrors of his own life; he needs to view them only tachistoscopically. At best, the topic of death is psychologically threatening and needs to be intermittently denied in order to maintain one's own mental balance and health. Denial is a necessary gyroscope in one's own psychic life.

Now to take the step from death to suicide (and to state my hypothesis about the reason for the relative barrenness of most suicide notes): In order for a person to kill himself he has to be in a special state of mind, a state of relatively fixed purpose (not gainsaying his ambivalence) and relative closed-mindedness. It is a psychological state which, while it permits suicide to occur (indeed facilitates suicide), obviously militates against insight or good communication. In other words, that special state of mind necessary to perform the suicidal deed is one which is essentially incompatible with an insightful recitation of what was going on in one's mind that led to the act itself.

Suicide notes are often like a parody of the postcards sent home from the Grand Canyon, the catacombs, or the pyramids—essentially unimaginative, *pro forma,* and not at all reflecting the grandeur of the scene being described or the grandeur of the human emotions that one might expect to be engendered by the situation. Melville, in his flawed masterpiece *Pierre,* described, in the language of genius, this special brand of emptiness:

> . . . we learn that it is not for man to follow the trail of truth too far, since by so doing he entirely loses the directing compass of his mind; for arrived at the Pole, to whose barrenness only it points, there, the needle indifferently respects all points of the horizon alike.
>
> By vast pains we mine into the pyramid; by horrible gropings we come to the central room; with joy we espy the sarcophagus; but we lift the lid—and no body is there!—appallingly vacant as vast is the soul of a man!

Admittedly it is difficult to select a prototypical suicide note, but my analysis of suicide note materials leads me to believe that such a note might sound rather like the pointedly empty conclusion of Ionesco's *The Chairs,* something to this effect:

> Ladies and Gentlemen: I am unhappy to be here today. I guess that I am gathered here to bespeak myself. What shall I say? I had it so clearly in mind just a short while ago. Now all I can say is that actions will have to speak louder than words. I sign this note as one who will soon no longer be himself. George.

In fact, actual suicide notes typically contain such phrases as "I love you. . . . I am sorry. . . . I am in pain. . . . I have lost the way. . . . Please don't blame yourself. . . . you drove me to this. . . . please be good to our child. . . . fix the spark plugs on the car. . . . don't come into this room. . . . " For one who seeks deep insights into the reasons for human self-destruction, the deep reasons why individuals intentionally end their own lives, these typical excerpts from genuine suicide notes are not very illuminating.

It is hypothesized that suicide notes cannot be the insightful documents which suicidologists would hope that they would be, mainly because they are written during a special psychological state, a state of focused purpose and narrow perception and psychodynamic denial. It is a state which, by its nature, precludes the individual's having access to the full ambivalent details of his own self-destructive drama and thus diminishes the possibility of his sharing with others (in a suicide note) what is truly going on in his mind.

In order to commit suicide one cannot write a meaningful suicide note; conversely, if one could write a meaningful note he would not "have to" commit suicide. Let me state the case in a highly figurative way: In almost every instance, one has to be, as it were, "intoxicated" or "drugged" in order to commit suicide, and it is well nigh impossible to write a psychologically meaningful document when one is in this special disordered state.[3]

However, by no means are all suicide notes dross or barren. There are many conspicuous exceptions in which the suicide note is filled with psychodynamic information, genuinely explaining the human reasons for the act and giving rather clear hints as to the unconscious reasons behind it. Occasionally a suicide note can serve an important "historical" role, as, for example, the suicide note of Percy W. Bridgman, the Nobel laureate in physics and famous American philosopher. His suicide note, dated August 20, 1961—reported by Holton in the *Bulletin of the Atomic Scientist* (1962)—written when he was 80 years old, is an indictment of the medical profession for their being loath to practice euthanasia on request. His note read: "It isn't decent for Society to make a man do this thing himself. Probably this is the last day I will be able to do it myself. p.w.b."

Bridgman had cancer and was in great pain. Earlier he had said that the "disease has run its normal course, and has now turned into a well-developed cancer for which nothing can be done . . . in the meantime there is considerable pain, and the doctors here do not offer much prospect that it can be made better." That he had cancer had been corroborated by two or three eminent physicians. He had asked them to give him a substance with which to end his life. They refused. The day before he shot himself he mailed to the Harvard University Press the index for the seven-volume collection of his complete scientific writings. In his earlier works he had discussed death. A few years before, in his book *The Way Things Are* (1959), writing about death he said: "If there is one thing which my own death is not it's a form of my own experience—when I am dead I no longer have experiences. The man who says 'I shall never die' cannot be refuted."

About one-third of those who commit suicide write suicide notes (Shneidman & Farberow, 1957a). Among those who commit suicide, what can we say psychologically about the note writers as compared with the nonwriters? We know from a previous study in Los Angeles (Shneidman & Farberow, 1960) that the distribution for sex, age, marital status, and socioeconomic status of the two groups has been found to be essentially the same. Further, on this point, Tuckman, Kleiner, & Lavell (1959) independently found—in a study of 165 notes collected in the Philadelphia area—that a "comparison of those who left notes with those who did not showed no significant difference between the two groups with respect to age, race, sex, employment, marital status, physical condition, mental condition, history of mental illness, place of suicide, reported causes or unusual circumstances preceding the suicide, medical care and supervision, and history of previous attempts or threats."

It is reasonable to assume that the contents of suicide notes vary according to who is expected to read the note—which can communicate a variety of messages, including apology, self-justification, revenge, anger, or even the wish to arouse curiosity or to create a mystery. What do some of the available data tend to show about the *addressees* of suicide notes? A survey was made of 906 suicide notes collected in the Los Angeles area in the 1940s and 1950s (Shneidman & Farberow, 1960). (This is the same set of notes from which the 33 genuine notes referred to elsewhere in this paper were selected.) The notes were examined in terms of the following categories of addressee, with the following findings. No addressee, 20%; to whom it may concern, 7%; police, 5%; spouse, 20%; parent, 6%; progeny, 8%; sibling, 3%; friend, 7%; a specific person, relationship not indicated, 15%; and other, 8%. Some additional results were as follows: More men than women had no addressee on their suicide notes or addressed their notes to their spouse; fewer men than women addressed their notes to their parents, children, or siblings. Not unexpectedly, the addressee differed among the various age groups: parents and friends as addressees sharply decreased after age 30; progeny as addressees increased after age 40; no addressee, increased after age 60; and, conversely, spouse as addressee decreased after age 60.[4]

Who, among those who commit suicide, writes suicide notes? Suicide note writers, I would currently hypothesize, are people who typically in their lives have a penchant for elaborating the obvious, explaining the apparent, belaboring the given, and repeating the unnecessary. There is probably a pervasive subtle redundancy in their life style. To a "Quarantine—Measles" sign such a person might add the words "Illness inside—please stay out." To a "House for Sale" sign, he might put the postscript "Owner moving, forced to sell." These addenda can be called "information duplication," for, after all, what can a suicide note pinned on the chest possibly add to the essence of information immediately conveyed by the hanging body itself? Seen in this light, a suicide note is one of the world's most "unnecessary" documents.

Erwin Stengel, in his book *Suicide and Attempted Suicide* says: "Whether the writers of suicide notes differ in their attitudes from those who leave no notes behind, it is impossible to say. Possibly they differ from the majority only in being good correspondents." The latter hypothesis, which Stengel seems to have mentioned in his book almost facetiously, has not so far been rigorously tested. It would seem to merit serious attention from students of suicide notes.

One can imagine at least two sets of motives for writing a suicide note: social motives, involving primarily the desire to have one's behavior understood by others, and personal motives, relating to the desire for self-expression for its own sake and to a number of secondary gains. In general, we cannot hope fully to understand suicide notes if we neglect the fact that the suicide note writer knows that he is writing a suicide note. In this light, we need to keep in mind that some persons will, each in his own idiosyncratic fashion, seek to exploit the latent possibilities in making oneself the momentary focus of attention. It is not always clear in reading a suicide note which were the primary motives at work in the production of the note.

A "good" suicide note would have to be written at least a fortnight before the act—in a more open frame of mind. But then of course it might not strictly be a suicide note but rather a journal or a diary. There are a few extensive diaries in the public domain of individuals who subsequently committed suicide. Two of them are reproduced in Ruth Cavan's book, *Suicide* (1928). One is by a young woman of 26 who kept a diary of over 50,000 words over a seven-year period and who subsequently committed suicide by shooting herself; the other is a diary kept by a young man, age 23, for a period of just over one and a half years. His last entry was on the day of his death before he drowned himself.

In Ponsonby's book, *English Diaries* (1923), there is a remarkable diary by the nineteenth-century painter B. R. Haydon covering a period of 26 years, from 1820 to 1846, including an entry about an hour before his suicide by cutting his throat and shooting himself in the head.

These diaries are "the real thing."[5] They permit one to see the life in its longitudinal workings. They are serial glimpses over extended time into what William James in his *Principles of Psychology* (1890) called "the recesses of feeling, the darker, blinder strata of character which are the only places in the world in which we catch real fact in the making, and directly perceive how events happen and how work is actually done."

Perhaps the most extensive personal document relating to suicide is the famous *Confessions* of Jean Jacques Rousseau (1781). The encyclopedias of this century (including the 1973 edition of the *Britannica*) invariably list Rousseau's death as a natural death, although Choron says that Rousseau "was rumored to have eventually committed suicide . . . what seems certain is that Rousseau talked suicide at length with David Hume whose ungrateful guest he was in 1776–1777." However, if one goes back to the early nineteenth century one finds that Rousseau's death is reported as a suicide. In a recent article, Fuller quotes extensively from a textbook on suicide written by a French physician, Jean Pierre Falret, in 1822 *(De l'hypochondrie et du suicide)*. The relevant section is as follows:

> . . . in some people the idea of suicide tortures them for months or even years. This affliction seems to have sapped the existence of the Geneva philosopher for a long time. Possessed of a happy temperament but gifted by a too high sensitivity Rousseau becomes affected by the miserable state he finds himself in and the most somber melancholia fills his heart. Apprehensive, fainthearted, timid, suspicious, he avoids the company of men because he believes they are all perverse, all his enemies. He seeks solitude and soon wishes for death. Let's look at some of his immortal writings to justify our assertion: "Here I am all alone on earth, without relatives, friends or society. Thus the most loving of men has been banished by a unanimous agreement. I have been in this painful situation for more than twenty years; it still seems like a dream to me. I have head pains and continuous indigestion. The least thing scares me, upsets me and saddens me. Since my body is only an embarrassment, an *obstacle* to my rest, I shall *seek* a way to divest myself of it, the sooner the better." This great writer accomplished his fatal project. The morning of the day Rousseau died, Madame De Stael reported. "He got up in his usual state of health, but he said he was going to see the sun for the *last time*." He had taken some coffee he himself had prepared before going out. He came in a few hours later and began suffering horribly. He *forbade* anyone to call for help or to notify anyone. A few days before this sad day Rousseau had noticed the vile inclinations of his wife toward a man of very low social condition. This had crushed him and he had spent eight hours on the edge of the lake in deep meditation.

If indeed Rousseau did commit suicide then his extended *Confessions* may well constitute the most remarkable and the most complete "suicide note" that we know. We shall need to study these documents—the confessions and the diaries—in greater detail to understand the psychological development of the suicidal drama.[6]

I move now from Rousseau to other philosophers for a brief epistemological aside—invoking the shades of Bacon, Kant, Hume, and especially Hegel. Hegel believed that the product of the interaction of thesis and antithesis, driven by the power of the negative, was a new synthesis. A contemporary psychodynamically-oriented psychologist would rather envisage the union of thesis and antithesis in terms of their continual coexistence, reflecting the psychological dualities in man (e.g., in many, simultaneous love and hate; in some few, at a special time, simultaneously wishing to live and wishing to die). For this state or condition I would propose the word *ambithesis.* I believe it to be the most typical state of mind, and paradoxically the least often represented, in suicide notes—for the reasons which I have outlined in this paper. I would propose five possible (epistemological) kinds of suicide notes.

1. Thetical. Those notes which assert a thesis; are declarative or testimonial. An example would be Percy Bridgman's note declaring that doctors should be permitted to practice euthanasia upon request.

> *Sample note*[7]*:* Dearest darling i want you to know that you are the only one in my life i love you so much i could not do without you please forgive me i drove myself sick honey please beleave me i love you again an the baby honey don't be mean with me please I have lived fifty years since i met you, I love you—I love you. Dearest darling i love you i love you. Please don't discraminat me darling i know that i will die dont be mean with me please i love you more than you will ever know darling please an honey Tom i know don't tell Tom why his daddy said good by honey. Can't stand it any more. Darling i love you. Darling i love you.

2. Antithetical. Those notes which rebut or deny a stated or implied thesis.

> *Sample note:* Good by Kid. You couldn't help it. Tell that brother of yours, When he gets where I'm going. I hope I'm a foreman down there. I might be able to do something for him.

3. Synthetical. Those notes which, in a new insight, combine (or attempt to combine) the basic tenets of a thesis and its antithesis.

> *Sample note:* To my wife Mary: As you know, like we've talked over before our situation, I'll always love you with all my heart and soul. It could

have been so simple if you had have given me the help that you alone knew I needed.

This is not an easy thing I'm about to do, but when a person makes a few mistakes and later tried to say in his own small way with a small vocabulary that he is sorry for what has happened and promises to remember what has happened and will try to make the old Bill come home again, and do his best to start all over again, and make things at home much better for all concerned, you still refuse to have me when you as well as I know that I can't do it by myself, then there's only one thing to do.

I'm sorry honey, but please believe me this is the only way out for me as long as you feel as you do—This will put you in good shape. Please always take care of Betty and tell her that her Daddy wasn't too bad a guy after all. With all the love that's in me.

Yes, Mommie, now you have your car and a lot more too, even more than you had hoped for. At least you are better off financially than you were 6 years ago. The only pitiful thing about the whole situation is the baby and the nice car that I bought with blood money. I only hope I do a good job of it. Then your troubles will be over with. I know this is what you have been hoping for a long time. I'm not crazy, I just love you too much!!!

I love you—Daddy—Goodbye forever.

4. Athetical. A suicide note which is lacking in "a point of view" and simply contains instructions or directions.

Sample note: Dear Mary. I am writeing you, as our Divorce is not final, and will not be till next month, so the way things stand now you are still my wife, which makes you entitled to the things which belong to me, and I want you to have them. Don't let anyone take them from you as they are yours. Please see a lawyer and get them as soon as you can. I am listing some of the things, they are: A Blue Davenport and chair, a Magic Chef Stove, a large mattress, an Electrolux cleaner, a 9 x 12 Rug redish flower design and pad. All the things listed above are all most new. Then there is my 30-30 rifle, books, typewriter, tools and a hand contract for a house in Chicago, a Savings account in Boston, Mass. Your husband, William H. Smith

5. Ambithetical. Those notes which present the simultaneous coexistence of a point of view and its opposite (contrary, contradictory, antinomy). Ambithetical suicide notes come closer to the psychological realities of how the person really feels. This type of suicide note—from which we learn most about suicide—is relatively rare. The expression of the ubiquitous ambivalence of the human spirit needs time for contemplation. That is why it is seen only on occasion in some extended journals, some few diaries, some rare series of letters, and among some special ambithetical authors such as Stendhal *(The Red and the Black)*, Tolstoy *(War and Peace)*, Hesse *(Narcissus and Goldmund* and "Klein and Wagner"), and especially Melville ("The Paradise of Bachelors and the Tartarus of Maids," Lucy and Isabel in *Pierre*, and the stark white dualities of good and evil which permeate *Moby Dick*). The key is in the conjunction.

It may well be that for Knowledge or Science the Hegelian model of attempting to unify opposites (spirit and nature, universal and particular, ideal and real, thesis and antithesis) into a transcending synthesis has its own special merits, but to describe the stream of an individual's inner psychological life, it may make more sense to think in terms of thesis—antithesis—ambithesis—not serially as Hegel believed, but flowing and concomitantly as Freud implied. Synthesis is itself an ideal; ambivalence is the human condition.

For reasons which the reader should now be able to understand, I have advertently chosen not to illustrate ambithesis with a suicide note, but shall instead quote a pivotal passage from Melville *(White-Jacket):*

> As I gushed into the sea, a thunder-boom sounded in my ear; my soul seemed flying from my mouth. The feeling of death flooded over me with the billows. The blow from the sea must have turned me, so that I sank almost feet foremost through a soft, seething foamy lull. Some current seemed hurrying me away; in a trance I yielded, and sank deeper down with a glide. Purple and pathless was the deep calm now around me, flecked by summer lightnings in an azure afar. The horrible nausea was gone; the bloody, blind film turned a pale green; I wondered whether I was yet dead, or still dying. But of a sudden some fashionless form brushed my side—some inert, soiled fish of the sea; the thrill of being alive again tingled in my nerves, and the strong shunning of death shocked me through.
>
> For one instant an agonising revulsion came over me as I found myself utterly sinking. Next moment the force of my fall was expended; and there I hung, vibrating in the mid-deep. What wild sounds then rang in my ear! One was a soft moaning, as of low waves on the beach; the other wild and heartlessly jubilant, as of the sea in the height of a tempest. Oh soul! thou then heardest life and death: as he who stands upon the Corinthian shore hears both the Ionian and the Aegean waves. The life-and-death poise soon passed; and then I found myself slowly ascending, and caught a dim glimmering of light.
>
> Quicker and quicker I mounted; till at last I bounded up like a buoy, and my whole head was bathed in the blessed air.

Up to this point, I have spoken about persons who have committed suicide. But if one is being pushed toward death, under the threat of a terminal disease or of execution, then apparently the psychological situation is quite different. Then one is forced from the outside to marshall one's psychic energies and, being so affected, can speak with passion and relevance. Witness the letters from the German concentration camps, and the letters written on the eve of their announced execution date by John Brown, Fiodor Dostoevsky (who was not executed), and Bartolomeo Vanzetti (all in Schuster's [1940] book of letters), and the poem, written in 1583 in the Tower of London by Chidiock Tichborne, a young nobleman who plotted against Queen Elizabeth I and who was caught, imprisoned, and beheaded. Of all these interesting pieces I reproduce only the second of the three verses from Tichborne's elegy:

> My tale was heard, and yet it was not told;
> My fruit is fall'n, and yet my leaves are green;
> My youth is spent, and yet I am not old;
> I saw the world, and yet I was not seen;
> My thread is cut, and yet it is not spun;
> And now I live, and now my life is done.

Here is another relevant quotation from the Danish psychiatrist Frederik F. Wagner (1960):

> It is interesting to note a striking difference between such letters and farewell letters of an entirely different category; letters from people who were convinced of facing an immediate, inevitable, unwanted death. In [Brocher's] *Letzte Briefe aus Stalingrad* (Last Letters from Stalingrad) (1954) the German soldiers openly express their feelings of despair and bitterness against their leadership, but even more often they dwell upon their "happy childhood," the "happy years" before the war or prior to the Hitler period, and first of all: their love for their relatives. In short: They stick to life. As an example of documents of particular high human quality can be mentioned the letters from members of the Danish resistance movement (1946) during the German occupation, written the night before their execution. These letters reveal a positive, dignified, often religious attitude towards life and a warm attachment to the family.

This special insight-giving quality is especially noteworthy in documents written by people who knew that they were dying of a fatal disease and who openly addressed themselves to their feelings about dying and death. What is to be noted about these documents is the amount of psychological information which they yield (in contrast to suicide notes). This may be because they were written over a period of time in which the individual has had an opportunity to experience (and to communicate) a variety of emotional states—including periods of denial. Whereas a level of denial characterizes the entire brief period of writing a suicide note, it would seem safe to assume that when a dying person is in a period of denial he simply does not turn to his manuscript. Thus the dying person's manuscript is composed during his more "lucid" periods. Recent articles of this genre include an article by a dying housewife (Helton, 1972), the personal report by a psychiatric social worker dying of cancer (Harker, 1972), reflections of a dying professor (Anon., 1972), and an account by a 30-year-old psychiatrist who discovered one day that he had acute myelogenous leukemia (Trombley, 1972). It is this last-named essay which is alluded to in the opening paragraph of this article as a contrast to a suicide note written by another person of the same age and occupation. The reader is encouraged to compare for himself that suicide note with Trombley's extended personal reflections and sharings. A few brief quotations must, in this context, suffice:

> . . . My reasons for writing this paper are to objectify and clarify my own feelings regarding my illness, to help crystallize my perspective on matters of living and dying, and to inform others in a subjective way about the psychological processes which take place in a person who has a life-threatening disease. . . . I have not yet found any enlightenment as to why people in our profession do not write about this. . . . In November 1966, I discovered that I had acute myelogenous leukemia. [p. 26] My initial reactions are difficult to describe and still more difficult to recall accurately. However, I do remember feeling that somehow the doctor's remarks could not be directed to me but must be about some other person. Of course, I shook off that feeling very soon during this conversation and the full realization of the import of this diagnosis struck me, I was steeped in a pervasive sense of deep and bitter disappointment. I thought that I had been maliciously cheated out of the realization of all the hopes and aims that I had accrued during my professional career. . . . The next subjective feeling I can clearly identify is that I was increasingly apprehensive following the diagnosis about my inevitable decreasing body efficiency and thus very likely my decreasing efficiency and interest in my work. . . . This engendered some little guilt over my anticipating not being able to do the job I had been doing. . . . Nonetheless, I did have pangs of remorse when I finally had to stop seeing long-term patients because my physical symptoms interfered too much with appointments. Surprisingly, I did not feel consciously angry or frightened by the knowledge that I had a life-threatening illness. [p. 27]
>
> I was gravely disappointed and terribly annoyed that this thing inside my body would interfere with my life, but at no time did I really feel, as one might put it, "angered at the gods" for having such sport with me. Nor did I find that I used denial as a defense to any extent early in the course of the illness, as I did later on when it appeared that some of the chemotherapeutic measures were having considerably good effect and I began to feel that I could go on interminably from drug to drug and not die of my disease. [p. 28]
>
> One almost amusing idea came to light through one of my supervisors, namely that some of my colleagues might very well be wishing that I would drop dead and get it over with rather than continue to torment them as I was. For others there was a heightened awareness of a close relationship that had never been verbalized in the past. This occurred with two

or three of my fellow residents and certainly we were all the better for it. Not only was there some clarification of feelings and a chance openly to discuss them between us, but also this produced a closer relationship. [p. 29]

People wrongly assume that a sick person should be "protected" from strong, and particularly negative feelings. The truth is that there is probably no more crucial time in a person's life when he needs to know what's going on with those who are important to him. [p. 30]

In the several months since the inception of my illness I became increasingly aware of a new sensitivity that had gradually but progressively developed in my interpersonal relationships, both with patients and with all my acquaintances. . . . One thing I noticed most pointedly was that I was very much more tolerant of the vagaries and inconsistencies of other people's attitudes and behavior than I had ever been before. . . . This heightened awareness of affect in others also extended to myself and I found that my own feelings were much more accessible to my conscious recognition than they had been in the past. I also found that all of my senses seemed more acute, though I believe that really I simply paid more attention to what was going on around me and, in a way, I found myself hungering for every sensory experience that I could absorb. In many ways the world seemed to offer more beauty and there was a heightened awareness of sounds and sights, which in the past I may have only casually observed or simply not have paid much attention to at all. [p. 32]

It would appear that the peace I made with myself during my illness and the maturing ability that I was developing to cope with life crises like this one, arose from several dynamic factors. One was the increasing capacity to sublimate the rage and aggression engendered by the impotency I felt regarding this invasion from within. . . . It was very seldom that I was conscious of any feelings of despair or depression. . . . Certainly there are rewarding aspects of facing life-threatening illness. I have learned much about the alterations in my own internal psychological processes, and the subtle metamorphosis in interpersonal relationships which have occurred and are still occurring. I wish that other people in my position would write also subjectively about this. Perhaps this paper may encourage it. [p. 33]

To return to suicide notes:

It seems as though we tend to confuse the drama of the suicidal situation with our own expectations that there be some dramatic psychodynamic insights in the communications written during the moments of that drama. But the fact remains that memorable (authenticated) words uttered *during* battle or *on* one's deathbed are relatively rare. It seems to be true also of suicide notes. Understandably, however, we continue to hope that any individual, even an ordinary individual, standing on the brink of what man has always conceptualized as life's greatest adventure and mystery, ought to have some special message for the rest of us. Western civilization has for centuries romanticized death (Shneidman,

1971b); we tend to read with special reverence and awe *any* words, however banal, that are part of a death-oriented document and thus we tend to think of suicide notes as almost sacred and expansive pieces of writing. And we are then understandably disappointed when we discover that, after all, suicide notes are always secular and usually constricted.

☐ Endnotes

[1]"The Bishop's Robe," *The New Yorker,* June 2, 1973, p. 39.

[2]A book of letters edited by Allport himself, *Letters from Jenny* (1965), is of especial psychological interest.

[3]A few words about "causes" of suicide may be useful. If one thinks, as one must, of a hierarchy or multiplicity of causes involving several layers—precipitating causes, secondary causes, sustaining or resonating causes, and primary causes—then it is clear that most suicide notes (and practically all newspaper accounts of suicide), when they touch upon causes at all, seem to deal solely with *precipitating* causes (e.g., ill health, being jilted, etc.), woeful conditions which happen to many people, most of whom do *not* commit suicide. This fact, in some large part, accounts for the relative shallowness of most discussions of (and many publications on) this topic and, further, for the somewhat "superficial" quality that one finds in most suicide notes.

[4]A separate paper on these data is to be published in the journal *Life-Threatening Behavior* by Arthur Ryskind, a UCLA student, to whom I am indebted for supplying the information cited in this paragraph.

[5]For a markedly contrary view on the usefulness of diaries, here is C. S. Lewis, from his extraordinary autobiography, *Surprised by toy* (1955) "If theism had done nothing else for me, I should still be thankful that it cured me of the time-wasting and foolish practice of keeping a diary. (Even for autobiographical purposes a diary is nothing as useful as I had hoped. You put down each day what you think important; but of course you cannot each day see what will prove important in the long run.)" Not much to gain from theism!

[6]My deep and abiding debt to Henry A. Murray (1949, 1959, 1967) should be obvious, for appropriately emphasizing the special usefulness of studying detailed data on a relatively few individuals in a multidisciplinary fashion over an extended period of time.

[7]This actual suicide note and the following three notes are from the appendix of *Clues to Suicide* (Shneidman and Farberow, 1957).

☐ References

Allport, G. W. (1965). *The use of personal documents in psychological science.* New York: Social Science Research Council.

Allport, G. W. (1965). *Letters from Jenny.* Harcourt, Brace & World.

Alvarez, A. (1972). *The savage god: A study of suicide.* Random House.

Anonymous. (1972, March). Notes of a dying professor. *Pennsylvania Gazette,* pp. 18–24.

Bjerg, K. (1967). The suicidal life-space: Attempts at a reconstruction from suicide notes. In E. S. Shneidman (Ed.), *Essays in self-destruction.* Internat. Science Press.

Bridgman, P. W. (1959). *The way things are.* Viking Press.

Capstick, A. Recognition of emotional disturbance and the prevention of suicide. *British Medical Journal, 1*:1–179.

Cavan, R. S. (1928). *Suicide.* New York: Russell & Russell.

Choron, J. (1972). *Suicide.* Scribner's.

Darbonne, A. R. (1969). Suicide and age: A suicide note analysis. *Journal of Consulting and Clinical Psychology, 33,* 46–50.

Farberow, N. L. (1957). Suicide and Age. In E. S. Shneidman & N. L. Farberow (Eds.), *Clues to suicide.* McGraw-Hill, 1957.

Frederick, C. J. (1969, March). Suicide notes: A survey and evaluation. *Bulletin of Suicidology,* 17–26.

Fuller, M. (1973). Suicide past and present: A note on Jean Pierre Falret. *Life-Threatening Behavior, 3,* 58–65.

Gottschalk, L. A., & Gleser, G. C. (1960). An analysis of the verbal content of suicide notes. *British Journal of Medical Psychology, 33,* 195–204.

Harker, B. L. (1972). Cancer and communication problems: A personal experience. *Psychiatry in Medicine, 3,* 163–171.

Helton, L. (1972, January 16). Soon there will be no more me. *Los Angeles Times, WEST Magazine,* pp. 8–13.

Holton, G. (1962, February). Percy Williams Bridgman. *Bulletin of the Atomic Scientist,* pp. 22–23.

Hood, R. W., Jr. (1970). Effects of foreknowledge of manner of death in the assessment from genuine and simulated suicide notes of intent to die. *Journal of General Psychology, 82,* 215–221.

Jacobs, J. (1967). A phenomenological study of suicide notes. *Social Problems, 15,* 60–72.

James, W. (1890). *Principles of psychology.* Henry Holt.

Kübler-Ross, E. (1969). *On death and dying.* Macmillan.

Lester, D. (1972). *Why people kill themselves.* Charles C Thomas.

Lewis, C. S. (1955). *Surprised by joy.* London: Fontana Books.

Melville, H. (1971). *Pierre or the ambiguities.* Northwestern-Newberry. (Original work published 1852).

Melville, H. (1970). *White-jacket.* Northwestern-Newberry. (Original work published 1850).

Mill, J. S. (1892). *System of logic.* London: George Routledge.

Morgenthaler, W. (1945). Letzte aufzeichnungen von selbstmorden. *Beheift fur scheizerischen zeitschrift fur psychologie und ihre anwendungen, No. 1.* Berne: Hans Huber.

Murray, H. A. (1949). Research planning: A few proposals. In S. S. Sargent & M. W. Smith (Eds.), *Culture and personality.* Basic Books.

Murray, H. A. (1959). Preparations for the scaffold of a comprehensive system. In S. Koch (Ed.), *Psychology: A study of a science: Vol. 3. Formulations of the person and the social context.* McGraw-Hill.

Murray, H. A. (1967). Autobiography. In E. G. Boring & G. Lindzey (Eds.), *A history of psychology in autobiography: Vol. 5.* Appleton-Century-Crofts.

Neuringer, C. (1961). Dichotomous evaluations in suicidal individuals. *Journal of Consulting Psychology, 25,* 445–449.

Neuringer, C. (1964). Rigid thinking in suicidal individuals. *Journal of Consulting Psychology, 28,* 54–58.

Neuringer, C. (1967). The cognitive organization of meaning in suicidal individuals. *Journal of General Psychology, 76,* 91–100.

Neuringer, C. & Lettieri, D. J. (1971). Cognition, attitude, and affect in suicidal individuals. *Life-Threatening Behavior, 1,* 106–124.

Ogilvie, D. M., Stone, P. J., & Shneidman, E. S. (1966). Some characteristics of genuine versus simulated suicide notes. In P. J. Stone et al. (Eds.), *The general inquirer: A computer approach to content analysis.* MIT Press.

Osgood, C. E., & Walker, E. G. (1959). Motivation and language behavior: A content analysis of suicide notes. *Journal of Abnormal and Social Psychology, 59,* 58–67.

Pasternak, B. (1959). *I remember: Sketch for an autobiography.* Pantheon.

Ponsonby, A. (1923). *English diaries.* London: Methuen.

Rousseau, J-J. (1954). *Confessions.* Penguin Books. (Original work published 1781).

Schuster, M. L. (Ed.) (1940). *Treasury of the world's great letters.* Simon & Schuster.

Shneidman, E. S. (1969). Logical content analysis: An explication of styles of "Concludifying." In G. Gerbner et al. (Eds.), *The analysis of communication content.* Wiley.

Shneidman, E. S. (1971a). Perturbation and lethality as precursors of suicide in a gifted group. *Life-Threatening Behavior, 1,* 23–45.

Shneidman, E. S. (1971b). On the deromanticization of death. *American Journal of Psychotherapy, 25,* 4–17.

Shneidman, E. S. (1971c). Review of Kübler-Ross's *On death and dying. Life-Threatening Behavior, 1,* 209–214.

Shneidman, E. S. (1973). *Deaths of man.* Quadrangle.

Shneidman, E. S., & Farberow, N. L. (Eds.) (1957a). *Clues to suicide.* McGraw-Hill.

Shneidman, E. S., & Farberow, N. L. (1957b). The logic of suicide. In *Clues to Suicide.* McGraw-Hill. (Also published in 1970), in *The psychology of suicide.* Science House.

Shneidman, E. S., & Farberow, N. L. (1957c). Some comparisons between genuine and simulated suicide notes in terms of Mowrer's concepts of discomfort and relief. *Journal of General Psychology, 56,* 251–256.

Shneidman, E. S., & Farberow, N. L. (1960). A sociopsychological investigation of suicide. In H. David & J. C. Brengelmann (Eds.), *Perspectives in personality research.* Springer.

Stengel, E. (1964). *Suicide and attempted suicide.* Penguin.

Tichborne, C. (1960). Elegy. Written in the Tower before his execution, 1586. In N. Ault (Ed.), *Elizabethan Lyrics.* Capricorn Books.

Tripodes, P. (1968). Reasoning patterns in suicide. Los Angeles, Suicide Prevention Center (mimeograph).

Trombley, L. E. (1972). A psychiatrist's response to a life-threatening illness. *Life-Threatening Behavior, 2,* 26–34.

Tuckman, J., Kleiner, R. J., & Lavell, M. (1959). Emotional content of suicide notes. *American Journal of Psychiatry, 116,* 59–63.

Wagner, F. F. (1960). Suicide notes. *Danish Medical Journal, 7,* 62–64.

Weisman, A. D. (1972). *On dying and denying.* Behavioral Pubs.

21

CHAPTER

Self-Destruction: Suicide Notes and Tragic Lives

> The path to my fixed purpose is laid
> with iron rails, whereon my soul is
> grooved to run.
> Herman Melville, *Moby Dick* (Chapter 37)

There is probably no description of suicide that contains as much insight in as few words as that found in the opening paragraph of *Moby Dick:* ". . . a damp, drizzly November in my soul." In its essence, that is what most suicide is: a dreary and dismal wintry storm within the mind, where staying afloat or going under is the vital decision being debated. In about one fourth of these occasions where a suicide is going to be committed, the individual will write something about that debate. Those documents—suicide notes—have something of the fascination of a cobra: they catch our eyes, yet we are ever conscious that some serious threat may lurk in them.

As rutters, suicide notes are cryptic maps of ill-advised journeys. A suicide note, no matter how persuasive it seems within its own closed world, is not a model for conducting a life. When one examines suicide notes, one can only shudder to read these testimonials to tortuous life journeys that came to wrecked ends. They fascinate us for what they tell us about the human condition and what they warn us against in ourselves.

Reprinted from E. Shneidman, *Voices of Death.* New York: Harper & Row, 1980, pp. 41–76. With permission.

My own long-term sustained study of them is admittedly a somewhat arcane pursuit. It would be like someone's contemporary fascination with alchemy, phlogiston or the inheritance of acquired characteristics, or with the notion that the world is flat, or that the earth is the center of the universe, or the proof that Bacon really wrote Shakespeare's plays—all flawed ideas. The difference that may make my obsession with suicide notes seem legitimate is that I know that suicide notes—like the many schizophrenic diaries I have read—are flawed rutters. I have never read a suicide note that I would want to have written.

But what can we actually learn about suicide from suicide notes? In the last twenty-five years, my answers to this question have undergone some radical changes. I have held three different positions on the relationship of suicide notes to suicidal phenomena.

My original view on the value of suicide notes dates from that special day in 1949 when I unexpectedly came across several hundred suicide notes in the vaults of a coroner's office. Since then, almost without a flagging of interest, I have been fascinated with suicide notes as perhaps the best available way of understanding suicidal phenomena. I believed that it was possible to unlock the mysteries of suicidal phenomena by using suicide notes as the keys. When one addresses the question: "Why do people take this trip?" (i.e., commit suicide), one can reasonably look upon suicide notes as psychological rutters and search them for clues as to how the tragic outcome of that life's voyage might have been averted. It would seem that suicide notes, written as they are in the very context of the suicidal act, often within a few minutes of the death-producing deed, would offer a special window into the thinking and the feeling of the act itself. In no other segment of human behavior is there such a close relationship of document to deed.

My subsequent counter reaction to that view was a (somewhat exaggerated) jump to an almost opposite position. In that position I believed that suicide notes, written as they were by individuals in a state of psychological constriction and of truncated and narrowed thinking, could hardly ever—by virtue of the state in which they were composed—be illuminating or even important psychological documents. Admittedly, that point of view had a touch of "overkill" in it.

I now believe that suicide notes, by themselves, are uniformly neither bountiful nor banal, but that they definitely can have a great deal of meaning under certain circumstances, specifically when they are put into the context of the detailed life history of the individual who both wrote the note and committed the act. In those instances—where we have both the suicide note and an extended life history—the note will then illuminate many aspects of the life history, and conversely, the life history can make many key words of the note come alive and take on special meanings that would otherwise have remained hidden or lost. My present view is thus an amalgamation of my two previous views.

To readers who know their philosophy, this process will remind them of the ideas of the German philosopher Georg Wilhelm Friedrich Hegel. Hegel believed that all thought and development of ideas proceeded in a certain way. Specifically, the process begins with an affirmation of an idea (which he called the "thesis"), then it gives way to its opposite (the "antithesis"), and then the two are united by a new idea which combines them (the "synthesis"). This process (which may take minutes or years or decades or centuries), repeated over and over, endlessly, Hegel called the "dialectic." (This idea influenced Friedrich Engels and Karl Marx in their "dialectical materialism.") What has happened over the last quarter century in relation to my own thoughts about suicide notes has unconsciously mirrored some aspects of this basic dialectical process and might be called a "dialectical suicidology."

☐ I

The findings of many previous investigations over the past century—starting with Brierre de Boismont's systematic study in 1856—have been extraordinarily diverse and diffuse. As a whole, these studies of suicide notes tell us that the suicidal person—specifically as compared with the nonsuicidal person—is likely to think in terms of dichotomous logic, separating everything in his world into two mutually exclusive categories (like perfect and nothing, life and death), and to be constricted and focused in his thinking; to think in terms of specific instructions (as opposed to broad or philosophic generalization), writing to his survivors-to-be as though he were going to be alive to supervise his wishes; to avoid intellectualizing (i.e., to avoid thinking about how he is thinking), dealing more with raw feeling than with rational thought; to be concerned with blaming, both others (the expression of hostility) and oneself (the expression of guilt or shame); and to be concerned with love—the various aspects, nuances and shading of affection, affiliation, devotion and either romantic or erotic love.

The figures vary as to the percentage of individuals who commit suicide who also leave suicide notes, ranging from 15 percent to over 30 percent. Who, among those who commit suicide, writes suicide notes? Except for knowing that note writers and non-note writers are essentially similar in terms of all the major demographic variables—age, race, sex, employment status, marital status, physical condition, history of mental illness, place of suicide and history of previous suicidal attempts—we know very little about the psychology of suicide-note writing. The distinguished suicidologist Erwin Stengel, in his scholarly book *Suicide and Attempted Suicide* (1964) said: "Whether the writers of suicide notes differ in their attitudes from those who leave no notes behind, it is impossible to say. Possibly they differ from the majority only in being good correspondents." That sounds like as reasonable an explanation as any.

Studies of suicide notes have dispelled at least one myth about suicide: that suicidal acts are uniformly motivated by a single formula. Of course, no one commits suicide who is not, in some way and to some heightened extent, intellectually or emotionally distraught, but these perturbations can take the form of the passions of unrequited love, intellectual self-assertion, shame and guilt related to disgrace, the wish to escape from the pain of insanity, the wish to spare loved ones from further anguish, and a sense of inner pride and autonomy connected to one's own fate and the manner of one's own death. All these psychological threads, and more, are found in suicide notes.

Suicidal acts are very complicated psychological events—never mind their social, sociological or anthropological components. "Just" from a psychological point of view, there are many underlying, resonating and sustaining causes (together with a multiplicity of precipitating events) that come together in each suicidal event. Nevertheless, we occasionally find a suicide note in which one particular emotional state will figure so clearly that it will seem to characterize (or at least to dominate) that particular suicidal act. In these cases we are almost beguiled into believing that this single emotion was the sole (if not the primary) cause of the act itself. Here are some examples.

Hate

In the now famous meeting of Freud and others in Vienna in 1910—the only meeting of the psychoanalytic group specifically on the topic of suicide—Wilhelm Stekel enunciated what was to become the orthodox psychoanalytic view. He said: "No one kills himself except as he wishes the death of another" (Friedman, 1967). Suicide was seen by the early psychoanalysts primarily as hostility directed toward the ambivalently viewed loved person who had been introjected into one's own unconscious mind—what I have called "murder in the 180th degree."

It is certainly not difficult to find evidence of hostility in contemporary suicide notes that would seem to support this hypothesis. The following hate note is from a most unusual set of suicide notes. Between 1934—the year after Fiorello La Guardia became mayor of New York City and began to reform the police department—and 1940, in a half-dozen years, ninety-three New York City policemen committed suicide. Only two papers have been written about this strange epidemic (Friedman, 1975). Among these ninety-three police suicides, nineteen left suicide notes. Here is one of the shortest and one of the angriest, written by a thirty-seven-year-old patrolman who was in a bar waiting for his sergeant, whom he had planned to kill. After a long wait, he wrote this hate-laden note and then shot himself.

> To whom concerned: Goodbye you old prick and when I mean prick you are a prick. Hope you fall with the rest of us, you yellow bastard. May the precinct get along without you.

Love

Currently, most suicidologists believe that suicide is not motivated by hostility alone, but that there are many other emotional states—such as dependency, shame, guilt, fear, despair, frustration, loss of autonomy and especially feelings of hopelessness and helplessness—that can be the basic psychological ingredients of suicide. Love, especially frustrated love, seems to play as great a role in as many cases of suicide as does hate. A young man of thirty-five wrote the following contemporary note:

> My Darling, To love you as I do and live without you is more than I can bear. I love you so completely, wholeheartedly without restraint. I worship you, that is my fault. . . . Without you life is unbearable. This is the best way. This will solve all our problems. . . . If it is possible to love in the hereafter, I will love you even after death. God have mercy on both our souls. He alone knows my heartache and love for you.

Here is a love suicide note from a European woman of the last century who was the daughter of a very famous man. Consider, in the following brief suicide note by Eleanor Marx, (Kapp, 1977) the youngest of Karl Marx's three daughters—whose sister also committed suicide—the complicated and overladen meanings of the word "love." One needs to keep in mind her tremendously complicated and psychologically tortured relationship with her famous father. For example, she did not learn until she was an adult that her father had had an illegitimate son by one of the dear friends of the family—and she immediately had to make a close psychological relationship with this person. Also keep in mind that her suicide note is addressed to her lover of several years, an unpredictable person who had had numerous affairs with other women, which she tolerated because she loved him. But there was a last straw which broke her heart. This man, Edward Aveling, had, without telling her, secretly married another woman. For Eleanor, that was the ultimate betrayal and rejection. Her note reads: "Dear, It will soon be over. My last word to you is the same that I have said during all these long, sad years—love."

She drank prussic acid in her apartment. It is unclear today whether Aveling arranged for her to have the poison or whether there was a suicide pact, from which he fled. What is clear is the ambiguity of that key word, "love." It can be read to mean bitterness, regret, accusation, disappointment, tenderness, nostalgia, impotent rage or helplessness at being duped or traduced.

An important key to suicide is to recognize that its cause is neither love nor hate; rather, it is the simultaneous presence of *both* of them as well as other emotions. This stage of being able to experience contradictory emotions at the same time toward the same person, called *ambivalence,* is illustrated in this short suicide note: "Dear Betty: I hate you. Love, George."

Shame and Disgrace

Some suicides seem to be related particularly to a sense of shame, "loss of face," disgrace or a sense of dereliction of duty. Prideful people especially seem vulnerable to these motions. An example is the suicide of Dr. Paul Kammerer, an eminent Viennese biologist. His experiments with Alytes, the midwife toad (called that because the male toad wraps the fertilized eggs around his legs and carries them until they are hatched), attempted to prove the inheritance of certain acquired characteristics, specifically friction (or nuptial) pads on the front paws of the male toad, which helped him hold the female during mating. He had done fifteen years of very careful work, breeding and observing these toads, when it was discovered that injections of India ink had been made into the paws of the demonstration specimens, thus producing false results. Although it is not known whether he, or a laboratory assistant attempting to be helpful, did the forging, Kammerer was a ruined man.

In the woods near Vienna, in 1926, six weeks after he was accused, Kammerer shot himself through the head. Here is a translation of the suicide note found beside his body:

> Letter to whosoever finds it:
>
> Dr. Paul Kammerer begs not to be brought to his home so that his family might be spared the sight. It would be the simplest and cheapest way to use the body in a dissecting laboratory of a university. This would also be most agreeable to me since, in this way, I would render science at least a small service. Perhaps my esteemed colleagues will discover in my brain a trace of the qualities they found absent in the expressions of my intellectual activities while I was alive. Whatever happens to the corpse—burial, crema-

> tion or dissection—its owner belonged to no religious denomination and wishes to be spared any kind of religious ceremony which would probably be refused to him in any event. This is not animosity against any individual priest who is as human as the rest of us and often a good and noble person (Koestler, 1972).

There are several interesting details in this lugubrious document. The sense of shame, repentance and restitution are evident. His attitude toward himself as already a corpse is striking, but his inability to see himself as dead—Freud had written that no one can truly imagine his own death, but always remained a spectator—is seen in the contradiction that he does not care what happens to the corpse, but that he (the living man? the corpse? and if the corpse, what difference does it make?) wishes to be spared a religious ceremony. And there is a sense of counteraction: he rejects others before they reject him, as in his phrase ". . . which would probably be refused to him in any event."

And what is not in the note: statements of affection and wishes for forgiveness from his family, warmth, love. The note is largely a set of instructions: to the person who finds his body to the pathologist who dissects his brain and to the priest who may or may not be good enough to conduct a tender ceremony. Finally, one can also infer that on an unconscious level, he views himself as a kind of priest of science who is as human as anyone and is really a good and noble person.

It seems to make most sense to view Kammerer's suicidal act as an overwhelming concatenation, in a disturbed individual, of several emotional surges in addition to the overarching shame: anxiety, anger, depression, hopelessness, guilt, rejection; in other words, heightened general perturbation. All suicidal deaths are complicated events, but Kammerer's suicide seems more complex and more mysterious than most.

Fear—Specifically of Recurring Insanity

Occasionally we find a suicide note that is rational in its irrationality, reflecting an act that we regret but nonetheless can understand. Virginia Woolf drowned herself in a small river, the Ouse, near her home in Sussex, England. She was a gifted woman, a literary celebrity, author of several novels in her special style emphasizing the flow of consciousness. She was also an editor, the founder, with her husband, of the Hogarth Press (which, among other famous books, printed Freud's works in English) and a key member of the so-called Bloomsbury group—a veritable who's who of creative individuals all concerned with the search for things good, true and beautiful.

In short, she was the hub of a radiant literary-philosophic wheel. But with all this, she still suffered—whether from genes or psychodynamics one cannot tell—crippling periods of mental incapacitation. In anyone, especially in a mature intellect, one of the most awesome fears is the niggling threat of losing one's hold on reality, of losing one's mind or going crazy. In 1941, these symptoms or presentiments began to reappear in Virginia Woolf. What they foreboded was simply too much for her to contemplate enduring, for herself and others. Here is her suicide note, addressed to her husband of almost thirty years:

> Dearest,
>
> I feel certain I am going mad again. I feel we can't go through another of those terrible times. And I shan't recover this time. I begin to hear voices, and I can't concentrate. So I am doing what seems the best thing to do. You have been in every way all that anyone could be. I don't think two people could have been happier till this terrible disease came. I can't fight any longer. I know that I am spoiling your life, that without me you could work. And I know you will. You see I can't even write this properly. I can't read. What I want to say is that I owe all the happiness of my life to you. You have been entirely patient with me and incredibly good. I want to say that—everybody knows it. If anybody could have saved me it would have been you. Everything has gone from me but the certainty of your goodness. I can't go on spoiling your life any longer.
>
> I don't think two people could have been happier than we have been. (Bell, 1972)

That note is both fearful and tender. She cannot bring herself to live through another period of psychosis, and more than that, she does not wish to burden her dear husband. The note, beginning with the reason for her desperate act, is then filled with feelings of hopelessness, concern, gratitude and love. The negative emotions are sparked by the desperation relating to her fears of her imminent madness. A significant part of that kind of malady is the inability to share one's secret terror—itself a symptom of the disturbed state of mind—with those who might have been the rescuers.

Traumatic Rejection and Self-Abnegation

The sense of total rejection, in a personality that already deprecates itself, is often a root cause of self-destruction. The cast of characters in the following tragedy is as complicated as it is well known. Fanny Imlay, later Fanny Imlay Godwin, had a star-crossed life seemingly from the moment she was conceived. Her genealogy is a bit complicated but bears careful tracing. She was born in 1794, the illegitimate daughter of Mary Wollstonecraft, who was a famous feminist—the author of *The Rights of Women*—and of an American Revolutionary War captain named Imlay. Her mother then married William Godwin, a famous pamphleteer and political philosopher and novelist (he wrote *Caleb Williams*), and died a few days after having given birth to her half-sister, Mary Wollstonecraft Godwin (later the author of *Frankenstein*), who became the second wife of the poet Percy Bysshe Shelley. Thus Fanny was Shelley's half-sister-in-law—and in love with him. All her short life she was the odd one: illegitimate, half orphaned, excluded from the excitement of her half-sister's life, unnoticed or rejected by the beautiful Shelley, unemployed because of her famous but unsavory relatives, and living with the legacy of her own mother's suicide attempt when she was a young woman. In 1816, at age twenty-two, Fanny Godwin poisoned herself in an inn at an english seaside resort. This is her suicide note:

> I have long determined that the best thing I could do was to put an end to the existence of a being whose birth was unfortunate and whose life has only been a series of pains to those persons who have hurt their health in endeavoring to promote her welfare. Perhaps to hear of my death may give you pain, but you will soon have the blessing of forgetting that such a creature ever existed. (Peck, 1927)

The key words in this painful note are "being" and "creature." She is not a woman or a person or a human; she is just a biological thing that never should have been born. This is a note filled with nothingness; an overpowering sense of void and worthlessness. And to her mind, without love to fill that void, she might as well be dead.

In 1817, the year after Fanny's suicide, Shelly wrote a poem entitled "On Fanny Godwin."

> Her voice did quiver as we parted,
>   Yet knew I not the heart was broken
> From which it came, and I departed
> Heeding not the words then spoken.
>   Misery—O Misery,
>   This world is all too wide for thee.

"Credo" Suicide Notes

Some few suicide notes are written as creeds. They are essays about suicide itself, specifically about a man's moral and legal right to take his own life if he so chooses. The most famous piece of "credo" suicidal writing is not contained in a suicide note but in the essay "On Suicide" by the eighteenth-century Scottish philosopher David Hume. So controversial was it considered that it was not published until a year after his death.

In his essay, Hume—who died a natural death (apparently of cancer) at age sixty-five—sought to decriminalize suicide. In current terms, he might say that where the victim is oneself, it is an act within a consenting adult, and thus there is, in either the legal or the moral sense, no victim. Hume asserted that suicide is no crime; that there is no culprit; and, certainly, there is no sin.

Elton Hammond was an English eccentric who committed suicide at age thirty-three in 1819. Hammond was on the fringe of the literary life of eighteenth-century England (Hammond, 1869). He was somewhat peculiar, perhaps even insane. (He once announced to his sister that he was going to be greater than Jesus Christ.) But the main point here is not Hammond's mental health, but the clear way in which, in his suicide note, he stated a man's right to ownership of himself. It is an anti-clerical, anti-authoritarian credo.

It is likely that a man like Hammond would have known of Hume's essay. The similarities in thought and language between the two documents strongly suggest this possibility. But Hammond goes Hume one better; he is not only writing about his beliefs about suicide, he is putting his life where his mind is.

Here is his suicide note.

> TO THE CORONER AND THE GENTLEMEN WHO WILL SIT ON MY BODY
>
> Norwood, 31st Decr. 1819.
>
> Gentlemen,
>
> To the charge of self-murder I plead not guilty. For there is no guilt in what I have done. Self-murder is a contradiction in terms. If the King who retires from his throne is guilty of high treason; if the man who takes money out of his own coffers and spends it is a thief, if he who burns his own hayrick is guilty of arson; or he who scourges himself of assault and battery, then he who throws up his own life may be guilty of murder,—if not, not.
>
> If anything is a man's own, it is surely his life. Far, however, be it from me to say that a man may do as he pleases with his own. Of all that he has he is a steward. Kingdoms, money, harvests, are held in trust, and so, but I think less strictly, is life itself. Life is rather the stewardship than the talent. The King who resigns his crown to one less fit to rule is guilty, though not of high treason; . . . the suicide who could have performed the duties of his station is perhaps guilty, though not of murder, not of felony. They are all guilty of neglect of duty, and all, except the suicide, of breach of trust. But I cannot perform the duties of my station. He who wastes his life in idleness is guilty of a breach of trust; he who puts an end to it resigns his trust,—a trust that was forced upon him,—a trust which I never accepted, and probably never would have accepted. Is this felony? I smile at the

ridiculous supposition. How we came by the foolish law which considers suicide as felony I don't know; I find no warrant for it in Philosophy or Scripture.

I would rather be thrown naked into a hole in the road than that you should act against your conscience. But if you wish to acquit me, I cannot see your calling my death accidental, or the effect of insanity, would be less criminal than a jury's finding a £10 Bank-of-England note worth thirty-nine shillings, or premeditated slaying in a duel simple manslaughter, both of which have been done. But should you think this is too bold a course, it is less bold to find me guilty of *felo de se* when I am not guilty at all, as there is no guilt in what I have done? I disdain to take advantage of my situation as culprit to mislead your understandings, but if you, in your consciences, think premeditated suicide no felony, will you, upon your oaths, convict me of felony? Let me suggest the following verdict, as combining liberal truth with justice:—"Died by his own hand, but not feloniously." If I have offended God, it is for God, not you, to enquire. . . . I am free to-day, and avail myself of my liberty. I cannot be a good man, and prefer death to being a bad one—as bad as I have been and as others are.

I take my leave of you and of my country condemning you all, yet with true honest love. . . . God bless you all!

Elton

As a footnote to this suicide document, it is sad to relate that the coroner's jury did not accede to Hammond's request; they rendered a verdict of suicide by virtue of insanity—exactly what Hammond did not wish. (But this was done, in part, because Hammond's friend Henry Crabb Robinson did not turn over Hammond's letter to the jury, hoping, perhaps, to save his reputation.)

☐ II

We have raised the question: What can we learn from suicide notes? Obviously, they often contain a great deal of interesting descriptive material, particularly of emotional states. But are they the full and explicating documents that would satisfactorily "explain" a suicide? The fact that a dozen and a half research studies by a score of qualified investigators over the past twenty years have *not* produced the new, important breakthroughs of information that one could legitimately expect from that amount of effort raises questions about their usefulness.

Overall, one might say that suicide notes are relatively barren compared with what we had hoped to find in them (Shneidman, 1973). It seems as though we tend to confuse the drama of the suicidal situation with our own expectations that there be some dramatic psycho-dynamic insights in the communications written during the moments of that drama. But the fact remains that memorable (authenticated) words uttered *during* battle or *on* one's deathbed are rare. It seems to be true also of suicide notes. Understandably, however, we continue to hope that even an ordinary individual, standing on the brink of what man has always conceptualized as life's greatest adventure and mystery, ought to have some special message for the rest of us. Western civilization has for centuries romanticized death; we tend to read with special reverence and awe *any* words, however banal, that are part of a death-oriented document.

Perhaps suicide notes, by themselves, cannot be what we wanted them to be—for the plain and simple reason that they are written by a person whose mind (by virtue of being suicidal) is usually, tunneled, overfocused, constricted and narrowed on a single goal.

A tragically precise and insightful description of tunneling and constriction is contained in the verbalization of the young woman who jumped from a balcony.

> . . . I went into a terrible state. . . . I was so desperate . . . That's the *only* way to get away from it. The *only* way to lose consciousness. . . . everything just got very dark all of a sudden, and *all* I could see was this balcony. Everything around it just *blacked out*. I was just like a *circle*. That was *all* I could see, just the balcony . . . and I went over it. . . . [Italics added.]

As we read these chilling words we can practically visualize the constriction of her mind's focus, almost as the diaphragm of a fine camera closes down to its essential linear circle. And while this is happening, the mind's lens is adjusting to sharpen the focus on but a single objective. The objective is escape, specifically escape from intolerable emotion. It is at that precise moment of maximum constriction and focus that the picture is snapped; it is at that same moment when, as it were, the mind snaps and the act occurs.

Several suicidologists and literary writers have commented on the role of constriction in suicide. Margarethe von Andics (von Andics, 1947) wrote a book about suicide (one hundred suicide attempts in Vienna in the 1940s) in which she emphasized the narrowing of the scope of consciousness that was characteristic of the suicidal state; Erwin Ringle, also of Vienna, has written extensively, since 1958, of what he calls the presuicidal syndrome, placing great emphasis on constriction (Ringel, 1976).

The contemporary English poet, novelist and critic A. Alvarez, who wrote an excellent book on suicide, *The Savage God,* has described what he calls "the closed world of suicide" in the following way:

> Once a man decides to take his own life he enters a shut-off, impregnable but wholly convincing world . . . where every detail fits and every

> incident reinforces his decision. . . . Each of these deaths has its own inner logic and unrepeatable despair. . . . [Suicide is] a terrible but utterly natural reaction to the strained, narrow, unnatural necessities we sometimes create for ourselves. (Alvarez, 1972).

Boris Pasternak, the famous author, writing of the suicide of several young Russian poets, has stated:

> A man who decides to commit suicide puts a full stop to his being, he turns his back on his past, he declares himself bankrupt and his memories to be unreal. They can no longer help or save him, he has put himself beyond their reach. The continuity of his inner life is broken, and his personality is at an end. And perhaps what finally makes him kill himself is not the firmness of his resolve but the unbearable quality of this anguish which belongs to no one, of this suffering in the absence of the sufferer, of this waiting which is empty because life is stopped and can no longer feel it. (Pasternak, 1959)

Because this sense of constriction exists in the suicidal person, is it any wonder that suicide notes, written at the very moment when an individual has lost touch with his own past, are taken up with minutiae and are in other ways relatively arid and psychologically barren?

Thus we see the relative barrenness of many—but not all—suicide notes can be psychologically explained. In order for a person to kill himself, he has to be in a special state of mind, a state of relatively fixed purposes (not to deny an ever-present ambivalence) and of relative constriction of the mind. It is a psychological state that, while it permits (indeed, facilitates) suicide, obviously militates against good insight or good communication. In other words, that special state of mind necessary to perform the suicidal deed is one which is essentially incompatible with an insightful recitation of what was going on in one's mind that led to the act itself. Suicide notes often seem like parodies of the postcards sent home from the Grand Canyon, the catacombs or the pyramids—essentially *pro forma,* not at all reflecting the grandeur of the scene being described or the depth of human emotions that one might expect to be engendered by the situation.

To state the case strongly: In order to commit suicide, one cannot write a meaningful suicide note; conversely, if one could write a meaningful note, one would not have to commit suicide. Or to put it in another way: In almost every instance, one has to be relatively intoxicated or drugged (by one's overpowering emotions and constricted logic and perception) in order to commit suicide, and it is well nigh impossible to write a psychologically meaningful document when one is in this disordered state.

Suicide notes, *by themselves,* may not tell us everything we want to know. Life is like a long letter and the suicide note is merely a postscript to it and cannot, by itself, be expected to carry the burden of substantiating for the total document.

☐ III

There is a vital reciprocity between suicide notes and the lives of which they are a part. This statement—my current position—is the synthesis of my two previous attitudes: the thesis that suicide notes by themselves are uniformly bountiful; and the antithesis that suicide notes have to be constricted and pedestrian documents. Suicide notes definitely can have a great deal of meaning (and give a great deal of information) when they are put in the context of the life history of the individual who both wrote the note and committed the act. In this situation—where we have *both* the suicide note and a *detailed* life history—then the note will illuminate aspects of the life history, and conversely, the life history can make many key words and ideas of the suicide note come alive and take on special meanings that would otherwise have remained hidden or lost. It is close to the art of biography.

Here are five suicide notes written by one woman (who committed suicide by barbiturate overdose) and many details of her life, to which these notes were but the final words.

In this case—Natalie, who killed herself at age forty—there were, in addition to her suicide notes, literally hundreds of separate personal documents and other records. They included the following: Early school records, teachers' notes to her parents, school physicians' reports, school evaluations, college records, several psychological tests, numerous questionnaires which she had completed, dozens of her letters and miscellaneous personal documents by the score. In all, there were over one hundred separate documents, including her suicide notes. (It took me many months to find them.)

We begin at the tragic end, with excerpts from the police report of her death:

> On arrival, went through house into bathroom where victim was observed lying on the floor, head resting on a pillow, toward the west, feet pointed toward the east. Victim was dressed in a green bathrobe; was cold to the touch, rigor mortis having started to set in. On the pillow it was noted there was a stain, caused by a purge from the victim's mouth. Photographs of the scene were taken.
>
> There was one small brown bottle with the label bearing prescription number and "One capsule at bed time . . ." This bottle was empty. Also a small plastic container was received with the label inside the cover reading "One tablet 4 times daily, regularly . . ." This container was also empty.

Undersigned spoke to [name and address], who stated he was victim's father. He further said that approximately two weeks ago, victim told him that she was going to commit suicide. He said he talked her out of the notion at that time, and did not figure she would make any further attempt on her life. He further said victim had been in ill health since her divorce and had been treated by a psychiatrist, address unknown; also that the victim had filed a will which is currently in the possession of her attorney.

While at location, victim's husband, [name], who gave address same as victim's, employed at Eastern Steel Corp., arrived and stated he would take care of his two children, Betty, 15 years; and Nancy, 10 years.

The investigating officer reported finding five suicide notes. I have made a few changes in identifying details:

1. To her adult friend:

   Rosalyn—Get Eastern Steel Co.—Tell them and they will find Bob right away. Papa is at his business. Betty is at the Smiths—Would you ask Helene to keep her until her Daddy comes—so she won't know until he comes for her. You have been so good—I love you—Please keep in touch with Betty—Natalie.

2. To her eldest daughter:

   Betty, go over to Rosalyn's right away—Get in touch with Papa.

3. To her ex-husband, from whom she was recently divorced:

   Bob—I'm making all kinds of mistakes with our girls—They have to have a leader and everyday the job seems more enormous—You couldn't have been a better Daddy to Nancy and they do love you—Nancy misses you so and she doesn't know what's the matter—I know you've built a whole new life for yourself but make room for the girls and keep them with you—Take them where you go—It's only for just a few years—Betty is almost ready to stand on her own two feet—But Nancy needs you desperately. Nancy needs help—She really thinks you didn't love her—and she's got to be made to do her part for her own self respect—Nancy hasn't been hurt much yet—but ah! the future if they keep on the way I've been going lately—Barbara sounds warm and friendly and relaxed and I pray to God she will understand just a little and be good to my girls—They need two happy people—not a sick mixed-up mother—There will be a little money to help with the extras—It had better go that way than for more pills and more doctor bills—I wish to God it had been different but be happy—but please—stay by your girls—And just one thing—be kind to Papa [*his* father]—He's done everything he could to try to help me—He loves the girls dearly and it's right that they should see him often—Natalie

   Bob—this afternoon Betty and Nancy had such a horrible fight it scares me. Do you suppose Gladys and Orville would take Betty for this school

> year? She should be away from Nancy for a little while—in a calm atmosphere.

4. To her ex-father-in-law:

> Papa—no one could have been more kind or generous than you have been to me—I know you couldn't understand this—and forgive me—[The lawyer] has a copy of my will—Everything equal—the few personal things I have of value—the bracelet to Nancy and my wedding ring to Betty—But I would like Betty to have Nana's diamond—have them appraised and give Betty and Nancy each half the diamonds in the band. Please have somebody come in and clean—Have Bob take the girls away immediately—I don't want them to have to stay around—You're so good Papa dear—

5. To her two children

> My dearest ones—You two have been the most wonderful things in my life—Try to forgive me for what I've done—Your father would be so much better for you. It will be harder for you for awhile—but so much easier in the long run—I'm getting you all mixed up—Respect and love are almost the same—Remember that—and the most important thing is to respect yourself—The only way you can do that is by doing your share and learning to stand on your own two feet—Betty, try to remember the happy times—and be good to Nancy. Promise me you will look after your sister's welfare—I love you very much—but I can't face what the future will bring.

A number of sad observations can be made about these suicide notes. The despairing writer of them seems so pushed, so weary, so harried, so beaten by life. She has capitulated. Not atypically, the notes—especially the first two—contain directions, words like "get," "ask," "tell," "go." The disposition of affection is curious: It can be seen in different forms of the salutation and the complimentary close. The only use of "dear" or "dearest" is with her children and her ex-father-in-law. Words of love are reserved only for her neighbor-friend and for her children. There is no note to either of her living parents, both of whom resided nearby.

Her note to her ex-husband is a painful *mea culpa*. She takes all blame and pleads to him—a man who drank quite a bit and was impossible for her to live with—to be good to their children. In an amazing turn-about, she asks that the new stepmother and her ex-husband provide a stable home for her girls.

Her life can be retraced from the available materials. The conditions of her birth were noted as "absolutely normal." She was breast fed until she was two months old. As an infant, she slept soundly.

At the age of five and a half she was given dancing lessons. There is a note that she was very enthusiastic and showed decided ability. When Natalie was six, her mother wrote to a friend that "Edgar Guest's poems are her great favorites." In that same letter, the mother wrote: "I have tried to use a lot of common sense and have answered every question to the best of my ability because she is an understanding child and will listen to reason. I have not had to stimulate a desire to learn because she always wanted to know everything her older playmates knew and she would try to learn voluntarily."

She had a brother, who was eight years older than she. Later she would say about him that "he could never make a living."

When Natalie was six years old, in the first grade, she was given an individual intelligence test. One item that she missed—although she scored extremely high overall, with an I.Q. of over 153, which put her in the extremely superior category—was this one: "Yesterday the police found the body of a girl cut into 18 pieces. They believed that she had killed herself. What is foolish about that?" Her nonprophetic answer was "She wouldn't kill herself." The psychologist noted, however, her general alertness and her extremely logical mind.

A very important event occurred in Natalie's life when she was seven; her father deserted her mother. Later in her life, she noted, with obvious sadness, that *"My father never came to see me except once."*

The records of her childhood medical examinations are interesting. One, written by a school physician when she was eight, states that she was "somewhat nervous, bordering on irritability," and that she had some loss of hearing in her right ear. A school record when she was eleven notes that her last name had been changed to reflect the fact that her mother had divorced and remarried. The teacher's report states that she was a "youngster with an understanding and reasoning little mind that at times surprises her family" and that "her courtesy and tact are remarkable."

At age twelve there are several items of interest. She suffered from numerous headaches and had glasses prescribed. She reported that she still had disturbing eye strain even with glasses. She experienced her menarche; she was a straight A student (in the seventh grade) and indicated that she wanted to go to college and that she would also like to be a dancer. Her hearing loss had increased and she was somewhat sensitive about it; she would not admit this difficulty to any of her teachers. Her main teacher reported that although she was extremely bright, she "shrinks from opportunities for leadership." At about this time, she wrote a letter in which she indicated that her new stepfather was devoted and kind to her and her brother. Perhaps this helps to explain her unusual attitude to her girls' new stepmother (in the note to her ex-husband).

She finished high school and went on to college for three years but did not graduate. At college she developed a close, lasting student-teacher relationship with a distinguished professor; she wrote detailed letters to him for years. At the age of twenty-five, having, in her own words been "an unsuccessful secretary," her "ultimate goal" was to "be a successful homemaker." She married and in the two following years lived in five different cities. Understandably, she wrote that "it is hard to develop interests in any one place." She became pregnant almost immediately after getting married.

There is a gap in the records for five years. At age thirty she had two children and reports a "great tendency to worry and extreme nervousness." Her husband was drinking rather heavily. There was a dramatic change in her own physical and psychological state. She reported that she was "too tired even to wash the windows." She also reported a sharp pain in her side, which her doctor told her was due to "neurotic tendencies." She wrote that she was "chronically worn out and tired and very unhappy in the marriage."

There is a painful letter to her favorite college professor, written when she was about thirty-five:

> . . . Until I was 25 I didn't know there were such things as problems in this world, but since then with the exception of my two lovely children and my perfect relationship with my mother, I've had just one struggle from another, made one blunder after another. My husband and I bicker constantly. I've wanted to divorce him a thousand times and still I know that is not the solution. We were both raised in broken homes and we both love our children too much. He comes home drunk at night far too often. He can't afford it. He refuses to look at the bills and says "Why haven't you saved money?" I have no one to talk to. I feel like I'm cornered. . . . My mother's youngest brother and my nearest neighbor both committed suicide in one month [about a year before].

In this same communication, writing about her misfortunes in general, she said this about her father: "I adored my father from afar. Our occasional meetings were unsatisfactory. My father is a very brilliant man—however *he has little use for me*—He lives 20 minutes away but has been in our home only once for a few minutes in the past two years." Those lines strike a key theme in her broken life. She said that she was reading Menninger's *Man Against Himself*—a book about suicide.

In another letter she wrote of her children:

> Our little ones are nice, but the eldest still bites her fingernails and fights constantly with her younger sister. She is the result of my selfishness. . . . Well, I've poured out my heart and I'm a little ashamed. In my heart I've never doubted that I can be happy, relaxed, useful human being, but it's taking such a long time to get there.

Four years later, when Natalie was thirty-nine, she separated from her husband, because—from another letter—of "his violent temper, his selfishness and his drinking." Nine months later she was divorced. Four months after the divorce was final (and he had already remarried), she was dead of suicide.

What deep psychological strains motivate such an act? When we read about her life, especially the subtleties of interaction with her father, we can see the malignant beginnings of her self-abnegating attitudes. At the end, she is so frantic that she will give anything, make any votive offering, including her life, to achieve the feeling of childhood love.

In her suicide she reenacted her own earlier life drama—the yearning for her parents to be together—and in this misdirected symbolic sacrifice, instead of giving her children a (seemingly) united home, she, in the most traumatic way possible, deprived them of their own mother. Her aspirations—to be her father's favorite, to be accepted and not abandoned, to care for and not reject her own children (as she had been rejected and not cared for), to be symbolically reunited with her father in a happy home, to sacrifice herself so that some of the problems of her children might be solved—were no better realized in her death than they were in her life.

Natalie's suicide note to her children is filled with contradictions and inconsistencies. (We remember that when she was tested as a child, the psychologist called her extremely logical.) In the suicide note, the implicit logical arguments flow back and forth, between assertion and counterassertion, never with any resolution. Here are some examples: She says, in effect, you will stay with your father, you should love your father, I know that you cannot love your father but at least you must respect him. She then almost free-associates to the word "respect" and argues, rather lamely, that love and respect are almost the same anyway, and in case that argument is not persuasive (which it is not), then one should, at least, respect one's self. The logic wanders.

Another sad example: She says to her children, You must stand on your own two feet, but she also implies that the point of her removing herself from their lives is so that they can be reunited with their father—as, probably, she unconsciously yearns to be reunited with her father.

To tell one's children in a suicide note to remember the happy times certainly has some contradictory element in it, on the very face of it. I love you so much, she says, but the end result of her actions is to make them orphans. She adds, I can't face what the future will bring, but she then takes her life largely because of the haunting, inescapable past. And finally, there is her statement, "I'm getting you all mixed up," which obviously betokens the confusion not in their minds but in her own.

The connections between suicide notes and other aspects of a life seem inescapable with Natalie. The first has to do with Natalie's passivity, her fear of aggression and her fear of violence. In her suicide note she says that the children have to have a leader; when she was twelve, her teacher reported that she shrank from opportunities for leadership. It would appear that all her life she wanted love given to her; in her childhood, and as a wife and mother, she was afraid to stand up for her legitimate rights. She feared and hated quarreling. In the note she said, about the girls, that one afternoon they had "such a horrible fight it scared me." Indeed it must have—adding to her feelings of helplessness and hopelessness, feelings that are part of the suicidal scene.

Another connecting thread can be found between the poignant item contained in the letter she wrote around age thirty-five in which she says, "I adored my father from afar. . . . however *he has little use for me,"* and all the pleading for her children in her suicide notes. In her note to her friend she says: "Please keep in touch with Betty"; and to her ex-husband: "Nancy misses you so . . . [and] needs you desperately . . . [and] really thinks you didn't love her . . . be good to my girls." If one substitutes her name for her girls', one can read the notes as though they were addressed to her own father, whom she could not bring herself—out of a mixture of hostility, rejection and yearning—to contact. At the end, her love is expressed to her ex-father-in-law: "You're so good Papa dear." Finally, in a state of psychological bankruptcy, she tells her children: "Your father would be so much better for you." She is depleted, tired, exhausted, burned out. "I can't face what the future would bring," she says. For her, it would be more of the same. The notes *and* the life both tell us so.

It should now be evident that suicide notes written, as they are, as part of the life that they reflect, can have a great deal of meaning (and give us a great deal of scientific and clinical information) when they are examined in light of the details of the full life history of which they are the penultimate act. By putting a suicide note within the context of the life history of the individual (who both wrote the note and committed the act), one can find that many words, ideas, emotional proclivities, styles of reaction, modes of thinking, etc., that characterized that life are reflected in the specific details of the suicide note. And conversely, many words, phrases, ideas, passions, emphases, etc., contained in the suicide note are extensions of those very same threads that had previously characterized the life. Living or dying, a particular individual has a certain consistency, a certain "unity thema," a certain "trademark," which he or she will show in work style, in play style and in life style, whether celebrating life in a poem of love or contemplating death in a note of suicide.

There is a bizarre but fascinating and incredibly inventive novel, *The Dwarf* (1945), by the contemporary Swedish author Pär Lagerkvist—winner of the 1951 Nobel Prize in literature—about an aberrant and evil dwarf (in a medieval Italian prince's court), which, by sheer coincidence, contains uncanny and tragic parallels to an actual contemporary case that I know. Indeed, the gruesome similarities (in what a sadistic monster can do to a sensitive child) between that honored work of fiction and the actual case are so striking that I have decided to present the two in tandem. My purpose is not to focus on the monsters, but rather on their victims. First, let us read some passages from the novel. It begins:

> I am twenty-six inches tall, shapely and well proportioned, my head perhaps a trifle too large. My hair is not black like the others', but reddish, very stiff and thick, drawn back from the temples and the broad but not especially lofty brow. My face is beardless, but otherwise just like that of other men. My eyebrows meet. My bodily strength is considerable, particularly if I am annoyed. When the wrestling match was arranged between Jehoshaphat and myself I forced him onto his back after twenty minutes and strangled him. Since then I have been the only dwarf at this court.

One of the several subplots in *The Dwarf* concerns the prince's young daughter, Angelica. Here is an excerpt:

> There is a great difference between dwarfs and children. Because they are about the same size, people think that they are alike, and that they suit each other; but they do not. Dwarfs are set to play with children, forced to do so. It is nothing less than torture to use us dwarfs like that. But human beings know nothing about us.
>
> My masters have never forced me to play with Angelica, but she herself has done so. That infant, whom some people think so wonderful with her round blue eyes and her little pursed mouth, has tormented me almost more than anyone else at court.
>
> We visit her dolls which have to be fed and dressed, the rose garden where we have to play with the kitten. . . . She can sit and play with her kitten for ages and expect me to join in. She believes that I too am a child with a child's delight in everything. I! I delight in nothing.

And then the dwarf's revenge on the child:

> Once I crept into her room as she lay sleeping with her detestable kitten beside her in bed and cut off its head with my dagger. Then I threw it into the dungheap beneath the castle window. She was inconsolable when she saw that it was gone, and when everybody said that of course it must be dead, she sickened with an unknown fever and was ill for a long time, so that I, thank goodness, did not have to see her.

And finally, the dwarf's ultimate revenge on Angelica when she had grown up to be a young woman: He informs the prince, his master, that Angelica is being visited by a lover, who is, of all people, the scion of the prince's hated rival family. The prince is furious.

> "Impossible!" he maintained. "Nobody can come into the town over the river, between the fortresses on both banks where archers keep watch night and day. It is absolutely unthinkable!". . .
>
> "Yes, it is unthinkable," I admitted . . . but think if the criminal had already slipped away! Of if both had fled! The horrible suspicion sent me flying over the courtyard as fast as my legs could carry me, and up the stairs to Angelica's door.
>
> I put my ear against it. No sound within! Had they fled? I slipped inside and immediately recovered my composure. To my joy I saw them sleeping side by side in her bed, by the light of a little oil lamp that they had forgotten to extinguish.
>
> Now I heard the prince and his men on the stairs, and presently he came in followed by two sentinels. Livid with wrath he snatched the sword from one of the sentinels and with a single blow severed Giovanni's head from his body. Angelica woke up and stared with wild dilated eyes as they dragged her gory lover from her couch and flung him on to the muckheap outside the window. Then she fell back in a swoon and did not recover consciousness as long as we remained in the room.

In the town there is a plague; Angelica suffers a rather peculiar and different malady:

> Angelica cannot be sick of this plague. Her malady is the same as that which she once had as a child. I do not quite remember when, nor the exact circumstances. She has always been rather sickly, for reasons which could not possibly affect anybody else's health. Ah, now I remember. It was when I cut off her kitten's head.

Finally, Angelica is driven to despair:

> Angelica has drowned herself in the river. She must have done it yesterday evening or last night, for nobody saw her. She left a letter behind which leaves no doubt that she killed herself in that manner. Throughout the day they have been searching for her body, all the length of the river where it flows through the beleaguered city, but in vain. Like Giovanni's it must have been carried away by the tides.
>
> There is a great to-do at the court. Everybody is upset and cannot realize that she is dead. I see nothing extraordinary about the letter, and it changes nothing—certainly not the crime which was committed and which everybody condemned unanimously. It contains nothing new.
>
> I had to hear it again and again until I know it almost by heart. It runs something like this:

I do not want to stay with you any longer. You have been so kind to me, but I do not understand you. I do not understand how you could take my beloved away from me, my dear one who came so far from another country to tell me that there was a thing called love.

As soon as I met him, I knew why life had been so strangely difficult up to then.

Now I do not want to stay here, where he is not, but I shall follow him. I shall just lay myself down to rest on the river, and God will take me where I am to go.

You must not believe that I have taken my life, for I have only done as I was told. And I am not dead. I have gone to be joined forever to my beloved.

I forgive you with all my heart.

Angelica.

The Princess is convinced that she is the cause of Angelica's death. This is the first time I have ever known her to take any interest in her child. She scourges herself more than ever to efface this sin, eats nothing at all, and prays to the Crucified One for forgiveness.

The Crucified One does not answer.

Now let us turn to a real-life tragedy: the suicide of a twenty-three-year-old woman. I shall call her Dolores. This occurred in the 1970s, in a large city in the United States, in a motel room. She had brought with her a copy of Alvarez's *The Savage God* (in which he discusses the suicide of the poet Sylvia Plath). She registered under the name "Marilyn Plath." She hanged herself from the shower. She left this suicide note:

Forgive me. It was too late for me to be repaired. No one is to blame. I love you all. I want to be buried here. I am a broken doll. I have been to too many doll hospitals. They couldn't repair me. So dear doctor and Gregor, you were working against the impossible. How can a doll that has been through a mangler be repaired? I love you all for your great loving effort. Remember me with happiness for now I shall have no more pain.

Some few weeks before that eventful day, she had spontaneously written another personal document, a sort of essay of anguish, which she had entitled "What Is Depression?" Here it is verbatim:

Depression is feeling revulsion from one's mother as a child. Depression is hoping to be the greatest love in someone's life and realizing it will never be so. Depression is knowing that although Maria, my nana as a child, loved me she went along all the way with the very strong mistress of the house, my charming mother, who constantly punished me for small reasons and instructed my nana to do the same. Depression is knowing that my family loved me but was told how bad I was, so love was limited. Depression is fear of having wanted to reach out to my mother and getting rejection in return. Depression is caring but beginning to stop reaching out.

> Depression is being a showpiece, the best dressed little girl. Who could say she hadn't the perfect mother? She dressed you so well—you have the nicest clothes—what a lucky girl you are to have such a wonderful mother. Depression is being noticed by my mother in public and ignored by her in private. Depression is knowing that I am being blackmailed by a little brother who knows he is the chosen one and having to do as he says. Depression is knowing that father loved me but never stood up for me—my mother was the master of the house. Depression is hearing over and over the story of my birth. The disappointment experienced by my mother of having had a girl. Depression is not really knowing if I was such an awful child—not being certain I couldn't have been such a revulsion without doing some great wrong. Depression is not remembering the wrong things. My father slept with a gun under his pillow—my mother told me I had access to it one day—that I pointed it at my mother and that it was taken away. I was about 3 and don't remember. *Depression was the killing of my dog and the murder of my doll by my brother.* [Italics added.] Depression is the development of hate, knowing that whatever I do I won't be loved. Depression was the encouragement of my parents telling my teacher to constantly punish me if I did anything incorrectly. Depression was being caned at school and beaten at home for having had to be caned at school. Depression is doing everything to be loved—but my mother saw to it that no one was going to love me. Depression is seeing love happening and suddenly disappearing. Depression is hearing that my brother makes my family so happy and I am a constant crown of thorns. Depression is my brother convincing me that if I put sugar in my hands bees will make honey for me—Depression is being stung and having my mother laugh heartily for my brother's cleverness and my stupidity. Depression is hearing this hilarious story repeated over and over. Depression is the fright of being stung by a bee for the first time and wanting to be held and comforted and receiving laughter at my stupidity. Depression is knowing in life there is no real love—that love will die or the person will leave me.
>
> There is so much more but I don't want to think anymore right now—but I hate her and all the people who couldn't love me just for me. They would just begin to love and then they would meet her and the love for me would stop almost immediately. I am never going to let her take anyone from me again. I will do anything however wrong to prevent this—however drastic. I will stop at nothing.

This remarkable psychological document is a painfully shrill cry of hate and hurt. It is the wail of the psychologically rejected child; the lament of the unfavorite sibling.

Dolores was born in a major city in South America. Her parents were well-to-do and sent her to a fancy school—where she was beaten. After she finished high school in her native country, she came to the United States, attended a large university and had a lover, named Gregor. He was a tender man and extremely solicitous of Dolores's feelings.

For some months before she died she was in psychotherapy. The following is a summary of some of her early memories as related to me by her therapist:

> When she was born, in the hospital, her mother refused to look at her because she was not a boy. Dolores knew this well because her mother reminded her of it again and again, but also because she was also told this by the nurse when she was old enough to remember. Her mother did not look at her until she brought her home and then she was taken care of by this nana. Dolores has distinct memories back to about the age of four. Those crucial memories were somewhere between four and six. The critical memory is that she had a doll. It was an ordinary doll, nothing very special about it, but she absolutely adored it. One day she couldn't find this doll. They lived in a large house which had a walled-in garden and wooden pickets all the way around the garden, and she couldn't find her beloved doll and went out and there she saw, on top of one of those pickets, just the head of her doll impaled on the fence. The rest of it her impish brother had destroyed. [The brother verified that memory to the therapist.] But her feeling was that he had killed her doll and her dog and she said that over and over.
>
> There is another memory which goes back to that time. These memories were also verified by her brother. This other memory—which dates back to a very young age—is of her grandmother's house, which was apparently not too far away from their house. Across from her grandmother's house there was a cemetery. Dolores remembers going often to the cemetery when she was very despairing, having been punished by her mother. At the age of four or five she would go to the cemetery whenever there was a funeral and she would sit and watch the mourners and all the beautiful flowers and she would say to herself, Oh, I wish someone would love me enough to care. She remembers her feelings of rejection as early as that.

The skeins of death were woven into her life almost from the beginning. Could it be that she was responding to her mother's unconscious (or even conscious) messages that things would be better if she, Dolores, were dead? A miserable childhood and the subtle parental cruelties of a lifetime can be a lethal potion.

When she was a young adult, her lover's concern and devotion could not pierce the impenetrable wall of Dolores's fixed feelings of being unlovable. In her distorted view of life, no one could give her enough love. Even her intense positive relationship with her psychotherapist was, not unexpectedly, contaminated with a fatal drop of deep childhood ambivalence.

The key imagery is that of the broken doll. The "broken doll" in the suicide note directly parallels the "murder of my doll" in the life history. In the same sense that the doll of her childhood was hopelessly destroyed and could never be repaired, she felt that neither could she—

another broken doll that had been through life's mangler—be propped up enough to live.

Although there was no actual dwarf in her life, her mischievous little brother, encouraged by the mother, was the impish and sadistic figure in her childhood. Like the dwarf, he was a monster. There were also other symbolic monsters in her life (such as her unbearable feelings of rejection), which finally broke her delicate spirit.

In these two cases, then, we can begin to appreciate the reciprocal relationships between the suicide notes and the lives themselves.

☐ References

Alvarez, A. (1972). *The savage god: A study of suicide.* New York: Random House.

Bell, Q. (1972). *Virginia Woolf—A Biography.* London: Hogarth Press; New York: Harcourt, Brace, Jovanovich.

Friedman, P. (Ed.) (1967). *On suicide.* New York: International Universities Press.

Friedman P. (1967). Suicide among police: A study of 93 suicides among New York City policeman, 1934–1940. In Ed. S. Shneidman (Ed.), *Essays in self-destruction.* New York: Science House; and M. F. Heiman (1975). Police suicides revisited. *Suicide, 5,* 5–20.

Kapp, Y. (1977). *Eleanor Marx.* New York: Pantheon.

Koestler, A. (1977). *The case of the midwife toad.* New York: Random House.

Lagerkvist, P. (1945). *The Dwarf* (A. Dick, Trans.). L. B. Fisher Publishing Corp.

Pasternak, B. (1959). *I remember: Sketch for an autobiography.* New York: Pantheon.

Peck, W. E. (1927). *Shelley: His life and work, Vol. I* (p. 493). Boston: Houghton, Mifflin Co. London: Chatto and Windus, Ltd.

Ringel, E. (1976). The presuicidal syndrome. *Suicide and Life-Threatening Behavior, 6,* 131–149.

Robinson, H. C. 1989. *The diary reminiscences and correspondence of Henry Crabb Robinson, Vol. III,* Chap. 5 (1869). London: Macmillan and Co.

Shneidman, E. S. (1973). Suicide notes reconsidered. *Psychiatry, 36,* 379–394.

Stengel, E. (1964). *Suicide and attempted suicide.* London: Penguin.

von Andics, M. (1947). *Suicide and the meaning of life.* London: William Hodge & Co.

22

CHAPTER

Letters of Enforced Death Versus Suicide Notes

When one is contemplating suicide, one is obviously on one's own and is likely to be in the grip of ambivalences (above love and hate, life and death) at their neurotic worst. It is thus little wonder that the documents of death under these circumstances—suicide notes—are sometimes filled with trivia and psychologically inconsequential thoughts and ideas, as well as with the negative side of the inner life: hostility, revenge, shame, guilt, fear, dependency, self-deprecation and so on. Rarely is the suicidal state the moment to be noble. Suicide is one's own doing and displays both the desperation and the neurotic elements that make the act seem "reasonable" when it is committed. The suicidal person is always in psychological pain, wishing to escape intolerable emotional distress.

The threat of being executed is psychologically entirely different from suicide. The menace comes from the *outside*, from a powerful "other," and the villains are real. In this circumstance there is little time to be neurotic; one has to marshal all one's inner forces against the palpably murderous enemy. Ambivalences are put aside; the mind is clear. If one is to write at all, the task is straightforward: It is to pen one last communiqué, unencumbered by trivia, to one's loved ones. Execution notes are, by and large, unusual psychological documents—unusual in their lucidity, their compassion for loved ones, and the expression of a sense

Reprinted from *Journal of Psychology and Judaism*, 1995, *19*, 153–160. With permission.

of peace. To characterize these last notes or farewell letters, we need to reach back to old-fashioned phrases like "righteous indignation" and "the courage of one's own convictions."

In this situation of great duress, when one *knows* that one is going to be killed soon, the human personality tends to husband itself, gathering together all possible psychological energy. There is no time for petty emotion. One is beyond hope and thus—having been flung, alive (at least for a little while), over those dangerous rapids (of having been sentenced to death)—one can be beyond fears for oneself. In that quiet pond—just before the fatal catastrophic waterfall ahead—one can disengage oneself from the usual anxieties, aspirations and views of one's "ordinary" life, with its daily stresses and "unlimited time," and, for a fleeting moment, rise, unencumbered, to a state of being at true peace with oneself. Then it is possible, with the trappings of life's neurotic pressures fallen away, to write a last letter that is complete, rounded off, filled with genuine compassion for others and signed boldly. Thus these letters often have an unusual clarity, maturity, and profundity.

People who are about to die think intensively about themselves. They think about being alive and what the world will be like after they are dead. In a very understandable and psychologically legitimate way, they mourn themselves. This phenomenon—self-mourning or auto-mourning—occurs not only with the threat of execution, but also with the forebodings of a life-threatening disease, like cancer or leukemia or AIDS.

Psychologically, a police state—and, in extreme form, a concentration camp—is a place where slavery is practiced. The master-slave relationship—whimsical or sadistic control, without accountability, over the welfare and the very life of another human being—often brings out the absolute worst in man. The opportunity, and with it the temptation, to be cruel (and to think of the other human being as less than a human being) is simply too beguiling. To enslave another person (through the power, say, of barbed wire, whips and weapons) debases the masters, reducing them to beasts.

Psychopathic genocide—icy planning of mass murder without a qualm of conscience—has never been seen on the scale in which it occurred in this century. In his searing book, *The Twentieth Century Book of the Dead,* (1972), Gil Elliot documents the unspeakable arithmetic of the 110 million people—"a nation of the dead"—who have been murdered by organized state governments since 1900. The villains have been certain segments among the Russians, Chinese, Turks, Poles, nationalistic or tribal Arab and African groups, and many others, including especially those archvillains the Nazis.

Understandably, very few documents that were written by the victims of the Nazi concentration camps have survived. Three fragmentary diaries are reproduced in a publication called *Amidst a Nightmare of Crime* (Bezwinska, 1973). The title was requested by one of the anonymous murdered writers. The booklet is published by the State Museum of Oswiecim (Auschwitz). Here is how one of the manuscripts was found: "On October 17, 1962—about twenty years after—in the course of a search conducted in the vicinity of the ruins of crematorium III at Birkenau, a jar was found buried in the ground near the gas chamber . . . a roll of papers was found in the jar, which proved to be a small notebook . . . Altogether there were 65 leaves in the jar. The leaves in the notebook were covered with writing on both sides. . . . 40% of the text was illegible. The manuscript, except for one page in Polish, is written in Yiddish . . ." It speaks for six million Jews. It tells of unimaginable barbarities and atrocities. Here is the very last entry of one diary:

> Today in crematorium III 600 boys were brought in the middle of a bright day 600 Jewish boys aged from 12 to 18, very thin; their feet were shod in worn out shoes or wooden clogs. The boys looked so handsome and were so well-built that even these rags did not mar their beauty. This happened in the latter part of October [1944]. They were brought by 25 SS men, heavily burdened with grenades. When they came to the square the SS men gave the order for them to undress in the square. The boys noticed the smoke belching from the chimney and at once guessed that they were being led to death. They began running hither and thither in the square in wild terror, tearing their hair, not knowing how to save themselves. Many burst into horrible tears; there resounded dreadful lamentation. An SS man beat the defenseless boys horribly to make them undress. His club broke even owing to that beating. So he brought another and continued the beating over the heads until violence became victorious. The boys undressed, instinctively afraid of death, naked and barefooted they herded together in order to avoid the blows and did not budge from the spot. One brave boy approached the SS man and begged him to spare his life, promising he would do even the hardest work. In reply he hit him several times over the head with a thick club. Many boys ran in a wild hurry . . . Others scurried naked all over the big square in order to escape from death. The SS man called the Unterscharfuhrer [Corporal] with a rubber truncheon to his assistance. The young clear boyish voices resounded louder and louder with every minute, when at last they passed into bitter sobbing. This dreadful lamentation was heard from very far. We stood completely aghast as if paralyzed by this mournful weeping. With a smile of satisfaction, without a trace of compassion, looking like proud victors, the SS men stood and dealing terrible blows drove them into the bunker. The Unterscharfuhrer stood on the steps and should anyone run too slowly to meet death he would deal a murderous blow with the rubber truncheon. Some boys, in spite of everything, still continued to scurry hither and thither in the square, seeking salvation. The SS men followed them, beat and belabored them, until they had mastered the situation and

> at last drove them into the bunker. Their joy was indescribable. Did they not have any children ever?

Sardonically, one has to admit that in a certain evil way, the Nazis were even-handed, capable of treating their own citizens and soldiers with a callousness that most people usually reserve only for their worst enemies. An extensive example of the Nazis' ruthlessness with their own can be seen in the handling of the last letters of doomed soldiers to their loved ones (Brocher, 1961). In August 1942, the German Sixth Army invaded Russia up to the Volga River, opposite Stalingrad. By September, the Russians were beginning to counterattack; in November, a Russian tank army made a pincer movement around the 240,000 German troops. The Sixth Army was trapped and—under Hitler's direct command—was left there to perish. In January 1943, when food and ammunition (and time) were obviously running out, the German soldiers were told that there would be one last airplane flying out and that they might write one letter. But under an order issued by Hitler's headquarters, there was never any intention of delivering the mail. It was merely a device to ascertain the morale of the troops. In fact, the letters were so critical of the German Supreme Command that Goebbels had the results suppressed. Eventually the letters were found by the Allied forces.

The German Sixth Army was destroyed by the Russians on February 2, 1943. Most of the men died. Here are excerpts from two of those last letters:

> I shall never return. Break it to our parents gently. I am deeply shaken and doubt everything. I used to be strong and full of faith; now I am small and without faith. I will never know many of the things that happen here; but the little that I have taken part in is already so much that it chokes me. No one can tell me any longer that the men die with the words "Deutschland" or "Heil Hitler" on their lips. There is plenty of dying, no question of that; but the last word is "mother" or the name of someone dear.

> They told us this morning that we could write. Just one more I say, for I know definitely that this will be the last time. You know that I always wrote to two people, two women, to the "other one" and you . . . Today, however, when fate gives me the choice of writing to one person only, my letter goes to you, who have been my wife for six years. The last letter of the man whom you loved is directed to you. So keep me alive in your memory as the man who recalled only at the very end that he is your husband and who asks your forgiveness; more, asks you to tell everyone you know, Carola included, that I found my way back to you at the moment which will take you away from me forever.

Here, from another source (Gollwitzer et al., 1956, pp. 173–175), are some notes written in the same year by a twentieth-century Czechoslovakian journalist, Julius Fucik. He was arrested by the Gestapo on April 24, 1942, and executed on September 8, 1943, in Berlin. An unknown person somehow rescued the notes and letters he wrote during his incarceration.

> . . . Hopes drop away silently, gone limp like wilted leaves. Poetic souls when they see this sometimes fall prey to longing. Winter prepares man for its rigors as it prepares a tree, Believe me, this has taken nothing, absolutely nothing, from the joy that is in me and that heralds itself each day with some Beethoven theme or other. Man does not become smaller even when he becomes shorter by a head. And my ardent wish is that when all is over you will remember me not with sorrow, but with precisely that joy with which I always lived.

That letter was addressed to his parents just after he had heard that he was to be shot. He then wrote a note, "To the Survivors," which contains a basic request that stands as the plea of all the victims: ". . . I ask for one thing: you who will survive this era, *do not forget*. Forget neither the good men nor the evil. Gather together patiently the testimonies about those who have fallen." His last written sentence was: "Mankind, I loved you. Be vigilant!"

Fucik's letter to his parents invokes an arboreal imagery of life as a tree, wilting, dying, that is often seen in letters written before executions. Here is another, written a year later by Nikolaus von Halen—lawyer, businessman, poet and anti-Nazi—a few minutes before he was executed by the Nazis in October 1944, at the age of thirty-nine (Gollwitzer et al., 1956, p. 18). This brief letter, written with manacled hands, was addressed—as many last letters are—to his beloved mother:

> Now I have overcome the last little tremor that seizes the top of the tree before it falls. And with this I have attained the goal of humanity. For we can and must endure consciously that which plants undergo without consciousness.
>
> Adieu. They are coming to get me.
>
> A thousand kisses. Your son

The archenemy of forests is fire. Here are some excerpts from the letter by a forty-year-old jurist and high-ranking official (before the Nazi regime), Peter, Count Yorek von Wartenburg, who was an outspoken anti-Nazi (ibid, pp. 133–134). He was executed in August 1944. He wrote to his mother and his wife. Here are the first and last paragraphs of his letter to his wife—which illustrate again the pride a person can take in his own victimization when he believes he is right.

> We have probably come to the end of the beautiful, rich life we have lived in common. For tomorrow the People's Court will sit in judgment on me

and the others. I hear that the army has expelled us: they can take our garments, but not the spirit in which we acted. And in this spirit I felt myself in union with my forebears and my brothers and also with my comrades . . . Though in appearance my death is an inglorious, even shameful one, I tread this last path erect and unbowed, and I hope only that you will not see this as arrogance and delusion. We meant to kindle the torch of life. And now a sea of fire engirds us—and what a fire!

Baron Alexis von Roennen was a colonel of the German Army. From the beginning of National Socialism, he regarded it and Hitler as a disaster for Germany. His own conscience prevented him from taking an active role in the preparation of the attempted coup on Hitler's life (on July 20, 1944, when a bomb was placed within a briefcase beneath the table at command headquarters), but his ties to the leaders of that attempt, as well as his known anti-Nazi sentiments, served as sufficient grounds for his arrest and execution. The letter that follows was written to his mother the night before he was executed. (Gollwitzer, Kuhn, & Schneider, 1956, pp. 279–282).

Berlin, October 11, 1944. Evening

My own beloved Mama:

Today for a very special reason the notion came to me to write you once again, although a short letter to you is enclosed with my previous letters of farewell. I have no fear at all. Father used to tell me that our grandfather on his deathbed refused a soothing medicine with the words, "Everything must be endured." He stood sovereign over death—it was quite magnificent.

For a week now I have been awaiting death from day to day; right now, for example, I expect it tomorrow. I take pleasure in the sunshine and I have tried to free myself from the world only insofar as I have given up reading and, as much as possible, keep my thoughts away from all political and military matters. Aside from thoughts about my little brood [his wife and two small children], I am a completely happy man—a phenomenon that has often been found astonishing here . . .

Death now means nothing to me; yet how gladly would I have gone home *with* my little brood, whom I can no longer care for and protect. But whenever such earthly thoughts come to me, the Lord reminds me that according to human probability I should in any case not have been beside them in time of stress, and that, above all, He is a far better protection . . .

I know that you will never abandon my dearest one [his wife]and that you will keep in mind especially her infinitely tender heart, which has such need of love and likewise holds all of you so dear. For this, and for all the boundless love of nearly forty-two years, I thank all of you, and especially you, my indescribably beloved mother, from the depth of my heart.

No child has ever received a richer or deeper love from his mother than

Your Allechi

> With infinite gratitude I thought today of the splendid childhood that your love above all else made for me in Mitau and Wilkajen. Everything is in a golden glory, with you at the center.

When a person was a Nazi victim, it did not much matter whether he was Junker or Jew. After the war, a few individuals—inspired by the discovery of the farewell letter of Baron von Roenne—decided to make a collection of farewell letters of the Nazi victims. In the foreword to that volume, called *Dying We Live,* Reinhold Neibuhr, the eminent theologian, wrote: "This collection of farewell letters proves what a refining fire the flames of martyrdom are. Non-German readers will learn from reading these letters that it is impossible to indict a whole nation and that in the same nation which generated and succumbed to Nazism there were the spiritual resources which made these heroic lives and deeds possible." In the great counterbalance of life, these fragile missives, containing ephemeral and lofty thoughts on thin and torn paper, have had to serve as the best available antidote for the unspeakable barbarities that prompted their writing.[1]

A collection of letters of a similar genre—written before execution—is *De Sidste Timer (The Last Hours)* (1945). It is a book of letters written by Danish patriots—members of the Danish resistance movement—on the night before they were executed by the Nazis, who were then occupying their country.

Kim Malthe-Bruun, a young Danish seaman, was shot by a firing squad on Sunday, April 8, 1945. A few weeks after his arrest, in December 1944, he wrote the following letter, which was smuggled out of prison and delivered to his mother. He was twenty-one years old.

> . . . The Gestapo is made up of very primitive men who have gained considerable skill in outwitting and intimidating feeble spirits . . .
>
> Now listen, in case you should find yourself someday in the hands of traitors or of the Gestapo, look them—and yourself—straight in the eye. The only change that has actually taken place consists of the fact that they are now physically your masters. Otherwise they are still the same dregs of humanity they were before you were captured. Look at them, realize how far beneath you they are, and it will dawn upon you that the utmost that these creatures can achieve is to give you a few bruises and some aching muscles . . .

What we particularly notice about many of the foregoing letters, especially when we contrast them with suicide notes, are the ties to loved ones. A Danish psychiatrist, Frederick Wagner (1960), has observed this striking difference between suicide notes and letters of farewell. He pointed out that in a farewell letter one finds a great love of relatives; that the writers, in their last written words, stick to life and "reveal a positive, dignified, often religious attitude toward life and a warm attachment to the family."

Endnote

[1]There are several lugubrious books, reflecting millions of murders, filled with letters of Nazi victims. These include: *Dying We Live* and *Amidst a Nightmare of Crime*, cited above; *The Last Hours: Farewell Letters of Danish Patriots* (Copenhagen: Berlingske Forlag, 1945); *I Never Saw Another Butterfly: Children's Drawings and Poems from Terezin Concentration Camp* (New York: McGraw-Hill, n.d.); and Terrence Des Pres, *The Survivor* (New York: Pocket Books, 1977). Des Pres's book contains a comprehensive bibliography of survivors of the concentration camps.

References

Bezwinska, J. (Ed.) (1973). *Amidst a nightmare of crime*. Publications of the Panstwowe Muzeum w Oswiecimiu.

Brocher, K. (Ed.) (1961). *Last letters from Stalingrad (Letze Briefe aus Stalingrad)* (F. Schneider & C. Gullans, Trans.). The Hudson Review, Inc.

Elliot, G. (1972). *The twentieth century book of the dead*. New York: Charles Scribner's Sons.

Gollwitzer, H., Kuhn, K., & Schneider, R. (Eds.) (1956). *Dying we live*. (R. C. Kuhn, Trans.) New York: Pantheon.

Wagner, F. F. (1960). Suicide Notes. *Danish Medical Journal, 7*, 62–64.

IV

SUICIDE
Section C: Administrative and Programmatic

Apart from his long stretch at the UCLA Neuropsychiatric Institute (1970–1988) where he was happy to be a professor without any special administrative duties, Shneidman's career included three bursts of programmatic and administrative efforts: co-founder and co-director of the Los Angeles Suicide Prevention Center (LASPC), 1955–1966; charter chief of the National Institute of Mental Health (NIMH) Center for the Studies of Suicide Prevention, in Bethesda, Maryland, 1966–1969; and founder of the American Association of Suicidology in 1968.

Perhaps the major pioneering administrative effort in Shneidman's life was his work at the LASPC. This was a joint effort with his partner, Norman Farberow. He and Farberow, and psychiatrist Robert E. Litman, were the troika that pulled suicide prevention onto the modern stage. Separately and collectively they represented the three interwoven aspects of modern suicide work: research, training, and clinical service. The LASPC was the first such comprehensive center in the world. Their indispensable patron was Harold M. Hildreth, then at NIMH. Shneidman has written: "The excitement of those early days at the LASPC is hard to describe. It was like sitting on the seat of a racing covered wagon, galloping into unknown territory, dust flying all around, with the reassuring anxious and friendly faces of fellow pioneers on all sides. The dangers were from ravines and flash floods and our judgment in choosing wrong trails. Every day seemed like a new high adventure."

In 1966, Dr. Stanley Yolles, Director of the NIMH, asked Shneidman to come temporarily to Bethesda to draft a proposal for a national program in suicide prevention. After a month, during the exit interview, Yolles invited him to organize and head the program he had designed. Without thought, Shneidman politely refused. Yolles is reported to have said, "All right, but you'll never again have the opportunity to paint on a national canvas." Shneidman took the position. In fewer than three years (1966–1969), under the leadership of the NIMH center, the number of suicide prevention centers in the U.S. increased from three to about 200. A NIMH Fellowship program in Suicidology was established at Johns Hopkins University, the *Bulletin of Suicidology*—later *Suicide and Life-Threatening Behavior*—was begun, and the American Association of Suicidology was founded. Hundreds of research grants on various aspects of suicide were supported.

Regarding "suicidology," one day Shneidman was discussing with Yolles his intention to start an American Association of Suicidology. Yolles had no objection to the idea, but indicated his reservations on purely etymological grounds, pointing out that the word had a Latin root and a Greek suffix. Shneidman responded: "You're absolutely right. That's what my friends in sociology tell me." Yolles laughed and said "Touché!"

The AAS was started in Chicago in 1968. At the first meeting there was a panel consisting of a who's who of suicide: Erwin Stengel, Karl Menninger, Louis Dublin, Jacques Choron, Paul Friedman, Lawrence Kubie, and Robert Havighurst. One notable change in the composition of the AAS in the past thirty years is the inclusion of nonprofessional volunteers and of survivors. Chapter 25, "Some Reflections of a Founder," was a paper given in San Francisco in 1987, at a joint meeting of the American Association of Suicidology (AAS) and the International Association of Suicide Prevention.

23

CHAPTER

The Los Angeles Suicide Prevention Center: A Demonstration of Public Health Feasibilities

What a Suicide Prevention Center could feasibly achieve is the theme of this paper. Based on five years' experience in Los Angeles, the authors list 12 points which they believe they have demonstrated as feasible and which such a center could undertake. Furthermore, they indicate why they feel a specialized center is needed.

The Suicide Prevention Center opened its telephones and its doors in Los Angeles to patients on September 1, 1958, in an abandoned and structurally condemned building on the grounds of the Los Angeles County General Hospital. Since then the center has moved to newer quarters near the center of the city. It is supported entirely by a Title 5 demonstration grant from the National Institute of Mental Health, United States Public Health Service, administered through the Department of Psychiatry of the University of Southern California School of Medicine. The

---

Reprinted from *American Journal of Public Health*, 1965, 55, 21–26 (With N. Farberow). With permission.

The authors are co-directors, Suicide Prevention Center, Los Angeles, California.

This paper was presented before a Joint Session of the Health Officers, Epidemiology, Mental Health, and Statistics Sections of the American Public Health Association at the Ninety-First Annual Meeting in Kansas City, Mo., November 13, 1963.

opening of the Suicide Prevention Center was preceded by a decade of interest, study, and concern with the topics of suicide and suicide prevention by us and a small group of collaborators, notably Drs. Robert Litman and Norman Tabachnick. From 1955 to 1958, our work was supported by a research grant from the National Institute of Mental Health. In large measure our present center grew out of our experience under that research grant, especially the experience of being unable, in clear conscience, to conduct pure research on the wards of a large hospital without being, at the same time, deeply involved with direct and consultative life-saving services. Our research grant was preceded by six years of investigations, primarily with suicide note materials that we had discovered in the vaults of the Los Angeles County Coroner's office and later with matched nonsuicidal materials we had begun to generate ourselves.

How far we have come since the day in 1949 when we discovered those hundreds of genuine suicide notes in the coroner's files is not for us to say, but we do believe that it would be most appropriate—now, five years after the formal establishment of the Suicide Prevention Center—to give some public accounting of our activities to date.

If we have a demonstration project, what have we demonstrated? Primarily, we believe that we have demonstrated certain important *feasibilities*. Webster's Dictionary defines "feasible" as "capable of being done or carried out; practicable, possible; reasonable or capable of being used or dealt with successfully." The remainder of this paper is a brief discussion of each of several feasibilities. As an overview, we shall list a dozen of them now.

We propose that our experiences at the Suicide Prevention Center in Los Angeles over the last several years have demonstrated *the feasibility of:*

1. Preventing suicide.
2. Discovering prodromal clues to suicide.
3. Doing social research on this topic.
4. Using active therapeutic techniques, often involving the "significant other."
5. Acting as a consultation service for established health agencies.
6. Working with a chief medical examiner-coroner, especially by use of the "Psychological Autopsy" procedure.
7. Having an around-the-clock service.
8. Employing a truly multiprofessional approach.
9. Re-conceptualizing some time-worn (and inadequate) concepts of suicide and death.
10. "Un-booing" some unnecessary taboos.

11. Showing the desirability of establishing regional training centers.
12. Operating a specifically focused suicide prevention center.

And now for a few words about each.

1. *The feasibility of preventing suicide*—We might say that if we have learned anything from our decade of work on this topic, we have learned that, happily, most individuals who are acutely suicidal are so for only a relatively short period, and that, even during the time they are suicidal, they are extremely ambivalent about living and dying. If the techniques for identifying these individuals before rash acts are taken can be disseminated, and if there are agencies, like the Suicide Prevention Center, in the community that can throw resources in on the side of life and give the individual some temporary surcease or sanctuary, then after a short time most individuals can go on, voluntarily and willingly, to live useful lives. We know that it is feasible to prevent suicide.

Everybody dies; the only question is when, not if. Suicidal deaths are premature and *un*timely. At the Suicide Prevention Center we have demonstrated that in practically every case they need not occur; that they are *un*necessary. Nor does the individual who commits suicide limit his rash act to himself. Suicides often, by the very nature of their death in our society, put their skeletons in their survivors' closets. From this we see why suicide is a community mental health problem, responsible for the perturbation in many people, a perturbation made visible perhaps years later, in the clinics and the hospitals.

2. *The feasibility of generating communicable prodromal clues of suicide*—The essential nature of suicides is not clearly understood. It is not a single disease entity. In our work at the Suicide Prevention Center and the Veterans Administration Central Research Unit for the Study of Unpredicted Death, we have used various technics in pursuit of information: retrospective studies of committed suicides, psychological autopsies, cross-sectional studies of "nowalive" patients, and prospective studies of individuals who have attempted or threatened suicide. These studies reveal that most persons go through discernible prodromal phases during which they reveal, consciously or unconsciously, their potentially suicidal tendencies. This communication is sometimes explicit, sometimes it is cryptic and in code, and even sometimes the communicator is unaware of the significance of his own behaviors. Our task is to make the content and nature of these prodromal clues explicit, as people in cancer prevention have publicized such clues of malignancy as "bleeding from an aperture": or "an unhealing skin blemish." Our studies have indicated that one primary target group for this information is the physician, in that at least two-thirds of the individuals who commit suicide have seen

a physician within three months prior to the act. We estimate that "cries for help"—attempts and threats—in relation to suicide occur at least 500,000 times a year in the United States. We believe that the experiences of the staff at the SPC, and the many other individuals who have trained with us, have demonstrated the feasibility of communicating knowledge about known prodromal clues of suicide to other professional and interested lay people.

3. *The feasibility of doing social research on this topic*—If we accept the notion that service and training improve largely to the extent that they receive nourishment from research findings, then a comprehensive program of suicide must include not only the saving of lives today but the investigation of why different individuals take their lives—so that more lives may be saved more expeditiously tomorrow. The question is, is it possible (i.e., permissible) to do meaningful research in this area.

Our experience at the SPC, in the Veterans Administration, with the local state and national health agencies, and indeed our experience with press, radio, and television people, all indicate the growing feasibility of both large- and small-scale research and clinical activities on the topic of suicide. The recent publication of Dr. Dublin's book, "Suicide: A Sociological and Statistical Study," underlines the timeliness of concerted effort in this area.

4. *The feasibility of using active therapeutic techniques*—A fundamental assumption in the clinical operation of the Suicide Prevention Center has been that it would involve essentially short-term treatment, viewing the suicidal situation as a crisis period. For this reason, the center serves primarily as a resource where immediate attention for the emergency is provided by means of diagnostic and referral services. It was recognized that this would be necessary in order to attend to the needs of many people rather than to focus on the long-term treatment of just a few. This dictates our need for active intervention. Most of our cases are persons in conflict with their "significant others" and the suicidal situation is the resultant of interpersonal (or dyadic) tensions. To work only with the one party neglects the significant others and makes the treatment procedure incomplete.

We have been active also in involving friends, family, community agencies, and in recommending hospitalization where we assess the lethality risk as high and the potential-rescuers' capacities as not adequate.

5. *The feasibility of acting as a consultation service for established health agencies*—To operate as a short-term emergency clinic requires close integration and liaison with other resources within the community to whom patients can be sent for various appropriate longer-term therapeutic, rehabilitative, or environmental care. The Suicide Prevention Center has established liaison with and integrated closely with other agencies in the

community, especially the health officers, the police and sheriff's departments, Welfare Planning Council, the medical and psychiatric societies, State Department of Mental Hygiene, and others. In addition, there has been contact with over 50 health and welfare agencies in our county who, having heard of the center, telephone for consultation or are a resource for direct referrals for extended treatment. At first there was reluctance on the part of many social agencies to accept individuals with even the lowest risk of suicide. However, with referrals that included an evaluation of suicidal potential and the knowledge that consultation by telephone would be readily available, a greater willingness has occurred among the agencies in accepting referrals. Also the demonstration of the capability of our own staff in working with suicidal persons encouraged workers in other agencies to do the same.

6. *The feasibility of working with great mutual usefulness with the chief medical examiner-coroner, especially by use of the "Psychological Autopsy" procedure*—Special mention should be made of the liaison with Dr. Theodore Curphey, the Los Angeles county chief medical examiner-coroner. With him, as deputy coroners, many of the staff of the Suicide Prevention Center work closely. Vital services and research functions are carried out in the Coroner's Office through the investigation of cases of equivocal deaths, that is, cases in which the mode of death was not clear but possibly suicidal. We call this process the "Psychological Autopsy." The staff members investigate the cases by obtaining a psychological picture of the deceased by sympathetically interviewing survivors (especially concerning the victim's motivations in relation to lethal outcome) and adding this information to the other data available to the coroner, allowing him to make a more meaningful certification as to the mode of death. Through the Coroner's Office also much important research data have been gathered for use in various investigations into suicide in the community. Dr. Curphey has reported the therapeutic effects of our contacts with these bereaved survivors.

7. *The feasibility of having an around-the-clock service, using other-than-fully professional personnel*—The Suicide Prevention Center operates with a relatively small staff, fewer than a dozen full- and part-time professionals—not counting trainees in various fields. Although the center began as an 8:00 a.m. to 5:00 p.m., Monday through Friday operation, it soon became clear that a 24-hour service would have to be provided to the community. We have met this problem by carefully selecting and thoroughly training young people—mostly graduate students in the field of psychology, psychiatry, nursing, sociology, social work, and other related fields, whom we call our clinical associates—who have already assumed a professional attitude and who are trainable in attitudes, procedures, and techniques required in working with suicidal persons.

8. *The feasibility of employing a truly multiprofessional approach*—At the SPC we like to feel that we are a congenial staff of individuals from various disciplines and points of view working together. The disciplines represented include nursing, social work, psychiatry, psychology, and others. Each, of course, has his special skills, but what needs to be noted is that our experience has demonstrated that members of each specialty can, independently—feeling free to ask consultation from each other—deal appropriately with suicidal patients, calling upon our common funds of knowledge.

9. *The feasibility of re-conceptualizing some time-worn (and inadequate) concepts of suicide and death*—We believe in the importance of both relatively short-span empirical research with almost immediate applicability and payoff, and also in the advisability of long-range research thinking where the potentiality of pay-off may be more problematic but the implications of the payoff more exciting. In the field of suicide and death, we are concerned about the serious questions of *definition* and *classification.* The usual coroner's classification which divides all deaths into four crypts (natural, accidental, suicide, and homicide) is a remarkably *a*-psychological classification in that it omits the role of the individual in his own demise. Although it is a classification which is required by custom based on the habit of centuries, it often is inconsistent and contradictory when applied to special cases. We need new thoughts on this topic. Furthermore, our time-honored classification of suicidal behaviors into committed suicide, attempted suicide, and threatened suicide groups obviously combines as "suicidal" a number of very different forms of behavior (in relation to both intention and motivation) which can, with profit, be separated and designated more clearly. Appropriate taxonomies of suicide and death need to be made the explicit topic of reflection and investigation.

At our center, we have established a subunit which we have called the Center for the Scientific Study of Suicide. To this center, distinguished Fellows representing various disciplines are invited to "contemplate suicide"—i.e., to study, to think, and to apply their particular wisdoms to the manifold problems of suicide prevention. We have had scholars interested in cognitive, phenomenological, and sociological approaches, among others, to suicidal phenomena. The feasibility of so providing multidisciplinary cross-fertilization within the setting of the SPC has been clearly demonstrated.

10. *The feasibility of "un-booing" some unnecessary taboos*—Recently, a book entitled "Taboo Topics" was published. The theme of this book and of the chapter on suicide within it is that given concerted effort and "derring do," given what Professor Osgood of Illinois called "the ability to run uphill," given the internally accepted assignment that a neglected topic

merits investigation or that a problem area begs to be solved—given all these, then the feasibility of what we shall call "un-booing" some unnecessary taboos becomes manifest. At the Suicide Prevention Center we have reflected as to whether we just happened to "come along at the right time" or whether we had played some active role in creating a more permissive *zeitgeist* in relation to suicide study. We believe an accurate appraisal would probably indicate both. But we have learned in our work over the past several years that one need not run scared and that, with proper obeisance to the social amenities, one can, in the service of suicide prevention, conduct clinical and research activities, some of which, at first blush, might seem taboo.

11. *The feasibility of establishing some regional training centers*—Of equal importance with the existence of a suicide prevention agency in a community is the training and education of both lay and professional personnel in relation to suicide prevention. Like fire prevention, it is everybody's problem. Recognizing this, the Suicide Prevention Center in Los Angeles has placed appropriate emphasis upon training and educational activities, directed toward pre- and postprofessional persons, and toward the public at large. In line with our recognition of the importance of the training function we have encouraged professional persons who are interested in establishing suicide prevention centers in their own communities throughout the United States to come to our center and to spend time with us, receiving intensive training especially in clinical procedures relating to the assessment of lethality and to appropriate referral and therapeutic techniques. We have established regularly scheduled courses in these procedures. But we know that the problem of training in this country is well beyond the capacity of our energies, and we now see the advisability and the feasibility of training trainers; that is, of sharing all we know with a half-dozen or a dozen groups spread through the various major regions of our country who might, with us, serve as regional training centers and regional resource agencies, as more and more local communities recognize their need and responsibility to establish their own suicide prevention agencies.

12. *The feasibility of operating a specifically focused suicide prevention center*—It is legitimate to ask why there should be a separate suicide prevention center. We know that in most communities there are already available facilities such as hospitals, clinics, social work agencies, professional persons, and more recently, emergency psychiatric centers. Cannot these resources be used optimally to take care of suicidal persons? Our advocacy of a separate suicide prevention center is consistent with our belief that the suicidal crisis has unique features, relating especially to the dramatically heightened intra- and interpersonal crisis in which life and death frequently hang in the balance. Focused resources are

needed for these focused emergencies. The suicide prevention center is conceived as an emergency psychosocial first aid center—we have compared it with a lifeguard station on a dangerous beach—with its special resources and specially trained personnel geared to meet the specific needs of both the individual and his significant others at the moments of special crisis. Suicide is, of course, not only the individual's problem. It is the family's problem, and it is the community's problem. We have referred to the ugly backwash of disrupted mental health created in the family and in the community by a suicidal death. Society faces its legitimate challenge of meeting the suicidal person's needs quickly and efficiently. Justice Benjamin Cardozo, in 1923, stated: "A cry of distress is a summons to rescue." This ringing statement can stand as the credo of an enlightened democratic society, whose keystone lies in its heightened evaluation of each human life.

We believe that there is a new and vocal group in America: it includes all of us who are passionate about the need and the feasibility of effectively reducing the unnecessary present suicide rates. The place for each of us to do this is in *our* community. The time is *now.*

24

CHAPTER

The NIMH Center for Studies of Suicide Prevention

This brief and informal description of the NIMH Center for Studies of Suicide Prevention focuses on its current goals and the actual and potential resources which it hopes to offer to individuals and institutions concerned with suicide prevention throughout the country.

As Dr. Stanley F. Yolles, Director of NIMH, has indicated in the Foreword of this BULLETIN, the Center for Studies of Suicide Prevention was established within the NIMH to support the development of the Nation's capability to prevent suicide. Within the NIMH, the Center for Studies of Suicide Prevention (along with the National Center for Prevention and Control of Alcoholism, the Center for Studies of Narcotics and Drug Abuse, and the Center for Studies of Metropolitan and Regional Mental Health Problems) represents a new concept for NIMH functioning. These centers focus on substantive areas of concern, embracing, as it were, a conceptual catchment area. Thus, the Center for Studies of Suicide Prevention is the focus of NIMH for self-destructive phenomena and their prevention.

The concept of the "operating" or "total" center is a new one within the NIMH. In practice, it means that all activities relating to suicide are, so to speak, housed under one administrative roof. Specifically, this means that the Center for Studies of Suicide Prevention will be concerned with a va-

Reprinted from *Bulletin of Suicidology*, 1967, *1*, 2–7. With permission.

riety of procedures, including training, demonstration, and the support of research relating to suicide. Concretely, it means that applications to NIMH for support in the field of suicide and suicide prevention should now be sent to the NIMH Center for Studies of Suicide Prevention, whether they reflect training, research, demonstration, or pilot enterprises as their primary focus. Operationally, this will involve a single suicide-prevention review committee which will appropriately process (and submit to the National Advisory Mental Health Council) all applications which come to the NIMH concerned with suicide and suicide prevention.

The goal of the NIMH Center for Studies of Suicide Prevention is to effect a reduction in the suicide rate in this country. Suicide is now the leading cause of unnecessary and stigmatizing deaths, and a comprehensive national suicide-prevention program is a first order of mental health business.

In overview, the Center for Studies of Suicide Prevention will have five basic functions:

1. The center will serve as the focal point within the Institute to coordinate and direct activities throughout the Nation in support of research, pilot studies, training, information, and consultation aimed at furthering basic knowledge about suicide, and improving techniques for helping the suicidal individual.
2. The center will compile and disseminate information and training material designed to assist mental health personnel, clergy, police, educators, and others in obtaining a better understanding of suicidal actions and learning to utilize research findings.
3. The center will assist in developing and experimenting with the variety of regional and local programs and organizational models to coordinate emergency services and techniques of prevention, case finding treatment, training, and research.
4. The center will maintain liaison with studies and programs on suicide prevention undertaken by other agencies, both national and international.
5. The center will promote and maintain the application of research findings by State and local mental health agencies.

In the planning which preceded the establishment of the Center for Studies of Suicide Prevention in its present form, a 10-point comprehensive national suicide-prevention program was outlined. The 10 aspects of a comprehensive national suicide-prevention program follow:

1. *A program of support of suicide-prevention activities in many communities throughout the Nation.* In suicide prevention, as in many other fields, needs usually run ahead of knowledge; urgency for service often precedes understanding. A comprehensive program for suicide prevention

can therefore include immediate application of present knowledge, with the goal of saving lives. Just as there are fire stations throughout our country, there ought to be suicide-prevention centers in every part of the land. Communities throughout the country should be encouraged to establish some kind of suicide-prevention activity. We need immediately to initiate new life-saving activities. Even in our present state of knowledge, before we know all that we are going to learn, we know enough to feel confident that we can apply currently known facts and principles with a reasonable anticipation of reducing the suicide rate. The Community Mental Health Centers will, in many cases, furnish an excellent vehicle for relating suicide-prevention activities to organized community programs.

It should be recognized that there will undoubtedly be a variety of organizational and funding models for suicide-prevention activities, each growing out of the needs and peculiarities of the local community. Some suicide-prevention units will be operated in conjunction with a general hospital, some with an emergency room, a psychiatric clinic, or a welfare bureau, and some will operate autonomously. NIMH's responsibility may best be discharged by its serving in a consultative capacity to requesting communities as they plan the services especially suited to their needs. In addition, the NIMH Suicide Prevention Center might act in a consultant capacity to the Comprehensive Mental Health Centers in relation to suicide prevention.

2. *A special program for the "gatekeepers" of suicide prevention.* An important key to suicide prevention lies in detection and diagnosis. One of the most important findings from past experience is that practically every person who kills himself gives some verbal or behavioral clues of his intention to do so. These prodromal clues are often in "code," are cryptic or disguised, but nonetheless they are clues, and one can learn to recognize them. These are the "handles" to prevention. In practice, a variety of people hear the presuicidal clues—spouse, friend, neighbor, clergyman, policeman, bartender, physician, employer, etc.; however, it is a most important fact that over 65 percent of all individuals who commit suicide have seen a physician (usually a general practitioner) within 4 months of the event. It is therefore crucial to have a program for physicians in detecting and diagnosing potential suicides.

Special programs, tailor-made for clergymen, policemen, educators, and others, should also be prepared. It is planned to produce training materials addressed to these target groups in the form of appropriate brochures, long-playing records, films, and special publications.

3. *A carefully prepared program in massive public education.* This is probably the most important single item for effective suicide prevention and at the same time one of the most difficult to put into practice in ways

which would be both acceptable and effective. One major avenue to the reduction of suicidal deaths is to use the lay citizen for first-line detection and diagnosis. A rough model of such lay cooperation may be found in cancer detection, wherein more and more citizens know the prodromal clues for cancer. The same model, with appropriate changes, might well be adopted in suicide prevention.

A study of mass public education might be done initially in a few carefully preselected communities. This study should involve experts in epidemiology, biostatistics, and especially in the communication media. This type of study should be preceded by a long-term comprehensive study of the actual state of suicidal (and suicidal equivalent) incidents in those areas. Public education should include planned and careful use of all the public media: schools, TV, newspapers, radio, advertisements, placards. Such education should be carried on in appropriate usual and unusual places, such as doctors' offices, pool halls, public lavatories, etc.

One or two cities might be selected for large-scale pilot projects (or one or two sections of cities might be selected with equal catchment areas). The effects and effectiveness of such a program of public education should be observed through scientifically controlled studies. This can be achieved, in part, by selecting other cities (or sections of cities) which are comparable, in terms of the major variables, to the experimental cities.

Although such a program of mass public education would seem to be very important in any full-scale assault on the problem of suicide, the unanticipated effects of publicizing and popularizing the topic of suicide prevention would have to be constantly appraised during any mass-education efforts. We do not know what either the short-term or the long-term effects of such a program might be. These effects, in turn, become a legitimate subject for serious study in which consultants in sociology would play an important role.

4. *A special program for followup of suicide attempts.* We know that about 8 out of 10 people who commit suicide have previously attempted or threatened it, but the data relating to the percentage of people who have attempted or threatened suicide, who subsequently commit suicide are contradictory and equivocal. The primary purpose of this program would be to prevent the committing of suicide. Some people who commit suicide do so the first time they attempt it, but the more common pattern is that of a series of attempts, with increasing lethality. Too many reports of suicide are of individuals who have been previously sewn up or pumped out and released, only to complete the task within hours. Like the program for the gatekeepers and the support of suicide-prevention centers and the program in public education, this program also is

meant to "nibble" at the suicide problem and to help effect a reduction in the suicide rate.

These studies might be conducted in two or three preselected sites where the conditions are propitious for success, especially in cooperating hospitals, police departments, and public health facilities. The actual followup could be done by a variety of types of personnel, including public health nurses, social workers, psychologists, etc. The data already available from the work of Robins, Tuckman, and Stengel would serve as beginning for further and better understanding.

There is great confusion about the relationship between attempted suicide and committed suicide. (This confusion exists largely because clinicians and investigators fail to think in terms of lethality. A suicidal event—whether a threat, an attempt, or a commission—is best understood in terms of its lethal intention, rather than method.) We need to know the characteristic of those attempters who are highly lethal, as opposed to the characteristics of those with low lethality. Obviously, prevention of suicidal deaths lies in dealing with the former.

It might be well to pattern the followup procedures for suicide attempts roughly after that of VD or TB followup, and look forward to the time when suicide attempt followup can be built into the Public Health Service. The followup could be seen as "post-crisis followup" and would be a legitimate aspect of a comprehensive approach to suicide prevention. It is known that the most dangerous period after a suicide attempt occurs within 3 months. A followup procedure might be one effective way of saving some lives.

5. *An active NIMH program of research and training grants.* This aspect of the comprehensive suicide-prevention program would include stimulating, catalyzing, promoting, and supporting especially promising and needed research projects. Also, training grants should be made available for special training in suicide prevention, for regional training activities, symposia, etc.

Pedestrian and repetitious studies especially should be avoided in the awarding of research grants. On the other hand, there are several special current interest and research areas in suicide where research might very well be supported and interest in these areas might be stimulated. These include: Adolescent and child suicides; biochemistry of suicide, including the study of stress and depression; stressful interpersonal relationships and suicide; cognitive aspects of suicide; the study of accidents, homicide, and self-destructive life styles; intensive longitudinal personality studies, especially relating to inimical behaviors; suicide and terminal illness; the effects of environmental deprivation and stress; studies of the use of volunteer personnel; studies of various organizational and funding patterns for suicide-prevention activities; studies of "psychological autopsies"; and the investigation of equivocal and unequivocal deaths.

It is anticipated that further information relating to developments, plans, and availability of NIMH grant support will be prepared for this BULLETIN from time to time.

6. *A redefinition and refinement of statistics on suicide.* It is generally agreed that current statistics on suicide are grossly inadequate and that comparisons of suicidal incidents between cities, between States, and between countries, based on available figures, are at best sometimes inaccurate and often obfuscatory and misleading. The current inaccuracies are due to many reasons, including the following: (a) confusion as to how to certify equivocal deaths, for example, those which lie between suicide and accident; (b) dissembling on the part of police and physicians who wish to protect the family, and public officials who wish to protect the reputation of their community; (c) inaccurate recordkeeping, where the data that could be known and ascertained simply is not accurately tabulated; (d) the inadequacies of the present concepts. More will be said of this last point in the paragraphs below.

Two additional points should be made in relation to statistics: An opportunity exists in this program to introduce improved classifications and to conduct pilot studies to determine (for the first time) the veridical suicide rates in some selected communities; and further, the specter exists that unless there is a refinement of the concepts related to self-destruction, there will never be accuracy of reporting, because the present concepts are simply not strong enough accurately to reflect the events which they are purported to represent.

The NIMH Suicide Prevention Advisory Committee might suggest new concepts, a comprehensive program for uniform national recordkeeping, and refinement and redefinition of statistics on self-destruction.

7. *The development of a cadre of trained, dedicated professionals.* There do not exist, at present, trained professionals in sufficient number to man the proposed and projected projects in suicide prevention. There is an acute need for the creation of a core of individuals who might then direct and staff the suicide-prevention programs in the NIMH central office, in the regional offices, and in the communities throughout the country. It should be pointed out that what is being proposed here is that individuals be given sufficient training in the basic ideas, facts, and skills relating to suicide and suicide prevention so that they can then act more meaningfully in their administrative and technical capacities. This aspect of the NIMH suicide-prevention program will be implemented by establishing multidisciplinary fellowships in suicidology. These individuals must be carefully selected from those who have either done research in suicide or evinced a special interest in this field, and then given special

opportunities for further training in suicidology. There is every reason to believe that such a program should be multidisciplinary. It would strengthen the program to have people with M.D.'s, Ph.D.'s, M.S.W.'s, and M.P.H.'s in such a program. The Ph.D.'s should come from a number of fields, especially psychology and sociology. The multidisciplinary aspect is especially important in that a variety of points of view are desired, a catholicity of interests is necessary, and the goal of this training is to provide administrative leadership, not primarily to create therapists in suicide prevention.

8. *Governmentwide liaison and national use of a broad spectrum of professional personnel.* This item is more a statement of attitude and approach than a blueprint for specific action. Self-destruction draws from, and adversely affects, many areas. A comprehensive and meaningful program of suicide prevention should obviously include coordination between NIMH and other units such as those concerned with cancer, accidents, child development, the military services, rural problems, environmental deprivation, etc. Just as there should be liaison between NIMH and other governmental agencies, there should be interaction among a variety of professions. What this field needs most is ideas, and no one profession holds a tight lien on thought. A comprehensive program should include the planned use of bright and interested people from a variety of fields including psychology, psychiatry, sociology, epidemiology, anthropology, linguistics, philosophy, law enforcement, religion, social work, education, and health education.

9. *A special followup program for the survivor-victims of individuals who have committed suicide.* It is not inaccurate to state that, from the point of view of the survivor, there are two kinds of deaths: all the deaths from cancer, heart ailment, accident, etc., on the one hand, and suicidal deaths on the other. If one stops to consider the kind of grief-work and mourning an individual experiences on the death of a loved one who dies from a natural or accidental cause on the one hand and then thinks of the kind of grief one has to live with for the rest of her life if his parent or spouse has committed suicide, the contrast is clear. The individual who commits suicide often sentences the survivor to be obsessed for the rest of his life about the suicidal death. The suicide puts his skeleton in the survivors' psychological closets. No other kind of death in our society creates such lasting emotional scars as does a suicidal death. A comprehensive suicide-prevention program should attend to the psychological needs of the stigmatized survivors, especially children who survive a parent who has committed suicide.

Although this aspect of the program is not especially directed toward reducing suicide, it nevertheless relates to the survivors of the suicidal death and is directly in the center of mental health concern. Today each citizen enjoys many rights in this country; we would hope that among these rights he might be granted the right to lead an unstigmatized life, especially a life unstigmatized by the suicidal death of a parent or a spouse.

Studies of the effects of suicides on survivors need to be done. Two kinds of studies immediately suggest themselves: retrospective studies of individuals one of whose family has committed suicide 1, 5, 10, or 20 years ago; and prospective studies of those who have experienced the suicide of a member of the immediate family in the very recent past. These studies would record the effects on the survivor through the years.

We do not at present know the "cost" of each suicide in terms of the deleterious mental effects on the survivors—how many survivors of a father's or a mother's suicide subsequently need mental hospitalization or other mental health care. To ascertain what these facts are, we need to develop special ways for effectively helping individuals who have suffered this kind of traumatic loss. Just as there are better and worse ways of responding, for example to the loss of a limb or to blindness, so we must develop better ways to help survivors respond to the grim facts of suicide in their family and thus to reduce the overall mental health toll.

Special research projects should be elicited, encouraged, and supported in the field of suicidal sequelae—that is, the effects of suicide on the survivors, and efforts should be made to mollify these effects.

10. *A rigorous program for the evaluation of the effectiveness of suicide-prevention activities.* Although, in the individual case, suicide can best be seen as reflecting "a damp, dismal November in the soul," it also seems to be so that, in the large, suicide rates vary with such items as the Nation's position in relation to peace and war; changes in the economic state of the Nation (prosperity or depression); changes, in any one locale, in the percentage and the role of ethnic minorities, etc. All this is to say that it is an extremely thorny methodological problem in epidemiology to test or to prove the effectiveness of a program in suicide prevention. Nevertheless, efforts to evaluate effective suicide-prevention activities must, from both a scientific and moral point of view, be a part of a comprehensive suicide-prevention program from its very beginning. Without this feature of rigorous evaluation there can be no accounting by NIMH, either to itself or to Congress, or to the scientific communities.

This aspect of the program can be implemented best by consultation with people in biometry, in epidemiology, in sociological methodology, in research design, and in statistics.

The basic issues in a suicide-prevention program are encompassed in this question: What can a local suicide-prevention program do that will lower the suicide rate of the people of that community, and how can we find out whether this is being accomplished?

In general, three levels of prevention might be envisaged: primary prevention, in which the goal is to make it unnecessary for the suicidal crisis ever to occur; secondary prevention, which has to do with the effective treatment of an existing suicidal crisis; and tertiary prevention, which relates to the reduction in the amount of disability in the survivor caused by the irreversible suicidal event.

A priori, there are two kinds of criteria for judging the effectiveness of suicide-prevention programs. The primary, and by far the more important criterion, is the reduction of suicidal deaths (and the unequivocal demonstration thereof). The secondary criteria (a large and potentially fruitful field for development) would include outcomes short of or different from the clear-cut demonstration of the saving of a life, but nonetheless relevant to the entire area of suicide prevention—especially as suicide prevention lies embedded in the larger field of mental health. As a beginning, one might suggest the following as possibly relevant secondary criteria: a decrease in the lethality of an individual; an increase in his mental health or psychological well-being; a decrease in the taboo or stigma of suicide; an increase in the amount of coordination among the mental health agencies in the community; improved conceptualizations and methods for gathering data; increased dissemination of information relating to suicide prevention. This area is of sufficient importance to merit some separate comments at a later time.

A program for evaluation cannot be tacked on to research efforts, but it must be built into the program from the beginning. The evaluation aspect of a comprehensive suicide-prevention program is critical, both scientifically and morally, and will be one of the initial—and sustained—features of the program.

The 10-point program for suicide prevention here outlined is a mutual enterprise whose successful development depends on the active interest, support, and activities of suicidologists throughout the country. In our mutual concern with suicidal phenomena and suicide prevention, we elicit your best help and invite your most earnest cooperation.

25

CHAPTER

Some Reflections of a Founder

When I was in Vienna for the International Association for Suicide Prevention (IASP) meeting in 1985, I saw a stunning exhibition of the art, music, architecture, politics, and psychology of Vienna from 1870 to 1930 at the Kunsterhaus. The exhibition was called *Traum und Wirklichkeit*—"Dream and Reality." For me, the joint meeting of the American Association of Suicidology (AAS) and the IASP in San Francisco could be summed up with this brief sentence: *Ein Traum ist Wirklichkeit geworden*—"A dream has become reality." I was heartened to note the presence of many members from abroad (27 different countries) and from 36 separate states of the United States.

☐ The Founding of the AAS

From 1966 to 1969, between my previous stay at the Los Angeles Suicide Prevention Center and my subsequent stints at Harvard and UCLA, I was at the National Institute of Mental Health (NIMH), serving as the first Chief of the Center for Studies of Suicide Prevention. In 1966 there were three suicide prevention centers in this country; by 1970 there were over 200. Dozens of research projects around the country were supported by the NIMH Center. The *Bulletin of Suicidology,* which later metamorphosed into *Suicide and Life-Threatening Behavior,* was begun. It was a lively period

Reprinted from *Suicide and Life-Threatening Behavior,* 1988, *18,* 1–12. With permission.

of considerable activity. It became evident to me that the time had come for a national organization relating the study of suicide and suicide prevention. I was determined to try to begin with a special meeting of the best available suicidologists in the country (and one from England). With the help of an old friend, Professor William E. Henry at the University of Chicago, a meeting was scheduled in Chicago on March 20, 1968. I believe that there was as much suicidological talent and experience at that table that day at the Conrad Hilton Hotel as has ever been assembled in one place. The group consisted of Jacques Choron, Louis I. Dublin, Paul Friedman, Robert Havighurst, Lawrence Kubie, Karl Menninger, and Erwin Stengel. They were all then in their 70s and 80s; only Dr. Menninger and Professor Havighurst, bless them, are alive today.

That meeting was a kind of "reconvening" of the famous meeting in Freud's apartment in Vienna in 1910—the meeting of Freud, Adler, Jung, Stekel, and Oppenheim. The 1910 meeting is reported to us in English in Paul Friedman's 1967 edited book *On Suicide,* which was my point of departure. In my comments at the 1968 meeting, I noted that the 1910 meeting was unusual in a number of ways. It was the only meeting held by the Vienna psychoanalytic group on the topic of suicide; the meeting was chaired not by Freud but by Adler; it was held on the temporal threshold (within 1 year) of the splintering of that group; it was the occasion of the first enunciation by Wilhelm Stekel of the psychodynamic formulation that the yearning of the death of the self is the mirrored wish for the death of another; it seemed to stimulate Freud's own thoughts on death and suicide; and it focused on the adolescent and on the role of education in suicide prevention. In all, this was a remarkable set of overt and latent threads.

In addition, in the report of the 1968 meeting, I addressed the issue of what was then new in suicidology. In this effort, I listed and discussed some 18 items, which I am emboldened to summarize here:

1. A new permissiveness to discuss and study suicide and death.
2. A focus on suicide prevention, including its elaborations, especially postvention.
3. Changes in concepts of death, especially (since Menninger) "partial death" and my concept of "subintentioned death."
4. Changes in the format and uses of the death certificate—a forerunner of the concept of the psychological autopsy.
5. An increased understanding of the varieties of intention in self-destruction.
6. A recognition of the pivotal place of ambivalence in suicide.
7. An appreciation of the key role of the significant other in suicide and of the usually dyadic nature of suicide.

8. The role of affective states other than hostility in suicide, especially hopelessness and malignant pessimism.
9. A growing appreciation of the role of age in the human life cycle as it touches suicide.
10. The usefulness of explicating suicidality along the dimensions of perturbation and lethality.
11. An emphasis on the delineation and dissemination of the prodromal clues to suicide—a pivot in the whole prevention movement.
12. The implications of advances in medical techniques related to suicide.
13. The impact of the massive secularization of death and the enormous spiritual and psychological problems created by it.
14. Some new looks at old masters, especially Freud and Durkheim, and the possibility and the obvious challenge to come to this topic through some new portals.
15. Significant changes in the public practice of suicide prevention, especially in the services that ought to be provided.
16. Changes in the patterns of financial and community support for suicide prevention activities.
17. A growing emphasis on assessment, especially of the effectiveness of interventional efforts.
18. The recent appearance of suicide professionalism and the possible role of a new profession, suicidology.

The AAS was founded at the meeting in Chicago. I was blessed with the special help of Avery Weisman, whose counsel was indispensable to me. Of course, I conferred with my mentor Henry Murray. At my request, Calvin Frederick, who was then with me at NIMH, prepared a constitution and a set of by-laws patterned more or less after those of the multidisciplinary American Orthopsychiatric Association. By the end of that day, our dream of an AAS, in our minds at least, was a reality. One year later at our second meeting in New York City, I found myself president. Happily, the organization soon had a life of its own. If the association were to have a motto, it would be "Research, Training, Service."

I now have the pleasure of listing the subsequent presidents of the AAS since 1969: Seymour Perlin, Avery Weisman, Norman Farberow, Jerome Motto, Robert Kastenbaum, Richard McGee, Nancy Allen, Robert Litman, Betsy Comstock, Bruce Danto, Calvin Frederick, Ronald Maris, James Selkin, Gwendolyn Harvey, Joseph Thigpen, Alan Berman, Pamela Cantor, Cynthia Pfeffer, Elizabeth Jones, and President-Elect Charlotte Sanborn—a *Who's Who* of American suicidology (including, I am pleased to note, a second generation of the younger professionals and workers in our field). What is evident is that the AAS has moved from being an organization of only psychologists and psychiatrists to being truly multidisciplinary. It includes nurses, social workers, sociologists, and health educators; even more, it reflects the role of volunteers and of help-lines, and the issues of accreditation and of standards. The list of presidents is varied, vibrant, and multitalented, and provides a good augury for our multidisciplinary future.

The topic for the IASP-AAS joint meeting was "Then and Now." What have I seen over the past 40 years in American suicidology? My reflections divide themselves into two categories: those about the phenomena of suicide itself, and those about the practice of suicide prevention within the larger social setting.

The Phenomena of Suicide

In relation to suicidal phenomena (the events themselves), I have seen no great change, nor would I expect to see one in so relatively short a time. By definition, the ubiquities are still there. The basic roots of anguish, psychological pain, thwarted emotions—hate, love, shame, guilt (who has said them better than Shakespeare almost half a millennium ago and Melville a century ago?)—have not changed. Of course, the phenotypic details vary, but the unity themes sound the same old chords. As a small example: Two years ago, with permission, I personally collected all the suicide notes for Los Angeles County for the calendar year 1984. They read pretty much the same as the suicide notes that Norman Farberow and I collected from that same office almost 40 years before. I do believe that the meaning of death and suicide *do* change, as Aries (1975/1981) has so persuasively shown us in *The Hour of Our Death* (a book that covers the past millenium), but the interval between 1968 and 1988, even with everything that has happened in the world, is merely a blip on the screen of these timeless topics. The ubiquities remain.

But the *study* of suicide is another matter. We have seen an expansion of what I consciously tried to promote in my brief tenure at NIMH—an advertent and tenacious multidisciplinarity. I assure you that I do not take credit for this expansion; I simply note its presence and call it to our attention. Today, there are *many* legitimate approaches to the study of suicide, among which can be listed the following:

1. The literary and personal-documents approach, including the use of suicide notes and suicide diaries. I am currently especially interested in the potentialities for concerted, cooperative studies of the recently published *Inman Diary* (Aaron, 1985), and, along these lines, who

has told us more about the inside of suicide than Dostoyevsky, Tolstoy, Flaubert, Melville, and Kate Chopin?

2. Theological and philosophical approaches, where our late friend Jacques Choron was so effective.
3. The demographic approach—an indispensable background for further work—where one thinks of John Graunt, Johann Sussmilch, and Louis I. Dublin.
4. The sociocultural approach—for example, between Japan and the United States (in this connection, see Iga's *The Thorn in the Chrysanthemum* (1986).
5. The sociological approach, with several members of the AAS at its intellectual forefront.
6. The dyadic, interpersonal, familial approaches—our recent leaders have had much to say here.
7. The psychodynamic approach, exemplified by Freud, Menninger, and several of our past presidents.
8. The psychological approach, emphasizing psychological pain, constriction, and thwarted needs, as explicated by Henry Murray.
9. The psychiatric approach—the mental illness and disease approach, focusing on depression.
10. The constitutional and genetic approach, involving both cohort and DNA studies.
11. Biological and biochemical approaches, with currently ambiguous but potentially thrilling potentialities.

12–15. Legal, ethical approaches; the preventional approach; systems theory approaches; and political, global, and supernational approaches. I have eschewed naming notable AAS members in connection with these only because I fear to omit many who should be included.

But one can clearly see that the study of suicide is a never-completed circle, containing many legitimate sectors or fields or approaches. The only illegitimate approach to this multidisciplinary pie is for someone to plant a fork in one spot and pronounce that *that* sector, *that* way of looking at things, is the whole pie. But this point is too obvious to belabor. The blessing of our lives is that we have come upon this field that was nascent, dormant, and quiescent, and in our own lifetimes have awakened it so that it has become a legitimate area for concern and for scholarly study. Nowadays, one can say "I am a suicidologist" and hold one's head high.

Speaking of the various sectors of the suicidal pie, in my own recent publications I have aimed, in some small way, to clarify the *psychological* sector of this fascinating etiological circle. In pursuit of this intellectual venture, I have developed a set of 10 commonalities of suicide (Shneidman, 1985). I see these as phenomenologically self-evident, and I find these psychological characteristics in every case (historical or current) that I look at, because I have the capacity to translate every instance into those terms. The 10 commonalities are as follows:

1. The common *purpose* of suicide is to seek a solution.
2. The common *goal* of suicide is the cessation of consciousness—the unbearable flow of intolerable mind content.
3. The common *stimulus* in suicide is intolerable psychological pain. Every suicide can be understood in terms of pain—unbearable psychological pain, idiosyncratically defined.
4. The common *stressor* in suicide is frustrated psychological needs. In Henry Murray's (1983), *Explorations in Personality,* we have served to us, on a golden platter, an explication of some 30 psychological needs. It is thwarting or blocking of certain needs—critical in the makeup of *that* individual—that causes the pain that pushes the suicide. I believe that it is necessary to understand this need system in order to understand an individual case of suicide.
5. The common *emotion* in suicide is helplessness-hopelessness. This seems not only evident from developmental psychology, but also avoids the unnecessary sibling rivalry among the relevant emotions: guilt, shame, fear, and Stekel's hostility.
6. The common *cognitive state* in suicide is ambivalence. The pervasive presence of wanting to stop unbearable pain and wanting to survive in a state of less pain—in other words, ambivalence—is universally documented.
7. The common *perceptual state* in suicide is constriction. One has to be mindful of and deal with that word "only": "the only thing I could do"; "the only way to commit suicide." Dealing with constriction is a first order of preventional business.
8. The common *action* in suicide is egression. There are ways of substituting more benign egressions or blocking the exits, including getting the gun.
9. The common *interpersonal act* in suicide is communication of intention. Not secrecy or withdrawal, but communication, albeit in code, is the hallmark of committed suicide.
10. The common *consistency* in suicide is with lifelong coping patterns. Individuals are enormously loyal to themselves and their own armamentaria, even (or especially) in their dying. This is seen in a careful examination of an anamnestic record in the nuances of egressions (e.g., leaving home, quitting a job, ending a marriage, etc.).

This compilation has been further refined into a theoretical model. In its schematic form, it is a suicidal cube (see Figure 25-1). The three sur-

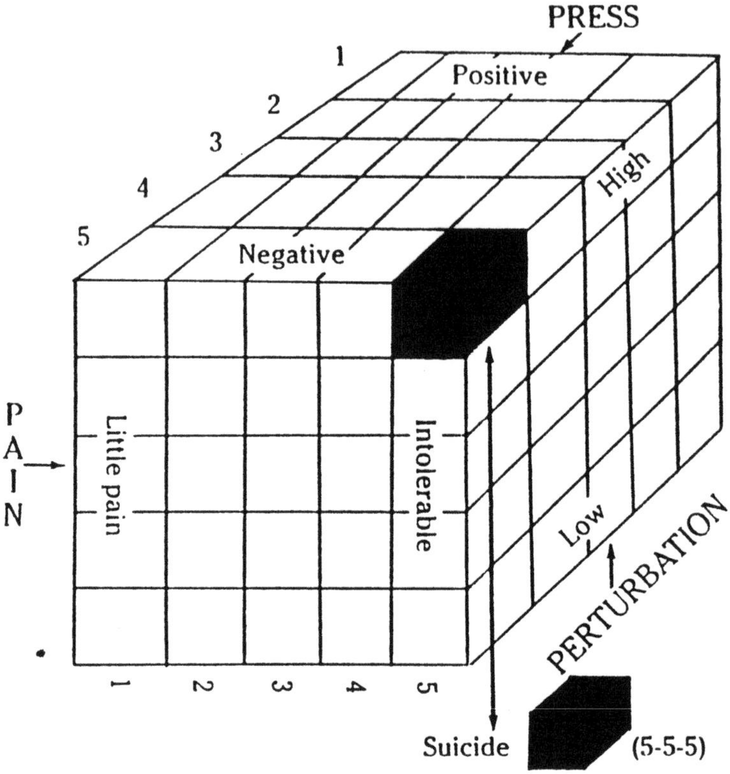

FIGURE 25-1. A theoretical cubic model of suicide.

faces of the cube are labeled "pain," "perturbation" (consisting of constriction and a penchant for precipitous action), and "press." "Press," from positive to negative, is Murray's (1938) term for everything that is done to an individual before (or to which) he or she responds. It includes DNA, parents, siblings, school, events, and chance. In this model, the suicidal cubelet (blackened in the figure) is in the right-hand corner, indicating the maximum concatenation of pain, perturbation, and (negative) press.

The implications for research would seem to be endless: to make comparisons, from the general (nonsuicidal) literature of psychiatry and psychology (perception, memory, learning, etc.) between and among pain and perturbation, pain and press, and press and perturbation, including their near-synonyms. All it takes is a careful, scholarly examination of the entire professional literature—a task that I am on the threshold of beginning.

The implications of this cubic model for treatment would seem to be obvious: Reduce (in reality or by reconceptualizing) the psychological pain a bit, and/or widen the opportunities for choice, and/or constrain the proclivity for irreversible action, and/or diminish the negative press. That is the utterly straightforward and relatively simple way in which lives can be saved: Mollify the pain, the perturbation, or the negative press. No one commits suicide in a nonsuicidal combination.

☐ Suicidology Within the Larger Social Setting

I turn now to the second category of my reflections—specifically, the changing place of suicidology within the also-changing social matrix. I have reflected about the impact of social policy on suicide acts and on suicide prevention activities. There are some generalizations that one can make about suicide and public policy in this country. In this, I am following the lead of Professor Shirley Zimmermann at the University of Minnesota in her recent book on family policy (Zimmermann, 1988). Four hypotheses are offered:

1. The more identifiable the risk, the more closely targeted the public (and legislative) response to relieve it will be. Thus it follows that suicidologists have a clear responsibility to identify, delineate, and disseminate (in ordinary language) the common clues to suicide.
2. The more organized and intense the political activity on behalf of potential victims, the more likely it is that public policy will concern itself with that problem. In this regard, it makes good tactical sense for us to focus on certain targeted groups, such as suicide among the young.
3. The more elevated the status of the potential victims (i.e., if it is likely to touch *us*), the more intense the public policy response will be, and vice versa. In this country today, we are only now becoming sufficiently alarmed about AIDS (acquired immune deficiency syndrome) because we realize that it is more than a malady of the "four H's": homosexuals, Haitians, hemophiliacs, and heroin addicts. It is because we fear that the disease may jump out of the containment of these groups and involve ordinary and "good citizens" that concern about AIDS is becoming widespread. In suicide, also, we are not egalitarian about death; we mourn the suicide of the talented, the beautiful, or the young more than that of the untalented, the homely, or the old. Here again, it is a strategic point to place an emphasis on youth suicide prevention and the use of young spokespersons. Nor is there anything nefarious in reciting these social realities.
4. The more congruent the prevention strategies are with current political and policy trends, the more active the political and policy response

on that topic will be. Here especially, there are some palpable changes to be seen in this country over the past 40 years.

It gives me no pleasure to report that there are, in fact, fairly solid cross-sectional empirical data on this last topic. A systematic study of the 50 states of the United States, in a study done by Zimmermann (1988) using 1980 and 1982 total data, correlated the amounts of expenditures for education and public service programs with suicide rates and teenage birth rates, state by state. The results clearly demonstrate a statistically significant *negative* correlation between per capita state public welfare expenditures and suicide: The lower the expenditure for public welfare within the state, the higher the suicide rate; the more generous the expenditure, the lower the suicide rate. Obviously one of the things needed is more than a modicum of government (both state and federal) support to effect a truly meaningful reduction in suicidal deaths.

Since the 1940s, when I first turned to (and then never turned away from) the joint topics of suicide and suicide prevention, I have been a suicidologist in this glorious country under the administration of nine presidents: Roosevelt, Truman, Eisenhower, Kennedy, Johnson, Nixon, Ford, Carter, and Reagan. It seems clear enough to me that more liberal federal leaderships tend in general to tolerate and support a variety of approaches, including sociological and psychological approaches, to what we call our social problems, including suicide; conversely, more conservative federal leadership—on a generally *reduced* overall level, specifically in the case of suicide—tends to emphasize biological and medical solutions, with the implied locus of blame in the person rather than in the social structure, and thus tends to cut down on the necessary catholicity of approaches.

One insufficiently recognized culture hero in America is Jonas Salk. If there has been a swing in this country in suicidology in the last 30 years, it has been from Freud to Salk: Biologicize the problem, concentrate on one disease, find the virus, and develop the vaccine—that is the current American way. This is an unarguably marvelous solution when one is dealing with *infantile* paralysis, but it is a model that in all likelihood is not applicable if one is dealing with a case of *hysterical* paralysis. And who is to say that suicide, paradigmatically speaking, is not more like the latter than the former? I finally believe that suicide is not a disease; it is, rather, a bio-socio-psycho-philosophical malaise.

A sad but curious fact is that the same people who talk about prayer in our schools—which seems clearly unconstitutional as I understand that noble document—also want to practice a flawed form of social Darwinism toward the less advantaged, in which a crisis or failure (e.g., suicide) is seen as the individual's own fault, and in which the larger group, sociobiologically speaking, might well be rid of that unadapting individual. At its heart, this attitude is opposed to suicide prevention. We are well advised to believe that this anachronistic 19th-century frontier philosophy imposed on a late 20th-century complex society is too costly for good conscience.

One obvious conclusion to draw from all this is that the *dramatis personae* along the Potomac are indeed keenly relevant to our public policies and the resulting suicide prevention programs that flow from them—both their magnitude and their nature—as they filter down to the states and cities. In relation to suicide prevention, I am convinced that we must wait until 1989, after the next presidential inauguration, for any really meaningful action to be effected.

Ernest Hilgard's (1986) recent comprehensive volume, *Psychology in America,* contains a chapter subheading that has caught my attention: "Topics that Become Centers of Excitement." Although he does not discuss suicide, in my mind that is what the suicide prevention movement has been in America: a topic that has become a center of excitement. For honesty's sake, I need to add that I did not quote Hilgard's subheading in its entirety. It is actually "Topics that Become Centers of Excitement over a Short Time Span." I hope that this is not going to be true for the suicide prevention movement or for the AAS, and I have reasons to believe that it will not be so, although certain subinterests (e.g., the current tactical focus on youth suicide) may very well wax and wane over the next few years.

Our broader hope is that the general concern with suicide prevention across the board, having been established, will endure. But I believe that this endurance will not happen on its own, and that we must all work to see that new conceptualizations, decent research efforts (both nomethetic and idiographic), and informed training programs ensure the continuance of suicidology. These are a few of my reflections about suicide, suicide prevention, the AAS over the 1968–1988 interval, and its role for the rest of this century. I hope that readers have found these remarks either interesting or provocative, preferably both.

☐ Remarks from 1968 AAS Meeting

I now have the pleasure of quoting some very special, albeit brief remarks made at the first meeting of the AAS in 1968. Here are their voices, expressing various points of view.

Jacques Choron:

Not sufficient attention has been paid to the difference between the death of another person, even of a loved one, and what I could call my own death. My death is something entirely different than the death of another person. A therapist who deals with a potentially suicidal patient or who is talking about the notions of death of the patient may help to re-establish communication between the patient and the therapist. It may also have diagnostic value in the sense that it may help us to establish the lethality of the patient.

Lawrence Kubie:

And finally as an act of desperation they slash their wrists a little bit, sometimes accidentally going too deep; they take whatever drugs they happen to have on hand; and they must all come into our statistics on suicide. But what the patient is trying to do is save his life. Many acts of self-injury which are lumped together under the concept of suicide do not have self-extinction as their goal.

Erwin Stengel:

The psychoanalytic contribution to suicide research has been mainly concerned with the intrapsychic dynamics of self-destructive tendencies. This has been both its strength and its limitation. It has until recently not concerned itself with the external world, apart from those objects which by introjection become parts of the inner world. Zilboorg's discovery of the role of the broken home in suicide proneness was a brilliant observation deduced from the study of intrapsychic processes and confirmed by clinical and epidemiological studies.

Louis Dublin:

The lay volunteer was probably the most important single discovery in the 50-year history of suicide prevention. Little progress was made until he came into the picture, for he alone apparently was qualified to make the live and fruitful contacts with the person in distress. He had the time and the qualities of character to prove that he cared. With proper training he can make a successful approach to the client. He can through direct friendly contact discover the principal cause of his difficulties and by his knowledge of the community services which are available for useful referral, he can often tide his client over his crisis.

Karl Menninger:

I think that it is important to distinguish between suicide as a form of death and suicide as an attempt at expression of something within one—helplessness, desperation, fear, the other emotions. The organism says, "Anything rather than suicide; anything rather than have to give up the most precious thing of all—namely, my life. Sickness, yes, even neurosis, even crime, but not that awful oblivion, that awful ultimate nothingness." The suicidal gesture is thus a cry not only of distress, not only a cry for help, not only a prayer, one might say, but it is a pleading: "I want to live; help me to find a way to live."

☐ Concluding Remarks

My final remarks are purely personal reflections. The nature of my childhood and then later of my being a parent conspired together to give me a certain psychodynamic orientation toward living systems. Thus, it was quite natural for me to view the AAS as a child of mine. I delight in having sired it; I am fiercely proud of what it has become; and I am entirely happy now to have it live on, unencumbered by any unnecessary meddling by me. It seems the natural thing to do: to give a living system—a little human being, a group, a center, or an association—the breath of life and then, after an appropriate period of devoted nurturing, to let it have an independent existence (with, of course, never-ending strings of concern and love, but not of control). This has been my life in suicidology. I have found it worth living, and would gladly live it again if the chance were offered me.

☐ References

Aaron, D. (Ed.). (1985). *The Inman diary: A public and private confession.* (Vols. 1 and 2). Cambridge, MA: Harvard University Press.

Aries, P. (1981). *The hour of our death.* New York: Knopf. (Original work published 1977).

Friedman, P. (Ed.). (1967). *On suicide.* New York: International Universities Press.

Hilgard, E. (1987). *Psychology in America: A historical survey.* San Diego, CA: Harcourt Brace Jovanovich.

Iga, M. (1986). *The thorn in the chrysanthemum: Suicide and economic success in modern Japan.* Berkeley and Los Angeles: University of California Press.

Murray, H. A. (1983). *Explorations in personality.* New York: Oxford University Press.

Shneidman, E. S. (1985). *Definition of Suicide.* New York, Wiley.

Zimmerman, S. (1988). *Understanding family policy.* Newbury Park, CA: Sage.

IV

SUICIDE
Section D: Clinical and Community

The proof of the suicidological pudding is in the "ventions"—as in prevention, intervention, and postvention. In other words, the main payoff of all our research and training activities lies primarily in making our *clinical* efforts more effective. That is what counts in everyday society. The four pieces in this section relate to three community and clinical aspects of suicidology: prevention at a public level; prevention and intervention as seen in two chapters on psychotherapy; and a comment on the issue of rational suicide.

Shneidman's career in suicidology has been both intellectual and practical. In Chapter 26, "How to Prevent Suicide," Shneidman, with Philip Mandelkorn, a writer for *Time* magazine, presents a public affair document. It was one of the first attempts (1962), while Shneidman was at NIMH, to meet the responsibility of prevention efforts at the community level.

Chapter 27 (on psychotherapy) contains prescriptive advice for the psychotherapist, suggesting a focus on the assessment of the patient's lethality and on the therapist's countertransference (and of the advisability of consultation if there are difficulties in that countertransference). Implied in the paper is that all psychotherapy cures of suicidal patients are transference cures. A brief case history is given.

Chapter 28 lists some twenty aphorisms about suicide and suggests their implications for psychotherapy. The special focus of this paper is on *constriction* as a potentially life-threatening condition that may require special attention from the therapist. It repeats several ideas of the previous paper but comes at the topic from a different direction and shows some of the special aspects of psychotherapy with suicidal patients from a new light.

Chapter 29 is a brief comment on the topic of rational suicide. Shneidman does not think that we can usefully debate this issue; rather, the main question is how we intervene, not whether a suicide is rational or not.

26

CHAPTER

How To Prevent Suicide

Before you finish reading this page, someone in the United States will try to kill himself. At least 60 Americans will have taken their own lives by this time tomorrow. More than 25,000 persons in the United States killed themselves last year, and nine times that many attempted suicide. Many of those who attempted will try again, a number with lethal success. And here's the irony: Except for a very few, all of the people who commit suicide want desperately to live.

At one time or another almost everyone contemplates suicide. It is one of several choices open to man. Yet any debate of suicide's sin or merit is best left to the academicians, the theologians, and the philosophers. Few suicidal persons would listen closely. Most of these deeply troubled men, women, and children are submerged in their own despair.

No single group, nor color, nor class of people is free from self-inflicted death. Rich or poor, male or female, Christian or Jew, black or white, young or old—to some extent every category of man suffers death by suicide. However, there appear to be some statistical differences. In the United States, the number of men who kill themselves is three times higher than that of women (though women attempt suicide more often than men); whites twice that of Blacks; college students half again as much as their non-college counterparts (for collegians, suicide is the third leading cause of death—only accidents and cancer take more lives);

Reprinted from Public Affairs Pamphlet. New York: Public Affairs Pamphlets, 1967, No. 406 (With P. Mandelkorn). With permission.

single people twice that of those married; and among adults, it is more frequently the elderly who kill themselves.

Suicides are much less accurately reported in some places than others; nevertheless, suicide is among the ten leading causes of death in the United States. Of every 100,000 persons in this country, each year 11 choose suicide. In contrast, Hungary has 26.8 suicides per 100,000; Austria, 21.7; Czechoslovakia, 21.3; Finland, 19.2; West Germany and Sweden, 18.5; Switzerland, 16.8; Japan, 16.1; and France, 15.5. Most other countries report suicide rates lower than the United States, including Italy, 5.3, and Ireland, 2.5.

The most typical American suicide is a white Protestant male in his forties, married with two children. He is a breadwinner and a taxpayer. The sorrow his untimely preventable death brings to his family cannot be totaled, but the financial burden on his family and community is considerable. Costs begin with the city or county ambulance fee. The cost of the coroner's time and facilities soon follows. Widows' and survivors' benefits and insurance must be added. Then there is the heightened probability of subsequent indigent relief. Recent studies indicate that the surviving children of suicide victims more often require mental health care. Mental and physical care for a suicide's survivors usually must be provided by the city or county to whom the suicide has irrevocably bequeathed this responsibility.

Over the years, a suicide can cost his community at least $50,000. Counting all the taxes that he would have paid over the next quarter century, in the end, a suicide may cost his community a great deal more.

☐ Why Do People Kill Themselves?

For troubled men, each day is different. Why do men kill themselves? This is the first question asked by anyone who knew the person who committed suicide. Certainly he was tragically upset. But this alone does not explain why he took his own life. So many other people carry heavier burdens in their daily lives, yet persevere. What made this person different from those others? Why did he give up? Men have been puzzled by suicide for centuries. Only in the last 50 or 60 years, however, have any scientifically tenable explanations taken shape.

One theory still highly regarded today was proposed initially by the French sociologist Emile Durkheim, late in the 19th century. Suicide, he asserted, is the result of society's strength or weakness of control over the individual. According to Durkheim, there are three basic types of suicide, each a result of man's relationship to his society. In one instance, the "altruistic" suicide is literally required by society. Here, the customs or rules of the group demand suicide under certain circumstances. Historically, Japanese committing hara-kiri are examples of altruistic suicides. Hindu widows who willingly cremated themselves on the funeral pyres of their husbands were also examples of altruistic suicide. In such instances, however, the persons had little choice. Self-inflicted death was honorable; continuing to live was ignominious. Society dictated their action and, as individuals, they were not strong enough to defy custom.

Most suicides in the United States are "egoistic"—Durkheim's second category. Contrary to the circumstances of an altruistic suicide, egoistic suicide occurs when the individual has too few ties with his community. Demands, in this case to live, don't reach him. Thus, proportionately, more men who are on their own kill themselves than do church or family members.

Finally, Durkheim called "anomic" those suicides that occur when the accustomed relationship between an individual and his society is suddenly shattered. The shocking, immediate loss of a job, a close friend, or a fortune is thought capable of precipitating anomic suicides; or, conversely, poor men surprised by sudden wealth, have also, it has been asserted, been shocked into anomic suicide.

As Durkheim detailed the sociology of suicide, so Freud fathered psychological explanations. To him, suicide was essentially within the mind. Since men ambivalently identify with the objects of their own love, when they are frustrated the aggressive side of the ambivalence will be directed against the internalized person. Psychoanalytically, suicide can thus be seen as murder in the 180th degree.

While these perceptive men, half a century ago, evolved their own distinctive theories to explain suicide, authorities today are melding these theories. As an outgrowth of Durkheim's original thinking, sociologists now feel they can explain suicide in the United States as partly resulting from the peculiarities of this culture. Dr. Herbert Hendin has written that suicide is a "barometer of social tension." The psychologists meanwhile understand suicide in terms of various levels of pressure on men, which sometimes parlay into suicide. Thus, a primary cause for suicide might be a traumatic experience during early childhood or youth, a physical handicap, or any of various fundamental psychological disturbances. An individual may be so affected by any of these primary problems, that his outlook, manner of thought, or perspective will sustain further impetus to commit suicide.

With these underlying tensions pulsing inside a person who is already somewhat suicidal, the end of a love affair, a failed examination, a serious illness, almost any unfortunate experience can precipitate an attempt at self-destruction.

☐ Suicide Notes

Fortunately, no one is 100 per cent suicidal. Psychologists today realize that even the most ardent death wish is ambivalent. People cut their throats and plead to be saved at the same moment. Suicide notes often illustrate the fatal illogic of the suicidal person, the mixing of cross-purposed desires: "Dear Mary, I hate you. Love John." "I'm tired. There must be something fine for you. Love Bill." These simple, but pathetic messages are actual suicide notes. Like the iceberg's tip above the surface, they hint at the awesome mass below. When a man is suicidal, his perspective freezes. He wants to live, but can see no way. His logic is confused, but he cannot clear his head. He stumbles into death, still gasping for life, even in those last moments when he tries to write down how he feels.

Though overflowing with genuine emotion, a suicide note is usually written with a specious logic that demonstrates the confusion of its author. These notes often instruct someone to do something in the future. There is the implication that the suicidal person will be there to insure that his orders are carried out. Other notes reflect a sad desire to punish persons close to the suicide, as if he would be able to observe the pity and tears he has created. Employing bizarre logic, still others identify their own death with suffering, and kill themselves because they are suffering.

No one knows what it is like to be dead. At best, one can only imagine what it would be like if one were alive to watch—an invisible personality—at one's own funeral. Often, such an attractive fantasy intoxicates the suicidal mind, and tips the scale to death. But until the very moment that the bullet or barbiturate finally snuffs out life's last breath—while the ground is rushing up—the suicidal person terribly wants to live. No doubt, he also wants to die. But it is an ambivalent wish—to die and to live. Until he dies, a suicide is begging to be saved. Before his death, the suicidal person leaves a trail of subtle and obvious hints of his intentions. Every suicide attempt is a serious cry for help.

This cry can be heard, and suicide can be prevented—reason enough for communities to establish suicide prevention services. Since people who kill themselves also want to live, and since their acute suicidal states are temporary—that is, given the opportunity to clear their heads, almost all would choose to live—help should be offered to the suicidal. The increasing financial cost of a suicide to a community simply underscores compassion's plea for suicide prevention. And there is yet another reason.

☐ Prevailing Attitudes

The victims of suicide are not only those who die by their own hands. The families—the wives or husbands, brothers and sisters, parents and especially the children—of a suicide are undoubtedly stigmatized. There is an onus associated with suicide that has nothing to do with the loss of life. A suicide in the family irrevocably affects the relatives. The mode of death forever after is mentioned by the family in whispers, if it is mentioned at all. They would rather their loved ones die of almost any other cause, no matter how painful or expensive. There is a taint, a stigma, an

Facts and fables on suicide*

FABLE:	People who talk about suicide don't commit suicide.
FACT:	Of any ten persons who kill themselves, eight have given definite warnings of their suicidal intentions.
FABLE:	Suicide happens without warning.
FACT:	Studies reveal that the suicidal person gives many clues and warnings regarding his suicidal intentions.
FABLE:	Suicidal people are fully intent on dying.
FACT:	Most suicidal people are undecided about living or dying, and they "gamble with death," leaving it to others to save them. Almost no one commits suicide without letting others know how he is feeling.
FABLE:	Once a person is suicidal, he is suicidal forever.
FACT:	Individuals who wish to kill themselves are "suicidal" only for a limited period of time.
FABLE:	Improvement following a suicidal crisis means that the suicidal risk is over.
FACT:	Most suicides occur within about three months following the beginning of "improvement," when the individual has the energy to put his morbid thoughts and feelings into effect.
FABLE:	Suicide strikes much more often among the rich—or, conversely, it occurs almost exclusively among the poor.
FACT:	Suicide is neither the rich man's disease nor the poor man's curse. Suicide is very "democratic" and is represented proportionately among all levels of society.
FABLE:	Suicide is inherited or "runs in the family."
FACT:	Suicide does not run in families. It is an individual pattern.
FABLE:	All suicidal individuals are mentally ill, and suicide always is the act of a psychotic person.
FACT:	Studies of hundreds of genuine suicide notes indicate that although the suicidal person is extremely unhappy, he is not necessarily mentally ill.

*From Shneidman, E. S. & Farberow, N. L. (1961). *Some facts about suicide.* Washington, DC: PHS Publication No. 852, U. S. Government Printing Office.

aura of shame that envelops the family of the suicide and marks even the closest friends and associates. The guileless remark, "her father committed suicide," is never forgotten by anyone who hears it. Suicide is never totally forgiven.

People have been killing themselves since the beginnings of recorded history, probably ever since there has been the species. Yet the action has always been condemned, with only occasional and specific exceptions, by most other men. And suicide is still very much taboo today.

Probably the present attitude stems from the long history of suicide's condemnation. Suicide is and always has been an action that contradicts the valuation of human life, a basic democratic and social ethic. Throughout the years, various societies have responded to this insult by many crude and cruel means. The bodies of suicides have been dragged through the streets, hung naked upside-down for public view, and impaled on a stake at a public crossroads. The dead man could not be punished, of course. But his widow and children could be. Early English practice was to censure the suicide's family formally, deny the body burial in the church or city cemetery, and confiscate the survivors' property.

As a violation of one of the Ten Commandments, suicide has been called a crime against God, a heinous offense punishable in hell, of course, but also in man's courts.

☐ Some Enlightenment

With the rise of humanism in the 18th century, attitudes toward the suicidal person shifted. He came to be seen, not as a malicious criminal, but as a lunatic. As such, he fared little better, though. The mentally disturbed have been treated as society's pariahs until only recently. Even today, they are not fully accepted.

But times and attitudes have changed. Scientists have come to take a more enlightened stand on suicide, notably in the last few decades. Although the act of suicide is still socially taboo in the Western world, fortunately education and mental health advances have encouraged its study, and the effective treatment of the suicidal has begun. Most of the early state laws outlawing suicide and punishing attempts have subsequently been revoked. Those still on the books are rarely enforced. The courts have begun to interpret suicidal deaths as results of mental disturbance. In the wake of current professional studies and news articles on their findings, the public is beginning to realize that suicides can be prevented.

Suicide Prevention Services

Americans have begun to *hear* the cries for help from their troubled relatives, neighbors, and friends. Suicide prevention services are being developed throughout the country. In 1966 the federal government established a national Center for Studies of Suicide Prevention within the National Institute of Mental Health (NIMH). Its purposes are many. The Center concentrates on catalyzing more active suicide prevention activities across the land. Both impetus and information are offered to those communities considering suicide prevention. The Center supports further research into suicide—its clues, its causes, and, hopefully, its prevention. By emphasizing suicide research and training and by encouraging the growth of suicide prevention activities, it aims, hopefully, in the not too distant future, to reduce the number of suicides in the United States.

Finally, suicide prevention has become a science. Suicidology now attracts professionals of varied disciplines—psychology, psychiatry, sociology, social work, nursing, health education, and public health among others. Currently, Fellowships in Suicidology are being offered at Johns Hopkins University supported by a five-year grant from NIMH.

Early History

The path to this achievement was first roughly cut by devoted laymen and then it took years of paving. Motivated by the compassion of their usually non-professional founders, the first suicide prevention services in the United States began operating early in this century. Probably the original, and still well-known, suicide prevention operation is the National Save-A-Life League established in 1906 in New York City by the late Baptist minister Harry Warren. His son, Harry Warren, Jr., now heads the League, essentially a lay organization. Boston's Rescue, Incorporated, is a church-sponsored suicide prevention service, organized in 1959 by Catholic Father Kenneth Murphy. Rescue, Incorporated, employs the volunteer services of 70 clergymen and professionals. Suicidal persons who have learned about these organizations through the local press frequently call them. The counselors then try to arrange personal interviews, use the basic techniques of psychological therapy, and, if necessary, refer the troubled callers on for psychiatric care.

These agencies have been effective, but hardly sufficient. With thousands of people intentionally killing themselves in this country every month, the need for more systematic suicide prevention on a national scale is obvious.

The Los Angeles Center

The first step in this needed direction was made in Los Angeles in 1958. This prototype professional suicide prevention center was founded by two clinical psychologists, Doctors Edwin S. Shneidman and Norman L. Farberow. Nine years earlier, they had stumbled on hundreds of carefully filed suicide notes in the Los Angeles Coroner's office. This find moved them to compare the actual suicide notes with hundreds of others that were obtained from non-suicidal persons who had been requested to write suicide notes. The investigators soon learned that they could easily distinguish the authentic from the fictitious notes. The underlying logic in the authentic suicide notes was more bizarre, the imminence of death more certain.

Their studies, moreover, clearly indicated that persons planning suicide unconsciously signal their intentions before they act. Thus, the investigators realized that most suicides could be detected—and prevented.

With federal grants from the NIMH, the Los Angeles center slowly grew into the first full-scale, scientifically-oriented suicide prevention operation. It has a staff of psychiatrists, psychologists, and social workers, plus a number of carefully selected and trained lay volunteers who help man the telephones. The Los Angeles center's operation has become so widely known that during a typical month more than 500 persons contact the 24-hour suicide prevention service for help.

In recent years, suicide prevention activities have quickly spread across the country. In 1958 there were three comprehensive suicide prevention centers in operation. Today, less than a decade later, there are 90 functioning in 26 states. The trend continues. Hundreds of new services will be operating before another decade passes. The reason that so many are going to such lengths is easy to explain: *the lives of people who are suicidal can be saved.*

Clues to Suicide

Almost everyone who seriously intends suicide leaves clues to his imminent action. Sometimes there are broad hints; sometimes only subtle changes in behavior. But the suicide decision is usually not impulsive. Most often, it is premeditated. Although it might be done on impulse, and to others appears capricious, in fact, usually suicide is a decision that is given long consideration. It is not impossible, then, to spot a potential suicide if one only knows what to look for.

Fully three-fourths of all those who commit suicide have seen a physician within at least four months of the day on which they take their lives. When people are suicidal, a state of mind that comes and goes, there is no single trait by which all of them can be characterized. Always, however, they are disturbed, and often they are depressed. They feel hopeless about the direction of their lives and helpless to do anything about it. Under the mammoth weight of their own pessimism, they sink to their death.

Usually their attitude reflects itself in various verbal or behavioral "clues." Most obvious are the self-pitying cries of those who threaten, "I'm going to kill myself." They usually mean it, at least unconsciously. They just haven't decided how or when. If conditions in the suicidal person's life do not change, he will soon set the time and choose the method of his death. *All verbal indications should be taken seriously.* Dejected or angry asides such as "I want to die. This is the last straw . . . my family would be better off without me. . . . I won't be around much longer for you to put up with"—all are real clues to suicide, and too seldom taken as such.

There are also behavioral hints, some quite obvious. A suicide attempt, no matter how feeble or unlikely to succeed, is the starkest testimony of the suicidal state. "She just wanted attention," is the exasperated comment which often follows a suicide attempt. Indeed, that is exactly what she wanted. Without it, she may well succeed in her next attempt. Four out of five persons who kill themselves have attempted to do so at least one time previously. Of course, there are less pointed behavioral clues to suicide. Though not so readily discerned, they predict a suicide quite accurately. Once a person has finally decided to kill himself, he begins to act "differently." He may withdraw to become almost monklike and contemplative. He may drastically reduce eating or refrain from conversation and ignore normal sexual drives. He may either sleep more soundly or suffer from insomnia. He may have a will drawn up, or, often, act as if he were going on a long and distant trip. In the final days of his life, frequently he gives away what for him have been highly valued material possessions. College students give away their skis, watches, and cameras. Wealthier men and women make outright money grants of cash to relatives and friends.

Occasionally, the situation itself may be the final straw, and is the crucial indicator of imminent suicide. People already suffering from suffocating depressions often kill themselves on learning—or believing erroneously—they have a malignant tumor. Singly, any of these rather unexpected acts or remarks is not particularly significant, but clustered, they predict suicide.

These are the clues to suicide. They are not too difficult to recognize. But it is not so easy to determine just how close the troubled person actually is to a suicide attempt. Trained professional or volunteer staff members of any suicide prevention service can predict a suicide with more than chance accuracy.

☐ The Phone Rings

Active suicide prevention begins when the telephone rings. Surprisingly few calls are made by cranks. Of all the calls received at the well-publicized Los Angeles suicide prevention center, fully 99 per cent are sincere. A third of them are made by people who, though distressed, are far from actually attempting to take their lives. At least 10 per cent of all calls are made by people moderately to seriously suicidal, and of these one out of six callers is on the verge of death.

When a worried man or woman calls the publicized telephone number of the suicide prevention service just to talk to someone, to share his problems, the staff person on duty begins immediately to assess the caller's degree of "lethality." Cold statistics help at the outset. The staffman knows that elderly, single men are more apt to commit suicide than young married women callers. He tries to evaluate the *stress* the person making the call is under. He asks questions gauged to uncover whether the caller is stable or not, if he has a history of suicide attempts, what his *life style* is, and if there are any symptoms that would indicate that suicide is imminent. Finally, and most important, the staff member must discover just how specific is the caller's *plan* to kill himself. Has he planned the day and hour of his suicide? And just how will he accomplish it? Here, it is important to know which method the caller has chosen; shooting one's self with a gun that lies loaded in the next room at the moment of the call is a much more lethal scheme than a vague plan to purchase some sleep medicine at a drug store.

A person who is vaguely considering ending it all may be quite serious. But the suicidal situation is not yet urgent. By contrast, an old man, depressed and lonely, withdrawn and confused, who plans suicide at a specific time with a gun or barbiturates now in hand presents a suicidal situation of extreme urgency to the suicide prevention worker.

These cases are the most serious at the moment of call. Here, the telephone therapist cannot hope to solve all the problems that a deeply troubled person faces. But even this highly imminent suicide can be averted, because suicidal crises can be managed. Professionally trained people who work in suicide prevention services realize that their goals must be limited. For the suicide prevention staff worker the primary goal is to stop the caller from killing himself, not to remake his personality. In most cases, the caller is suffering from any of a wide range of psychological problems, sometimes coupled to body ills. But curing all the caller's troubles, no matter how serious, is not the major intention of a suicide prevention service. When a man is foundering, a lifeline must be thrown to him. It is neither the time nor the task of the rescuer to teach the drowning man to swim or to improve his stroke. Thus, suicide prevention need have only limited mental health goals. Similarly, an active suicide prevention service has a limited goal. It provides a ready contact between the community's highly disturbed citizens and the established helping agencies which are available for them.

When a person calls to say that he or she is contemplating suicide, the voice of the suicide prevention worker on the other end can become the caller's lifeline. Callers have shot themselves to death while talking to a suicide prevention worker. Others have held loaded pistols to their temples.

The first telephone interview often spells the difference between life and death. The staff person who answers the phone must immediately establish some continuing communication with the caller, maintaining even the most tenuous of relationships. ("How did you get into this trouble?" he'll ask the caller. "What are some of the solutions that you've thought about?") At the same time, he begins to determine the lethality of the suicidal situation. ("Have you thought how you would do it?" "When?") As communication continues, the staff member must work toward establishing rapport with the caller while keeping the interview from becoming simply conversational. In fact, the caller must be made to feel he is being interviewed by a sympathetic, knowledgeable authority who can help.

If the situation is highly critical, the staffer must come up with an answer right there on the telephone. Frequently, with suicidal persons, life has lost its shadings. Every issue is either black or white, yes or no, life or death. Sometimes the caller can be persuaded to see his problem in a broader perspective. In other cases, the staff therapist might be able to "arrange" things for the suicidal caller. Simply setting up an interview with a staff psychiatrist, psychologist, social worker, or volunteer may provide the tension relief needed to ease a critical suicidal situation.

☐ The Suicidal Crisis

Suicidal crises almost always concern two people: the suicidal person and the "significant other." The telephone therapist must determine who this is: father, wife, mother, lover, or whoever. Then an interview is arranged, if possible, to see both. It does little good to counsel a suicidal person who will return a few hours later to the relationship which has just driven him to the brink of self-inflicted death. The "significant other" person in his life must be made aware of the situation, and, if possible, become involved in the life-saving efforts. In most cases, these "others" show surprise, concern, and a willingness to help—at least to some extent; in some cases, they must be disregarded or even circumvented.

Sometimes, really only a little help is needed during the period of the suicidal crisis. A person who verges on suicide also clings to life. All of his problems cannot be erased in a telephone call during the middle of the night to a staffman at a suicide prevention service. Should the posture of the "significant other" momentarily shift in this crucial relationship, there is no guarantee that the story will have a happy ending. But the suicide, for the moment, has been averted. Fortunately, people are not permanently suicidal. Even for those whose daily lives are as gloomy as the black despair inside their minds, the suicidal mood ebbs and flows like the tides.

☐ Suicide Research

Study of suicide begun during the early part of this century has evolved into study of its prevention. Authorities from a number of widely varying disciplines are contributing to man's knowledge on suicide. Research continues along avenues seemingly far apart. But their goals essentially are the same: to save lives and to improve mental health. While a range of specialists continues to refine the overall methods of suicide prevention, still another group of scientists is searching for the chemical links between man's mental and physiological circumstances.

One aim is to develop effective antidepressant drugs. NIMH Director Dr. Stanley F. Yolles believes that these drugs will help save the lives of potential suicides who are suffering from blinding depressions. Three-quarters of them visit physicians within months of taking their lives. By training physicians to spot the clues to suicide and arming them with such drugs, suicidal crises can be postponed and suicides can be averted.

Of course drugs will not stop all suicides. However, if they help postpone the irrevocable act, suicide prevention activities will do the rest. Anthropologists, sociologists, health educators, philosophers, and social workers today work along side psychiatrists and psychologists in suicide prevention centers. Together, these professionals continue to shed new light on the subject even as they save the lives of the troubled people calling for help. Research continues on many fronts. For example, investigators are studying the relationship of sleep to suicide. Some people escape into long and peaceful sleep just before they kill themselves. Others suffer from insomnia. The key seems to lie in the quality of sleep and the individual's attitudes toward his own sleep.

Another body of research probes the tendency to suicide that may be related to an individual's peculiarities of reasoning. Suicide notes clearly indicate that many suicides are at least in part the result of faulty reasoning. Those whose thoughts are without shades of meaning will not consider depression a passing mood. When *life* is black, *death* is the only answer. Still others regularly employ a spurious logic which can trip them over life's edge.

Today's newly operating suicide prevention services are helping to explain why men kill themselves. Combined with biochemical advances toward eliminating depression, suicide prevention has begun to take effect. All of these activities aim at reducing the suicide rate in the United States. Before that happens, the nation's suicide rate may very well appear to rise. As suicide prevention takes hold across the country, more accurate and standard methods of reporting suicides will become the practice. *Reported* suicide totals will rise for a while.

☐ Accurate Reports Needed

At present, suicide is not uniformly reported. What constitutes suicide in one county, city, or state is often not the same for the coroner in the neighboring area. Some coroners report as suicides only those deaths which are accompanied by suicide notes. In all cases, coroners and physicians are under pressure in their communities to certify suicides as accidental or natural deaths.

The families of suicide victims are loath to have self-inflicted death accurately reported. Many of them petition coroners to change their rulings to accidental or natural death. In three-quarters of these cases insurance money hangs in the balance. Some life-insurance policies will not pay their face value for death by suicide.

One method of improving suicide reporting is by "Psychological Autopsy." This procedure was begun by Dr. Theodore Curphey, Los Angeles Chief Medical Examiner-Coroner. The coroner may invite members of the local suicide prevention service to investigate a death if he is uncertain about certifying it as an accident or a suicide. Since it is now known that suicidal persons almost invariably leave clues to their intentions days or weeks before they act, these "death investigation teams" often accurately uncover the true mode of death. The clues are gleaned by carefully assessing the information gathered from interviewing members of the deceased's family, friends, co-workers, physicians, and others.

Death investigation teams attempt to discover whether the deceased actually *intended* to die during those last days of his life. If the investigators learn that prior to death the deceased was very depressed, had seen a physician recently, and had spoken or acted in such a way that had indicated he was suicidal, this can be established.

Sometimes, what appear to be suicides are actually accidental deaths. Death investigation teams in these cases help the family survivors avoid the stigma of suicide. But it is equally important that death by suicide be accurately certified. The scientific community demands accurate death certification, a crucial ingredient in further research. Suicide prevention requires honest reporting. Recording suicides accurately is fair to all citizens, and ultimately will help to improve the community's mental health.

☐ Sub-intentioned Death

There is still another aspect of death which does not appear on death certificates today. This is the "sub-intentioned" death. Among the modes of death listed today—natural, accident, suicide, and homicide (called the NASH classification)—there is no space for the sub-intentioned death. But authorities now realize that those same pressures which work fatally on the victims of suicide sometimes move more subtly.

No one knows how many accidental and natural deaths are caused by the sub-intentioned wish to die. Some people want to die, but have not reached that state where they will act consciously on a suicidal desire. Instead, they begin to live more carelessly and unconsciously imperil their lives. A chronically ill person who stops taking his life-saving medicine is an example. Depressed college students who drive recklessly are others. Fate, they seem to be saying, will make the crucial decision. But they are giving death the edge.

Generally today, these deaths are ruled as accidental. But it has been proposed that the prior attitude of the victim toward his death be assessed as *intentioned, sub-intentioned,* or *unintentioned*—and thus reported on the death certificate in addition to the usual cause and mode of death.

Some people are eating away at their own lives. If they do not have the resolve to commit suicide overtly, they can still offer up their lives to chance. Sooner or later, many of them will succeed in killing themselves . . . or *permit* some disease to kill them. Whether these sub-intentioned deaths are called accidental or natural, they are nonetheless results of death-oriented behavior. Suicide prevention efforts can also save many of these death-prone persons.

☐ Community Service Planning

There is no doubt that carefully established suicide prevention services pay off in lives and money saved. Community mental health improves as a result. Each community should tailor a suicide prevention service to its own needs. It should be emphasized that there is no single pattern or organization yet proved to be overall better or more successful than another. A suicide prevention service can be organized to operate autonomously or as a unit of the community's mental health facilities. It can be part of an emergency hospital or tied to the local university or mental health clinic. However, it seems evident that the apparent pattern for the future is that many suicide prevention services will be an integral part of the community's comprehensive mental health center—a logical site for them. In any case, suicide prevention requires planning, interest, and time.

Ideally, any new service will be staffed with at least one, and, hopefully, two professional persons such as psychiatrists, psychologists, or psychiatric social workers. A professional psychiatric consultant should be available to the service at least for a few hours each week.

The rest of the staff may be non-professional volunteers. Experience has proved that lay volunteers can be very effective staff members *if* they are *carefully selected,* and *rigorously trained.* Generally, housewives who are mature, usually over 40, and have weathered psychological storms within their own lives, are potentially good members. For example, women who have lost children through accident or disease and have since adjusted to these personal tragedies often are compassionate, resilient, and unafraid staff members. As a rule, it may be a good idea not to select people who have suffered psychotic breakdowns or who themselves at one time attempted suicide, or who appear overzealously interested in suicide.

A suicide prevention service cannot open shop all at once like a supermarket. Rather, the entire process, if it would be successful, must be gradually and tactfully woven into the community. From the beginning, the organizers must solicit help—at the very least, cooperation—from the city or county medical authorities. The hospitals, the coroner's office, and the police chief should know about the beginning of any suicide prevention service. In fact, suicide prevention needs their help. This is reasonable, since the new service ultimately will ease police and hospital emergency room work loads. But on occasion, the suicide prevention service will have to call on them for help. The local press, radio, and television should be informed about what's afoot and asked to cooperate. If a story breaks before the budding suicide prevention service is ready, this premature news could be disastrous.

Of course, the city government must know what plans are being made. If city officials are not the initial sponsors of such a community service, certainly their endorsement should be heartily pursued. Without local cooperation, successful suicide prevention is practically impossible.

☐ Obtaining Funds

It is certainly impossible without adequate funds. There is no avoiding the hard fact that effective suicide prevention costs money. Of the various suicide prevention services now in operation across the country, budgets range from the most modest at $10,000 per year (for one coordinator and small staff) to that of the Los Angeles Center which spends $300,000 annually for research, training, and the services of its professional staff members.

A carefully planned service will turn to every possible avenue for funds. Since the local citizenry will gain the most, they might be approached to help finance a new suicide prevention service. Local philanthropies, local government, and private citizens usually will contribute. There are many foundations in the country which aim their grants toward local mental health undertakings.[1] Suicide prevention services might also qualify for federal aid. As a component of a comprehensive community mental health center, a new suicide prevention activity might qualify for NIMH construction and staffing funds under the Community Mental Health Services Act of 1963 (P.L. 88–164). Requests for federal support for suicide prevention, research, training, and demonstration (but not for direct services) may be sent to the Center for Studies of Suicide Prevention at the NIMH, Chevy Chase, MD.

☐ Staff Training

Once the plans are off the ground, the local service staff must be trained. The team core of two professionals will find visits to currently operating suicide prevention operations both educational and stimulating. After a relatively brief period of such indoctrination, these core members will be able to select and train their volunteers. Their training, which must be allotted at least three months time, might consist of required study of the literature on suicide coupled to more active indoctrination. In one form of training, called psychodrama, volunteers assume the roles of various types of suicidal persons and hold conversations with the staff therapist. Another method employs tapes of actual calls to operating suicide prevention services. A tape is stopped in the midst of the conversation, and a volunteer is asked how he would continue the handling of the call. By starting the tape again he can immediately check his response with that of an expert.

A name for the service must be selected—one that is easy to remember and comes straight to the point. Here, perhaps, it is better to be direct. Suicide should not be euphemized. The words *suicide prevention* could well be part of the organization's name, whether it is called a clinic, service, unit, office, corporation, foundation, institute, bureau, or center. A deeply troubled person on the verge of self-destruction usually has neither the patience nor the inclination to search through the telephone book trying to find the name of the organization designed to save his life. It would be a good idea to have the emergency suicide prevention telephone number listed at the front of the telephone book together with other emergency numbers.

Well before the service is ready to take calls, local community sources should be informed. Local physicians, clergymen, police, government officials, and businessmen's clubs should be told. At the same time, the science writer for large newspapers or the city editors for smaller papers should be informed. The public will learn quickly about the new service.

☐ A Beginning

Then calls will begin, and lives will be saved—which is, after all, the purpose of suicide prevention.

Today, hundreds of thousands of people are frightened and alone. They live in what Melville called ". . . a damp, drizzly November of my soul." For them it seems that death is closing in. They see no other way. Active, increasingly effective suicide prevention services offer the suicidal person a fresh grasp on life. They promise no panacea. Life's burdens will continue. But troubled men can persevere. The services now spreading across the country can show him that life is not so narrow—and, more importantly, that death is not the answer.

Suicide is a tragic and unnecessary waste. Fortunately now, it can, with appropriate measures, be prevented.

What To Read

Readers interested in further study of the subject are referred to the following books which discuss suicide and its prevention from various points of view:

Choron, J. (1963). *Death and western thought.* New York: Collier Books.
Dublin, L. (1963). *Suicide: A sociological and statistical study.* New York: Ronald Press.
Farberow, N. L. & Shneidman, E. S. (Eds.) (1961). *The cry for help.* New York: McGraw-Hill.
Feifel, H. (Ed.) (1961). *The meaning of death.* New York: McGraw-Hill.
Menninger, K. (1938). *Man against himself.* New York: Harcourt Brace.
Resnik, H. L. P. (Ed.) (1968). *Suicidal behaviors.* Boston: Little, Brown & Company.
Shneidman, E. S. & Farberow, N. L. (Eds.) (1957). *Clues to suicide.* New York: McGraw-Hill.
Shneidman, E. S. (Ed.) (1967). *Essays in self-destruction.* New York: Science House.
Stengel, E. (1964). *Suicide and attempted suicide.* Baltimore: Penguin Books.

Endnote

[1]Brand, J. L. (n.d.). *Private support for mental health: A study of the support, by foundations and other private national granting agencies, for mental health and related disciplines.* Washington, DC: U. S. Government Printing Office, Public Health Service Publication No. 838, 35¢. This pamphlet gives the name, address, assets, types of support, and fields of interest in mental health for each of 142 foundations.

27

CHAPTER

Psychotherapy with Suicidal Patients

It seems logical that before we consider what the psychotherapy of a suicidal person ought to be that we have some common understanding of the suicidal state itself. Of course, everybody agrees that suicide is an enormously complicated term, encompassing a wide variety (and different ranges) of dysphoria, disturbance, self-abnegation, resignation, terror-cum-pain—to mention but a few inner states that are involved. . . .

Suicide is the human act of self-inflicted, self-intended cessation (i.e., the permanent stopping of consciousness). It is best understood as a bio-socio-psychologico-existential state of malaise. It is obviously not a disease and just as obviously a number of kinds of trained individuals other than physicians can help individuals who are in a suicidal state.

If we are to escape many of the current somewhat simplistic notions of suicide (especially those which totally equate a disease called suicide with a disease called depression), then we need to explicate what the suicidal state of mind is like. Our key source in this can be the ordinary dictionary—eschewing any nomenclature of technical and, especially, technically diagnostic terms. In the dictionary there are words, e.g., angered, anguished, cornered, dependent, frustrated, guilty, helpless, hopeless, hostile, rageful, shamed, that will help us in our understanding. For us, in

Reprinted from T. B. Karasu & L. Bellak (Eds.), *Specialized Techniques in Individual Psychotherapy*. New York: Brunner/Mazel, 1980, pp. 305–313. With permission.

this chapter, two less common (but ordinary) dictionary words—*perturbation* and *lethality*—will be the keystone words of our understanding.

Perturbation refers to how upset (disturbed, agitated, sane-insane, discomposed) the individual is—rated, let's say, on a 1 to 9 scale. Lethality refers to how lethal the individual is, i.e., how likely it is that he will take his own life—also rated on a 1 to 9 scale.

At the outset, I need to indicate what kinds of suicidal states I am talking about in order to indicate what kinds of psychotherapy are appropriate for them. We can arbitrarily divide the seriousness (or risk, or lethality, or suicidality) of all suicidal efforts (actions, deeds, events, episodes)—whether verbalizations (ordinarily called threats) or behaviors (ordinarily called attempts)—into three rough commonsense groupings: low, medium and high. In this chapter, I shall focus on the suicidal events or deeds of *high* lethality, where the danger of self-inflicted death is realistically large and imminent; what one might ordinarily call high suicide risks. Of course, a suicide act (deed, occurrence, event, threat, attempt) *of whatever lethality* is always a genuine psychiatric situation and should be treated without any iatrogenic elements. Thus, in the treatment of the suicidal person there is almost never any place for the therapist's hostility, anger, sardonic attitudes, daring the patient, or pseudo-democratic indifference.

By focusing solely on the *psychotherapeutic* approaches to high suicide risks, it should be obvious at the beginning that this chapter is a moiety—omitting entirely (and advertently) the lively areas of treatment suicidal individuals receive by means of chemical, electrical or institutional modalities.

Theoretically, the treatment of an acutely highly suicidal person is quite simple: It consists, almost by definition, of lowering his lethality level; in practice, this is usually done by decreasing or mollifying his level of perturbation. In short, we defuse the situation (like getting the gun), we create activity of support and care around the person, and we make that person's temporarily unbearable life just enough better so that he or she can stop to think and reconsider. *The way to decrease lethality is by dramatically decreasing the felt perturbation.*

Working intensively with a highly suicidal person—someone who might be assessed as 7, 8 or 9 on a 1 to 9 scale of lethality—as distinguished from someone of moderate or low lethality, is different from almost any other human encounter, with the possible exception of that of working intensively with a dying person—but that is another story. Psychotherapy with an intensely suicidal person is a special task; it demands a different kind of involvement. The goal is different—not that of increasing comfort, which is the goal of most ordinary psychotherapy, but the more primitive goal of simply keeping the person alive. The rules are therefore different, and it follows (or rather precedes) that the theoretical rationale is different.

At this juncture, I wish to make a distinction among *four* psychologically different kinds of human encounters: conversation (or "ordinary talk"); an hierarchical exchange; psychotherapy or a "professional exchange"; and, finally, clinical suicidology or working psychologically with a highly lethal person.

In ordinary talk or conversation, the focus is on the surface content (concrete events, specific dates, ordinary details); on what is actually being said; on the obviously stated meanings; on the ordinary interesting (or uninteresting) details of life. Further, the social role between the two speakers is one in which the two participants are essentially equal. Each participant has the social right to ask the other the same questions which he or she has been asked by the other. The best example of ordinary talk is two friends conversing with one another.

In a hierarchical verbal exchange the two participants are socially, and hence psychologically, unequal. This difference may be imposed by the situation, such as the exchange between a military officer and an enlisted person, or it may be agreed to by the two involved parties, such as between a physician and a patient. In either instance, the two are not psychologically equal. For example, an officer or a physician can ask an enlisted person or a patient, respectively, certain personal questions to which a rational response is expected, that the person of "lower status" could not ask the other person in return without appearing impertinent or aberrant. Yet most of the talk is still on the surface, concerning the real details of everyday life.

In a professional psychotherapeutic exchange the focus is on feelings, emotional content and unconscious meanings, rather than on what is apparently being said. The emphasis is on the latent (between-the-lines) significance of what is being said more than on the manifest and obvious content; on the unconscious meanings, including double-entendres, puns, and slips-of-the-tongue; on themes that run as common threads through the content, rather than on the concrete details for their own sake. Perhaps the most distinguishing aspect of the professional exchange (as opposed to ordinary talk) is the occurrence of transference, wherein the patient projects onto the therapist certain deep expectations and feelings. These transference reactions often stem from the patient's childhood and reflect neurotic patterns of reaction (of love, hate, dependency, suspicion, etc.) to whatever the therapist may or may not be doing. The therapist is often invested by the patient with almost magical healing powers, which, in fact, can serve as a self-fulfilling prophecy and thus help the interaction become therapeutic for the patient. In this paragraph, the use of the words therapist and patient already implies that, of the two parties, one has tacitly agreed to seek assistance and the other has agreed to try to give it. The roles of the two participants, unlike those in a conversation, are, in this respect, not co-equal. A therapist and a patient could not simply exchange roles.

In working as a clinical suicidologist with an individual who is highly suicidal, the focus is again different. In this situation, the attention is primarily on the lethality. Most importantly, what differentiates this modality of therapy from any other psychotherapy is the handling of the transference feelings. Specifically, the transference (from the patient to the therapist) and the countertransference (from the therapist to the patient)—especially those positive feelings of affection and concern—can legitimately be much more intense and more deep than would be seemly or appropriate (or even ethical) in ordinary psychotherapy where time is assumed to be endless and where it is taken for granted that the patient will continue functioning in life.

Working with a highly suicidal person demands a different kind of involvement. There may be as important a conceptual difference between ordinary psychotherapy (with individuals where dying or living is not *the* issue) and psychotherapy with acutely suicidal persons as there is between ordinary psychotherapy and ordinary talk.

The main point of working with a lethally-oriented person—in the give-and-take of talk, the advice, the interpretations, the listening—is to increase that individual's psychological sense of possible choices and sense of being emotionally supported. Relatives, friends and colleagues should, after they are assessed to be on the life-side of the individual's ambivalence, be closely involved in the total treatment process. Suicide prevention is not best done as a solo practice. A combination of consultation, ancillary therapists and the use of all the interpersonal and community resources that one can involve is, in general, the best way of proceeding.

Recall that we are talking about psychotherapy with the highly suicidal persons—not one of low or even medium lethality. With this in mind—and keeping in mind also the four psychological components of the suicidal state of mind (heightened inimicality, elevated perturbation, conspicuous constriction of intellectual focus, and the idea of cessation as a solution)—then relatively simple formula for treatment can be stated. That formulation concentrates on two of the four psychological components, specifically on the constriction and the perturbation. Simply put, the way to save a highly suicidal person is to decrease the constriction, that is, to widen the range of possible thoughts and fantasies (*from* the dichotomous two—either one specific outcome or death—*to* at least three or more possibilities for admittedly less-than-perfect solution), and, most importantly—without which the attempt to broaden the constriction will not work—to decrease the individual's perturbation.

How does a psychotherapist decrease the elevated perturbation of a highly suicidal person? Answer: by doing anything and almost everything possible to cater to the infantile idiosyncrasies, the dependency needs, the sense of pressure and futility, the feelings of hopelessness and helplessness that the individual is experiencing. In order to help a highly lethal person, one should involve others; create activity around the person; do what he or she wants done—and, if that cannot be accomplished, at least move in the direction of the desired goals to some substitute goals that approximate those which have been lost. Remember that life—and remind the patient of this fact (in a kindly but oracular way)—is often the choice among lousy alternatives. The key to functioning, to wisdom and to life itself is often to choose the least lousy alternative that is practicably attainable.

Taken down to its bare roots, the principle is: To decrease lethality one puts a hook on perturbation and, doing what needs to be done, pulls the level of perturbation down—and with that action brings down the active level of lethality. Then, when the person is no longer highly suicidal—then the usual methods of psychotherapy (which are not the subject for this chapter) can be usefully employed.

As to how to help a suicidal individual, it is best to look upon any suicidal act, whatever its lethality, as an effort by an individual to stop unbearable anguish or intolerable pain by "doing something." Knowing this usually guides us as to what the treatment should be. In the same sense, the way to save a person's life is also to "do something." Those "somethings" include putting that information (that the person is in trouble with himself) into the stream of communication, letting others know about it, breaking what could be a fatal secret, talking to the person, talking to others, proferring help, getting loved ones interested and responsive, creating action around the person, showing response, indicating interest, and, if possible, showing deep concern.

I conclude with an example—actually a composite of several actual highly suicidal persons I have known.

☐ Case Study

A young woman in her 20s, a nurse at the hospital where I worked, asked me pleadingly if I would see her teenage sister whom she believed to be highly suicidal. The attractive, younger woman—agitated and tearful but coherent—told me (in the privacy of my office) that she was single, pregnant and determined to kill herself. She showed me a small automatic pistol she had in her purse. Her being pregnant was such a mortal shame to her, combined with strong feelings of rage and guilt, that she simply could not "bear to live" (or live to bear?). Suicide was the *only* alternative, and shooting herself was the *only* way to do it. Either she had to be unpregnant (the way she was before she conceived) or she had to be dead.

I did several things. For one, I took out a sheet of paper and—to begin to "widen her blinders"—said something like, "Now, let's see: You could have an abortion here locally." ("I couldn't do that.") It is precisely the "can'ts" and the "won'ts" and "have to's" and "nevers" and "always" and "onlys" that are to be negotiated in psychotherapy. "You could go away and have an abortion." ("I couldn't do that.") "You could bring the baby to term and keep the baby." ("I couldn't do that.") "You could have the baby and adopt it out." ("I couldn't do that.") "We could get in touch with the young man involved." ("I couldn't do that.") "We could involve the help of your parents." ("I couldn't do that.") and "You can always commit suicide, but there is obviously no need to do that today." (No response.) "Now first, let me take that gun, and then let's look at this *list* and rank them in order and see what their advantages, disadvantages and implications are, remembering that none of them may be perfect."

The very making of this list, my professional and nonhortatory and nonjudgmental approach already had a calming influence on her. Within 15 minutes her lethality had begun to deescalate. She actually rank-ordered the list, commenting negatively on each item, but what was of critical importance was that suicide, which I included in the total realistic list, was now ranked third—no longer first or second.

She decided that she would, reluctantly, want to talk to the father of her child. Not only had they never discussed the "issue," but he did not even know about it. But there was a formidable obstacle: He lived in another city, almost across the country and that involved (what seemed to be a big item in the patient's mind) a long distance call. It was a matter of literally seconds to ascertain the area code from the long distance operator, to obtain his telephone number from information, and then—obviously with some trepidation and keen ambivalence for her—to dial his number (at university expense), with the support of my presence to speak to him directly.

The point is not how the issue was practically resolved, without an excessive number of deep or shallow interpretations as to why she permitted herself to become pregnant and other aspects of her relationships with men, etc. What is important is that it was possible to achieve the assignment of that day: to lower her lethality.

In general, any suicidal state is characterized by its transient quality, its pervasive ambivalence, and its dyadic nature. Psychiatrists and other health professionals are well advised to minimize, if not totally to disregard, those probably well-intentioned but shrill writings in this field which naively speak of an individual's "right to commit suicide"—a right which, in actuality, cannot be denied—as though the suicidal person were a chronic univalently self-destructive hermit.

A number of special features in the management of a highly lethal patient can be mentioned. Some of these special therapeutic stratagems or orientations with a highly lethal patient attend to or reflect the *transient, ambivalent* and *dyadic* aspects of almost all suicidal acts.

1. A continuous, preferably daily, monitoring of the patient's lethality rating.
2. An active out-reach; being willing to deal with some of the reality problems of the patient openly, where advisable; giving direction (sans exhortation) to the patient; actively taking the side of life. It relates to befriending and caring.
3. Use of community resources including employment, Veterans Administration (when applicable), social agencies, and psychiatric social work assistance.
4. Consultation. There is almost no instance in a therapist's professional life when consultation with a peer is as important as when he is dealing with a highly suicidal patient. The items to be discussed might include the therapist's treatment of the case; his own feelings of frustration, helplessness or even anger; his countertransference reactions generally; the advisability of hospitalization for the patient, etc.
5. Hospitalization. Hospitalization is always a complicating event in the treatment of a suicidal patient but it should not, on those grounds, be eschewed. Obviously, the quality of care—from doctors, nurses and attendants—is crucial. Stoller (1973), discussing one of his complex long-range cases, says: ". . . there were several other factors without which the therapy might not have succeeded. First, the hospital. The patient's life could not have been saved if a hospital had not been immediately available *and a few of the personnel familiar with me and the patient."*
6. Transference. As in almost no other situation and at almost no other time, the successful treatment of a highly suicidal person depends heavily on the transference. The therapist can be active, show his personal concern, increase the frequency of the sessions, invoke the "magic" of the unique therapist-patient relationship, be less of a *tabula rasa,* give "transfusions" of (realistic) hope and succorance. In

a figurative sense, I believe that Eros can work wonders against Thanatos.

7. The involvement of significant others. Suicide is most often a highly charged dyadic crisis. It follows from this that the therapist, unlike his usual practice of dealing almost exclusively with his patient (and even fending off the spouse, the lover, parents, grown children), should consider the advisability of working directly with the significant others. For example, if the individual is married, it is important to meet the spouse. The therapist must assess whether, in fact, the spouse is suicidogenic; whether they ought to be separated; whether there are misunderstandings which the therapist can help resolve; or whether the spouse is insightful and concerned and can be used by the therapist as an ally and co-therapist. The same is true for homosexual lovers, for patient and parent, etc. It is not suggested that the significant other be seen as often as the patient is seen, but that other real people in the suicidal patient's life be directly involved and, at the minimum, their role as hinderer or helper in the treatment process be assessed.
8. Careful modification of the usual canons of confidentiality. Admittedly, this is a touchy and complicated point, but the therapist should not ally himself with death. Statements given during the therapy session relating to the patient's overt suicidal (or homicidal) plans obviously cannot be treated as a "secret" between two collusive partners. In the previous example of the patient who opened her purse and showed me a small automatic pistol with which she said she was going, that day, to kill herself, two obvious interpretations would be that she obviously wanted me to take the weapon from her, or that she was threatening me. In any event, I told her that she could not leave my office with the gun and insisted that she hand her purse to me. She countered by saying that I had abrogated the basic rule of therapy, namely that she could tell me anything. I pointed out that "anything" did not mean committing suicide and that she must know that I could not be a partner in that kind of enterprise. For a moment she seemed angered and then relieved; she gave me the gun. The rule is to "defuse" the potentially lethal situation. To have left her with a loaded gun would also leave her with a latent message.
9. Limitation of one's own practice to a very few highly lethal patients. It is possible to see a fairly large number of moderate and low-rated lethal patients in one's patient load, but one or two *highly* lethal patients seem to be the superhuman limit for most therapists at any given time. Such patients demand a great deal of investment of

psychic energy and one must beware of spreading oneself too thin in his or her own professional life.

Working with highly suicidal persons borrows from the goals of crisis intervention: not to take on and ameliorate the individual's entire personality structure and to cure all the neuroses, but simply to keep him or her alive. That is the *sine qua non* without which no human being can function—and no therapy would have meaning.

☐ Reference

Stoller, R. J. (1973). *Splitting.* New York: Quadrangle Books.

28

CHAPTER

Aphorisms of Suicide and Some Implications for Psychotherapy

The author proposes twenty aphorisms—essential truths—about suicide. From these, some theoretical implications about the psychological nature of suicide as well as some practical implications for psychotherapy with highly lethal individuals are derived. In addition, some general suggestions for management of suicidal persons are given.

☐ I. Introduction

No one can speak with total objectivity about a topic as complicated as suicide. Thinking about death and self-destruction can be endlessly intriguing—and always has important subjective elements. Even if one were to limit one's discourse to the objective statistics and demographic facts about suicide, that in itself would imply a statement of one's view of things. It is probably best for anyone who seeks to discuss suicide to show his flags and allegiances explicitly, saying, as it were, "Here are some of my views on this matter." Such a presentation has the advantage of the author sharing with the reader where he stands, what his beliefs are, and who—vis-a-vis suicide—he is (Shneidman, 1973).

The driving thought behind this essay is that psychotherapy is most effective when it flows from understanding, that remediation follows defi-

Reprinted from *American Journal of Psychotherapy*, 1984, *38*, 319–328. With permission.

nition. This assertion might seem too obvious to belabor, but the present difficulties and inefficiencies in treating, as one example, schizophrenia—where we do not definitely know its cure, its causes, and (most importantly) its nature, if it is an "it" which clearly it is not—should alert us to the importance of clear conceptualization. This paper cannot seek to solve the problem, but it hopes to clarify the issue, specifically to comment on suicide in such a way as to yield direct implications for intervention.

The comments will take the form of aphorisms. An aphorism is a pithy short statement stating a general doctrine or truth. It is a maxim or saying; a principle expressed tersely in a few telling words. Historically—see the article on aphorisms in the *Encyclopaedia Britannica* (1973)—aphorisms are closely tied to the development of medicine.

> The name was first used in the *Aphorisms of Hippocrates*, a long series of propositions concerning the symptoms and diagnosis of disease and the art of healing in medicine. . . . The first aphorism, perhaps the best known of all, runs as follows: "Life is short, art is long, opportunity fleeting, experimenting dangerous, reasoning difficult; it is necessary not only to do oneself what is right, but also to be seconded by the patient, by those who attend him, by external circumstances."

In the Western world at large probably the most acclaimed set of aphorisms are those philosophic ruminations of Pascal (1623–1662) known as the *Pensées* (1657–58). In those notes and fragments Pascal posits and then discusses the "Bet Situation," by which he means the bet on whether or not God exists. In a series of aphorisms he gives arguments for betting on the side of His existence.

In our own time the famous English novelist John Fowles—*The Collector, The Magus, The French Lieutenant's Woman, The Ebony Tower*, etc.—has written a set of contemporary aphorisms entitled *The Aristos* (1964), in which he also (like Pascal) creates aphorisms about death, immortality, and the Bet Situation. Not unexpectedly, his truths are quite different from those of Pascal.

It is obvious that one way to define and to discuss a topic is to do so aphoristically. In a set of aphorisms there is usually, if not a thread of logic, then at least a flow of thought from one aphorism to the next, building a general point of view. That is what I hope to do with my aphorisms on suicide.

☐ II. Aphorisms about Suicide

1. There are two basic, albeit contradictory, truths about suicide: (A) Suicide should never be committed when one is depressed (or dis-

turbed or constricted); and (B) almost every suicide is committed for reasons that make sense to the person who does it.

2. We can empathize with every person who has committed suicide and yet we should seek to thwart every suicidal plan that has not yet been consummated.
3. There is no such act as a rational suicide; but every suicide is a rational act—except possibly one committed by an actively psychotic person.
4. Suicide is both a logical and psychological phenomenon. As a logical thought disorder it is fueled by an individual's emotional turmoil and grounded in his psychological history.
5. The primary thought disorder in suicide is that of a pathological narrowing of the mind's focus, called constriction, which takes the form of seeing only *two* choices: either something painfully unsatisfactory *or* cessation.
6. There is nothing intrinsically wrong (or aberrant) in thinking about suicide; it is abnormal only when one thinks that suicide is the *only* solution.
7. The chief shortcoming of suicide is that it unnecessarily answers a remediable challenge with a permanent negative solution. In contrast, living is a long-term set of resolutions with oftentimes only fleeting results.
8. Wilhelm Stekel and the other early psychoanalysts (1910 and after) overstated the case when they proclaimed that no one commits suicide who has not wished the death of another; that suicide is basically hostility directed toward the image of a loved one incorporated within the psyche. Not only is this explanation often off the mark but even more the individual who commits suicide usually does not even wish to kill himself.
9. Suicide should not be misunderstood as hostility directed toward the introjected love object; but rather suicide is better understood as anguish over the plight of the writhing self.
10. When suicide is a hostile act, it is often not the hostility of the perpetrator but rather the hostility of the significant others who have provoked or permitted the act.
11. The central issue in suicide is not death or killing; it is, rather, the stopping of the consciousness of unbearable pain which—unfortunately—by its very nature entails the stopping of life.
12. If tormented individuals could somehow stop consciousness and still live, why would they not opt for that solution? In suicide, "death" is not the key word. The key words are "psychological pain."
13. If the pain were relieved then the individual would be willing to continue to live. Nobody yearns to embrace "that skeleton with a

scythe astride a white horse"; we just want to get out of the way of its stampeding hooves that hurt us.

14. As a psychological disorder suicide relates specifically to unmet or frustrated needs, such as the need for acceptance, achievement, dignity, self-regard, clear conscience, safety, and succorance. There are many pointless deaths, but never a needless suicide. Every suicide act is addressed to certain unfulfilled needs.
15. Suicide is not only a reaction to unmet needs, but also the need for important psychological freedoms, such as freedom from pain, freedom from guilt, freedom from shame, freedom from rejection and aloneness. When these freedoms are traumatically violated, an individual who realistically lacks "a court of appeal" may take matters into his own hands and remove his consciousness from the painful scene.
16. Much of what has been written about suicide is relatively useless for actual prevention. There can be little meaningful practical research on suicide until the obfuscating categories of "attempted suicide" and "threatened suicide" are eschewed and the continua of "perturbation" and "lethality" are understood and employed.
17. Suicide is not a "right" any more than is the "right to belch." If the individual feels forced to do it he will do it. That capacity for untoward action cannot be taken away.
18. A definition of suicide should never be undertaken lightly. Much—especially implications for individual rescue and for global survival—depends upon it. The task of defining suicide is worthy of a separate book.
19. With some few clear exceptions, I am against suicide committed by other people but I want to reserve that option for myself.
20. Nietzsche said that "The thought of suicide is a great consolation; by means of it one gets successfully through many a bad night." I can say that the topic of suicide has been a great preoccupation that has kept me up more nights than I care to remember.

☐ III. Theoretical Implications

There are certain notions on which the aphorisms rest (that are propaedeutic to them) and certain notions which flow out of them (that are implications of them). For purposes of this discussion they need not be separated. At least five relatively important general notions about suicide can be delineated:

A. That suicide is best understood not so much as a movement toward death as it is a movement away from something and that something is always the same: intolerable emotion, unendurable pain or unacceptable anguish. Reduce the level of suffering and the individual will choose to live.

B. That suicide is best understood not so much in terms of some sets of nosological boxes—e.g., depression or any of the labels in *DMS-III*—but rather in terms of two continua of general personality functioning: perturbation and lethality. Everyone is omnipresently rateable (by oneself or by others) on how disturbed he is (perturbation) and how deathfully suicidal he is (lethality). To say that an individual is "disturbed" or "suicidal" simply indicates that there is an elevation in that individual's perturbation and lethality levels, respectively. Moreover, it often happens that an individual is highly perturbed but not suicidal. It infrequently occurs that an individual is highly lethal but not perturbed. Experience has taught us the important fact that it is neither possible nor practical in an individual who is highly lethal and highly perturbed to attempt to deal with the lethality directly, either by moral suasion, confrontational interpretations, exhortation or whatever. (It does not work any better in suicide than it does with alcoholism.) The most effective way to reduce elevated lethality is by doing so indirectly, that is by reducing the elevated perturbation. Reduce the individual's anguish, tension, and pain and his level of lethality will concomitantly come down, for it is the elevated perturbation that drives or fuels the elevated lethality.

C. That suicide is best understood not so much as a psychosis, a neurosis or a character disorder but rather as a more-or-less transient psychological constriction of affect and intellect. Synonyms for constriction are a tunneling or focusing or narrowing of the range of options usually available to *that* individual's consciousness when the mind is not panicked into dichotomous thinking: either some specific (almost magical) total solution *or* cessation. The range of choices has narrowed to two—not very much of a range. The usual life-sustaining images of loved ones are not only disregarded, they are not even within the range of what is in the mind. Boris Pasternak, writing of the suicidal deaths of several young poets, described life-threatening constriction in this way:

> A man who decides to commit suicide puts a full stop to his being, he turns his back on his past, he declares himself to be bankrupt and his memories to be unreal. They can no longer help or save him, he has put himself beyond their reach. The continuity of his inner life is broken, and his personality is at an end. And perhaps what finally makes him kill himself is not the firmness of his resolve but the unbearable quality of his anguish which belongs to no one, of this suffering in the absence of the sufferer, of this waiting which is empty because life has stopped and no one can feel it. (1959)

One of the most dangerous aspects of a suicidal state (high lethality/high perturbation) is the presence of constriction. Any attempt at rescue or remediation has to deal almost from the first with the pathological constriction.

D. That suicide is best understood not so much as an unreasonable act (or a defect in cognition) but as a reaction to frustrated psychological needs. These needs—taken from the monumental work on personality by Henry A. Murray (1938)—include the needs for affiliation, avoidance (of pain), succorance,[1]—among many others. A suicide is committed because of frustrated or unfulfilled needs. In an even wider sense the systems theorist Ludwig von Bertalanffy—emphasizing that self-destruction is intimately connected with man's symbolic and psychological world—says:

> The man who kills himself because his life or career or business has gone wrong, does not do so because of the fact that his biological existence and survival are threatened, but rather because of his quasi-needs, that is, his needs on the symbolic level are frustrated. (1965)

Given that there are no suicides in the absence of thwarted needs, if one will but address the frustrated needs, the suicide will then not have to occur (Shneidman, 1980a).

E. That suicide is best understood not so much in relation to the idea of a reified Death as it is in terms of the idea (in the mind of the chief protagonist) of "cessation," specifically when cessation—the complete stopping of one's consciousness of unendurable pain—is seen by the suffering individual as a solution, indeed the perfect solution, of life's painful and pressing problems. The moment that the idea of the possibility of stopping consciousness occurs to the mind as the answer or as the way out in the presence of unusual constriction and elevated perturbation and high lethality, then the active suicidal scenario has begun.

With these several theoretical supplements (of the twenty aphorisms) in mind, we can now turn to the main point of this brief paper, namely, the implications for psychotherapy of this general point of view.

☐ IV. Implications for Psychotherapy

Initially I had developed implications for each of the twenty aphorisms but in the end it seems both tedious and somewhat repetitious to present them in this fashion. Instead, I decided to combine my twenty sets of working notes into one amalgam or synthesis of what seemed to me to be the most important implications for therapy from the view of suicide implicit in the aphorisms. The careful reader can easily match the implications for therapy with one or more aphorisms.

Some of the implications for psychotherapy are:

1. The therapist should ascertain the separate levels of the patient's perturbation and lethality (on a scale of 1 to 9) and make a day-to-day assessment of each of them. A lethality rating of 7, 8 or 9 indicates that the patient may be hazardously suicidal and that special measures need to be taken.

2. With a highly lethal suicidal person the main goal is, of course, to reduce the elevated lethality. The most important rule to follow is that *high lethality is reduced by reducing the patient's sense of perturbation.* One way to do this is by addressing in a practical way those in-the-world things that can be changed, if ever so slightly. In a sensible manner, the therapist should contact (preferably by telephone) the patient's spouse, lover, employer, government agencies, etc. In these contacts the therapist acts as ombudsman for the patient, promoting his interests and welfare. The subgoal is to reduce the real-life pressures that are driving up the patient's sense of perturbation.

A psychotherapist decreases the elevated perturbation of a highly suicidal person by doing almost everything possible to cater to the infantile idiosyncrasies, the dependency needs, the sense of pressure and futility, the feelings of hopelessness and helplessness that the individual is experiencing. In order to help a highly lethal person, one should involve others; create activity around the person; do what he or she wants done—and, if that cannot be accomplished, at least move in the direction of the desired goals to some substitute goals that approximate those which have been lost. Remind the patient that life is often the choice among lousy alternatives. The key to well functioning is often to choose the least lousy alternative that is practicably attainable.[2]

The basic principle is this: To decrease lethality one puts a hook on perturbation and, doing what needs to be done, pulls the level of perturbation down—and with that action brings down the active level of lethality. When the person is no longer highly suicidal—then the usual methods of psychotherapy can be usefully employed.

As to how to help a suicidal individual, it is best to look upon a suicidal act as an effort to stop unbearable anguish or intolerable pain by "doing something." Knowing this usually guides us as to what treatment should be. In the same sense the way to save a person's life is also to "do something." Those "somethings" include putting that information (that the person is in trouble with himself) into the stream of communication, letting others know about it, breaking what could be a fatal secret, talking to the person, talking to others, proferring help, getting loved ones interested and responsive, creating action around the person, showing response, and indicating concern.

3. It is vital to counter the suicidal person's constriction-of-thought by attempting to widen the angle of the mental blinders and to increase the number of options, certainly beyond the two options of either having some magical resolution or being dead. An example may be useful. A teenage college student, demure, rather elegant (and somewhat wealthy) was encouraged to come to see me. She was single, pregnant, and suicidal, with a formed suicidal plan. Her challenge to me was that I somehow, magically, had to arrange for her to be the way she was before she became pregnant, virginal in fact, or she would have to commit suicide. Her being pregnant was such a mortal shame to her, combined with strong feelings of rage and guilt, that she simply could not "bear to live." At that moment suicide was the *only* alternative for her.

I did several things. For one, I took out a sheet of paper and—to begin to "expand her blinders"—said something like, "Now, let's see: You could have an abortion here locally." ("I couldn't do that.") (It is precisely the "can'ts" and the "won'ts" and "have to's" and "nevers" and "always" and "onlys" that are negotiated in psychotherapy.) "You could go away and have an abortion." ("I couldn't do that.") "You could bring the baby to term and keep the baby." ("I couldn't do that.") "You could have the baby and adopt it out." ("I couldn't do that.") "We could get in touch with the young man involved." ("I couldn't do that.") "We could involve the help of your parents." ("I couldn't do that.") and "You can always commit suicide, but there is obviously no need to do that today." (No response.) "Now, let's look at this list and rank them in order of your preference, keeping in mind that none of them is exactly what you want."

The very making of this list, my nonhortatory and nonjudgmental approach already had a calming influence on her. Within a few minutes her lethality had begun to deescalate. She actually rank-ordered the list, commenting negatively on each item. What was of critical importance was that suicide was now no longer ranked first or second. We were then simply "haggling" about life—a perfectly viable solution.

The point is not how the issue was eventually resolved or what interpretations were made as to why she permitted herself to become pregnant, other aspects of her relationships with men, etc. What is important is that it was possible to achieve the assignment of that day: to lower her lethality by widening her range of visible and realistic options including, but not limited to, the choice between suicide and one other unrealistic choice.

4. The mental pain of the suicidal person relates to the frustration or blocking of important psychological needs, that is, needs deemed

to be important by that person. It should be the therapist's function to help the patient in relation to those thwarted needs. Even a little bit of improvement can save a life. Oftentimes just the possibility of a small amount of gain gives the perturbed individual enough hope and comfort to divert the suicidal course. In general, the goal of psychotherapy is to increase the patient's psychological *comfort.* One way to operationalize this task is to focus on the thwarted needs. Questions such as "What is going on?" "Where do you hurt?" and "What would you like to have happen?" can usefully be asked by a therapist helping a suicidal person.

The psychotherapist can focus on feelings, especially such distressing feelings as guilt, shame, fear, anger, thwarted ambition, unrequited love, hopelessness, helplessness, loneliness. The key is to improve the external and internal situations a J.N.D. (Just Noticeable Difference). This can be accomplished through a variety of methods: ventilation, interpretation, instruction, and realistic manipulation in the world outside the consultation room. That last means to do things, involve significant others, and invoke agencies. All this implies—when working with a highly lethal person—a heightened level of interaction during the period of elevated lethality. The therapist needs to work diligently, always giving the suicidal person realistic transfusions of hope until the perturbation intensity subsides enough to reduce the lethality to a tolerable, life-permitting level.

A highly suicidal state is characterized by its transient quality, its pervasive ambivalence, and its dyadic nature. Psychotherapists are well advised to minimize, if not totally to disregard, those probably well-intentioned but shrill writings in this field which naively speak of an individual's "right to commit suicide"—a right which in actuality cannot be denied.

A dozen other special features in the management of a highly lethal patient can be mentioned. Some of these special therapeutic stratagems or orientations reflect the *transient, ambivalent,* and *dyadic* aspects of almost all suicide acts.

1. *Monitoring.* A continuous (preferably daily) monitoring of the patient's lethality.
2. *Consultation.* There is almost no instance in a psychotherapist's life when consultation with a peer is as important as when one is dealing with a highly suicidal patient.
3. *Hospitalization.* Hospitalization is always a complicating event in the treatment of a suicidal patient but it should not, on those grounds, be eschewed. Obviously, the quality of care—from doctors, nurses, and attendants—is crucial. Stoller (1973), discussing one of his complex long-range cases, says:

> . . . there were several other factors without which the therapy might not have succeeded. First, the hospital. The patient's life could not have been saved if a hospital had not been immediately available *and a few of the personnel familiar with me and the patient* (Italics added.)

4. *Transference.* The successful treatment of a highly suicidal person depends heavily on the transference. The therapist can be active, show his personal concern, increase the frequency of the sessions, invoke the magic of the unique therapist-patient relationship, be less of a *tabula rasa,* give transfusions of (realistic) hope and nurturance. In a figurative sense I believe that Eros can work wonders against Thanatos.
5. *The involvement of significant others.* Suicide is often a highly charged dyadic crisis. It follows from this that the therapist, unlike his usual practice of dealing almost exclusively with his patient (and even fending off the spouse, lover, parents, grown children), should consider the advisability of working directly with the significant other. If the individual is married, it is important to meet the spouse. The therapist must assess whether, in fact, the spouse is suicidogenic; whether the patient ought to be separated from the spouse; whether there are misunderstandings which the therapist can help resolve; or to what extent the spouse is insightful and concerned. At the minimum the role of the significant other as hinderer or helper in the treatment process needs to be assessed.
6. *Careful modification of the usual canons of confidentiality.* Admittedly this is a touchy and complicated point, but the therapist should not ally himself with death. Statements given during the therapy session relating to the patient's overt suicidal (or homicidal) plans should not be treated as a secret between two collusive partners.

Working with highly suicidal persons borrows from the goals of crisis intervention: not to take on and ameliorate the individual's entire personality structure and to cure all the neuroses but simply to keep the person alive. That is the *sine qua non* without which all other psychotherapy could not have an opportunity to function.

☐ Summary

An aphorism is a pithy short statement stating a general truth. This article presents twenty aphorisms about suicide. One example: "There are many pointless deaths, but never a needless suicide." What is implied is that every suicide is an effort to redress certain unfulfilled, thwarted or frustrated psychological needs. (These include the needs for affiliation, avoidance of pain, succorance—among some twenty psychological needs that have been identified.) The psychotherapeutic implication of this particular aphorism is fairly obvious: Reduce the sense of frustration or effect *some* satisfaction of the frustrated needs of the suicidal individual and the elevated level of perturbation will be mollified sufficiently so as to drop below the lethal threshold of suicidal action. For the twenty aphorisms about suicide, some implications for response and the management of suicidal persons are suggested in order to prevent suicide. In addition a few general suggestions are offered for the management of suicidal persons.

☐ Endnotes

[1]A partial listing of Murray needs includes the following: the need for abasement, achievement, affiliation, aggression, autonomy, counteraction, defendance, deference, dominance, exhibition, harm-avoidance, pain-avoidance, inviolacy, nurturance, order, play, rejection, sentience, sex succorance and understanding.

[2]This paragraph and the following two are paraphrased from Shneidman (1980b).

☐ References

Bertalanffy, L. von (1965). Comments on aggression. In I. G. Sarason (Ed.), *Psychoanalysis and the study of behavior,* (p. 114). Princeton: Van Nostrand.

Encyclopaedia Britannica. 14th Edition 1973 (Vol. 2, p. 109) Chicago: William Benton.

Fowles, J. (1964). *The aristos.* Boston: Little, Brown.

Murray, H. A. (1938). Explorations in Personality. New York: Oxford University Press. Reprinted in Shneidman, E. S. (Ed.) (1981). *Endeavors in psychology: Selections from the personology of Henry A. Murray.* New York: Harper and Row

Pascal, B. (1657–58). *Pensées.*

Pasternak, B. (1959). *I remember: Sketch for an autobiography.* New York: Pantheon.

Shneidman, E. S. (1973). Suicide. In *Encyclopaedia Britannica* (Vol. 21, pp. 383–386). Chicago: William Benton.

Shneidman, E. S. (1980a). A possible classification of suicidal acts based on Murray's need system. *Suicide Life-Threat. Behav., 10,* 175–181.

Shneidman, E. S. (1980b). Psychotherapy with suicidal patients. In T. B. Karasu & L. Bellak (Eds.), *Specialized techniques in individual psychotherapy.* New York: Brunner/Mazel.

Stoller, R. J. (1973). *Splitting.* New York: Quadrangle Books.

29

CHAPTER

Letter to the Editor: Rational Suicide and Psychiatric Disorders

To the Editor: Because Conwell and Caine quote me appositely in their Sounding Board article "Rational Suicide and the Right to Die" (Oct. 10 issue) (Conwell & Caine, 1991, Letter to the Editor): I am emboldened to comment on their remarks. They write:

> The concept of rational suicide is elusive and controversial. A pioneer in the study of suicidal behavior, Edwin Shneidman, captured this quality when he said, "It is not a thing to do while one is not in one's best mind. Never kill yourself when you are suicidal." (Shneidman, 1986)

Of course, I believe that. What I am not so sure about is what follows in their article.

The burden of their presentation is that the crux of suicide prevention lies in the diagnosis (and treatment) of affective disorders. I do not believe this is necessarily so. Forty years of practice and research as a suicidologist have led me to believe that the assessment and treatment of suicidal persons is best conceptualized not in terms of psychiatric nosologic categories (such as one finds in the *Diagnostic and Statistical Manual*), but rather in terms of psychological pain and thresholds for enduring that pain.

Reprinted from *New England Journal of Medicine*, 1992, *326*, 889. With permission.

Some suicidal persons have psychiatric disorders. Many suicidal persons are depressed. Most depressed patients are not suicidal. (One can live a long, unhappy life with depression.) But it is undeniable that all persons—100 percent—who commit suicide are perturbed and experiencing unbearable psychological pain. The problem of suicide should be addressed directly, phenomenologically, without the intervention of the often obfuscating variable of psychiatric disorder.

In human beings pain is ubiquitous, but suffering is optional, within the constraints of a person's personality. Just as it is important to distinguish between the treatment of physical pain and the treatment of suffering (Cassell, 1991), so there are also important differences between the diagnosis of depression and the assessment of psychological pain. A focus on mental illness is often misleading. Physicians and other health professionals need the courage and wisdom to work on a person's suffering at the phenomenological level and to explore such questions as "How do you hurt?" and "How may I help you?" They should then do whatever is necessary, using a wide variety of legitimate tactics (Shneidman, 1984), including medication, to reduce that person's self-destructive impulses. Diagnosis should be adjunctive to a larger understanding of the person's pain-in-life.

☐ References

Cassell, E. J. (1991). *The nature of suffering: And the goals of medicine.* New York: Oxford University Press.

Conwell, Y., & E. D. Caine (1991). Rational suicide and the right to die—reality and myth. *New England Journal of Medicine, 325,* 1100–1103.

Shneidman, E. S. (1984). Aphorisms of suicide and some implications for psychotherapy. *Am J Psychother., 38,* 319–328.

Shneidman, E. S. (1986). Some essentials of suicide and some implications for response. In A. Roy (Ed.), *Suicide* (pp. 1–16). Baltimore: Williams & Wilkins.

IV

SUICIDE Section E: Psychological Autopsy and Postvention

Shneidman helped to create two other major endeavors in suicidology—the psychological autopsy, which is intended to clarify the psychological nature of a death; and postvention, pertaining to the care of the bereaved.

The concept of investigating deaths which are uncertain as to mode of death—natural, accident, suicide, or homicide—is at least as old as the work of John Graunt of London in the 17th century. The recent history of this procedure focuses around the LASPC, which is reported in Chapter 30 in this section. In the 1950s, the Chief-Coroner and Medical Examiner of Los Angeles County, Theodore J. Curphey, asked the leaders at the LASPC—Shneidman, Farberow, and Litman—

to assist him with coroners' cases which were ambiguous as to mode of death, usually between accident and suicide. These were cases which depended on the decedent's *intention.* The Center's three leaders were designated as deputy coroners and went to the scenes of death, where they gently interviewed a number of key survivors, and then reported back to Dr. Curphey in a setting that was strictly non-partisan, that is, no one had a brief for one mode of death or another (e.g., accident or suicide). Shneidman labeled this clinical-scientific investigatory procedure the psychological autopsy. This chapter, first published in 1977, provides an outline for the psychological autopsy procedure and makes suggestions for the improvement of the contemporary certificate of death.

Chapter 31 is a general comment on psychological autopsies. It notes that the psychological autopsy is about intention: What was the person's intention vis-à-vis the death?

Chapter 32 is an example of a psychological autopsy, carried out in an adversarial setting, an Army court martial. Everything, except a few names, is verbatim. The bare facts were that an army officer was charged with the murder of his wife and faced a lifetime sentence in Leavenworth federal prison. The defense—in whose behalf Shneidman was an expert witness—believed that her death was a suicide, and that the officer had been wrongly accused. It is instructive to read the various experts' differing opinions, to take in Jerome Motto's model report, to see the extraordinary letter from the decedent's mother, and to note Shneidman's testimony on the stand as he holds his ground on behalf of the accused.

After a suicide has been committed, the tragedy is not over. Shneidman has coined the word postvention to refer to those activities that can assuage the grief and mollify the mourning processes of the survivor-victims. Chapter 33, on the care of the bereaved, sets forth the differences that distinguish professional sessions with survivors from ordinary condolence conversations.

30

CHAPTER

The Psychological Autopsy

It is probably best to begin by defining a psychological autopsy and its purposes, then to discuss some related theoretical background and ways of actually performing psychological autopsies. The words *psychological autopsy* themselves tell us that the procedure has to do with clarifying the nature of a death and that it focuses on the psychological aspects of the death. Two ideas, important to understanding the psychological autopsy, need to be discussed. The first is what I have called the NASH classification of deaths; the second is the idea of *equivocal* deaths.

From the beginning of this century (and with roots that can be clearly traced back to Elizabethan times), the certification and recordkeeping relating to deaths have implied that there are four *modes* of death. It needs to be said right away that the four modes of death have to be distinguished from the many *causes* of death listed in the current *International Classification of Diseases and Causes of Death* (World Health Organization 1957, National Center for Health Statistics 1967). The four modes of death are natural, accidental, suicide, and homicide; the initial letters of each make up the acronym NASH. Thus, to speak of the NASH classification of death is to refer to these four traditional modes in which death is currently reported. Contemporary death certificates have a category which reads "Accident, suicide, homicide, or undetermined"; if none of

---

Reprinted from L. I. Gottschalk et al. (Eds.), *Guide to the Investigation and Reporting of Drug-Abuse Deaths.* Washington, DC: USDHEW, U.S. Government Printing Office, 1977, pp. 179–210. With permission.

these is checked, then a "natural" mode of death, as occurs in most cases, is implied.[1]

It should be apparent that the cause of death stated on the certificate does not necessarily carry with it information as to the specific mode of death. For example, asphyxiation due to drowning in a swimming pool does not automatically communicate whether the decedent struggled and drowned (accident), entered the pool with the intention of drowning himself (suicide), or was held under water until he was drowned (homicide).

It so happens that a considerable number of deaths—the estimate is between 5 and 20 percent of all deaths that need to be certified—are not clear as to the correct or appropriate mode. These unclear or uncertain deaths are called *equivocal* deaths. The ambiguity is usually between the modes of suicide or accident, although uncertainty can exist between any two or more of the four modes.

The main function of the psychological autopsy is to clarify an equivocal death and to arrive at the correct or accurate mode of that death. In essence, the psychological autopsy is nothing less than a thorough retrospective investigation of the *intention* of the decedent—that is, the decedent's intention relating to his being dead—where the information is obtained by interviewing individuals who knew the decedent's actions, behavior, and character well enough to report on them.

Drug-related deaths can be among the most equivocal as to the mode of death. Proper certification often necessitates knowledge of the victim over and beyond standard toxicological information, including such questions as what dosage was taken (related to the exact time of death and the time at which autopsy blood and tissue samples were taken); the decedent's weight and build; the decedent's long-term drug habits and known tolerances; the possible synergistics of other ingested materials, notably alcohol, or the effects of certain combinations like hydromorphone (Dilaudid) and Methedrine; and the role of lethal action of drug overdoses, for example, morphine sulfate (morphine) as opposed to the quicker acting diacetyl morphine (heroin).

□ Historical Background

In 1662 John Graunt, a London tradesman, published a small book of observations on the bills of mortality that was to have great social and medical significance. By this time the weekly bills were consolidated at the end of each year, and a general bill for the year was published. Graunt separated the various bits of information contained in these annual bills and organized them into tables. When the available data on deaths were believed accurate, Graunt then focused on individual causes of death. He next turned to the subject of population estimation. Finally he constructed a mortality table, the first attempt to organize data in this manner. Of greatest significance was his success in demonstrating the regularities that can be found in medical and social phenomena when one is dealing with large numbers. Thus, John Graunt demonstrated how the bills of mortality could be used to the advantage of both the physician and government (Kargon, 1963).

In 1741, the science of statistics came into existence with the work of a Prussian clergyman, Johann Süssmilch, who made a systematic attempt to correlate political arithmetic, or what we now call vital statistics. From this study came what was subsequently termed the "laws of large numbers," which permitted extended use of the bills of mortality to supply important data in Europe as well as in the American colonies. Cassedy (1969) says that Süssmilch's "exhaustive analysis of vital data from church registers . . . became the ultimate scientific demonstration of the regularity of God's demographic laws" (p. 110).

For many years no provisions existed anywhere in the American colonies for anything comparable to the London bills of mortality (Cassedy, 1969). At first there was no necessity for detailed records since communities were small, but something better than hearsay or fading memories was needed as towns grew larger. The birth of newspapers in the British sections of America, about the year 1700, provided a means of remedying this situation. Some editors went to the trouble of obtaining information from local church and town records. They accumulated long lists to which summaries were added, which together were loosely called "bills of mortality." Issued in a variety of publications, the bills became the earliest systematized American death certificates.

Meanwhile, back in England, "the London Bills of Mortality remained among the eternal verities for Englishmen" (Cassedy 1969, p. 118). Londoners were sure to find the bills on sale in each parish each week. Bills with lists of cases of various diseases printed on the back brought twice the price of the regular bills. The American colonists had relatives or friends send copies to them: "Just as John Graunt had found the English doing, the early Americans used the bills as grist for conversation if for nothing else" (Cassedy 1969, p. 118). Few in the colonies even knew of Graunt's statistical applications to the bills of mortality for years after his book was published. Not until William Douglass commented upon statistical method in his history of the British colonies in North America, published in 1751, did the colonists begin to make use of Graunt's methods.

The fact that no colonial bills were published during the seventeenth century may be attributed to printing priorities and especially to lack of legislative requirements. Though a printing press had begun operation in

Cambridge, Massachusetts, in 1638, the next half century saw the introduction of only four more. These few presses were generally kept running at capacity turning out government documents. Though the government of each colony required the registration of all vital statistics, none of them made any provision for the information to be published. Thus the publication of anything resembling the London bills was left to private enterprise. Despite the spread of colonial newspapers and the existence of a few church bills of mortality, British publications remained the colonists' best sources of vital statistical information (Cassedy, 1969).

The use of such nonstandardized death records continued into the nineteenth century. Recognition of the need for informed medicolegal investigation in England led to a series of reforms aimed at improving the quality of death registration. In 1836 Parliament enacted a bill requiring the recording of all deaths. Under the terms of this act, notification of the coroner was not required unless the cause of death was one included in a special category. This system of death certification and registration was to ensure that those special deaths that came under the coroner's jurisdiction were in fact reported. The new certification system was designed to utilize the data on causes of death for statistical purposes as well as to prevent criminal practices. The medical explanation of the death was the essential information required for statistical determination. A curious aspect of the law, however, was that doctors were specifically enjoined to include no information on the mode of death on the death certificate.

The English 1836 registration act was amended in 1874 to require that personal information on the death be submitted to the registrar of the district within five days of its occurrence by the nearest relative of the deceased who was present at the death or in attendance during the last illness. A fine was to be levied for noncompliance. The new law also required a registered medical practitioner present during the last illness to complete a certificate stating the cause of death to the best of his knowledge and belief.

In 1893 a Select Committee on Death Certification of the House of Commons attempted to correct the shortcomings of the previous legislation, particularly "the carelessness and ignorance of the persons certifying, the absence of medical attendants during the last illness and the indefinite character of the disease itself" (Abbott, 1901). That committee made a series of ten recommendations, the most important of which were the following:

1. That in no case should a death be registered without production of a certificate of the cause of death signed by a registered medical practitioner or by a coroner after inquest.

2. That in each sanitary district a registered medical practitioner should be appointed as public medical certifier of the cause of death in cases in which a certificate from a medical practitioner in attendance was not forthcoming.
3. That a medical practitioner in attendance should be required personally to inspect the body before giving a certificate of death.
4. That a form of a certificate of death should be prescribed, and that in giving a certificate a medical practitioner should be required to use such a form.

The United States Congress, trailing behind the British Parliament, enacted no standard registration act until 1903. Prior to that date, any attempts at standardization were left to the individual states.

In Massachusetts deaths were reported on sheets of paper measuring 18 by 24 inches, with approximately forty records to a page. Information asked for (but not always provided) included date of death, date of record, name of deceased, sex, marital status, age, residence, disease or other cause of death, place of death, occupation, place of birth, and names and birthplaces of parents. These questions are generally to be found on all records of that period. The California form added only a line for the signature of the attending physician or coroner. New Jersey requested the same information but asked for a more detailed explanation of the cause of death. This was optional, however, and the space provided for it was usually left blank. The New York form, the most comprehensive of its time, also required data concerning the burial.

These early death registrations lacked many significant data: cause of death and place of death were often omitted, and no questions were asked regarding an autopsy report or the time and manner of the death, relevant information needed for statistical purposes and criminal investigation.

When the United States Census Bureau was making its preparations for the 1880 census, it decided to rely upon registration records instead of mortality enumerations, wherever possible, and made a study of state and local forms to determine where these registration records were adequate to its purpose. Wide variation was noted in the ways in which items were worded and data recorded. The study revealed the inherent disadvantages of allowing each state to enact its own registration system without guidelines provided by some central authority (Colby, 1965). Therefore, with the aid of the American Public Health Association, the Census Bureau developed what may be termed a model death certificate and prescribed its use by the states, but the use of a standard certificate for the registration of deaths was not approved by Congress until 1903.

The Death Certificate

The impact of the death certificate is considerable. It holds a mirror to our mores; it reflects some of the deepest taboos; it can directly affect the fate and fortune of a family, touching both its affluence and its mental health; it can enhance or degrade the reputation of the decedent and set its stamp on his postself career. But if the impact of the death certificate is great, its limitations are of equal magnitude. In its present form the death certificate is a badly flawed document.

Today most states follow the format of the U.S. Standard Certificate of Death. Most relevant to our present interests is the item which reads: "Accident, suicide, homicide, or undetermined (specify)." When none of these is specified, a natural mode of death is, of course, implied. Only two states, Delaware and Virginia, have made all four modes of death explicit on the death certificate (and have included a "pending" category as well). Curiously enough, Indiana included four modes of death on the death certificate form from 1955 to 1968, but then revised the form in 1968 and now provides no item for mode of death; nor, surprisingly, does the current Massachusetts death certificate contain an accident-suicide-homicide item.

In addition to the U.S. Standard Certificate, the International Classification of Diseases and Causes of Death plays a major role in determining the way a specific death may be counted—and thus in the apparent change in causes of death statistics from decade to decade. For example, the definitions of suicides and accidents were changed in the Seventh Revision (1955) and Eighth Revision (1965) of the International Classification, and the numbers of suicides and accidents changed along with the definitions. When the Seventh Revision was put into effect for the data year 1958, the death rate for suicides increased markedly over 1957. In part, one can find the explanation in this paragraph (National Center for Health Statistics 1965a):

> About 3.3 percent of the total suicide rate for 1958 as compared with that for 1957 resulted from the transfer of a number of deaths from accident to suicide. In 1958 a change was made in the interpretation of injuries where there was some doubt as to whether they *were* accidentally inflicted or inflicted with suicidal intent. Beginning with the Seventh Revision for data year 1958, "self-inflicted" injuries with no specification as to whether or not they were inflicted with suicidal intent, and deaths from injuries, whether or not self-inflicted, with an indication that it is not known whether they were inflicted accidentally or with suicidal intent, are classified as suicides. The change was made on the assumption that the majority of such deaths are properly classified as suicide because of the reluctance of the certifier to designate a death as suicide unless evidence indicates suici-

> dal intent beyond the shadow of a doubt. The magnitude of the comparability ratios for suicide varied considerably with means of injury, from 1.02 for suicide by firearms and explosives to 1.55 for suicide by jumping from high places.

It would seem that this redefinition led to an apparent 55 percent increase from one year to the next in suicides by jumping from high places. Even more interesting is the official observation that the death certifier would be reluctant to indicate suicide "unless evidence indicates suicidal intent beyond the shadow of a doubt." Clearly the certifier plays an important role in the process of generating mortality data. It is he who makes the subjective judgment of what constitutes conclusive evidence of the decedent's intent. The Eighth Revision (National Center for Health Statistics, 1967), which made the category "Undetermined" available, introduced still further problems, apparently shifting many suicidal deaths to the Undetermined category.

What is urgently needed is an exploration and description of the current practices of certifying deaths, especially deaths by suicide. We need a uniform system that would eliminate such inconsistencies or confirm the differential unequivocally, as for example, 10.9 deaths by suicide per 100,000 population for Idaho versus 20.2 for Wyoming. What is required is a correctional quotient for each reporting unit—county, state, and nation. Until such information is obtained, available suicide statistics are highly suspect.

At the turn of the century, an early reference book of the medical science (Abbott, 1901) urged reliable death registration bookkeeping and listed the following as "objects secured by a well-devised system":

1. Questions relating to property rights are often settled by a single reference to a record of death.
2. The official certificate of a death is usually required in each case of claim for life insurance.
3. Death certificates settle many disputed questions in regard to pensions.
4. They are of great value in searching for records of genealogy.
5. A death certificate frequently furnishes valuable aid in the detection of crime.
6. Each individual certificate is a contribution *causa scientiae.* Taken collectively, they are of great importance to physicians, and especially to health officers, in the study of disease, since they furnish valuable information in regard to its causes, its prevalence, and its geographical distribution.

At least three more functions for the death certificate might be added to the half-dozen listed in 1901:

7. The death certificate should reflect the type of death that is certified—brain death (a flat electroencephalographic record), somatic death (no respiration, heartbeat, reflexes), or whatever type is implied.
8. The death certificate should include space for the specification of death by legal execution, death in war or military incursions, death by police action, and others of that sort.
9. Perhaps most importantly, the death certificate should abandon the anachronistic Cartesian view of man as a passive biological vessel on which the fates work their will. Instead, it should reflect the contemporary view of man as a psycho-socio-biological organism that can, and in many cases does, play a significant role in hastening its own demise. This means that the death certificate should contain at least one item on the decedent's intention vis-à-vis his own death.

In the Western world death is given its administrative dimensions by the death certificate. See Figure 30-1. It is the format and content of this document that determine and reflect the categories in terms of which death is conceptualized and death statistics reported. The ways in which deaths were described and categorized in John Graunt's day and earlier set deep precedents for ways of thinking about death, and they govern our thoughts and gut reactions to death to this day. Deaths were then assumed to fall into one of two categories: There were those that were truly adventitious—accidents, visitations of fate or fortune (called natural and accidental)—and there were those that were caused by a culprit who needed to be sought out and punished (called suicidal and homicidal deaths). In the case of suicide, the victim and the assailant were combined in the same person, and the offense was designated as a crime against oneself, a *felo de se*. England did not cease to classify suicide as a crime until 1961, and in the United States it remains a crime in nine States.

The historical importance of certifying the mode of death—that is, of the coroner's function—can now be seen: It not only set a stamp of innocence or stigma upon the death, but also determined whether the decedent's estate could be claimed by his legal heirs (natural or accidental death) or by the crown or local lord (a suicide or a murder). That was certainly one important practical effect of the death certificate. The NASH categories of death were implied as early as the sixteenth century in English certification, and this submanifest administrative taxonomy of death has beguiled most men into thinking that there *really* are four kinds of death, which, of course, is not necessarily so at all.

Although it may be platitudinous to say that in each life the inevitability of death is an inexorable fact, there is nothing at all inexorable about our ways of dimensionalizing death. Conceptualizations of death are manmade and mutable; what man can make he can also clarify and

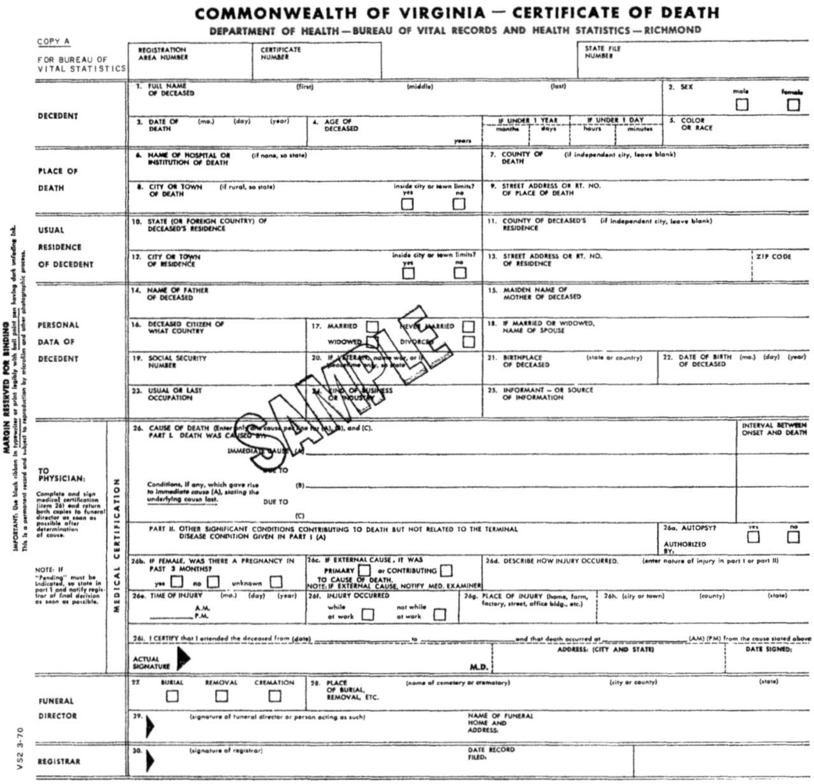
COMMONWEALTH OF VIRGINIA — CERTIFICATE OF DEATH

DEPARTMENT OF HEALTH — BUREAU OF VITAL RECORDS AND HEALTH STATISTICS — RICHMOND

COPY A

FOR BUREAU OF VITAL STATISTICS

REGISTRATION AREA NUMBER | CERTIFICATE NUMBER | STATE FILE NUMBER

DECEDENT

1. FULL NAME OF DECEASED (first) (middle) (last)
2. SEX male ☐ female ☐
3. DATE OF DEATH (mo.) (day) (year)
4. AGE OF DECEASED years | IF UNDER 1 YEAR months days | IF UNDER 1 DAY hours minutes
5. COLOR OR RACE

PLACE OF DEATH

6. NAME OF HOSPITAL OR INSTITUTION OF DEATH (if none, so state)
7. COUNTY OF DEATH (if independent city, leave blank)
8. CITY OR TOWN OF DEATH (if rural, so state) inside city or town limits? yes ☐ no ☐
9. STREET ADDRESS OR RT. NO. OF PLACE OF DEATH

USUAL RESIDENCE OF DECEDENT

10. STATE (OR FOREIGN COUNTRY) OF DECEASED'S RESIDENCE
11. COUNTY OF DECEASED'S RESIDENCE (if independent city, leave blank)
12. CITY OR TOWN OF RESIDENCE inside city or town limits? yes ☐ no ☐
13. STREET ADDRESS OR RT. NO. OF RESIDENCE | ZIP CODE

PERSONAL DATA OF DECEDENT

14. NAME OF FATHER OF DECEASED
15. MAIDEN NAME OF MOTHER OF DECEASED
16. DECEASED CITIZEN OF WHAT COUNTRY
17. MARRIED ☐ NEVER MARRIED ☐ WIDOWED ☐ DIVORCED ☐
18. IF MARRIED OR WIDOWED, NAME OF SPOUSE
19. SOCIAL SECURITY NUMBER
20. IF VETERAN, name war, or if peacetime only, so state
21. BIRTHPLACE OF DECEASED (state or country)
22. DATE OF BIRTH OF DECEASED (mo.) (day) (year)
23. USUAL OR LAST OCCUPATION
24. KIND OF BUSINESS OR INDUSTRY
25. INFORMANT — OR SOURCE OF INFORMATION

SAMPLE

MEDICAL CERTIFICATION

TO PHYSICIAN: Complete and sign medical certification (item 26) and return both copies to funeral director as soon as possible after determination of cause.

NOTE: If "Pending" must be indicated, so state in part I and notify registrar of final decision as soon as possible.

26. CAUSE OF DEATH (Enter only one cause per line for (A), (B), and (C).
PART I. DEATH WAS CAUSED BY:
IMMEDIATE CAUSE (A)
DUE TO
Conditions, if any, which gave rise to immediate cause (A), stating the underlying cause last. (B)
DUE TO
(C)
INTERVAL BETWEEN ONSET AND DEATH

PART II. OTHER SIGNIFICANT CONDITIONS CONTRIBUTING TO DEATH BUT NOT RELATED TO THE TERMINAL DISEASE CONDITION GIVEN IN PART I (A)
26a. AUTOPSY? yes ☐ no ☐ AUTHORIZED BY:
26b. IF FEMALE, WAS THERE A PREGNANCY IN PAST 3 MONTHS? yes ☐ no ☐ unknown ☐
26c. IF EXTERNAL CAUSE, IT WAS PRIMARY ☐ or CONTRIBUTING ☐ TO CAUSE OF DEATH. NOTE: IF EXTERNAL CAUSE, NOTIFY MED. EXAMINER
26d. DESCRIBE HOW INJURY OCCURRED. (enter nature of injury in part I or part II)
26e. TIME OF INJURY (mo.) (day) (year) ________ A.M. P.M.
26f. INJURY OCCURRED while at work ☐ not while at work ☐
26g. PLACE OF INJURY (home, farm, factory, street, office bldg., etc.)
26h. (city or town) (county) (state)
26i. I CERTIFY that I attended the deceased from (date) ________ to ________ and that death occurred at ________ (AM) (PM) from the cause stated above
ACTUAL SIGNATURE ▶ M.D. | ADDRESS: (CITY AND STATE) | DATE SIGNED:

FUNERAL DIRECTOR

27. BURIAL ☐ REMOVAL ☐ CREMATION ☐
28. PLACE OF BURIAL, REMOVAL, ETC. (name of cemetery or crematory) (city or county) (state)
29. ▶ (signature of funeral director or person acting as such) | NAME OF FUNERAL HOME AND ADDRESS:

REGISTRAR

30. ▶ (signature of registrar) | DATE RECORD FILED:

MARGIN RESERVED FOR BINDING

IMPORTANT: Use black ribbon in typewriter or print legibly with ball point pen having dark unfading ink. This is a permanent record and subject to reproduction by microfilm and other photographic process.

VS2 3-70

FIGURE 30-1. U.S. Standard Certificate of Death Form

change. Indeed, changes in our conceptualizations of death are constantly occurring, notwithstanding the NASH notions of death have held on for centuries after they became anachronistic. Each generation becomes accustomed to its own notions and thinks that these are universal and ubiquitous.

From the time of John Graunt and his mortuary tables in the seventeenth century, through the work of Cullen in the eighteenth century and William Farr in the nineteenth century, the adoption of the Bertillon International List of Causes of Death in 1893, and the International Conference for the Eighth Revision of the International Classification of Diseases as recently as 1965 (National Center for Health Statistics, 1965b), the classification of causes of death has constantly been broadening in scope. The changes are characterized primarily by attempts to reflect additions to knowledge, particularly those contributed by new professions as they have developed—anesthesiology, pathology, bacteriology, immunology, and advances in obstetrics, surgery, and most recently, the behavioral sciences.

☐ Purposes of the Psychological Autopsy

As long as deaths are classified solely in terms of the four NASH categories, it is immediately apparent that some deaths will, so to speak, fall between the cracks, and our familiar problem of equivocal death will continue to place obstacles in our path to understanding human beings and their dying. Many of these obstacles can be cleared away by reconstructing, primarily through interviews with the survivors, the role that the deceased played in hastening or effecting his own death. This procedure is called "psychological autopsy," and initially its main purpose was to clarify situations in which the mode of death was not immediately clear.

The origin of the psychological autopsy grew out of the frustration of the Los Angeles County Chief Medical Examiner-Coroner, Theodore J. Curphey, M.D., at the time of the reorganization of that office in 1958. Despite his efforts, which were combined with those of toxicologists and nonmedical investigators, he was faced with a number of drug deaths for which he was unable to certify the mode on the basis of collected evidence. As a result he asked the Los Angeles Suicide Prevention Center to assist him in a joint study of these equivocal cases, and it was this effort—a multidisciplinary approach involving behavioral scientists—which led to my coining the term "psychological autopsy" (Curphey, 1961, 1967; Litman et al., 1963; Shneidman, 1969, 1973; Shneidman & Farberow, 1961).

In the last few years, especially with the interesting and valuable work of Litman and colleagues (1963), Weisman and Kastenbaum (1968), and Weisman (1974), the term "psychological autopsy" has come to have other, slightly different meanings. At present there are at least three distinct questions that the psychological autopsy can help to answer:

1. Why did the individual do it? When the mode of death is, by all reasonable measures, clear and unequivocal—suicide, for example—the psychological autopsy can serve to account for the reasons for the act or to discover what led to it. Why did Ernest Hemingway "have to" shoot himself (Hotchner, 1966)? Why did former Secretary of Defense James Forrestal kill himself (Rogow, 1963)? We can read a widow's explicit account of how she helped her husband, dying of cancer, cut open his veins in Lael Tucker Wertenbacker's *Death of a Man* (1957). Some people can understand such an act; others cannot. But even those who believe they understand cannot know whether their reasons are the same as those of the cancer victim or his wife. What were their reasons? In this type of psychological autopsy, as in the following type, the mode of death is clear, but the reasons for the manner of dying remain puzzling, even mysterious. The psychological autopsy is no less than a reconstruction of the motivations, philosophy, psychodynamics, and existential crises of the decedent.

2. How did the individual die, and when—that is, why at that particular time? When a death, usually a natural death, is protracted, the individual dying gradually over a period of time, the psychological autopsy helps to illumine the sociopsychological reasons why he died at that time. This type of psychological autopsy is illustrated by the following brief case from Weisman and Kastenbaum (1968):

> An 85-year-old man had suffered with chronic bronchitis and emphysema for many years but was alert and active otherwise. He had eagerly anticipated going to his son's home for Thanksgiving and when the day arrived he was dressed and ready, but no one came for him. He became more concerned as the hours went by. He asked the nurse about messages, but there were none, and he finally realized that he would have to spend the holiday at the hospital. After this disappointment the patient kept more and more to himself, offered little, and accepted only minimal care. Within a few weeks he was dead.

The implication here is that the patient's disappointment and his resignation to it were not unrelated to his sudden downhill course and his death soon afterward, that is, if his son had come to take him out for Thanksgiving, the old man would have lived considerably longer than he did. This man's death like some others—voodoo deaths, unexplained deaths under anesthesia, and self-fulfilling prophecy deaths, for example—must be considered subintentioned. There can be little doubt that often some connection exists between the psychology of the individual and the time of his death (Shneidman, 1963).

There is, of course, a wide spectrum of applicability of this concept. When a person has been literally scared to death by his belief in the power of voodoo, the role of the victim's psychological state seems fairly obvious; and it is difficult to believe that there was no psychological connection between the fatal stroke of Mrs. Loree Bailey, owner of the Lorraine Motel in Memphis, and the assassination of Martin Luther King, Jr., at the motel 3 hours earlier. But in many other cases any relationship between the individual's psychological state and the time of his death seems difficult or impossible to establish.

As an example of the problems raised by this concept, consider the following case, reported in the *New York Times* of June 26, 1968:

WIDOW, 104, DIES IN COTTAGE
SHE ENTERED AS 1887 BRIDE

> Mrs. John Charles Dalrymple, 104 years old, died here [Randolph Township, New Jersey] yesterday in the cottage to which she came as a bride in 1887.
>
> Her husband brought her in a sleigh to the house, which she was to leave next week to make way for the new Morris County Community College. . . .

The main question here, as in Weisman and Kastenbaum's case of the old man who was left alone on Thanksgiving, is: might even this person have lived at least a little longer had she not suffered the psychologically traumatic threat of being dispossessed from the home where she had lived for eighty-one years? Or does the question in this particular case tax one's common-sense credulity?

3. *What is the most probable mode of death?* This was the question to which the psychological autopsy was initially addressed. When cause of death can be clearly established but mode of death is equivocal, the purpose of the psychological autopsy is to establish the mode of death with as great a degree of accuracy as possible.

The typical coroner's office, whether headed by a medical examiner or by a lay coroner, is more likely to be accurate in its certification of natural and accidental deaths than of those deaths that might be suicides. Curphey (1961) says, "A major reason for this, of course, is that both the pathologist and the lay investigator lack sufficient training in the field of human behavior to be able to estimate with any fair degree of accuracy the mental processes of the victim likely to lead to suicidal death. It is here that the social scientists, with their special skills in human behavior, can offer us much valuable assistance" (p. 112).

The professional personnel who constitute a death investigation team obviously should hold no brief for one particular mode of death over any other. In essence, the members of the death investigation team interview persons who knew the deceased—and attempt to reconstruct his lifestyle, focusing particularly on the period just prior to his death. If the information they receive contains any clues pointing to suicide, their especially attuned ears will recognize them. They listen for any overt or covert communications that might illuminate the decedent's role (if any) in his own demise. They then make a reasoned extrapolation of the victim's intention and behavior over the days and minutes preceding his death, using all the information they have obtained.

☐ Conducting the Psychological Autopsy

How is a psychological autopsy performed? It is done by talking to some key persons—spouse, lover, parent, grown child, friend, colleague, physician, supervisor, coworker—who knew the decedent. The talking to is done gently, a mixture of conversation, interview, emotional support, general questions, and a good deal of listening. I always telephone and then go out to the home. After rapport is established, a good general opening question might be: "Please tell me, what was he (she) like?" Sometimes clothes and material possessions are looked at, photographs shown, and even diaries and correspondence shared. (On one occasion, the widow showed me her late husband's suicide note—which she had hidden from the police!—rather changing the equivocal nature of the death.)

In general, I do not have a fixed outline in mind while conducting a psychological autopsy, but, inasmuch as outlines have been requested from time to time, one is presented below with the dual cautions that it should not be followed slavishly and that the investigator should be ever mindful that he may be asking questions that are very painful to people in an obvious grief-laden situation. The person who conducts a psychological autopsy should participate, as far as he is genuinely able, in the anguish of the bereaved person and should always do his work with the mental health of the survivors in mind.

Here, then, are some categories that might be included in a psychological autopsy (Shneidman, 1969):

1. Information identifying victim (name, age, address, marital status, religious practices, occupation, and other details)
2. Details of the death (including the cause or method and other pertinent details)
3. Brief outline of victim's history (siblings, marriage, medical illnesses, medical treatment, psychotherapy, suicide attempts)
4. Death history of victim's family (suicides, cancer, other fatal illnesses, ages at death, and other details)
5. Description of the personality and life-style of the victim
6. Victim's typical patterns of reaction to stress, emotional upsets, and periods of disequilibrium
7. Any recent—from last few days to last twelve months—upsets, pressures, tensions, or anticipations of trouble
8. Role of alcohol or drugs in (a) overall life-style of victim, and (b) his death
9. Nature of victim's interpersonal relationships (including those with physicians)

10. Fantasies, dreams, thoughts, premonitions, or fear of victim relating to death, accident, or suicide
11. *Changes* in the victim before death (of habits, hobbies, eating, sexual patterns, and other life routines)
12. Information relating to the "life side" of victim (up-swings, successes, plans)
13. Assessment of intention, that is, role of the victim in his own demise
14. Rating of lethality (described in the final section of this chapter)
15. Reaction of informants to victim's death
16. Comments, special features, and so on.

In conducting the interviews during a psychological autopsy, it is often best to ask open-ended questions that permit the respondent to associate to relevant details without being made painfully aware of the specific interests of the questioner. As an example: I might be very interested in knowing whether or not there was a change (specifically, a recent sharp decline) in the decedent's eating habits. Rather than ask directly, "Did his appetite drop recently?" a question almost calculated to elicit a defensive response, I have asked a more general question such as, "Did he have any favorite foods?" Obviously, my interest is not to learn what foods he preferred. Not atypically, the respondent will tell me what the decedent's favorite foods were and then go on to talk about recent changes in his eating habits—"Nothing I fixed for him seemed to please him"—and even proceed to relate other recent changes, such as changing patterns in social or sexual or recreational habits, changes which diagnostically would seem to be related to a dysphoric person, not inconsistent with a suicidal or subintentioned death.

In relation to a barbiturate death where the mode of death is equivocal (between suicide and accident), it might be callous to ask the next of kin, "Did your husband (wife) have a history of taking barbiturates?" A more respectful and productive question might be, "Did he (she) take occasional medication to help him (her) sleep at night?" If the response to this question is in the affirmative, one might then ask if the respondent knows the name of the medication or even the shape and color of the medication. If one determines that the deceased in fact had a history of taking sleeping medication, one might then ask if the decedent was accustomed to having some occasional alcoholic beverages prior to going to sleep. If these facts can be brought into the open, it may well be that one can then establish the quantity of the medication and alcohol content that the decedent was taking immediately prior to his death. The general method of questioning is one of "successive approaches," wherein the respondent's willingness to answer one question gives permission to ask the next one. That is the general way that one would inquire, if it were relevant, into, say, drug patterns of behavior. Where suicide or homicide is a possible mode of death, it is rather important to know whether or not the decedent was into drugs, a habitual user, or a dealer, on what terms he was with his dealer, and so forth.

☐ Functions of the Psychological Autopsy

The questions should be as detailed (and lines of inquiry pursued) only as they bear on clarifying the mode of death. All else would seem to be extraneous. And to do this depends, of course, on having established rapport with the respondent.

The results of these interviewing procedures are then discussed with the chief medical examiner or coroner. Because it is his responsibility to indicate (or amend) the mode of death, all available psychological information should be included in the total data at his disposal. Since a sizable percentage of deaths are equivocal as to mode precisely because these psychological factors are unknown, medical examiners and coroners throughout the country are robbing themselves of important information when they fail to employ the special skills of the behavioral scientists in cases of equivocal deaths. The skills of behavioral scientists should be employed in the same way as the skills of biochemists, toxicologists, histologists, microscopists, and other physical scientists. The time has long since passed when we could enjoy the luxury of disregarding the basic teachings of twentieth century psychodynamic psychology and psychiatry. Certification procedures (and the death certificates on which they are recorded) should reflect the role of the decedent in his own demise, and in equivocal cases this cannot be done without a psychological autopsy.

The retrospective analysis of deaths not only serves to increase the accuracy of certification (which is in the best interests of the overall mental health concerns of the community), but also has the heuristic function of providing the serious investigator with clues that he may then use to assess lethal intent in living persons.

And there is still another function that the psychological autopsy serves: In working with the bereaved survivors to elicit data relative to appropriate certification, a skillful and empathic investigator is able to conduct the interviews in such a way that they are of actual therapeutic value to the survivors. A psychological autopsy should never be conducted so that any aspect of it is iatrogenic. Commenting on this important mental health function of the psychological autopsy, Curphen (1961) has stated:

> The members of the death investigation team, because of their special skills, are alert in their interviews with survivors to evidences of extreme guilt, serious depression, and the need for special help in formulating plans for solving specific problems such as caring for children whose parents committed suicide. Since we noted this phenomenon, the coroner's office has, in some few cases, referred distraught survivors of suicide victims to members of the team specifically for supportive interviews even when the suicidal mode of death was not in doubt. [p. 116]

This therapeutic work with the survivor-victims of a dire event is called *postvention* and has been presented in some detail elsewhere (Shneidman, 1967, 1971, 1973).

A large university hospital in the East (which has asked not to be identified, but to which I am appropriately beholden) conducts what they call "psychiatric inquests" on those (rare) occasions when a patient commits suicide or makes a serious suicide attempt. A staff psychiatrist, emphasizing the therapeutic aspects of the psychological autopsy procedure, stated that "the inquest is a kind of postvention, designed primarily for the benefit of a shocked and grieving staff." He stated further that, for them, there are essentially three main purposes of such a procedure: "(1) To review with those responsible for the patient, the status of the patient prior to the act, and to determine what course of clinical management would more likely have led to its anticipation and prevention; (2) To facilitate expression of feeling appropriate to the event on the part of staff members; and (3) To determine whether dissemination of the results of the inquest would serve an educational purpose, and arrange for this (e.g., grand rounds) when appropriate." Further, he states that these meetings "should be small enough to exclude those interested primarily in the sensational aspects of the event in question, and should include only those whose presence would serve one of the above purposes."

Following, reprinted with permission, are verbatim reports (except for a few minor changes to disguise identity) of two psychiatric inquests from that university hospital setting.

> **Case 1.** A 32-year-old male graduate student took his life by drug overdose. He had first been hospitalized in 1974 for treatment of strychnine poisoning and was discharged eight days later with a diagnosis of cyclothymic personality. He was readmitted late the same year with depression and paranoid delusions, both of which cleared rapidly on Triavil (a combination of the major tranquilizer-antipsychotic agent perphenazine– and the tricyclic antidepressant amitriptyline), was discharged after a two-week hospitalization, and was followed in the outpatient clinic by a resident who had undertaken his care only one week before the discharge date. Gradual improvement was reported, although the absence of the su-

pervisor (who was aware of the suicide risk and would have questioned termination of treatment) leaves the reported improvement open to question. Two months later the patient said that he had discontinued his medications because they slowed him down and that he was confident about his work, feeling well, and would not try suicide again. He was discharged from outpatient treatment at his request, with the assurance that he could call back if he needed further help. He did not contact the clinic again, but three days before his death called his faculty advisor, made accusations against a fellow graduate student, and requested a departmental inquiry. He was advised to go on a vacation but went instead to another city, where it was reported that he spent two days praying in a chapel, returned to his boardinghouse, ate supper, and took a fatal drug overdose. Those commenting on the case stressed the questionable aspects of taking at face value the statements of the patient which led to his discharge from the clinic. Furthermore, the patient sent out danger signals in his last call to his faculty advisor.

Case 2. An 18-year-old male patient spent three months on the child psychiatry service two years prior to committing suicide. He had been evaluated for a mild aortic stenosis about which he and his family were greatly concerned. During his first admission, he showed fragmentation, loose associations, grimacing, and bizarre movements. Within three months of treatment with haloperidol (a major tranquilizer with antipsychotic properties), milieu therapy, and psychotherapy, he improved enough for discharge to outpatient treatment. Haloperidol was discontinued three weeks prior to his discharge from the hospital. He was carried as an outpatient for six months. About a month prior to readmission looseness of associations and paranoid ideation recurred, and he was reported by his family to have wandered nude out of his house. His school performance declined, and he said he had strange thoughts and could not trust anyone. He refused to take the haloperidol which was again prescribed for him. Upon readmission to the hospital he appeared disorganized, suspicious, and regressed. Two months later he had improved sufficiently to warrant a reduction of the haloperidol which he had been given since admission, but he again regressed and was placed on higher doses of haloperidol by a staff supervisor. His bizarre behavior, open sexual advances to staff and patients, and age combined to necessitate a transfer to a ward where he could be more appropriately managed. There it was reported that he accepted seclusion when required, seemed to respond to medications, but was in general withdrawn and regressed. He was angry at his therapist, who had informed him of his departure some months hence, and on the day of his suicide made known a desire to cut off his penis. Later that day he struck an attendant, spent some time in seclusion, and shortly after his release from seclusion left the ward undetected and went to the tenth floor where, finding an unguarded window, he jumped to his death. After the event it was revealed in a patient meeting that he had informed another patient of his intention and had given away his radio. The discussion pointed out the strong suicide potential of young disturbed males, the risks of multiple therapists and multiple absences, the hazards of disagreement about diagnosis, prognosis, and treatment method.

☐ Suicide Statistics: Some Questions

In relation to suicide statistics in the United States, we know that accurate figures do not now exist. There is widespread confusion and considerable difference of interpretation as to how to classify deaths. For example, what is considered suicide in one locality is often reported as accidental death in another. The factors that determine decisions of coroners and medical examiners must be made clearly visible as attempts are made to develop criteria for gathering vital baseline data in the area of suicide.

There is an urgent need to explore and describe present practices of reporting suicides and the degree of consistency or inconsistency of such reporting in the United States. Until such information is obtained, it will be impossible to interpret the available statistics. The coroners and medical examiners are the keys to the meaningful reporting of statistics on suicide.

It is believed that it is of the highest priority that an investigation be focused around the following questions directly related to this problem:

1. What percentage of all deaths are autopsied?
2. Who, at present, are the certifying officials, officers, or agencies? Are these medical examiners, physicians in the community, sheriffs, coroners? How are they selected? How trained?
3. What are the present official criteria given to certifying officials in various jurisdictions to guide them in reporting a death as suicide?
4. What are the present actual practices of certifying officials in reporting suicidal deaths? To what extent are these practices consistent with or different from the official criteria?
5. By what actual processes do the certifying officials arrive at the decision to list a death as suicide?
6. How often are autopsies performed? Who determines when an autopsy is to be performed? Are the services of a toxicologist and biochemist available?
7. What percentage of deaths are seen as equivocal, or undetermined, or as a combination of two or more modes (for example, accident-suicide, undetermined)?
8. What are the criteria for special procedures in an equivocal death?
9. How much of the total investigation of a death is dependent upon the police reports? What is the relationship of the coroner's investigation to the local police department?

10. When, if ever, are behavioral or social scientists involved in the total investigatory procedure of a death?
11. What percentage of certifying officials in the United States are medically trained? Does medical training significantly influence the way in which deaths are reported?

From data dealing with these questions, based on appropriate sampling from regions and taking into account rural-urban differences, size of municipalities, and so on, appropriate agencies could then address themselves to a number of important general questions, including the following:

- What local, state, regional, or other differences emerge in the practices of reporting the various modes of death?
- What are the general implications from the data for the accuracy of present death statistics, especially the statistics for each separate mode?
- What suggestions can be made for improvement in conceptualization, practice, and training which point toward more accurate and meaningful reporting?

☐ Suggestions for the Conceptual Improvement of the Death Certificate

The current NASH classification of death grew out of a seventeenth century way of thinking about man (as a biological vessel who was subject to whims of fate) and tended to leave man himself out of his own death. Twentieth century psychology and psychiatry have attempted to put man—conscious and unconscious—back into his own life, including the way in which he dies. The NASH classification of modes of death is not only apsychological but it tends to emphasize relatively unimportant details. For example, it is essentially a matter of indifference to a human being whether a light fixture above him falls and he is invaded by a lethal chandelier (accidental mode), or someone about him coughs and he is invaded by a lethal virus (natural mode), or someone shoots a gun at him and he is invaded by a lethal bullet (homicidal mode), if the fact is that he does not wish (intention) any of these events to occur.

In order to avoid the inadequacies of this conceptual confusion, it has been proposed that all human deaths be classified among three types: intentioned, subintentioned, and unintentioned (Shneidman, 1963, 1973).

An *intentioned* death is any death in which the decedent plays a direct, conscious role in effecting his own demise. On the other hand, an *unin-*

tentioned death is any death, whatever its determined cause or apparent NASH mode, in which the decedent plays no effective role in effecting his own demise—where death is due entirely to independent physical trauma from without, or to nonpsychologically laden biological failure from within.

But most importantly—and, in a fashion I believe to be characteristic of a sizable percentage of all deaths—*subintentioned* deaths are deaths in which the decedent plays some partial, covert, or unconscious role in hastening his own demise. The objective evidences of the presence of these roles lie in such behavioral manifestations as, for example, poor judgment, excessive risk-taking, abuse of alcohol, misuse of drugs, neglect of self, self-destructive style of life, disregard of prescribed lifesaving medical regimen, and so on, where the individual fosters, facilitates, exacerbates, or hastens the process of his dying.

That individuals may play an unconscious role in their own failures and act inimically to their own best welfare and even hasten their own deaths seems to be well documented in the psychoanalytic and general clinical practice. This concept of subintentioned death is similar, in some ways, to Karl Menninger's concepts of chronic, focal, and organic suicide (1938). Menninger's ideas relate to self-defeating ways of continuing to live, whereas the notion of subintentioned cessation is a description of a way of stopping the process of living. Included in this subintention category would be many patterns of mismanagement and brink-of-death living which result in death. In terms of the traditional classification of modes of death (natural, accidental, homicide, and suicide), some instances of all four types can be subsumed under this category, depending on the particular details of each case.

Confusion also discolors and obfuscates our thinking in the field of suicide. Currently there is much overattention paid to the categories of attempted, threatened, and committed suicide. These categories are confusing because they do not tell us with what intensity the impulse was felt or the deed was done. One can attempt to attempt, attempt to commit, or attempt to feign, and so on. One can threaten or attempt suicide at any level of intensity. What is needed is a dimension which cuts across these labels and permits us to evaluate the individual's drive to self-imposed death. We propose a dimension called *lethality,* defined as the probability of a specific individual's killing himself (i.e., ending up dead) in the immediate future (today, tomorrow, the next day—not next month). A measure of the lethality of any individual can be made at any given time. When we say that individual is suicidal we mean to convey the idea that he is experiencing an acute exacerbation (or heightening) of his lethality. All suicide attempts, suicide threats, and committed suicides should be rated for their lethality. The rule of thumb would be that beyond a certain point one must be wary of the danger of explosion into overt behavior.

What is suggested is that, *in addition* to the present NASH classification, each death certificate contain a new supplementary item which reflects the individual's lethality intent. This item might be labeled *Imputed Lethality* (recognizing its inferential character) and would consist of four terms, one of which would then be checked. The terms are: *High, Medium, Low, Absent,* and would be defined as follows.

High lethality: The decedent definitely wanted to die; the decedent played a direct conscious role in his own death; the death was due primarily to the decedent's openly conscious wish or desire to be dead, or to his (her) actions in carrying out that wish (e.g., jumping rather than falling or being pushed from a high place; he shot himself to death; he deliberately interrupted or refused lifesaving procedures or medical regimen).

Medium lethality: The decedent played an important role in effecting or hastening his own death. Death was due in some part to actions of the decedent in which he played some partial, covert, or unconscious role in hastening his own demise. The evidences for this lie in the decedent's behaviors, such as his carelessness, foolhardiness, neglect of self, imprudence, poor judgment, provoking others, disregard of prescribed lifesaving medical regimen, active resignation to death, mismanagement of drugs, abuse of alcohol, tempting fate, asking for trouble, and so on, where the decedent himself seemed to have fostered, facilitated, or hastened the process of his dying, or the date of his death.

Low lethality: The decedent played some small but not insignificant role in effecting or hastening his own demise. The same as medium above, but to a much lesser degree.

Absent lethality: The decedent played no role in effecting his own death. The death was due entirely to assault from outside the body (in a situation where the decedent played no role in causing this to happen), or death was due entirely to failure within the body (in a decedent who wished to continue to live).

The item on the certificate might look like this:

IMPUTED LETHALITY (Check One):
High Medium Low Absent
(See Instructions)

The reasons for advocating the suggestion are as follows: First, this classification permits reflection of the role that the dead individual played in his own dying, in hastening his own death; the ways in which he might have participated in his own death, and so on. Next it is more fair. At present, individuals of higher social status who commit suicide are more likely to be assigned the mode of accidental or natural death than are individuals of lower social status who no more evidently commit suicide. If the term is to have any meaning at all, it should be fairly used across the board, measured by the individual's intention. Finally, the lethality intention item provides an unexampled source of information by means of which biostatisticians, public health officials, and social scientists could assess the mental health of any community. It is obvious that the number of deaths that are caused, hoped for, or hastened by the decedents themselves is a measure of the prevalence of psychological disorder and social stress. At present we do not have this measure, and we need it.

It might be protested, inasmuch as the assessments of these intention states involve the appraisal of unconscious factors, that some workers (especially lay coroners) cannot legitimately be expected to make the kinds of psychological judgments required for this type of classification. To this, one answer would be that medical examiners and coroners throughout the country are making judgments of precisely this nature every day of the week. In the situation of evaluating a possible suicide, the coroner often acts (sometimes without realizing it) as psychiatrist and psychologist, and as both judge and jury in a quasi-judicial way. This is because certification of death as suicide does, willy-nilly, imply some judgments or reconstruction of the victim's motivation or intention. Making these judgments—perhaps more coroners ought to use the category of Undetermined—is a part of a coroner's function. But it might be far better if these psychological dimensions were explicit, and an attempt, albeit crude, made to use them, than to have these psychological dimensions employed in an implicit and unverbalized (yet operating) manner. The dilemma is between the polarities of the presently used oversimplified classification, on the one hand, and a somewhat more complex, but more meaningful classification, on the other. The goal should be to try to combine greatest usefulness with maximum meaningfulness.

In Marin County, California, the coroner's office assessed each death processed by that office in terms of *both* the traditional NASH classification of mode of death and the lethality intention of the decedent. For a two-year period, 1971–1972 (978 cases), the breakdown was as follows.[2]

Natural deaths (630): high lethality intent, none; medium lethality, 33 (5%); low, 37 (6%); absent, 560 (89%).

Accidental deaths (176): high lethality intent, 2 (1%); medium, 77 (44%); low, 40 (22%); absent, 57 (33%).

Suicidal deaths (131): high lethality intent, 131 (100%).

Homicidal deaths (37): high lethality intent, none; medium, 20 (54%); low, 9 (24%); absent, 8 (22%).

Four deaths were of unknown origin.

The first thing we notice is that *some* natural, accidental, and homicidal deaths were classified as having *some* degree of lethal intention. If the medium-intention and low-intention categories are combined, then over one-fourth (26%) of all natural, accidental, and homicidal deaths (216 in 843) were deemed to be *subintentioned.* If one then adds the suicidal deaths, in which the decedent has obviously played a role in his own death, then only 64 percent of all deaths (625 in 978) were deemed to have been totally adventitious; conversely, 36 percent were deemed to have had some psychological components.

Also of special interest in these Marin County data is the finding that coroners can, with apparently no more difficulty than they experience in assigning deaths to the NASH categories, simultaneously (and by essentially the same process of inference and induction) assign deaths to intentional categories as well. It is an important pioneer effort and deserves widespread emulation.

In summary, the following points may be emphasized:

Causes. The classification of causes of death has been rather well worked out and is consistent with contemporary knowledge. There is currently an international classification which has wide acceptance.

Modes. The modes of death have not been stated explicitly and have not been too well understood. In general, four currently implied modes of death—natural, accidental, suicidal, and homicidal—suffer from the important deficiency of viewing man as a vessel of the fates and omitting entirely his role in his own demise.

Intent. The addition of the dimension of lethal intention serves to modernize the death certificate, just as in the past, advances have been made from the teachings of bacteriology, surgery, anesthesiology, immunology, and so forth. The time is now long overdue for the introduction of the psychodynamics of death into the death certificate. The addition of a single item on imputed lethal intent (High, Medium, Low, Absent) would provide an appropriate reflection of the psychological state of the subject and begin, at last, to reflect the teachings of twentieth century psychology. In this way we might again permit the certification of death to reflect accurately our best current understanding of man.

☐ Endnotes

[1]See U.S .Standard Certificate of Death, Figure 1.

[2]I am especially grateful to Keith C. Craig, coroner's deputy, Marin County, California, for his interest and help in supplying these data.

References

Abbott, S. W. (1901). Death certification. In A. H. Buck (Ed.), *Reference handbook of the medical sciences.* New York: William Wood.

Cassedy, J. H. (1969). *Demography in early America.* Cambridge, MA: Harvard University Press.

Colby, M. (1965). The significance, evolution, and implementation of standard certificates. *American Journal of Public Health, 55,* 596–599.

Curphey, T. J. (1961). The role of the social scientist in the medicolegal certification of death from suicide. In N. L. Farberow & E. S. Shneidman (Eds.), *The cry for help* (pp. 110–117). New York: McGraw-Hill.

Curphey, T. J. (1967). The forensic pathologist and the multidisciplinary approach to death. In E. S. Shneidman (Ed.), *Essays in self-destruction* (pp. 110–117). New York: Science House.

Hotchner, A. E. (1966). *Papa Hemingway: A personal memoir.* New York: Random House.

Kargon, R. (1963). John Graunt, Francis Bacon, and the royal society: the reception of statistics. *Journal of Historical Medicine, 18,* 337–348.

Litman, R. E., Curphey, T. J., Shneidman, E. S., et al. (1963). Investigations of equivocal suicides. *Journal of the American Medical Association, 184,* 924–929.

Menninger, K. A. (1938). *Man against himself.* New York: Harcourt, Brace.

National Center for Health Statistics (1965a). Mortality trends in the United States, 1954–1963. *Vital and Health Statistics.* PHS Pub. No. 1000. Series 20. No. 2. Public Health Service. Washington, DC: U.S. Government Printing Office.

National Center for Health Statistics (1965b). Report of the U.S. delegation to the International Conference for the Eighth Revision of the International Classification of Diseases, Geneva, Switzerland, July 6–12. *Vital and Health Statistics.* PHS Pub. No. 1000. Series 4. No. 6. Public Health Service. Washington, DC: U.S. Government Printing Office.

National Center for Health Statistics (1967). *Eighth Revision International Classification of Diseases, Adapted for Use in the United States.* PHS Pub. No. 1693. Public Health Service, Washington, DC: U.S. Government Printing Office.

Rogow, A. A. (1963). *James Forrestal: A study of personality, politics and policy.* Los Angeles: Boulevard Bookshop.

Shneidman, E. S. (1963). Orientations toward death: A vital aspect of the study of lives. In Robert W. White (Ed.), *The study of lives* (pp. 200–227). New York: Atherton.

Shneidman, E. S. (1967). Sleep and self-destruction: A phenomenological study. In E. S. Shneidman (Ed.), *Essays in self-destruction* (pp. 510–539). New York: Science House.

Shneidman, E. S. (1969). Suicide, lethality, and the psychological autopsy. In E. S. Shneidman & M. Ortega (Eds.), *Aspects of Depression* (pp. 225–250). Boston: Little, Brown.

Shneidman, E. S. (1971). Prevention, intervention, and postvention of suicide. *Annals of Internal Medicine, 75,* 453–458.

Shneidman, E. S. & Farberow, N. L. (1961). Sample investigations of equivocal deaths. In N. L. Farberow & E. S. Shneidman (Eds.), *The cry for help.* New York: McGraw-Hill.

Weisman, A. D. (1974). *The realization of death: A guide for the psychological autopsy.* New York: Behavioral Publications.

Weisman, A. D., & Kastenbaum, R. (1968). The psychological autopsy. *Community Mental Health Journal Monograph No. 4.* New York: Behavioral Publications.

Wertenbaker, L. T. (1957), *Death of a man.* New York: Random House.

World Health Organization (1957). *Manual of the International Statistical Classification of Diseases, Injuries, and Causes of Death.* Based on the Recommendations of the Seventh Revision Conference, 1955. Geneva: World Health Organization.

31

CHAPTER

Comment: The Psychological Autopsy

I wish to make some comments relative to the report of the USS *Iowa* incident (Poythress, Otto, Darkes, & Starr, 1993).

In general, it can be said that there are four kinds of death investigations: the medical autopsy, the forensic investigation, the statistical or demographic report, and the psychological autopsy. Unfortunately, the forensic investigation and the statistical report are often confused with (or passed off as) a psychological autopsy. A brief description of each type of death-follow-up procedure might be useful.

1. Autopsy. The autopsy involves inspection and partial dissection of a dead body to learn the cause of death, the nature and extent of disease, and where possible, the mode of death. It is an examination by a physician–pathologist (and ancillary personnel). It is objective; it reports the facts—the weight of the brain, alcohol content of the blood, appearance of the liver, and so forth. The pathologist acts as an amicus curiae, specifically as a friend to the state, reporting the findings concerning a particular dead person for public and archival record. The autopsy is not adversarial; it does not pull for one particular mode of death over another or for the indictment of a particular individual.

2. Forensic investigation. The forensic investigation relates to the physical evidence surrounding the death. It may include a plethora

---

Reprinted from *American Psychologist*, 1994, *39*, 75–76. With permission.

of relevant details: windows open, doors locked, trajectory of bullets, powder marks, fingerprints, handwriting analyses, personal documents (suicide notes, threatening letters, cashed checks, etc.). Although these facts can be centrally relevant in either criminal or civil cases and need to be done as thoroughly as possible, a report of forensic details is, of course, not an autopsy at all—and certainly not a psychological autopsy—but an *investigation.* Often these investigations in civil suits, conducted as they are in an adversarial situation and paid for by one side or another, are "gumshoe" investigations, contaminated by conscious or unconscious bias, in which data are sometimes selectively reported or even deliberately perverted.

3. Statistical or demographic reports. If one is interested in, for example, the prevention of suicide, then it is obvious that knowledge of past patterns of behavior of individuals who have committed suicide can be a useful tool. These patterns might be called *prodromal indices* or *premonitory signs.* They make up the now well-known "clues to suicide" (Shneidman & Farberow, 1957). What may not be so obvious is that the statistical truths about a large number of committed suicides do not necessarily tell us anything about any particular case. The frequent error in this field is to confuse statistics with individual events and then to argue that because this individual does (or does not) have certain desiderata characteristic of a group, suicide must have (or must not have) occurred. Statistics are made up of individual cases; an individual case is not controlled by statistics. To argue from statistics to an individual case is a tyro's error. An example from my experience: In a recent criminal case (in which a man was accused of murdering his wife) the "expert witness" for the prosecution seriously argued that the wife could not have committed suicide because she was in the nude, and there was no record in his jurisdiction of a woman (in that age range) committing suicide whilst nude; hence, the husband must be guilty of homicide (Shneidman, 1993b). One must be on the alert for this kind of reverse reasoning. In any event, the citation of statistical and demographic data, even when cogent and sensible, is clearly not a psychological autopsy—although it was so asserted in the case cited above.

4. Psychological autopsy. The clarification of the mode—natural, accident, suicide, homicide—of some deaths devolves on the *intention* of the decedent in relation to the death (suicide, by definition, is an intentioned death). The psychological autopsy was devised to assist certifying officials to clarify deaths that were initially ambiguous, uncertain or equivocal as to the mode of death (Curphey, 1961; Litman, Curphey, Shneidman, Farberow, & Tabachnick, 1963; Shneidman, 1969, 1973, 1977, 1993b). A psychological autopsy is a consultation to the chief medical examiner,

coroner, or certifying official. It should be as objective as an autopsy. It is something of a contradiction to talk about an adversarial psychological autopsy that, for example, interviews the survivors on only one side of a litigation or has a monetary or an ego-centered stake in one outcome or another. Simply put, the psychological autopsy seeks to make a reasonable determination of what was in the mind of the decedent vis-à-vis his or her own death. It does this by looking at lifestyle, behavioral history, as well as the characterogical elements that contribute to that history: the degree of ambivalence, the clarity of cognitive functioning, the amount of organization or obsession, the state of turmoil or agitation, and the amount of psychic pain (Shneidman, 1993a). A psychological autopsy is a behavioral science impartial investigation of the psychological (motivational, intentional) aspects of a particular death. It legitimately conducts interviews (with a variety of people who knew the decedent) and examines personal documents (suicide notes, diaries, and letters) and other materials (including the autopsy and police reports) that are relevant to the *psychological* assessment of the dead individual's role in the death. Often the results cannot be stated with certainty. The psychological autopsy is not a gumshoe operation. I believe that a detective, a prosecutor, or a "hired gun" psychologist (or psychiatrist) cannot properly conduct a psychological autopsy. In the recent past, regrettably, we have seen misrepresentations of the psychological autopsy procedure by avid expert witnesses who seek to cloak themselves with the honorific aura of an impartial procedure. The court or the attorneys have a responsibility to clarify what the psychological autopsy procedure actually is before anyone involved in the courtroom proceedings is permitted to claim that it has been used.

☐ References

APA's expert panel in the congressional review of the USS *Iowa* incident. *American Psychologist, 48,* 8–15.

Curphey, T. J. (1961). The role of the social scientist in the certification of death by suicide. In E. Shneidman & N. Farberow (Eds.), *The cry for help* (pp. 110–117). New York: McGraw-Hill.

Litman, R. E., Curphey, T. J., Shneidman, E., Farberow, N., & N. Tabachnick. (1963). Investigations of equivocal suicides. *Journal of the American Medical Association, 184,* 924–929.

Poythress, M., Otto, R. K., Darkes, J., & Starr, L. (1993). *American Psychologist, 48,* 8–15.

Shneidman, E. (1969). Suicide, lethality, and the psychological autopsy. In E. Shneidman & M. Ortega (Eds.), *Aspects of depression.* (pp. 225–250). Boston: Little, Brown.

Shneidman, E. (1973). *Deaths of man.* New York: Quadrangle.

Shneidman, E. (1977). The psychological autopsy. In L. A. Gottschalk, F. L. McGuire, E. C. Dinovo, H. Birch, & J. F. Heiser (Eds.), *Guide to the investigation and reporting of drug-abuse deaths* (pp. 42–56). Washington, DC: U.S. Department of Health, Education and Welfare.

Shneidman, E. (1993a). Suicide as psychache. *Journal of Nervous and Mental Disease, 181,* 147–149.

Shneidman, E. (1993b). *Suicide as psychache.* Northvale, NJ: Jason Aronson.

Shneidman, E., & Farberow, N. (Eds.). (1957). *The cry for help.* New York: McGraw-Hill.

32

CHAPTER

An Example of an Equivocal Death Clarified in a Court of Law

☐ Prefatory Note

This chapter is an illustration of the principle of *res ipsa loquitur:* "The facts speak for themselves." In this chapter the documents—investigation reports, consultation reports, newspaper accounts, court testimony, letters—speak for themselves and convey their messages directly to the reader. In this sense, I hardly wrote this chapter; I merely assembled it. In this fascinating case, I was not so much the author as I was the amanuensis.

In all that follows, only the names of the attorney, Mr. Dan R. Hyatt, the consultant psychiatrist, Jerone A. Motto, M.D., and my own name are real. The others are fictitious. Also, all dates, places, and other identifying demographic details have been changed. I have obtained permission from the principal parties of the defense to write this account, and they have seen this text before it was printed.

Reprinted from *Suicide as Psychache*. Northvale: Jason Aronson, Inc., 1993, pp. 211–246. With permission.

The Charge

A few years ago I received a long-distance telephone call from an attorney asking me if I might be interested to help in a court-martial case involving an army officer who had been charged with murdering his wife. The attorney's lucid presentation of the tenuous and questionable details in the official charges led me to agree, then and there, to testify for the defense. I shall begin by reproducing a local newspaper account—which I did not see until some time afterwards—which sets forth the serious charges brought against the officer.

CAPTAIN CHARGED IN DEATH

ARMYVILLE, Sept. 22—A five-man court-martial panel was seated Wednesday in the trial of an army officer who is accused of slaying his wife in their Armyville apartment last July.

Capt. Joseph P. Campbell, 33, is charged with premeditated murder in the shooting death of Peggy Scott-Campbell on July 12. The 30-year-old woman was killed by a single blast from a 12-gauge pump shotgun.

The case, being heard before Judge (Col.) George D. Maris, is expected to last two weeks and involve dozens of witnesses and a trip to Los Angeles to hear testimony from an expert on suicide.

In his opening statement, Dan R. Hyatt, a civilian attorney who is representing Campbell, said he would prove that Scott-Campbell had suicidal tendencies. Also representing Campbell is Maj. James Purdich.

Prosecuting attorney Maj. Stanley Bates told the panel that the Campbells, who had been married about five years, were having marital problems and had discussed separation and divorce only hours before the shooting.

Bates said he would present evidence to show that following the argument, Scott-Campbell went to a nearby pizzeria where she was well known. She stayed late, he said, to help with the dishes. She left for home, but returned a few minutes later, telling the owner she had too much to drink. She asked that a cab be summoned to take her back to the couple's apartment.

Bates said he would introduce evidence that would indicate that Campbell beat her after she returned home and cut her five times with a knife. Bates told the court that Campbell later retrieved a shotgun from the bedroom, took her into the bathroom near the living room, and shot her in the chest.

Campbell woke up a neighbor and told him his wife had shot herself, Bates told the court.

In his opening statement, Hyatt said Scott-Campbell had made several prior suicide attempts. On the night she died, he said, Campbell had awakened to find her in the bathroom shower stall cutting her abdomen with a knife. His shotgun was sitting nearby, Hyatt said.

> He said that when Campbell attempted to move the shotgun she grabbed the barrel with her right hand and pulled it toward her. The gun discharged.
>
> Hyatt challenged the prosecution to prove that Campbell beat his wife. No witnesses, he said, ever saw Campbell strike his wife, although the bruises noted in the autopsy of the 130-pound woman could not be accounted for, he said.
>
> Hyatt termed the cuts on Scott-Campbell's body as "hesitation marks" and said a doctor would testify that such marks are often inflicted by suicide-prone people.
>
> "Why should he (Campbell) shoot his wife intentionally when she was trying to commit suicide?" Hyatt asked during his opening remarks.
>
> Prosecutors told the court that the case would be based on circumstantial evidence from investigators and forensic experts.

In summary, the events were as follows: Peggy Scott-Campbell, age 30, is dead as a result of a shotgun wound to her chest. Her husband, army Capt. Joseph Campbell, age 33, asserts that the gun was accidentally discharged as he sought to take it from his wife who was in the process of attempting suicide by cutting herself in the abdomen (while seated in the shower of their apartment bathroom). The government charges that, following a domestic quarrel, he willfully murdered his wife by deliberately shooting her and then cutting her abdomen to make the event appear like a suicide attempt. He is being tried by a court-martial.

The Issues

To either the ordinary observer or the trained investigator, the nature or mode of a death is usually self-evident. Each death falls into one of four modes: natural, accidental, suicide, or homicide (NASH). In some cases, however, the mode of death is not so clear; it is equivocal. Then what usually occurs is a more intensive investigation of the physical evidence of the case, including fingerprints, toxicological reports, and so forth. But sometimes the designation of the correct mode of death depends not on the physical evidence but on what the dead person had in mind. Did she take pills to die or just to sleep? Did he jump off the balcony, did he fall, or was he pushed? Did he mean to pull the trigger or was he just cleaning his gun? You can see that one has to distinguish between an investigation of the physical evidence in a case as opposed to a psychological investigation that focuses on the decedent's *intentions* vis-à-vis his or her own death. We shall be interested, in this case, to see whether or not the military investigator and the prosecuting attorney were able to make and maintain this distinction.

There is a further important distinction between a psychologically oriented report and a *psychological autopsy.* (Inasmuch as I coined the phrase "psychological autopsy," I feel that I am entitled to help define it).

The next section of this chapter contains the "Pre-Trial Report of the Military Special Investigator." In the first paragraph of that report, the investigator states: "This is in part a psychological autopsy because it attempts to use pertinent background information to arrive at an understanding of deceased's state of mind at the time of her death." Here, at the outset, he confuses a psychologically slanted report with a psychological autopsy. (This is only the first of several serious errors in this flawed report.) His report is *not* a psychological autopsy. He misunderstands what a psychological autopsy is.

A psychological autopsy is neither a procedure done exclusively from police or medical records nor a procedure conducted in an adversarial situation (where one sets out to prove one mode of death over another). A police officer or prosecutor cannot conduct a psychological autopsy. It would be as though one performed a physical autopsy with the bias of proving a homicidal mode of death, rather than ascertaining the facts and permitting those facts to lead one to an unbiased conclusion.

The psychological autopsy should always be done as an *amicus curiae,* specifically as an impartial consultant to the medical examiner-coroner. A hired gun cannot do it. The purported use of the psychological autopsy by either defense or prosecution in either criminal or civil trials is, as far as I can see, a misappropriation of the name of what is essentially a neutral scientific process, in which the self-announced expert witness tries to cloak himself with the honorific label of a procedure he did not conduct and probably does not understand.

The main function of the psychological autopsy (Curphey 1961, 1967; Clark and Horton-Deutsch 1992; Litman 1963; Shneidman 1969, 1973, 1977; Weisman 1974) is to clarify the *mode* of death in cases where the mode appears unclear. The usual uncertainties lie between suicide and accident. The logical setting for the psychological autopsy is the medical examiner-coroner's office where deaths are certified.

The psychological autopsy was developed in the late 1950s as a joint enterprise between the staff of the Los Angeles Suicide Prevention Center and Theodore J. Curphey, M.D., Chief Medical Examiner-Coroner of Los Angeles County. It was Dr. Curphey who recognized the direct relevance of behavioral science data in clarifying deaths that were equivocal as to mode. At his request, the LASPC assembled a multidisciplinary behavioral science team to conduct psychological autopsies of equivocal deaths.

By definition, the psychological autopsy focuses on the decedent's *intentions* in relation to his or her own death. By definition, all deaths, in addition to being classified in terms of the traditional NASH categories of death, may also be designated as intentioned, subintentioned, or unintentioned (Shneidman 1963, 1973). The psychological autopsy supplements the traditional autopsy, forensic findings, toxicological results, police reports, criminal investigations, and the like. It concentrates on the decedent's personality, character, behavior, history, habits, and self-destructive tendencies.

Putting the human drama aside, what we have in this case is a psychological enigma within a legal context. The goal is not only to establish what mode of death should appropriately be placed on the decedent's death certificate, but also (and primarily) to ascertain the guilt or innocence of an accused. In either way of conceptualizing this process, the issue is to rule out suicide and then render a decision between two modes of death: accident or homicide. If homicide, then there is a perpetrator and he should be punished; if accident, then there is no perpetrator and the individual accused in these proceedings is free of charges. The situation is made more complicated by the fact that the death in question occurred within a suicidal context, that is, the decedent was apparently attempting to take her own life (in an effort of unknown lethality) when the fatal event, homicide or accident, took place.

☐ Pre-trial Report of the Military Special Investigator

What follows in this section is a paraphrased and excerpted presentation of the "Report of Consultation in the Matter of Peggy Scott-Campbell (deceased) dependent wife of Capt. Joseph Campbell." The report was written by Perry N. Olds, a special agent of the Army Office of Special Investigation. The ten-page single-spaced typed report is divided into thirteen sections.

1. Introduction. This report was prepared for the Criminal Investigation Division to better understand the deceased's manner of death. The key issue is whether she was attempting suicide or whether she died from homicide that was subsequently reported otherwise. Materials used included photographs, witness statements, background information on both the decedent and the accused, correspondence, and so forth. The investigator states: "This is in part a psychological autopsy. . . ." (I have already commented on this in the section above.) The investigator indicates the number of violent deaths he has previously analyzed—approximately 1,000 suicides and 460 homicides.

2. Location and Date of the Incident. The date, time, and place of the event are indicated. Neighbor's names—all Army officers—are indicated.

3. The Presenting Event. Witnesses stated that around 3:00 AM on the given date, Captain Campbell went to his neighbors and is reported to have said: "Peggy was hurt and he needed me to call an ambulance." "Peggy had tried to kill herself." "Peggy had shot herself." A neighbor ran to Campbell's place, where he found the deceased lying on the floor between the couch and the bathroom door. He could not detect a pulse. An ambulance was called. Medical and law enforcement personnel arrived soon thereafter.

4. The Initial Story by Captain Campbell. Witness reported that when Campbell came to his door, his eyes were red, he was crying and seemed confused. Another witness reported that Campbell said that Peggy "was trying to cut herself up" and he tried to get the shotgun (which she had put there by the shower stall) away from her, but "she grabbed it and pointed it toward herself and it went off."

During those early morning hours, after the death, Campbell told a military investigator about the events early that afternoon and evening. When he returned home in the late afternoon she was drinking a beer. She had spent the day watching rented videos. He prepared a barbecue while she continued watching TV. After eating, they watched some TV and played a computer game. While playing she drank some brandy and began to get intoxicated. She became angry with him and turned the computer off. He calmed her down and they talked about how they were not getting along. She told him that she felt trapped and wanted to return to school.

Around 10 P.M. he said he was tired and wanted to go to bed. She announced she was going out to a pizza parlor (which was a favorite place of hers). Some hours later, around 1 A.M., she returned. He did not want to get up, but she pulled the sheets off him. He then got up and went into the living room. It was obvious that she had been drinking. He then went back to bed. A little later he heard her talking to herself. He got up to see what was happening. He looked through the house and saw the light in the bathroom. When he opened the bathroom door he saw her sitting in the shower stall. He noticed a cut on her abdomen and blood in the shower basin. He also noticed his shotgun. It was propped up against the shower ledge. When he tried to reach for the shotgun she grabbed it by the barrel, and, as she pulled the gun toward herself, it discharged.

Campbell took the shotgun into the living room, put it down by the couch, and ran next door, where he told his neighbors that he needed help. He then ran back to his house and moved Peggy from the shower stall to the living room, where he placed her on the floor. The gun was in the way, so he took it back to the back room. By this time, neighbors were attempting first aid on Peggy. The ambulance had been called. A neighbor suggested he step aside. He went into his bedroom where he changed his bloodsoaked shirt and pants.

5. The Crime Scene. The criminal investigation agents reported the crime scene as "a real mess." In the bedroom the agents observed what they believed to be bloodstains on the pillows, on the bedspread, on the fitted (bottom) sheet, and on the wall next to the bed. They also reported some damp washcloths with blood on the floor. In addition, they reported finding a trail of blood from the bedroom into the bathroom, and what they called "drag bloodstains" from the bedroom to the living room. They reported finding blood in places where Campbell denied having been subsequent to his contact with his wife's blood.

6. The Autopsy. An autopsy of the deceased was conducted by a forensic pathologist. He reported a number of findings, including a contact shotgun wound, which would indicate that the barrel was against her skin. The direction of fire was approximately level. On her lower abdomen there were four stab wounds. One of the cuts had numerous pricks around it. These the autopsy surgeon indicated might have been caused by "taunting" (tentative cuts on the body before a deep cut is made). In addition, there were multiple bruises on the extremities and the back of her head. He identified sixty bruised areas, with a majority being less than four hours old at the time of her death. There was a bruise on her chin. He also noted scars on both wrists and in each elbow. He reported her blood alcohol level was .10—actually it turned out to be .17—and no other drugs in her body. "The manner of death was ruled homicide."

7. Victimology. The following information is given in this section: the place and date of the decedent's birth. There are indications that she had a somewhat dysfunctional childhood. Her stepfather describes her as "rebellious," "subject to mood swings," "high-strung," "unhappy," and stated that she had made several suicide attempts. Her military medical records indicate "a history of affective disorders since her early adolescence." Her symptoms reportedly included "severe dysphoria, sleep and appetite disturbance, tension and nervousness, irritability, anger with episodic aggression and suicidal ideation."

The marriage was apparently rocky. The stepfather reported that when alcohol was involved, "The situation could become very violent." For the three months preceding her death, Peggy had been seen by a military clinical psychologist for complaints of depression and stress. The psychologist indicated that Peggy needed regular contact with psychiatric and psychological services for her mood swings and depressive episodes.

When her husband was away on military maneuvers—once for a period of three months—she volunteered at a military hospital, but reportedly became bored and lonely and drank heavily. After his return her drinking continued, and he reportedly drank (sometimes heavily) on the weekends and was reportedly hot-tempered when he drank.

8. Was Deceased Attempting Suicide on the Date of Her Death? The key question is whether or not Peggy was attempting suicide when her husband discovered her. Four issues will be addressed: her mental status on the evening of her death, the fact that she was nude at the time of her death, the use of multiple methods in a suicide attempt, and the nature and extent of her injuries.

9. Deceased's Mental Status. There is a history of affective disorder, somatic complaints, and alcohol abuse. On the date of her death, three facts are undisputed: that she was at home with her husband on the fateful afternoon and evening except for her visit to the pizza parlor; that she did leave her home that evening driving her own car, and that she returned in the small hours, brought by taxi; and that at the time of her death she was intoxicated. There is no indication that she was in a depressive mood swing during this period. Apparently the situation began to deteriorate when she became angry while they were playing a computer game in the early evening.

Would deceased have been sufficiently depressed to become suicidal? It seems unlikely that she was. She was unhappy in the marriage. It would not come as a surprise to her to be engaged with her husband in a discussion of the marriage and the possibility of their separating. This would argue against an impulsive suicide. In addition, a separation "would allow her to solve her problems." Based on all that is known . . . it is more likely that she would have been belligerent and hostile rather than retiring and self-punitive. In short, there is nothing to support a contention that she was in a mental state that would have led to self-destructive behavior; however, this remains an ambiguous issue.

10. Deceased's Nudity at the Time of Her Death. At the time of her death she was nude. What was the significance of this point? A review of 150-plus female active-duty and dependent suicides revealed none in which the person was nude at the time of her death. "Her reported nudity at the time she was reported to be attempting suicide is thus highly unusual and correspondingly improbable."

11. Multiple Methods. Suicides involving multiple methods—in this case, cutting and shooting—are not common. It does not make sense that she would have taken both the knife and the gun into the bathroom with her, "Because if she had set aside the plan to kill herself in favor of a gesture, then why take the shotgun?" "If she anticipated the cutting to fail even before doing it (hence taking the shotgun into the bathroom), why did she not just go ahead and shoot herself first without attempting to stab herself to death?"

12. The Nature and Extent of Her Injuries. According to military records, suicide by cutting is rare, and when it occurs the cuts are on the wrists or throat. "Multiple wounds to the abdomen are noteworthy by their absence." Furthermore, "The use of a shotgun is . . . relatively rare among women." The pathologist reported that the wound was a contact wound, which means that the barrel of the gun was pressed against her body. "The circumstances described by Captain Campbell make this highly improbable." Finally, the large number of fresh bruises on the deceased "clearly suggest aggressive contact within four hours of her death," something not accounted for by Campbell's report of the event.

13. Summary. "Taken in toto, Campbell's description of the fatal events appear to be contradicted by fact, logic, and probability. What is suggested is that on the evening (of the death), a violent contact occurred between deceased and Campbell during the course of which he shot her with the shotgun. The circumstances further suggest that following the shooting, Campbell placed deceased in the shower stall and staged the scene to conform to the story he intended to tell. He was favored in this design by virtue of her unstable personality and the fact that she had made suicide gestures in the past. Based on the foregoing, it is my professional opinion that Captain Joseph Campbell shot deceased with the shotgun and attempted to conceal the true facts of the event by staging the scene he subsequently reported."

/ signed /
Perry N. Olds
Special Agent
Office of Special Investigations
U.S. Army

Report of Psychiatric Consultant for the Defense

Captain Campbell's lawyer, Mr. Dan Hyatt, contacted two expert witnesses, Jerome A. Motto, M.D. and me. Dr. Motto is professor of psychiatry at the University of California at San Francisco and past president of the American Association of Suicidology. For a number of tactical and practical reasons, Dr. Motto did not testify in person at the trial—held in another state. However, in my court testimony, I alluded to his report and read portions of it into the record, so that in this way, it figured in the trial. It is presented here with a few elisions. I consider it a model consultation report.

Consultation Report

The problem at hand is the determination of the mode of death of Peggy Scott-Campbell. The question addressed is whether her death on July 23, 1990 was an accident in the course of thwarting her suicide attempt, or whether other issues played a role.

In order to form the basis for answering the question at hand, four preliminary questions are addressed: (1) Was Peggy Scott-Campbell the kind of person who would resort to suicide under adverse circumstances; (2) Was she being subjected to significant emotional stress at the time of her death; (3) Was there a precipitating event or circumstance that could reasonably have provoked a suicidal act at the time of her death; and (4) would Captain Campbell's character and behavior pattern be consistent with either premeditated or impulsive homicide?

1. Was she vulnerable to suicidal impulses or behavior? The record is very consistent as regards the emotional vulnerability of Mrs. Scott-Campbell. Her medical record indicates an ongoing affective disturbance since early adolescence. In 1984 she complained of severe dysphoria, anger with episodic aggressiveness, and suicidal thoughts. She was diagnosed at that time as suffering from a major depressive disorder with borderline personality traits. The recommendation that she have a psychiatric evaluation and follow-up treatment with anti-depressive medication was not implemented. Nor was the recommendation that she be seen for psychiatric and psychological treatment.

Mrs. Scott-Campbell is said to have exhibited outspoken suicidal behavior on at least four occasions. . . . These events are given varying dates by different informants, but the episodes themselves appear to be discrete and separate experiences. Some were related by Mrs. Scott-Campbell to confidants, and others are noted in Army medical records.

In addition to specific suicidal behaviors, there is virtual unanimity among those who knew her best that she was moody, emotionally volatile, prone to act impulsively and violently, and moved to intense feeling states by seemingly minor issues. The most provocative of these issues were apparently feelings of being criticized, ignored, or in some way devalued. Examples are numerous, such as Mrs. Scott-Campbell's own description (on tape) of the altercation with her friend Marlene, and the episode in which she is said to have kicked in the bathroom door after Capt. Campbell retreated there to escape her angry outburst.

2. Was she under significant emotional stress? Mrs. Scott-Campbell made no secret of her discontent with army life, with "not fitting in" with the separations entailed or with other army wives, or with the "homebody" nature of her husband, leading to repeated consideration of divorce. Her persistently heavy drinking underscored her inability to find a stable adjustment; at the same time she apparently felt guilty about her behavior. She was heard to repeat "I'm sorry—I'm sorry—" when in an intoxicated state. She confided that Captain Campbell treated her well and that she wanted to reward him with a party. Though emotionally very immature, she was intelligent enough to know that sooner or later her repeated drunkenness and violent outbursts would catch up with her—that it was only a matter of time, and that time might be getting short. For a person with intense rejection sensitivity, the threat of being abandoned would constitute an ever-increasing emotional pressure in addition to her underlying insecurity and dissatisfaction with her life.

3. Was there a precipitating event? A recurrent theme in the available data regarding Mrs. Scott-Campbell's behavior is the sequence of (1) argument, (2) withdrawal by Captain Campbell, (3) drinking by Peggy Scott-Campbell, (4) guilt, depression and contrition on the part of Mrs. Scott-Campbell. In one such previous sequence, Mrs. Scott-Campbell came home from a bar, told Captain Campbell she was going to cut her wrist, and when he tried to calm her down, she hit him with a chair. On the night of her death, this sequence seems to have been repeated. . . . Whatever the facts were, they went beyond the usual pattern of returning from a drinking episode feeling depressed, and calling someone to talk, or even making suicidal threats. Mrs. Scott-Campbell was unable to get Captain Campbell to respond to her that night, even to placate her, and combined with the progressive dissatisfaction of her life and the depression and guilt she was prone to express after drinking, this experience of "being ignored" could easily have triggered a characteristic violent act. In this instance the act was directed at herself, but her disorganization and ambivalence created only preparation for a lethal act (loaded gun, cutting of abdomen).

4. Would his character be consistent with homicide?

Any effort to determine the likelihood of a given behavior by a given individual must take into account that person's behavioral history, as well as the characterological elements that contribute to that history. In short, the best predictor of behavior is past behavior.

In Captain Campbell's case, those who knew him on a day-to-day basis could hardly be more consistent in their impressions: "loving and supportive," "good natured," "least prone to violence," "Violence is not in him. He is not capable of violence," "Absolutely no way he could have done anything to hurt Peggy," and the like.

While it appears to be sophisticated to be skeptical of such unequivocal statements, it is difficult to document contradictory evidence. Mrs. Scott-Campbell's multiple bruises are only a mild example of what one sees in chronic heavy drinkers, as falls and bumping into objects are so common. Even cracked ribs, severe facial bruises, and head trauma are not uncommon. She stated that some bruises on her arm were from his trying to stop her from swinging a broken glass at him. In short, Captain Campbell's apparent need to be protective of his wife under the most provocative conditions, and to reflect this demeanor toward the rest of the world as well, is a virtually unanimous perception, and the record gives us nothing substantial to question it.

Comment on report of Investigator Olds. Investigator Olds recapitulates the events surrounding Mrs. Scott-Campbell's background and death, and then asks whether she would have been "sufficiently depressed to become suicidal." The question is irrelevant. The nature of her pathology is not depressive but characterological. This is familiar to persons engaged in the field of suicide prevention, although lay persons and even some professionals continue to consider suicide a function of depression rather than psychological pain.

Investigator Olds's subsequent three questions are based on epidemiological comparisons that are interesting but likewise irrelevant. Though some of the numbers can be challenged, the most important issue in this analysis is that such issues as nudity, methods used, and the nature and extent of injury are unique to each individual. The degree of ambivalence, clarity of cognitive functioning, how organized and obsessive the individual is, his or her state of turmoil and agitation, and so forth, are the determinants of behavior. What another or a thousand others have done plays no essential role in understanding a given individual's behavior. In the present instance, an intoxicated, frustrated, angry, disorganized individual is involved. Trying to create a scientific aura by judging how common a given pattern appears is simply sophistry.

In short, I believe Investigator Olds's data are interesting, as is his discussion, but they are of no significance whatever in the individual instance under consideration. Thus an opinion based on such considerations is little more than speculation and fertile imagination.

Summary and Conclusions.

In summary, Mrs. Scott-Campbell was a person with a lifelong emotional vulnerability, manifested by extremes of reactivity, a very low threshold for psychic pain, and limited behavioral control. She required a great deal of emotional support and in its absence had repeatedly demonstrated a pattern of self-destructive behavior. In suicide prevention language, she would be regarded as "chronically suicidal," implying that even at her best level of functioning she was vulnerable to becoming suicidal in adverse circumstances, especially if a perceived rejection was involved.

Captain Campbell demonstrated an inexplicable ability, perhaps a need, to protect and nurture this emotionally vulnerable young woman. The record is replete with observations documenting his consistency in this regard. No evidence is available of traits that would contradict this.

The circumstances surrounding Mrs. Scott-Campbell's death are entirely consistent with her patterns of behavior and with Captain Campbell's efforts to protect her from her own lack of control. I find nothing in the record to indicate otherwise, and regard undocumented hypotheses to the contrary as speculative. Though the documented record can mislead us, I feel that it provides a better basis for sound judgment than hypotheses without documented support.

Jerome A. Motto, M.D.
Professor of Psychiatry
University of California, San Francisco

☐ Two Consecutive Newspaper Reports of the Trial

These two accounts were written on the second and third days of the court-martial and published (the following days) in the local newspaper.

Testimony Given in Trial

ARMYVILLE, September 23—Murder defendant Capt. Joseph P. Campbell lowered his head Thursday while a criminal investigation agent testified about photographs he took where Campbell's wife died last July.

Special Agent Jerome Beach took the photos shortly after the death of Peggy Scott-Campbell on July 26. The 30-year-old woman died in the couple's Armyville apartment from a single shotgun wound to the chest. Her husband is being charged with premeditated murder.

The trial, before Judge (Col.) George D. Maris entered its second day Thursday and is expected to last into next week.

The defense plans to argue that Scott-Campbell's death could have been an accident or suicide.

In opening statements Wednesday, Campbell's attorney, Dan Hyatt, told the five-man court-martial panel that Campbell was attempting to take the sawed-off shotgun from his wife when it accidentally discharged.

Two photos introduced Thursday by the prosecutor Major Stanley Bates showed a shower basin half filled with blood and water. The bathroom was next to the living room in the couple's apartment. The government also offered into evidence the death weapon, a 12-gauge shotgun, a blood-stained blue T-shirt worn by Campbell, and an empty liquor bottle found in the living room. Beach testified that an empty bottle of Ativan, an anti-anxiety drug similar to Valium, was found on the couple's living room table.

In an opening statement Wednesday, Hyatt said his client awoke in the early morning of July 23 to find his wife in the bathroom shower stall cutting her abdomen with a knife. A shotgun was sitting nearby.

Oscar Christol, a fingerprint expert for the U.S. Army Criminal Investigations Laboratory, testified that it could not be determined if Scott-Campbell could have grabbed the gun barrel.

Christol said that when he received the shotgun, its barrel and grip were covered with paper sacks. That preservation method could have destroyed a palm print, he said

In testimony late Wednesday, a key witness described Campbell as "a teddy bear."

"I have never seen him mad," said First Lieutenant William Lambert, referring to Campbell. "He was always telling jokes. He's the one who would always pick you up."

Lambert lived in the same apartment building where Scott-Campbell died. He testified that Campbell awakened him about 3 A.M. the night of the shooting.

"He was panicking," said Lambert, referring to the events of July 23. "He said, 'Peggy's hurt. Call an ambulance. She tried to kill herself.' "

Lambert testified that he accompanied Campbell to the couple's apartment, where he found the victim with a "quarter-sized hole in her chest." Lambert said he administered mouth-to-mouth resuscitation, but was unable to inflate the victim's lungs.

Lambert testified that Campbell, with the help of Captain Alice Adams, a friend of Lambert's, called an ambulance to the scene.

Later, Lambert testified, an emergency medical technician examined the victim and shook his head. Campbell then began crying, Lambert said.

Adams testified Wednesday that while waiting for the ambulance, Campbell told her that the weapon went off when he tried to pull the shotgun from his wife.

"I can't live without her. I can't believe my baby is gone," Adams said Campbell told her while waiting for the ambulance.

Antonio Mondello, owner of the pizzeria, testified Wednesday that Scott-Campbell, a regular customer, came into the restaurant, had several drinks, and left about 12:30 A.M.

"She was in an OK mood," Mondello testified. "She had a couple of beers."

The restaurant owner called for a taxi, he said. "She was the same old Peggy—cheerful. She helped me wash dishes," Mondello said.

Adams said that Scott-Campbell was in good spirits that evening and remembered her returning to the apartment building about 1 A.M.

"You could tell that she had been drinking," she said. "But she was in an OK mood and not angry."

Lambert testified that Campbell "appeared to be in shock" and "alternated from calm to crying," following the shooting.

According to Lambert, Campbell told him that he saw his wife holding a knife and the shotgun, and that he tried to take the shotgun away from her when it fired.

"He kept repeating, 'I did not murder her. I did not murder her,' " Lambert said.

Experts Testify in Trial

ARMYVILLE, Sept. 25—Two blood-spatter experts originally hired—but never called to testify—by the prosecution, testified late Thursday afternoon on behalf of an army officer accused of killing his wife last July.

Capt. Joseph P. Campbell, 33, is charged with premeditated murder in the July 23 death of Peggy Scott-Campbell. Scott-Campbell, 30, died in the couple's apartment from a single shotgun blast.

Leon Aron and Albert Hawkins, forensic blood-spatter specialists at the Minnesota State Crime Laboratory, testified that their analysis of bloodstains enabled them to reconstruct the shooting scene. They told the five-man court-martial panel that Campbell's statements to military investigators did not contradict their findings.

Campbell has maintained he awoke in the early hours of July 23 to find his wife in the bathroom shower, cutting her stomach with a knife. Witnesses testified earlier that Scott-Campbell had been drinking heavily that night. Campbell said he saw his 12-gauge pump shotgun nearby. Campbell told investigators he was attempting to remove the gun when his wife grabbed the barrel. It discharged, striking her in the chest.

Campbell told Criminal Investigation Command agents he carried her into the living room, put her on the floor behind the couch, then summoned help.

"There were no inconsistencies in what we read in (criminal Investigation Command) reports," Aron said.

Aron said he and his colleague used the bathroom in the couple's apartment to stage a reenactment of the shooting. Aron said they used Campbell's statements to investigators to determine if the physical positions that Campbell and his wife were purportedly in at the time of the shooting were possible.

Aron and Hawkins testified that events can often be reconstructed by analyzing the shape, size, and distribution of bloodstains. Aron said, however, they could not determine if the shooting was a homicide.

Aron and Hawkins were first hired by the prosecution, which believed that Scott-Campbell was shot in the couple's bedroom before her body was carried into the living room. No evidence has been offered during the trial to support that theory.

The prosecution, led by Major Stanley Bates, continued to call witnesses Friday. The case, which began Wednesday, is expected to wind up next week.

On Friday, prosecution witness Perry N. Olds, investigative consultant from the Office of Special Investigations in Washington, testified he found nude suicides highly unusual. Olds said suicides involving multiple methods like knife and gun were also uncommon.

Olds said he was drawing on data from other military suicide cases. Those cases include service members and dependents, he said.

Prosecution and defense attorneys were expected to fly Saturday to Los Angeles to take a deposition from Dr. Edwin Shneidman, founder of the American Association of Suicidology.

☐ A Letter from the Decedent's Mother

Here is an unsolicited letter to the court from the mother of the decedent—the mother-in-law of the man charged with murdering her daughter. What, offhand, would one expect to find in it? I cannot forbear commenting that it is one of the most extraordinary suicidological documents I have seen in my professional career.

To Whom It May Concern:

It is probably not necessary to state that I have spent hundreds of hours thinking about the tragedy of my daughter's death and how such a thing could have occurred. I have been extremely reluctant to put any kind of statement into words for two reasons: First, any comprehensive picture of my daughter would fill a novel, and second, due to the necessity of brevity, I am concerned that something I say might be taken out of context of the entire picture. I cannot, however, see Joe's life go down the drain without making a statement about how his account of that night could be true. I, of course, not having been there, cannot know for certain what is true, nor can anyone but Joe himself. There are, however, some facts which are pertinent to the possibility of the truth of his statements.

In taking Joe's scenario at face value, it is likely that he thought Peggy was actually attempting suicide. It is my opinion that it is more likely that she was making another plea for help, not seeking to actually die. She would have, at least, have left a note for her mother if she had actually intended death to result from her actions. She was seeking help (relief from her unceasing emotional pain) in some form which would not require hospitalization/lock-up. She had resisted all Joe's efforts to persuade her to seek professional help because of this fear of being locked up in a mental ward. The fear was not irrational. It came about because I had admitted her to the mental ward of a major medical hospital after a similar (but milder) "show" of suicide attempt when she was in her late teens.

Self-infliction of abdominal stab/slash wounds is a pretty dramatic and unusual method of gaining attention, however, each successive "plea" must be different and more dramatic than those preceding it, since said preceding attempts have obviously failed to bring relief. Peggy had a relatively high physical pain threshold, although low emotional pain threshold, which, together with the alcohol level and possibility of pills, could very well explain the bizarre nature of this particular plea for help.

It was very difficult for me to admit Peggy to the hospital that time they locked her up, and she was very angry with me for a long time. It was my thinking at the time that the experience would deter her from ever seeking attention in such a dangerous way again. In retrospect, she should have been referred for professional psychological counseling, not treated with fear tactics. This was not recommended nor done and the long-term result has been her subsequent unnecessary death and the possible complete ruin of her husband's life. I believe Joe loved her deeply and sought, to the best of his ability and knowledge, to help her and to protect her from herself.

Joe had no idea of the depth or duration of depression and social maladjustment with which he was attempting to deal. He knew only what she told him and what he, an untrained observer, could see for himself. She could not tell him what she did not herself know or understand. I myself, although I tried, was never able to understand what made her tick and I think it would have taken an extremely sensitive, experienced psychologist, with great gifts of insight and wisdom, to figure it out.

Joe's entire life is on the line here and, unless there's something significant I don't know, I think unfairly. He loved Peggy deeply. He put up with a great deal, and did it with unbelievable patience and acceptance. He stayed with her when any other man would have thrown his hands up in despair and walked out long ago. He gave her the only real happiness she ever had in her life. I think that frightened her. She could never understand how he could love her since she was never able to love herself, but

Joe saw, knew and loved the depth, intrinsic goodness, and love of all creation that was the true Peggy beneath the surface of terrible depression and inability to cope with life, with which she suffered her entire life. She had a desperate need to be loved and accepted because of her inability to understand her own self worth. She was convinced she wasn't worth loving. This is what made her go to such desperate measures to prove otherwise, at any cost. The cost was great indeed.

There is nothing that can bring my daughter back. The *only* solace is that she is at peace now in God's love—the first peace she has ever known. My sister wrote me that as she was praying her rosary, she felt Peggy's presence, bringing her an overwhelming sense of joy such as she had not felt in years. She said she thought that Peggy wanted to share *her* joy with us. I was very moved by this and, at first, concerned that I had not felt her presence. In thinking about it, I believe it is because I have not worked through my grief yet, particularly all the guilt I feel over what I might have done differently to have kept this terrible tragedy from happening. I have a lot of thinking and praying to do over this yet, but there is one thing I do know. I don't want to add a second tragedy to the oppressive burden of guilt I already have, and condemning Joseph unjustly for Peggy's death would do just that.

I, frankly, don't think there should even be a trial. I don't think Joe is guilty of anything except negligence in handling the gun in trying to take it away from her. It is regrettable and he knows better, but how many of us would have done any better under such circumstances? A larger negligence may have been in somehow not getting her professional help, or at least telling me of the seriousness of what was going on. I might have been able to discern the urgency of the situation and done something about it. Then again, I may not have understood the gravity at all. I'm sure Joe would have sought help if he had understood how serious the situation was becoming and the possible repercussions. Hindsight is always 20/20.

I have been under a great deal of pressure from my family not to get involved, to just "wait and see what happens." In fact, I just received a letter from my mother in which she clearly stated her feelings that to say anything in defense of Joe would be a betrayal of Peggy. So, against all advice and in the knowledge of possible repercussions, I am writing this letter for two reasons. First, I feel I know Joseph very well and I do not believe that he would hurt Peggy, let alone kill her, even in anger, *no matter what she had done.* I do not say this naively. I know they have gotten into it a few times, when both had been drinking, and there were some blows meted out from both sides. What I'm saying is that he could not coolly, maliciously hurt her. And the idea of premeditation is so preposterous as to not even be worthy of comment. Second, Peggy loved Joe very much, despite what she may have done that might make it appear otherwise. She was driven by emotional problems that were not her fault and which she could not control. I do not believe that Peggy would want Joe's life ruined. He has suffered enough already for any unwitting part he played in this tragedy. To lose his military career, for which he spent many years in preparation, is a severe blow. He has lost his wife he loved and misses her desperately. He is suffering untold pain from the guilt he feels over what he should or should not have done differently at the time, as well as not having somehow forced her to get help before it came to what it did. Is this not enough? I think it is.

Respectfully,
/ signed /
Maria E. Scott

☐ Excerpts from My Testimony, with Comments

The following is an excerpt of my responses to questions from Mr. Dan Hyatt, counsel for the defense.

Hyatt: *The army investigator, Mr. Olds, has testified earlier in this case. He offered an opinion that it was unusual to see two instrumentalities when either attempting or committing suicide. Do you have an opinion with respect to that statement?*

Ess: *Yes. In a picayune way he is right. But in an overall way he is howlingly wrong. I'll tell you about each of those if I may.*

Hyatt: *Please.*

Ess: *Suicide itself, fortunately, is an event of infrequent occurrence. So that you can make tabulations of methods and all sorts of things. A lot of events are infrequent, but if the incontrovertible evidence is that the person has done it, then you can't say that the person has not done it simply because it is infrequent. Using two methods is much more infrequent than using one. That's true. But then to argue from that to this particular case is a tyro's error. It's a mistake that freshmen, undergraduates in my Death and Suicide course at UCLA, make of going from statistics to an individual case. Statistics are an interesting background for a case but they don't tell you about that case. Here we are talking about this case.*

Hyatt: *Mr. Olds also testified that he thought it was very rare based on his study of army personnel and their dependents, his data base, that it was very rare to find a dependent female to commit suicide or attempt to commit suicide in the nude. Do you have an opinion about that?*

Ess: *Yes, Well, I would say to him, "That's true. That's absolutely true. But you're really not seriously making an argument that that has a bearing on this case, are you?" And if he said "Yes," my already low opinion of him would drop precipitously.*

Hyatt: *What value do you see of statistical information such as that offered by Mr. Olds in determining the cause of death?*

Ess: *In a particular case?*

Hyatt: *Yes.*

Ess: *None. It's background material.*

Hyatt: *Is the utilization of statistics in the manner testified to by Mr. Olds a scientifically acceptable method, or is that data reasonably relied upon by other experts in your field as a means of drawing a conclusion?*

Ess: *If your question is, is it a scientifically credited method the way he has done it, the answer is no.*

Hyatt: *And why would that be?*

Ess: *The technical response is that in these matters, in suicidology, the confusion of statistical-demographic-epidemiological-numerical data with the etiology or outcome of any particular individual case, to make a judgment about that individual case on the basis of statistics is a methodological error.*

Hyatt: *Why is it a methodological error?*

Ess: *Because it has things backwards. It isn't that the statistics generate the case; it is that the cases taken in long series or large numbers generate the statistics. To say that it is rare is not to say that it did not occur.*

Hyatt: *What do you say when you hear that Peggy Campbell was nude on the evening of her death?*

Ess: *I would say, "Gee whiz, isn't that unusual." But then to argue as he did that it couldn't be suicide on that account is a howler. It boggles the mind. Where did his logic go?*

Hyatt: *And would you have the same opinion as to the use of two instrumentalities?*

Ess: *Yes, sure. What is persuasive is the whole history of her lifetime. . . .*

My courtroom exchanges with Maj. Stanley Bates, the deposing counsel for the prosecution, had, in my mind, a somewhat eerie quality. Against all the evidence that I could see, he held firmly to the view that Captain Campbell had murdered his wife in the bedroom and dragged her body into the bathroom and then cut her abdomen to disguise the deed. He completely endorsed Mr. Olds's report—the heart of the prosecution's case. In addition, there was what seemed to me a mildly bizarre twist: He insisted on meeting with me privately before he cross-examined me. Mr. Hyatt and I acceded to this request. But in that private session, in response to a question from me about his marital status—I had said, "Tell me something about yourself," and instead of finessing or parrying my somewhat impertinent question, as I expected him to do, considering the circumstances—he told me about his recent divorce. He then pressed me to believe his view of the case. He seemed to be to be muddleheaded, not too well prepared, and curiously immature for an Adjutant General officer.

Back in the courtroom, I was not very sympathetic to his flawed view of the case. He saw the accused as guilty and wanted to convict him. But he had neither the facts on his side nor the tools in his head, but he had the fervor of his convictions and confusions. I could see him carrying contaminated water in some other cases, and that troubles me. Of course—as I have stated and implied in my testimony above—I consider Mr. Olds's crucial investigation report to be badly flawed, bordering on incompetence.

Here is a brief verbatim excerpt of the exchanges between Major Bates and me.

Bates: *For the record also, I would like to back up to where we started to do this. And I'll log an objection to this for the reasons that we've just discussed. Doctor, a physical autopsy is something that you make by gathering facts to render a professional judgment on the mode of death. Is that correct?*

Ess: *I beg your pardon. You said a physical autopsy.*

Bates: *No sir. I said a psychological autopsy.*

Ess: *No. For the record, you said physical, if I may say so.*

Bates: *My question is that is it your testimony that in a psychological autopsy you gather facts to make a professional judgment on the mode of death?*

Ess: *Yes.*

Bates: *And that psychological autopsies are sometimes undetermined?*

Ess: *Yes.*

Bates: *And that they can be an accurate determination of the mode of death?*

Ess: *I didn't hear you. Did you say accurate or inaccurate?*

Bates: *Can be an accurate determination of the mode of death.*

Ess: *Yes.*

Bates: *Is it your testimony that the psychological autopsy can always be correct?*

Ess: *No. It is just more information.*

Bates: *Would it be important to rely upon . . . strike that. Is it not important to have accurate facts in relying upon, to rely upon accurate facts to make a psychological autopsy?*

Ess: *Yes.*

Bates: *And if these facts were inaccurate, it could significantly affect the determination through the psychological autopsy?*

Ess: *Well, the psychological autopsy stands alongside the investigation of the physical facts. It doesn't rest upon them. I think that is part of the confusion here.*

Bates: *I would like to object at this point. And see if you can perhaps just answer the question. Would you like for me to restate it, sir?*

Hyatt: *What is the basis for your objection?*

Bates: *He's not answering the question.*

Ess: *Well, you don't understand the psychological autopsy, Major. You truly don't.*

Bates: *I would object to this also. Is it not important in making a psychological autopsy . . . I'll strike that. Doctor, did you generate a written report in this case?*

Ess: *No.*

☐ Additional Newspaper Accounts

DEPOSITION OFFERED IN TRIAL

ARMYVILLE, Sept. 30—A noted authority on suicide described a military wife who was shot to death last year as "terribly unhappy," and suicide-prone.

A videotape featuring Dr. Edwin Shneidman, founder of the American Association of Suicidology, was played Thursday in the premeditated murder trial of Capt. Joseph P. Campbell. The defendant, 33, is charged with slaying his wife, Peggy Scott-Campbell, in the bathroom of their apartment July 23. The 30-year-old woman died of a chest wound from a 12-gauge pump shotgun.

Campbell told military investigators that he found his wife of five years in the shower stall, cutting her abdomen with a knife. His shotgun was nearby.

Witnesses have testified that Campbell said his wife grabbed the barrel of the gun when Campbell tried to remove it. It discharged, striking her in the chest.

The defense is trying to prove that Scott-Campbell was shot accidentally while attempting suicide.

Shneidman's deposition was taken in Los Angeles on Monday. A court-martial panel of five officers is hearing evidence in the courtroom of Judge (Col.) George D. Maris.

Shneidman evaluated the psychological autopsy report of Dr. Jerome Motto, a psychiatrist and professor at the University of California in San Francisco. Motto is a consultant for the defense.

Shneidman said he believed Scott-Campbell was attempting to kill herself on the night she died.

"If she had survived that episode—this is a terrible thing to say about a fellow human being—she would be dead by her own hands in a year or two," he testified.

Shneidman said he based his conclusions in part on a letter written by Scott-Campbell's mother on her son-in-law's behalf.

Earlier this year, Maria E. Scott wrote a "To whom it may concern" letter to the court stating that when her daughter was a teenager, she had admitted her to a hospital mental ward.

"She had resisted all Joe's efforts to persuade her to seek professional help because of this fear of being locked up in a mental ward," Scott wrote. "He loved Peggy deeply," the letter also said.

Although only portions of the letter were admitted into evidence, Scott also added, "I, frankly, don't think there should even be a trial. I don't think Joe is guilty of anything except negligence in handling the gun in trying to take it away from her."

"In forty years, I never read a document like this," Shneidman said, referring to the letter.

Shneidman disputed prosecution testimony offered last week by Perry N. Olds, an army criminal investigator. Olds testified that statistics show that nude suicides and suicides involving two instruments of destruction were highly unusual.

Shneidman agreed, but told the court that statistics cannot be applied to individual cases.

Also played Thursday was the videotaped deposition of Beverly Simkins, a former counselor at the Armyville education center.

For a time, Simkins said, Scott-Campbell worked with her. Simkins said the woman experienced wide mood swings and eventually quit her job at the center and became almost reclusive. Scott-Campbell also drank excessively, she testified. She described the victim's husband as a peaceable man who was devoted to his wife.

Prior to deploying to Panama, Simkins said, Campbell came to her office and asked that she look out for his wife.

Winifred LeClerq, who described herself as a close friend of the Campbells, testified Thursday that Scott-Campbell would sometimes telephone her at night to discuss personal problems.

"She felt like she wasn't worth anything or had no reason for living," LeClerq said.

The defense rested Thursday afternoon. Prosecution rebuttal witnesses were scheduled to begin testifying later Thursday.

Tape Reveals Wife's Anguish

ARMYVILLE, Oct 2—"I was playing with the shotgun the other day. . . . "

The voice belonged to Peggy Scott-Campbell, a military spouse who has been dead since July 23. Her words, laughter, and song filled a courtroom Thursday afternoon and brought tears to the eyes of the man accused of killing her.

For Capt. Joseph Campbell, it was a voice from the grave.

Campbell sobbed quietly as he listened to a cassette tape she had made months before when he was in Panama. The tape, however, was never mailed, and Campbell, who returned to the United States in May, had never heard it.

Until Thursday at his murder trial.

The tape became an unusual and spellbinding piece of evidence. . . .

The 33-year-old officer was charged with premeditated murder in the shotgun death of his 30-year-old wife. Scott-Campbell was fatally wounded in the bathroom of the couple's apartment.

The shotgun is the same one to which she referred in the tape recording.

Campbell claimed he found his wife, a woman with a history of mental problems, in the bathroom, cutting herself with a knife. His sawed-off shotgun was nearby. He told authorities that when he tried to remove the gun, she grabbed the barrel and pulled it to her chest, causing it to discharge.

Military investigators confiscated the tape, along with other evidence, shortly after the shooting. Campbell's attorney said his client has had access to the recording, but found it too painful to hear.

On Thursday, the 45-minute tape spoke to the court. It portrayed a lonely, frightened woman who missed her husband and feared he might be killed. Her words also revealed an angry, depressed personality that was having trouble coping with life.

At the same time, the tape unveiled a side of Scott-Campbell that was fun loving and playful.

On the tape she tells Campbell repeatedly that she loves him and, at one point, she mentions the shotgun. She also asks where he keeps the shells.

But Scott-Campbell doesn't dwell on the gun. She talks about many other things, like their dog getting into the garbage, her trip to a Chinese restaurant, the laundry, and a possible vacation when he returns from Panama.

"You've only been gone a little over two weeks," she says on the tape. "It seems like a year."

"I'm doing better than some of these other women. They're freaking out or crying all the time."

"Oh, babe, I can't wait until you get home."

"It's no fun going to bed. Nobody to tuck me in. Nobody to turn out the lights."

"I'm lonely. I'm miserable without you. I'm scared."

"It's hard being here without you. It's hard being anywhere without you."

"I did make the bed once since you were gone, but mostly the sheets are up around my ears. I want to reach out and touch your foot, but there's no foot."

"At least my heart is with you. My heart is with you every second, every moment of every day and minute you're over there. I just hope you understand."

She asks what Bible passage Campbell was reading before he was deployed to Panama, adding, "I really want to know."

"I have not been sleeping that great, honey, and when I do sleep, it's horrible."

Suddenly she puts on some music, a collection of songs from the 1960s. She mentions that she tries not to watch the television news. Against a backdrop of Sonny and Cher singing "I Got You Babe," she talks of a television special she watched, dedicated to servicemen in Panama.

"I cried during the whole thing. It was really moving."

"I just want you home now. I'm so scared of losing you."

Her voice is pleading, almost a cry.

"Joe, I swear I'll never take you for granted again."

"Come home to me. You've got to come home to me."

She stops the music and sings a song to her husband. It's a strange song to come from a troubled woman, but she sings it with feeling.

It's titled "I'm the Happiest Girl in the Whole U.S.A."

Newspaper Account of the Verdict

Captain Acquitted in Trial

ARMYVILLE, Oct. 1—An officer charged with the shotgun slaying of his wife last July was found innocent Friday by a five-man court-martial panel.

The panel's verdict came after about three hours of deliberation that brought to an end a court-martial that lasted more than a week.

Capt. Joseph Campbell had been charged with premeditated murder in the death of Peggy Scott-Campbell on July 12. Campbell had told investigators that he walked in on his wife while she was trying to kill herself in the bathroom of their apartment. Campbell said he found her cutting her abdomen with a knife. He said he saw his shotgun lying nearby.

When he attempted to remove the gun, Campbell said she grabbed the barrel and put it to her chest, causing it to discharge.

When Judge (Col.) George Maris read the verdict, Campbell threw back his head and emitted an audible sigh. His mother, Elizabeth Campbell, began crying loudly.

Campbell first hugged his two attorneys, Dan Hyatt, a civilian from Portland, Oregon, and Major James Purdich, a military attorney.

When Campbell embraced his mother, he broke into tears.

"I'm glad it's over. It's been a long time," he said. "It kind of restored my faith in the system. I loved my wife very much. I'm sorry she had to be dragged through this, too."

Chief prosecutor Maj. Stanley Bates would not comment on the verdict.

In closing arguments Friday morning Bates told the panel that Campbell was anything but a peaceful "teddy bear" as defense witnesses sometimes characterized him.

"She (Scott-Campbell) was not greeted by a teddy bear. She was greeted by a bear with fangs."

He later referred to Campbell as a "grizzly bear, a peaceable person like most who can be pushed into violence."

Citing Scott-Campbell's drinking problems, her belligerent attitude, and her habit of ignoring housecleaning, Bates argued that she had pushed her husband over the brink.

"He's angry. He tolerated a lot for a long time," he said.

Bates said that the couple had an argument the evening prior to Scott-Campbell's death about separation and divorce, during which the woman mentioned returning to school.

Scott-Campbell later went out alone to a nearby pizzeria. Bates told the panel an angry Campbell waited up for his wife. When she returned, he charged that Campbell beat her and then took her into the bathroom and shot her.

After pulling the trigger, Bates said that Campbell attempted to cover up the crime by cleaning the bathroom and changing clothes. Bates argued that under the circumstances it would have been impossible for the woman to grab the gun and pull it to her chest.

Hyatt, in his closing arguments, said the charges brought against Campbell were unwarranted.

Regarding the murder charge, Hyatt remarked, "Why would you kill someone who is in the process of killing themselves?"

Hyatt said that a tape recording made by Scott-Campbell proved the couple loved each other very much. The defense attorney said the government had failed to prove that Campbell was guilty.

"They proved beyond a reasonable doubt this man is innocent," he said.

Hyatt described Scott-Campbell as a "very fragile human being." Evidence established that while a teenager, she had been locked up in a hospital mental ward. In a letter, her mother told the court that Scott-Campbell was reluctant to seek professional help for fear of being locked up again.

At the time of her death her blood alcohol content tested .17. Campbell's blood tested zero alcohol.

The trial began September 21 and involved a trip by attorneys to Los Angeles where a deposition was taken from Edwin Shneidman, a noted authority on suicide.

☐ Newspaper Account of Subsequent Developments

Top Army Lawyer Called Irresponsible by Defense

ARMYVILLE, Oct. 8—The civilian attorney of an officer acquitted last week of killing his wife has accused the Corps' top lawyer of being irresponsible by bringing a premeditated murder charge against his client.

Dan Hyatt, a lawyer from Portland, Oregon, also accused Col. Robert Bakersfield, the staff judge advocate of the Corps, of refusing to consider evidence that surfaced following an Article 32 investigation of Capt. Joseph Campbell. The evidence could have altered the charges, Hyatt said.

A Corps spokesman said that Bakersfield would not respond to the accusation.

Campbell, 33, was charged with the killing of Peggy Scott-Campbell, 30, with a 12-gauge shotgun inside their off-base apartment. A five-member court-martial panel acquitted the ten-year army veteran following a seven-day trial. The trial involved travel by prosecution and defense lawyers to both U.S. coasts to obtain videotaped depositions.

Hyatt asserted that Bakersfield ignored Article 32 investigation findings that recommended a charge of involuntary manslaughter be filed.

"Given the evidence as to Captain Campbell's intent, I felt it extremely unlikely that premeditation existed or could be proven by the government," wrote Lt. Col. George R. Pasteur, the investigating officer who conducted the Article 32.

An Article 32 investigation is similar to a civilian grand jury investigation.

Pasteur, after listening to three days of testimony concluded in the Article 32 report that "the charges and specifications are not in the proper form. The government barely produced minimum evidence which would indicate premeditation on the part of Captain Campbell."

Pasteur, an artillery officer, stated that the evidence warranted a charge of involuntary manslaughter instead.

Hyatt, citing trial costs that he said would exceed $250,000, claimed that filing the charge of premeditated murder constituted an "irresponsible exercise of power" by Bakersfield and Major Stanley Bates, who was chief prosecuting attorney.

Bates was unavailable Friday for comment.

Hyatt accused Bakersfield of failing to consider new evidence which included:

- Testimony from two blood-spatter experts that proved Scott-Campbell was shot in the bathroom of the couple's apartment, not the bedroom as the government believed. Hyatt said the experts, originally hired by the government for $25,000, were never called to testify by the prosecution.
- Answers from Campbell to thirty-five additional questions posed by the Criminal Investigation Command.
- A letter from Mrs. Maria Scott, Scott-Campbell's mother, outlining her daughter's psychological history, which included a stay in a mental ward. She said her son-in-law loved her daughter and would not have killed her.

"The idea of premeditation is so preposterous as to not even be worthy of comment," she wrote.

Campbell has said that he found his wife in the bathroom cutting her abdomen with a knife and that the shotgun was lying nearby. He said that when he tried to remove the shotgun, his wife grabbed the barrel and put it to her chest, causing it to discharge.

Hyatt said Bakersfield would not even look at the new evidence.

"He refused to take (the evidence) to the General (Corps Commander, Lt. Gen. Jonathan M. Faubus), and that was irresponsible," Hyatt said. "I think he's got a duty to the general to keep him apprised of continuing developments in the case. That shows a real bias."

Faubus was the convening authority.

"In my fifteen years of practice, I haven't seen a case that was such a gross overstatement of the charge," said Hyatt, a Vietnam veteran who specializes in military law. "There is no more serious charge than premeditated murder, and there was not evidence to support it."

In the military, a premeditated murder conviction carries an automatic sentence of life imprisonment.

Hyatt said that the military justice system is fair. "But it's also a system where abuse of power occurs with regularity."

"With Joseph, you've got basically a grieving widower," Hyatt said. "Can you imagine the horror of facing the prospect of having to spend the rest of your life in prison because this one person (Bakersfield) said, 'Well, I think he's guilty'?"

In a related action, Campbell filed a complaint Thursday with the Corps Inspector General, requesting an inquiry into the conduct of the Criminal Investigation Command and the prosecution's handling of this case. In it, he claims that the prosecution withheld what he says appears to be *a suicide note written by Scott-Campbell just before she died.* [Italics added]

A Corps spokesman said the Inspector General acknowledged receipt of Campbell's complaint and has advised him to pursue it through appropriate legal channels.

The note, which Campbell said he discovered when he went to the Criminal Investigation Command's evidence room to retrieve his personal property, reads:

"Joe, I love you. You have nothing else but sleep on your mind. I have something a little more important than that on my mind. I'm a fool."

She wrote, "I love you" seven times, and then continued, "I'm so scared. I'm crazy. I think I drink too much. I think I'm an alcoholic. I know I am. I don't know what to do. I'm just like daddy I guess. I'm crazy. Just like him. I'm just so scared baby." In larger script she wrote, "I know I'm not stupid! Military is free." She drew ten lines under the word "free."

Campbell said the note shows his wife's state of mind at the time and could have aided in his defense. Hyatt, contacted late Friday, said he spent two full days at the Criminal Investigation Command office and never came across the letter.

☐ Summary

In summary, five items (of fact and inference) can be listed.

- Joseph Campbell is out of the army, honorably discharged, back in his home state, trying to pick up the pieces of his shattered life.
- The court-martial not-guilty verdict implied that Campbell definitely did not commit murder, that his wife was in the process of attempting suicide, and that the death was accidental—a rare case of an accidental death within a suicidal context. (After the trial, a revised death certificate was issued that changed the mode of death from homicide to accident.)

- To the extent that the testimony regarding the personality of the deceased wife played a role in the court's decision, the court-martial also functioned as a psychological autopsy investigation.
- The question of the irresponsibility of the Army Criminal Investigation Command and the prosecution's handling of the case (in bringing an unwarranted charge of premeditated murder) was never resolved.
- The further question of whether or not the prosecution knew about (and advertently withheld) the wife's suicide note (which would have absolved the husband at the outset) has not been answered. However, the very presence of this vexing question about the prosecutor's behavior raises the specter of the potentiality for breakdowns in the military criminal justice system that is frightening to contemplate.

References

Clark, D. C., and Horton-Deutsch, S. L. (1992). Assessment in absentia: The value of the psychological autopsy for studying antecedents of suicide and predicting future suicides. In R. W. Maris et al. (Eds.), *Assessment and prediction of suicide*, New York: Guilford.

Curphey, T. J. (1961). The role of the social scientist in the medicolegal certification of death from suicide. In N. L. Farberow & E. S. Shneidman (Eds.), *The cry for help* (pp. 110–117). New York: McGraw-Hill.

Curphey, T. J. (1967). The forensic pathologist and the multidisciplinary approach to death. In E. S. Shneidman (Ed.), *Essays in self-destruction*, (pp. 463–474). New York: Science House.

Litman, R. E., Curphey, T. J., Shneidman, E. S., et al. (1963). Investigations of equivocal suicides. *Journal of the American Medical Association, 184*, 924–929.

Shneidman, E. S. (1969). Suicide, lethality and the psychological autopsy. In E. S. Shneidman & M. Ortega (Eds.), *Aspects of Depression*, (pp. 225–250). Boston: Little, Brown.

Shneidman, E. S. (1973). *Deaths of man*. New York: Quadrangle.

Shneidman, E. S. (1977). The psychological autopsy. In L. I. Gottschalk (Ed.), *Guide to the investigation and reporting of drug abuse deaths* (pp. 42–56). Washington, DC: USDHEW, U.S. Government Printing Office.

Weisman, A. D. (1974). *The realization of death: A guide for the psychological autopsy*. New York: Jason Aronson.

33

CHAPTER

Postvention: The Care of the Bereaved

Grief and mourning are not diseases, but their deleterious and inimical effects can often be as serious as though they were. The recently bereaved person is typically bereft and disorganized. Long-standing habit patterns of intimate interpersonal response are irreversibly severed. There is a concomitant gale of strong feelings, usually including abandonment and despair, sometimes touching upon guilt and anger, and almost always involving a sense of crushing emptiness and loss. In light of these psychological realities it comes as no surprise that individuals who are acutely bereaved constitute a population "at risk" (Kraus & Lillienfeld, 1959; Young, Benjamin & Wallis, 1963; Rees & Lutkins, 1967; Parkes & Fitzgerald, 1969; Stein & Susser, 1969; Parkes, 1964, 1970, 1971, 1972).

Excluding Freud's indispensible paper, "Mourning and melancholia," published in 1917 (Freud, 1957), much of the important work on this topic has been done only since 1944 (Lindemann, 1944; Bowlby, 1961; Caplan, 1964; Lifton, 1969; Silverman, 1972; Weisman, 1972; Shneidman, 1974). In general, these studies point out that grief and mourning may have serious physical and psychological concomitants (in the way of heightened morbidity and even a greater risk of death), and they explicate some of the dimensions of bereavement as well as ways of helping the bereaved.

Reprinted from R. O. Pasnau (Ed.), *Consultation in Liaison Psychiatry.* New York: Grune and Stratton, 1975, pp. 245–256. With permission.

This chapter will not be an attempt to replow the ground so fertilely turned by others, especially Parkes in his chapter "Helping the bereaved" in his book *Bereavement* in which he discusses the role of the funeral director, the church, the family doctor, and self-help organizations, among others (Parkes, 1972). Instead, the discussion will be limited to what I know best, namely, my own work with bereaved persons.

A specific example will be useful at the outset. Here are some excerpts from a taped session with a young adult widower whom I had seen for several months after his wife died. She was a university student (whom I came to know in a course on death and suicide that I taught). She died of scleroderma. This session is three years after her death.

Dr. S: *Now to start with, your relationship with Edith was unusual in that you knew she was ill from the beginning.*

Mr. H: *That's correct, I first met her ten years ago, she was 18. It was just after her illness had been diagnosed and her parents, if I remember correctly, told me about it when they saw that we were becoming serious, after we had been courting for some time. And I really didn't know exactly what the disease was, I mean as far as life span was concerned. I wonder why I didn't try to find out more. Maybe I was afraid; I don't know. I knew her life would be shortened, but I don't think I really allowed myself to think about it or to find out exactly what it was. It was terminal about eight years after. I have thought about it, because it seems to me strange of my not pursuing it. She was the first girl I guess I really had a good meaningful relationship with, and I think I might have been very frightened to find out the truth. But I didn't want to know . . . The more I think of it the more I really realize I think I blocked a tremendous amount out.*

Dr. S: *Her death was not totally unexpected to you. When she came into the hospital, she was struggling and you knew she was failing. How were you told that she was dead, and then what happened?*

Mr. H: *The doctor that had been attending her told me when I came in that morning to see her, and he brought me aside. He took me somewhere. I think he gave me a tranquilizer. I was extremely impressed with him. I was probably in shock, but I remember the clear thing I did feel was some sense of relief that I don't have to wait any longer. That incredible waiting that I realized I had been going through was suddenly over. But then there was this, I don't know . . . I went home alone from the hospital, alone, really alone. I really don't recall what happened the rest of the day. I think that a good friend of ours stayed with me that night. I was feeling very freaked out. I must have gone around for maybe a week or so before I really began to feel the loneliness and her loss. I finally stopped running around taking care of everybody, and really felt the mourning, really felt her loss. It was a feeling inside of having an incredible emptiness. I felt sort of at a loss, kind of wondering how my life was going to continue. How it possibly could go on. Everything sort of like disintegrated. Sort of like a piece of me just was kind of lost.*

Dr. S: *What helped you the most?*

Mr. H: *I don't know that there's any one thing that helped me the most. Perhaps Susan probably has helped a lot. Even though it was after a year, she forced me to the issue of dealing with Edith, really moving her out of the apartment and started showing me things. About six months after Edith died, I went around and grabbed everything that had anything to do with her and put them in boxes and shoved them in the closets; but still Edith was in the closet. She was still there. We moved things around the apartment to make it different. I started doing some of those things, but she just kept saying that she really felt it wasn't her place, that it was still Edith's. She wanted it to be hers. So she did force me a great deal.*

Dr. S: *Did you get rid of all her things?*

Mr. H: *Oh, no. As a matter of fact we have some pottery that Edith had made that we use, that I had never thought of using before.*

Dr. S: *Do you sleep in the same bed that you had before?*

Mr. H: *Yes, but I've moved the bed in the room and I sleep on the other side of the bed. I've told Susan that the bed used to be in a different location and I never made anything of it. I did this about six months after Edith died, before I met Susan. I did a few things, painted one of the walls, and a few things like this, rearranged the furniture. But there was still the other thing. It was very hard for me to commit myself to Susan. This was a big problem. This is over two years now. We've been married for several months and had been going together for two years. I took all that time to make a commitment.*

Dr. S: *Why was that?*

Mr. H: *I don't know. I searched in myself a lot for what it was. And I wasn't really able to grab it. I'm sure that part was really there. A part of it was the holding on. I'm sure that was also a large part of it. I don't think it was until Susan and I were married that we went through all the boxes in the closets, took all the stuff and decided either to throw it away or use it, to get it out of the closet, literally and figuratively.*

Dr. S: *Did you make any inquiries as to Susan's state of health?*

Mr. H: *Susan is very healthy. I don't recall. I might have asked her, but I'm conscious of the fact that I certainly noticed her health. She's also younger than I am by a few years and I thought of that. You know what that means. I think part of that means that I don't want to live longer. I don't want her to die before I do. I'm sure that's there. I'd be surprised if it weren't.*

Dr. S: *I knew Edith and then I knew you. How did that work out?*

Mr. H: *Well, I think I came to you; I'm not sure if it was because you knew her. I think that was part of it, because you did know her and you knew me through her. But I think it was because of you yourself. I felt you were the type of person who could help me.*

Dr. S: *In what way?*

Mr. H: *I can't recall, whatever, but I think that some of the things that you said at the time helped me, helped to alleviate my desperation that I felt. A few times I did come in I was feeling pretty desperate. Completely kind of lost and floundering. But that worked out . . .*

Definition and Purpose of Postvention

I prefer to think of the work with the bereaved person as a process that I have called *postvention:* those appropriate and helpful acts that come *after* the dire event itself (Shneidman, 1964, 1970, 1974). The reader will recognize prevention, intervention, and postvention as roughly synonymous with the traditional health concepts of primary, secondary, and tertiary prevention, or with the concepts of immunization, treatment, and rehabilitation. Lindemann has referred to "preventive intervention." It would be simpler to speak of postvention.

As I have described in *Deaths of Man,* postvention consists of those activities that serve to reduce the aftereffects of a traumatic event in the lives of the survivors (Shneidman, 1974). Its purpose is to help survivors live longer, more productively, and less stressfully than they are likely to do otherwise. I will attempt to summarize my observations in the following paragraphs.

Reactions of Survivor Victims

It is obvious that some deaths are more stigmatizing or traumatic than others: death by murder, by the negligence of oneself or some other person, or by suicide. Survivor victims of such deaths are invaded by an unhealthy complex of disturbing emotions: shame, guilt, hatred, perplexity. They are obsessed with thoughts about the death, seeking reasons, casting blame, and often punishing themselves.

The investigations of widows by Parkes are most illuminating (Parkes, 1972). The principal finding of his studies is that independent of her age, a woman who has lost a husband recently is more likely to die (from alcoholism, malnutrition, or a variety of disorders related to neglect of self, disregard of a prescribed medical regimen or common-sense precautions, or even a seemingly unconscious boredom with life), or to be physically ill, or emotionally disturbed than nonwidowed women. The findings seem to imply that grief is itself a dire process, almost akin to a disease, and that there are subtle factors at work that can take a heavy toll unless they are treated and controlled.

These striking results had been intuitively known long before they were empirically demonstrated. The efforts of Lindemann, Caplan, and Silverman to aid survivors of "heavy deaths" were postventions based on the premise of heightened risk in bereaved persons (Lindemann, 1944; Caplan, 1964; Silverman, 1972). Lindemann's work, which led to his formulations of acute grief and crisis intervention, began with his treatment of the survivors of the tragic Coconut Grove nightclub fire in Boston in 1942 in which 499 people died (Lindemann, 1944). Silverman's projects, under the direction of Caplan, have centered around a widow-to-widow program (Caplan, 1964; Silverman, 1972). These efforts bear obvious similarities with the programs of "befriending" practiced by the Samaritans, an organization founded by the Reverend Chad Varah (1966) and most active in Great Britain (Varah, 1966).

Death a "Disaster"

A case can be made for viewing the sudden death of a loved one as a *disaster* and, using the verbal bridge provided by that concept, learning from the professional literature on conventionally recognized disasters—those sudden, unexpected events, such as earthquakes and large-scale explosions, that cause a large number of deaths and have widespread effects. Wolfenstein has described a "disaster syndrome": a "combination of emotional dullness, unresponsiveness to outer stimulation and inhibition of activity. The individual who has just undergone disaster is apt to suffer from at least a transitory sense of worthlessness; his usual capacity for self-love becomes impaired" (Wolfenstein, 1957).

A similar psychological contraction is seen in the initial shock reaction to catastrophic news—death, failure, disclosure, disgrace, the keenest personal loss. Studies of a disastrous ship sinking by Friedman and Lum and of the effects of a tornado by Wallace both describe an initial psychic shock followed by motor retardation, flattening of affect, somnolence, amnesia, and suggestibility (Friedman & Lum, 1957; Wallace, 1956). There is marked increase in dependency needs with regressive behavior and traumatic loss of feelings of identity and, overall, a kind of "affective anesthesia." There is an unhealthy docility, a cowed and subdued reaction. One is reminded of Lifton's description of "psychic closing off" and "psychic numbing" among the Hibakusha, the survivors of the atomic bomb dropped on Hiroshima:

> Very quickly—sometimes within minutes or even seconds—Hibakusha began to undergo a process of "psychic closing off"; that is, they simply ceased to feel. They had a clear sense of what was happening around them, but their emotional reactions were unconsciously turned off. Others' immersion in larger responsibilities was accompanied by a greater form of closing off which might be termed "psychic numbing" (Lifton, 1969).

☐ Postvention: An Ongoing Therapy

Postventive efforts are not limited to this initial stage of shock; they are more often directed to the longer haul, the day-to-day living with grief over a year or more following the first shock of loss. Typically postvention extends over months during that critical first year, and it shares many of the characteristics of psychotherapy: talk, abreaction, interpretation, reassurance, direction, and even gentle confrontation. It provides an arena for the expression of guarded emotions, especially such negative affective states as anger, shame, and guilt. It puts a measure of stability into the grieving person's life and provides an interpersonal relationship with the therapist that can be genuine, in that honest feelings need not be suppressed or dissembled.

Parkes distinguishes four phases in the bereavement process: numbness, yearning/protest, disorganization, and reorganization—but in general we ought to view "stages" of recovery from death (and especially we need to view the so-called stages of the dying process) with a liberal and flexible mind (Parkes, 1970).

Characteristics of the Postventive Session

In order to appreciate the nature of postvention, it is necessary to touch upon some important characteristics of the interaction between the bereaved victim and the therapist,[1] specifically the difference between a *conversation* (or "ordinary talk") and a *professional exchange*—recognizing that postventive efforts should be of the latter sort. This distinction is exceptionally elementary, but because this understanding is at the very heart of effective postventive work, these rudimentary ideas need to be made explicit. The differences between the two can be charted in the form of some contrasts between ordinary talk (e.g., "I'm so sorry to hear about the death." "Please accept my most sincere condolescences." "Time will heal the wounds.") and a professional exchange.

Conversation	Professional Exchange
1. Content	
Substantive content, i.e., the talk is primarily about things, events, dates—the surface of the world.	Affective (emotional) content, i.e., the exchange focuses (not constantly but occasionally) on the feelings and the emotional tone of the patient, sometimes minimizing the "facts."
2. Level	
Manifest level, i.e., conversation focuses on what is said, the actual words that are uttered, the facts that are stated.	Latent level, i.e., the professional person listens for what is "between the lines," below the surface, what is implied, not expressed or only unconsciously present.
3. Meanings	
Conscious meanings, i.e., in ordinary speech we deal with the other person as though what was said was meant and as though the person were "a rational man" and that he "knows his own mind."	Unconscious meanings, i.e., there is a whole flow of the mind that is not immediately available at any given moment to the person and that there are unconscious meanings and latent intentions in human exchanges. We listen for double entendre, puns, hidden meanings, latent implications, and so on.
4. Abstraction	
Phenotypic abstraction, i.e., there is concern with the ordinary interesting details of life, where no set of details necessarily bears any relationship to any other set.	Genotypic abstraction, i.e., the therapist is always looking for congruencies, similarities commonalities, *generalizations* about the patient's psychological life. These constitute the understanding of the therapist (and are the reservoir of his possible interpretations to the patient).
5. Role	
Social role, i.e., in a conversation or ordinary discourse people are co-equals (like neighbors or friends) or depend on the prestige of age, rank, status, and so on, but essentially the relationship is between two people who have equal right to display themselves.	Transference, i.e., a professional exchange is not talk between two co-equals. Rather it is a very special kind of exchange between one person who wishes help (and tacitly agrees to play the patient's role) and another person who agrees to proffer help (and thus is cast in the role of physician, priest, father, magician, witch doctor, helper). Much of what is effective in the exchange is the patient's "transference" onto the therapist. Some of the effectiveness of the therapeutic exchange lies in the power of the "self-fulfilling prophecy."

Another retrospective example may be useful. Late one afternoon a beautiful 19-year-old girl was stabbed to death by an apparent would-be rapist in a government building. Within an hour her parents were shattered by the news given to them by two rather young, well-meaning but inexperienced policemen. The victim was the couple's only child. Their immediate reactions were shock, disbelief, overwhelming grief, and mounting rage, most of it directed at the agency where the murder had occurred.

A few days later, right after the funeral, they were in the office of a high official who was attempting to tender his condolences when the mother said in an anguished tone: "There is nothing you can do!" To which, with good presence of mind, he answered that while it was true that the girl could not be brought back to life, there was something that could be done. Whether he knew the term or not, it was postvention that he had in mind. He brought them, personally, to my office.

I began seeing the parents, usually together, sometimes separately. The principal psychological feature was the mother's anger. I permitted her to voice her grief and to vent her rage (sometimes at me), while I retained the role of the voice of reason: empathizing with the parents' state, recognizing the legitimacy of their feelings when I could but not agreeing when in good conscience I could not agree. I felt that I was truly their friend, and I believed that they felt so too. I had insisted that each of them see a physician for a physical examination. A few months after the brutal murder, the mother developed serious symptoms that required major surgery, from which she made a good recovery. The situation raises the intriguing (and unanswerable) question in my mind whether or not that organic flurry would have occurred if she had not suffered the shock of her daughter's death (Rahe, 1972). In the year following her daughter's death the mother had two extended hospitalizations. Several months after the tragedy the parents seemed to be in rather good shape, physically and emotionally, everything considered. They still had low-level grief and no doubt always will. Here is an edited verbatim portion of a session exactly one year after the death.

Dr. S: *Is today a year?*

Mrs. A: *Exactly one year. And just about this time when she was killed . . .*

Dr. S: *Where are you both today? Can you sketch the course of your grief?*

Mrs. A: *Well, at first it was extremely intense. It was actually a physical pain. For a couple of months I went around and it hurt—it actually hurt in here. And I felt like I was carrying the world on my shoulders and inside of me.*

Mr. A: *I don't think the pain was physical, it was . . .*

Mrs. A: *No, it wasn't. I mean I felt it physically, but it was a mental pain too.*

Mr. A: *There are times when the pain is still there. It's hard to describe it, it's just there, feeling of pain. I guess it's part of sorrow. We had a very bad day yesterday, much more so than today.*

Mrs. A: *You can't just cut off 19 years in one day. It was like losing an arm or a leg or a head or something. Or a head, because you can do without an arm, and you learn to do in a way, without a daughter. It sounds trite when you say it that way.*

Mr. A: *I think one of the things that has happened in the past year is that, as far as I'm concerned, I don't think I've discussed it too much, but I'm more capable of facing the situation, of thinking about it. I used to try to put it out of my mind. For a while there, the hardest thing I had to do was look at her picture.*

Dr. S: *Do you still have that in your house, do you have it displayed?*

Mrs. A: *Yeah.*

Mr. A: *We have one in our bedroom on the bureau. It stays there all the time, but, uh, I don't get a shock anymore when I look at her picture.*

Mrs. A: *I still turn around to look when I see blonde hair bobbing up and down and I still turn to look, and then I realize how stupid it is. She couldn't look like that anymore. A little girl lives down the street, that I sometimes see, and she walks like she walked. And it still plays tricks, I still look to see if it's her. And sometimes the other children say or do something and it's always in the back of our minds, always in the back of my mind anyway. I think these meetings with you have been very good for us, because there was someone we could talk to. And someone that could show—in a way—take a different viewpoint. How can we see beyond our noses when we're so grief stricken and, oh, I don't know.*

Mr. A: *That's what I was trying to bring out a while ago, that is that you've helped us, me in facing the truth.*

Dr. S: *How was that done?*

Mr. A: *I don't know; just the fact that I was discussing rather freely and maybe . . .*

Mrs. A: *And we thought we could tell you anything and you wouldn't be angry or, I don't know exactly how to say it, but I always felt we could talk to you and we could tell you exactly what we thought and not face any recriminations or anything like that.*

Dr. S: *Speaking of anger and recriminations, there was a time—isn't this so—that you were just terribly angry?*

Mrs. A: *Yes.*

Dr. S: *What has happened to that anger?*

Mrs. A: *It's dissipated. At first, in the beginning, I was ready to kill everybody and anybody.*

Dr. S: *Including me.*

Mrs. A: *Including you because you represented the government to us.*

Mr. A: *No, really?*

Mrs. A: *Yes, in a way he did because I blamed the government for her death. I still feel that somebody here helped. Somebody here helped, and he must know. Whoever it is; who helped, did his part in getting her killed. By not patroling the building, by not doing—a sin of omission is just as big as a big sin of comission. I mean they knew darn well that the building was not safe.*

Dr. S: *So there are still certainly reservoirs of anger and blame.*

Mrs. A: *At the time I wanted the murderer caught and killed. Now I would just like him stopped, but I don't want him killed. Will that bring her back? But people were afraid of us. They were afraid to talk to us.*

Mr. A: *Some still are.*

Mrs. A: *Some of them still are because they didn't know what to say. It was a difficult thing; it's a difficult thing for most people to find words of sympathy. What do you tell parents whose daughter is killed like that? Another thing that in a way you taught me is to take one day at a time.*

Dr. S: *How did I teach you that?*

Mrs. A: *I don't know how, but that's what I've been doing, taking one day at a time. You were able really to show us in a proper perspective. That's one of the things you did; you were always the one to look at things in a straight manner. How could we when we were so prejudiced about anything—I mean about what happened to her. We are so close to the forest, we can't see the trees.*

Mr. A: *I think you've also managed to curtail her anger in general to a certain extent. Because she was mad at the whole world at the time—any reason. She'd get mad, get ready to prosecute her soup.*

Dr. S: *Have there been some changes in your general character?*

Mrs. A: *I think so, I've probably been a little bit more tolerant.*

Dr. S: *What do you think will happen now in the next year or two?*

Mrs. A: *We get more used to it. I suppose. He will become more resigned to it; that she isn't here, she won't come back, and that going to the cemetery won't hurt so much. But I try not to make this a special day because what's to celebrate? But it is in a way a special day.*

Dr. S: *It is an occasion to memorialize.*

Mrs. A: *It was sad to come home last night and find my husband was crying.*

Mr. A: *It was just a defense mechanism. I was crying to keep you from crying, so you would feel sorry for me for a change.*

Mrs. A: *I suppose in a way it made me less intolerant of other people. But what a price to have to pay. What a pity. All those years. There is something so final now. I used to feel that there was continuity, that she would have children and in a way live on. My husband is the last of his line. The last male of his line. The last one of his family.*

Mr. A: *It's the end of the name anyway.*

Dr. S: *There is a sense of being cut off from the future, isn't there?*

Mr. A: *I imagine there is going to be a lot of hurt when we have to attend weddings or births.*

Mrs. A: *Somehow it is very hard to think that when you die, that's the end. But it's not as bad as I used to be afraid of death. I am no longer afraid of death personally. It's no longer such a terrible thing. It was terrible, I suppose, because it was unknown. Another time I would have been afraid when I went into the hospital. I was so unafraid that I believed the doctor when he told me before the operation that it wasn't going to hurt. How naive can you be? I wanted to believe it. I don't think, I mean, I'm sure, I could not have gone through this past year without my husband.*

Dr. S: *I think you have helped each other in a marvelous way.*

Mrs. A: *I'm really sure that I could never have come through it.*

Mr. A: *Except for one time when she almost walked out on me.*

Mrs. A: *That's different. That didn't count. To get through the impossible days and even longer nights. We weren't perfect, and she was not perfect. Of course, no one will ever bring up any of her faults now.*

Dr. S: *That's so. One doesn't speak ill of the dead.*

Mrs. A: *No. Everybody, when they do talk about her, glosses over any of her faults. No one wants to talk about them. I don't know of anyone who has voluntarily brought up her name but you. Why is there such a taboo? It's been a whole year.*

Dr. S: *Do you feel more than a year older?*

Mr. A: *Very much. We were discussing this not too long ago, and we both felt we had missed out on middle age, that we went from youth to old people.*

Dr. S: *Really. You feel that way?*

Mrs. A: *Most of the time I feel so old and I caught myself talking to my brother and I said when we were young, and he said, "Hey, you are talking about a couple of years ago."*

Dr. S: *Well, what we need to work on is to bring back the sense of youthful middle age.*

Mrs. A: *I don't thing that will ever come back. I always felt inside that I was about 19 or 20 and now I feel 60 years old. I said we could talk to you and tell you anything. You have taught us a great deal, and not to worry about recriminations.*

Mr. A: *There were times when I felt that you were trying to make her mad at you.*

Dr. S: *I never did that. I have always liked you.*

Mrs. A: *I always felt that you liked me. It was that feeling. I remember the look on your face when I showed you her picture. I will never forget it.*

Dr. S: *I can't describe what went through me.*

Mrs. A: *You showed it. It was like hitting you, and you absolutely recoiled as though I had hit you. I miss you when I don't see you.*

Dr. S: *How often do you think we ought to meet now? Should we make the next meeting in a month?*

Mrs. A: *They've been almost about a month apart.*

Mrs. A: *I would hate to think about our meetings finishing, ending.*

☐ Principles of Postvention

What can be noted in this exchange are some general principles of postventive work:

1. In working with survivor victims of abrasive death, it is best to begin as soon as possible after the tragedy, within the first 72 hours if that can be managed.
2. Remarkably little resistance is met from the survivors; most are either willing or eager to have the opportunity to talk to a professionally oriented person.
3. Negative emotions about the decedent or about the death itself—irritation, anger, envy, shame, guilt, and so on—need to be explored, but not at the very beginning.
4. The postvener should play the important role of reality tester. He is not so much the echo of conscience as the quiet voice of reason.
5. Medical evaluation of the survivors is crucial. One should be constantly alert for possible decline in physical health and in overall mental well-being.
6. Needless to say, pollyannish optimism or banal platitudes should be avoided—this statement being a good example.
7. Grief work takes a while—from several months (about a year) to the end of the life, but certainly more than three months or six sessions.
8. A comprehensive program of health care on the part of a benign and enlightened community (or a first-rate hospital) should include preventive, interventive, and *postventive* elements.

☐ Endnote

[1]The person who systematically attempts to help the bereaved individual is either a therapist or is acting in the role of a therapist. He cannot escape this role. This is not to say that many others—relatives, dear friends, organization (e.g., church) members, neighbors—do not play important, perhaps the most important, roles.

References

Bowlby, J. (1961). Processes of mourning. *International Journal of Psychoanalysis, 42,* 317–340.
Caplan, G. (1964). *Principles of preventive psychiatry.* New York: Basic Books.
Freud, S. (1957). Mourning and melancholia. In *The standard edition of the complete psychological works of Sigmund Freud* (Vol. 14). London: Hogarth Press.
Friedman, P., & Lum, L. (1957). Some psychiatric notes on the *Andrea Doria* disaster. *American Journal of Psychiatry, 114,* 426–432.
Kraus, A., & Lilienfeld, A. (1959). Some epidemiologic aspects of the high mortality rate in the young widowed group. *Journal of Chronic Disease, 10,* 207–217.
Lifton, R. (1964). *Death in life: Survivors of Hiroshima.* New York: Vintage.
Lindemann, E. (1944). Symptomatology and management of acute grief. *American Journal of Psychiatry, 101,* 141–148.
Lindemann, E. & Greer, I. (1972). A study of grief: Emotional responses to suicide. In A. Cain (Ed.), *Survivors of suicide.* Springfield, IL: Thomas.
Lindemann, E., Vaughn, W. T., & McGinnis, M. (1972). Preventive intervention in a four-year-old child whose father committed suicide. In A. Cain (Ed.), *Survivors of suicide.* Springfield, IL: Thomas.
Parkes, C. (1964). Bereavement and mental illness. *British Journal of Medical Psychology, 38,* 1–26.
Parkes, C. (1970). The first year of bereavement. *Psychiatry, 33,* 442–467.
Parkes, C. (1971). Psychosocial transitions: A field for study. *Social Sciences Medicine, 5,* 101–115.
Parkes, C. (1972). *Bereavement.* New York: International Universities Press.
Parkes, C., & Fitzgerald, R. (1969). Broken heart: A statistical study of increased mortality among widowers. *British Medical Journal, 1,* 740–743.
Rahe, R. H. (1972). Subjects' recent life changes and their near-future illness reports. *Annals of Clinical Research, 4,* 250–265.
Rees, W., & Lutkins, S. (1967). Mortality of bereavement. *British Medical Journal, 4,* 13–16.
Shneidman, E. S. (1974). *Deaths of man.* New York: Penguin.
Shneidman, E. S. (1964). Sleep, suicide and death. *Journal of Consulting Psychology, 28,* 95–106.
Shneidman, E. S. (1970). Recent developments in suicide prevention. In E. S. Shneidman (Ed.), *The psychology of suicide.* New York: Science House.
Silverman, P. (1969). Intervention with the widow of a suicide. In A. Cain (Ed.), *Survivors of suicide.* Springfield, IL: Thomas.
Stein, Z., & Susser, M. (1969). Widowhood and mental illness. *British Journal of Preventive Social Medicine, 23,* 106–110.
Varah, C. (1966). *The samaritans.* New York: Macmillan.
Wallace, A. (1956). *Tornado in Worcester: An exploratory study of individual and community behavior in an extreme situation.* Washington, DC: National Research Council.
Weisman, A. D. (1972). *On death and denying.* New York: Behavioral Publications.
Wolfenstein, M. (1957). *Disaster: A psychological essay.* New York: Macmillan.
Young, M., Benjamin, B., & Wallis, C. (1963). The mortality of widowers. *Lancet, 2,* 454–456.

PART

V

DEATH

Death is superordinate to suicide. Suicide is only one category among the four universally recognized modes of death: Natural, accident, suicide, homicide—what Shneidman has called the NASH categories of death. Some notions of death are always involved in the suicidal scenario. It makes sense for a suicidologist to study the topics of death, grief and mourning.

Shneidman spent the majority of his career at UCLA as a Professor of Thanatology, studying death and dying. (Since 1988, he has been Professor of Thanatology Emeritus.) For several years—in addition to his seeing suicidal persons at UCLA—he worked on the oncology wards of the UCLA Center for Health Sciences, endeavoring to assist terminal patients to die better, and trying to help their survivors survive better—better, that is, than if they had not interacted with him at all. The fact that all the cancer patients were dying unwillingly permitted new insights into why suicidal people would electively seek out their own demise. Every suicidologist is a potential thanatologist.

There are four chapters in this part. Chapter 34, "Orientations Toward Death" is, by Shneidman's own account, his favorite publication. Perhaps this is because he wrote it expressly for a Festschrift for Henry Murray's 70th birthday in 1963, *The Study of Lives* edited by Robert W. White. In this chapter, Shneidman proposes three categories of death to supplement the four traditional NASH types: Intentioned deaths (all suicides), subintentioned deaths, and unintentioned deaths. The most interesting category is the subintentioned death group. These are deaths that can include some natural, many accidental, and even some homicidal deaths. A subintentioned death is one in which the decedent has played some covert, indirect, latent, unconscious role in his or her demise. Such deaths are not totally natural, not entirely accidental, not wholly adventitious—and yet they are not conscious suicide either. This concept appropriately makes the decedent a participant in the death, when the facts warrant this designation. It psychologizes death. The last section of this chapter is a psychological autopsy of the death of a giant fictional character, the immortal Captain Ahab, the tormented protagonist of Melville's *Moby-Dick.*

Chapter 35 was written while Shneidman was on sabbatical leave at the Karolinska Institute in Stockholm, in 1978, working with his dear friend, oncologist-psychiatrist Loma Feigenberg. Here Shneidman pours out his heart about specific characteristics of psychotherapy with terminal patients, focusing especially on the intense positive transferences and countertransferences that often occur in that setting. The paper also deals with the ways in which thanatological psychotherapy is special and how it differs from psychotherapy with persons who are not dying.

Chapter 36—the last chapter of Dr. Shneidman's most recent book—relates primarily to suicide as a way of death and reflects on the life-saving role that others can play in saving a potentially suicidal person's life. But Shneidman ruefully reflects that, in the final analysis, it is the suicidal individual who must play the vital role in sustaining the drama and living to another day.

Chapter 36 is the dedication (in *Voices of Death*) to his "late beloved parents"—some deeply sentimental reflections he had while wandering through an ancient Greek cemetery in his sixties. These themes of attachment and gratitude touch almost all his work.

34

CHAPTER

Orientations Toward Death: A Vital Aspect of the Study of Lives

It is both stimulating and depressing to contemplate the fact that at this period in man's history, when, at long last, one can find a few genuine indications of straightforward discussions and investigations of death, these pursuits come at the time of man's terrible new-found capacity to destroy his works and to decimate his kind. For these reasons, it may be said that a special kind of intellectual and affective permissiveness, born out of a sense of urgency, now exists for man's greater understanding of his own death and destruction.

For the past few years, a number of us engaged in activities related to the prevention of suicide have habitually looked upon instances of suicidal phenomena as manifestations of a major scourge, involving, as they inevitably do, untimely death for the victim and generally stigmatized lives for the survivors. My own special interest in the classification of death phenomena is one outcome of this group concern with suicidal behaviors.[1] The purpose of this paper is to stimulate a rethinking of conventional notions of death and suicide. A further purpose is to attempt to create a psychologically oriented classification of death phenomena—an ordering based in large part on the role of the individual in his own demise.

Reprinted from R. W. White (Ed.), *The Study of Lives*. New York: Atherton Press, 1963, pp. 200–227. With permission.

Reflections on death, including suicide, are found in some of man's earliest written works. Death and suicide have been depicted and reified in various ways; numerous misconceptions have grown up around these topics. These proliferated intellectual overgrowths are not the specimens that we wish to describe here. Rather, we have to see them as encumbering underbrush that must be cleared away before we can come to the heart of the problem. This is the task to which I now turn.

"Idols," or False Notions About Death and Suicide

This section might have been entitled "A Few Aphorisms Concerning the Interpretation of Suicide and the Nature of Death." Such a heading would, of course, be a minor variation of a theme in Bacon's *Novum Organum*. As in Bacon's day, there are "idols and false notions which are now in possession of the human understanding." Bacon enumerated four classes of "idols" (or fallacies): Idols of the Tribe, Idols of the Cave, Idols of the Market Place, and Idols of the Theater. Of particular interest to us in the present context are the Idols of the Cave—"the idols of the individual man, for everyone . . . has a cave or den of his own, which refracts and discolors the light of nature" (Bacon, 1620). In respect to suicide and death each person figuratively builds for himself, in relation to the cryptic topics of life and death, his own (mis)conceptual vault of beliefs, understandings, and orientations—"Idols of the Grave," as I will call them. Further, I would propose five subcategories of these Idols of the Grave, specifically as they concern: (1) the role of classification or taxonomy in treating dying or suicidal people; (2) the classification of suicidal phenomena; (3) the relationships between suicidal and death phenomena; (4) the classification of death phenomena; and (5) the concept of death itself.

The Idol That Maximally Effective Programs of Prevention and Treatment Can Be Developed in the Absence of Taxonomic Understanding

Although one's associations to the word taxonomy—the discipline whose purpose it is to develop concise methods for classifying knowledge—are primarily to the fields of botany and zoology, I wish to focus on the role of taxonomy in the healing arts and sciences. It has been axiomatic in these disciplines that definitive therapies or cures stem from accurate diagnosis and that accurate diagnoses can hardly exist in the absence of meaningful (including taxonomic) understanding of the phenomena. Before one can meaningfully and efficiently treat, protect, and help, one must understand; paradoxically, however, the heart of understanding lies in meaningful classification. In the area of mental health (especially in the areas concerning death and suicide), meaningful taxonomies would seem to be the professionals' *sine qua non* for effective diagnosis, prevention, and treatment. All this is not to imply that there have not been classifications of death and suicidal phenomena but rather to suggest that we must continue to attend to the classificatory aspect of our enterprise if we mean to increase, over the years, our effectiveness—an effectiveness which must rest on expanded understanding.

The Idol That the Present Classifications of Suicidal Phenomena Are Meaningful

The use of an illustration may be the best introduction to this topic. A woman of around thirty years of age was seen on the ward of a large general hospital after she had been returned from surgery. She had, a few hours before, shot herself in the head with a .22 caliber revolver, the result being that she had enucleated an eye and torn away part of her frontal lobe. Emergency surgical and medical procedures had been employed. When she was seen in bed subsequent to surgery, her head was enveloped in bandages, and the appropriate tubes and needles were in her. Her chart indicated that she had attempted to kill herself, the diagnosis being "attempted suicide." It happened that in the next bed there was another young woman of about the same age. She had been permitted to occupy the bed for a few hours to "rest prior to going home, having come to the hospital that day because she had cut her left wrist with a razor blade. The physical trauma was relatively superficial and required but two stitches. She had had, she said, absolutely no lethal intention, but had definitely wished to jolt her husband into attending to what she wanted to say to him about his drinking habits. Her words to him had been, "Look at me, I'm bleeding." She had taken this course after she had, in conversation with her husband, previously threatened suicide. Her chart, too, indicated a diagnosis of "attempted suicide."

Common sense should tell us that if we obtained scientific data from these two cases—psychiatric anamnestic data, psychological test data, etc.—and then grouped these materials under the single rubric of "attempted suicide," we would obviously run the risk of masking precisely the differences which we might wish to explore. Common sense might further tell us that the first woman could most appropriately be labeled as a case of "committed suicide" (even though she was alive), and the second woman as "nonsuicidal" (even though she had cut her wrist with a razor blade). But, aside from the issue of what would be the most appropriate diagnosis in each case, it still seems evident that collating these two cases—and hundreds of similar instances—under the common heading of "attempted suicide" might definitely limit rather than extend the range of our potential understanding.

Individuals with clear lethal intention, as well as those with ambivalent or no lethal intention, are currently grouped under the heading of attempted suicide: we know that individuals can attempt to attempt, attempt to commit, attempt to be nonsuicidal. All this comes about largely because of oversimplification as to types of causes and a confusion between modes and purpose. (The law punishes the holdup man with the unloaded or toy gun, precisely because the victim must assume that the bandit has, by virtue of his holding a "gun," covered himself with the semantic mantle "gunman.") One who cries "help" while holding a razor blade is deemed by society to be suicidal. Although it is true that the act of putting a shotgun in one's mouth and pulling the trigger with one's toe is almost always related to lethal self-intention, this particular relationship between method and intent does not hold for most other methods, such as ingesting barbiturates or cutting oneself with a razor. In most cases the intentions may range all the way from deadly ones, through the wide variety of ambivalences, rescue fantasies, cries for help, and psychic indecisions, all the way to clearly formulated nonlethal intention in which a semantic usurpation of a "suicidal" mode has been consciously employed.

It may not be inaccurate to state that in this century there have been two major theoretical approaches to suicide: the sociological and the psychological, identified with the names of Durkheim and Freud, respectively. Durkheim's delineation of etiological types of suicide—anomic, altruistic, and egoistic—is probably the best-known classification (Durkheim, 1951). For my part, I have often felt that this famous typology of suicidal behaviors has behaved like a brilliantly conceived sociologic motorcycle (anomie) with two psychological sidecars, performing effectively in textbooks for over half a century, but running low on power in clinics, hospitals, and consultation rooms. This classification epitomizes some of the strengths and shortcomings of any study based almost entirely on a social, normative, tabular, nomothetic approach. It is probably fair to say, however, that Durkheim was not so much interested in suicide per se as he was in the explication of his general sociological method.

Freud's psychological formulation of suicide, as hostility directed toward the introjected love object—what I have called "murder in the

180th degree" (1924a, p. 220; 1924b, pp. 162–163)—was more a brilliant inductive encompassment than an empirical, scientific particularization. This concept was given its most far-reaching exposition by Karl Menninger, who, in *Man Against Himself* (1938), not only outlined four types of suicide—chronic, focal, organic, and actual—but also proposed three basic psychological components: the wish to kill, the wish to be killed, and the wish to die.

Neither of these two theoretical approaches to the nature and causes of suicide constitutes the classification most common in everyday clinical use. That distinction belongs to a rather homely, supposedly commonsense division, which in its barest form implies that all humanity can be divided into two groupings, suicidal and nonsuicidal, and then divides the suicidal category into committed, attempted, and threatened.[2] Although the second classification is superior to the suicidal-versus-nonsuicidal view of life, that it is not theoretically or practically adequate for understanding and treatment is one of the main tenets of this paper. It may well be that the word suicide currently has too many loose and contradictory meanings to be scientifically or clinically useful.

The Idol That Living and Dying Are Separate

Living and dying have too often been seen erroneously as distinct, separate, almost dichotomous activities. To correct this view one can enunciate another, which might be called the psychodynamics of dying. One of its tenets is that, in cases where an individual is dying over a period of time, which may vary from hours to years in persons who "linger" in terminal illnesses, this interval is a psychologically consistent extension of styles of coping, defending, adjusting, interacting, and other modes of behavior that have characterized that individual during most of his life up to that time. Feifel says, "A man's birth is an uncontrolled event in his life, but the manner of his departure from life bears a definite relation to his philosophy of life and death. We are mistaken to consider death as a purely biological event. The attitudes concerning it and its meaning for the individual can serve as an important organizing principle in determining how he conducts himself in life" (Feifel, 1959, p. 128). How an individual dies should no less reflect his personal philosophy, the goodness of his personal adjustment, his sense of fruition, fulfillment, self-realization. Feifel further states that ". . . types of reactions to impending death are a function of interweaving factors. Some of the significant ones appear to be . . . the psychological maturity of the individual; the kind of coping techniques available to him; variables of religious orientation, age, socioeconomic status, etc.; severity of the organic process; and the attitudes of the significant persons in the patient's world" (Fiefel, 1959, p. 126).

Dr. Authur P. Noyes is reported to have said, "As we grow older, we grow more like ourselves." I believe that this illuminating but somewhat cryptic remark can also be taken to mean that during the dying period, the individual displays behaviors and attitudes which contain great fealty to his lifelong orientations and beliefs. Draper says, "Each man dies in a notably personal way (Draper, Dupertuis, & Coughley, 1944, p. 74). Suicidal and/or dying behaviors do not exist *in vacuo*, but are an integral part of the life style of the individual (Curphey, 1961, pp. 110–117; Farberow & Shneidman, 1961, pp. 118–128).[3]

The Idol That the Traditional Classification of Death Phenomena Is Clear

The *International Classification of the Causes of Death* lists 137 causes, such as pneumonia, meningitis, malignant neoplasms, myocardial infarctions[4]; but, in contrast, there are only four commonly recognized *modes* of death: *natural death, accident, suicide,* and *homicide*. In some cases, cause of death is used synonymously to indicate the natural cause of death. Thus, the standard U.S. Public Health Service Certificate of Death has a space to enter cause of death (implying the mode as natural) and, in addition, provides opportunity to indicate accident, suicide, or homicide. Apparently, it is implied that these four modes of death constitute the final ordering into which each of us must be classified. The fact that some of us do not fit easily into one of these four crypts is the substance for this section.

The shortcoming of the common classification is that, in its oversimplification and failure to take into account certain necessary dimensions, it often poses serious problems in classifying deaths meaningfully. The basic ambiguities can be seen most clearly by focusing on the distinctions between natural (intrasomatic) and accidental (extrasomatic) deaths. On the face of it, the argument can be advanced that most deaths, especially in the younger years, are unnatural. Perhaps only in the cases of death of old age might the termination of life legitimately be called natural. Let us examine the substance of some of these confusions. If an individual (who wishes to continue living) has his skull invaded by a lethal object, his death is called accidental; if another individual (who also wishes to continue living) is invaded by a lethal virus, his death is called natural. An individual who torments an animal into killing him is said to have died an accidental death, whereas an individual who torments a drunken companion into killing him is called a homicidal victim. An individual who has an artery burst in his brain is said to have died with a cerebral-vascular accident, whereas it might make more sense to call it a cerebral-vascular natural death. What has been confusing in this traditional approach is that the individual has been viewed as a kind of biological *object* (rather than psychological, social, biological organism), and as a consequence, the role of the individual in his own demise has been omitted.

The Idol That the Concept "Death" Is Itself Operationally Sound

We come now to what for some may be the most radical and iconoclastic aspect of our presentation so far, specifically the suggestion that a major portion of the concept of "death" is operationally meaningless and ought therefore to be eschewed. Let the reader ask the question of the author: "Do you mean to say that you wish to discuss suicidal phenomena and orientations toward death without the concept of death?" The author's answer is in the affirmative, based, he believes, on compelling reasons. Essentially, these reasons are epistemological, that is, they have to do with the process of knowing and the question of what it is that we can know. Our main source of quotable strength—and we shall have occasion later to refer to him in a very different context—is the physicist Percy W. Bridgman. Essentially, his concept is that death is not experienceable, that if one could experience it, one would not be dead. One can experience another's dying and another's death and his own dying—although he can never be sure—but no man can experience his own death.

In his book *The Intelligent Individual and Society.* Bridgman states this view as follows:

> There are certain kinks in our thinking which are of such universal occurrence as to constitute essential limitations. Thus the urge to think of my own death as some form of my experience is almost irresistible. However, it requires only to be said for me to admit that my own death cannot be a form of experience, for if I could still experience, then by definition it would not be death. Operationally my own death is a fundamentally different thing from the death of another in the same way that my own feelings mean something fundamentally different from the feelings of another. The death of another I can experience; there are certain methods of recognizing death and certain properties of death that affect my actions in the case of others. Again it need not bother us to discover that the concept of death in another is not sharp, and situations may arise in practice where it

> is difficult to say whether the organism is dead or not, particularly if one sticks to the demand that "death" must be such a thing that when the organism is once dead it cannot live again. This demand rests on mystical feelings, and there is no reason why the demand should be honored in framing the definition of death. . . . My own death is such a different thing that it might well have a different word, and perhaps eventually will. There is no operation by which I can decide whether I am dead; "I am always alive." (Bridgman, 1938, pp. 168; Bridgman, 1955, pp. 234–235.)

This pragmatic view of death—in the strict philosophical sense of pragmatism—is stated most succinctly (in a side remark about death) by the father of pragmatism. Peirce, in discussing metaphysics, says:

> We start then, with nothing, pure zero. But this is not the nothing of negation. For *not* means *other than,* and *other* is merely a synonym of the ordinal numeral *second.* As such it implies a first; while the present pure zero is prior to every first. The nothing of negation is the nothing of death, which also comes *second to,* or after, everything. (Hartshorne & Weiss, 1931–1958, p. 148)

In literature this concept of death as nothingness seems to have appeared early and remained.

Two further thoughts on death as experience. Not only, as we have seen, is death misconceived as an experience, but (1) it is further misconceived as a bitter or calamitous experience, and (2) it is still further misconceived as an *act,* as though dying were something that one had to do. On the contrary, dying can be a supreme passivity rather than the supreme act or activity. It will be done for you; dying is one thing that no one has to "do."[5]

In addition to this philosophical aspect of the situation, there is also the reflection that one's own death is really psychologically inconceivable. Possibly the most appropriate quotation in this connection is from the twentieth-century giant of depth psychology. In his paper on "Thoughts of War and Death," Freud wrote:

> Our own death is indeed unimaginable, and whenever we make the attempt to imagine it we can conceive that we really survive as spectators. Hence the psychoanalytic school could venture on the assertion that at bottom no one believes in his own death, or to put the thing in another way, in the unconscious every one of us is convinced of his own immortality. (1924c, pp. 304–305)[6]

Indeed, the word "death" has become a repository for pervasive logical and epistemological confusions—"Idols of the Dead." The first order of business might well be to clarify the concepts presently embedded in our current notions of death. For my part, I would wish to eschew, where possible, the concept of death and, instead, use concepts and terms which are operationally viable. This is the text of the present section, the content of the next section, and the burden of this paper.

Cessation, Termination, Interruption, and Continuation

In the preceding section, I have been critical of some current concepts relating to suicide and death. In this section I wish to propose a tentative psychological classification of all behaviors involving demise. Two sets of key concepts are involved: the first is made up of the terms cessation, termination, interruption, and continuation; the second, of the terms intentioned, subintentioned, unintentioned, and contraintentioned. At this point, our first tasks are those of definition.

Cessation

The key concept in this paper is the idea of "cessation."[7] In this context, cessation has a psychological, specifically introspective referent. Our definition of "cessation" is that it is the stopping of the potentiality of any (further) conscious experience. "Death"—some form of termination—is the universal and unbiquitous ending of all living things; but only man, by virtue of his verbally reportable introspective mental life, can conceptualize, fear, and suffer cessation. Cessation refers to the last line of the last scene of the last act of the last drama of that actor. It should be immediately obvious that different individuals—and any particular individual at different times—can have a variety of attitudes and orientations toward their cessations. The next section contains an explication of possible orientations toward cessation. Cessation is used here not as a synonym for the word death, but rather as its operationally defined substitute. Also, in order to have a shorthand term for cessation, I shall use the term, "Psyde," referring, so to speak, to the demise of the psychic processes—the final stopping of the individual consciousness, as far as we know.[8]

Termination

The concept of "termination"—which is defined as the stopping of the physiological functions of the body—is needed because there can occur the stopping of the potentiality of conscious experience (cessation) which is not temporally coincident with the stopping of the functions of the body. Our shorthand word for termination is "Somize," referring to the demise of the soma. Consider the report of the following incident: A young man was, while riding as a passenger on a motorcycle, hit by an automobile and thrown several yards through the air. He landed on his head at a curbside. At the hospital, this case was regarded as remarkable, because, although his skull was crushed and although he showed no evidence of any conscious experience and even had a rather complete absence of reflexes, he was kept alive for many days by means of intravenous feeding, catheter relief, and many other life-extending pieces of mechanical apparatus. Eventually he "expired." The conceptual point to be made in this context is that he suffered cessation the moment that his head hit the pavement. So, although he had ceased, he had not terminated, in that he continued to breathe. No one would have thought to suggest that he be buried or cremated as long as he was still breathing. A further point can be made: the operational definition (or criterion) for termination can be put at the stopping of the exchange of gases between the human organism and his environment, i.e., an individual may be said to be terminated when, if a mirror is put to his mouth, there is no frosting on the glass—the subsequent growth of his beard or other activities do not matter.[9] If cessation relates to the psychological personality, then termination has to do with the biological organism. It is useful to distinguish between cessation and termination. We all know that it is possible for an individual to put a gun to his head, planning to "blow his brains out" (termination) and yet *believe* that he will be at his own funeral, that he will be able to check whether or not his widow follows the instructions in his suicide note (without cessation). In order not to be entrapped by the confusion that exists in many minds concerning these two concepts, we must clarify them in our own.

Interruption

The third concept of this group is that of interruption, which relates not to termination but to cessation. If cessation has to do with the stopping of the potentiality of any conscious experience, then interruption is in a sense its opposite, in that "interruption" is defined as the stopping of consciousness with the actuality, and usually the expectation, of further conscious experiences. It is a kind of temporary cessation. The best example of an interruption state is being asleep; others are being under an anesthetic, in an alcoholic stupor, in a diabetic coma, in an epileptic seizure, and, on another level, being in a fugue, amnesic, or dissociative state. The primary purpose of introducing the notion of interruption states is to provide a concept whereby data—especially those which could be obtained from experimental situations—might serve as paradigms, analogues, models, or patterns for certain cessation conditions. For example—and more will be said about this later—it might be possible to devise paradigms having to do with sleep behavior that will give us fresh leads and new insights into suicidal behaviors, which a direct approach would not yield.

Continuation

When one works with suicidal people clinically and investigates, through "psychological autopsies," cases of suicide, one often gets the impression that individuals who, in point of fact, have killed themselves, have not necessarily "committed suicide." That is to say, in some cases, it seems that the person's intention was not to embrace death but rather to find surcease from external or internalized aspects of life. In the context of this paper, we shall call the process of living "continuation." "Continuation" can be defined as experiencing, in the absence of interruption, the stream of temporally contiguous conscious events. From this point of view, our lives are made up of a series of alternating continuation and interruption states.

One might find a group of nonlethally oriented "suicide attempters"—each of whom wished to postpone cessation—who, individually, might manifest quite different patterns of orientation toward continuation. The nuances of these patterns might well include the following: (1) patterns of ambivalence (coexistent wishes to live and to die, including rescue fantasies, gambles with death, and cries for help); (2) the state of hopefulness or hopelessness, and accompanying feelings of psychological impotence; (3) patterns of self-righteousness, indignation, inner resourcefulness, defeat, and ennui; (4) orientations toward the next temporal interval, whether one of blandness, inertia, habit, interest, anticipation, expectation, or demand; (5) intensity of thought and action in relation to continuation, ranging from absent (no thought about it), through fleeting fantasy, concern, obsession, and rash behavior outburst, to deliberate performance. Continuation is the converse of cessation. It would be important to know, in any particular case, how an individual's attitudes toward continuation interacted with his orientations toward cessation. In addition to this, we could say that a comprehensive study of suicidal phenomena should include concern for nonsuicidal phenomena and such perverse questions as what a specific individual has to live for or why a specific individual does not commit suicide.

Basic Orientations Toward Cessation

The operation which gives meaning to the phrase "basic orientation toward cessation" has to do with the role of the individual in his own demise. By "role of the individual" is meant his overt and covert behaviors and nonbehaviors which reflect conscious and unconscious attributes relevant to his cessation. These include at least the following: his attitudes and beliefs about death, cessation, hereafter, and rebirth; his ways of thinking; his need systems, including his needs for achievement, affiliation, autonomy, and dominance; his dyadic relationships, especially the subtleties of dependencies and hostilities in relation to the significant people in his life; the hopefulness and hopelessness in the responses of these people to his cries for help; the constellation and balance of ego activity and ego passivity; his orientations toward continuation states. To know these facts about a person would well require a comprehensive psychological understanding of his personality.

Four subcategories relating to the role of the individual in his own demise are suggested: intentioned, subintentioned, unintentioned, and contraintentioned.

Intentioned

By intentioned, I refer to those cases in which the individual plays a direct and conscious role in his own demise. These cases do not refer to persons who wish for "death" or termination, but rather to those who actively precipitate their cessation. (Of course, cessation cannot be avoidance by anyone. The entire issue is one of timing and involves postponing and hastening.) In terms of the traditional categories of death, no presently labeled accidental or natural deaths would be called intentioned, some homicidal deaths might be called intentioned, and most (but, importantly, not all) suicidal deaths would be called intentioned. In relation to the term "suicide," intentioned cases may be said to have *committed* suicide. Using the word "Psyde" to represent cessation, we can list a number of subcategories: (1) Psyde-seekers; (2) Psyde-initiators; (3) Psyde-ignorers; and (4) Psyde-darers.

1. Psyde-Seeker

A Psyde-seeker is one who, during the time that he can be so labeled, has consciously verbalized to himself his wish for an ending to all conscious experience and behaves in order to achieve this end. The operational criteria for a Psyde-seeker lie not primarily in the method he uses—razor, barbiturate, carbon monoxide—but in the fact that the method *in his mind* is calculated to bring him cessation; and, whatever his rescue fantasies or cries for help may be, he does the act in such a manner and site that rescue (or intervention) is realistically unlikely or impossible. In all, he has a predominantly unambivalent intention or orientation toward cessation during that period. The phrase "during that period" is meant to convey the notion that individuals' orientations toward cessation shift and change over time.[10] A person who was a Psyde-seeker yesterday and made a most serious suicidal act then, could not today be forced to participate in activities that might cost him his life. It is known clinically—as supported by our experience at the Suicide Prevention Center—that many individuals are "suicidal" for only a relatively brief period of time; so that if they can be given appropriate sanctuary, they will no longer seek Psyde and will wish to continue to live as long as possible.

2. Psyde-Initiator[11]

A Psyde-initiator is a Psyde-seeker, but sufficiently different to warrant a separate label. A Psyde-initiator believes that he will suffer cessation in the fairly near future—a matter of days or weeks—or he believes that he is failing and, not wishing to accommodate himself to a new (and less effective and less virile) image of himself, does not wish to let "it" happen to him. Rather *he* wants to play a role in its occurrence. Thus he will do it for himself, at his own time, and on his own terms. In our investigations at the Veterans Administration Central Research Unit for the Study of Unpredicted Death we find, on occasion, a case in which an older person, hospitalized in a general medical hospital, in the terminal stages of a fatal disease will, with remarkable and totally unexpected energy and strength, take the tubes and needles out of himself, climb over the bed rails, lift a heavy window, and throw himself to the ground several stories below. What is most prototypical about such an individual is that, when one looks at his previous occupational history, one sees that he has never been fired—he has always quit. In either case, the person ends up unemployed, but the role he has played in the process is different.[12]

3. Psyde-Ignorer

Consider the following suicide note: "Good-by, kid. You couldn't help it. Tell that brother of yours, when he gets to where I'm going, I hope I'm a foreman down there; I might be able to do something for him." Although it is true that suicide notes which contain any reference to a hereafter, a continued existence, or a reunion with dead loved ones are relatively very rare, it is also true that some people who kill themselves believe, as part of their total system of beliefs, that one can effect termination without involving cessation. They seem to ignore the fact that, so far as we know, termination always involves cessation. One can note that even those in our contemporary society who espouse belief in a hereafter as part of their religious tenets, still label a person who has shot himself to death as suicidal. This is probably so primarily because, whatever *really* happens after termination, the survivors are still left to live (and usually to mourn) in the undeniable physical absence of the person who killed himself. Thus, this subcategory of Psyde-ignorer, or, perhaps better, Psyde-transcender, contains those persons who, from our point of view, effect their own termination and cessation but who, from their point of view, effect only their termination and continue to exist in some manner or another.

This paragraph is not meant to necessarily deny a (logical) possibility of continuation after cessation (life after death), but the concept of Psyde-ignoring (or something similar to it) is a firm necessity in any systematic classification of this type; otherwise we will put ourselves in the untenable position of making exactly comparable (1) a man's shooting his head off in the belief and hope that he will soon meet his dead wife in heaven and (2) a man's taking a trip from one city to another with the purpose and expectation of being reunited with his spouse. Obviously, these two acts are so vastly different in their effects (on the person concerned and on others who know him) that they cannot be equated. Therefore, independent of the individual's convictions that killing oneself does not result in cessation but is simply a transition to another life, we must superimpose our belief that cessation is necessarily final as far as the human personality which we can know is concerned.

4. Psyde-Darer

A Psyde-darer is an individual who, to use gamblers' terms, bets his continuation (i.e., his life) on the objective probability of as few as five out of six chances that he will survive. Regardless of the outcome, an individual who plays Russian roulette is a Psyde-darer at that time. In addition to the objective probabilities that exist, the concept of a Psyde-darer also involves subjective probabilities of the same order of magnitude. Thus, a person with little skill as a pilot who attempts to fly an airplane, or one with unpracticed co-ordination who attempts to walk along the ledge of a roof of a tall building, may be classified as a Psyde-darer. The rule of thumb is that it is not what he does, but the background (of skill, prowess, and evaluation of his own abilities) against which he does it, that matters. In a sense the Psyde-darer is only a partial, or fractional, cessation-seeker; but since each lethal fraction contained within the gambling situation is completely lethal, it seems most meaningful to classify such an act within the intention category.

Subintentioned

Subintentioned cessation behaviors relate to those instances in which the individual plays an indirect, covert, partial, or unconscious role in his own demise. That individuals may play an unconscious role in their own failures and act inimically to their own best welfare seem to be facts too well documented from psychoanalytic and general clinical practice to ignore. Often cessation is hastened by the individual's seeming carelessness, imprudence, foolhardiness, forgetfulness, amnesia, lack of judgment, or other psychological mechanisms. This concept of subintentioned demise is similar, in some ways, to Karl Menninger's concepts of chronic, focal, and organic suicides, except that Menninger's ideas have to do with self-defeating ways of continuing to live, whereas the notion of subintentioned cessation is a description of a way of stopping the process of living. Included in this subintention category would be many patterns of mismanagement and brink-of-death living which result in cessation. In terms of the traditional classification of modes of death (natural, accident, homicide, and suicide), some instances of all four types can be subsumed under this category, depending on the particular details of each case. In relation to the term suicide, subintentioned cases may be said to have *permitted* suicide.

Subintentioned cessation involves what might be called the psychosomatics of death: that is, cases in which essentially psychological processes (like fear, anxiety, derring-do, hate, etc.) seem to play some role in exacerbating the catabolic or physiological processes that bring on termination (Gengerelli & Kirkner, 1953) (and necessarily cessation), as well as those cases in which the individual seems to play an indirect, largely unconscious role in inviting or hastening cessation itself (Wolfgang, 1959). The Psyde groups for the subintentioned category are, tentatively, as follows: (1) Psyde-chancer; (2) Psyde-hastener; (3) Psyde-capitulator; and (4) Psyde-experimenter.

1. Psyde-Chancer

The Psyde-darer, Psyde-chancer, and Psyde-experimenter are all on a continuum of chance expectation and chance possibility of cessation. The difference lies in the combination of objective and subjective probabilities. If a Psyde-darer has only five chances out of six of continuing, then a Psyde-chancer would have chances significantly greater than that, but still involving a realistic risk of cessation. It should be pointed out that these categories are largely independent on the method used, in that most methods (like the use of razor blades or barbiturates) can, depending on the exact place of the cut, the depth of the cut, and the realistic and calculated expectations for intervention and rescue by others, legitimately be thought of as intentioned, subintentioned, unintentioned, or contraintentioned—depending on these circumstances. Individuals who "leave it up to chance," who "gamble with death" (Weiss, 1957), who "half-intend to do it" are the subintentioned Psyde-chancers.

2. Psyde-Hastener

The basic assumption is that in all cessation activities the critical question (on the assumption that cessation will occur to everyone) is when, so that, in a sense, all intentioned and subintentioned activities are hastening. The Psyde-hastener refers to the individual who unconsciously exacerbates a physiological disequilibrium so that his cessation (which would, in ordinary terms, be called a natural death) is expedited. This can be done either in terms of the "style" in which he lives (the abuse of his body, usually through alcohol, drugs, exposure, or malnutrition) or, in cases where there is a specific physiological imbalance, through the mismanagement of prescribed remedial procedures. Examples of the latter would be the diabetic who "mismanages" his diet or his insulin, the individual with cirrhosis who "mismanages" his alcoholic intake, the Berger's disease patient who "mismanages" his nicotine intake. Very closely allied to the Psyde-hastener is the Psyde-facilitator, who, while he is ill and his psychic energies are low, is somehow more-than-passively unresisting to cessation, and "makes it easy" for termination (and accompanying cessation) to occur. Some unexpected deaths in hospitals may be of this nature. The excellent recent paper of Weisman and Hackett explores this area (Weisman & Hackett, 1961).

3. Psyde-Capitulator

A Psyde-capitulator is a person who, by virtue of some strong emotion, usually his fear of death, plays a psychological role in effecting his termination. In a sense, he gives in to death or he scares himself to death. This type of death includes voodoo deaths; the type of death reported among Indians and Mexicans from southwestern United States railroad hospitals, where the patients thought that people who went to hospitals went there to die, and being hospitalized was thus cause in itself for great alarm; and some of the cases reported from Boston by Weisman and

Hackett. All these individuals play a psychological role in the psychosomatics of their termination and cessation.

4. Psyde-Experimenter

A Psyde-experimenter is a person who often lives "on the brink of death," who consciously wishes neither interruption nor cessation, but—usually by use of (or addiction to) alcohol and/or barbiturates—seems to wish a chronically altered, usually befogged continuation state. Psyde-experimenters seem to wish to remain conscious but to be benumbed or drugged. They will often "experiment" with their self-prescribed dosages (always in the direction of increasing the effect of the dosage), taking some chances of extending the benumbed conscious states into interruption (coma) states and even taking some chances (usually without much concern, in a kind of lackadaisical way) of running some minimal but real risk of extending the interruption states into cessation. When this type of death occurs, it is traditionally thought of as accidental.

Unintentioned

Unintentioned cessation describes those occurrences in which, for all intents and purposes, the person psychologically plays no significant role in his own demise. He is, at the time of his cessation, "going about his business" (even though he may be lying in a hospital), with no conscious intention of affecting or hastening cessation and no strong conscious drive in this direction. What happens is that "something from the outside"—the outside of his mind—occurs. This "something" might be a cerebral-vascular accident, a myocardial infarction, a neoplastic growth, some malfunction, some catabolism, some invasion—whether by bullet or by virus—which, for him, has lethal consequences. "It" happens to "him." Inasmuch as all that anyone can do in regard to cessation is to attempt some manipulation along a temporal dimension (i.e., to hasten or to postpone it), one might suppose that unintentioned is synonymous only with "postponer," but it appears that there are other possible attitudes—welcoming, accepting, resisting, disdaining, etc.—all within the unintentioned category.

In terms of the traditional categories of death, most natural, accidental, and homicidal deaths would be called unintentioned, and no presently labeled suicidal deaths would be so called. In relation to the term "suicidal," unintentioned cases may be said tc have *omitted* suicide.

The Psyde categories for unintentioned cessation are: (1) Psyde-welcomer; (2) Psyde-acceptor; (3) Psyde-postponer; (4) Psyde-disdainer; and (5) Psyde-fearer.

1. Psyde-Welcomer

A Psyde-welcomer is one who, although playing no discernible (conscious or unconscious) role in either hastening or facilitating his own cessation, could honestly report an introspective position of welcoming the end to his life. Very old people, especially after a long, painful, debilitating illness, report that they would welcome "the end."

2. Psyde-Acceptor

The slight difference between a Psyde-welcomer and a Psyde-acceptor lies in the nuance of activity and passivity that distinguishes them. The Psyde-acceptor is one who has accepted the imminence of his cessation and "is resigned to his own fate." In this, he may be relatively passive, philosophical, resigned, heroic, realistic, or mature, depending on "the spirit" in which this enormous acceptance is made.

3. Psyde-Postponer

Most of the time most of us are acute Psyde-postponers. Psyde-postponing is the habitual, indeed the unthinking, orientation of most humans toward cessation. The Psyde-postponer is one who, to the extent that he is oriented toward or concerned with cessation at all, wishes that it would not occur in anything like the foreseeable future and further wishes that it would not occur for as long as possible. (This Psyde-postponing orientation should not be confused with the ubiquitous human fantasies of immortality.)

4. Psyde-Disdainer

Some individuals, during those moments when they consciously contemplate cessation, are disdainful of the concept and feel that they are above being involved in the cessation of the vital processes that it implies. They are, in a sense, supercilious toward death. It may well be that most young people in our culture, independent of their fears about death, are habitually Psyde-disdainers, as well they might be—for a while (Schilder & Wechsler, 1934; Nagy, 1959).

5. Psyde-Fearer

A Psyde-fearer is one who is fearful of death and of the topics relating to death. He may literally be phobic about this topic.[13] He fights the notion of cessation, seeing reified death as a feared and hated enemy. This position may be related to conscious wishes for omnipotence and to great cathexis to one's social and physical potency. Hypochondriacs, fearing illnesses and assault, are perhaps also Psyde-fearers. (A person who, when physically well, is a Psyde-fearer might, when physically ill, become a Psyde-facilitator.)

Imagine five people, all older men on the same ward of a hospital, all dying of cancer, none playing an active or unconscious role in his own cessation. Yet it is still possible to distinguish among them different orientations toward cessation: One wishes not to die and is exerting his "will to live" (Psyde-postponer); another is resigned to his cessation (Psyde-acceptor); the third is disdainful of what is occurring to him and will not believe that death can "take him" (Psyde-disdainer); still another, although not taking any steps in the direction of hastening his end, does at this point in his illness welcome it (Psyde-welcomer); and the fifth is most fearful about the topic of death and the implication of cessation and forbids anyone to speak of it in his presence (Psyde-fearer).

Contraintentioned

It is, of course, possible to shout "Fire!" in the absence of a conflagration, or "Stop thief!" in the absence of a crime. It is also possible, figuratively or literally, to shout or to murmur—the intensity of the cry does not seem to matter in some cases—"Suicide!" in the clear absence of any lethal intention. (I shall, of course, eschew the words "suicide attempt" and "suicide threat," having already indicated that either of these can range from great lethal intent, through ambivalent lethal intent, to no lethal intent.) One common result of shouting "Fire!" or "Stop thief!" is that these calls mobilize others; indeed, they put society (or certain members of society) in a position where it has no choice but to act in certain directions. An individual who uses the semantic blanket of "Suicide!" with a conscious absence of any lethal intention, I shall term as one who has employed contraintentioned—advertently noncessation—behavior. From a strictly logical point of view, it might be argued that contraintentioned behaviors belong within the unintentioned category. I believe, however, that there are sufficient reasons to warrant a separate category, if only to point up the fact that individuals can usurp the labels and the semantic trappings of death, especially of suicide and, at the same time, have a clear, conscious intention not to commit suicide and not to run any risk of cessation.

Among the contraintentioned individuals there are, by definition, no cessation or related postmortem states and hence no comparable traditional modes of death. In relation to the term suicide, contraintention cases may be said to have *remitted* (in the sense of having "refrained from") suicide.

The Psyde subcategories that we distinguish among the contraintentioned cases are (1) Psyde-feigner and (2) Psyde-threatener.

1. Psyde-Feigner

A Psyde-feigner is one who feigns or simulates what appears to be a self-directed advertent movement toward cessation. Examples are the ingesting of water from a previously emptied iodine bottle or using a razor blade with no lethal or near-lethal possibility or intent. Psyde-feigning involves some overt behavior on the part of the individual.

2. Psyde-Threatener

A Psyde-threatener is a person who, with the conscious intention of avoiding cessation, uses the threat of his cessation (and the other's respect for that threat) with the aim of achieving some of the secondary gains which go with cessation-oriented behavior. These gains usually have to do with activating other persons—usually the "significant other" person in the neurotic dyadic relationship in which the individual is involved.

Two additional comments, both obvious, should be made about contraintentioned behavior. The first is that what are ordinarily called "suicide attempts" may range in their potential lethality from absent to severe.[14] I do not wish to imply for a moment that all so-called suicide attempts should be thought of as contraintentioned; quite the contrary. Thus, each case of barbiturate ingestion or wrist cutting, or even of the use of carbon monoxide in an auto, must be evaluated in terms of the details of that case, so that it can be assessed accurately—as of that time—in terms of its intentioned, subintentioned, unintentioned, and contraintentioned components. The second comment is that those who work with people who have "attempted suicide," especially those people seen as having manifested contraintentioned behavior, must guard against their own tendencies to assume a pejorative attitude toward these behaviors. It is all too easy to say that an individual *only* attempted suicide or to dismiss the case as beneath the need for human compassion, if one assesses the act as contraintentioned. It should be obvious that no act which involves, even merely semantically, cessation behavior is other than a genuine psychiatric crisis. Too often we confuse treatment of suicidal individuals with attending to the physical trauma, forgetting that meaningful treatment has to be essentially in terms of the person's personality and the frustrations, duress, fears, and threats which he experiences in his living relationships. An unquestioned contraintentioned act merits fully as much professional attention as any other maladaptive behavior; a cry for help should never be disregarded, not only for humanitarian reasons, but also because we know that the unattended cries tend to become more shrill, and the movement on the lethality scale from cry to cry is, unfortunately, in the lethal direction.

It might be protested, inasmuch as the assessments of these intentioned states and Psyde categories involve the appraisal of *unconscious* factors, that some workers (especially lay coroners) cannot legitimately be expected to make the kinds of psychological judgments required for this type of classification. To this, one answer would be that coroners throughout the country are making judgments of precisely this nature every day of the week. In the situation of evaluating a possible suicide, the coroner often acts (sometimes without realizing it) as psychiatrist and psychologist and as both judge and jury in a quasi-judicial way. This is because certification of death as suicide does, willy-nilly, imply some judgments or reconstruction of the victim's motivation or intention. Making these judgments—perhaps more coroners ought to use the category of "undetermined"—is an inexorable part of a coroner's function. My position is that it is much better for these psychological dimensions to be made explicit and an attempt, albeit crude, be made to use them, than to have these psychological dimensions employed on an implicit and unverbalized level. The dilemma is between the polarities of a usable, oversimplified classification, on the one hand, and a complex, but more meaningful classification, on the other. The goal would be to try to combine greatest usefulness with maximum meaningfulness.

☐ An Example of an Equivocal Death

It might be most appropriate to conclude this paper by presenting, by way of example, some excerpts from a singularly interesting case. The study I have chosen is taken from a uniquely comprehensive study of death and lives by Herman Melville. It is the case of the equivocal death—was it accident, suicide, or what?—of Melville's tortured, obsessively possessed, fury-driven, cetusized man: Captain Ahab of the *Pequod*.[15]

The procedure called the "psychological autopsy" (used at the Suicide Prevention Center) involves obtaining psychological data about the behaviors and statements of the deceased in the days before his death; from this information an extrapolation of intention is made over the moments of, and the moments directly preceding, his cessation. In the case of Captain Ahab, I shall proceed as though I were preparing a report for an imaginary Nantucket coroner, including some sort of recommendation as to what labelings would be the most appropriate on his imaginary death certificate. The focus will be an attempt to come to some kind of resolution concerning Ahab's intention types and Psyde categories. But first, some facts: specifically how did the end of his life occur?

Facts

For Ahab's death, we have the following account (from Chapter 135) of his last actions: "The harpoon was darted; the stricken whale flew forward; with igniting velocity the line ran through the groove;—ran foul. Ahab stooped to clear it; he did clear it; but the flying turn caught him round the neck, and noiselessly as Turkish mutes bowstring their victim, he was shot out of the boat, ere the crew knew he was gone. . . ." On first thought, it might sound as though Ahab's death were pure accident, an unintentioned death, the cessation of a Psyde-postponer; but let us see where our second thoughts lead us. Perhaps there is more.

Background

It is possible to view *Moby Dick* as a great, sonorous Mahlerlike symphony—*Das Lied von der See*—not primarily about the joy of life nor the pessimism engendered by a crushing fate, but rather as a dramatic and poetic explication of the psychodynamics of death. And, within the context of this thought, is it not possible that Moby Dick, the great *white* whale, represents the punishment of death itself? In Chapter 28, when Ahab makes his first appearance on the *Pequod* at sea, the word "white" is used three times in one paragraph to describe Ahab: a head-to-toe scar on Ahab's body, "lividly whitish"; an allusion to a "white sailor," in the context of Captain Ahab's being laid out for burial; and "the barbaric white leg upon which he partly stood." Everywhere, reference to the pallor of death; and if there is still any question, the case for "white death" is made explicit in the discussion of the whiteness of the whale (Chapter 42), in which we are told: "It cannot well be doubted, that the one visible quality in the aspect of the dead which most appalls the gazer, is the marble pallor lingering there; as if indeed that pallor were as much like the badge of consternation in the other world, as of mortal trepidation here. And from that pallor of the dead, we borrow the expressive hue of the shroud in which we wrap them. Nor even in our superstitions do we fail to throw the same snowy mantel round our phantoms; all ghosts rising in a milk-white fog—Yea, while these terrors seize us, let us add that even the king of terrors, when personified by the evangelist, rides on his pallid horse."

And if the great white whale is death, then is not the sea itself the vessel of death? Melville sets this tone for his entire heroic narrative in his stunning opening passage:

> Call me Ishmael. Some years ago—never mind how long precisely—having little or no money in my purse, and nothing particular to interest me on shore, I thought I would sail about a little and see the watery part of the world. It is a way of driving off the spleen, and regulating the circulation. Whenever I find myself growing grim about the mouth; whenever it is a damp, drizzly November in my soul; whenever I find myself involuntarily pausing before coffin warehouses, and bringing up the rear of every funeral I meet; and especially whenever my hypos get such an upper hand of me, that it requires a strong moral principle to prevent me from deliberately stepping into the street, and methodically knocking people's hats off—then, I account it high time to get to sea as soon as I can. This is my substitute for pistol and ball. With a philosophical flourish Cato throws himself upon his sword; I quietly take to the ship. . . .

And again, much later, in the description of the blacksmith (Chapter 112), we read:

> Death seems the only desirable sequel for a career like this; but Death is only a launching into the region of the strange Untried; it is but the first salutation to the possibilities of the immense Remote, the Wild, the Watery, the Unshored; therefore, to the death-longing eyes of such men, who still have left in them some interior compunctions against suicide, does the all-contributed and all-receptive ocean alluringly spread forth his whole plain of unimaginable, taking terrors, and wonderful, new-life adventures; and from the hearts of infinite Pacifics, the thousand mermaids sing to them—"Come hither, broken-hearted; here is another life without the guilt of intermediate death; here are wonders supernatural, without dying for them. Come hither! bury thyself in a life which, to your now equally abhorred and abhorring, landed world, is more oblivious than death. Come hither! put up *thy* grave-stone, too, within the churchyard, and come hither, till we marry thee!"

If any case is to be made for subintention—Psyde-chancing, Psyde-hastening, Psyde-capitulating, Psyde-experimenting behavior patterns—then, at the least, two further background issues need to be involved: the concept of unconscious motivation and the concept of ambivalence. Ahab's chronicler would not have, in principle, resisted the concept of subintention, on the grounds of its involving unconscious motivation, for (in Chapter 41) he says:

> Such a crew, so officered, seemed specially picked and packed by some infernal fatality to help him to his monomaniac revenge. How it was that they so aboundingly responded to the old man's ire—by what evil magic their souls were possessed, that at times his hate seemed almost theirs; the White Whale as much their insufferable foe as his; how all this came to be—what the White Whale was to them, or how to their unconscious understandings, also, in some dim, unsuspected way, he might have seemed the gliding great demon of the seas of life—all this to explain, would be to dive deeper than Ishmael can go. The subterranean miner that works in us all, how can one tell whither leads his shaft by the ever shifting, muffled sound of his pick?

That which is most sharply and most accurately characteristic of the subintentioned person—namely, the ubiquitous ambivalence, the pervasive psychological coexistence of logical incompatibles—is seen vividly in the following internal dialogue of life and death, of flesh and fixture (as reported in Chapter 51) within Ahab:

> Walking the deck with quick, side-lunging strides, Ahab commanded the t'gallant sails and royals to be set, and every stunsail spread. The best man in the ship must take the helm. Then, with every mast-head manned, the piled-up craft rolled down before the wind. The strange, upheaving, lifting tendency of the taff-rail breeze filling the hollows of so many sails, made the buoyant, hovering deck to feel like air beneath the feet; while still she rushed along, as if two antagonistic influences were struggling in her—one to mount directly to heaven, the other to drive yawningly to some horizontal goal. And had you watched Ahab's face that night, you would have thought that in him also two different things were warring. While his one live leg made lively echoes along the deck, every stroke of his dead limb sounded like a coffin-tap. On life and death this old man walked.

And within Ahab, toward Moby Dick, there were deep ambiguities.

Method

In any psychological autopsy it is important to examine the method or the instrument of death and, especially, the victim's understandings and subjective estimations of its lethal works. Ahab was garroted by a free-swinging whale line. We are warned (in Chapter 60) that ". . . the least tangle or kink in the coiling would, in running out, infallibly take somebody's arm, leg, or entire body off . . ."; we are forewarned ". . . of this man or that man being taken out of the boat by the line, and lost"; and we are warned again, "All men live enveloped in whale lines. All are born with halters round their necks; but it is only when caught in the swift, sudden turn of death, that mortals realize the silent, subtle, ever-present perils of life." Ahab knew all this; nor was he a careless, accident-prone man. The apothecary knows his deadly drugs; the sportsman knows the danger of his weapons; the whaler captain—that very whaler captain who, instead of remaining on his quarterdeck, jumped to "the active perils of the chase" in a whaleboat manned by his "smuggled on board" crew—ought to know his whale lines.

Questions

Having described the precise circumstances of Ahab's death, and having mentioned some background issues deemed to be relevant, I would now pose some questions concerning his demise: Was Ahab's death more than simple accident? Was there more intention than unintention? Was Ahab's orientation in relation to death entirely that of Psyde-postponing? Are there discernible subsurface psychological currents that can be fathomed and charted, and is there related information that can be dredged and brought to the surface? Specifically, can Ahab's death be described as victim-precipitated homicide; that is, is this an instance in which the victim stands up to subjectively calculated overwhelming odds, inviting destruction by the other? Let us see.

Extracts

Ahab led a fairly well-documented existence, especially insofar as the dark side of his life was concerned. *Moby Dick* abounds with references to various funereal topics: sleep, coffins, burials, soul, life-after-death, suicide, cemeteries, death, and rebirth.

But—as in a psychological autopsy—we are primarily interested in interview data from everyone who had known the deceased, especially in what our informants can tell us about Ahab's personality, insofar as his orientations toward death are known. It should be recognized that in some important ways Captain Ahab's psychological autopsy will be a truncated and atypical one, especially with respect to the range of informants; there is no information from spouse, parents, progeny, siblings, collaterals, neighbors; there are only mates, some of the more articulate shipboard subordinates, captains of ships met at sea, and, with terrifying biblical certitude, Elijah.

As we know, all the possible informants, listed below, save Ishmael, perished with Captain Ahab and are technically not available for interview. Only Ishmael's observations are direct; all else is secondhand through Ishmael, colored by Ishmael, and perhaps with no more veridicality than Plato's reports of Socrates. We shall have to trust Ishmael to be an accurate and perceptive reporter.

Our primary informant, Ishmael, reflected about Captain Ahab in twenty-five separate chapters (specifically chapters 16, 22, 27, 28, 30, 33, 34, 36, 41, 44, 46, 50, 51, 52, 73, 100, 106, 115, 116, 123, 126, 128, 130, 132, and 133). Starbuck, the chief mate of the *Pequod,* is next: there are nine separate encounters with, or reports about, his captain (in chapters 36, 38, 51, 118, 119, 123, 132, 134, and 135). Next is Stubb, the second mate, with seven separate anecdotes (to be found in chapters 28, 31, 36, 73, 121, 134, and 135). All the others are represented by one or two bits of information apiece: Elijah (in chapters 19 and 21); Gabriel of the *Jeroboam* (Chapter 71); Bunger, the ship's surgeon of the *Samuel Enderby* (100); the blacksmith (113); the Captain of the *Bachelor* (115); Flask, the third mate (121); the Manxman (125); and the carpenter (127).

Knowing that the limitations of space simply do not permit me to document the essence of each informant's remarks, either with appropriate quotations or abbreviated résumés, how can I summarize all the data? Perhaps my best course would be to concentrate on the general features that one would look for in any psychological autopsy. Thus, the information distilled from interviews with Ishmael, Starbuck, Stubb, and all the others, might, in a dialogue of questions and answers, take the following form.

1. Hidden psychosis? Not at the beginning of the voyage, but certainly at the end (and indeed from Chapter 36 on—"the chick that's in him picks the shell. 'Twill soon be out.") the madness in Ahab was blatant, open, known. His monomania was the official creed of his ship. Along with his other symptoms, his psychiatric syndrome was crowned with a paranoid fixation. But what matters in Ahab is not so much the bizarrely shaped psychological iceberg which many saw above the surface, but rather the hugeness of the gyroscopically immovable subsurface mass of other-destruction and self-destruction. We know the poems about fire and ice. Ahab is a torrid, burning, fiery iceberg.
2. Disguised depression? Ahab was openly morbid and downcast. His was not exactly psychotic depression, nor can we call it reactive depression, for it transcended the bounds of that definition. Perhaps best

it might be called a "character depression," in that it infused his brain like the let-go blood from a series of small strokes in the hemisphere.
3. Talk of death? The morbid talk of death and killing runs through reports about Ahab like an *idée fixe*.
4. Previous suicide attempts? None is reported.
5. Disposition of belongings? Ahab, after forty solitary years at sea, had little in the way of self-possessions or interpersonal belongings. His wife, he said, was already a widow; his interest in the possible profits from the voyage was nil: his withdrawal from meaningful material possessions (and his loss of joy with them) is perhaps best indicated by his flinging his "still lighted pipe into the sea" and dashing his quadrant to the deck—both rash acts for a sailor-captain.

In Ahab's conscious mind, he wanted to kill—but have we not said that self-destruction can be other-destruction in the 180th degree? Figuratively speaking, the barb of the harpoon was pointed toward him; his brain thought a thrust, but his arm executed a retroflex. Was his death "accident"? If he had survived his psychodynamically freighted voyage and had returned unharmed to Nantucket's pier, *that* would have been true accident. Men can die for nothing—most men do: but some few big-jointed men can give their lives for an internalized something: Ahab would not have missed this opportunity for the world.

What further evidence can be cited bearing on the issue of subintentioned cessation? With his three harpooners before him, with their harpoons turned up like goblets, Ahab (in Chapter 36) commands them, in this maritime immolation scene, as follows: " 'Drink, ye harpooneers! drink and swear, ye men that man the deathful whaleboat's bow–Death to Moby Dick! God hunt us all, if we do not hunt Moby Dick to his death!' " Kill or be killed; punish or be retributed: murder or suicide—how the two are intertwined.

In Arab's case, we have no suicide note or other holograph of death, but, *mirabile dictu,* we do have (in Chapter 135) Ahab's last thoughts:

> I turn my body from the sun. . . . Oh, lonely death on lonely life! Oh, now I feel my topmost grief. Ho, ho! from all your furtherest bounds, pour ye now in, ye bold billows of my whole foregone life, and top this one piled comber of my death! Towards thee I roll, thou all-destroying but unconquering whale; to the last I grapple with thee; from hell's heart I stab at thee; for hate's sake I spit my last breath at thee. Sink all coffins and all hearses to one common pool! and since neither can be mine, let me now tow to pieces, while still chasing thee, though tied to thee, thou damned whale! *Thus,* I give up my spear!

What is to be particularly noted in this is the prescience of Ahab. "I spit my last breath at thee," he says. How does he know that it is to be his *last* breath? Where are the sources of his premonitions? What are the contents of his subintentions? Does this not remind us of Radney, the chief mate of the *Town-Ho* (Chapter 54) who behaved as if he "sought to run more than half way to meet his doom"? Is this not exactly what the tantalizer says to his "all-destroying but unconquering" executioner in cases of victim-precipitated homicide?

Recommendation

It is suggested that Captain Ahab's demise was goal-seeking behavior that made obsessed life *or* subintentioned death relatively unimportant to him, compared with the great press for the discharge of his monomania of hate. He dared, and made, that murderous death-white whale kill him. He could not rest until he was so taken. (Did Satan *provoke* God into banishing him?) Ahab invited cessation by the risks that he ran; he was a Psyde-chancer. He permitted suicide. Consider Ahab's psychological position: what could he have done, to what purpose would any further voyages have been, if he *had* killed the symbol of his search? It was, from Ahab's point of view, the time; and in his unconscious wish, it was the "appropriate death." *In nomine ceti albini!*

Endnotes

[1]At the Suicide Prevention Center (supported by the U. S. Public Health Service) and at the Central Research Unit for the Study of Unpredicted Deaths (supported by the Veterans Administration), both in Los Angeles. The group includes Norman L. Farberow, Robert E. Litman, and Norman Tabachnick.

[2]This important distinction was made by Farberow (1950) and supported by Rosen, Hales, and Simon (1954).

[3]A practical extension of this belief is contained in the "psychological autopsies" that the professional staff of the Suicide Prevention Center conducts in connection with the Los Angeles County Coroner's Office in the certification of equivocal or possible suicidal deaths.

[4]*International Classification of the Causes of Death.*

[5]I am indebted to Professor Abraham Kaplan of the Philosophy Department of the University of California at Los Angeles for this insight and information.

[6]Miguel de Unamuno, who is probably as nonpsychoanalytic as it is possible for a cultivated twentieth-century human to be, says, in his chapter entitled "The Hunger for Immortality" in *The Tragic Sense of Life*: "It is impossible for us, in effect, to conceive of ourselves as not existing, and no effort is capable of enabling consciousness to realize absolute unconsciousness, its own annihilation."

[7]The term "cessation" is used in this present sense by Bridgman on at least two occasions, both in *The Intelligent Individual and Society* (1938, pp. 169, 225).

[8]I am indebted to Professor James Diggory, of the Psychology Department of the University of Pennsylvania, for suggesting this term to me.

[9]"I know when one is dead and when one lives; She's as dead as earth. Lend me a looking glass; if her breath will mist or stain the stone, Why, then she lives." (Shakespeare, xxxx, Act V, Scene 3).

[10]The Psyde-states described herein are meant to describe only the *current* status (vis-à-vis cessation) of the individual. Thus, one would, in any complete description of an individual, need also a biphasic taxonomy that describes the relatively chronic, pervasive, charactero-logical, "presuicidal" aspects of his psychological make-up.

[11]This concept of the initiator was developed primarily by Mrs. Calista V. Leonard of the staff of the Veterans Administration Central Research Unit and is described in her article, "A Theory of Suicide: The Implementor" (unpublished paper, Veterans Administration Central Research Unit, Los Angeles, California, 1962). *See also* the section of the unaccept-ing patient in Shneidman, Farberow, and Leonard (1962).

[12]Three very different examples of Psyde-initiators—all eminent men—are contained in the following: Wertenbaker (1957, pp. 174–181); Hemingway (1962, p. 283); Holton (1962). It is interesting to contrast Hemingway's attitude toward his failing body with that of Zinsser (1940, pp. 200–201).

[13]For example, W. A. Swanberg [*The meaning of death* (pp. 79–98). New York: McGraw-Hill Book Co, Inc. 1961, p. 455] says: "Hearst . . . had a violent aversion for mortality, and there was an unwritten law never to mention death in his presence."

[14] At the Los Angeles Suicide Prevention Center, the staff has evolved procedures for as-sessing "suicidal potentiality." *See* Litman and Farberow (19xx), and Tabachnick and Far-berow (19xx).

[15]The reader is referred to Henry A. Murray's masterful psychological studies of Melville (Murray, 1949, 1953; Stern, 1960, pp. 25–34; Chase, 1962, pp. 62–74).

☐ References

Bacon, F. (1620). *Novum Organum.*

Bridgman, P. W. (1938). *The Intelligent Individual and Society.* New York: Macmillan.

Bridgman, P. W. (1955). *The Way Things Are.* Cambridge, MA: Harvard University Press.

Chase, R. (Ed.) (1962). *Melville: A Collection of Critical Essays.* Englewood Cliffs, NJ: Prentice-Hall.

Curphey, T. J. (1961). The role of the social scientist in the medicolegal certification of death from suicide. In *The Cry for Help* (pp. 38–57). New York: Dover.

de Unamuno, M. (1921). The hunger for immortality. In *The Tragic Sense of Life* (pp. 110–117). New York: McGraw-Hill.

Draper, G., Dupertuis, C. W., & Caughley, J. L. (1944). *Human Constitution in Clinical Medicine.* New York: Hoeber.

Durkheim, E. (1951). *Suicide.* J. A. Spaulding and G. Simpson (trans.). Glencoe, IL: The Free Press. Originally Published as *Le Suicide* (1897).

Farberow, N. L. (1950). Personality patterns in suicidal mental patients. *Genetic Psychology Monographs, 42,* 3–79.

Farberow, N. L., & Shneidman, E. S. (1961). Sample investigation of equivocal suicidal deaths. In *The Cry for Help* (pp. 118–128). New York: McGraw-Hill.

Feifel, H. (Ed.) (1959). *The Meaning of Death.* New York: McGraw-Hill.

Freud, S. (1924a). The psychogenesis of a case of homosexuality in a woman. In *Collected Papers,* Vol. 2. London: Hogarth Press.
Freud, S. (1924b). Mourning and melancholia. In *Collected Papers,* Vol. 4. London: Hogarth Press.
Freud, S. (1924c). Thoughts on war and death. In Collected Papers, Vol. 6. London: Hogarth Press.
Gengerelli, J. A., & Kirkner, F. J. (Eds.) (1953). *Psychological Factors in Human Cancer.* Berkeley, CA: University of California Press.
Hartshorne, C., & Weiss, P. (Eds.) (1931–1958). *Collected Papers of Charles Sanders Pierce,* Vol. 6. Cambridge, MA: Harvard University Press.
Hemingway, L. (1962). *My Brother, Ernest Hemingway.* New York: World Publishing.
Holton, G. (1962). Percy Williams Bridgman. In *Bulletin of the Atomic Scientists, 17(2),* 22–23.
Litman, R. E., & Farberow, N. L. (1961). Emergency evaluation of self-destructive potentiality. In N. L. Farberow & E. S. Shneidman (Eds.), *The Cry for Help* (pp. 48–59). New York: McGraw-Hill.
Menninger, K. (1938). *Man Against Himself.* New York: Harcourt, Brace & Co.
Murray, H. A. (1949). Introduction. In *Pierre, or The Ambiguities* (pp. xiii–ciii). New York: Hendricks House.
Murray, H. A. (1953). In nomine diaboli. In *Moby-Dick Centennial Essays* (pp. 3–29). Dallas, TX: Southern Methodist University Press. (Reprinted from *New England Quarterly, 24,* 1951, pp. 435–452.)
Nagy, M. (1959). The child's view of death. In H. Feifel (Ed.), *The Meaning of Death.* New York: McGraw-Hill, pp. 79–98.
Rosen, A., Hales, W. M., and Simon, W. (1954). Classification of 'suicidal' patients. *Journal of Consulting Psychology, 18,* 259–362.
Schilder, P., & Wechsler, D. (1934). The attitudes of children toward death. *Journal of Genetic Psychology, 45,* 406–451.
Shakespeare, W. *King Lear.*
Shneidman, E. S., Farberow, N. L., & Leonard, C. V. (1962). Suicide-Evaluation and treatment of suicidal risk among schizophrenic patients in psychiatric hospitals. In *Medical Bulletin MB-8.* Washington, DC: Veterans' Administration, Department of Medicine and Surgery.
Stern, M. R. (Ed.) (1960). *Discussions of Moby Dick.* Boston: D. C. Heath & Co.
Swanberg, W. A. (1961). *Citizen Hearst.* New York: Charles Scribner's Sons.
Tabachnick, N. D., & Farberow, N. L. Emergency evaluation of self-destructive potentiality. In N. L. Farberow & E. S. Shneidman (Eds.), *The Cry for Help* (pp. 60–77). New York: McGraw-Hill.
Weisman, A. D., & Hackett, T. P. (1961). Predilection to death: Death and Dying as a Psychiatric Problem. *Psychosomatic Medicine, 23(3),* 232–256.
Weiss, J. M. A. (1957). The gamble with death in attempted suicide. *Psychiatry, 20,* 17–25.
Wolgang, M. E. (1959). Suicide by means of victim-precipitated homocide. *Journal of Clinical and Experimental Psychology and Quarterley Review of Psychiatry and Neurology, 20,* 335–349.
Zinsser, H. (1940). *As I Remember Him.* Boston: Little, Brown & Co.

Discussions[1]

AVERY D. WEISMAN, M.D.:
Department of Neurology and Psychiatry, Harvard Medical School, and the Department of Psychiatry, Massachusetts General Hospital, Boston, Massachusetts, U.S.A.

As one of America's leading authorities on suicide, Dr. Edwin Shneidman is understandably impatient with the prevalence of false notions about death and suicide. In fact, he thinks that the word *suicide* is too ambiguous to be either scientifically or clinically significant. He also wants to avoid the term *death* and to replace it with operational terms. Like other investigators of suicide and death, he is deeply aware that the line that divides living from dying is often difficult to determine. Semantic confusion, oversimplification, prejudice, and unexamined assumption impose still further obstacles to understanding.

Dr. Shneidman's central concept is that of *cessation.* It refers to conscious experience. An analogous concept, *termination,* applies to physiological functions. The relation of cessation to termination is approximately that between psychic death and physical death. While termination presumably puts an end to conscious experience, it is possible for cessation to occur without concomitant termination. This distinction underscores the contrast between extinction of individual consciousness and objective death as an inescapable fact of nature.

Dr. Shneidman focuses on the concept of cessation, and shows how people may, knowingly or not, bring about or delay their own cessation. Thus, there are cessation-fearers, cessation-ignorers, cessation-postponers, and so forth. According to the degree in which a person's conscious motivation participates in his own cessation, he distinguishes between intentioned, subintentioned, unintentioned, and contraintentioned acts.

Concepts of Death

It is extremely difficult to learn what people think about death and dying. Not only are most people burdened by assumptions and prejudices which have been uncritically absorbed in the course of life, but their personal attitudes toward death are likely to change as they grow older, fall sick, and are themselves threatened with death.

The concept of cessation allows us to recognize how people affirm the reality of death at various stages of life and under different circumstances. Patients are not expected to say *what* death means to them, or *how* they expect to die. Although Dr. Shneidman's classification of cessation behavior is largely contingent upon reports and observations made by sophisticated, observant investigators, the choice of category is broad enough to reduce unwarranted inferences. He demonstrates that *cessation attitudes are not necessarily suicidal, nor is there a specific cessation attitude for suicide.* With equal relevance, cessation attitudes are both vital and lethal, covering a wide range of comprehensive versions of life as well as death.

Perhaps the most prevalent concept of death is that it is an unmitigated evil, never to be sought, always to be avoided as long as possible. Although cessation and termination cannot be postponed indefinitely, most people also believe that suicide is wrong—far more than those who believe that suicide is a sickness. Even sophisticated thinkers find that death is deplorable, and that hastening the inevitable is a sign of disability or defeat, not merely of disease. In Dr. Shneidman's sense, most of us are *doomed* to be cessation-postponers and cessation-fearers. Mankind concedes the universality of objective death, but still regards personal extinction either as an illusion or a tragic fault. Because Dr. Shneidman shows that the inner attitude of suicidal patients cannot be reduced to a single formula, he urges us to think again about our conventional notions of life and death.

Appropriate Death

In 1961, Dr. Thomas Hackett and I reported a group of patients who approached death with a minimum of anxiety and conflict.[2] Several of our patients anticipated death as a fitting solution to their problems. It was apparent that for some people death is not deplorable, but desirable as a means of attaining resolution of conflict, fulfillment of desire, and rewarding quiescence. We termed this concept *appropriate death.*

Although we were quite explicit about our meaning, so strong are the forces of habit and prejudice that the concept of appropriate death has been misunderstood in different ways. First, it is not intended to be merely a poetic metaphor, or a sentimental afterthought when someone has died. Second, appropriate death has no etiological significance. It is not a conspiracy of emotional, social, and biological forces that come together and dispose patients to an unwelcome death. Third, we understood that because the world is filled with so many needless and meaningless deaths it is difficult to imagine that death can ever be either acceptable or appropriate. The judgment about whether or not death was appropriate could not be made with finality, nor could we dogmatically declare that death was wholly acceptable to our patients. We defined an appropriate death as one in which there is reduction of conflict, compatibility with the ego ideal, continuity of significant relationships, and consummation of prevailing wishes. In short, an appropriate death is one which a person might choose for himself, had he an option. Death is therefore a harmonious end point of motivated acts within the context of the ego ideal. It is not merely conclusive; it is consummatory.

It is quite simple to define appropriate death in whatever way we choose. It is another matter when we try to discover if there are appropriate and acceptable deaths among patients who are not "predilected" to death and who manage to survive.

We can ask a hypothetical question: If no one died until he chose to, who would ever be ready for death? For the vigorous, healthy adult, the question is clearly unthinkable, because his affiliation with life is so strong. However, there are other people, for example, the chronically ill and the extremely aged, in whom the margin between life and death is obscure. They may be quite willing to slip into oblivion, without being either depressed or suicidal. But to be willing to die is not equivalent to being able to die. Death may be acceptable, and not appropriate, or it may be appropriate, and not acceptable. We have known a patient who survived a series of hazardous operations for brain abscess. Despite numerous postoperative complications, he recovered. Three weeks after hospital discharge, he committed suicide. Evidently, his "drive to survive" persisted during his hospital weeks, but collapsed shortly after discharge! What kind of cessation was this? Had he died in the hospital, his death would have been subintentioned or unintentioned. He was a cessation-acceptor at this time. After discharge, he became a successful cessation seeker. We may speculate that he was not suicidal in the hospital because he was cared for with unusual dedication and was not expected to fulfill social obligations. After discharge, however, he was once again a homeless drifter, living on the margins of life. No one can tell if this patient, deep in his mind, expected to destroy himself, nor can we be sure whether he was a cessation-welcomer or a cessation-fearer. In other words, although Dr. Shneidman has provided us with a valuable system of taxonomy, it is still not quite operational. We require quite a bit of understanding of a patient's attitude toward survival before we can appraise his attitude toward extinction.

Any concept of death is a version of life. The range of possible deaths is a catalogue that depicts many kinds of acceptability and appropriateness. Because there is a difference between cessation and termination, some kinds of death may be highly appropriate in the interpersonal and intrapersonal dimension, without involving a suitable impersonal or biological termination. We have studied several patients in whom social and emotional factors were consistent with both an acceptable and appropriate death, and yet they did not die. Naturally, we do not understand the specific biological, social, and emotional conjunction that eventuates in death. The concept of appropriate death does not require this kind of information. It does require that cessation and termination have a meaning in the life style of a patient, that a patient does not die merely as a passive victim of a disease, and that dying is a positive act that protects his responsibility.

Suicide and Appropriate Death

What is the relation of suicide to appropriate death? Is it not an appropriate death that a suicidal patient wants to bring about? Does each variety of cessation correspond to a different context in which death is appropriate? Suicidal patients seek harmony, relief, and resolution of conflict. They apparently choose to extinguish themselves in order to find an idealized version of life.

Despite their similarities, suicide and appropriate death differ. There are, to be sure, many illustrious men who have chosen to terminate their life rather than to survive with diminished creative powers. There are many other instances in which murder may be defensible. Whether a man's life is always his to dispense with is a moral question, and cannot be decided by psychiatrists or psychologists. Knowledge of the psychopathology of suicide is still rudimentary, but we have reason to believe, with Dr. Shneidman, that self-destruction may be "murder in the 180th degree." In other words, a suicidal act may replace and relieve a homicidal phantasy. Moreover, suicidal impulses are inconstant. A man who is suicidal today may find the idea unthinkable tomorrow. In suicide there are critical phases; one part of a person takes over the autonomy of the rest, and decrees its extinction—usually in opposition to his life style, his ego ideal, and the longitudinal meaning of his life.

A suicidal patient has *appropriated* death, without achieving an appropriate death. The availability of suicide carries many people through sleepless nights, but I doubt if many people choose suicide, quietly and dispassionately, as the culmination of a life plan. Any of us may choose suicide rather than suffer the tyranny of disease or despotic forces, but those people who do destroy themselves are usually suffering from an inner agony, not an external crisis.

The statement, "I have nothing more to live for," may be a sentiment expressed by someone whose feasible work is done, or, in contrast, an utterance wrung out in a moment of despair. Despite verbal similarity, one statement is an expression of quiescence, the other, of pain. This is the interface where Dr. Shneidman's work and our own will meet. We are deeply appreciative of the contributions that he and his colleagues have made to these basic problems.

KARL MENNINGER, M.D.:
The Menninger Foundation, Topeka, Kansas, U.S.A.

There is much in the lives of individuals and communities that is puzzling: bickerings, hatreds, and fightings over trivia, useless waste and self-destructiveness. People extend themselves to injure others, and expend time, trouble, and energy in shortening that pitifully small recess from oblivion which we call life. As if lacking aught else to destroy or failing to accomplish it, many turn their weapons directly upon themselves.

Death Instinct

It was such observations as this that led Sigmund Freud to the formulation of the theory of a drive toward self-destruction which he called the death instinct. There exist from the beginning in all of us strong propensities toward self-destruction and these come to fruition as actual suicide only in exceptional cases where many circumstances and factors combine to make it possible.

Freud makes the further assumption that the life and death instincts—let us call them the constructive and destructive tendencies of the personality—are in constant conflict and interaction just as are similar opposing forces in the concepts of physics, chemistry, and biology. To create and to destroy, to build up and to tear down, these are the anabolism and the catabolism of the personality, no less than of the cells and the corpuscles—the two directions in which the same energies exert themselves.

These forces, originally directed inward and related to the intimate problems of the self, continuously tend to be directed outwardly, focused on other environmental objects. Managed with sufficient skill and with the maintenance of a certain balance and control, this may resolve in growth, development, social integration. An incomplete turning outward of the self-directed destructiveness *and* also of the constructiveness with which we are—by hypothesis—born, results, of course, in permanent lack of development. Instead of dealing with people such individuals avoid them. Instead of fighting their enemies, such individuals fight themselves; instead of loving friends or music or the building of a house, such persons love only themselves. Hate and love are the emotional representatives of the destructive and constructive tendencies.

But no one evolves so completely as to be entirely free from the upsurge of the self-destructive tendencies; indeed, the phenomena of life, the behavior peculiar to different individuals, may be said to express the result of the measures taken to control these conflicting factors. An equilibrium of sorts, oftentimes very unstable, is achieved, maintained until disturbed by new developments in the environment which cause a rearrangement with perhaps a quite different outcome.

Freud repeatedly emphasized that the manifestations of the self-destructive instinct were never nakedly visible. In the first place, the self-destructive instincts get turned in an outward direction by the very process of life, and in the second place, they get neutralized in the very process of living. Self-destruction in the operational sense is a result of a return, as it were, of the self-destructive tendencies to the original object. It is not *quite* the original object as a rule, because the object of redirected aggression, aggression reflected back upon the self, is usually the body. And since a part of the body may be offered up as a substitute for the whole, this partial suicide, as we have called it, is a way of averting total suicide. But if that part of the body is a vital part, the partial suicide becomes actual suicide.

On this basis we can understand how it can be that some people kill themselves quickly and some slowly and some not at all, why some contribute to their own deaths and others withstand valiantly and brilliantly external assaults upon their lives to which their fellows would have quickly succumbed. So much of this, however, takes place automatically and unconsciously that it will seem at first blush like an impossible task to dissect the details of a particular bargain or compromise between the life and death instincts.

Early in my professional career I was impressed with the central position in all psychiatry held by the phenomenon of suicide. It is considered irrational in most cultures; in some societies it is unknown; it is strangely overprevalent in certain very civilized countries. It increases with prosperity. Rationalized as it may be by intellectuals, its occurrence is always somewhat uncanny, incredible, inexplicable. It is a little difficult for survivors to conceive of anyone having been *quite* so hopeless, *quite* so heartless, *quite* so unrealistic. It is, indeed, a last act, an irreparable, irreversible, final blow. Its dreadfulness, its aggressive impact, is felt by relatives and friends and physicians, which, of course, was partly its victim's intent.

Three Components in the Suicidal Act

First of all suicide is obviously a *murder*. In the German language it is, literally, a murder of the self (*Selbstmord*), and in all the earlier philological equivalents the idea of murder is implicit.

But suicide is also a murder committed *by* the self as murderer. It is a death in which are combined in one person the murderer and the murdered. We know that the motives for murder vary enormously; so do the motives for wishing to be murdered, which is quite another matter and not nearly as absurd as it may sound. For since in suicide there is a self that submits to the murder and would appear to be desirous of doing so, we must seek the motives of this strange submission.

If the reader will picture to himself a battlefield scene in which a wounded man is suffering greatly and begs someone to kill him, he will readily appreciate that the feelings of the *murderer* would be very different, depending upon whether he were a friend or a foe of the wounded man; those of the man who desires to be murdered, that is, to be put out of his agony, however, would be the same in either case.

In many suicides it is quite apparent that one of these contributing factors is stronger than the other. One sees people who want to die but cannot take the step against themselves; they fling themselves in front of trains, or like King Saul and Brutus, they beseech their armor bearers to slay them.

Probably no suicide is consummated unless—in addition to these wishes to kill and be killed—the suicidal person also wishes to die—using the word "wish" here to relate to the resultant of motivational factors, conscious and unconscious wishes. Many suicides, in spite of the violence of the attack upon themselves and in spite of the corresponding surrender, paradoxically seem to be unwilling to die. Every hospital intern has labored in the emergency ward with would-be suicides, who beg him to save their lives. The fact that dying and being murdered achieve the same end so far as personal extinction is concerned, leads the practical-minded individual to think, "If a person wants to murder himself, or if he feels so badly about something that he is willing to be murdered, then he surely must want to die." But the illustration just given is only one of many indications that this is not so. Murdering or being murdered entails factors of violence, while dying relates to a surrender of one's life and happiness. In attempted suicide the wish to die may or may not be present, or may be to quite a variable degree, as Shneidman has described in his concepts of cessation, termination, interruption, and continuation. Freud emphasized the fact that instincts were never conscious and that we should not equate the death instinct with the wish to die or the life instinct with the wish to live. What I am proposing is that many other factors enter the formula. Stengel and others have pointed out how a certain amount of playacting is always involved whereby the drama of suicide is played with a childish and unrealistic King's X cross: "It really isn't going to happen even though I am doing it." "I am doing it not to end all but to portray all." "I am showing what I have suffered." "I am dramatizing the need I have for help." Such feelings as this represent a wish to live, despite the actions which seem to indicate a wish to die.

Suicide must thus be regarded as a peculiar kind of death which entails three basic internal elements and many modifying ones. There is the element of dying, the element of killing, and the element of being killed. Each is a condensation for which there exist complexes of motive, unconscious and conscious. What we call a suicide is for the individual himself an attempt to burst into life or to save his life. It may be to avoid some thing far more dreadful, to avoid committing murder or going mad. After all the reasoning processes of the suicidally impelled person cannot be expected to be logical or rational or even consistent. From my own point of view the suicidal determination—determination, I say, in fantasy, not enactment, not motivation—the suicidal determination as such, the surrender of all hope, is a final catastrophe of dissolution which the organism so greatly dreads. In a sense suicide is a flight from death, using death in a very broad sense.

Some Additional Comments on Methods and Prevention

In the end each man kills himself in his own selected way, fast or slow, soon or late. We all feel this, vaguely; there are so many occasions to witness it before our eyes. The methods are legion and it is these which attract our attention. Some of them interest surgeons, some of them interest lawyers and priests, some of them interest heart specialists, some of them interest sociologists. All of them must interest the man who sees the personality as a totality and medicine as the healing of the nations.

I believe that our best defense against self-destructiveness lies in the courageous application of intelligence to human phenomenology. If such is our nature, it were better that we knew it and knew it in all its protean manifestations. To see all forms of self-destruction from the standpoint of their dominant principles would seem to be logical progress toward self-preservation and toward a unified view of medical science.

Koji Sato, Ph.D.:
Department of Psychology, Kyoto University, Kyoto, Japan

It is a great pleasure for me to add some comments to Dr. Shneidman's stimulating paper. I have been thinking of the death of Zen masters. Even Zen masters have their individuality, and their ways of leaving this world are different from one another. I wrote for our journal *Psychologia*—an International Journal of Psychology in the Orient—a paper entitled "Deaths of Zen masters" (Vol. 7, Nos. 3, 4, 1964). Master Gempo Yamamoto's way of passing away is specially interesting in Shneidman's classification. After the Master reached his ninetieth birthday, he was thinking of closing the curtain of his puppet show in this world. He began fasting a number of times. But his disciples begged him to live more. At last, at the end of 1960, he seemed to leave this world and began fasting. Seigen Tanaka, one of his layman disciples, begged him to stop fasting, but was struck by the old Master with all his might. Tanaka, however, succeeded in persuading him to stop it for the reason that it was the end of the year and the Master's death would make much trouble to many people. Next year Tanaka visited the Master on May 28, and the Master said, "I was thinking of leaving today; it is the day of my master's death: I have nothing to say, just hold my hand," and grasped his hand firmly. When Tanaka told him that he would come again on June 5, the Master laughed, saying, "I will see you at the main hall of Ryutakuji Temple." At one o'clock on the night of June 3, the Master requested a cup of wine from his attendant monk, took it and showed his enjoyment. After ten minutes he said briefly: "I am going out on a journey, prepare my clothing," and lay down and passed away at 1:15 A.M. in his ninety-sixth year. Someone said it was suicide, but it is quite sure it was not a usual suicide. The fruit was ripe enough. Usually ripe fruits fall down unintentionally, but this fruit fell down intentionally, being ripe enough.

ROBERT E. LITMAN, M.D.: Chief Psychiatrist, Suicide Prevention Center, Los Angeles, California; Clinical Associate Professor of Psychiatry, School of Medicine, University of Southern California, Los Angeles, California, U.S.A.

Shneidman applies psychodynamic concepts to the classification of deaths. The result is a new scientific view of self-destruction avoiding the sociolegal connotations of suicide.

The academic reader will enjoy this essay for its polished literary style and marks of philosophic erudition. But style should not obscure the essential content, which is a bold proposal that the prevailing classification of death, honored by centuries of use, should be discarded as unclear in favor of a new classification which assigns the deceased into categories according to his orientation toward death.

The traditional classification of death has served the sociolegal need to assign blame for every death, either to God (natural, accident) or man (homicide, suicide). By analogy with homicide, suicide might be "justifiable" (as in heroic self-sacrifice), "excusable" (as in simple carelessness), or "culpable" (a deliberate social wrong). The concept of the role of the individual in his own demise cuts across these categories and serves a different need, that of furthering the scientific understanding of self-destruction.

Is Suicide a Useful Term?

Shneidman suggests, "It may well be that the word *suicide* currently has too many loose and contradictory meanings to be scientifically or clinically useful."

This is a statement with which I must agree. As a term, *suicide* leads more to scientific confusion than to clarity. In clinical practice the word *suicide* has an affectual shock value which is useful in a few limited communication situations but often leads to ambiguous discourse and misunderstanding between practitioners. In talking about suicidal behavior, it promotes clarity if the clinician specifies whether the given act, thought, impulse, or affect was mildly suicidal, moderately suicidal, or seriously suicidal. Suicide is not a unitary syndrome, but rather a collection of different acts by dissimilar people for various motives.

However, I do not feel that the community is ready for a new taxonomy of death. Rather we should encourage the legal profession, coroners, and police officials to use the customary and accepted classifications more consistently and conscientiously. By contrast, behavioral scientists working in the vanguard of research on self-destruction do need new designs for ordering their observations. To classify certain people as "death-seekers," "death-darers," "death-experimenters," etc., is dramatically descriptive and stimulates new views of human lives and deaths.

Is It Dynamic?

"The operation which gives meaning to the phrase 'basic orientation toward cessation' has to do with the role of the individual in his own demise. By 'role of the individual' is meant his overt and covert behaviors and nonbehaviors which reflect conscious and unconscious attributes relevant to his cessation."

By his concept "role of the individual" Shneidman ties "orientation" to behavior (and nonbehavior). These behaviors are understood to reflect all the multidetermined complexity of shifting drives and defenses ambivalently balanced against each other. Obviously the whole purpose of this classification is to introduce psychodynamic concepts into the descriptive terminology of death. For this effort the essay deserves general recognition and evaluation.

Probably the greatest difficulty from the standpoint of personality dynamics involves Shneidman's snapshot focus on a limited unit of time. By tying "orientation" to action behavior, the concept freezes psychodynamics at one particular moment of time, that moment appropriate to the behavior "relevant to his cessation." Although this focus on a segment of time and a segment of behavior-action is in some respects artificial and does not do justice to the complexity of total personality, it provides a tremendous gain in clarity and, we hope, in useful diagnostic divisions. A difficulty in the path of clinical application is that over periods of time patients tend to change, sometimes rapidly, in their orientations and behaviors.

Did Ahab Commit Suicide?

When a seagoing vessel or an airship is lost, there is an inquiry to determine what happened and to assign blame. In this context the traditional suicide concepts retain some validity. Some of us may serve as consultants for such investigations. What should we say if it is learned that a disaster with great loss of life occurred as a direct result of certain unusual actions of the captain, actions that contradict the lifelong habits, training, ethical attitudes, and responsibilities of the captain? What if, before the event, the captain behaved strangely, with symptoms of depression and even madness? We would ask ourselves, was the captain suicidal? If we do our duty conscientiously, some such deaths will be labeled suicide.

Then what of the crew and passengers? Are not all of us who travel in automobiles, ships, and airplanes death-chancers? In order to live with any freedom of action, we must constantly consciously place our lives somewhat in jeopardy, chancing death one way or another.

In my opinion, Captain Ahab was more than a death-chancer (which we all are); he was at least a death-darer. There is good evidence that he was, during the last moments of his life, a death-seeker. Was his death accidental? A board of inquiry to whom the facts were disclosed, as Shneidman has reported them, might well consider carefully, deliberate at length, and then conclude that this death was "probable suicide." Then, having completed the legal requirement, the board could seek further scientific enlightenment by reconstructing the Captain's orientation toward his own cessation and that of his ship and its crew.

☐ Reply

Edwin S. Shneidman

These words are not rebuttal or even clarification; they should be considered, rather, simply as an addendum. I feel that everything that needs to have been said has already been included in the comments to my paper, and that I have nothing to add but my deep feelings of gratitude and pleasure.

When I first read these comments to my paper, my primary reaction was an affective one. I was emotionally moved, especially by the tinges of a pervasive feeling that I was reading about someone who was already dead. I experienced a transcendent narcissism that was quickly and mysteriously transformed into feelings of concomitant depression and humility. It may be that part of this feeling stemmed from the fact that this essay was written by me during a period the passing of which I have constantly mourned. Specifically, it was written in 1961–1962, the year of the greatest intellectual excitement of my life, when I was privileged to be a U. S. Public Health Service Special Research Fellow at Harvard University, studying with that incomparable man, Professor Henry A. Murray; and this feeling was also based in part on the fact that these ideas are already old ones for me—and in that sense represent some of my "dead" thoughts.

As I think about my own essay, and the insightful and generous comments that have been made about it, I believe that my own interests—which began with the discovery of several hundred suicide notes in the vaults of the Los Angeles Coroner's Office in 1949—have moved from (1) a specific concern with suicide, to (2) a broader interest in death, and currently to (3) a deep interest in and concern with what I consider to be a still wider topic, namely, inimical patterns of living. By this I have in mind the multitudinous ways in which an individual can reduce, truncate, demean, narrow, shorten, or destroy his own life. I personally prefer not to talk about "substitute suicide," but, rather, straightforwardly, to talk about inimical patterns of behavior—of which killing oneself is the most extreme. My own current interests concern the various orientations to life, of which one's orientations to death are one significant aspect. Growing out of my own thoughts on cessation, interruption, and altered continuation, one facet of my own current research work has to do with aspects of interruption, specifically with the intensive study of the sleep patterns of a small number of suicidal and nonsuicidal subjects night-by-night over the period of the past three years. In a book which I am currently editing, called *Essays in Self-Destruction* (to be published this year by Holt, Rinehart and Winston), I have a chapter entitled "Sleep and Self-Destruction," in which I give a first report of some of the relationships between interruption patterns and orientations toward cessation. I can also report that my interests in Melville has been intensified one-hundredfold by my thoughts about orientations toward life and death subsequent to my writing the Ahab section of this paper. I have, in the last several months, read through the eleven novels and collections of stories by Melville, cataloguing every reference to any aspect of cessation, interruption, or altered continuation—I now have a few thousand such punch cards—and attempting to relate what Melville did in each of his books to what was going on in his own life at the time, specifically, his own partial deaths, withdrawal from society, decrease in public productivity, etc. I feel that the labors involved in this hobby have already come to a meaningful fruition in my own increased understandings of human nature, and I would hope someday to publish on this topic.

Endnotes

[1]These discussions originally appeared in a reprinting of "Orientations toward death" in The International Journal of Psychiatry, 1966, *2*, 190–200.

[2]Weisman, A., & Hackett, T. (1961). Predilection to death: Death and dying as a psychiatric problem. *Psychosomatic Medicine, 23*, 232–256.

35

CHAPTER

Clinical Thanatology and Psychotherapy: Some Reflections on Caring for the Dying Person

The relationships between "ordinary psychotherapy" and clinical thanatology—the latter relating to working with dying patients and their survivors—are explored. The two authors had, in print in the last year, quite independently asked the question: "It is (clinical thanatology) psychotherapy?" As background, this paper delineates four kinds of verbal interaction: Conversation or ordinary talk; hierarchical exchanges; psychotherapy; and thanatological exchanges. The main part of the paper is an explication of eight special characteristics of thanatological exchanges. They include comments on time, transference, aspirations and empathy, among others. It is felt that clinical thanatology deserves a special emphasis and a separate designation.

We begin with a personal note: It struck us as an extraordinary coincidence that each of us, in our respective recent publications about our work with dying persons had, independently, written a section entitled "Is this psychotherapy?" (Feigenberg, 1977; Shneidman, 1978). The occasion of our working together for a month at the Radiumhemmet of the Karolinska Hospital[1] provided an opportunity to discuss, in somewhat extensive fashion, this question which we both deem to be an interesting and thought-provoking one: Is what we clinical thanatologists do when

Reprinted from *Omega*, 1979, *10*, 1–8 (With L. Feigenberg). With permission.

we psychologically care for (or work with) a dying person properly to be called psychotherapy? Or, to put it another way: Is the close psychological relationship with a dying person one which merits special rules, understandings and concepts, to the extent that it ought even have labels of its own? That question is the issue for this exploratory joint paper. We would like to share these thoughts with others, especially those who have had direct experience working with dying persons.

Dying and Various Verbal Modes of Intervention

On the face of it, commonsense tells us that doing intensive psychological work with a person who is dying *is* different from working with any other kind of person. We need to state at this point—not a digression—that by a "dying" person we mean an individual who believes, in whatever way, or knows that he or she is in an inexorable life-threatening situation and that the probabilities of surviving are extremely remote, and that there is not an "indefinite" or extended (macrotemporal) period of time in which to live. In "dying," the essential point is not the nature of the disease or injury, but the individual's emotional state of mind, the phenomenological sense that one is in an imminently life-threatening situation. Psychologically, this is what dying is.

We might, at this point, mention cancer as only one example of what we mean, simply because cancer is often identified (and confused) with dying. The facts are that approximately half the people who have cancer are cured or have remissions (and are not dying), but some are, in fact, deemed to be incurable (after all sorts of vigorous treatment regimens) and are then living "on borrowed time," knowing their days are limited, and they can be said to be "dying." Obviously, from whatever cause of disease, such individuals are in a special psychological state, marked by many problems and moods, but certainly by a discernable amount of realistic dysphoria, fear and concern.

There is a demonstrable and important difference that needs to be identified and attended to between working psychologically with a dying person and the ordinary use of psychotherapy—or, at the least, a broadening of the concept of psychotherapy itself.

In a recent book, *Illness as Metaphor* (1978), Susan Sontag (who has had cancer) invoked the image of two worlds: the world of the well and the world of the ill:

> Illness is the night-side of life, a more onerous citizenship. Everybody who is born holds dual citizenship, in the kingdom of the well and in the

> kingdom of the sick. Although we prefer to use only the good passport, sooner or later each of us is obliged, at least for a spell, to identify ourselves as citizens of the other place.

We would quibble a bit with her way of putting it. We would like to add a "third world" to this scheme: the world of the dying. There is admittedly a keen difference between being well and ill (feeling bad and having pain), but there is an even greater difference—a vastly greater one—between being ill and dying. The psychological distance between knowing that one has an illness (and is expected or hopes to recover) and understanding that one has a mortal enemy is enormous. "Being ill" and "dying" are quite different.

Quite obviously, both psychotherapy (with an emotionally disturbed person who is not physically ill) and working with a dying person usually involve a verbal exchange between two persons in a face-to-face relationship. To the extent that this is so, our first task is then to explicate the various types of verbal exchanges.

In principle, it may be said that there are at least four different kinds of human (essentially verbal) communication. They can be described briefly as follows:

☐ Communication Exchanges

Ordinary Talk or Conversation

In this kind of exchange, which makes up most of human discourse, the focus is on the surface content (concrete events, specific details, abstract issues, questions and answers of content). The individuals are talking about what is actually being said: the obvious, stated meanings, and the ordinary interesting (or uninteresting) details of life. Further, the social role between the two participants is one of essential equality, sometimes tempered somewhat by considerations of age, status or prestige. But each of the two parties has the social right to ask the other the same kind of questions which he or she has been asked. Some examples of ordinary talk might be two friends conversing with one another about the events of the day, or two lovers whispering intimate thoughts to one another, or two businessmen closing a deal, or two neighbors simply chatting.

Hierarchical

In this kind of exchange the entire focus (like in a conversation) is on the manifest content—on what is being said—but the situation is marked by an explicit or tacit acknowledgement by the two parties that there is a significant difference of status between them; one of them is "superior" to the other. Questions asked or suggestions made or information transmitted or orders given by one would seem inappropriate if attempted by the other party. Examples would be the verbal exchange between a supervisor and subordinate, between an army officer and enlisted man, or between an oncologist and a patient in the doctor's office. The officer can order the enlisted man, but not vice versa; the doctor can examine the patient, but not vice versa. The doctor-patient relationship is an hierarchical one in that a doctor and a patient do not exchange roles.

Professional (e.g., Psychotherapy)

Here the focus is on feelings, emotional content and unconscious meanings, rather than primarily on what is apparently being said. The emphasis is on the latent (between-the-lines) significance more than on the manifest and obvious content; on unconscious meanings, including double-entendre, puns and slips of the tongue; on themes that run as common threads through the content rather than on the concrete details for their own sake. Perhaps the most distinguishing aspect of the professional exchange (as opposed to ordinary talk) is the occurrence of "transference"—wherein the patient projects onto the therapist certain deep expectations and feelings. These transference reactions often stem from the patient's childhood and reflect earlier patterns of reaction (of love, hate, dependency, suspicion, etc.) to whatever the therapist may or may not be doing. The therapist (like the doctor) is often invested by the patient with almost magical healing powers, which, in fact, can serve as a self-fulfilling prophecy and thus help the interaction become therapeutic for the patient. The roles of the two participants, unlike those in a conversation, are not co-equal. The situation is hierarchical but the focus is not on the manifest content.

Thanatological

A person who systematically attempts to help a dying individual achieve a psychologically comfortable death (or a more "appropriate" death or an "ego-syntonic" death)—given the dire, unnegotiable circumstances of the situation—is acting in a special role. (This is not to say that many others—doctors, nurses, relatives, dear friends, church members, neighbors—cannot also play extremely important roles.) If the distinction between a conversation and a professional exchange is crucial, certainly the distinction between working with dying persons as opposed to working with any other kind of individual is a vital one. Working with a dying person demands a different kind of involvement. Our position is that there may be as important a conceptual difference between ordinary psychotherapy and working with dying persons as there is between ordinary psychotherapy and ordinary talk. Below, we have attempted to limn out some of the important nuances of these differences.

☐ Clinical Thanatology

Here are some of the main elements which we believe distinguish thanatological work from other forms of human interaction, including ordinary psychotherapy.

The Unique Nature of the Existential Confrontation

An exchange between any two people is always, in a sense, an existential event. Consider the very nature of the existential situation with a dying person: it is between two human beings, one of whom (the patient) is currently struggling with dying and the other (the clinical thanatologist) who is not dying, but *both* are, without any question, going to share the common fate of dying someday—and both know *that.* The thanatological situation is certainly a unique one, where both individuals share a common vital problem. (This is not so in working with, say, a schizophrenic or suicidal or neurotic patient.) That fact, in itself, seems to set working with a dying person apart from usual psychotherapy. "Doctor, doctor, will I die? Yes my dear and so shall I." This is not suggested as necessarily something to say to a patient; it is simply a statement of the nature of life.

The Dimension of Time

In psychotherapy we usually assume that there is unlimited time. We attempt to "work through" problems with the implicit understanding that the patient will continue to live—it is hoped better adjusted. In the dying situation, an irrevocable series of changes, from what has been to what may be, takes place along the dimension we call time. When a person is dying, the passage of time creates anxiety. Moreover, time does not pass uniformly and the experiences of sudden accelerations or decelerations lead to further feelings of insecurity, threat and helplessness.

The perception of time alters and disintegrates in the process of dying. The habitual and conventional idea of time as a linear process is broken up by the patient into sections, a relevant measure being the intervals between meals, visits, or medications. The subjective experience of time is filled with special inner experiences and becomes increasingly disconnected with the chronological time of those around the dying person and thus loses much of its usual significance.

The Possibility of Intense Transference

We believe that it is therapeutic if the dying person develops rather strong feelings of essentially positive transference toward the clinician who is seen as being potentially helpful "in the business of dying." That helper then becomes an admittedly exaggerated "key figure" in the dying person's remaining days.

The nature and intensity of the dying person's positive transference is indeed another key feature which distinguishes thanatological work from ordinary psychotherapy. The clinical thanatologist helps the dying person through this most important "rite-de-passage." We therefore feel that it is permissible, in fact desirable, to create a situation of intense transference from the very beginning which might, in ordinary psychotherapy appear to be unseemly or contraindicated. There is something ineffibly special (and sometimes rather dramatic) in the transference that occurs with a dying person.

Negative transference—feelings of anger or dislike or jealousy—may arise, and perhaps the handling of it, because of the very situation that the patient is in, further distinguishes thanatological work from ordinary psychotherapy. Fear of negative transference is only one of the reasons why many physicians eschew working psychologically with dying persons.

Of course, where there is strong transference there is also countertransference; the thanatologist's genuine positive feelings of liking and concern for the welfare of the patient; and there is also an unavoidable psychological price: the vulnerability and grief over the eventual loss. One cannot ever invest without running the risk of loss. Dealing with dying persons is abrasive psychological work and the clinician is well-advised to have good support systems in his or her own life: loved persons, dear friends, congenial work and peer consultants.

The Goals Are Limited

Because for the dying person time is limited, the goals for the thanatologist are more finite. The omnipresent goal is the psychological *comfort* of the person, with, as a general rule, as much alleviation of felt physical pain as possible. Full psychological insight is not the goal. There is no rule that states that an individual must die with any certain amount of self-knowledge. In this sense, every life is incomplete. The goal is to make a dire situation go as well as possible; to give psychological succor; to permit the tying-off of loose ends; to lend as much stability to the dying person as it is possible to give.

The thanatologist needs to be able to tolerate incompleteness and lack of closure. No one ever untangles all the varied skeins of another's intrapsychic life; to the last second there are psychical creations and recreations that require new resolutions. Total insight is an abstraction. There is no golden mental homeostasis.

The Importance of Empathy

Without empathy one cannot really understand another person. Empathy partly has to do with identification and should be present in all psychotherapy. In the doctor-patient relationship empathy is important and a desirable component.

Empathy is comprehending another person, feeling one's way into and sharing the other's reality ("If I were he . . ."). It involves identification and at the same time a maintained awareness of one's own feelings. Empathy is essentially a feeling of warmth and emotional involvement; it is beyond simple befriending; it is true caring. In the process of dying, pity may be abrasive, sympathy of little use, whereas empathy is a necessary condition for really helping the dying person. To the best of one's ability, through an open relationship, one should try to comprehend who the dying person is and what, in dialogues at every level, that person wishes to convey.

The Special Place of Flexibility

In the care of the dying person, flexibility is paramount; to use a fixed system would be to misconstrue the art. One is not trying to help the patient to function better "afterwards," but to make the limited life that is left bearable, meaningful and self-fulfilling as possible. This calls for maximal flexibility in relation to the psychological and biological manifestations of dying.

Psychotherapy is a disciplined undertaking. You meet at a fixed place, at scheduled hours, the patient sits or lies in the same place, and one usually has a program in mind for months ahead. Systematic work is done, guided by the therapist. On the other hand, for those who work with dying persons, everchanging pictures pass before the mind's eye. These pictures are evocative, causing psychological events to occur in both minds, albeit in different respects. Some of these are, by their very nature, anxiety provoking, but also linking one person to the other, making a common bond. The clinician needs to be as flexible as his own personality and controlled countertransference will permit.

The Importance of Being Concerned with the Significant Others

Death is seldom a uni-person event. In the dying scene there are two classes of persons: the person who dies and those who continue to live and are left to mourn and grieve. The algebra of death's suffering is a complicated equation. But more important than this theoretical point is the demonstrated fact that widows and widowers, especially in the first year after the death of their spouse, suffer pain and are seriously ill more often (requiring hospitalization) and more of them die (from a wide variety of causes) than non-bereaved men and women of their same age and general status. Mourners are, to use a public health expression, a population "at risk." It follows from this that working with a dying person ought almost always to include someone's also working with the mourner-to-be, both before the death of the loved one and after, for perhaps a year or so, at decreasing intervals.

The Ambience of the Dying Scene

Typically, dying persons become sicker, bed-ridden, tired and weak, and begin to take on the signs of approaching death. Depending upon the circumstances, the clinical thanatologist will, during these weeks or days or hours, witness another human being's down-hill course toward death. During this onerous process, one would naturally follow the patient's own moods (and content) more and more, With each visit, the clinician will meet unexpected questions, fresh memories that the dying person has never talked about before, and also expressions of a variety of emotions—rebellion, aggression, grief, submission, fear, ennui, etc. The thanatologist will resonate to the patient's expressions. Depending on the circumstances and the "dying trajectory," the thanatologist will change the schedule and come more and more often, toward the end as frequently as more than once a day. The drama of the dying scene can be shared by talk or by sitting nearby without saying a word.

And so the question remains: Is clinical thanatology sufficiently different in the persons involved, in its requirements for empathy and flexibility, in its relationships to time, in its content and in its goals to warrant a special designation? We are inclined to believe that it is. We can see the prefiguring of a new and separate art, discipline, specialty, practice or emphasis. It does not matter what it is called (someone will coin a felicitous term), so long as it is practiced more often by people working with dying persons in health-care settings, whether in hospitals, hospices, or (more and more) in the person's own home.

Endnote

[1]Gratitude is expressed to the Swedish Cancer Society for making this collaboration possible.

References

Feigenberg, L. (1977). *Terminalvård: En metod för psychologisk vård av döende cancer patienter.* Lund: Liber Läromedel (published in English by Brunner/Mazel under the title of *Terminal friendships: Psychiatric care of the dying* in 1979).

Shneidman, E. S. (1978). Some aspects of psychotherapy with dying persons. In C. A. Garfield (Ed.), *Psychosocial aspects of terminal patient care.* (pp. 201–218) New York: McGraw-Hill.

Sontag, S. (1978). *Illness as a metaphor.* New York: Farrar Straus and Giroux.

36

CHAPTER

Final Thoughts and Reflections

The suicidal act is both a moving away and a moving toward. Psychache, psychological pain, is what the individual wishes to escape; peace is what the person seeks and moves toward. In suicide, the two goals are merged as one: Escape from pain *is* relief—that is how peace is defined. The unbearable pain is transformed into peace; the suffering is taken away. At least, that is what the suicidal person thinks and hopes.

To a suicidal individual, to be unconscious means to be in a state of tranquil quiet, a nothingness and oblivion that is total and complete. Problems are not merely taken care of; there are no problems, and, even better, there is no consciousness of the possibility of problems—or of anything else.

Suicide is an effort to "get away from it all." It is the ultimate escape. Jean Baechler, a contemporary French social scientist, in his book *Suicides* discusses "escapist suicides" as the centerpiece of his presentation. "To commit a suicide of flight is to escape by taking one's own life from a situation sensed by the subject to be intolerable" (1979, p. 66). The action of suicide is an exiting, a departure from a painful life. The act of suicide says: In case of fire (of unbearable negative emotions) use this Exit.

Even in Hell this is so. A concentration-camp prisoner wrote about his thoughts while in the camp: "I look at those hanging and am jealous of the peace that they know." Speaking of Hell, by and large the idea of Hell does not ordinarily enter into suicide. On the contrary, there are some

Reprinted from *The Suicidal Mind.* New York: Oxford University Press, 1996, pp 157–166. With permission.

few suicides—committed out of the pain of grief—in which the idea of reunion with departed loved ones, in heaven or some other peaceful haven, is in the mind of the suicidal person. But most suicides—as is clear from reading a large number of suicide notes—are disappointingly secular. The destination (or concern) is not to *go* anywhere, except *away.* The goal is to stop the flow of intolerable consciousness; not to continue in an afterlife or an eternity. "Escape" does not mean to escape from one torture chamber to enter another. In suicide the goal is to achieve a peace of mindlessness.

The clinical problem with suicide—the challenge for the potential rescuer—is to wrestle with the fact that the goals of escape and peace *are* beguiling to the suicidal person. If they were not, the person would not be suicidal. One must recognize and deal with the fact that continuance in life is automatically burdened with returns to duty and pain.

Ever since I first read this passage as a young man, I have always admired Thomas Mann's genius for catching this life-and-death counterpoise. The key passage is from his first novel, *Buddenbrooks,* written when he was all of 25.

> Cases of typhoid take the following course.
>
> When the fever is at its height, life calls to the patient: calls out to him as he wanders in his distant dream, and summons him in no uncertain voice. The harsh, imperious call reaches the spirit on that remote path that leads into the shadows, the coolness and peace. He bears the call of life, the clear, fresh, mocking summons to return to the distant scene which he has already left so far behind him, and already forgotten. And there may well up in him something like a feeling of shame for a neglected duty; a sense of renewed energy, courage and hope: he may recognize a bond existing still between him and that stirring, colorful, callous existence which he had thought he had left so far behind him. Then, however far he may have wandered on his distant path, he will turn back—and live. But if he shudders when he hears life's voice, if the memory of that vanished scene and the sound of that lusty summons make him shake his head, and make him put out his hand to ward off as he flies forward in the way of escape that is opened to him—then it is clear that the patient will die. (1952, Part XI, Ch. 3)

That is a perfect description of the inner workings of the suicidal debate, how the awful work is actually done.

What is warded off is psychological pain. But what is critical is the individual's unwillingness to endure pain, the larger characteristics that make a person the person he or she is, the sense of identity, and especially that person's ideal self and ideal identity. In other words, how the person privately and secretly really views himself or herself. I quote here from my colleague, Robert Litman (1995): "People commit suicide because they cannot accept their pain, because the pain does not fit in with their concept of themselves, with their personal ideal. So for me, the long-range treatment of chronically suicidal people includes helping them change their self concept so that they can learn to acknowledge that their pain, while unique to them, is not radically different from everyone else's pain, and their personhood is basically pretty much the same as everybody else's personhood."

Some nonsuicidal people believe that they are pretty much the same as everybody else. But in suicide, there is often the feeling that one's pain is somehow special and greater than the pain and suffering of others, making it unendurable in a special way—bordering on a feeling of grandiosity. This is so because suicidal people tend to cut themselves off from human contact and are talking only to themselves. They think that their suffering and their dying are unique. They imagine their funeral and their mourners—in effect, an existence in this world, at least for a while, after their own death; that they will be remembered, not forgotten; that they stay alive in the minds of others.

Dying is the one thing—perhaps the only thing—in life that you don't have to do. Stick around long enough and it will be done for you. And dying is also the only thing you have to do. There is no If to death. The only questions in dying are when and where and how. Suicide names the time, the place, and the method. Suicide is the only kind of death in which the individual supplies most of the details for the death certificate. Suicide—for all the noble-born literary heroes and all the Thomas Chattertons and all the Archduke Rudolfs and all the Sylvia Plaths who have committed it—is a lonely act, a desperate and, almost always, unnecessary one. Most of us have thought about it. It touches all the social strata, the highest and the lowest, all races, both sexes, all age groups, each with its own special obligations.

Almost every one of us has serious obligations in life, but there is only one *obligatory* from which there is *no* escape—to die. Admittedly, to die well is a most difficult thing to do. To die by suicide is to die before one's time; it almost never gets applause—except, perhaps, in grand opera. There is no "courtly suicide," with the possible exception of doing so at the request of one's liege or lord, but suicide on command is hardly the type of suicide that happens nowadays. In World War II, Field Marshall Erwin Rommel was ordered by Hitler to commit suicide, but the onus here is on the demented Hitler.

By curious contrast, the other leader of our then wartime enemy made what is perhaps the most impactful suicide *prevention* statement of this century, perhaps of recorded history. In the rescript of capitulation on August 14, 1945, in which Emperor Hirohito, by unprecedented radio broadcast—almost none of his subjects had ever heard his voice before—ordered his loyal subjects to surrender, he touched on the two main antidotes to suicide: the sense of futurity; and the redefining of the key term, variously defined by the person as unbearable, unacceptable, intolerable, unendurable. With great prescience the Emperor commanded all members of his nation-family:

> It is according to the dictates of time and fate that we have resolved to pave the way for a grand peace for all the generations to come by enduring the unendurable and suffering what is unsufferable. (Hanson, Herndon, & Langsdorf, 1947)

He ordered his people to live.

Sometimes the most difficult thing in the world is to choose to endure life. But even when there is no choice, as in a natural death in old age, dying *well* is among the most challenging feats of life: To die with some sense of grace, panache, good manners, or thanatological breeding—especially when one is frightened and in pain—can be the crown of one's life. Of course, the physical pain can and should be treated, but there is no handy morphine drip for psychological pain that, to be effective, does not, at the same time, alter who we are. To die naturally will, in the course of time, occur to most of us, but to die "well," to accept one's mortality and not hasten one's death may be the most difficult act in a life.

To "will the obligatory"—a phrase from Otto Ranks (1932)—is to accept the immutable cycles of Nature, especially human nature, and to understand that (whether or not you believe that there is any existential purpose or meaning to life, or a spiritual extension beyond it) no one, absolutely no one, escapes being finite and mortal. And knowing this brute fact, then to accept it, to *will* it, and not be in an unnecessary state of angst or terror or rebellion over it can be a remarkable and in many ways a truly human feat of courage and grace.

This book propounds the view that suicide stems from psychological pain, and that that pain comes from frustrated psychological needs peculiar to each person. But the suicidal person must also have the desire or drive to escape the unbearable pain of these frustrated needs. What then is the "psychological soil" in which the suicidal mind malignantly flourishes? While we can agree on the central role of psychache, we must still speculate on the causes of the reactions of the suicidal mind. Are these predilections fostered in early childhood, or can they arise for the first time during adulthood? We know a great deal about the more or less immediate psychological circumstances that surround suicide, but there is no easy answer to the enigma of the "root causes" of a lower threshold for withstanding the psychological pains associated with suicide.

I am totally willing to believe that suicide can occur in adults who could not stand the immediate pain of grief or loss that faced them, independent of a good or bad childhood or good or bad parental care and love. But I am somewhat more inclined to hold to the view that the subsoil, the root causes of being unable to withstand those adult assaults lie in the deepest recesses of personality that are laid down in rather early childhood. In my view, these speculations are illustrated by the three clinical cases in this book.

Each of our three acquaintances—Ariel, Beatrice, and Castro—reports that they were unhappy in childhood. Those are two key words in any life, unhappy and childhood. Suicide never stems from happiness—it happens because of the stark absence of it. In this century, especially in the latter half, we tend to identify happiness with the mere absence of pain and the presence of creature comforts—good food, fine wine, expensive clothes. But in relation to *suicide,* genuine happiness has an almost magical aura to it. Or, to put it another way, unhappiness reflects the lost joys of an unrealized childhood. Early childhood especially is the time when we can—unrestrained by realistic and adult rules and actualities—fantasize about what we would optimally like to have happen within ourselves and between ourselves and our parents. Secret inner pacts can be made and savored. These fantasies give a magical quality, a special happiness, an ecstasy and consuming exuberance that one can experience only in a childhood that is essentially benign.

Those are the benchmarks; anything less than that is pain. And, once lost, or once glimpsed but never experienced, they strike in too deep, and leave such a scar that nothing can every make them right. One feels old and burdened long before any wrinkles appear; and, as Melville (1849) said, the airs of paradise cannot erase them.[1] It is not possible to be robbed totally of one's childhood, but what does happen can seem to be just as bad. One can have one's childhood vandalized. Perhaps—I do not know—every person who commits suicide, at *any* age, has been a victim of a vandalized childhood, in which that preadolescent child has been psychologically mugged or sacked, and has had psychological needs, important to *that* child, trampled on and frustrated by malicious, preoccupied, or obtuse adults. I tend to believe that, at rock-bottom, the pains that drive suicide relate primarily not to the precipitous absence of equanimity or happiness in adulthood, but to the haunting losses of childhood's special joys.

The role of parents, relatives, friends, physicians, therapists, artisans, helpers, and good samaritans—and even books—in life is clear to everyone. We could not get through life without the help of others. But after infancy, a vast part of life is a do-it-yourself proposition. It is not inaccurate to assert that even in the best of therapies, the patient's role—the don't-do-it-yourself part of it—is vital to the success of the whole process. In this spirit I invite the reader (as has been implicit throughout this book) to reflect, to examine your own needs, how your mind is in dialogue with those ongoing needs, and to generate the self-help that might flow from such introspective insight, aided by the conceptual tools provided in these pages.

Having just asserted that each of us has to play a vital role in keeping ourselves alive, it is not, in my view, a contradiction now to say that there are times in life when we cannot do some vital things for ourselves and it is prudent on those occasions to seek the help of others. One of the themes of this book is that there is much we can do to understand our own tendencies, thoughts, and impulses toward suicide in an effort to turn those self-destructive impulses into lifesaving self-knowledge. A big part of what we can do for ourselves is to get appropriate professional help when we need it—to recognize that certain crises we cannot effectively handle alone.

The happy fact is that there are thousands of people who have been helped, their lives saved, by the intervention of therapy by psychologists, psychiatrists, physicians, suicide prevention workers, and others. It would be a sad misreading of this book to believe that—in relation to suicide and its admittedly dire consequences—there is not a large place for realistic hope of a life-prolonging outcome.

In this book, I have proposed the view that suicide is prevented by changing our perception of the situation, and by redefining what is unbearable. Perceiving that there are other possible ways of seeing things, redefining the impossible, bearing the unbearable, swallowing the undigestible bolus of shame or guilt. What has saved Beatrice Bessen is her willingness, albeit reluctant, to consider the possibility of renegotiating her perception of her parents and rethinking their role in her life.

Here, in the United States, we have never had a Sun-God Emperor or a tyrannical dictator to whom we have been taught total obedience from childhood, and whose every order we must unhesitatingly obey. Each of us is our own monarch. As long as we are alive, we democrats can say, as Melville did, "The queenly personality lives in me, and feels her royal rights." What we are talking about here is our conscience, our selves, our view of what amount of psychological pain we will put up with. It is our independent personhood, whose voice we follow, and if, in the flux of things, she orders us to die, we are doomed—unless an autonomous part of us can summon the will and the energy to answer, "I don't have to do it," or someone else, a friend or acquaintance, restrains our hand and guides us to help.

Every single instance of suicide is an action by the dictator or emperor of your mind. But in every case of suicide, the person is getting bad advice from a part of that mind, the inner chamber of councilors, who are temporarily in a panicked state and in no position to serve the person's best long-range interests. Then it is time to reach outside your own imperial head and seek more qualified and measured advice from other voices who, out of their loyalty to your larger social self, will throw in on the side of life, and—to use a Japanese image—will urge the chrysanthemum, not the sword.

All this is consistent with deep beliefs I have held for years. Suicide involves both inner disturbance and the idea of death as escape. But it is simply good sense not to commit an irrevocable suicide during a transient perturbation in the mind. Suicide is not the thing to do when you are disturbed and your thinking is constricted. There is a short aphorism or maxim that captures this lifesaving truth: Never kill yourself while you are suicidal. You can, if you must, think about suicide as much as your mind wishes and let the thought of suicide—the possibility that you could do it—carry you through the dark night. Night after night. Day after day, until the thought of self-destruction runs its course, and a fresh view of your own frustrated needs comes into clearer focus in your mind and you can, at last, pursue the realistic aspects, however dire, of your natural life.

Endnote

[1]Moody, stricken Melville expressed his lament and his psychological insights, at age 29:

> Cold, bitter cold as December and bleak as its blasts, seemed the world then to me; there is no misanthrope like a boy disappointed; and such was I with the warm soul of me flogged out by adversity. . . . Talk not of the bitterness of middle-age and after life; a boy can feel all that, and much more, when upon his young soul the mildew has fallen; and the fruit, which with others is only blasted after ripeness, with him is nipped in the first blossom and bud. And never again can such blights be made good; they strike in too deep, and leave such a scar that the air of Paradise might not erase it.

References

Baechler, J. (1979). *Suicides* (p. 66). New York: Basic Books.

Hanson, H. A., Herndon, J. G., & Langsdorf, W. G. (Eds.) (1947). *Fighting for freedom: Historic documents* (p. 358). Philadelphia: John C. Winston Co.

Litman, R. E. (May 13, 1995). Personal communication.

Mann, T. (1952). *Buddenbrooks*. New York: Alfred A. Knopf. (Originally published in 1901).

Melville H., (1849). *Redburn*. New York: Harper & Bros.

Rank, O. (1932). (Ch. 2). *Art and the artist*. New York: Alfred A. Knopf.

37

CHAPTER

Dedication (to Parents)

To my late beloved parents, who only vaguely appreciated that they were the golden sacrificial bridge from a Czarist *shtetl* to an American university. Once, after their deaths, when I was in Athens, I sought for their noble prototypes among the voiceless lifesize grave reliefs in the ancient Karameikos cemetery, but I learned then that they really lie in my own heart's vault of treasures and that their voices, even in death, speak to me continuously on the beat of my pulses.

Reprinted from *Voices of Death*. New York: Harper & Row. 1980. With permission.

Bibliography: The Complete Works of Edwin S. Shneidman

□ 1943

The experimental study of the appraisal interview. *Journal of Applied Psychology, 27,* 186–205.

□ 1946

Information form useful in vocational counseling. *Occupations, 25,* 108–109.

A short method of scoring the Minnesota Multiphasic Personality Inventory. *Journal of Consulting Psychology, 10,* 143–145.

□ 1947

The Make A Picture Story Projective Personality Test: A preliminary report. *Journal of Consulting Psychology, 11,* 315–325.

Psychodrama and the MAPS Test. *Journal of Projective Techniques, 11,* 1–26 (with E. Fantel).

□ 1948

Schizophrenia and the MAPS Test. *Genetic Psychology Monographs, 38,* 145–223.

☐ 1949

The Make-A-Picture-Story (MAPS) Test. New York: Psychological Corporation.

The Guilford-Shneidman-Zimmerman Interest Survey. Beverly Hills, CA: Sheridan Supply Company (with J. P. Guilford & W. W. Zimmerman).

Some Comparisons among the Four Picture Test, Thematic Apperception Test, and Make a Picture Story Test. *Journal of Projective Techniques, 13,* 150–154.

☐ 1951

Thematic Test Analysis. New York: Grune & Stratton (with K. B. Little & W. Joel)

☐ 1952

The case of Jay: Psychological test and anamnestic data. *Journal of Projective Techniques, 16,* 297–345 and 444–475.

Manual for the MAPS Test. *Projective Techniques, 17,* 1–92.

☐ 1954

Validity of MMPI Interpretations. *Journal of Consulting Psychology, 18,* 425–428. Reprinted in E. I. Megargee (Ed.), *Research in clinical assessment.* New York: Harper and Row. Also in G. S. Welshe & W. G. Dahlstrom (Eds.) (1956). *Basic readings on the MMPI in psychology and medicine.* Minneapolis: University of Minnesota Press (with K. B. Little).

☐ 1955

Acute paranoid schizophrenia in a veteran. In A. Burton & R. E. Harris (Eds.), *Clinical studies in personality.* New York: Harper and Brothers.

The validity of thematic projective techniques interpretations. *Journal of Personality, 23,* 286–294. Reprinted in E. I. Megargee (Ed.) (1968), *Research in clinical assessment.* New York: Harper and Row (with K. B. Little).

Attempted, threatened and completed suicide. *Journal of Abnormal and Social Psychology, 50,* 230 (with N. L. Farberow).

☐ 1956

Clues to suicide. *Public Health Reports, 71,* 109–114 (with N. L. Farberow).

Some relationships between the Rorschach technique and other psychodiagnostic tests. In B. Klopfer (Ed.), *Developments in the Rorschach technique* (Vol. 2). New York: World Book Company.

☐ 1957

Some comparisons between genuine and simulated suicide notes. *Journal of General Psychology, 56,* 251–256 (with N. L. Farberow).
A method for educing the present correlates of perception: An introduction to the method of successive co-variation. *Journal of General Psychology, 57,* 113–120.
Clues to suicide. (Ed.). New York: McGraw-Hill Book Company (with N. L. Farberow). Translated into Japanese.

☐ 1958

Some relationships between thematic and drawing materials. In E. F. Hammer (Ed.), *The clinical application of projective drawings.* Springfield, IL: C. C. Thomas.
A Nisei woman attacks by suicide. In G. Seward (Ed.), *Clinical studies in culture conflicts.* New York: Ronald Press (with N. L. Farberow).
Suicide and the police officer. *Police, 2,* 51–55 (with N. L. Farberow).
Some relationships among thematic projective tests of various degrees of structuredness and behavior in a group situation. *Journal of Projective Techniques, 22,* 3–12 (with C. L. Edgar).
TAT heroes of suicidal and non-suicidal subjects. *Journal of Projective Techniques, 22,* 211–228 (with N. L. Farberow).

☐ 1959

Congruencies among interpretations of psychological test and anamnestic data. *Psychological Monographs, 73.* 1–42. Reprinted in E. I. Megargee (Ed.) (1969), *Research in clinical assessment.* New York: Harper and Row (with Kenneth B. Little).
Suicide and death. In H. Feifel (Ed.), *The meaning of death.* New York: McGraw-Hill Book Company (with N. L. Farberow).
Conversations about suicide: A review of Bosselman's *Self-destruction. Contemporary Psychology, 3,* 329–330.
Current aspects of the problem of validity: Suggestions for the delineation of validational studies. *Journal of Projective Techniques, 23,* 259–262.

☐ 1960

Suicide of the aged. Report to the U.S. Senate Sub-Committee on Problems of the Aged and Aging (Part IV, pp. 970–980).
A socio-psychological study of suicide. In H. David & J. D. Brengelmann (Eds.), *Perspectives in personality research.* New York: Ronald Press (with N. L. Farberow).
The MAPS Test with children. In A. I. Rabin (Ed.), *Projective techniques for children.* New York: Grune & Stratton.
Psycho-logic: A personality approach to patterns of thinking. In J. Kagan & G. Lesser (Eds.), *Current issues in thematic apperceptive fantasy.* Springfield, IL: C. C. Thomas.

The Travis Projective Pictures. In O. Buros' *Fifth mental measurement yearbook.* New Brunswick, NJ: Rutgers University Press.

The logical, psychological and ecological environments of suicide. *California's Health, 17,* 193–196.

The clergy's responsibility in suicide prevention. In *Preventive mental hygiene and the clergy.* Oakland, CA: Alameda County Mental Health Service.

☐ 1961

Suicide: The problem and its magnitude. Washington, DC: V.A. Medical Bulletin 7 (with N. L. Farberow).

Some facts about suicide: Causes and prevention. Washington, DC: U.S. Government Printing Office. P.H.S. Publication No. 852. (with N. L. Farberow & C. V. Leonard).

The cry for help (Ed.). New York: McGraw-Hill Book Company (with N. L. Farberow). Translated into Japanese and Spanish.

A suicide prevention center. In J. H. Masserman (Ed.), *Current psychiatric therapies.* New York: Grune & Stratton (with R. E. Litman & N. L. Farberow).

The case of El. *Journal of Projective Techniques, 25,* 131–154.

A suicide prevention center. *American Journal of Psychiatry, 117,* 1084–1087 (with R. E. Litman & N. L. Farberow).

☐ 1962

Suicide: Evaluation and treatment of suicidal risk among schizophrenic patients in psychiatric hospitals. Washington, DC: V.A. Medical Bulletin No. 8 (with N. L. Farberow).

Suicide: Some classificatory considerations. In *Special treatment situations.* Des Plaines, IL: Forest Hospital Publications.

Projections on a triptych; or a hagiology for our time. *Journal of Projective Techniques, 26,* 379–387.

☐ 1963

Suicide among general medical and surgical hospital patients with malignant neoplasms. Washington, DC: V.A. Medical Bulletin No. 9 (with N. L. Farberow).

The logic of politics. In M. A. May & L. Arons (Eds.), *Television and human behavior.* New York: Appleton-Century-Crofts.

Suicide: Trauma and taboo. In N. L. Farberow (Ed.), *Taboo topics.* New York: Atherton Press.

Orientations toward death: A vital aspect of the study of lives. In R. W. White (Ed.), *The study of lives.* New York: Atherton Press. Reprinted in *International Journal of Psychiatry, 2,* 167–188; also in H. Resnik (Ed.), *Suicidal Behaviors.* Boston: Little Brown and Company. Translated into Japanese.

A look into the dark: A review of Meerloo's *Suicide and mass suicide. Contemporary Psychology, 8,* 178–180.

Investigations of equivocal suicides. *Journal of the Amreican Medical Association, 184,* 924–929 (with R. E. Litman, T. J. Curphey, N. L. Farberow, & N. D. Tabachnik).
The suicidal patient and the physician. *Mind, 1,* 69–75 (with N. L. Farberow & R. E. Litman).

☐ 1964

Pioneer in suicidology: A review of Louis I. Dublin's *Suicide: A sociological and statistical study. Contemporary Psychology, 9,* 370–371.
Some reflections of personality explorers, 1938–1963. *Journal of Projective Techniques, 28,* 156–160.
Suicide, sleep and death: Some possible intercorrelations among cessation, interruption and continuation phenomena. *Journal of Consulting Psychology, 28,* 95–106.
Tranquilizers and suicide in the schizophrenic patient. *Archives of General Psychiatry, 11,* 312–321 (with S. Cohen, C. V. Leonard, & N. L. Farberow).
Premiers secorrs lors de crises suicidairees. *Medicine et Hygiene, 22,* 633–637 (with R. E. Litman & N. L. Farberow).

☐ 1965

Projective techniques. In B. Wolman (Ed.), *Handbook of clinical psychology.* New York: McGraw-Hill Book Company.
The Los Angeles Suicide Prevention Center: A demonstration of public health feasibilities. *American Public Health Journal,* 21–26 (with N. L. Farberow).
Suicide Prevention Telephone Service. *Journal of the American Medical Association, 192,* 21–25 (with R. E. Litman, N. L. Farberow, S. M. Heilig, & J. Kramer).
Some reflections on death and suicide. *Folia Psychiatrica et Neurologica Japonica, 19,* 317–325.

☐ 1966

The logics of communication: A manual for analysis. China Lake, CA: U.S. Naval Ordnance Test Station (with P. Tripodes).
Review of D. J. West's *Murder followed by suicide. American Journal of Psychiatry, 123,* 501–502.
Suicide prevention around the clock. *American Journal of Orthopsychiatry, 36,* 551–558 (with N. L. Farberow, R. E. Litman, C. Wold, S. M. Heilig, & J. Kramer).
Foreword, Japanese edition of *Clues to suicide* (O. Kenshiro & S. Makota, Trans.).
Case history and hospitalization factors in suicides of neuropsychiatric hospital patients. *Journal of Nervous and Mental Disease, 142,* 32–44 (with N. L. Farberow & C. Neuringer).
Suicide among adolescents. *California School Health, 2,* 1–5.
Suicides of children and adolescents: A national problem. *Technical assistance project proceedings of a conference on depression and suicide in adolescents and young adults.* Montpelier, VT: Department of Mental Health.

1967

How the family physician can prevent suicide. *Physicians Panorama, 5,* 5–10 (with L. H. Dizmang).

Multiple MMPI profiles of suicidal persons. *Psychological Reports, 21,* 401–404 (with A. Devries).

A major cause of death among the young: Self-destruction. *Social Service Outlook, 7,* 13–14.

Description of the NIMH Center for Studies of Suicide Prevention. *Bulletin of Suicidology, 1,* 2–7.

Some current developments in suicide prevention. *Bulletin of Suicidology, 1,* 31–34.

Essays in self destruction. (Ed.). New York: Science House. Translated into Japanese.

Sleep and self-destruction: A phenomenological approach. In E. S. Shneidman (Ed.), *Essays in self-destruction.* New York: Science House.

How to prevent suicide. *Public Health Pamphlet* No. 406. New York: Public Health Pamphlets (with P. Mandelkorn).

1968

Suicide: Psychological aspects. *International encyclopaedia of the social sciences.* New York: Crowell-Collier.

Suicidal phenomena: Their definition and classification. *International encyclopaedia of the social sciences.* New York: Crowell-Collier.

First training record in suicidology. Chevy Chase, MD: National Institute of Mental Health.

The Suicide Prevention Center of Los Angeles. In H. Resnik (Ed.), *Suicidal behaviors.* Boston: Little, Brown and Company (with N. L. Farberow).

Suicide prevention: A current national view. In N. L. Farberow (Ed.), *Proceedings: Fourth international conference for suicide prevention.* Los Angeles: Del Mar Publishing Company.

The deaths of Herman Melville. In H. P. Vincent (Ed.), *Melville and Hawthorne in the Berkshires.* Kent, OH: Kent State University Press.

Preventing suicide. *American Journal of Nursing, 65,* 111–116. Reprinted in D. Mereness (Ed.), *Readings in public health Nursing.* Dubuque, IA: W. C. Brown Company; also in J. P. Gibbs (Ed.), *Suicide.* New York: Harper and Row.

The role of nonprofessional volunteers in a suicide prevention center. *Community Mental Health Journal, 4,* 287–295 (with S. M. Heilig, N. L. Farberow, & R. E. Litman).

Orientations toward cessation: A reexamination of current modes of deaths. *Journal of Forensic Sciences, 13,* 33–46.

Suicide prevention: The hospital's role. *Hospital Practice, 3,* 56–61.

Classifications of suicidal phenomena. *Bulletin of Suicidology, 2,* 1–10.

1969

Aspects of depression. (Ed.). Boston: Little, Brown and Company (with M. Ortega).

Suicide, lethality and the psychological autopsy. In E. S. Shneidman & M. Ortega (Eds.), *Aspects of depression.* Boston: Little, Brown and Company.

On the nature of suicide. (Ed.). San Francisco: Jossey-Bass.

The suicidal death. In A. H. Kutscher (Ed.), *But not to lose.* New York: McGraw-Hill Book Company.

Logical content analysis: An explication of styles of concludifying. In G. Gerbner et al. (Eds.), *The analysis of communication content.* New York: John Wiley and Sons.
Some characteristics of genuine versus simulated suicide notes. In P. J. Stone et al. (Eds.), *The general inquirer: A computer approach to content analysis.* New York: John Wiley (with D. M. Ogilvie & P. J. Stone).

□ 1970

The psychology of suicide. New York: Science House (with N. L. Farberow & R. E. Litman).

□ 1971

The National Suicide Program. In J. Zusman & D. Davidson (Eds.), *Organizing the community to prevent suicide.* Springfield, IL: C. C. Thomas.
"Suicide" and "Suicidology": A brief etymological note. *Life-Threatening Behavior, 1,* 260–264.
On the deromanticization of death. *American Journal of Psychotherapy, 25,* 4–17.
Prevention, intervention and postvention of suicide. *Annals of Internal Medicine, 75,* 453–457.
Perturbation and lethality as precusors of suicide in a gifted group. *Life-Threatening Behavior, 1,* 23–45.

□ 1972

Prevention of suicide: A challenge for community service. In S. E. Golann & C. Eisdorfer (Eds.), *Handbook of community psychology and mental health.* New York: Appleton-Century-Crofts.
Death and the college student. (Ed.). New York: Behavioral Publications.
Death and the college student. In H. Feifel (Ed.), *New meanings of death.* New York: McGraw-Hill Book Company.
The creative artist and the savage god: A review of A. Alvarez's *The savage god. Psychotherapy and Social Science Review, 6,* 19–22.
Can a young person write his own obituary? *Life-Threatening Behavior, 2,* 262–267.

□ 1973

Deaths of man. New York: Quadrangle/New York Times Book Company. New York: Penguin Books, 1974. Translated into Japanese. Nominated for the National Book Award in Science, 1973.
Suicide. *Encyclopaedia of Psychology.* Port Washington, NY: Dushkin Publishing Company.
Suicide. *Encyclopaedia Britannica.* Chicago: William Benton.
Who owns the patient? In L. S. Bermosk & R. J. Corsini (Eds.), *Critical incidents in nursing.* Philadelphia: W. B. Saunders.
Suicide notes reconsidered. *Psychiatry, 36,* 379–395.

□ 1974

Community programs in suicidology. In S. Arieti (Ed.), *American Handbook of psychiatry.* New York: Basic Books.

□ 1975

Psychiatric emergencies: Suicide. In A. Freedman, H. Kaplan & B. Sadock (Eds.), *Comprehensive textbook of psychiatry, revised edition.* Baltimore: Williams & Wilkins Company.

Postvention: Care of the bereaved. In R. O. Pasnau (Ed.), *Consultation-liaison psychiatry.* New York: Grune & Stratton.

□ 1976

Suicide: An overview. A psychological theory and recent developments. *Psychiatric Annals, 6,* 9–121 (not inclusive).

Some psychological reflections on the death of Malcolm Melville. *Suicide and Life-Threatening Behavior, 6,* 231–242.

Death: Current perspectives. (Ed.). Palo Alto, CA: Mayfield Publishing Company.

Suicidology: Contemporary developments. (Ed.). New York: Grune & Stratton.

□ 1977

The psychological autopsy. In L. I. Gottschalk et al. (Eds.), *Guide to the investigation and reporting of drug abuse deaths.* Washington, D.C.: USDHEW, U. S. Government Printing Office.

Aspects of the dying process. *Psychiatric Annals, 7,* 25–40.

Foreword to C. Hatton, S. Valente, & A. Rink (Eds.), *Suicide: Assessment and intervention.* New York: Appleton-Century-Crofts.

□ 1978

Some aspects of psychotherapy with dying persons. In C. A. Garfield (Ed.), *Psychosocial aspects of terminal patient care.* New York: McGraw-Hill Book Company.

□ 1979

Clinical thanatology and psychotherapy: Some reflections on caring for the dying person. *Omega, 10,* 1–8 (with L. Feigenberg).

Risk writing: A special note about Cesare Pavese and Joseph Conrad. *Journal of the American Academy of Psychoanalysis, 7,* 575–592.

A bibliography of suicide notes, 1856–1979. *Suicide and Life-Threatening Behavior, 9,* 57–59.

☐ 1980

Voices of death. New York: Harper and Row. New York: Bantam Books, 1981. Translated into Japanese, Swedish and German.
Death: Current perspectives (Second ed.). (Ed.). Palo Alto, CA: Mayfield Publishing Company.
A genuine classic in suicidology: Review of Jean Baechler's *Suicides. Contemporary Psychology, 25,* 108–109.
Foreword, in L. Feigenberg, *Terminal Care.* New York: Brunner/Mazel.
Psychotherapy with suicidal patients. In T. B. Karasu & L. Bellak (Eds.), *Specialized techniques in individual psychotherapy.* New York: Brunner/Mazel.
A possible classification of suicidal acts based on Murray's need system. *Suicide and Life-Threatening Behavior, 10,* 175–181.

☐ 1981

Suicide thoughts and reflections, 1960–1980. (Ed.) New York: Human Sciences Press.
Endeavors in psychology: Selections from the personology of Henry A. Murray. (Ed.). New York: Harper and Row.
Suicidal behaviors. In J. F. Fries & G. E. Ehrlich (Eds.), *Prognosis: Contemporary outcomes of disease.* Bowie, MD: Charles.
Commentary. In D. Yannella & H. Parker (Eds.), *The endless, winding way in Melville: New charts by Kring and Carey.* Glassboro, NJ: The Melville Society.

☐ 1982

On "Therefore I must kill myself." *Suicide and Life-Threatening Behavior, 12,* 52–55.
The suicidal logic of Cesare Pavese. *Journal of the American Academy of Psychoanalysis, 10,* 547–563.
Aspects of the personological system of Henry A. Murray. *Personality and Social Psychology, 8,* 604, 617–619.

☐ 1983

On abolishing death: An etymological note. *Suicide and Life-Threatening Behavior, 13,* 176–178.
Review of *Lifelines: Clinical perspective on suicide* by E. L. Bussak, S. C. Schoonover, & A. D. Gill, *New England Journal of Medicine, 308,* 108–109.
Reflections on contemporary death. In J. Stillion (Ed.), *Proceedings. Forum for Death Education and Counseling.*

☐ 1984

Death: Current perspectives (3rd ed.). (Ed.). Palo Alto, CA: Mayfield Publishing Company.

Aphorisms of suicide and some implications for psychotherapy. *American Journal of Psychotherapy, 38,* 319–328.

Personality and "success" among a selected group of lawyers. *Journal of Personality Assessment, 48,* 609–616.

Suicide prevention. *Encyclopaedia of psychology.* New York: John Wiley.

Make-A-Picture-Story (MAPS) Test. *Encyclopaedia of psychology.* New York: John Wiley.

Henry A. Murray. *Encyclopaedia of psychology.* New York: John Wiley.

Epilogue to C. Haskell (Ed.), *Cancer treatment, second edition.* Philadelphia: W. B. Saunders.

Remembrance of Mort Meyer. *Journal of Personality Assessment, 48,* 558–559.

☐ 1985

Definition of suicide. New York: John Wiley.

Some thoughts on grief and mourning. *Suicide and Life-Threatening Behavior, 15,* 51–55.

Forem des sterbens und thanato-therapie. In I. Spiegel-Rosing & H. Petzold (Eds.), *Die begeitung sterbender: Theorie und praxis der thanato-therapie.* Paderborn, Germany: Junfermann Verlag.

Some psychological reflections of Herman Melville. *Melville Society Extracts, 64,* 7–9.

☐ 1986

Some essentials of suicide and some implications for response. In A. Roy (Ed.), *Suicide.* Baltimore: Williams & Wilkins.

Melville's cognitive style: The logic of Moby-Dick. In J. Bryant (Ed.), *A companion to Melville studies.* Westport, CT: Greenwood Press.

MAPS of the Harvard Yard. *Journal of Personality Assessment, 50,* 436–447.

Foreword to Mamoru Iga, *The thorn in the chrysantheum: Economic success and suicide in contemporary Japan.* Berkeley and Los Angeles: University of California Press.

Review of new perspectives in schizophrenia, M. N. Menuck and M. V. Seeman (Eds.). *New England Journal of Medicine, 314,* 795.

☐ 1987

At the point of no return. *Psychology Today,* March, 54–58.

Dying, denying and willing the obligatory. In M. B. Freeman (Ed.), *Social change and personality: Essays in honor of Nevitt Sanford.* New York: Brunner/Mazel.

A psychological approach to suicide. In G. R. VanderBos & B. K. Bryant (Eds.), *Cataclysms, crises and catastrophes: Psychology in action.* American Psychological Association Master Lecture Series. Washington, D.C.: American Psychological Association.

Approaches and commonalities of suicide. In R. F. W. Diekstra (Ed.), *Attitudinal factors in suicidal behavior and its prevention.* Leiden: Swets & Zeitlinger/Brill.

Suicide and suicide prevention. In R. Corsini (Ed.), *Concise encyclopaedia of psychology.* New York: John Wiley.

☐ 1988

Foreword, in A. Leenaars, *Suicide notes.* New York: Behavioral Science Press.
Reflections of a founder. *Suicide and Life-Threatening Behavior, 18,* 1–12; also in R. Maris (Ed.), *Understanding and preventing suicide.* New York: Guilford Press.

☐ 1989

A multidisciplinary approach to suicide. In D. Jacobs & H. Brown (Eds.), *The Harvard sourcebook of suicide.* New York: International Universities Press.
The Indian summer of life: A preliminary study of septuagenarians. *American Psychologist, 44,* 684–694.

☐ 1990

The suicidal psycho-logics of *Moby-Dick.* In S. Deats & L. Lenker (Eds.), *Youth suicide prevention: Lessons from literature.* New York: Human Sciences Press.

☐ 1991

[Autobiography] A life in death: Notes of a committed suicidologist. In C. E. Walker (Ed.), *The history of clinical psychology in autobiography.* Pacific Grove, CA: Brooks/Cole.
The commonalities of suicide across the life-span. In A. Leenaars (Ed.), *Life span perspectives of suicide.* New York: Plenum.
Foreword to Alan Berman and David Jobes' *Adolescent suicide: Assessment and intervention.* Washington, D.C.: American Psychological Association.
Foreword to Bruce Bongar & Eric Harris' *The suicidal Patient: Clinical and legal standards for professional psychological practice.* Washington, D.C.: American Psychological Association.

☐ 1992

A conspectus for conceptualizing the suicidal scenario. In R. Maris, L. Berman, J. Maltsberger, & R. Yufit (Eds.), *Assessment and prediction of suicide.* New York: Guilford Press.
What do suicides have in common? A summary of the psychological approach. In B. Bongar (Ed.), *Dangerous intersections: The assessment and management of suicide in clinical practice.* New York: Oxford University Press.
Comment on rational suicide and the right to die. *New England Journal of Medicine, 326,* 889.

1993

Suicide and psychache. *Journal of Nervous and Mental Disease, 181,* 147–149.

Suicide as psychache: A clinical approach to self-destructive behavior. Northvale, NJ: Jason Aronson, Inc.

Some controversies in suicidology: Toward a mentalistic discipline. *Suicide and Life-Threatening Behavior, 23,* 292–298.

1994

Comment: The psychological autopsy. *American Psychologist, 49,* 76–77.

The psychology of suicide: Revised edition. Northvale, NJ: Jason Aronson, Inc. (with N. Farberow and R. E. Litman).

Clues to suicide reconsidered. *Suicide and Life-Threatening Behavior, 24,* 395–397.

The Inman diary: Some reflections. In A. Leenaars, J. Maltsberger, & R. Neimeyer (Eds.), *Treatment of suicidal people.* London: Taylor and Francis.

Six Melville poems. Los Angeles, CA: BB Communications (privately printed).

1995

Death: Current perspectives, fourth edition. Los Gatos, CA: Mayfield Publishing Company (edited with J. Williamson).

Letters of enforced death versus suicide notes. *Journal of Psychology and Judaism, 19,* 153–160.

1996

Foreword, in J. T. Maltsberger and M. Goldblatt (Eds.), *Essential papers on suicide.* New York: New York University Press.

The suicidal mind. New York: Oxford University Press.

1997

The suicidal mind. In R. Maris, M. Silverman, & S. Canetto (Eds.), *Review of suicidology, 1997.* New York: Guilford Press.

1998

"Suicide" in the *Encyclopaedia Britannica,* 1777–1997. *Archives of Suicide Research, 4,* 189–199.

Obituary: Evelyn Hooker (1907–1996). *American Psychologist, 53,* 480–481.

Some further reflections on suicide and psychache. *Suicide and Life-Threatening Behavior, 28,* 245–250.

The best psychological book on suicide. A retrospective review of Karl A. Menninger's *Man against himself. Contemporary Psychology, 43,* 161–164.

Suicide on my mind: Britannica on my table. *The American Scholar, 67,* 93–104.

☐ 1999

Perturbation and lethality: The inimical twins of suicide. In D. Jacobs (Ed.), *Harvard Medical School guide to suicide assessment and intervention* (pp. 83–97). Cambridge, MA: Harvard Medical Publications.

The TAT: A paradise of psychodynamics. In M. Gieser & M. Stein (Eds.), *Evocative images: The thematic apperception test and the art of projection.* Washington, D.C.: American Psychological Association (in press).

The psychological pain assessment scale: A first report. *Suicide and Life-Threatening Behavior 29,* (in press).

☐ 2000

Comprehending suicide: Landmarks in suicidology. Washington, D.C.: American Psychological Association (with John T. Maltsberger). (in preparation).

INDEX

For Product Safety Concerns and Information please contact our EU
representative GPSR@taylorandfrancis.com
Taylor & Francis Verlag GmbH, Kaufingerstraße 24, 80331 München, Germany

www.ingramcontent.com/pod-product-compliance
Ingram Content Group UK Ltd.
Pitfield, Milton Keynes, MK11 3LW, UK
UKHW022005180926
475701UK00003B/203
* 9 7 8 1 5 8 3 9 1 0 1 1 5 *